2

THE CHILD'S PATH TO SPOKEN LANGUAGE

↓ Pg 8 'what is language'

John L. Locke

THE CHILD'S PATH
TO SPOKEN LANGUAGE

Harvard University Press

Cambridge, Massachusetts

London, England

Second printing, 1995

First Harvard University Press paperback edition, 1995

Library of Congress Cataloging-in-Publication Data

Locke, John L.
  The child's path to spoken language / John L. Locke.
    p.   cm.
  Includes bibliographical references and index.
  ISBN 0-674-11640-2 (cloth)
  ISBN 0-674-11639-9 (pbk.)
  1. Language acquisitions. 2. Biolinguistics. I. Title.
P118.L618   1993
401'.93—dc20   92-34661
                                                   CIP

To my brother
Edward Nash Locke

ACKNOWLEDGMENTS

One of the most rewarding things about scholarly life is the way colleagues help each other think their way through complex issues. I have been the recipient of some excellent advice from colleagues in several fields, and this book is the better for it.

The central thrust of the book is developmental biolinguistics—the biology of language development—and over the last decade my thoughts in this area have been greatly influenced by the papers, lectures, and personal remarks of Michael Studdert-Kennedy, who, to my benefit, has also offered detailed suggestions on the manuscript.

I have come to see spoken language in the context of social cognition, and I am greatly indebted to Leslie Brothers for exposing me to the richness of this magnificent subject. She helped me to understand the neurophysiology of face processing and to appreciate the linkage between this area, related neural specializations, and social development more generally.

Much of this book deals with differences and similarities between humans and other primates, and I am indebted to Marc Hauser for interpretations of the primate literature and for many intense discussions of animal behavior. Marc also commented on an early draft of the manuscript, as did Aniruddh Patel, a doctoral student in evolutionary biology at Harvard. Ani is a master at the art of gentle correction, and through his assistance some of my misstatements of biological fact were painlessly put right. This book deals with the development of language that is spoken, and I also wish to thank Michael Lynch for commenting on issues relating to vocal development.

I shall forever remember the seven students in the inaugural class of the Graduate Program in Communications Sciences and Disorders at the MGH Institute of Health Professions, who uncomplainingly made their way through an early draft of the manuscript as their course reading requirement in the Ontogeny of Spoken Language—Belinda Campbell, Kathleen Hegarty, Ellen Meisel, Stacey Pappas, Deborah Proia, Susan Smith, and Kara Sullivan, emergent scholars all. Many of these same individuals, in their capacity as itinerant xerographers to the lab, made frequent trips to area libraries to obtain obscure references.

I am pleased to acknowledge the assistance of several research assistants in the Neurolinguistics Laboratory, especially Gretchen Johnson, whose literary suggestions caused the text to read more smoothly; Lee Sullivan, who assisted with the references; and Katerina Leftheri, who prepared some of the figures.

The writing of this book took me away from other projects. Sandra Sumner, my very able administrative assistant at the MGH Institute of Health Professions for the last nine years, made that possible by doing many things for me. I am grateful to Sandi for this, and also to the James S. McDonnell Foundation for supporting the cost of several of the studies reported herein.

I would like to recognize several individuals at Harvard University Press—Angela von der Lippe for her encouragement in the initial stages, and Linda Howe for her judicious editing.

Finally, I wish to thank Michael Smith, my colleague and close friend over a period of nearly two decades, for his gentle encouragement, and for his careful reading and wise editing of the entire book. One Saturday morning in May, after an enjoyable breakfast at the Magnolia Beach Cafe, he offered up what I take to be the perfect compliment, given what I was trying to do: "It's as though the kid wrote this book!"

CONTENTS

To speak of "language acquisition" is to imply that language is an extraneous object of knowledge for children which is first "acquired" and then spoken. The contrary is equally plausible: in learning to speak children learn a language.

Elena Lieven and John McShane,
"Language Is a Developing Social Skill"

1

A BIOLINGUISTIC APPROACH
TO LANGUAGE DEVELOPMENT

About a year after birth, humans do something other living creatures never do. They speak. How the infant develops the means to take this first step, while revealing the readiness to plunge even more deeply into linguistic communication, is the subject of this book.

It is easy to say, as some have, that humans possess a capacity for spoken language. Who among us would doubt that we do, when every group of people—wherever situated, however isolated—speaks? But just how the infant comes to possess and use its phonological and referential capacity is another matter. And it is here that our glibness wanes and the need for systematic inquiry begins.

It would be considered a scientific breakthrough if we could learn how hominids came to possess an interest in vocal behavior and evolved the capacity for spoken language. And yet, the ontogenetic equivalent of this question has yet to be resolved *or even recognized* as a problem by contemporary linguistics and psychology. A step toward resolution will be attempted here as I examine the perceptual, social, vocal, neural, and cognitive capabilities of the human infant, identifying the environmental circumstances under which neonates begin to deal *in,* and learn to deal *with* vocal sounds. I will also describe the developmental path subsequently followed to languages that are spoken.

In this chapter, I will set down some of the parameters of biolinguistic thinking. These parameters relate to questions a biolinguist would naturally want to ask and the predispositions and biases a person with such a perspective would bring to the study of language development in children. We want to know what accounts for the infant's ability to detect and process environmental stimulation that is relevant to language. Our inclination would be to place great value on social communication, since that provides the function and the context for language behavior. We will naturally be curious about the genetic transmissibility of neural and vocal structures that are available or can be commandeered for linguistic use. Questions about the development of linguistic capacity naturally will intensify our curiosity about phylogeny; this and other theoretical business will cause us to look at selected findings on nonhuman primates, songbirds, and other animals. The ways in which these animals negotiate with their environments suggest generalizations about our own behavior and reveal which aspects of our capacities are species-specific and tightly linked to language per se.

A biolinguistic perspective will not allow us to believe that the capacity for spoken language accrues to children purely because they belong to a species that has this capability and are frequently exposed to a range of speech behaviors. The child needs to obtain its own copy of the capacity for spoken language. How it does this is hard to say, but the question is no less magnificent than asking how our species came to speak, though it is more empirical and, let us hope, a great deal more tractable. We need to know how it is that infants can differentiate linguistic behavior from behavior that is not linguistic. One accepts that genes and environmental stimulation interact to produce linguistic capacity, but acceptance of this is no reason not to try to understand it. Quite to the contrary, it is precisely because of its pervasively factual status that we must try to explain when and how genes and stimulation collaborate.

It is inaccurate to say that "language" develops. What is true is that developing children increasingly take on and manifest the capacity for language. Language development is therefore a preeminently biological matter. It will take the child a year to start talking, but on every day of that year a variety of language-related mechanisms will inch their way toward efficient action. Vocal and manual motor systems, auditory, ocular, and other systems will rise to a greater readiness to interpret and act upon ambient stimulation. These mechanisms are mixed in with a number of others that have little direct relationship to language. Our many tasks as theorists thus include sorting this out.

A number of theorists have made the argument that environmental stimulation cannot explain the child's rapid learning of complex linguistic rules, and therefore that in an unspecified place inside of young humans some "innate" knowledge of language is stored. But if every normally developing member of our species has a significant preadaptation for languagelike behaviors, what is the nature of this preadaptation? Can it be influenced? If we want to see it, where do we look? If we knew more about the neural prerequisites for language, could we say from morphometric or functional evaluations, other things being equal, that this brain is better for language than some other brain?

It has been common in recent years for psycholinguists (for example, Morgan, 1986) to discuss "the input to the child." What is this input? One gets the impression that the input to the child is taken to be the "output" of those speaking within the child's earshot. Or is it the utterances of those who are addressing the child directly? Certainly anyone intent on understanding the correspondence between the child's experience and its behavior will need to know a great deal about this. But is it not true that infants only pay attention to the stimulation that interests them? If so, which of the things said in the vicinity of infants is to be counted as relevant linguistic experience? Should we admit manual gestures and eye movements into evidence? How can we investigate the child's development of language if we ignore the child's actions— its sensory and motor behavior, social interactions, and mental activities?

It appears that many infants are "born with" some awareness of what language sounds are or ought to be like. It is in this connection that some scholars have used the word "innate," regarding early phonetic biases as a preeminently genetic matter. But there are problems with this interpretation. Birth gives the fetus a change of climate and scenery—and provides observers with an unprecedented opportunity to see and hear it—but this event is not the beginning of the infant's life, and it is now quite seriously considered possible that some things may be learned about the physical form of language before birth.

In this chapter I take a look at the explanatory burdens that are taken on by theories of language acquisition and ask how well existing theories explain the eagerness with which children naturally embark upon the path leading to spoken language. I then preview a theory of the empowerment and elaboration of the human infant's species-characteristic capacity for spoken language. This theory represents a distinct departure from the way many of us have thought about language development in the past, and it differs from all conventional treatments of this subject.

Theories of Language Development

We are in dire need of good developmental theories, for as George Miller has said, "we already know far more about language than we understand" (1990, p. 7). If they are to behave responsibly, our theories of language development have a lot of work ahead of them. They must explain how it is that children develop the affective, social, perceptual, motoric, neural, cognitive, and linguistic capabilities required for the efficient use of spoken language. They must be able to describe the nature of the environmental and genetic interactions that produce these capabilities. They must be able to explain the emergence of linguistic structures, and the social conditions under which various linguistic behaviors are deployed. One hopes that theories of language development will make it possible to understand variations in the developmental path taken by particular infants—to understand why some children progress quickly and others slowly, and why some take a particular path to language and their peers a different one.

In the study of language, we embrace the very definition of what it means to be human and to be a developing member of the species. Children negotiate their animate and inanimate world according to resources possessed and conditions operative at the moment. Although they are the source of the utterance data with which developmental linguistic theories deal, children are not data generators. The child's purpose in life is not to supply raw material for theory builders. Rather, it is to approach the world on child terms, and react adaptively to its own changing propensities and capabilities.

What we must explain, according to Lieven and McShane (1978), "is that children begin to do something: to speak" (p. 919). The simple truth of this is undeniable, and yet when we examine the literature, we find theories of language development and entire books on the child's acquisition of language that pay no attention to how the infant's learning mechanisms develop and say nothing about how infants come to evince interest in linguistic behavior.

I am not criticizing these works. As far as I can tell, they meet the theoretical need, as they define that need, fairly well. Some seek to account for the order in which phonological contrasts or syntactic structures emerge. Others deal with the organization of lexical semantics or the manner in which linguistic knowledge is deployed in social interactions. But as different as they are, existing theories of language development have a common property. They take the child's talking as their point of departure, and I take this event as an explanatory challenge.

I believe there is a tremendous amount of developmental linguistic turf that is unclaimed by any existing theories. For this reason, I do not expect my theoretical forays into these neglected areas to compete with or replace extant linguistic theories of language development. Their goals are just too different from mine.

A Complementary Approach

Although I believe that more can be understood about language within a biolinguistic approach, much of what I will propose is new and does not yet have an empirical track record of its own. I will ask readers to consider some fresh hypotheses about the way language comes about, and why it is expressed by children in the ways it is. There is a temporary—though not inconsiderable—price to be paid in this. We will need to set aside many of our present conceptions about what language is and devote some thought to the *infant's* view of linguistically behaving people.

In this book, I will propose an explanation of how the infant becomes linguistically enfranchised, and thus deposit it on the doorstep of the theories that take the child ever more deeply into phonology, morphology, syntax, semantics, and rules for the effective use of spoken language in social communication. As a psychobiological matter, this aim *anticipates* the child's derivation and application of linguistic grammars. Though there is a deep, functional joint and a degree of superficial overlap between communicative and grammatical domains, these domains are of fundamentally different kinds. But at some point after the infant becomes lexically referential, the functions of social cognition begin to converge with those of grammatical analysis, and even on specific linguistic substance there will be particular areas of shared responsibilities. These include the infant's use of prosody—the natural changes in vocal pitch, intensity, and timing—as a bridge to words and syntax.

The Path to Language

According to the theory I will develop in succeeding chapters, the human infant travels along a path that is not itself linguistic but which—save for cerebral insult or environmental dirty tricks—will naturally lead to spoken language. This result will come as a pleasant surprise, but the infant has no inkling of this when it starts down the path.

The depth and breadth of the path to spoken language is laid down by genes operating in favorable chemical environments and by interactions between cortical cells. The curvature and ultimately the length of the path, and the child's adherence to it, are dictated by the genome in collaboration with the social interactions that characterize our species, and in collaboration with other factors that are equally biological. In "precapacious" infants of immature brain and inexperienced mind, the component capabilities and processes—the precursors to language—*potentially* matter because the child reaches full linguistic capacity gradually, step by step. Development will not proceed apace unless infants enjoy the kind of success in vocal communication that is enabled by cognitive, social, and motoric developments of one kind or another.

Much is experienced along the way; there are many things for the infant and its caregivers to do, and many flags and beacons to keep the infant on course. All parties will use face and voice to communicate feelings, attitudes, and intentions. Eye and hand movements will be used to isolate the objects of their attention. There are social roles and vocal tunes to be played, and countless opportunities for both sides to indulge in a variety of phonetic accommodations. Spoken language arises within these rich experiences and grows from them, but to the human infant the behavior of speaking is interesting in and of itself. This natural interest is the infant's passport to languages that are spoken and is therefore a fact that biolinguistics must explain.

In speaking of the anticipatory aspect of my own model of language I do not mean to diminish the qualitative contribution to linguistic structure of the specific path infants take to language. Language is simply the way it is because it was invented and acquired by humans, who gave it perceivable, producible properties and built systems of linguistic cues that would be easily manipulable and socially useful. How could it be otherwise? Infants haul into the act of speaking all their perceptual biases and motoric dispositions, and execute our natural languages imperfectly—as natural as the structure of these systems may already be—because of their particular sensitivities and constraints at the moment. In later chapters, the infant, as child, will be followed a short distance into language precisely so these effects can be observed. In ways I never imagined when I began to write, we will witness the hookup between the social-vocal domain and the species-specific specialization broached by computational-grammatical theories (Chapter 9).

What Is "It"?

On one level, one could hardly disagree with George Miller's declaration that the child "learns the language because he is shaped by nature to pay attention to it, to notice and remember and use significant aspects of it" (1965, p. 20). Indeed, most treatments of language acquisition seem content to take the child's interest in language as their point of departure and then proceed to document the timing and sequence of language development: the age of first words, the order in which syntactic structures are acquired and expressed, and so on. But we are left with a vital question: Why does the child do any of this? What motivates the child to pay attention to speech, to respond to it? If the child is "shaped by nature to pay attention to it," we might ask, what is "it"?

To the infant, "it"—in the first instance—is the appearance of familiar faces releasing familiar voices that are modulated by moving mouths in coordination with expressive eyes. In my view, infants do not really set out to learn language. Instead, they study the movements of faces and voices—the observable displays of talkers—and gradually accommodate to and reproduce these behaviors. They do this not because they know about language and understand its importance, but because they have a deep biological need to interact emotionally with the people that love and take care of them. If infants continue to do these things while experiencing appropriate advances in motoric and cognitive functions, one day we will consider them to be children and their utterances to be speech. But there is much that separates this developmental stage and the initial experiences of the fetus and neonate.

An Active View

How do infants "get" language? Is linguistic capacity bestowed upon the infant, a genetic gift from its parents? If so, is the social environment totally innocent, the key players simply standing by while genes do their work? Or is ambient stimulation needed to trigger, perhaps even to empower the child's constitutional potentialities? By either account there is work to be done by industrious genes or stimulating parents. But what is the role of the infant itself?

We speak easily about the child's *acquisition* of language, and certainly acquisition is a favorable result, but I am unconvinced that it is the process by which infants come to know a great deal of what listeners take to be linguistic. It can be argued that infants do not "get" language and do not behave acquisitively. I believe the young infant is unaware of anything linguistic that is "out there" to be acquired, and that Michael Studdert-Kennedy got it absolutely right when he said that "language is not an object, or even a skill, that lies outside the child and has somehow to be acquired or internalized. Rather it is a mode of action into which the child grows because the mode is implicit in the human developmental system" (1991, p. 10).

If we are to leave no ontogenetic stone unturned, we cannot go far without dislodging a massive boulder: we must give the human infant some specific reasons to start down the path to spoken language in the first place. I believe that when we know what causes infants to do the things that lead to language, we will understand more about their *motivation to speak,* which must surely be considered the central factor in linguistic ontogeny. We also stand to learn a great many other things about how infants arrive at the functional point where they know and use language.

No one doubts that language acquisition is allowed by species-characteristic capabilities supported by congenial environments. But this implies a passivity that does not exist. Susan Oyama has said that "fate is constructed, amended and reconstructed, partly by the emerging organism itself. It is known to no one, not even the genes" (p. 121). The evidence shows that infants enter extra-uterine life with many strong perceptual biases and motoric dispositions already nudging them toward linguistically relevant patterns of stimulation. But I contend, further, that the infant is an active, even zealous force in building its capabilities and in shaping the flow of ambient stimulation.

In a nurturant world, the infant's own behavior prompts and configures much of the physical, social, and vocal information that is used to construct a linguistic system. This is empirically true, as I will attempt to demonstrate in the chapters that follow. It is also logically necessary, for as Marilyn Shatz has pointed out, "if the environment to which the organism was exposed changed at just the rate at which the organism learned and according to the order in which information was to be acquired, there would be no need for the organism to be equipped with means for selecting what was to be learned when. Simply moving through the appropriately changing environment over time would provide the necessary varied input for learning to occur over time" (1985, p. 214). But as Shatz argues, executive control over language acquisition is likely to reside in the child, the "program host," and cannot be entrusted to the environment because to do so would jeopardize language development.

As we shall see in Chapter 7, human infants, like other animals, actively seek out and selectively work for patterns of stimulation that influence their neural and, therefore, conceptual and perceptuomotor development. Neural and perceptual capacities for spoken language are empowered by genes, nurturant environments, and active, stimulus-seeking infants. From conception, the organism acts upon its environment—structures it as well as responds to it. How we address the infant is greatly influenced by its own behavior:

how the infant looks at us, what noises it makes, and what it does with its face, eyes, and hands. The infant's brain expects to take on the behaviors that lead to spoken language, but it also depends on appropriate stimulation, much of which is elicited or supplied directly by the infant itself.

Continuity

In the last ten or fifteen years there has been a steady accumulation of evidence that the ontogeny of spoken language in children rests upon their earlier vocal and gestural behaviors as infants. Books such as *The Transition from Prelinguistic to Linguistic Communication* (Golinkoff, 1983) and *Precursors to Early Speech* (Lindblom and Zetterstrom, 1986) attest to this interest. But important issues have been left unresolved. We need to know if behaviors heralding the emergence of language are incipient or "proto-forms" of language itself, and we need to know which nonlinguistic cognitive capabilities are required for language. Clearly, we may shed light on these issues by studying species that lack a full-fledged linguistic capacity and by looking at children who have just one thing that is very different about them.

If the growth of behavioral capacity is gradual and continuous, then the child's developmental course will be cluttered with major and minor events that may be regarded as precursors to advances occurring later. It is imperative that we investigate these precursors and yet this area is not without risks. First, we have what is essentially a perceptual problem for scholars. For example, when theorists speculate on the evolution of human language, they immediately run into a wall of disbelief. The reason is that evolution is a great tinkerer, gradually building new capabilities from available parts. A behavioral capability that is precursive to language will be one of these "parts," in effect, a nonlinguistic part, and as such will automatically seem unrelated to language. When we are told, for example, that bimanual coordination may have paved the way to language (MacNeilage, 1986)—however plausible this might be—we still are left wondering how coordinated use of the hands led to language as we think of it now.

A second problem has to do with brain development. If global factors operate to slow the overall rate of brain development, they also may slow the maturation of neural machinery that is dedicated specifically to spoken language. This will be revealed in the form of delayed language and deficits in a number of other things the brain does. Some of these deficits—indeed, the ones we are most likely to witness—will be in functions that appear to be linguistically relevant, such as auditory memory. There will then be the temptation to conclude that language development depends upon the maturation of auditory memory systems, even though the relationship may be epiphenomenal. I will say more about this in Chapter 10.

What are the ontogenetic parts assembled and used in the development of language? After Mundy and Sigman (1989), I will define "precursor" as an earlier, simpler skill that is associated with the subsequent development of a later capacity, but which is not, itself, an expression of that capacity. Like phylogenetic precursors, the ontogenetic factors that activate, reinforce, and empower the capacity for spoken language are not, and therefore do not look, linguistic. If they were linguistic, it could be said at that point in the infant's development that the capacity for language was already operative and therefore the factors proposed were not in fact facilitating or enabling. In principle, a precursor could enable a later behavior or merely facilitate it. According to Alberts and Decsy, facilitative precursors include "stimuli that accelerate maturation. Such precursors have no effect on *whether* a particular feature develops, nor on *which* features develop. They influence only *when* they are manifested" (1990, p. 573, authors' italics).

Which children will be first to achieve linguistic competence is likely to be evident early in the emergence of language, during the period when first words typically appear. For the most part, the child that speaks early, and attains a fifty-word vocabulary while relatively young, is unlikely to stumble or slow down appreciably during later stages of language acquisition (Nelson, 1973). We may therefore assume that mechanisms responsible for the vocal learning and reference required for single word production are the same as or more likely correlated with mechanisms responsible for later developments in the realm of phonology, morphology, syntax, and semantics. The age of first words, in turn, is correlated with events and neural advances occurring in the first year. To understand the source of the child's capacity for spoken language, therefore, we need to know about the infant's development from our earliest opportunity to observe it—typically, from birth. This effort requires us to examine the infant's initial orientation to the human voice, a matter that will be considered in the next chapter.

Uniquely Human?

For centuries, scholars have been unable to resist the impulse to proclaim that language is unique to humans. In 1637, Descartes made a statement to this effect. Among contemporary thinkers, Philip Lieberman has built an entire book around the proposition (Lieberman, 1991). If humans are so obviously different from animals, why does this need to be proclaimed anew by each generation? One possibility stems from religious beliefs, the Christian tradition holding that humans are categorically different from animals, since the former have souls and the latter do not. Anthropological and psychological thinking have apparently been influenced by spiritual teachings of this sort (Gibson, 1990). A second possibility comes from the historical belief, traceable to the ancient Greeks, that humans are the only rational creatures in the universe (Hauser, 1992b).

I think there may be a more concrete reason for persistent recitations of the uniqueness doctrine: we have never been able to put our finger on the nature of the linguistically relevant difference or differences between human and nonhuman primates, and lacking a more specific idea about where the functional differences lay, we could only restate the premise in its most general form. In any case, through the years these reiterations have provoked several animal behaviorists to try to teach chimpanzees to speak (Hayes, 1951), sign (Gardner and Gardner, 1969; Terrace, 1979), or use artificial languages (Premack, 1972) or computerized systems of augmentative vocal communication (Savage-Rumbaugh, 1990). Though at least one ape comprehends some words and commands (Savage-Rumbaugh, 1988), the ability to control expressive speech now seems to be ruled out. Data continue to come in on the question of signed or alternative symbol systems, but it is clear that the question has shifted from nonhuman primates' learning of *spoken* language to their ability to acquire *any other kind* of language.

As special as our linguistic talents and capacities may make us feel, it is unclear to me what scientific benefit attaches to the claim that language is uniquely human. Our linguistic facility certainly seems to set us apart from other species, but the capacity for grammatical behavior rests on social cognition and the neural capabilities associated with motor coordination. Within these domains, many animal species appear to possess the capability for one or more component behaviors, although they lack other requisite abilities. One significant value of interspecific comparisons is that they may isolate those of our capabilities that are indispensable to language and thereby reveal which ones are optional or unrelated.

Comparative Studies

Do human babies differ from infant monkeys and apes as much as human adults differ from mature primates? After all, we share a great percentage of our DNA (Miyamoto et al., 1988) and have some similar physical structures and behavioral mechanisms. According to Kathleen Gibson, "comparative infantile behavior remains a largely untapped research area" (1990, p. 117), although the book in which her chapter appears represents a step in the right direction. The few comparative studies we do have reveal parallels in the ontogeny of human and nonhuman primates and suggest that with continued development the human child surpasses the primate or moves onto different tracks. Nonhuman primates have capabilities that humans could never match, but in other areas, including social communication, humans appear to possess certain of the primate's capabilities and then some.

Scarr (1983) has pointed out that behavioral similarities between species are generally greater among the young. In the early postnatal period, human behavior is panmammalian. Until eighteen months, by her estimate, much of it is panprimate. The sensorimotor skills of nonhuman primates are remarkably like those of human infants, and at three years the parallels may greatly outweigh the differences (Hayes and Nissen, 1971). Of course, an important difference between human and nonhuman primates, as Bruner (1977) has advised, relates to the flexible use and combinatorial quality of sensorimotor schemes, rather than the schemes themselves.

Many of the capabilities we share with primates are the first to develop in the human infant, just as they also were the earliest to evolve. For example, nonhuman primate socialization revolves around affective signaling by voice and face; so do the interactions of human young. Both groups of primates retain their capacity to communicate at that level, but humans additionally take on the more arbitrary and codified means of communicating that we term "linguistic." In effect, aspects of our babies' social cognition resemble theirs, but for us there is a next grammatical step, while for nonhuman primates there is not.

I propose that we can learn a great deal more about the child's development of spoken language by conducting a range of comparative studies. By "comparative studies" I mean to include variations within our own species, such as children who differ in important physical ways or who are growing up in unusual environments. We can also look elsewhere within the animal kingdom for behaviors that correspond or seem analogous to putative linguistic precursors in humans. We are human primates, so it is not surprising that we might occasionally cast a sidelong glance at our "cousins," as some people call monkeys and apes, to see how they develop. Even studies of phylogenetically disparate species, such as songbirds, can suggest to us some things about what we humans are doing and, conceivably, how we might be doing them.

Animal behaviorists have come up with various rebuttals to the linguistic uniqueness claims. One (Greenfield and Savage-Rumbaugh, 1990) goes something like this: if we humans have neural machinery that is responsible for language and little else, if we share a large percentage of our genetic material with chimpanzees (King and Wilson, 1975), and if, as seems certain, language is a polygenic function (Studdert-Kennedy, 1991), then we may not be alone in having capabilities for representation, communication, and many of the operations that contribute to linguistic capacity.

In my view, there is a biolinguistic question that is ontogenetically more important than whether nonhuman primates can be taught to speak or to sign. That question is, how do humans acquire language? If scholars had asked what human and nonhuman primates have in common, they might have spent their time more usefully. Do human infants ever do any of the things that nonhuman primates do? If so, do infants achieve those things before they go on to other things? For even if primates cannot acquire or use a complex vocal code like human language, they naturally communicate their feelings and intentions with vocal and gestural signals. In my view, the more we know about this the more we may understand about the first leg of the species-typical developmental path human infants follow to language. This is the ontogenetic equivalent of the evolutionary approach, which studies apes in order to understand the origins of our own species.

Intraspecific Comparisons

Precedents for comparative studies within our species were established long ago, when researchers (such as Lenneberg, 1962, 1967) described the development of children whose environmental or physical circumstances threatened to alter the developmental course that normally leads to language. And now, when developmental psycholinguists want to identify cognitive prerequisites to language, they often choose to study infants with Down syndrome (Smith and Oller, 1981) or preterm babies with very low birthweight and depressed Apgar scores (Jensen et al., 1988). If my colleagues and I want to estimate the role of audition in vocal development, we look at infants who are deaf or temporarily aphonic or reared by parents who are mute (Oller and Eilers, 1988; Locke and Pearson, 1990; Sachs, Bard, and Johnson, 1981). To understand the role of vision, we analyze the utterances of blind children (Mulford, 1983, 1988). To estimate social contributions, we study language in the neglected or the abused (Fromkin et al., 1974). If we are interested in the role of the vocal tract or motor systems, we document the developmental course of infants with aglossia or cleft palates or focal brain lesions (MacKain, 1984; O'Gara and Logemann, 1985; Marchman, Miller, and Bates, 1991). By virtue of being human, all these individuals have the gross capacity for spoken language, but some will be unable to realize or express that capacity fully.

Continuity of development implies the presence of precursors, and yet, when we begin to investigate precursors to spoken language—in our own young and analogously in other animals—we immediately find that this is not a straightforward matter. First we must identify candidate precursors. Then we must figure out how to

interpret research identifying variables (such as sight) that normally *facilitate* language development but fail to *impede* it when
that variable is absent or disordered. In the sweeping "uniqueness
of language" arguments, with their absolute claims—for example,
that "we" have a lot of linguistic capacity and "they" none of it—
there is a point to be made about the development of language
within our own species. Psycholinguists commonly ask, "If X is a
factor enabling the development of language and Subject #1 has
little or no X, how is it (as is often the case) that the child in fact
got language?" For X, one may substitute hearing, a tongue, a left
hemisphere, normal social relations, and so forth. This is a tough
kind of question to answer, and I am not sure it has ever been
seriously addressed.

My response would be that humans have a strong neural specialization for spoken language, and that like other robustly preadapted behavioral capacities, it takes a lot of physical or environmental interference to knock it down. Each factor that facilitates
language does so in combination with others. Just as the brain is
plastic, so also is the language learning system capable of reorga-
nizing itself in the face of impediments and malfunctions. Language
knowledge and linguistic communication may seem to survive serious sensory and environmental obstacles, but under a different
flag, as it were, with a different allocation of cerebral resources,
mode of phonological and syntactic processing, and organization of
linguistic knowledge. Our conclusion, then, would not be that X
had *no* effect on language; rather, it had a significant *qualitative*
effect on language but no discernible effect on the rate of learning
or size of vocabulary. The type of qualitative effect could vary
owing to differences in the nature of linguistic organization, the
form of internal representations, and the combination of other processing and implementation strategies.

If our interest were limited to humans, we would be prepared to
accept that all humans with a reasonably normal nervous system
possess the capacity for spoken language. As long as the infant has
access to nurturant talkers, it will realize this capacity. Researchers
can look for natural variations in the sensory, motoric, cognitive,
affective, and social domains, individually and in interaction with
one another, and try to relate these variations to certain aspects of
language development and usage. But if the variations are slight,

they may be masked by the robustness of the child's linguistic capacity.

If biolinguists wish to know upon which other capabilities spoken language rests, and why nonhuman primates lack linguistic capacity, then it will be necessary to identify facilitating and enabling factors. This can be somewhat circular, of course, because data from nonhuman primates may help us to determine what the functional precursors to language are in the first place. Moreover, this precursors business can be complicated. For example, in humans we know that if infants have a very small tongue or a lesion in the speech areas of their brain, they may still learn to talk intelligibly because they come from a long line of talkers. Presumably, these defective or missing components would not seriously impair any other species that had a similar lineage. But other animals do not come from a long line of talkers, and that is why their vocal tract, perceptual ability, and other capabilities matter a great deal.

We also need to keep in mind that sensory information is vitally important to all those who can pick it up and process it, who grew up with sensation *being there*. Vision is important to those who see. To show that speech can be comprehended by audition alone does not mean that sighted people are unaffected by visual cues; we know that their interpretation of spoken messages is greatly influenced by eye movements and facial expression, not to mention visible articulatory activity. We also know that the content of a sighted child's initial lexicon is affected by his ability to see lip movements. Showing that a blind child has acquired language is only to say that it must have done so *differently*. If we wish to understand these differences, we must conduct studies of language processing in visually impaired adults.

What will we find? First, by analogy to studies of congenitally deaf adults we can be reasonably certain that in the neural development of blind infants "visual cortex" was up for grabs. Almost certainly a big piece of it would now be owned by the ears. Evoked potentials research would be expected to show this. Behavioral studies may reveal differences in sensitivity to vocal cues that normally signal one's intention to yield or take the floor, message interpretations that are differently attuned to affective information, and a host of "subtle" effects in the way phonological language is processed.

Just as language has several "parts"—phonology, morphology, and syntax, and multiple modes of manipulation and deployment, including speech acts, conversation, and discourse (Snow and Pan, 1993)—its precursors will inevitably be of various sorts and may do their developmental work combinatorially with other precursors. The grand capacity for spoken language, then, is pluralistic, enabled by developments in multiple domains—affective, perceptual, social, vocal, neural, and conceptual. Experience and maturation in these domains empower and enrich, and thereby fully constitute the capacity needed for acquisition of spoken language.

If this is true, however, it seems that we must recognize the existence of a resolving mechanism in the equation, an overseer capable of surveying the assemblage of component parts and insinuating them into roles that produce the grand, species-typical result. According to this view, it might not matter if an infant lacked one of the parts as long as oversight operations were working effectively to coordinate the individual actions of other parts. I suspect that developmental linguistic capacity includes a function of this sort and that language is not, therefore, the sum of its component capabilities. The overall plan for language is implemented by way of these capabilities, much as a tinkerer builds new things from available parts and is stumped only when there is too little of the right material to work with.

A Note on Phylogeny

When the human infant travels the path to spoken language, its behavior—and certainly that of its mother—may suggest some things about how our present way of doing socially communicative business evolved in the species. Finding out how something is, ontogenetically, implies how it might have arisen in evolutionary history and this is intriguing enough in its own right. But my fascination with the relationship between the two is not limited to an interest in phylogeny itself. Rather, when one thinks about how language "takes off" in the infant, one naturally wonders how linguistic capacity may have evolved, and this too begins to look like an ontogenetic matter. (I will speculate further on evolutionary issues throughout this book but especially in the final pages of Chapter 11.)

The Dual Specializations of Human Language

After spending several years reading the animal literature, asking what capabilities we share with other animals, particularly non-human primates, or what we have that they lack, I came to realize something about human language: either it is the product of two highly specialized informational systems or it is due to no such systems at all. As the latter proposition is clearly false, in succeeding chapters I will attempt to develop the thesis that humans have a dual specialization for spoken language. That is, language sits atop two domains of information processing that conjointly gather, analyze, and control all the behavior required by linguistic communication.

Phylogeny has supplied modern humans with specialized phonetic encoding and decoding devices that permit speech communications at the rate of twenty to thirty phonemes per second (Liberman et al., 1967). Nonspeech sounds presented at this rate tend to fuse into a continuous buzz or hum, unlike the perceptibly discrete sounds and syllables of speech. For this and a host of other reasons, it is clear that speech, as so many have said, is "special." But linguistic ontogeny requires more. If we have a coldly analytical and computational system that deals with linguistic grammars it must have access to lots of warmly social behavior, from vocalizations to facial gestures and eye movements. For this we require a set of more personal and interactive capabilities, which nudge infants toward the activities associated with speaking, encourage a modest level of indulgence in like activities, and refer utterance data for appropriate analysis. I hope to demonstrate later that this dual specialization thesis accounts for a number of disparate facts about language development that currently have no uniformly accepted explanation.

If we can learn how to read Nature, she undoubtedly will have a great deal to say about the various factors that influence the course and rate of language development. Natural variations are among the few clues we can use to identify developmentally influential factors. In the last chapter I will look at genetic and neuromorphometric variations that may account for interchild variability in language development, including delays, and the types of damage that can produce linguistic disorders.

*   *   *

In this chapter I have drawn the broad outlines of what I hope will prove to be a biologically responsible and psycholinguistically useful framework for studying the infant's development of linguistic capacity. The framework is complementary to extant ontogenetic theories of language, which for the most part seek to account for various structural or functional aspects of language per se. These theories do not attempt to explain the human infant's gravitation toward behavior that will ultimately be called linguistic or the psychobiological empowerment of the capacities needed to speak.

According to the view adopted here, the human infant does not, and cannot, acquire language as such, but it can begin to travel along a path that, unbeknownst to it, naturally leads to spoken language. I take this to be a critical issue, for unless the infant is motivated to be like people who talk, unless it recognizes that we experience different feelings and thoughts than it experiences, there is simply no reason for the infant to work later at any of the things that language learning requires.

Fair consideration of this approach may require some readers to momentarily set aside their present conceptions about what language is and to attempt to think about what the infant sees and hears when people behave linguistically. The baby studies and is tempted to fall in with talking people for reasons that have less to do with abstract codes for the expression of rational information than with its immediate need for attachment and nurturance.

Ever since the discovery of a continuity between sensorimotor aspects of fetal life and the attainment of linguistic mastery, still to be richly chronicled, we have become able to document—and can now begin to explain—transitions from numerous antecedent behaviors and capabilities to later ones, which ultimately will include orthodox language. Continuity has thus licensed the comparative study of humans infants with atypical anatomies and physiologies or unusual social circumstances. It has also made theoretically useful the comparative analysis of data from other animals who have some of the same, or analogous capabilities. This enables us to be enlightened and allows our theories to be enriched, as never before, by certain of the findings on nonhuman primates and songbirds.

2

FACES AND VOICES:
THE PERCEPTUAL PATH
TO SPOKEN COMMUNICATION

An animal ethologist once asked, "What is it like to be a bat?" (Nagel, 1974), and a recent book by several senior primatologists contains a chapter entitled "What Is It Like to Be a Monkey?" (Cheney and Seyfarth, 1990). These are intriguing questions. Certainly we do not know how bats and monkeys experience the world. But neither do we know what it is like to be a human infant. From a sensory and perceptual standpoint, we might well ask, What is it like to be a baby?

It seems to me unlikely that infants will or could acquire linguistic knowledge without a strong orientation to the cues given off by conversing people. They must tune into the behaviors associated with speaking. I think, then, that the greatest burden on any developmental linguistic theory is to explain why infants pay attention to *the things people do when they use spoken language.* Affective communication is evident at birth. Here, the newborn's face and voice convey information about emotional and physical health as they will continue to do, uninterrupted by the acquisition of language, throughout its life as a child and adult.

In this chapter I will begin to address factors influencing the neonate's orientation to the physical cues given off when people speak, for this perceptual focus encourages the development of the human infant's capacity to interpret the vocal and articulate sounds of others. Because speech cues are embedded in the stream of signals to which prelinguistic infants naturally pay attention, spoken language is made learnable by a synergism between species-typical perceptual biases and the stimulation provided by ambient vocal activity.

Though "instinct" has been contrasted with "learning" for decades, there are several problems with such a neat polarity. First, behaviors that pass as "instinctive" reflect environmental effects, and possibly early learning, that has already taken place (Gottlieb, 1991a, 1991b). Second, ethological research suggests that genetic information actually complements the process of learning (Gibson, 1990). The seemingly "innate" perceptual biases found in young animals is what causes them to pay special attention to certain sensory patterns and therefore to learn particularly about those things. In this sense, "instinct" could be said to guide, perhaps even to enable learning (Gould and Marler, 1987).

One need not look too hard for examples of "learning by instinct." Studies indicate that young honey bees have definite biases with regard to odors, colors, and shapes (Gould, 1984). And well they might; to survive bees need to know about the best sources of pollen and nectar. The sources are flowers, of course, and they are marked by odor, color, and shape. It is not the case, however, that these individual attributes are equally easy to learn about, that is, to associate with reinforcement. Indeed, training studies indicate that odor contrasts may be learned to greater than 90 percent accuracy in just one trial, whereas distinctions within the color and especially within the shape categories require additional training (Gould, 1984).

To understand how spoken language is acquired, we need to ask about the baby's attention to things people do while speaking. In perceptual approaches to language development, there has been a tendency to concentrate upon the *sounds* of speech. But speech sounds are intimately related to visual cues of various kinds. Whereas initially the voice may draw the neonate's attention to its source—the face—the mere appearance of the human face can focus the infant's attention on the vocal sounds of others. The visibly moving face also may stimulate infants to move their own faces, to vocalize, and to imitate the sounds of speech.

Prenatal Learning

Tanner has said that "many developmental events, from the re-
placement of fetal by adult hemoglobin to the appearance of conditioned responses, seem quite indifferent to the fact of birth; their
progression has to await the striking of some differently regulated
biological clock" (1974, p. 77). And yet, the traditional practice in
human development has been to treat birth as the beginning of
experience. But infants are exposed to linguistically relevant stimulation while still in the womb, and there is evidence to suggest
that infants react to prenatal stimulation in developmentally favorable ways. This evidence includes the finding that neonates can
generally distinguish between their own mother's voice and the
voice of another mother, and the observation that newborns seem
to prefer the language spoken by their mother to disparate languages.

Gilbert Gottlieb was among the first to show that behaviors evident very early in the life of an organism are not entirely determined by genetic factors or postnatal stimulation. They are also
influenced by experience that occurs prior to birth. This possibility
was not seriously entertained by behavioral scientists for most of
their history, an omission Michael Studdert-Kennedy (1986) has
ascribed less to theoretical motivation than to the fact that birth
was merely the first convenient opportunity for psychologists to
observe and study behavior. But there was never a scientific reason
to preclude prenatal learning. Indeed, the womb is a "sensational"
place where auditory, thermal, tactile, and other sources of sensory
stimulation, as well as opportunities for movement, occur at a developmental period in which much of the infant's processing machinery is already turned on. Moreover, the fetus' afferent nerves
are hooked up to a rapidly developing and impressionable brain. It
is conceivable, perhaps likely, that some critical decisions are made
for the infant during the final weeks of intrauterine life.

In Gottlieb's work, the environment for early learning was not
intrauterine but *in ovo,* for his classic experiments were conducted
with chicks and ducklings. If placed in an experimental situation
in which conspecific and heterospecific calls are equally available,
chicks typically approach the source of conspecific calls more fre-

quently than the source of heterospecific calls. Questioning whether this effect could be the result of prior learning, Gottlieb noted that duck embryos are capable of hearing at least five days before hatching and begin vocalizing three days before hatching.

Gottlieb reasoned that the duckling's preference for conspecific calls at hatching could be produced by experience with its own voice in the shell and by the greater similarity of its own voice to adult females of its own species. To test this, he temporarily "devoiced" one group of embryos by touching their syrinx with a glue-tipped hypodermic needle and in a control group merely touched the syrinx with a dry needle. At hatching, control chicks showed the usual conspecific effect, but the vocally deprived chicks, as expected, approached conspecific and heterospecific sources equally often (Gottlieb, 1978; see Gottlieb, 1991a, 1991b for a richer account).

Some mammalian fetuses are able to learn about voices too, even heterospecific ones. Vince (1979) stimulated a group of pregnant guinea pigs once a day with loudly played tape recordings of the feeding call of game bantam hens for two or three weeks prior to parturition. A second group of pregnant guinea pigs received no such exposure to bantam hen calls. Several hours after birth, the newborns in both groups were presented with bantam calls. There was less heart rate change in the animals who had received prenatal stimulation than in control animals, who experienced cardiac deceleration at their first hearing of bantam calls. These findings suggested that treated animals were already familiar with the calls from their prenatal exposure. This interpretation was reinforced in postnatal stimulation sessions in which experimental animals responded less to an additional series of bantam calls than control animals. Interestingly, Vince found that guinea pigs vocalized more to conspecific than to heterospecific vocal stimulation, even though the former was less familiar.

A conspecific effect was produced later by Vince and her colleagues (Vince, Billing, Baldwin et al., 1985), who recorded the bleats of pregnant ewes and played them to their newly born lambs. In general, it was found that neonatal heart rates were differently affected by bleats from the animal's own mother than by alien bleats. This selective reaction to the mother's voice was interpreted as a familiarity effect since intrauterine recordings showed that the mother's voice was significantly more intense than vocal sounds originating from outside the ewe.

The Fetal Environment: Where Human Experience Begins

> The fact that a particular capacity cannot be observed at birth does not warrant the assumption that this capacity is "learned" in the usual sense . . . Nor does our limited information about the prefunctional organization of human behaviour justify the assumption that heredity alone accounts for the infant's neuropsychological status at birth.
>
> P. H. Wolff, "Mother-infant Relations at Birth"

Studies reveal that the environment of the human fetus abounds with dynamic sensory stimulation (see review in Smotherman and Robinson, 1988), and the fetus is receptive to much of it. It has been estimated that at two months, the fetus is capable of tactile and vestibular function; at six months, auditory and visual function are possible (Gottlieb, 1971a). Although there is little to see in the womb, it now appears that the fetus has access to a great deal of sound.

FETAL HEARING

How well can the fetus hear? Can the fetus hear noises that originate within its mother? What about sounds whose source lies outside its host? Women who have sat near the bass drum of a symphony orchestra during their final trimester of pregnancy may have some ideas on this, especially if they received a few well-timed kicks!

In several studies (Murphy and Smythe, 1962; Wedenberg, 1965), fetal cardiac activity has been measured during the application of pure tones to the maternal abdomen. Beginning at about twenty-six weeks, heart rate is seen to decelerate significantly a few seconds after presentation of stimuli, especially those sounds in the lower frequency range.

For years, we have tested the auropalpebral reflex (an eye blink to loud sounds) in the human neonate. According to research reported by Birnholtz and Benacerraf (1983), this reflex can be elicited in the fetus. In their study, stimulation was provided by an electro-larynx—the buzzing device used by some individuals who have had their larynx removed—that was set off several inches from the mother's abdomen.[1] Using ultrasound, they continuously observed the fetus' eyelids during stimulus presentation. After about twenty-four to twenty-five weeks of gestation, and certainly by twenty-eight weeks, fetuses blinked to the tones. This occurred immediately, within a half second of the tone, and so forcefully that their blinks were called eye "clenches." These clenches are, thus, the human infant's first recorded facial expression.

Of the 680 fetuses tested between twenty-eight and thirty-six weeks of gestational age, only eight produced no observable eye clenching. Two of these subjects were later found to have severe deafness; the remaining six had a variety of central nervous system anomalies.

ACOUSTICS OF THE WOMB

The six- to seven-month-old fetus may be able to hear, but what is there to be heard? What is known of the intrauterine auditory environment? Using a hydrophone, one group of researchers recorded sound pressure levels near the ear of the fetus in sixteen pregnant women (Walker, Grimwade, and Wood, 1971). They found a fair amount of local noise, which averaged about 85 dB and came mainly from the sound of turbulent blood flow. Above this background, the maternal pulse rose by an additional 10 dB or so. There was also a small amount of extrauterine noise, especially at low frequencies where attenuation is the least.

The fetus can hear external sounds across a frequency range that includes the more intense vocal sounds in adult female voice. Measurements of adult female voice usually reveal a fundamental frequency of about 200 to 250 Hz. Querleu, Renard, and Crepin (1981) found that the mother's voice may rise above background noise by as much as 15 dB in that portion of the spectrum. This is quite sufficient to expose the normally hearing fetus to maternal voice.

---

1. The tone had spectral peaks at 250 and 850 Hz and an intensity level at the abdomen of about 110 dB; this was assumed to attenuate about 15 dB across the abdominal wall.

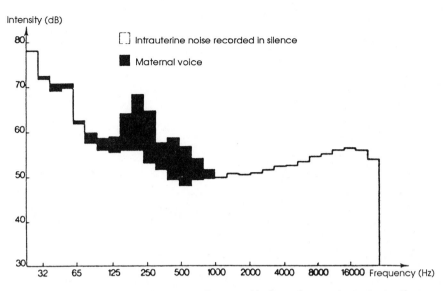

Figure 2.1. Intensity of maternal voice (darkened areas) against other intrauterine noise. Note the large voice-to-noise ratio in the vicinity of 250 Hz, the fundamental frequency of most vocally typical women.

Figure 2.1 is a display of their findings on one mother. In later work by Querleu (Querleu, Renard, and Versyp, 1985), it was found that when the mother speaks at an average intensity level of 60 dB—a conversational level—her voice is about 24 dB more intense than background activity. Female and male voices produced *ex utero* at the same intensity level tend to exceed background sound levels by about 8 to 12 dB.

Later work by a group of researchers in Western Ontario (Benzaquen, Gagnon, Hunse et al., 1990) produced substantially the same findings with a group of ten mothers. Intrauterine recordings were made while the mothers were silent and while they pronounced the number "ninety-nine." Figure 2.2 contains a display of their findings. It is evident that maternal vocalization was more intense than background noise over a range of frequencies extending from about 150 to 275 Hz. As in Querleu et al. (1981), the greatest peak seems to lie between 200 and 250 Hz, where the fundamental frequency of maternal voice usually falls. Listening to audio recordings from the uterus, Benzaquen et al. commented

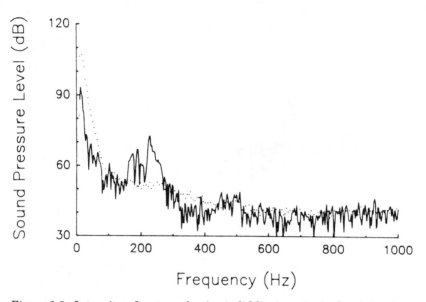

Figure 2.2. Intensity of maternal voice (solid line) against other intrauterine noise (dotted line).

that the pronunciation of ninety-nine "was slightly muffled but clearly audible above the background noise" (p. 487).

AUDITORY AND VOCAL LEARNING

The human fetus responds to sounds, including voices. But can it learn anything about the sounds or voices it hears? A French team (Lecanuet et al., 1986) exposed thirty-seven- to forty-week-old fetuses to three successive presentations of high-pass filtered (800 Hz) noise at just over 100 dB. Noise was presented with a loudspeaker positioned some 20 to 25 cm away from the maternal abdomen at the level of the fetus' head. The rate of cardiac response in quietly sleeping fetuses diminished significantly with stimulus repetition. This suggests that the fetuses adapted to the stimuli.

Is adaptation equivalent to learning? The evidence seems to suggest that it is (Bornstein, Pecheux, and Lecuyer, 1988). Indeed, a wide variety of studies suggests that infants who reveal decrements of attention on various tasks also seem to prefer complex stimulus arrangements, show advanced sensorimotor development, explore their environment rapidly, play in relatively sophisticated ways,

solve problems quickly, attain concepts efficiently, and excel at
oddity identification, picture matching, and block configuration
(Bornstein and Sigman, 1986).

To date, I believe there has been just one reported attempt to
induce and contemporaneously measure vocal learning prenatally.
Lecanuet, Granier-Deferre, and Busnel (1989) found that intrauterine vocal learning can occur and, surprisingly, may include
familiarization with individual speech sounds. The experiment required loudspeakers to be placed on the abdomens of women in their
last trimester of pregnancy. Then, during periods of low fetal heart
rate variability—when higher levels of attention might be available—either [babi] or [biba] was presented at 95 dB every four
seconds. After sixteen presentations of one stimulus, the second
stimulus was presented an equal number of times. One group of
prenatal subjects was exposed first to [babi] and the other heard
[biba] first.

Lecanuet and his colleagues calculated the mean heart rate per
second for the prestimulus and stimulus periods. They found significant decelerations during the first few seconds of a particular
stimulus. Then, as exposure to a stimulus continued, heart rate
returned to normal. When the stimulus was changed from "babi"
to "biba," or vice-versa, heart rates slowed again. In the [babi] →
[biba] group, the presentation of [babi] induced a cardiac deceleration in fifteen of the nineteen subjects. When the stimulus was
changed to [biba], sixteen displayed a deceleration. In the [biba] →
[babi] group, the presentation of [biba] induced a cardiac deceleration in ten of the fourteen subjects, and an equal number showed a
reduction of heart rate when [babi] was introduced.

MOTOR ACTIVITY

In Lecanuet et al. (1989), fetuses also reliably produced leg movements in response to the noise stimuli. This reflects a motoric capability that is present early in fetal life. Indeed, it has been found
that the first spontaneous movements of the fetus occur as early as
7.5 weeks of postmenstrual age (de Vries, Visser, and Prechtl, 1982).
By 15 weeks, these investigators were able to record sixteen movement patterns that closely resembled those observed in newborns.
Somersaults and lateral rotations were also observed during this
period, movements requiring organized limb and body control (Suzuki and Yamamuro, 1985). By its birth day, the human fetus is

yearning to get out of the womb and get moving. In fact, there is evidence to suggest that maternal labor is set in motion by signals from the hypothalamus of the fetus (McDonald and Nathanielsz, 1991).

For nonhuman primates, the day of birth is an active one indeed. Newborn rhesus monkeys have been observed to "deliver them- selves by grasping the mother's leg and pulling themselves from the birth canal . . . the mother makes little or no attempt to aid the neonate in its upward climb to her chest and nipple area . . . almost all the work is done by the baby" (Sackett and Ruppenthal, 1974, pp. 168–169). Nevertheless, we will see later that the motor capa- bilities of human primates develop far later than their sensory systems, an asynchrony that may have interesting implications for emotional and communicative development.

When an expectant mother is kicked by her fetus, and when a fetus learns something about the language spoken by its mother, it becomes obvious that each party affects the other long before birth. But perhaps the most dramatic demonstration of fetal influ- ence was provided by Sackett, Holm, and Landesman-Dwyer (1975). They found that monkeys pregnant with a male fetus were *bitten* significantly less often during pregnancy than those carrying a female fetus. This fetal sex effect began at about three to four months gestation age, when the hormonal requirements of a male fetus normally would first significantly "masculinize" its mother's blood with testosterone. Sackett et al. suggested that this may subtly decrease, in unspecified ways, the mother's perceived "at- tackability."

EARLY POSTNATAL EFFECTS

The intrauterine vocal learning seen in the preceding studies was measured while the fetuses were in the womb. To my knowledge, the other studies of fetal learning have tested the postnatal famil- iarity of prenatal stimulation.

Neonates respond preferentially to stimuli that are familiar. For example, newborns prefer the sound of maternal heart beats, which typically are experienced prior to birth, to their father's voice, which is not as likely to be heard prenatally (Panneton and DeCasper, 1984). If neonates respond in a familiar way to a stimulus that resembles a pattern experienced prior to birth, this may imply prenatal learning. On the basis of intrauterine sound recordings we should expect that female voices will be more familiar than, perhaps even "preferable" to, male voices, and research confirms this. Fifer and Moon (1989) found that newborns suck faster and longer to their mother's or another female's voice than to quiet. In an earlier study, Moon and Fifer (1988) found no more than a weak advantage of adult male voices over quiet, suggesting that both male and female voices are preferred to quiet and that the female effect is, in Moon and Fifer's words, "more potent."

There are reasons to believe that the preference for maternal voice stems from intrauterine experience, apart from or in collaboration with postnatal experience. Most neonates do not have selective access to their mother's voice; rather, they hear a sample of her voice along with the voices of nurses and other women and men. There is also evidence in animals that specifically prenatal experience can produce such effects. For example, Pedersen and Blass (1981) introduced a novel chemical odorant (citral) to the uterine environment of fetal rats. At birth, these rat pups attached to maternal nipples that also were painted with citral, whereas control pups did not.

The preference for maternal voice and the ability to discriminate between male and female speakers are important for several very different reasons. The prospects for nurturance vary across the two sexes, of course, but so do the cues to speech sounds. In speech, identical phonemes may be associated with different spectral cues in the speech of men and women (Peterson and Barney, 1952). One would expect infants to use vocal cues for sex identification, and they demonstrate this discriminative capability by at least two months of age (Jusczyk, Pisoni, and Mullennix, 1989) and continue to show it at seven months (Miller, Younger, and Morse, 1982).[2]

If distressed neonates are comforted by familiar experience, we might expect fussy babies to be calmed by intrauterine sounds. Analyses suggest that when the mother is silent frequencies below 125 Hz are the most intense of such sounds (Rosner and Doherty, 1979; Querleu et al., 1981). Perhaps this is why tones that are low in frequency are more soothing to infants than high frequency tones (Bench, 1969; Birns et al., 1965).

---

2. In principle, I suppose infants could also identify the sex of speakers from facial cues and intermodally activate the appropriate speech recognition program, but I know of no research that shows this.

Acoustic studies indicate that the maternal heart beat is some-what more intense than other low-frequency uterine noise (Querleu et al., 1981; Querleu and Renard, 1981) and for this reason alone we may suspect that the fetus can hear the beating of its mother's heart. If an audiotape of the heart beat is played to neonates, will they be soothed? Salk (1962) found that such treatment caused newborns to cry less and to gain more weight. Rosner and Doherty (1979) observed that an audiotape of intrauterine sounds caused newborns, especially fussy ones, to become significantly less active. In other studies, the maternal heart beat has also been found to effectively reinforce neonatal behavior and thereby to facilitate learning (DeCasper and Sigafoos, 1983; Panneton and DeCasper, 1984).

PRENATAL STIMULATION IN ONTOGENY AND PHYLOGENY

Prenatal stimulation probably affects a number of behaviors and behavioral capacities in the developing infant, several of which have been discussed recently by Fifer and Moon (1988).

Social Effects. Intrauterine exposure to maternal voice may en-courage attachment between the newborn child and the person who is its primary source of sustenance and care. Clearly, the newborn's preference for the voice of its mother selectively orients it to the source of that voice.

Neurodevelopmental Effects. As I will discuss further in Chapter 7, the cortex develops on a competitive basis. The brain's capacity to process information from a particular sensory modality is advan-taged, relative to other modalities, when developing organisms are selectively exposed to stimulation in that modality and not to other stimulation that might compete for the same neural "space." Intra-uterine exposure to sound and not light, other things being equal, should encourage selective development of auditory cortex, if not some more specific mechanism that processes conspecific vocal cues.[3]

---

3. Colleagues of mine at the Massachusetts General Hospital (Weaver and Rep-pert, 1989) experimentally exposed fetal mice to light and postnatally performed autoradiographs through the suprachiasmatic nuclei. They found that brain struc-ture was significantly altered by this prenatal exposure to visual stimulation.

Vocal Orientation. There are several thousand natural languages in the world.[4] All of them are spoken rather than signed, and yet the reasons for this phonological exclusivity have never been explained. Most explanations turn on the inefficiency of imagined alternatives, for example, that primarily visible systems frequently cannot be seen, and that manually encoded messages require hands that may be otherwise encumbered. Moreover, the temptation has been to assume that languages are spoken because speech works so very well. But children easily acquire and use signed languages, and signing is efficient—it conveys complex information accurately and speedily (Meier and Newport, 1990).

There is another possibility. Humans may have developed their communication systems around the modalities toward which their young are biased in early life. Because nonhuman primates make liberal use of the voice to convey information about affective states and the existence of predators, we may assume that prelinguistic hominids vocalized.[5] In addition, contemporaneous studies of kin recognition (Cheney and Seyfarth, 1980; Waser, 1977) and gestural activity (Hewes, 1981) suggest that hominids probably used vocal cues to identify each other and to distinguish acquaintances from strangers but made relatively little use of manual gestures.

Intrauterine exposure to maternal vocal stimulation may be responsible, at least in part, for infants' biases toward the human voice. As there is no visual stimulation during this period of vocal exposure, selective access to intrauterine voice may contribute to vocal primacy in the human neonate and ultimately to our species' capacity for phonetic processing.[6] The plausibility of this effect is suggested by studies revealing that early exposure to stimulation in one modality can interfere with processing of stimuli in another modality. For example, Lickliter (1990) exposed quail embryos to patterned visual stimulation. After hatching, the neonates were

4. When I used the term "natural languages" I refer to languages that have cropped up among normally hearing individuals and are learned spontaneously as a native language, i.e., not invented for special purposes.

5. One is naturally very curious to know whether the nonhuman primate fetus is sensitive to maternal voice given interspecies differences in capacity for vocal learning.

6. It would be interesting to look at the vocal preferences of normally hearing neonates who were born to signing (nonspeaking) mothers.

unusually responsive to species-specific visual cues; relative to un-treated chicks, the prenatally stimulated chicks were more likely to approach stuffed models of conspecific hens, although they dis-played reduced orientation to conspecific calls. In other words, pre-natal exposure to visual stimulation enhanced postnatal response to species-specific visual information and suppressed response to vocal stimulation. I will have more to say later about our species-characteristic bias toward languages that are spoken.

Prosodic Salience. Studies of intrauterine sound transmission and fetal hearing suggest that prenatal learning about spoken language could only be *vocal,* and that prosodic cues are probably the first to be perceived and learned by the neonatal human. The reason is that maternal voice is low-pass filtered; prenatal vocal learning is likely, therefore, to be oriented toward the lower frequencies of the voice, which bear prosodic information (DeCasper and Spence, 1986; Spence and DeCasper, 1987). This may be responsible for the in-fant's prosodic orientation, which mothers discover (or assume) and appeal to when they systematically vary pitch and durational cues in linguistically sensitive ways (Fernald, 1985, 1991; Fernald and Kuhl, 1987).

The Neonate's Sensitivity to Voice

Many accounts of language development ask how the infant ac-quires the adult's ability to perceive speech, but I am not sure that this is an appropriate task for theorists. Suzanne Langer (1988) has said that the brain does not wait for experience, that it develops in one direction or another whether it gets appropriate stimulation or not. The young human does not wait for language either. Infants know little of what is in store for them, so they pay attention to the things that are interesting; many of these stimuli—smells, movements, sounds, and shapes—will have little to do with lan-guage directly, but infants do not know this and are incapable of caring about it. What we need to explain is how the behaviors leading to something as ultimately complex as language get noticed and internally represented and analyzed—in spite of, or in addition to, all the other things on which the infant might focus its cognitive resources.

When the infant first becomes interested in language as we think of it, prosody and affect have long been its primary venue. How is this interest in voice initially revealed? Ironically, the evidence in favor of conspecific vocal preference is less strong than the evidence for the voice of a particular person, the mother. Does the human neonate possess a behavioral bias—a preference—for the voice of its species? There is precious little information on this; for some reason, there have been few attempts to compare neonatal reactions to human voice and to other types of sound.[7] The scanty evidence we do have lies in the neurophysiological realm, where there are indications from EEG studies (Molfese, Freeman, and Palermo, 1975) that different sides of the neonate's brain respond to human voice (vowels) and inanimate sounds (chords), and suggestions from monaural listening experiments using the sucking paradigm (Prescott and DeCasper, in submission) that maternal voice lateralizes differently from nonvocal sounds (heartbeats).

As I have mentioned, maternal voice—by virtue of its internal transmission—escapes the attenuation of abdominal tissue. Perhaps this is why, in the first few days of extrauterine life, neonates display a preference for the voice of their own mother. DeCasper and Fifer (1980) measured the nonnutritive sucking rate of day-old infants; during the same day the mothers were tape-recorded while reading a children's story. Then, a computer was programmed to play the mother's voice every time a neonate sucked with a longer (or shorter) than normal interburst interval, and another mother's voice when the intersuck interval was shorter (or longer) than the basal measurement. These newborn infants were thus in complete control of their listening material. DeCasper and Fifer found that they electively sucked at rates that exposed them to their own mother's voice significantly more often than to the voice of another mother.

The effect occurred in eight of the nine subjects. In the second part of DeCasper and Fifer's experiment, the reinforcement schedule was changed. Four of the subjects who earlier had heard their mother's voice whenever they sucked faster than normal now heard

7. Frankly I am amazed by this. I think we could do with some comparative studies of neonatal reactions to various animal and human voices, and some investigations in which male and female voices are directly pitted against each other.

it whenever they sucked slower than normal, and vice versa for the other woman's voice. This shift did not fool the subjects; they readily did whatever speeding up or slowing down was necessary to keep hearing their mother's voice.

Had the neonates become familiar with their mother's voice in the first few days of extrauterine life? This may seem unlikely since they had no more than twelve hours of postnatal contact with their mother prior to testing and came in contact with many other women (ward personnel) during that interval. However, technically speaking, twelve hours may be enough. Following the finding of a weak effect in earlier research (Simner, 1971), Martin and Clark (1982) observed that at just sixteen hours postnatally, their infant subjects reacted differentially to audio recordings of their own crying as opposed to that of other infants. If quiescent, infants were more likely to be set crying by the voices of other infants; if already crying, neonates were more likely to quit at the sound of their own presumably more familiar vocal cries. If this effect represents postnatal vocal learning, the newborn's preference for maternal voice may also represent postnatal learning.

The neonate's differential reaction to its own voice also suggests that voices in general are interesting to newborn infants. But it is not clear whether the learning of both the maternal voice and the neonate's own voice reflects a conspecific bias to pay attention to human vocalization or whether the baby's interest in its own voice is secondarily derived from a prenatally conditioned familiarity with maternal voice. If a species bias exists, it could be derived from prenatal exposure to a particular member of the species, the mother of the fetus. This would then represent the converse of what apparently happens with ducklings (Gottlieb, 1978). Whereas ducklings are drawn to the mother's voice because it resembles their own voice as heard *in ovo,* the human infant would be attracted to its own voice because it resembles the voice of its mother as heard *in utero.*

Finally, the literature suggests that two-day-olds may be able to learn the difference between a syllable and a short sequence of speechlike sounds. Moon and Fifer (1990) presented neonates of that age with alternations between sequences of [paet] and sequences of [pst]. In a counterbalanced design, if the infant initiated a sucking burst during either of the stimulus sequences, it was exposed either to the mother's voice or to quiet. In this way, [paet] or [pst] effectively became a cue to one contingency or the other. Moon and Fifer found that overall, babies initiated significantly more sucking bursts to the stimulus associated with the mother's voice than to the one associated with quiet.[8]

EXPERIENCE REQUIRED

I think it is significant that the neonates in DeCasper and Fifer's study did not *passively* register a preference for their mother's voice, merely orienting selectively to her voice when it was present. Quite to the contrary, DeCasper and Fifer's neonates learned the rate at which they would have to suck in order to hear their mother, and they expended the oral and respiratory energy[9] needed to get a supply of her voice. They learned the structure of the task and they did the work.

Recent research suggests that the more available speech is to the left cerebral hemisphere, the more newborns like it. In a study of two-day-olds (Prescott and DeCasper, in submission), if a Speech group sucked faster (or slower) than baseline rate, a low-pass filtered recording of a woman reading a passage was presented to the left or the right ear. The sucking of a Heartbeat group was similarly reinforced with a monaural presentation of a pregnant woman's heartbeat sounds. There was a significant *right ear* preference for prosody in that the relative frequency of interburst sucking intervals that resulted in right-ear reinforcement increased over baseline levels, and the relative frequency of interburst intervals resulting in left-ear reinforcements decreased from baseline levels. By the same analysis, there was a significant *left ear* preference for heartbeat. The neonates acted as if they wanted their left hemisphere to be stimulated by speech sounds and their right hemisphere to be stimulated by nonspeech sounds; they brought about this result through their own actions.

8. A similar result was not found with a second group of infants for whom the stimuli were the vowels [a] and [i]. I think differential responses to these stimuli would have made a somewhat more convincing case for linguistically significant vocal learning in that both are vocal and both can serve as phonological units. The other contrast pits a legitimate syllable ([paet]) against a nonsyllabic pattern ([pst]).

9. Exactly how much work they did is difficult to state in terms that most of us would understand. Among full-term neonates, mean peak pressures apparently vary from 50 to 100mmHg according to papers referenced in McGowan et al. (1991).

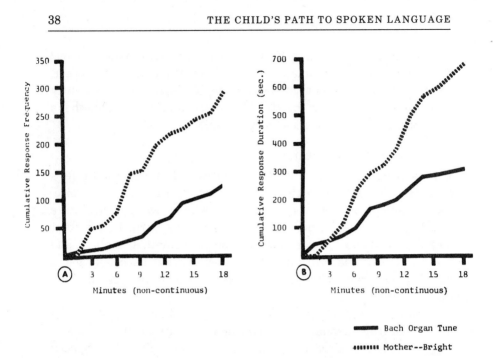

Figure 2.3. His master's voice. A thirteen-month-old boy's preference for his mother's voice over organ music. Panel A displays frequency of responses and panel B shows the duration of responses.

Other research shows that later, at twenty to thirty days of life, infants continue to favor, and to work for, the sound of their mother's voice (Mills and Melhuish, 1974; Mehler et al., 1978). Older infants also indicate a willingness to work for their mother's voice as opposed to music or to a stranger's voice. Friedlander (1968) installed a self-stimulation apparatus in the playpens of three infants at eleven to fifteen months, hooking up two cylindrical plastic knobs to one type of taped stimulation or another. To receive stimulation, the infants had to manually displace a cylinder in any direction, continuously, with a force exceeding two ounces in any direction. As Figure 2.3 reveals, one infant immediately set to work, displaying a preference for his mother's voice over the sound of music.

Glenn and Cunningham (1983) used a similar apparatus with Down syndrome and nonretarded children at the developmental ages of approximately nine and eighteen months. At both ages, subjects worked harder, operating the manipulandum more persistently for a children's rhyme than a piano tone and expending greater effort to hear a tape of their mother speaking to them than to hear a tape of her addressing one of the experimenters.[10]

Later in the chapter I will revisit the perceptual proactivity of infants. In the meantime, we might ask how far intrauterine vocal learning really goes. On the day of its birth, how much does Baby already know about the way we talk?

FETAL LEARNING OF SPECIFIC LANGUAGES?

Neonates do not merely prefer the resonance properties of their mother's voice. They also seem to prefer her vocal movements in effect—as we adult observers think of it—the *language* that she spoke when they were still in the womb. Jacques Mehler and his colleagues (Mehler et al., 1988; Bertoncini et al., 1989) have found that at four days of age, babies born in Paris of French-speaking women prefer the sound of French to Russian. Babies whose mother spoke a different language during pregnancy lack this preference for French over Russian; indeed, they give little evidence that they even discriminate these languages.

The finding of Mehler's group presumes that Russian and French can be differentiated on the basis of low frequency cues of the type that are generated by a mother's voice and carried through her tissues and fluids to the ear and brain of the fetus. To my knowledge, however, this has not been tested and in fact there have been few efforts to demonstrate the distinctiveness of languages in that restricted region of the spectrum that carries maternal fundamental frequency (Cohen and Starkweather, 1961; see, however, Fernald's [1989] interesting analyses of infant responses to low-pass filtered maternal prosody).

The neonate's preference for its native language would presumably be strongest at birth, since the effect implicates a familiarity derived from fetal stimulation. However, Mehler later reported that

10. At various places in the book I will take a look at the data from infants with Down syndrome, as I have here. In doing so I am aware that intergroup differences will frequently be difficult to interpret. Down children have many characteristics that differentiate them from normally developing infants, just as nonhuman primates differ from human ones in many ways. Nevertheless, it is helpful to see where populations such as these do *not* differ from "controls."

"the most recent results . . . show that the infant under twelve hours of age does not respond differentially to French and Russian utterances as do four-day-olds. Indeed, at that age there is no preference" (1989, p. 207). Obviously, more research of this type is needed on the very early postnatal reactions of infants.[11]

Visual Factors in Vocal Learning

Every speaker knows that spoken language can be transmitted by audition alone. We do not always look at our addressors—sometimes we are physically prevented from doing so—and often we cannot see our listeners. This does not mean, however, that there are no visual concomitants of speech, or that facial expressions are irrelevant. Indeed, it appears that some strictly auditory (for example, telephone) communications are essentially compensatory by their very nature; that both parties, aware that they cannot see each other, structure their discourse in fundamentally different ways (Argyle and Cook, 1976).

Visual factors are important to the ontogeny of vocal communication from the first postnatal seconds of life, and they continue to exert enormous influence on phonetic learning throughout infancy. I will launch our exploration of this issue by asking what difference it makes if the infant can see the individuals from whom it must learn about vocal movements and sounds, and the things to which they refer. Later, I will join those who speculate that visual factors may have played an evolutionary role in the emergence of linguistic capacity in the species.

There has been some research on the contribution of vision to vocal learning in songbirds. This research indicates that if a prospective tutor does not *look* like a conspecific, its song may be ignored and is unlikely to be imitated. In one study, N. S. Clayton (1988) placed either a young zebra finch or a young Bengalese finch in a cage with two adult males, which served as surrogate fathers

11. This does not eliminate the possibility that the mother's face originally became "special" because it was seen to be the source of her already familiar voice. Mills and Melhuish (1974) have stated that from the time of their birth, "babies will turn towards the source of a sound, and this orientation to a voice helps them to learn about faces . . . infants are more interested in their mother's face when she is talking" (p. 123).

and song tutors. One tutor was a zebra finch that had learned the song of Bengalese finches in its youth. The other tutor was a Bengalese finch that had learned to sing zebra finch. In other words, each tutor looked like (and was) one kind of finch but whistled the tune of another kind. Whose song, Clayton asked, will the young finches learn? Which of the two tutors will the young birds seek to copy? The answer was clear. The young finches learned the song of the conspecific, the bird that looked like a member of their own species (or at least looked like the young finch), even though it sang an alien tune.

How do young finches know, from looking, which birds are members of their species? One hint is available in Salzen and Cornell's (1968) study of chicks, which were dyed green or red just after hatching and reared with birds of the same color or in isolation from other birds. Eight days later, the chicks were placed at a choice point. One path led to a cage of red chicks, a second to a cage of green chicks, and a third to an empty cage. The socially reared chicks preferentially approached the cage containing chicks of a color that matched that of their companions and themselves. The chicks reared in isolation went toward their own color more often than toward the opposite color, but the effect was much weaker than in the socially reared chicks. With an additional adjustment, Salzen and Cornell found that this moderate effect may have been produced by self-perception, for it was obtained only in birds whose cage had a container of drinking water, which could conceivably have acted as a mirror. Chicks that drank from a pipette and were unable to see their own reflection showed no preference for birds of a similar color.

Clayton thought that conspecific effects such as hers suggested the likelihood of better rearing by an adult of one's own species and better quality interactions with conspecifics. This is congruent with an experiment (Eales, 1987) in which zebra finches learned the song of Bengalese finches, with which they were given a chance to interact, rather than their own species, which they could only see and hear in an adjacent cage. This suggests that to learn a song, finches must be able to *interact* with tutors during the sensitive phase of song learning.

Access to the vocalizations of one's species, then, may not be enough. The availability of appropriately interactive tutors are a telling part of the story. One presumes that the same is true of human infants; more will be said about their reaction to such visuo-social factors in the next chapter. But in the meantime we might ask some more specific questions about the *anatomy* of perception and social interaction. If vision is helpful, what must young learners have in their sights? Do feet or elbows or knees play a role?

The Linguistic Face

Perhaps the most salient sight to the newborn is the human face. Neonates eagerly address the face and keep careful watch on things that faces do. What biological purpose is served by this? I believe facial surveys such as these answer several very salient questions. One is whether the faces that are observed belong to humans and are therefore biologically equipped to offer nurturance and protection. And if they do, an additional question, answerable with facial configurations and movements, is whether these particular faces have a personal interest in providing for the baby's care.

But if they are to survive, it would be adaptive for the newborns of a social species such as our own to start up or join into a phatic communion with the mature humans who (optionally) surround them. Faces are avenues of communication that continuously signal the intentions and evaluations of others. How, but for facial and vocal signals, will neonates know which ambient events are potentially worrisome? Without the visible movements of the eyes and mouth, and the audible actions of the vocal tract, how will babies proceed to interact with others?

Faces are a major instrument of affective and social communication, and I believe faces play a developmental linguistic role: they help launch the normal neonate on a trajectory that, with other capabilities and experiences, will lead to the acquisition of spoken language. For the face not only conveys emotion directly, it is also the origin of the human voice. Because the mere sight of their mother's face is physiologically arousing (Field, 1979), infants who see the maternal face "talk" are likely to notice aspects of her speech. Even silent movements of the face, especially of the mouth and eyes, command the infant: PAY ATTENTION TO THIS ACTIVITY!

Let us examine a very special developmental role of the human face, the linguistic role. In the following pages I will propose that the physical cues associated with faces and voices conspire to promote and configure the infant's phonetic learning.

Evidence from various quarters suggests that voices and faces are linked on several levels of function, a linkage that is manifested in many ways. First, actions of the voice and face have the authority to reinforce, intensify, weaken, annul, or contradict the nominal message in a linguistic communication. Second, the capacity to store and retrieve information about faces and voices appears to develop in parallel in the human child. Third, voices and facial movements seem to have been functionally joined at several points in phylogenetic history, and certain of their actions now appear to share neural substrate, suffering similarly when that tissue is damaged.

"NONVERBAL" COMMUNICATION: RUBBISH OR RICHES?

Both the face and the voice convey social signals and serve as channels for emotional expression. Over a century ago, Charles Darwin observed that "the force of language is much aided by the expressive movements of the face and body" (1872, p. 354). With or without awareness, vocal and facial activity specify an intensity appropriate to the words used to convey thoughts. Working together or independently, voice and face cues intensify or weaken the illocutionary force of speech, and they may even contradict the nominal message (see Knapp, 1972, pp. 8–12, for a list of such effects). In cases of intended deception, these "paralinguistic" cues may also be the speaker's undoing (Ekman and Friesen, 1969).

Jonathan Miller (1990) has raised eloquent questions about the force of "nonverbal" communication—facial, vocal, gestural—in social exchanges outwardly manifested as "verbal." He asked what would be left over in verbal messages if nonverbal cues were eliminated: "For anyone who regards *language* as the canonical form of human communication, the answer would probably be 'Not much is left over' and the residue, such as it is, is either a redundant supplement to words—something which the telephone shows we can do without—or else a sadly impoverished alternative which we are sometimes compelled to use when circumstances make the ordinary use of words awkward or impossible" (p. 115, italics his).

But in reality, if speech were removed the leftovers would include "a rubbish heap of nudges, shrugs, pouts, sighs, winks and glances . . . the behavioural exhaust thrown out of the rear end of an extremely high-tech linguistic machine" (p. 115). Millers' own view is that "eliminating words and sentences exposes a level of communication of unsuspected richness, one in which human beings express their true meanings" (p. 113).

How does the field of linguistics value these rich sources of meaning? The answer is disappointing. Gesture, the use of the face and hands to convey feelings and thoughts, has been almost completely ignored. A major category of "nonverbal" vocal cues—prosody—has traditionally been relegated to the sidelines. A clue to the reasons emerged recently when Dwight Bolinger (1989) published a monograph arguing that intonation cannot be considered a grammatical matter because it is directly linked to emotion. Of course, the factors that cause prosody to be uninteresting to linguists make it unusually useful to babies and apparently to the adults who, by their speaking habits over the ages, have designed all our linguistic systems!

Historically, psycholinguists have not done much better than linguists. One reason is that they bought into linguistics as practiced, and therefore took on the aprosodic views of that discipline. Because most psycholinguists were trained in experimental psychology, they also tended to see their subject matter coldly, as did lab psychologists of the day. According to Lazarus (1991), "there was a perplexing resistance to emotion in mainstream academic psychology until the 1960s, especially during the heyday of behaviorism and logical positivism" (p. 4). Since theories of language acquisition were generally crafted by psycholinguists, these individuals carried their indifference to emotion directly into language with them. The result, of course, is theories that say nothing about the infant's interest in the things people do when talking.

Mapping onto cognitive science as they do, neurologists could hardly avoid making the same mistake. According to Le Doux (1992), neurology has followed psychology's lead by paying unusual attention to memory, attention, and perception, and rarely taking emotion seriously. Because cognitive models lack emotional and motivational components, neuroscientists have seen little reason to explain processes that are not integral to behavior as conceptualized.

Since linguistics has continued to ignore vocal and gestural communication, less is known about these aspects of language than about structural elements and grammar. This invites the inference that the latter are preeminently important in communication; it is easy to misinterpret "no evidence of an effect" as "evidence of no effect." But the flaws in just such an inference will become increasingly obvious as we witness again and again the communicative significance of prosodic and facial signals.

Because the face is the spatial origin of voice and face movements are responsible for many of the vocal modulations that make up speech, perhaps we should not be surprised to find a variety of visual effects in speech. What about speech without vision? When the telephone was first gaining currency, there was so much practical concern about this question that the British Post Office, the Bell Telephone Laboratories, and the Australian Post Office all commissioned studies of the effectiveness of vocal communication without visual cues. According to Argyle and Cook, the British Post Office "found that a considerable proportion of the population never use the telephone and, it is presumed, cannot" (1976, pp. 164–165).

Research shows that when they are in visual contact, listeners are better able to judge from the gaze patterns of speakers whether they are being told the truth. Speakers produce more different words and longer utterances when they can see their listeners, and they have an easier time with the coordination of turn taking (Argyle and Cook, 1976). In fact, interruptions occur least commonly when the listener's visual field is limited to the speaker's eyes (Argyle, Lalljee, and Cook, 1968).

Visuofacial processing plays a crucial role in the give and take of conversations. This is so deeply natural to speakers that they tend not to notice the amount of social *work* accomplished by their own transmission and reception of gaze signals. When Kendon (1967) made videotapes of seven people conversing with one other individual, he found that

> at points in the interaction where the speaker and auditor exchange roles, the speaker characteristically ends his utterance by looking at the auditor with a sustained gaze and the auditor characteristically looks away as he begins to speak. It is suggested that the speaker, by looking at the auditor, signals to him that he is ready for him to start speaking, as well as being able to see whether this signal has been

received. In looking away, the other person signals that he has accepted the "offer" of a change of role. (p. 60)

Not surprisingly, when conversors are denied visual access to these regulatory devices, they have more difficulty synchronizing speech turns (Argyle, Lalljee, and Cook, 1968).

In signed languages, although they are frequently referred to as *manual* languages, a great amount of regulatory and linguistic information is conveyed by movements of the face and eyes (Baker, 1977). In American Sign Language (ASL), the desire to take or yield the floor is expressed facially, and some lexical items are formed solely by facial gestures. Moreover, movements of the face lend a sense of "prosody" to signed messages, intensifying content generated by the hands. To comprehend ASL, then, it is necessary to watch the signer's face as well as his or her hands, and in any case it is considered socially rude not to look at the face while signing is going on (Baker, 1977).

Movements of the face and voice may be regarded as nonlinguistic behavior by social scientists, but to the developing infant they are not "non" anything. They attract and sustain the infant's attention to what will become a linguistically important stream of cues.

The Ontogeny of Face Identification and Perception of Facial Affect

NEONATAL ATTENTION TO THE HUMAN FACE

As I noted earlier, newborns pay close attention to the human voice as soon as they hear it after birth, and they are nothing if not fascinated by the face. Figure 2.4 contains four simple drawings that were shown to newborns at the age of nine minutes, before they saw any human faces that were not masked (Goren, Sarty, and Wu, 1975). The drawings were not presented statically but were moved across the neonates' visual field. These nine-minute-olds looked significantly longer at the reasonably normal, though still highly stylized one on the upper left than at the scrambled faces, which were nonetheless preferred to the unfilled outline of a face.

A research team headed by Mark Johnson and John Morton has replicated Goren et al., reported and clarified some of the later

Figure 2.4. Visual stimuli shown to newborns. Subjects looked longer at the pattern in the upper left panel.

developing effects, and resolved apparent discrepancies with a two-process theory of the ontogeny of face perception. By analogy, this theory may also say something of importance about the development of auditory and speech perception, and I will comment on that later on. In their initial experiment, Johnson and Morton used the Goren et al. stimuli with infants whose mean age was thirty-seven minutes. Like the original study, they found that a moving facelike pattern elicits more visual following behavior than does a nonface-like pattern (Johnson et al., 1990).

If nine- and thirty-seven-minute-old infants prefer the intact and properly oriented human face compared to other visual stimuli of similar complexity and type, how are we to understand the failures—too numerous to mention here—to find such effects in one-month-old infants? A second experiment by the same team (Johnson et al., 1992) reversed the earlier arrangement. This time schematic faces were displayed on a screen and the neonate's chair was rotated past them. Using this method, the investigators observed a *decline* in facial preference between four and six weeks of age, with a *return* to neonatal levels of performance by two months of age. What explains the loss and resumption of the infant's preference for faces? Why is there such an uneven developmental course?

Johnson and Morton (1991) have proposed a two-process theory in an effort to account specifically for the discontinuity. According to their theory, the newborn's preference for the face, which they call CONSPEC, represents knowledge of conspecific facial characteristics. This knowledge is "innate" in the sense that it comes to exist without specific exposure to faces. Morton and Johnson think the neuroanatomic substrate of CONSPEC is generally subcortical, more specifically in the superior colliculus, which appears to be involved in attention and orientation to stimuli. They also note that the retino-collicular pathway develops in advance of retino-cortical connections, which may not begin to function until about two months of age (Atkinson, 1984; Maurer and Lewis, 1979).

As that age and level of maturation draws near, the cortex begins to receive and process information about faces and by two months is able to do so. Then the second mechanism—CONLERN—kicks in, and the infant is able for the first time to learn about particular faces. The seemingly dormant interval in between, according to the theory, is neurologically unavoidable; the subcortex is shut down and the cortex has yet to fully assume its responsibilities.

From an operational standpoint, the initial face orientation mechanism (CONSPEC) does not itself do facial learning. Instead, it enables this learning by directing the infant's attention to the features of faces. The cortical structures associated with CONLERN, when they are able to receive and process patterned information from the eye, perform the infant's learning about particular faces.

If the "on again-off again" appearance of face preference behaviors need not pose explanatory problems for neurodevelopmental theories, as we have seen, such variability should not threaten existing conceptions of behavior development either. For as Fischer and Bidell (1991, 1992) have recently argued, skills and concepts usually do not burst onto the scene in full flower. Rather, they tend to emerge over a period of developmental time as progressions to ever more complex forms and decreasingly supportive contexts. Each step in the sequence represents a further expression of behavioral capacity, revealed gradually. This developmental framework, Fischer and Bidell note, "moves beyond arguments about whether or not a behavior shows a capacity. The behavior fits a point in an epigenetic pathway moving toward what eventually becomes a rich and powerful skill" (1992, p. 11). This avoids arguments over precisely when some particular capacity may be present.

EARLY FACIAL LEARNING

We have seen that within the first few days of life, neonates react to their own mother's voice differently than they do to the voices of other mothers. This effect might be the result of prenatal learning, as mentioned earlier. That it could also reflect postnatal experience is suggested by the fact that neonates respond to their own voice differently than they do to the voice of other neonates.

Similar preferences have been expressed for the mother's face. At the age of forty-five hours, the newborns in one study (Field et al., 1984) looked longer at the face of their mother than at the face of other adult females. Although this preference for the mother's face was particularly strong if they also heard her voice, the effect was statistically reliable even when the mother was silent at the time of test.[12] The investigators admitted, however, that they had ne-

12. Olfactory research also indicates that mothers typically smell more like their infant than they smell like other women—evidently not because of assimilation of odor, but because mothers and infants share a genetically mediated smell (Porter, Cernoch, and Balogh, 1985; Porter, Balogh, and Makin, 1988)—which leaves unclear how much if any learning is involved in other findings that two days after birth, mothers can olfactorily discriminate their own infant from other infants (see review in Fleming, 1990).

glected to, and logically needed to control for olfactory cues. The reason is that breast-feeding infants are very sensitive to their mother's odor and can discriminate her from other women using olfactory cues alone (MacFarlane, 1975; Balogh and Porter, 1986; Cernoch and Porter, 1985; Porter et al., 1992).[13]

Bushnell, Sai, and Mullen (1989) eliminated both odor and vocal cues and still obtained a reliable maternal face preference. In their research, forty-eight-hour-olds were presented with the live face of their own mother or a different mother. Looking time analyses revealed a significant preference for the mother's face in these two-day-old infants.

How could the newborn child learn the image of its mother's face so quickly? After all, it has been estimated that during daylight hours the newborn is not even visually alert more than 3 percent of the time (White and Held, 1966) and cannot see all that well anyway (Leehey et al., 1975). We can only assume that the face has been of such importance phylogenetically that at birth, the infant's first opportunity to look at and extract information from the face, there is something approaching one-trial learning. As Bushnell et al. (1989) have suggested, exposure to the pairing between the mother's face and her voice—already familiar from intrauterine exposure—may facilitate this preference.

Whatever the precise mechanisms, it appears that by the end of their second day of postnatal life most neonates recognize the face, voice, and odor of their mother. It is as though Nature has taken no chances on the neonate's bonding with the wrong person. Nature has also created safeguards so that mothers will not confuse their own child with someone else's. The evidence is that this happens rarely with nonhuman primate mothers, who seem to have an uncanny ability to identify their young even during unstable social circumstances (Nicolson, 1991). For example, pigtail macaque females who were separated from their infants at birth responded preferentially to them up to a month later (Sacket and Ruppenthal, 1974).

But let us return to the question of early facial learning that we raised earlier. If the subcortical CONSPEC is incapable of learning,

13. Though many of us get a fair amount of mileage out of exclamations such as *ah-ha, oh, wow, ah,* and so forth.

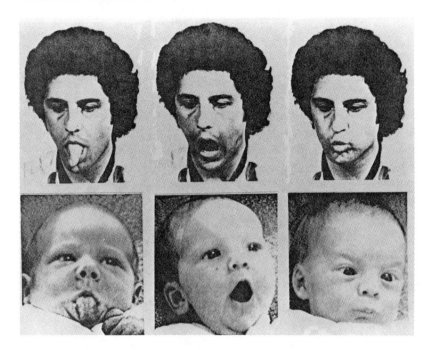

Figure 2.5. Stimulus faces of Andrew Meltzoff and a young mimic.

how do Morton and Johnson interpret neonatal preference for the mother's face? It is not clear that this finding can be accommodated by the two-process model, as currently structured, since in additional analyses of their data Johnson et al. found no positive correlation (indeed, a weakly negative one obtained) between age and the face preference over the 20- to 126-minute age range represented by their subjects (nor did Bushnell et al. [1989] find a positive correlation over a similar age range).

If CONSPEC had some learning potential, it could account for certain discrepancies that have turned up in studies of early facial imitation. A few years ago, Andrew Meltzoff startled Piagetian psychologists with the finding that neonates are capable of reproducing facial gestures immediately after birth (Meltzoff and Moore, 1977), even at forty-five minutes (Meltzoff, 1986). Inexplicably, by learning-based accounts, this behavioral capability is in place before the infant has had the opportunity to see its own face. Figure 2.5 shows a baby responding in kind to three of Meltzoff's facial configurations—tongue protrusion, mouth opening, and lip protrusion.

Though the finding has been replicated in at least seven independent labs since the original report (Meltzoff and Gopnik, 1989), there is no satisfactory explanation of how neonates do this in advance of what would seem to be the requisite experience. Meltzoff's own hypothesis, in less formal detail but in a way not inconsistent with the subcortical CONSPEC mechanism, invokes nonspecific constitutional factors. It is possible that these effects represent *contagion,* a social process by which a behavior spreads, more or less unconsciously, from one individual to nearby observers. Contagion is just now being addressed in an appropriately formal way by Brothers (in submission), who sees contagion as the beginning of a developmental progression that eventuates in the capacity to share in group life. Later, I will consider a similar two-process theory for the infant's evolving capability for speech perception, one that accounts for the infant's seemingly adultlike performance on a range of subtle contrasts prior to a great deal of phonetic exposure and in an early stage in the development of auditory cortex.

In the meantime we might ask: When neonates see their first faces, which facial parts are of the greatest interest? It seems logical that infants might first identify the species of other animals by looking at the appropriately contrastive features and then focus selectively on the moving parts that are capable of conveying attitudes and emotion. In very young infants there is a preference for facial boundaries that may assist with species identification. But I can find no reports of scanpath analyses with newborns, and therefore no indication of what they look at first or the order in which they apprehend individual structures.

Nevertheless, we do have indications of infants' looking preferences. Haith, Bergman, and Moore (1977) recorded the visual fixation patterns of infants while looking at their mother's face or at a strange male or female face (no familiarity effect was found). The infants were equally divided across three age ranges from three to eleven weeks. The mothers were to look at their baby without any expression ("still"), while gently swaying from one side to the other ("moving") or while continuously talking to the infant ("talking"). Measurements were made of the infants' visual fixations on the periphery of the face and on the eyes, nose, and mouth.

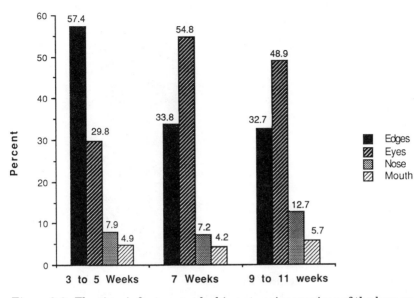

Figure 2.6. The time infants spent looking at various regions of the human face.

As Figure 2.6 reveals, all groups spent the least time looking at the mouth, about 4 to 5 percent, which is interesting in light of infants' strong tendency to imitate mouth movements. The next smallest amount of looking time involved the nose. The youngest infants spent the greatest amount of their time looking at the edges of faces and much less time fixated on the vicinity of the eyes. In contrast, the two older groups, who behaved similarly, spent less time on facial edges and more time in the eye regions.

Studies of rhesus monkeys reveal a similar looking preference for eyes—even in black and white photographs—whether the subjects are other rhesus monkeys, chimpanzees, humans, or schematic drawings, and regardless of facial expression (Keating and Keating, 1982). The eyes remained the primary visual target even when the monkeys were shown conspecific faces that were grinning or threatening, that is, "despite the presence of prominent mouth gestures" (p. 216).

Figure 2.7 depicts the fixations of two older groups of human infants for the still condition (moving was essentially the same as still) and the talking condition (Haith et al., 1977). I find it partic-

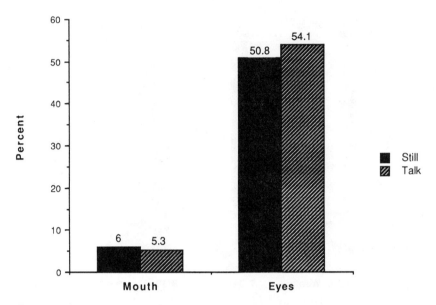

Figure 2.7. Changes in infants' visual attention for a speaking as opposed to a still face. Note the slight increase to the eyes when the mouth starts moving.

ularly interesting that when the adults talked, infants' visual fix-ations shifted slightly away from the mouth—a moving structure—to the eyes. The effect is not a huge one, but it intrigued the investigators; they commented that "there is no obvious reason why talking should enhance" the appeal of the eyes, a finding which "suggests that visual perceptual activity is not determined by visual stimuli alone" (p. 854).

When adults speak to babies, their eyes surely do not move as conspicuously as their jaw and lips. Perhaps the shift of attention from the mouth to the eyes occurs because talking is associated with increases in activity in the peri-orbital region. I am more intrigued, however, by the possibility that speaking is implicitly regarded as a personal act, and that information that supports (or disconfirms) one's words is expected to be available in the region of the eyes—those social organs that convey interest and excitement, enjoyment and joy, distress and anguish, fear and terror, shame and humiliation, and anger and rage (Argyle and Cook, 1976). Now if a speaker conveys any one of these emotions, I wonder why we should not naturally include the eyes—along with the tongue, lips, and jaw—as full-fledged members of the "articulatory" system.

The eyes (or other aspects of the face) may be important even in processing the more mechanical aspects of speech. Greenberg and Bode (1968) presented college students with a silent videotape of a person speaking monosyllabic words embedded in a short carrier phrase. In one condition, the speaker's entire face was visible. In a second condition, only the lips and mandible of the speaker could be seen. It was found that when vision was limited to the lips and mandible, lipreading performance was moderately though significantly reduced. There are other such studies of word reception, but I will not review them here because they unfortunately do not tell us what we would most like to know—how, in natural conversations, the quality of listeners' interpretations of intended meanings varies with visual access to speakers' eyes. To my knowledge, this incredibly rich domain has only been partially explored.

The Communication of Human Intentions

In reference to television, Marshall McLuhan is remembered for his observation that "the medium is the message." The meaning of this, he explained, is that "the 'content' of any medium is always another medium" (1964, p. 23). The physical content of human conversation is vocal and facial; purely by talking, adults display affective signals that attract the interest of babies. Moreover, simply by observing talkers, neonates get exactly what they want and are prepared to interpret in light of their own needs. For when speakers generate sentences, they produce utterances replete with vocal and facial affect. From the standpoint of the speaker the medium is talk, whether it is expected to be comprehensible or not. From the standpoint of the infant the thing conveyed is emotion, and it is completely intelligible on that level. The neonatal observer is well equipped to interpret alterations of voice and face, including mouth and eye movements, which express so directly our attitudes about infant listeners and the messages we want them to absorb.

Listeners cannot make useful sense out of most personally relevant utterances without knowing the intentions of speakers. They infer intentions in a variety of ways, usually by putting together a speaker's verbal and nonverbal actions with assumptions about the relevance of the speaker's behavior to their own life circumstance, and to the immediate situation in which both individuals happen to find themselves.

In an intriguing elaboration of Gricean assumptions, Sperber and Wilson (1988) argue convincingly that knowing a person's intention in speaking is frequently communicatively sufficient, in and of itself. The nominal content of the message may be redundant, vacuous, or unimportant for other reasons. "Communication is successful," they say, "not when hearers recognize the linguistic meaning of the utterances, but when they infer the speaker's 'meaning' from it" (p. 23). The special importance of this view of communication is that many of the cues used to infer intentions—facial and vocal gestures, situational facts—are transparently available to the linguistically naive observer. Even the family dog may sense that his masters are speaking angrily.

In discussions of the well-known Clever Hans phenomenon, psychologists and animal behaviorists have drawn attention to the subtlety of vocal and bodily cues that individuals give off unconsciously. Reconstructions of the case suggest that if Hans's trainer knew the correct answer, his horse picked it up, probably from a slight inclination of the trainer's head. But what came across as a "trick" in the Clever Hans case apparently was not a trick at all. Hans's trainer thought his horse actually knew the answers to the difficult questions he was posed. This is not surprising. Since in speaking our only intent is, in fact, to speak, we pay little attention to any nonspeech cues we might convey. In a discussion of the Clever Hans phenomenon, Stebbins (1990) has pointed out that "many nonverbal cues of the sort which might enable a nonhuman animal to respond appropriately without having genuinely acquired linguistic skills take place in ordinary human conversation. Some are redundant, and some not, but in most cases the presence of subtle cues vastly increases the ease of expression and understanding. Much human conversation would founder without them" (p. 271).

There is every reason to believe that human infants pick up and react to these cues, proving that they understand perhaps the most important information that can be conveyed to babies, information about speakers' (that is, prospective caregivers') emotions and intentions.

Although we are fond of stating that spoken messages are carried by waves of vocal prosody, from the infant's point of view, and perhaps even from the adult's, the situation is exactly the opposite. Prosody is not a by-product of sentences. In many cases, our only reason for speaking may be to reveal our intentions or feelings to others. But because civilized humans do not characteristically reveal these things vocally without speaking, we quickly assemble a few convenient sentences and express them, and while doing so the listener is exposed to the vocal signals that reliably convey our intentions. It will usually be completely redundant to say "I am angry with you!" if our voice also conveys this feeling. But speaking gives us the opportunity to literally *voice* our concerns.

Where I believe linguists and psycholinguists have given affective vocal communication too little of their attention, some primatologists believe that their colleagues may have done just the opposite. Primate vocal behaviors include discrete categories of vocalization, calls that appear to have "meaning" of some sort, as well as continuous or graded forms that convey emotionality. "Most calls probably contain both discrete and graded components," wrote one team of primatologists, "and overemphasis on the latter may discourage the experimental testing of the information content of the former" (Smith, Newman, and Symmes, 1982, p. 31). But human speech also contains linguistic and affective messages, and unlike the primatologists, I contend that overemphasis on discrete segmental contrasts has discouraged appropriate attention to graded variations of vocal affect and prosody.

There may be several reasons for this lack of interest in vocal affect and prosody, ranging from the lack of an appropriate notational system to problems of instrumental measurement and to some fundamentally mistaken notions about the "rational" or "logical" nature of "Man." Perhaps the primary etiology of this "prosodic neglect" is the fact that unlike other animals, humans do not commonly convey vocal affect without speaking; when they do speak, the mind is linguistically engaged and many of their affective signals are emitted unintentionally and unconsciously. Because linguists are human speakers with the implicit understandings of speech possessed by human speakers, they too are accustomed to sending and interpreting affective cues unconsciously. For this reason, it has probably been easy to confuse such a rich source of information about intentions and feelings with some minor property of spoken language.

My purpose here is neither to scold social scientists for past omissions nor to review the meager literature on vocal affect (Knapp, 1972, pp. 158–164). Let us proceed instead to examine those few studies that have used reasonably sophisticated acoustic analyses. In one study, Lieberman and Michaels (1962) asked speakers to record a set of sentences in such a way as to simulate eight different emotions (bored, fearful, and so on). Listeners were 85 percent correct in classifying the emotionality of the sentences. When frequency and amplitude information was edited out of the tapes, however, accuracy plunged to about half that level. In another study, Williams and Stevens (1972) studied the voice patterns of three actors who attempted to simulate emotions. Their analysis was largely qualitative and produced no clear acoustic patterning. Cosmides (1983) asked ten undergraduate volunteers to produce a standard phrase immediately after silently reading each of ten emotionally evocative selections from novels. Analysis of several acoustic parameters revealed that fundamental frequency was significantly correlated with emotions; other measures of frequency, duration, and amplitude were less closely associated with whatever emotional variation the passages evoked.

The most useful study on the vocal correlates of emotion was conducted by Ladd et al. (1985). These investigators assessed the relative contribution of fundamental frequency range, intonation contour, and voice quality on German listeners' affective judgments of three sentences. The sentences were recorded by a native German speaker and digitally resynthesized in order to vary the three acoustic characteristics. Listeners rated each sentence on an eight-category scale, which included different emotional states (for example, arrogant, emphatic, annoyed). Each of the three acoustic variables, as manipulated by the experimenters, had a significant effect on affective ratings. We need many more such studies of the acoustic attributes of voice that contribute to various emotions. One could well see threshold studies of adults with unilateral right hemisphere lesions or of children with developmental affective disorders.

ASSOCIATION OF FACES AND VOICES

From birth, infants' processing of visual patterns is influenced by the presence of sound (Mendelson and Haith, 1976). In the infant's own repertoire, certain facial expressions are grossly correlated with certain types of vocalization. As would be expected, smiling is positively correlated with playful vocalization and negatively correlated with fretting and crying (Lewis, 1969).

Undoubtedly the most thorough effort to explore infants' facial and vocal expressions naturalistically was that reported by Young and Decarie (1977). They observed nine- to twelve-month-olds in a range of emotionally evocative settings, cataloguing forty-two different facial expressions and ten vocal expressions. If each of the expressions in one modality occurred with each expression in the other modality, there would be 420 possible face-voice combinations. However, by my count Young and Decarie identified only 61 actually occurring combinations (14.5 percent) (for example, sad faces occurred in combination only with "soft wails" and "wails" and not with any of the other eight vocal expressions). Surely this suggests strong co-occurrence bonds for vocal and facial expression of emotions, as we would expect if the two shared neural substrate.

The neonate's orientation to faces and voices suggests that face-voice associations might be readily learnable in the first few days of life, but there seems to be no directly relevant research during this early period of development. It has been reported that talking increases the time three- to five-week-old infants look at the face (Bergman, Haith, and Mann, 1971, in Mendelson and Haith, 1976), but design details and the actual findings of this research do not seem to be readily available. At one to two months, infants are distressed by spatial separation of voice and face (Aronson and Rosenbloom, 1971).

There is some evidence that infants at three to seven months of age are able to associate particular faces and voices in a rudimentary way. When seated before two screens, one showing their mother's, and the other their father's immobile face, infants look longer at the face belonging to the voice they heard (Spelke and Owsley, 1979). This finding obviously could be due to infants' knowing the physical cues associated with the sexes (for example, hair length and fundamental frequency) rather than an awareness of particular face-voice associations within a sex.

One test of whether face and voice processing are closely related functions would be to see whether one activity primes or, contrarily, inhibits the other. In this regard, there is an indication that at four months, infants prefer to look at a human face after hearing a human voice and to look at an inanimate object after hearing a nonvocal sound, although the finding was weak and inconclusive (Spelke and Cortelyou, 1981).

My hunch is that associations between indexical face recognition and voice recognition can be learned in the first few days of life, though this remains to be demonstrated. I say this because prenatal learning of the mother's voice, and subsequent pairing of the mother's voice with her face, have not yet been ruled out as the means by which maternal face preferences are established. Moreover, there are the findings of a study of face preferences in infants who were observed from two through seven weeks of age (Carpenter, 1974). In this study, measurements were made of the time infants spent looking at the mother's face alone, the mother's face plus her voice, the mother's face with a stranger's voice, and parallel conditions for a stranger's face. Though details were sketchy, it was reported that (1) the mother's face received more attention than the stranger's face, regardless of which voice was heard, (2) each face was looked at longer if accompanied by a voice,[14] and (3) the mother's face without voice was looked at longer than the stranger's face with either voice. Carpenter concluded that "associations between the familiar face and voice had been learned" (p. 744).

RECOGNITION AND DISPLAY OF FACIAL AND VOCAL AFFECT

We have been discussing the infant's extraction of personal identity from facial and vocal information. Presumably, the critical cues are in the structure of the face and voice, though we do not know this— the cues could be spun off by speaking activities. What, then, of the *actions* of these social signaling systems? Faces and voices are the principal ways that we transmit our feelings, states, and intentions. When do infants begin to pick up on this; when and how do they begin to send signals back?

---

14. It would be interesting to know whether this represents a vocally induced interest in the eyes, as in Haith et al. (1977), or some sort of neural priming effect in which, for example, voice cells activate or alter the sensitivity of face cells, a matter I will revisit in Chapter 6.

Recognition of Facial Affect. How do infants know that facial expressions are correlated with particular emotions? Wittgenstein (1980) wrote that "We do not see facial contortions and *make the inference* that [the individual] is feeling joy, grief, boredom. We describe a face immediately as sad, radiant, bored, even when we are unable to give any other description of the features" (in Hobson, 1990, p. 116). There seems not, then, to be a developmental period during which infants come to associate the very basic facial expressions with the corresponding feelings. This is instantiated in the infant's own expressive behavior in simple ways. For example, smiling frequently co-occurs with playful vocalization and never occurs with crying. One is inclined to look at such elementary facts and ask how it could be any other way, but of course that is the point.

Early studies of infants' awareness of facial affect were conducted with still photos, and they came up with very conservative estimates. For example, one study of four- to six-month-olds revealed longer looking times for a slide depicting a facial expression of "joy" than an expression of "anger" or a "neutral" face (LaBarbera, Izard, Vietze et al., 1976). Other studies have placed the onset of these capabilities in the second half of the first year of life. Fortunately, recognition of facial affect has also been studied naturalistically. One group of investigators (Field, Woodson, Greenberg et al., 1982) found that at thirty-six hours, newborns held by an adult female experimenter reliably discriminated happy, sad, and surprised facial expressions (and according to looking time analyses, also imitated her expressions). Of course, findings such as these say nothing about infants' ability to understand the meaning or social significance of whatever expressions they do discriminate, which presumably develops over a longer period (Nelson, 1987).

Recognition of Vocal Affect. According to Morton's (1977) compendium of animal call data, variations in pitch and tonality among birds and mammals convey information about motivational state. It is no wonder, then, that the voice is affectively communicative in humans too, independently and in conjunction with lexical messages. However, we are more likely to discover these effects as participants in social communication than readers of scientific literature. There have been few studies of the vocal correlates of emotions in adults and even fewer investigations of the cues that adult listeners use to infer the emotional state of speakers. A review by Scherer (1979b) indicated that only the emotions of anger and grief or sadness had been studied frequently enough to be acoustically characterized with any confidence.

There have been even fewer studies of infants' awareness of vocal affect. I know of one that deals with "tone of voice." Culp and Boyd (1975) found that eight- and nine-week-old infants were able to discriminate a "harsh" from a "soft" voice when an adult female delivered the same poem under instructions to read in these different registers. Other studies of this kind are needed, but I would be particularly interested in measures of physiological change, such as vagal tone (Porges, 1991), because with autonomic measures, neither party need be unnaturally constrained or forced to perform. Adults can simply address infants with utterances having a range of emotional values and infants can respond or not as they naturally would.

There have been more studies of vocal attributes associated with nurturant maternal speech; some of these attributes undoubtedly convey affective information. In a study using an operant head-turning technique, it was found that four-month-olds prefer hearing the higher fundamental frequency and more exaggerated frequency variations associated with motherese—the speech mothers address to their infants—to ordinary mother-adult speech (Fernald and Kuhl, 1987). The investigators speculated that this listening preference might be due to the perceptual salience of radical frequency sweeps associated with inherent design features of the auditory system. Research with two-month-olds reveals a similar preference for rising as compared to falling intonations (Sullivan and Horowitz, 1983).

In this connection, it is of some interest that synthetic sound contours with extreme pitch variations evoke pleasant emotions in adult subjects, who associate them with happiness, interest, and surprise (Scherer, 1979a). Moreover, exaggerations of pitch seem to hold a certain universal appeal, presumably as a result of underlying biological mechanisms that have evolved to serve ontogenetic functions (Fernald, 1992a). Cross-linguistic studies indicate that large variations in vocal pitch are a key feature of motherese and occur in a number of disparate languages and cultures (Fernald and Simon, 1984; Fernald et al., 1989; Grieser and Kuhl, 1988).[15]

Fernald and Kuhl also saw merit in a second hypothesis, one that recognizes the affective properties conveyed to infants by maternal prosody. "The initial appeal of motherese," they write, "may lie in its affective expressive power, especially in the early months before adult speech has become linguistically meaningful to the infant" (1987, p. 291). This idea was developed further in Fernald (1992a), where a parallel was drawn between the human mother's use of intonation to transmit affective meaning to her infant and nonhuman primates' use of pitch, intensity, rhythm, and other "graded" vocal parameters to convey information about intentions and motivational states. This parallel, and some interesting cross-cultural research, bespeak a biological basis for mothers' manipulation of, and infants responses to, nonarbitrary relationships between intonation and affective meaning. These early sound-meaning associations include mothers' use of falling frequency contours when attempting to soothe a distressed infant, rising contours when attempting to engage attention or elicit a response, and rising-falling contours when seeking to maintain attention. Fernald has also reported evidence that infants, in fact, react to these manipulations as their mothers intend; regardless of the language spoken or the infants' understanding of the words, they pick up and mirror in their own facial activity at least the positive and negative affect that mothers intend to convey in their statements of approval and prohibition.

Fernald proposed a model of maternal prosody's changing role in the emergence of affective and linguistic sound-meaning relationships. According to this model, the vocal parameters that are manipulated in intonation are highly salient to newborns and initially communicate information about their mother's feelings and intentions. Later, intonation takes on additional functions; it begins to

15. Most of us have encountered or heard about someone's dog, which seems to respond appropriately to vocal questions such as "Do you want to go for a ride?" and commands such as "Roll over." I have always been amused by those of my fellow psycholinguists who comment that, in these cases, dogs are "just responding to your tone of voice" but at the same time act as though intonation could not possibly be an important factor in linguistic communication among humans.

signal the location of linguistic units in the otherwise continuous stream of speech and to facilitate comprehension of spoken language.

As Fernald notes, many linguists take lexical comprehension as the first, perhaps even the sole indication of emergent referential capability. But affect is information. And prosody conveys. What could be more informative than the vocal cues that tell listeners whether the signal is worth listening to, why the message is being generated, and—taken with the linguistic structures that are conveyed—what the speaker really means.[16] Indeed, from this perspective it can be argued that infants latch onto first those social signals that mean the most. Whether psycholinguistic theory officially takes note of this information or continues to ignore it is scarcely of any importance to children!

Recognition of Facial and Vocal Affect. How does the infant's discrimination of affective facial and vocal displays develop? Walker (1982) found that five- and seven-month-olds looked longer at vocally supported than at silent films, whichever of two emotions was conveyed. In a subsequent study (Walker-Andrews and Grolnick, 1983) she learned that five-month-old infants (but not three-month-olds) discriminated vocal enactments of happiness and sadness, and were able to recognize the association between vocal and facial expressions of these emotions from tape recordings and slides.

In a similar vein, Caron, Caron, and MacLean (1988) observed that facially transmitted emotions are detected by infants at a younger age if accompanied by voice than if conveyed silently. In a series of five experiments, Caron et al. presented infants at five and seven months of age with color videotape segments of women repeating standard sentence material under the instruction to act happy, sad, or angry. Tapes conveying a particular emotion were presented until infants' eye fixations indicated habituation, then were switched to tapes conveying a different emotion. It was found

16. And yet, we strongly associate our own voices with our sense of who we are personally. In his discussion of the etymology of "personality," Moses (1954) pointed out that "the word comes from the Latin *persona,* which originally meant the mouthpiece of a mask used by actors (*per sona:* the sound of the voice passes through). From the mask the term shifted to the actor; the "person" in a drama. The word eventually came to mean any person and finally "personality," but over the centuries it lost its symbolic connection with the voice" (p. 7).

that when vocal cues were available, inter-emotion discriminations occurred at younger ages than when the facial expressions were merely seen. Summing up their own data and the results of several other experiments, Caron et al. determined that the sad-happy discrimination was possible with vocal cues alone at three months, with vocal and visual cues at four to five months, and with facial cues alone at five months. Starting several months later, a similar progression seems to occur for the angry-happy discrimination. They concluded that "infants may first attend strictly to auditory information when differentiating emotional expressions, but as their visual resolving power increases they may come gradually to detect a concordance in temporal patterning between facial dynamics and voice, until finally they become able to discriminate emotions on a purely visual basis" (p. 615). This ontogenetic scenario will soon have a familiar ring to it, for the auditory to auditory plus visual to visual sequence parallels an evolutionary account (Andrew, 1963a, 1964; 1965) that will be taken up below. Indeed, there is some evidence that among adults the sight of a person speaking may convey more affective information than the sound of the speaker's voice (Levitt, 1964).

If movements of the voice and face convey information about an individual's feelings and intentions, can we say how much information is conveyed by each? Some information is available on the vocal side of the question. Mehrabian and Wiener (1967) attempted to estimate the capacity of these channels individually. They found that when the affective information in the words and the vocal "tone" of a message were in conflict, listeners' judgments of speaker attitude were more likely to be influenced by the tone, even when they were instructed to ignore tone and react only to content. The authors concluded that "the tonal component makes a disproportionately greater contribution to the interpretation of the total message than does the content" (p. 113).

Display of Facial and Vocal Affect. If facial and vocal affect are intimately linked, when infants transmit information over one channel they will generally send congruent information over the other channel. Malatesta, Davis, and Culver (1984) videotaped three- and six-month-old infants during interactions with their mothers. Facial expressions were classified using the discrete emotion-coding system developed by Carroll Izard. Vocal affect was classified independently by different coders using a system that anticipated four "hedonically" positive and negative expressions.

The analysis revealed little specificity of vocal expressions, producing nonspecific associations between facial and vocal expressions. However, agreement between the two modalities was observed for hedonic tone. It was found, for example, that the facial expressions of joy and surprise were both associated with the vocal category of "contentment/mild interest," and the facial expressions of anger, sadness, and pain were associated with "mild discomfort/displeasure/frustration." It was not possible to locate more specific face-voice associations because the vocal affective system in these three- to six-month-old infants was less differentiated than the facial system.

Vocal Recognition. It has been found that within forty-eight hours of birth, mothers are able to vocally identify their own infant from its crying (Formby, 1967). One presumes that this early ability, like the infant's recognition of its mother's voice, has been heavily valued in evolutionary history. And in at least one other species of primates, vervet monkeys, mothers are able to do the same thing when they hear the screams and grunts of their 2.5-year-old juveniles (Cheney and Seyfarth, 1980). To a limited extent, mothers and, indeed, all listeners can easily use vocalization to discern distress from other states, but even an infant's own mother is likely to have difficulty distinguishing one source of crying from another (Muller, Hollien, and Murry, 1974).

The Similar Developmental Course of Facial and Vocal Recognition

DEVELOPMENT OF FACE RECOGNITION

Most of us are able to recognize the faces of many different individuals, even if we haven't seen them for years. There is some research to confirm this. Bahrick, Bahrick, and Wittlinger (1975) found that up to thirty-five years after leaving high school, graduates could recognize the faces of their former classmates at over 90 percent accuracy, regardless of class size. How does this remarkable capacity develop?

The developmental course for face recognition and voice recognition is very similar. They rise together, fall at about the same chronological age, and return at about the same point to adultlike levels of performance. Carey and Diamond (1977) presented a stimulus recognition task to children at six, eight, and ten years of age. The stimuli were mixed sets of photographs of faces and houses presented either in upright or inverted orientation. On each trial, stimuli were presented for inspection and followed immediately by pairs of photos that contained target and distractor items. In children from six to ten years old, the investigators found little improvement in performance for inverted faces but did observe significant improvement for upright ones, which they attributed to an increasingly efficient means of utilizing configurational information.

Carey and Diamond got exactly the opposite effect for houses. Performance on upright houses remained essentially constant in children from six to ten years old, but there was significant improvement in children's recognition of inverted houses over this age range. They speculated that this pattern reflects an improvement in "encoding the piecemeal features of this relatively unfamiliar stimulus domain" (p. 312). This speculation received support in a second experiment in which children were asked to select from a pair of photographs either the one that looked the most like a target photo seen earlier or the one that depicted the same person. Under both instructions, six- and eight-year-olds were influenced more by shared articles of clothing than by shared facial expressions, while the opposite was true of ten-year-olds.

Carey, Diamond, and Woods (1980) gave facial memory tasks to children and adolescents from six to sixteen years of age. In the first experiment, a series of photographs of male adults were presented to six- and ten-year-olds. On each trial, three target photographs were shown for five seconds each. Then subjects saw three pairs of photographs, each composed of a target and a distractor photo, and were asked to select the target photo they had seen earlier. This was also done for a control set of pictures of houses, although the resulting data were not reported.

As in their earlier work, on half of the trials the stimuli were presented in their normal orientation and on the other half the faces and houses were inverted. The investigators found that inverted and upright photos were about equally recognizable to the six-year-olds, who recalled just over 60 percent correctly in both cases. But the ten-year-olds recalled significantly more upright than inverted photos.

In the second experiment, there were child and adolescent subjects, whose ages ranged from seven to sixteen years, and a group of adults. As expected, performance was the lowest at seven years, with no significant increases at nine years. Then there was an improvement at age ten and eleven, followed by a large decrement at twelve years. At fourteen, performance improved somewhat, though it did not reach the level that had been achieved by eleven-year-olds and was less than that of adult subjects. A final experiment extended the age range to sixteen years and, although no adolescent performance dip was observed, a failure of continued improvement was found in those ages. Figure 2.8 is a graph of the data from the first experiment.

Though one expects successful performance on a wide variety of cognitive tasks to increase as children mature and acquire more experience, Carey et al. asked what accounted for the improvement that occurred from six to nine years. They pointed to data from a tachistoscopic study (Leehey, 1976) revealing an increase in the left visual field advantage for facial stimuli over this age range. In addition, in terms of neurophysiology, they speculated that "maturational factors may be implicated in the development of the capacity to encode upright faces. By 'maturational' we mean a genetically programmed component to developmental change. For example, perhaps one limiting factor in the performance of children younger than age 9 is immaturity of the right posterior cortex. And perhaps hormonal upheavals at puberty might in some way affect right hemisphere involvement in the processing of unfamiliar faces" (p. 266). Continued interest in the performance dip at adolescence caused Carey and Diamond (1980) to examine the maturational hypothesis more comprehensively in other work. They noted that performance decrements at this approximate age have occurred on a few other tasks that appear to tap common cognitive capabilities and to implicate shared neural substrate.

DEVELOPMENT OF VOICE RECOGNITION
Aural identification of inanimate objects is less accurate than identification by sight. Some years ago, I listened with some regularity

% CORRECT

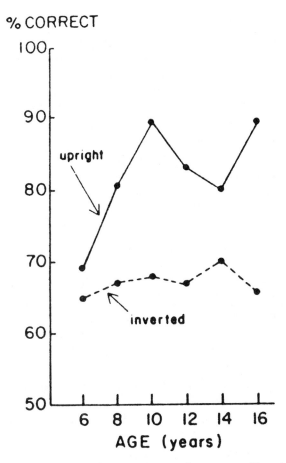

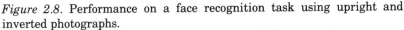

Figure 2.8. Performance on a face recognition task using upright and inverted photographs.

to a British radio program that played recordings of sounds made by common household implements and challenged listeners to identify the source. Caller's guesses were usually incorrect, even though the sounds were high frequency events in the listeners' daily lives. Once the implement was identified and it became possible to visualize the sound making activity, the acoustics suddenly seemed to fall into place.

Voice identification is not much better.[17] We are able to recognize

17. Though this capacity is created horizontally by permuting and stringing out a small number of segments. Of the segments most like voices, the vowels, the most

the voices of our closest associates and a few public figures, but this capability is far less efficient than face recognition. Our voices can even be somewhat variable—colds and laryngeal abuse may alter, or even cause us temporarily to lose our voice—but in critical ways our face remains a fairly stable index to our identity. In some circumstances, faces may even be able to override voices: Tiberghien and Clerc (1986) described a patient with prosopagnosia, a face recognition disorder, who could identify an unseen politician on television by voice alone, but lost this ability whenever the politician was visible as well as audible.

What about recognition of voices from one's personal past? There seems to have been little research on this, but I can supply an anecdote. Years ago there was a television program called "This Is Your Life" in which a famous person was subjected to a seemingly surprise review of his or her life. Before associates from bygone eras came out on the stage, they first said a few words over a backstage P.A. system to alert the honored person to their presence. As I watched, it seemed to me that the honoree was frequently unable to recognize the voices, even with the hints that were supplied, and yet he or she always appeared to remember the individuals once they walked on stage.

The identification of other individuals by voice has been the subject of some research on animals. Species other than our own have at least a limited facility for intraspecific vocal recognition. In bats (Gould, 1975) and monkeys (Waser, 1977) there is evidence that mothers recognize their young by voice alone. While we might suppose that recognition of one's own family members is due exclusively to exposure, there may be other ways that such a capability might emerge. We might ask if genetically related individuals have more in common, vocally, than those that are genetically unrelated. If they do, is this because their vocal tracts have similar twists and turns or because they have been exposed to, and have accommodated to each other? Is any of a speaker's vocal resonance—apart from articulatory and linguistic habits—acquired? It is quite amazing how little we have cared about and therefore know about this.

On logical grounds, the cues that could be used to identify a

---

usual vowel inventory in the world's languages has no more than five: /i e a o u/ (Maddieson, 1980).

person include articulatory as well as phonatory variations. Which
cues most reliably point to the individual who produced them? Our
vocabularies contain massive numbers of segmental strings,[18] so we
may suspect immediately that our limited ability to recognize individuals by voice is based largely on storage of suprasegmental
cues. Some investigators have tested voice recognition under normal circumstances and when articulatory cues were reduced by
filtering out high frequencies or playing tapes backwards (Bartholomeus, 1973; Bricker and Pruzansky, 1966). This research suggests that speech contributes less to the recognition of a person than
voice, confirming our suspicions.

Which vocal cues are the most useful in this regard? Computers
can identify people from a variety of acoustic measures, including
fundamental frequency, spectral patterns of vowels and nasal consonants, slope of the glottal source spectrum, voice onset time, and
word duration (Wolf, 1972). Which of these is useful to listeners is
another question, an unanswered one as far as I can tell. There are,
of course, perfectly good reasons to base personal identification on
phonatory properties rather than articulatory cues. For one thing,
the articulatory variations that could identify a speaker must be
kept to a minimum if intelligibility is to be maintained. And nuances of the voice, like subtle changes in the vowels (Fry, Abramson,
Eimas et al., 1962), are more likely to be perceived than are consonantal variations (Ladd et al., 1985). Vocal resonance then,
should, offer listeners better opportunities for inter-speaker discrimination.

I know of no studies of infants' awareness of the particular physical parameters that give voices their distinctive nature, but there
has been one study of children's ability to identify their peers.
Bartholomeus (1973) presented two nursery school classes and their
teachers with a face recognition and three voice recognition tasks.
In a *face naming* task, children were shown color photographs of
other students' faces and asked to supply the name. In a *voice
naming* task, they heard a tape recording of a phrase ("Hi, I go to

18. This study was conducted when I was at the Institute for Child Behavior and
Development at the University of Illinois. The sentences were constructed by my
research assistant at the time, Richard Cureton. I am indebted to William Brandy,
who made available subjects at the Danville Veterans Administration Medical Center, and Roberta Williams, who recorded the sentences and assisted with the testing.

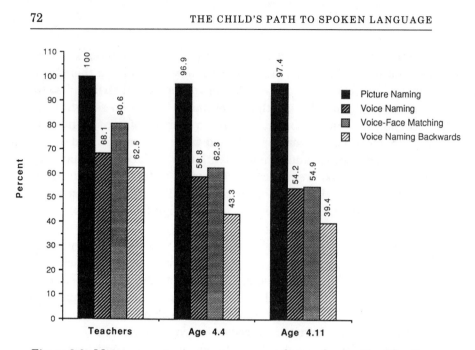

Figure 2.9. Mean percent correct responses on face and voice identification tests.

your school. Do you know who I am?") uttered by a dozen and a half of their peers and were asked to name the speaker. In a *voice naming backwards* task, this procedure was repeated but the tape was played in the reverse direction, which typically destroys intelligibility while preserving vocal distinctiveness. In a *voice-face matching* task, the children were presented with the same voice sample and asked to point to the speakers' picture from an array of photographs. Bartholomeus obtained the results shown in Figure 2.9. With the exception of a five-year, five-month-old girl (apparently the oldest child in the experiment) who obtained 100 percent on both face naming and voice-face matching, every subject performed more accurately on the face task than on all three of the voice tasks. Inferior performance on voice-naming apparently is not due to any special difficulty in retrieving the names that go with voices; performance on the voice-face matching task was just as poor.

When voice samples were played backwards, listeners were still able to identify speakers fairly well. Among the teachers, performance on the reversed tapes was 91 percent of that on tapes played normally, which agrees with data on other adults reported by Bricker and Pruzansky (1966; Figure 11). Because the articulatory cues that comprise idiolects, and therefore distinguish one speaker from another, are minimized by reversing the direction of speech playback, such a small decrement suggests that speakers are normally identified by vocal resonance arising naturally from their vocal tract morphology. If so, on these grounds alone we should expect the right hemisphere, which is relatively more responsible for suprasegmental cues, to contribute disproportionately to speaker identification when the face cannot be seen. Incidentally, among the child subjects in Bartholomeus (1973), tapes played in reverse were identified at 73 percent of normal performance. This greater decrement could mean that children are more reliant than adults on articulatory cues, but it could also mean that they were unusually confused, distracted, or perhaps even amused by this dramatic alteration of a normal circumstance.

Thanks particularly to a group of researchers led by Diana Van Lancker, we have some information on the ability of adults to recognize people from their voice. In one study (Van Lancker, Kreiman, and Emmorey, 1985), the voices of famous individuals were played forwards and backwards. When two-second samples were heard in the normal forward order, individuals were identified from a list of six with about 70 percent accuracy. When four-second samples were heard in reverse, accuracy declined to about 58 percent. Interestingly, some voices were identified equally well in forward and reverse orders, and one was identified more accurately in reverse (Richard Nixon). Other studies (listed in Table 5 of Van Lancker et al.) have found a performance decrement for reverse order listening ranging from 14 percent to 3.5 percent.

In a second study (Van Lancker, Kreiman, and Wickens, 1985), listeners were presented with famous male voices at either a normal rate or one that was a third faster or slower than normal. The voice recognition rate was about 68 percent correct in the normal condition, dropping to about 56 to 57 percent in the rate expanded and rate compressed conditions. Again, tampering affected some voices more than others. Compared to the normal case, the voices of some speakers were recognized slightly better when the rate was expanded (Nelson Rockefeller, Gerald Ford), while recognition of several others was unusually impaired by expansion (Johnny Carson, John F. Kennedy, Richard Pryor).

Some attention has been given to the development of vocal recognition ability. Mann, Diamond, and Carey (1979) gave a memory for voices test to subjects from six years of age to adolescence and adulthood. Twenty-two adult females, all native speakers of American English, recorded the sentences (for example, "He threw the ball") to be used as the targets and recognition items. On each trial, one or two speech samples were heard followed by a forced choice recognition test with either two or four alternative choices. Half the subjects heard the same speech material in both the inspection and recognition sets; the other half heard different utterances.

The investigators found that six-year-olds performed at chance while all other age groups exceeded chance performance. The pattern (shown in Figure 2.10) is remarkably like that observed in Carey and Diamond's earlier experiments on face recognition. Accuracy improved significantly between ages six and eight, and again between ages eight and ten. Performance then declined between ages ten and thirteen and returned to adult levels by age fourteen, paralleling the developmental course for face recognition seen in Figure 2.8.

Why do the developmental peaks and troughs of the voice recognition curve correspond so closely to the ages of maximal and minimal performance on face recognition? Aware of voice discrimination deficits in patients with cortical lesions (Assal et al., 1976), Carey and Diamond (1980) commented that "voice encoding shares neural substrate with face encoding," noting that vocal memory "also shares experiential influences with face encoding, since both are bases of person identification" (p. 38).

In search of support for a maturational hypothesis, Carey and Diamond (1980) surveyed the literature for some other cognitive capability that develops, experiences a temporary setback at adolescence, and suffers with focal brain damage. After an extensive search, Carey and Diamond found a study (Spreen and Gaddes, 1969) that used a task which logically draws on some of the same cognitive capabilities as voice memory, the Seashore Tonal Memory test. On the Seashore test, subjects hear a sequence of three to five tones, which are repeated immediately except that the frequency of one tone is varied. Listeners are to identify which tone in the

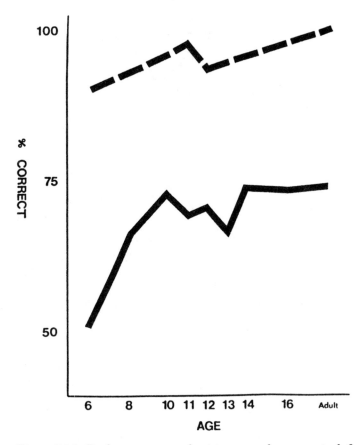

Figure 2.10. Performance on a short-term vocal memory task for test items (solid line) and practice items in which speakers differed in accent (broken line).

repetition is different. Just as in voice and face recognition, Spreen and Gaddes's findings reveal improvement from eight to thirteen, a dip at ages fourteen and fifteen, and another rise in performance by age eighteen. Significantly, Milner (1962) found impaired performance on the Seashore test in patients with right temporal lobectomies. These patients scored at about the same level as the nine-year-olds in Spreen and Gaddes.

These findings suggest that the dip in voice and face processing at adolescence may be associated with the neurological reorganization that is assumed to occur during that period of development.

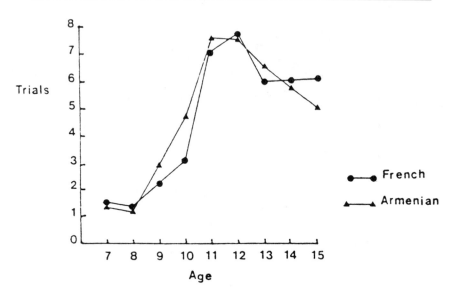

Figure 2.11. Mean number of trials required before intonation of French and Armenian phrases was correctly reproduced by monolingual English children and adolescents.

Some support for such a presumption is offered by the research of Levine (1985). She found that the left visual field advantage for unfamiliar faces that is revealed at ten, eleven, and twelve years of age is missing among fourteen-year-olds but present among adult subjects.

Developmentally, a similar result can be found in a pattern of results reported by Tahta, Wood, and Loewenthal (1981) for development of control over nonnative intonation, although in this case the direction of performance runs in the opposite direction. Tahta et al. examined the ability of seven- to fifteen-year-old monolingual English children to reproduce French and Armenian phrases with native-sounding prosody. Figure 2.11 shows the results. Based on the number of trials needed to reach a criterion level of learning, the best performance occurred at ages seven and eight, followed by a decline until age eleven, stabilization at age twelve, and an improvement at ages thirteen to fifteen. This pattern resembles the developmental course of face and voice recognition, suggesting that whatever cerebral organization occurs at adolescence is disruptive of at least two types of prosody. One type is the prosody that make one's language sound native; the other type includes the cues used in identifying people.

I take the foregoing studies as developmental support for a functional linkage between the indexical aspects of face and voice processing. It appears from the controls available that the rise, dip, and recovery of voice identification is not merely a vocal expression of a centrally located personal recognition ability; rather, it is related specifically to phonatory, and to a lesser degree articulatory cues. Mann et al. (1979) commented that "Faces and voices are both complex stimuli which convey important social information. Encoding of both plays a part in the ability to recognize and distinguish individual persons. These similarities make it plausible that the development of voice recognition may, in some respects, parallel the development of face recognition" (p. 154). And further, "whether there is . . . a direct tie between the development of voice recognition and changes in functioning of the right hemisphere has not yet been evaluated" (p. 162).

VISUAL EFFECTS IN SPEECH PERCEPTION

One very powerful visuofacial effect in speech perception is what is customarily called "lipreading." In the field of aural rehabilitation, where much has been written about lipreading, it was observed long ago that the lips were not the sole source of information about the speaker's message. It wasn't that the tongue or some other oral structure was more visible or contained more information. Rather, the organ of speech transmission was taken to be the face. In recognition of this, some aural rehabilitationists (for example, Pauls, 1947) recommended that lipreading be called by an anatomically neutral name: *speech reading*. By masking parts of the face, some research showed that structures other than the lips contributed to speech recognition (Greenberg and Bode, 1968; Berger, Garner, and Sudman, 1971). Summerfield (1979) experimentally affirmed the existence of extra-labial sources of visual input but was unable to judge whether the missing information was strictly articulatory, relating to lingual action and dentition, or associated with other characteristics or movements of the face.

I suspect that most people believe that "lipreading" is a compensatory means of taking in information about speech that is used by the hard of hearing only after a period of specialized training. In fact, we all do it. Lipreading is such a natural behavior, most of us may be unable to stop it. McGurk and MacDonald (1976) reported a very powerful perceptual link between facial movements and vocal perception, one so strong that it is seemingly indissoluble. In this phenomenon, now commonly called the "McGurk effect," the videotaped speaker is observed to articulate a syllable initiated at one place of articulation (for example, [ba]) but—through dubbing—the listener hears an initial consonant associated with a different point of articulation ([ga]). Frequently, the listener reports a conflation of the two sounds ([da]), which has an intermediate point of closure in the vocal tract. The striking thing about these illusions is that the perceiver is completely unaware that the information seen differs from the information heard, and there seems to be little that one can do to prevent these perceptual fusions except, of course, to blink or look away. One can scarcely imagine a more flagrant form of "the linguistic face" than these McGurk effects.

Following the original report a number of confirming accounts appeared in the literature (see Massaro, 1987), suggesting that speech perception was naturally bimodal, and that optical and auditory information about speech integrate automatically. Summerfield (1979) reasoned that for this integration to occur there must be a "common metric" within which the information from light and sound overlaps, as a reflection of their common origin in speech articulation, and enables their coherence. The common metric could be featural, Summerfield supposed, but would more likely be articulatory.

In the perception of speech, intersensory contributions are not limited to the content of light and sound. They also extend to the temporal relationship between these modalities. Many people report that when they see a vintage film they are extremely bothered if the sound is out of synchrony with the movement. The "bother" can be functional, as I learned several years ago when I presented eight older adult listeners with videotapes of a woman speaking sentences auditorily or visually, or with both auditory and visual cues that were either synchronous or asynchronous.[19] Unbeknownst to the

---

19. There may be other ways that the face promotes understanding of speech. For example, there is evidence that speech is easier to recognize if one knows the sex of

subjects, each sentence contained a key noun in initial, medial, or final sentence position (for example, "The *lamp* gave some light to the plants"; "The woman lighted the *lamp* with a match"; "She put a new wick in the *lamp*"). In all, there were nine lists of twenty-seven sentences.

The conditions of presentation were systematically varied. To test lipreading ability, one list was presented with visual cues alone. In a second list, visual cues were completely eliminated by a darkened screen, and the volume was turned down to a point where listeners would understand about half the key words (it turned out to be slightly fewer). All other lists were presented at this level so that visual cues would be needed for accurate recognition. To evaluate the degree to which observers could profit from visual support, one list of sentences was presented with visual and auditory cues in normal synchrony. The remaining six lists were presented asynchronously, with the auditory portion preceding or following the visual portion by 100, 200, or 300 msec. Listeners were instructed to repeat each sentence as best they could, though analyses were based exclusively on accuracy of key words.

As Figure 2.12 reveals, target words were identified correctly in just 3 percent of the cases when subjects could see but not hear the sentences. With weak audition alone, intelligibility increased to 43 percent, and when both cues were simultaneously available there was a multiplicative increase to 72 percent. This higher level of performance was threatened by the asynchronous conditions. When the sound preceded or followed the video portion by 100 msec, the reduction was slight, but a larger drop occurred when asynchronies were increased to 200 msec, an amount which approaches the average duration of American English syllables in running speech. An asynchrony of 300 msec caused a further decrease, bringing recognition in this circumstance to a sound-only level of accuracy, that is, completely wiping out the contribution of vision.

Infants are also bothered by audio-video asynchronies in speech. Dodd (1979) exposed ten- to sixteen-week-olds to the sight of a woman speaking. Her sounds were heard in time with her articu-

---

the speaker (Mullennix, Pisoni, and Martin, 1989; Johnson, 1990), and of course one can obtain such information by visual inspection of the face. It would be interesting to see if speech processing is speeded by sex information provided in this way.

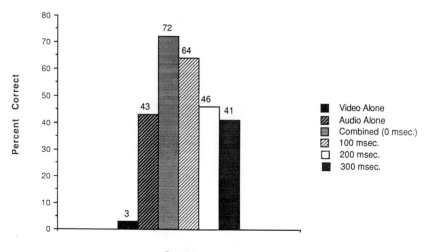

Figure 2.12. Sentence intelligibility when the speaker could be seen (video), heard (audio), seen and heard (combined), and when combined cues were out of synchrony by 100, 200, and 300 msec. Note that if the asynchrony was as much as 300 msec., vision contributed nothing to the recognition of speech from auditory cues alone.

latory movements or were delayed by 400 msec. Dodd found that ten of the twelve infants spent more time *not looking* at the speaker when her mouth movements and speech sounds were asynchronous than when movements and sounds occurred synchronously. A group analysis revealed that overall, infants were more than twice as likely to turn away from the screen when the speaker's articulatory movements and sounds were out of synchrony than when they were in perfect time. A similar finding has been obtained in four-month-olds using a slightly different method (Spelke and Cortelyou, 1981).

At four to five months, infants are aware of the visible articulatory gestures and audible frequency spectrum of vowels, for they react differently when gestures do or do not correspond to sound. In Kuhl and Meltzoff (1982), two groups of eighteen- to twenty-week-old infants watched a film of a woman repetitively articulating [i] and [a], which involve visibly different movements. While the film played, one group of infants heard the same vowel that the woman visibly articulated in the film or a different vowel. The other group of infants heard control stimuli which contained no formants but did have similar durations and amplitude contours. Infants who heard the intact vowels looked significantly longer at the face whose visible articulation matched the heard vowel than at the face whose articulation differed. No such effect occurred for control stimuli.

A report published in the following year suggests that these congruency effects may reflect a contribution of the left hemisphere, since in a similar study it was observed that five- to six-month-olds looked longer at filmed faces whose visible articulations matched the utterance heard (for example, [mama], [zuzu]) but *only if the infant was looking to the right* (MacKain et al., 1983). In older infants, support for this looking-time-as-linguistic-lateralization account was provided by a study of the time children spend looking at line drawings on a split screen (Mount et al., 1989). The investigators found that the correlation between percentage fixation time to the right and mean length of utterance increased between sixteen and twenty-one months, reaching a peak at twenty months ($r =$ .87) when there is generally a peak in the rate of children's lexical growth.

I am intrigued by infants' awareness of the temporal and spectral concordance between seen and heard speech movements. How do they get the cross-modal knowledge implied by their looking patterns? Through what epigenetic route do neonates come to know which of their own facial muscles to instruct when they want to imitate another person's tongue protrusion or mouth opening? "How," as Michael Studdert-Kennedy has so eloquently asked, "does the light get into the muscle?" One can only hope that in this decade of intense neuroscience research we will begin to get some answers fairly soon, for the neural operations associated with these activities appear to provide the biological foundation for social learning and, ultimately, the transmission of culture.[20]

From Faces and Voices to Speech

By now, readers may have surmised that I believe it can be a mistake to ask how or even when the infant "gets" language. The

20. Note that this is not the same as placing two types of vocalic information directly in competition, as would have been the case had syllables such as [bʌg]-[bɪg] been produced by different speakers or dissimilar tones of voice.

reason is that infants do not acquire language, at least in any direct fashion. Rather, they display and accomplish a number of behaviors along the way to language that are communicative, involve acquisitions, and seem increasingly symbolic. Infants smile and pout, coo and babble, and point with hands and eyes at objects that engage their attention. At some interval they will modulate their voice to referential effect. They may seem to use their vocal tract as a tool for social signaling. But no one of these separate acts will look very much like an expression of linguistic knowledge.

The infant participates competently in a social world comprising emotive faces and voices. How does it begin to deal with a linguistic world in which different movements of the same faces and voices serve as cues to spoken language? It might be helpful to think about how this transition might have occurred phylogenetically in the species. There have been many efforts to explain how the capacity for spoken language evolved, but we always remind ourselves that unless there was an exaptation, as Piatelli-Palmarini (1989) has suggested, it happened gradually. And it would have grown up out of the functions and structures that existed at the time (Pinker and Bloom, 1990), assembled from spare parts.

Nonhuman primates easily send and receive affectively encoded vocal and facial messages. Like humans, as we will see, they seem to process indexical information in the voice bilaterally and to process faces with disproportionate action of the right cerebral hemisphere. I think it can be assumed that our hominid ancestors had similar dispositions and neural specializations. As vocal communication evolved, it would have elaborated from an *affective base*. But at some point in our phylogeny, a duality must have crept in. And of course we know our present-day capability for affective vocal-facial communication, with right hemisphere control, was preserved. But with the retention and presumably continuous operation of these functions, there evolved a complementary capacity for symbolic communication with contralateral control mechanisms.

Ontogenetically, we need a story with a similar sequence of events. The ability to identify people by voice has its origins in prenatal and neonatal learning and seems to precede vowel learning and vowel discrimination. Babies are predisposed to process voice information, and the child retains these capabilities while also taking on the capacity to transmit and receive phonetically encoded messages. As Lamendella (1977) has observed, "the majority of the limbic functions acquired by the child remain part of the adult communication repertoire as a neurobehavioral framework into which linguistic communication is embedded" (p. 159).

It would seem that our theoretical task is not to explain how the infant starting from scratch becomes linguistic, but how it progresses from one vocal orientation to another. Adults process utterances for both their affective and their linguistic significance. Accordingly, on the way to spoken language I would suggest that infants graduate from a preoccupation with indexical and affective properties of the voice to a more comprehensive orientation that includes phonological information as well as the social-vocal cues tracked earlier.

We do not send a particular set of vocal messages in order to publicize information about our age, sex, body size, species, social class, or emotional state. These kinds of information are conveyed incidentally when we talk; though unintentionally so, linguistic vowels serve as the carriers. A [b] or [f] is unlikely to convey much personal information about speakers, but an [a] or [e] may express a great deal, not because it represents the phonemes /a/ or /e/ but because they are *vocal*. Vowels are resonant, and to the infant one presumes this is their initial value.

It seems, then, that language is *developmentally additive* in the sense that the multiplicity of cues that trip off phonetic categories are piled on top of the prosodic, affective, and speaker-identifying cues that form the infralinguistic core of our vocal messages. In a classic paper, Alvin Liberman (1970) pointed out that in the complex code that is speech, information about consonants and vowels resides in the structure of consonant-vowel transitions and is transmitted simultaneously. Somehow the listener processes this segmental information in addition to the countless cues, already residing in the vowels, that are associated with prosody, affect, and information about speaker identity. Figure 2.13 is a schematic display of the consonantal information in an adjacent vowel.

Liberman's demonstration, of course, was that vowels contain information about neighboring segments. In Figure 2.13, the [ae] in *bag* contains information about its consonantal neighbors, [b] and [g]. My point is that something analogous goes on in the infant's affective and indexical experience. For the infant the vowel speci-

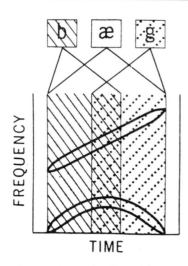

Figure 2.13. The parallel transmission model constructed by Liberman. Each segment, and particularly the vowel, contains information about itself and one or more of its phonetic neighbors.

fies a range of socially relevant pieces of information, for example, {+ adult}, {+ male}, {+ formal register}, and whatever there is to be known about the speaker's emotionality, health, and attitude. When segmental processing begins, this level of social transmission continues. Familiarity, age, sex, register, and emotionality are then taken out of the vowel along with information about [b] and [g].

How do infants juggle the multiplicity of cues? The seeds of an answer may be contained in the fact that we have separate neural mechanisms for prosodic patterns and individual speech sounds (see Chapter 6). Studies in which cues from these domains were co-varied suggest that consonant perception survives noticeable variations in stress. For example, Jusczyk and Thompson (1978) found that two-month-olds are sensitive to place of articulation contrasts among the voiced stops (bada-gada), and are also aware of contrasts between stressed and unstressed syllables (badá-báda). They also found that place discrimination occurred independent of stress or was sufficiently powerful to hold steady regardless of whether the stops appeared in a stressed (dabá-dága) or unstressed syllable (dába-dága).

The central question, though, is this: If infants are initially tuned in to prosody and vocal affect and then become more aware of vowel contrasts, do they have any difficulty in dealing with co-variations involving the two? Can one kind of information draw processing resources away from the other or divert the infant's attention from one type of contrast or perceptual mechanism to the other? Kuhl and Miller (1982) found that when one- to four-month-old infants were presented with contrasts between pitch contour (rising or falling) *or* vowel quality ([a] and [i]), they discriminated each with relative ease. However, when confronted with contrasts involving pitch *and* vowel quality, the vocalic contrast "won," that is, overrode pitch. This suggests that infants' bias toward the categorial differences between vowels may compete with cues that convey indexical or affective information, or even linguistic tones. It would be interesting to know whether infants lose some of their sensitivity to certain kinds of vocal information when they begin to recognize phonetic categories.

Working with two-month-olds, Jusczyk et al. (1989) asked several questions about the interrelationship between perception of vocally encoded "personal information" and phonetically encoded linguistic information. They conducted a series of experiments using the high amplitude sucking paradigm. Infants heard the syllables "bug" or "dug" spoken by a single male or female or by multiple speakers of both sexes. The test phase followed the habituation phase immediately or after a two-minute delay. In single talker conditions, listeners heard one of the speakers during the habituation phase and a different talker during the test phase, or a single speaker throughout. In multiple talker conditions, there were twelve different speakers, six male and six female, in the habituation and test phases of the experiments.

During "phonetic change" trials, subjects exposed to multiple talkers took longer to habituate, but they discriminated the syllables as well as subjects exposed to only a single talker. In other words, these two-month-olds were aware of the consonantal place information that varied across the twelve different voices but were able to "ignore" it. In the "talker change" condition, where infants were habituated with one voice and then presented with one of the opposite sex (with the syllable held constant), there was a significant change in sucking rate. But there was no indication that "talker variability" interfered with infants' ability to discriminate. a place contrast between voiced, syllable-initial stop consonants. This recreates in the lab what is of course true on the street: a multitude of people with a range of vocal qualities, rates of speech, and so forth produce the same words, which must be identified as the items intended regardless of their topographic variations.

Our ultimate concern, of course, is with the development of a linguistic vocabulary. What role, if any, does speaker information play in the buildup of internal representations? It would seem to be adaptive for infants to know the identity and intentions of those who are speaking to them, but maladaptive to store this information along with any new lexical items. When Jusczyk et al. (1989) inserted a delay between habituation and test phases of dug-bug trials, there was a significant change in sucking rate only in the single talker condition. For subjects in the multiple talker condition there was no significant increase in sucking rate following the delay. This seems counterintuitive, for if physical information about the stimuli faded during the delay, perceptions built up from exposure to many different speakers should be less tied to sensory cues and more resistant to decay than stimuli produced by a single voice.

As in the immediate test condition, infants in the talker change comparison heard the same syllable throughout habituation and test phases with a change only in the speakers' voices. Both within-gender and between-gender vocal comparisons were made. In the immediate test conducted earlier, recall that infants had resumed a fast rate of sucking when they heard a new voice of the same gender. The delay wiped out this effect; there was a significant increase in sucking only for the between-gender change of voice. It evidently took the more salient contrast between male and female voices to survive the delay interval.

To summarize, when two-month-olds' discrimination was tested with minimal memory load, consonantal contrasts and minor (within-gender) vocal variations were about equally discriminable. When memory load was increased, vocal variations had to be exaggerated or made more salient for performance to keep abreast of consonantal discrimination.

From Voices to Vowels

When children begin to treat the sounds of language as linguistic units, they have already been using them for a different purpose for some months. They have regularly used vocalization, on some level of consciousness, to convey their feelings and their intentions. They have preferentially responded to manipulations of vowel frequency and, less markedly, to vowel amplitude and duration, by mothers and other individuals who seek to make their speech (or their presence) interesting. Invaluably, voices—and therefore vowels—have conveyed indexical information about the age, sex, and state of mind of the individuals with whom the infant has come in contact.

Of course, vowels play an additional role that infants can initially know little about: they make a referential difference. Vowels distinguish words. How easily will the infant come to hear the melodious and emotional signals of its babyhood as members of phonological categories, as lexical communication requires?

THE CURIOUS NEGLECT OF THE VOWELS

We have generally assumed that, relative to consonants, vowels were fairly easy for children to produce. Many of the children that come into speech clinics appear to have the vowels down pat, seemingly speaking with the rhythm and prosody of their native language even when they have no more than a handful of consonantal forms. It appears, however, that some children may have difficulty getting into the vowels. Just how many we do not know, because consonants have been the central focus of most work on phonological development.

Stoel-Gammon was among the first to call attention to the neglect of vowels in accounts of phonological development (Stoel-Gammon, 1990; Stoel-Gammon and Herrington, 1990). The neglect has been so complete, and so persistent, that it calls for an explanation. Stoel-Gammon (1990) observed that "one reason vowels are often ignored is that vowel errors tend to be less discrete than consonantal errors; they are, in some sense, less perceptible and seem to be more difficult to transcribe reliably. In addition, dialectal differences in the pronunciation of vowels may make us more tolerant of variations in the production of target vowels" (p. 259). When vowels express dialectal variations, they potentially tell us something about where, when, and in what social circumstances a person grew up, and what level of education that person has attained—this in addition to "the usual" information about age, sex, affect, and personality! Little wonder that when acoustic analysis became illuminating enough to identify particular speakers, the records were referred to as "voice prints."

It is widely held in phonetics that consonantal movement patterns are more complex than vocalic ones and develop later; these facts are thought to account for the observation that consonant sounds generally take longer to master than vowel sounds. If we encounter exceptions to the modal pattern, therefore, we are likely to suspect that extra-motoric factors may be operating. One possibility, it seems to me, is related to a developmental reorientation that is logically necessary with vowels but which consonants would not require. But first, let us look at recent evidence on some possible exceptions to the general developmental pattern of vocalic superiority.

There have been a few case studies of unusual difficulties with vowel production in children having immature phonological systems. Stoel-Gammon and Herrington (1990) described a phonologically delayed girl who at three years, eight months, was 43 percent accurate on the consonants and 38 percent accurate on the vowels. Davis and MacNeilage (1990) described in some detail a young girl's emerging sound system with especial attention to the vowels (and to consonant-vowel interactions). They found that their subject's accuracy in producing vowels came no where near that which would be expected of adults. Based on a large sample of utterances, the girl's accuracy in producing English vowels varied from 15 to 89 percent correct, with a mean accuracy of 57 percent. No account of the girl's consonantal development was reported, however, so no direct comparisons between her production of consonants and vowels is possible.

What explains the poor vocalic performance of Davis and MacNeilage's subject? Let us pause for a moment to consider the child's situation prior to spoken language. When first observed, she was already using a minimum of several dozen words and during the succeeding six months of the study took on over seven hundred additional words. Because we are given no relevant information, we can only speculate that up to that point, she—like other infants—communicated by way of vocal affect and prosody (according to Davis and MacNeilage, even during the period of her burgeoning vocabulary about a fifth of the girl's recorded utterances were babbles). Since these "paralinguistic" attributes are carried almost exclusively by vowels, it is not implausible that the girl continued to convey and interpret affective information at the expense of the vowels as linguistic categories.

There may be an analogy here between affective-linguistic perception and duplex perception (Whalen and Liberman, 1987), in which under laboratory conditions one is able to hear simultaneously a synthetic phonetic element, such as an isolated formant transition, both as a chirplike auditory event and as a fully integrated segmental cue to place of articulation. In a somewhat analogous fashion, when listeners hear an utterance under socially natural conditions they normally develop a global impression of its meaning. But to a degree, they hear and judge the emotionality of the message separately. After all, in everyday life it is commonplace to hear verbal messages that seem insincere or sarcastic; as listeners, we know when vocal and facial emotionality does not fit with lexical content. I think this duality constitutes the *duplexity* of natural communication. Along with other types of evidence it seems to speak to a neural specialization that is brought to bear upon problems of social cognition and of language analysis (Locke, 1992a). I will spend more time on this problem in Chapter 9.

How do infants progress from "uniplex" to duplex perception? It would seem that some cognitive remodeling is called for, and it is conceivable that some infants have difficulty with the transition from vowel-as-voice to vowel-as-voice-*and*-linguistic-unit. In dynamical systems theory, such children may be said to experience difficulty shifting from one set of controlling parameters to another. At present, we know little about how these dual capabilities develop.

If the transition is not a smooth one, the vocalic progression from prespeech utterances to words may be discontinuous, for the vowels would long have functioned as vehicles for the expression of feeling states. Consonantlike sounds, on the other hand, would not have previously served as affective channels and will not be used to transmit linguistic and nonlinguistic information in parallel. For their part, children will not need to cope with the functional duality of consonants, and consonantal production would be expected to develop under a set of constraints different from those applying to vowels. But any child having difficulty with the transition from vowel as indexical and affective signal to vowel as linguistic unit will produce discontinuous acquisition data, as Davis and MacNeilage's subject may have, and will experience difficulty in the production of vowels, as their subject certainly did. Obviously, we need much more information on children's phonetic development in general, including vowels, consonants, vowel-consonant interactions, vocal affect and prosody, and we are greatly in need of data on young children's linguistic perception and social interpretation of speech that is directed to them.

Later I will take up findings by Davis and MacNeilage (1990) and by Stoel-Gammon (1983) which suggest that vowels may influence consonants more than consonants influence vowels, that is, that vowels seem to be *primary* in some sense. In the meantime, I will ask whether "paralinguistic" information merely shares the same vocal stream with linguistically encoded messages, or more intriguingly, if the rise and fall of a speaker's voice tells us, and babies, something about words and phrases.

THE USE OF PROSODY TO LOCATE WORDS

Certainly infants are aware of changes in vocal frequency, intensity, and time, as they are of variations in vocal quality. As we saw earlier, they prefer speech that has large sweeps of fundamental frequency, and this is what many mothers offer their babies. What does this do, if anything, for the development of linguistic comprehension? Infants pay attention to vowels, and one can hardly imagine a more helpful perceptual bias, for the vowel, by dint of its capacity to carry stress, is capable of highlighting other levels of language. According to Fernald's model (1991), infants at some point begin to use prosodic variations such as stress to find linguistic units in physically continuous streams of speech. This allows them to comprehend running speech, to develop vocabulary, and ultimately to put together a linguistic sound system.

Hirsh-Pasek et al. (1987) found that seven- to ten-month-old infants are sensitive to prosodic cues that correspond to clause boundaries. In their investigation, the infants were seated near two loudspeakers. One played speech that was interrupted *at* clause boundaries, for example, "Cinderella lived in a great big house / but it was sort of dark / because she had this . . ." The other speaker delivered speech in which interruptions were inserted *within* clause boundaries, for example, "Cinderella lived in a great big house, but it was / sort of dark because she had / this . . ." It was found that infants spent significantly more time looking toward the source of speech that had been interrupted at clause boundaries than toward the speaker playing within-clause interruptions. Intriguingly, in a follow-up study it was found that this effect applied only to "motherese"—speech that mothers address to their infants—and not to adult-directed speech (Kemler Nelson et al., 1989). This suggests that mothers may systematically manipulate prosody in such a way as to highlight clause boundaries for their babies.

It is likely, I think, that infants also use prosodic cues to identify words. In adults, this seems to be the case. Cutler and Carter (1987) examined dictionaries and frequency counts of English words to see if stress was sufficiently regular to assist linguistically naive listeners in their efforts to locate word boundaries, that is, to pick words out of a stream of continuous speech. Specifically, they looked at the incidence of content words that are monosyllabic or begin with strong syllables, such as *analogue* and *structure*. Usage frequency data revealed that 90 percent of content words are either monosyllables or begin with strong syllables, and the authors concluded that stress was potentially a reliable cue to word onset. One wonders whether other languages offer the same opportunities.

Do English-speaking listeners actually use stress cues to locate words? Cutler and Norris (1988) conducted an experiment to find out. First, they constructed a number of nonword disyllables that contained a real word as a strong or a weak syllable. For example, they heard the word *mint* in *mintayve*, where the second syllable was strong, and in *mintesh*, where the second syllable was weak. Listeners were to signal whenever they heard a nonsense construction that contained a real word. Cutler and Norris hypothesized that if listeners associate strong syllables with words, they would respond more quickly and accurately when the real word was stressed (for example, *mintesh*), and this is what happened, suggesting that syllabic stress tells listeners which phonemic strings they should use to initiate a search of their mental lexicon.

Infants find out about words in several different ways. One is that they hear them in acoustic isolation, thanks frequently to their mothers, who may be inclined to bracket citation forms with silence. Another is that infants hear a word in enough different phonetic contexts to eventually figure out which parts of the word belong to the lexical item itself and which more properly belong to its neighbors. And finally, one must suppose that infants, oriented as they are to stress differences in adult speech, identify words by following the trail of stress cues. For English, they will be right far more times than they are wrong if they follow a simple rule: if you want to find a word, look to the right of stressed syllable onsets.

Although it is unclear whether some children have difficulty with this rule, it is easy to see that the discovery of a great many words would be difficult for a child who did. In this connection, it should be recognized that, while children with specific language impairments have restricted lexicons (Leonard, 1982), they demonstrate no special difficulty in acquiring new lexical items when these appear in controlled sentence frames such as "Here's the ——" and "Watch the baby ——" (Leonard, Schwartz, Chapman et al., 1982). In light of these findings, it might be worth asking if specifically language impaired children have any particular difficulty dealing with prosody or using vocal frequency and stress as a springboard to other levels of language.

I should mention that movements of the eyes are not irrelevant to parsing. Indeed, speakers tend to glance at their listeners at the beginning and end of utterances (Levine and Sutton-Smith, 1973), and their level of gaze tends to rise rapidly at the beginning of a phrase boundary pause (Kendon, 1967). I think it likely that the listener-observer uses these ocular gaze patterns, along with vocal cues, to isolate linguistically coherent material.

By synthesizing findings from cross-sectional studies, it becomes possible to detect sequences in communicative development. In all normally developing infants, the facial transmission of emotion precedes the development of gestural communication, which in turn anticipates the emergence of lexical reference. If this sequence involves functional dependence, an infant with a disturbance of facial affect—as sender or receiver—may be at risk for the gestural and referential behaviors normally expected to come later. In this connection, clinical evidence indicates that autistic children, probably for neurological reasons, display reduced vocal and facial affect. As one might expect, autistic children also reveal reduced "indicating behaviors" such as showing and pointing (Attwood, Frith, and Hermelin, 1988), and a less than normal amount of referential looking and joint attention, which appears to retard (and to predict) linguistic development in this population (Mundy and Sigman, 1989; Mundy, Sigman, and Kasari, 1990).

PERCEPTION OF SPEECH SEGMENTS

In the early 1970s there was a great deal of interest in the perceptual sensitivity of neonates to synthetic-speech contrasts that correspond to the category boundaries of real-speech phonemes. When the nonnutritive sucking paradigm was developed and the finding of categorical perception was initially reported (Eimas et al., 1971), psycholinguists rushed to do studies to show that the major (that is, universal) speech contrasts were already operational soon after birth and, therefore, probably "prewired" into the human newborn's auditory or speech-processing mechanisms. I still recall a very senior psycholinguist saying at a conference in 1978 that if this work was relevant to language, we had better stop and take stock of what all this meant, since language *develops*. I will return to this point later after briefly visiting the work on infants' perception of segmental contrasts.

Studies of infants in the first few months of life reveal adultlike categorical discrimination for all major categories of consonantal features, including articulatory place, manner, and voicing, and differential response to a range of vocalic contrasts. In essence, the evidence from sucking studies is that when infants adapt to a phonetic element, they are best dishabituated by elements drawn from linguistically different phonetic categories. This is true at least with computer-synthesized laboratory speech, where the vocal carrier is aprosodic, unemotional, and unrecognizable.

Because there is little listening time in the first month or two, and since other animals can discriminate some of the same contrasts (see review in Moody, Stebbins, and May, 1990), several observers have commented that the human infant's perceptual biases seem to be "innate." And indeed, there is awareness of strong phonetic feature contrasts in the first few days of life. Using the high amplitude sucking paradigm, Bertoncini et al. (1987) presented French five-day-olds with artificially shortened CV syllables consisting of a burst portion followed by just 29 msec of voicing. The neonates discriminated [ba] from [da] and [ga], and also discriminated [ba] from [bi], [da] from [di], and [ga] from [gi]. There was a tendency for changes in sucking rate to be greater for vocalic than for consonantal changes, but this difference was not significant. In light of the subjects' extreme youth and inexperience, Bertoncini et al. suggest that "infants are born with an innate predisposition for extracting invariant acoustic properties . . . which provide a framework for perceiving the phonetic dimensions of speech" (p. 36).

It is more likely that infants are preadapted to process phonetic cues, and that even brief exposures to speech are sufficient to activate and stabilize their pre- or neonatal biases. That this preadaptation may include subcortical mechanisms is suggested by the subcortical processing of faces during the same period, by the relatively unimpaired course of perceptual development displayed by children at risk for language disorders (Swoboda, Morse, and Leavitt, 1976), and by one dramatic case of intact consonantal discrimination in an anencephalic infant (Graham et al., 1978).

DEVELOPMENT OF FUNCTIONAL PERCEPTION

Recently, questions have been raised about the developmental significance of experiments reporting categorical perception of synthetic speech by infants. According to Studdert-Kennedy (1991), those studies

seem to have no more than a general bearing on the specialized development of language. They are psychophysical studies, demonstrating that infants at, or soon after, birth have the capacity to discriminate and categorize certain acoustic patterns which occur in speech. They provide detailed support for a general observation, suggested by the fact that speech sounds are concentrated in the few octaves of the acoustic spectrum to which humans (and many other animals) are most sensitive: spoken language has evolved and develops within the constraints of prelinguistic auditory capacity. Surely it would be surpris-

ing if this were not so. We do not expect an animal to have a communication system that is not matched to its sensory capacities! (p. 16)

The relevant experiments confirm that what must be logically
true is also empirically true. But Studdert-Kennedy went on to add
an even more serious objection to functional interpretations of the
work on neonatal perception. Development generally proceeds from
the general to the specific, and complex structures evolve by differentiation of a larger entity into smaller parts or functions. We
should expect, then, that phonemes fall out of words, that is, that
they are made possible by the child's knowledge of words. If the
neonate's awareness of "phoneme-sized" contrasts were a functional
development, the psycholinguistic account would be exactly backwards both ontogenetically and phylogenetically.

Others have criticized the "nativistic account" of the early investigators on the grounds that it placed too little emphasis on experience. Since there are thousands of different languages in the
world, each having its own phonological system, there is much to
any particular language that is learned, and prelinguistic perceptual categories are modified or lost in the process. Let us turn, then,
to a functional model of perceptual development, one that starts
with the assumption that young infants are aware of acoustic variations that are more or less aligned to the requirements of speech,
but also assumes that listening experience is needed, that phonetic
and phonological experience is necessary to development of spoken
language.

A Model of Perceptual Development

When we systematically investigate perceptual development we
stand to find out to what degree the infant is aware of acoustic
energies that happen to be functionally significant at the level of
the phoneme, syllable, word, and higher-order linguistic units such
as phrases and sentences. A great deal rests on this; the theoretical
stakes are high. We may also learn if infants pay more attention
to certain phonetic patterns than to others. In principle, this could
explain selective effects in infants' learning by telling us why certain elements appear in the infant's speech before others. It also
offers clues about the completeness and grammaticality of utter-

ances produced in the presence of the child, for as Atkinson (1982) has advised, "if the child is devoting more attention, processing capacity, etc. to certain segments of an utterance, then the chances are that his perception of the rest of the utterances will be downgraded in some way. It seems inevitable in these circumstances that the child will be confronted with ungrammatical data which are not labelled as such. In terms of a traditional psychological distinction it is the *proximal* stimulus which is relevant for the learning procedure and not the *distal* stimulus" (p. 232, italics his).

A decade ago, several speech theorists, inspired by Gilbert Gottlieb's work with ducks mentioned earlier, created a model of perceptual development that contained provisions for separate processes—maintenance, learning, and loss (Aslin and Pisoni, 1980; Walley, Pisoni, and Aslin, 1981). Research supports the existence of these processes in the second six months of life, when experience maintains some early perceptual biases and alters or obliterates others.

MAINTENANCE AND LOSS

Infants remain able to distinguish phonetic features they discriminate in the early postnatal period if those features are functional components of language. The early discriminations that are maintained are "robust" spectral and temporal contrasts, such as the voiced-voiceless distinction between stop consonants (Burnham, 1986), that are very likely to be present in every language. Although infants initially reveal an awareness of these "universal" contrasts, it is not until the second six months of life that they reveal the emergent capacity to discriminate weak phonetic contrasts. During this interval, they demonstrate an environmental effect that is not strictly acquisitive but is nonetheless vital to the development of spoken language: the selective loss and readjustment of "fragile" postnatal perceptual categories that are not reinforced by exposure to the ambient language (Burnham, 1986; Werker and Pegg, 1992).

LEARNING

If the research of Lecanuet et al. (1989) is replicated, we will have to accept that segmental phonetic learning is possible prior to birth.

Recall that this French team placed loudspeakers on the abdomens of women in their last trimester of pregnancy (between thirty-five and thirty-eight weeks gestation) and presented either [babi] or [biba]. One group of subjects was first exposed to [babi] and the other to [biba]. Lecanuet and his colleagues obtained a significant cardiac deceleration during the first few seconds of stimulation, an effect which recurred when the stimulus was changed from [babi] to [biba] or vice versa. Though the effect may have been acoustic, it would at least be an acoustic effect that supports a phonetic contrast.

Because so much attention has been called to the infant's adult-like discrimination of consonantal contrasts in the first few months of life, some may draw the false impression that all the major phonetic contrasts are discriminable soon after birth and have no course of acquisition. This is not true. The ability to discriminate weak phonetic features, such as the place information in certain of the fricatives, tends to emerge during the second six months of life (Eilers and Minifie, 1975; Eilers, Wilson, and Moore, 1977).

Phonetic learning, loss, and and a variety of other perceptual readjustments traceable to ambient stimulation occur in the second six months of life. This may build on the very rapid cortical growth that occurs in the first six months (a matter to be taken up in Chapter 7). In his classic dissection studies, Conel (1939–1967) found a distinct peak in the rate of growth of motor cortex at approximately six months, at which age there is more dendritic branching in the left hemisphere in both motor and speech-motor areas than in the right hemisphere (Simonds and Scheibel, 1989). Other studies (Lecours, 1975; Yakovlev and Lecours, 1967) suggest that intra- and interhemispheric cortical association bundles begin to myelinate postnatally at about five to six months. Presumably the true developments in perceptual ability—those associated with specific patterns of ambient stimulation—take place as cortical matters. Phonetic perceptual capacities demonstrable in the neonate may be more reliant on subcortical structures. If so, newborns' preference for maternal voice quality and prosody, *and* categorical perception of synthetic speech material may occur subcortically. If so, there might be a temporary interruption in speech discrimination between the first month or two and the next several months, paralleling the course of face discrimination over the same period.

FEATURAL BIASES AND MEMORIAL CONSTRAINTS

I have talked of perceptual biases, physical patterns which selectively command the neonate's attention. To the degree that these biases correspond to linguistically important features, which they do, the components of language become easier to learn. This is the human equivalent to "learning by instinct." But Newport (1990) has argued that in addition it is critical that children possess a means of constraining the almost endless sea of raw data from which cues must be extracted if they are to synthesize an adultlike linguistic system. She suggests that limitations on short-term memory may naturally restrict linguistic samples, causing children to concentrate upon the smaller stretches that are likely to comprise functional units and eliminating the need to search through extensive mental corpora in order to locate critical linguistic cues. I think Newport may be right about the need for perceptual focus, but "constraints" may be unnecessary if the prosody of motherese accomplishes the same purpose, as was suggested by studies reviewed above (Hirsh-Pasek et al., 1987; Kemler Nelson et al., 1989).

Some have commented on the role of perceptual biases in sentential processing, although there is no consensus on their nature. Slobin (1973) has suggested that children pay special attention to the ends of sentences. Others have reported evidence to suggest that children are particularly aware of the beginnings of sentences (Newport, Gleitman, and Gleitman, 1977). It is obvious that we need additional investigation of children's perceptual orientation at the level of the phrase or sentence.

Perceptual Self-Determination

How can we know what stimulation constitutes an infant's perceptual environment? Surely we could begin by asking about the speech that is directed to the infant and produced in its presence. But others only generate the range of sounds to which the infant will then choose to react. Moreover, my guess is that no matter what they say, it is likely to be adequate. Scarr (1992) has argued that the reason parental behavior affects children less than genetics is that most well-meaning parents are *good enough*. Because of this good enough attribute, the differences between families are relatively benign. In all probability, the spoken language habits displayed in most homes is *good enough speech*. Experiential effects are therefore likely to be introduced by the infant itself. The infant's *effective* perceptual world is determined by what the infant notices. Infants are free to attend selectively to sound patterns whose physical characteristics appeal to their auditory and phonetic processing systems.

Infants proactively (a) attend to certain patterns of phonetic stimulation corresponding to perceptual biases present early in life, which are caused by interactions between genetic and early (intrauterine or neonatal) stimulation; (b) attend to stimulation provided by their own activity (see Gibson, 1966, for a discussion of the infant's perception of its own activity); (c) produce sounds, look at particular objects, and in other ways effectively solicit the phonetic, lexical, and semantic information upon which their own linguistic code will be constructed. Let us examine the evidence.

THE INFANT'S USE OF NONVERBAL CONTROL MECHANISMS

In the previous chapter I argued that infants play an active role in their own development. Some research implies that infants' own activity may cause their perceptual capacity to expand. I think the raw material for a nonlinguistic model for such effects may be available in the findings of Campos and Bertenthal and their associates (Bertenthal, Campos, and Barrett, 1984; Telzrow et al., 1987; Campos and Bertenthal, 1989; Bertenthal and Campos, in press; Kermoian and Campos, 1988), who have described some developmental effects of infants' emergent locomotor activity. This model may suggest a role for self-vocalization in the development of speech and speech monitoring systems. The behavior in question, crawling, seems to be at least partly responsible for:

1. *Visual-vestibular adaptation.* Infants learn through their own movement how to compensate posturally for changes in vestibular sensation. Bertenthal and Bai (1989) found that between seven and nine months, infants become able to right themselves, that is, adjust their posture to visually perceived alterations in the walls of a small test room.

2. *Visual attention to changes in the environment.* Infants who plan to move from A to B must identify any obstacles or special challenges that lie in the path between these points. As

infants begin to crawl, they are likely to become more interested in their physical environment.

3. *Social referencing.* Newly crawling infants expose themselves to a variety of risky situations before they are able to assess danger. For this reason, locomoting infants frequently look at their mother and reveal heightened awareness of maternal affect. They look at their mother more frequently after the beginning of crawling than before and are more affected by her facially expressed emotions (Bertenthal and Campos, 1990).

4. *Conceptual development.* When infants begin to locomote, they stop defining the physical environment in relation to their own location. This seems to encourage the developmental transition from egocentric (self-oriented) to allocentric (object-oriented) coding of the physical environment.

5. *Differentiation of emotions.* Crawling and walking typically elicit positive affect from parents, since these activities represent desirable stages of maturation and development. Parents also react to certain of their infant's movements with fear and alarm, which may be partly responsible for the acquired fear of heights. At times, infants will also become frustrated and angry because of various barriers to movement.

If locomotion serves the functions identified above, I suspect that vocalizing may have its own developmental effects, initially in the area of vocal imitation and ultimately in complex phonetic learning. More will be said about this in Chapter 5; some possible neural effects of self-produced activity are taken up in Chapter 7.

At the beginning of this chapter I asked what it was like to be a baby, since our own perceptual experience as an adult is a poor guide. It does not tell us what infants are likely to pay attention to, and it gives us little information about infants' interpretations of those things to which they do attend. If animals tend to learn about the things they pay attention to, we need to ask what the human infant focuses on when people are talking. We must also ask what cues are given off by the act of speaking. These displays contain all the language-pertinent information the environment has to offer.

The evidence is that humans begin to pay attention to and learn about the voice at a very early age, probably in the final trimester of gestation. At birth, the neonate is obviously oriented to conspecific voice, since it becomes aware of properties of its own voice and that of its mother within the first several days of life and seems already to prefer prosodic patterns associated with its mother's tongue. From its earliest opportunity, the infant seeks out the particular kinds of stimulation that it enjoys and that its brain may need in order to develop maximally. The development of vocal perception is therefore influenced by the infant's own activities.

Other cues given off by talking people include the visible movement patterns of the face. Newborns prefer facelike to nonfacelike stimuli and quickly learn to recognize their mother's face. They are also aware of facial movements, particularly mouth posturings of various kinds. Early in their infancy young humans express more interest in the eyes than in any other region of the face. This is adaptive, since the eyes are vital components of our social signaling system, revealing much about the objects of our attention and about our social intentions and attitudes. The human infant is more inclined to look at a pleasantly moving face than at one that is passive, and it prefers a voice that rises and falls to one with little tonal variation.

The human infant, then, is largely preadapted to indexical and affective communication; when family members speak, babies tend to look and listen. The movements of the articulators can frequently be seen, and they augment speech reception. The movements of the emotionally expressive parts of the face can also support an intended message or, in cases of deception, contradict it. Infants are aware of the correspondence between certain kinds of facial and vocal activity by as early as three to four months, which is not surprising since there appears to be a single neural system that coordinates the activities of these affective signaling systems.

Voices provide infants with information about the identity and social intentions of the individual who is speaking, but voices are not necessarily offered up just for that purpose. Rather, voices are supplied by the vowels (primarily) of people who are talking. At some point, the developing infant needs to recognize the linguistic significance of vowels while not losing its handle on their indexical and affective properties. How this occurs is unknown, and it is unlikely to be understood until more work is done on the development of vowels in the context of social communication.

Because infants are increasingly exposed to the distinctive phonetic stimulation of their linguistic community, some of their previous perceptual sensitivities naturally readjust. Some perceptual categories shift or fade out, while others are retained or slightly sharpened. How these behavioral changes are reflected in the brain is unknown, although in the first few years of life the brain loses some of the "experience expectant" synapses that are present at birth while experiencing a change in the efficacy of other synapses and an increase in dendritic branching.

The changes in perceptual behavior observed during and toward the end of the first year of life take place in the context of social interactions. The infant is not merely exposed, it experiences. These social interactions move the child along the path to spoken language.

3

THE SOCIAL CAPACITY
FOR SPOKEN LANGUAGE

Any function in the child's cultural development appears twice, or on two planes. First it appears on the social plane, and then on the psychological plane. First it appears between people as an interpsychological category, and then within the child as an intrapsychological category . . . Social relations or relations among people genetically underlie all higher functions and their relationships.

L. S. Vygotsky, "The Development of Higher Forms of Attention in Childhood"

Earlier I said that organisms tend to learn about the things to which they pay attention. In Chapter 2 I identified cues that attract infants to the social act of speaking and therefore draw them to the physical nature of speech. But I said little about any *in kind* responses by the infant to what it observes when people talk, or about any two-way communications of the kind that spoken language is *for*. Ultimately, one supposes that linguistic capacity is driven by the desire to convey, a desire that arises within a social framework whose function and structure are understood by the participants. One presumes that this framework is elaborated when the infant discovers that its intentions can literally be given voice and can be inferred by others when they are.

We also need to understand the referential experiences that promote first the comprehension of words and then the use of words that are comprehended. How do infants know what we are talking about? How do parents know what objects and activities engage the attention of their child, the names of which the child might wish to know? To get answers to questions like these, each party must analyze the superficial behaviors of the other. These analyses are performed in the fractions of a second in which glancing, reaching, pointing, and uttering take place. Mothers need to know that a thing being looked at by their baby is a thing that they should name. For their part, infants need to know that the sounds Mother says go with the thing they are looking at.

Social relationships are the context for communication and thus the context within which linguistic communication develops. In this chapter I will discuss the development of the social capacity for spoken language. In doing so, I will appeal to various sources of information, including findings on nonhuman primates as well as on our own species, and discuss data from clinical populations that include children who are blind or retarded.

We have all heard that language develops in a social context (Bruner, 1981), but what does "social" mean? Clearly, infants will need to spend some time observing individuals who are behaving linguistically. But language, as Studdert-Kennedy (1991) has said, is action, and it is revealed through interaction. So infants will need to interact with linguistically behaving individuals, not merely observe them.

Social interactions are guided by physical cues. Hahn defines social interaction as "the interlocking of behavior between two or more organisms by virtue of the cue functions that each behavior or act has for the other organism. Such cue or stimulus functions serve to attract, direct, synchronize, facilitate, or inhibit the social activities of another organism and thus shape the interaction" (1990, p. 65). The facial and vocal movements produced by people who are talking are the currency of social transactions. When infants immerse themselves in these sensory experiences, they take a path that leads to systems for encoding and classification and to more complex forms of communication. These systems, as *we* know, will facilitate management of the infant's physical and social environment, but this is a serendipitous byproduct enjoyed by fully developed individuals who are able to access and privately experience aspects of their linguistic knowledge. Benefits such as these make language worth using and "having," yet the infant cannot know this. What the infant does know is what it likes to experience, and it likes to experience faces, voices, and other stimuli provided by caregivers on whose assistance its very life, over a protracted period, vitally depends. Let us join up with the infant at that level of interaction and follow the trail to its linguistic consequences.

Affective Reactions to Facial Stimuli

To understand how it is that facial displays carry out their social function, we need to know what expectations we interpreters of facial messages bring to the task. What parts and movements of the face do we look at? Where in the face do we go to get our information? And how is it that friendly faces cause the infant to vocalize playfully? How does the sight of smiling faces ultimately contribute to vocal imitation?

Reactions to faces are very well defined in the primate world. Sackett (1966) showed pictures of conspecific animals to rhesus monkeys that had been reared in isolation; except for early feeding episodes, they never saw other monkeys. Nevertheless, they reacted very sharply to still color slides of conspecific monkeys with threatening expressions, and their behavior was marked by vocalization and a variety of "disturbances" such as withdrawal, rocking, huddling, and other fear reactions.

Young monkeys are also very sensitive to the gaze patterns of conspecific animals. Mendelson, Haith, and Goldman-Rakic (1982) presented infant rhesus monkeys with four color photographs of a conspecific animal. The subjects were tested at one, three, and seven weeks of life. The angle of viewing was adjusted so that it would appear to the subjects that the photographed monkey was looking away from them, to the left or right, or looking at them from the left or right. Each subject's visual activity was recorded with an infrared corneal-reflection technique. Mendelson et al. found that at one week of age, monkeys looked equally long at faces that were looking away from them and faces that were looking at them. At both of the older ages, however, the monkeys selectively averted their gaze when shown photographs of animals that seemed to look directly at them. These studies suggest that little experience is needed for development of these perceptuofacial social reactions.

A facial scan analysis revealed that the monkeys directed their attention to internal constituents of the faces,[1] devoting their longest looks to the closer of the two ears and the next longest looks to

1. A complication in the interpretation of these findings is that primates may decline to look directly at features of which they may nonetheless be aware.

the eyes. Among other things, this analysis revealed that the monkeys showed very little interest in the *mouth*. At all three ages, the monkeys paid this structure—the instrument of biting, vocalization, and several affective displays—less attention than the nose, eyes, forehead, and hair.

Apparently, monkeys and human infants are alike in this indifference to the mouth. Recall that in Figure 2.6 we displayed data by some of the same investigators (Haith et al., 1977), which indicated that human infants looked longer at all other regions that were studied—the edges of the face and the eyes and nose—than at the mouth. For some reason, the mouth, whether still or moving, is relatively less interesting to human and nonhuman primates, and yet human babies imitate mouth movements an hour after birth.

Since language develops out of social interactions, to understand the development of language we need to identify the factors and circumstances that promote socialization. These things will be at least as important to language as any other distal factors such as brain size or vocal tract configuration. According to Coe (1990), the socialization of young primates reflects several phylogenetic trends. First, with evolution there has been a reduction in the number of infants born in a litter and a lengthening of the interval between births. Gestation is about three to four months in prosimians, five to six months in monkeys, and eight months in the great apes. Correspondingly, maternal care lasts about three to six months in prosimians, six to twelve months in monkeys, and four to six years in the great apes. The protractedness of these periods makes more important the survival of each individual infant and lengthens the period of intimate mother-infant contact.

Among humans, there is an even greater period of gestation and a longer interval over which mothers see to the needs of the infant most recently born. This period of protracted nurturance strengthens initial feelings of attachment and encourages frequent interactions. These interactions, which include turn taking and joint visual attention, are vitally important to language, for they provide the necessary conditions for vocal learning and the emergence of reference.

Attachment, Turn Taking, and Joint Visual Attention

Jerome Bruner was right when, a decade ago, he told an interviewer that "learning is not simply the kid operating solo in a random environment. Learning is being part of a society, with that society trying somehow to keep the error rate down to a minimum by arranging manageable encounters" (1983, p. 41). In a more explicit reference to language, Bruner commented that "the early human capacity to recognize the constitutive rules of the language and the matching adult capacity to frame input to make it acceptable as input to this system—operate in unison as preadapted species-specific systems" (1981, p. 176). He envisioned negotiations between the child's Language Acquisition Device and its parents' Language Assistance System.

I believe that conversational exchanges are anticipated in the very earliest interactions, which occur within a nurturant framework between the infant's mother and itself. Kenneth Kaye sees similarities between this framework and that of other mother-infant dyads in the mammalian world: "It is neither the baby whale's propensities for swimming nor his mother's propensities for pushing him to the surface which guarantees his survival and his subsequent exposure to the necessary and sufficient experiences for whaleness. It is instead the perfect design of each partner's behavior for the other's" (1979, p. 193).

What is linguistically significant about mother-infant interactions? When infants become *attached* to their mothers many language-critical processes are encouraged: the desire to engage in playful vocalization, including vocal exploration, the emergence of turn taking and dialogue structure, and the desire to imitate vocal patterns. In turn, mothers who are attached to and feeling nurturant toward their infants provide them with a number of opportunities to learn. Among the other processes encouraged by attachment are the use of eye gaze and manual gestures to signal attentional focus and convey labels, and the use of voice to designate and convey. Attachment is a powerfully enabling construct that conspires with other factors to set it all in motion.

ATTACHMENT

In the first few weeks and months of life, infants normally develop a feeling of attachment to their mother (Bowlby, 1969). This emotional affiliation is woven with several strands of sensory stimulation, including the mother's voice and face and possibly her touch and smell. One can test for the presence of attachment in several ways. One can compare the infant's behavior when alone with its mother and alone with a stranger. And a more drastic test is to briefly separate the infant from its mother.

The story is similar in nonhuman primates. Infant monkeys tend to be tightly attached to their mother by the age of three to four weeks, at which time even brief separations can produce anxiety and depression (Rosenblum, 1978). They, like humans, also need a mechanism for remaining physically attached. Nonhuman primate mothers and infants quickly learn the sound of the other party, and use their voices to preserve or regain contact (see review in Nash and Wheeler, 1982). Adult females appear to produce certain types of vocalizations in the service of affiliation with other "bonded" females (Smith et al., 1982). One wonders if nonhuman primates also vocalize differently when "addressing" their infants, if there is an ape or monkey version of "motherese."

Attachment is both encouraged and sustained by affective communication. Bowlby (1969) has suggested that vocalization is the infant's instrument for maintaining maternal contact. He commented that "babbling . . . has the function of maintaining a mother-figure in proximity to an infant by promoting social interchange between them" (p. 289). In turn, it appears that vocal and referential learning are encouraged by the social and emotional ties between the infant and its mother or other caregivers.

How Do INFANTS BECOME ATTACHED?   In the first few days of life, infants respond preferentially to the sound, sight, and to some degree, the smell of their mother. They spend hours looking at her face, seeming to gaze directly into her eyes. When normal levels of maternal contact are unavailable or disrupted, neonates expand their ocular focus to include any other adults that happen to be nearby (Hittelman and Dickes, 1979). New parents respond readily to eye gazing and generally show an intense interest in the eyes of their neonate (Klaus, Trause, and Kennell, 1975). They also cater to their infant's interest in faces by making their own readily available for examination; they put their face near and in the proper orientation to the infant's own face (Papousek and Papousek, 1984).

As infants develop, they increasingly gaze at their mother. Farran and Kasari (1990) found that between six and twenty months, infants nearly double the time they spend looking at their mother's face, and this nearly doubles again between twenty and thirty-six months. Clearly, such an escalating investment of energy must be sustained by emotional benefits. There is an indication of this in infants' responses to inexpressive faces. In one experiment where mothers were instructed to look at their baby with a "poker face" (Tronick, Als, Adamson et al., 1978), the infants smiled less, slumped down in their seats, and looked away. The mothers reported that "they found it very difficult to sit still-faced in front of the infant and resist his powerful sallies and bids to interaction" (p. 10). In another study, maternal poker face significantly reduced three- and four-month-old's eye gaze at their mother (Berger and Cunningham, 1981).

In other research (Cohn and Tronick, 1983), mothers of three- and four-month-olds were asked to simulate depression by speaking in a monotone, keeping their faces expressionless, and minimizing body movement and tactile contact with their infant. Depression trials lasted three minutes and were either preceded or followed by control trials of the same duration in which the mother was to behave normally. Cohn and Tronick found that simulated depression caused infants to produce many more sober or negative facial expressions, which continued for at least the first minute after the mother had switched into her normal mode of relating.[2]

If the mother naturally has a poker face, infants may shop around for the facial activity they crave. In a description of the reactions of a sighted infant to her blind mother, Brazelton and his colleagues

2. Apparently either party can induce depression in the other. Brazleton (1961) described a case in which a somewhat deviant infant caused depression in its mother. The mother had eagerly looked forward to the birth and rearing of her son, but he either slept deeply or screamed continuously. The mother could neither rouse him in the former state nor quiet him in the latter. Eventually, she became so consistently depressed that she sought psychotherapy. In terms of other primates, Meier (1975) has conducted research indicating that rhesus monkey mothers reject their own neonates if they display low levels of activity and vocalization.

(Brazelton et al., 1975) noted that the girl "would glance only briefly at her mother's eyes and then avert her eyes and face from the mother as the mother leaned over to talk to her" (p. 146). In contrast, Brazelton et al. observed that the girl "greedily watched" the eyes and faces of the researchers.

The facial and vocal cues that express and reinforce attachment travel over a channel that will be used for speech. If the priming of this channel facilitates language learning, failures of attachment may interfere with vocal and referential learning and, if persistent, negatively affect the development of spoken language.

THE LESS ATTACHED   Thompson, Cicchetti, Lamb et al. (1985) evaluated facial and vocal affect in Down syndrome infants at nineteen months of age and in normally developing control infants at just over twelve and nineteen months. Infants were submitted to the Strange Situation, a procedure consisting of the following seven three-minute episodes:

1. Mother and baby alone in a playroom.
2. Entrance of stranger, who interacts with mother and baby.
3. Mother departs leaving baby alone with stranger.
4. Reunion of mother and baby (stranger departs).
5. Mother's second departure, leaving infant alone in playroom.
6. Stranger's return.
7. Second reunion of mother and baby (stranger departs).

During these episodes, observers classified facial displays of emotion on a six-point scale and vocal displays of emotion on a thirteen-point scale. Analyses of peak intensity and emotional range revealed that the Down syndrome infants showed consistently less facial and vocal affect than both groups of control subjects during all except the last episode. They were less distressed when their mother left the room and they regained their composure sooner when she returned. Down syndrome infants were slower to show even the attenuated changes they did reveal, and they exhibited a restricted range of emotional response. Overall, their emotional reactions were subdued and their socioemotional variability flat.

Figures 3.1 and 3.2 represent some of Thompson et al.'s data. Figure 3.1 shows that there was little change in vocal or facial affect with age and that the infants with Down syndrome were

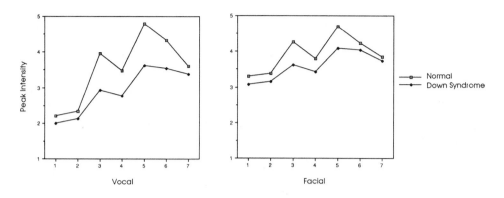

Figure 3.1. Vocal and facial displays of affect by normally developing and Down syndrome infants at nineteen months of age. It is evident that the normally developing infants were more intensely affective in both modes than the Down syndrome infants.

consistently less expressive in both modes. Figure 3.2 contains the same data displayed by group. Note that, since the scales used to rate vocal and facial affect were discommensurate, the useful comparison here is the vocal-facial relationship across the three groups. As the figure reveals, except for Episodes 1 and 2 (with mother; with mother and stranger), where there may have been more facial expressivity, among the normally developing infants there were similar scale values for vocal and facial affect. The Down syndrome

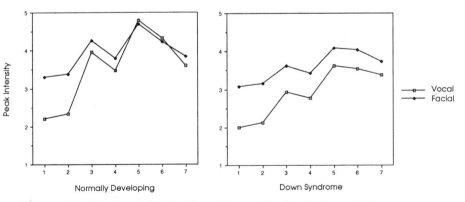

Figure 3.2. Vocal and facial affect of normally developing and Down syndrome infants. The Down syndrome infants were less affective vocally than facially by a somewhat greater margin than the control subjects.

infants, by comparison, were less overtly affective in the vocal than in the facial mode.

Thompson et al.'s analysis of social interactions revealed that Down syndrome infants were significantly less inclined to seek proximity to their mothers or to interact with them from a distance; overall they made fewer social bids for their attention or reactions. Retarded infants also exhibited less search behavior in Episode 5 than the normally developing controls.

Whatever its other values, and there are many, an affective bond is a channel over which emotion is routinely transmitted by voice and face. The same parties will employ this channel to convey linguistic knowledge using similar sets of cues. Attachment starts infants down the path that leads to language and therefore qualifies as a central element in our species-specific capacity for linguistic communication. At present, one can only guess whether this reduced vocal expressivity puts Down syndrome infants in particularly poor stead for languages that are spoken.

ATTACHED TO PHONOLOGY   Before we leave attachment and go on to other social issues I want to take up a question I raised earlier: Why is there a universal bias toward languages that are spoken? One might speculate that speech had an advantage over alternative systems from the start, since voice and vocalizing faces already contain the information—affect and person-identifying—that babies naturally attend to and are prepared to process. The infant begins postnatal life pretuned to that information, relying heavily upon vocal and facial cues as specific points of attachment to his mother. To be assured of a measure of success from the start, it makes excellent biological sense for any other would-be communicative system to "piggy back" onto this open channel—to take immediate advantage of the species-characteristic commitment to maternal-infant attachment by embedding new information in the same stream of cues—and that is what our ancestors did when they invented spoken language. This poses no threat to either the extant attachment system or the new code, since voice quality and prosody may be manipulated independent of articulatory activity. In principle, this gives phonological languages a "naturalness" not shared by systems of encoding in which information about the speaker—

age, sex, identity, mood, credibility, intentions—are conveyed via wholly different muscles and perceptual mechanisms.

VOCAL TURN TAKING

Unlike signed languages, in which signals can overlap without loss of intelligibility (Baker, 1977), speech generally requires that participants take turns, since one cannot efficiently speak and listen simultaneously.

THE VALUE OF VOCAL TURN TAKING IN LINGUISTIC DEVELOP-MENT   The specific reasons for vocal turn taking become clear when one asks why either partner might value the vocal sounds made by the other. As we have seen, infants crave the sight of a friendly face and go out of their way to catch a glimpse of one. They also are willing to expend a great amount of energy in order to hear a familiar voice. It is not surprising, then, that infants are disposed to suspend or to withhold vocalization when their mother is talking.

In nurturant cultures, mothers pay close attention to the voice of their infant from the first postnatal moments (Donovan, Leavitt, and Balling, 1978; Donovan and Leavitt, 1983; Murray, 1985). They use vocal information to identify their infant and gain information about its health and emotional state. Mothers also treat their infant's vocalizations as social signals when they adjust their own utterances to conform to those of their infant.

Some of the silent intervals in bouts of parent-infant vocalization may be introduced by the infant in an attempt to hear the utterances and thereby to know the feelings of the caregiver to which it is attached. Barrett-Goldfarb and Whitehurst (1973) measured the listening preference of four one-year-olds for their father's voice or their mother's voice. Then they recorded the infants' vocalization while playing first one tape and then the other. Significantly, in three of their four one-year-old subjects, the preferred voice was associated with greater suppression, that is, more attention, than the nonpreferred voice. In the fourth subject, the preferred (and more suppressing) voice was the same in seven of eight sessions. Though this research should be replicated with a larger sample, the implication is clear: babies will turn off their own voice if that increases access to the voice of a person they want to hear more.

Turn taking is important to the development of spoken language in several ways. Although it is a manifestation of the desire to hear one another's voice, turn taking also provides a temporal framework for more complex forms of social and emotional communication. Turn taking facilitates vocal learning by encouraging learners to attend to and reproduce model utterances, and by providing mothers with the opportunity to monitor the phonetic quality and semantic significance of their infant's reproductions. Kenneth Kaye (1977) has said that "turn-taking is more than just a characteristic of language, whether learned or unlearned; it is a necessity for the *acquisition* of language. A child will be able to extract little information from adult utterances, or from the mismatch between his own utterances and those of adults, unless there is some high probability he and they are talking about the same thing" (p. 93). Kaye added that "there needs to be temporal proximity between the trials of the learner and the model. Timing is crucial in the effect of any feedback—reinforcing, comparative or corrective—upon learning. Thus dialogue ought to be acquired or built into the system first, so that the specifics of language, object manipulation, social ritual, or whatever can then be learned efficiently. Put this way, we can think of *dialogue as a necessary context for language acquisition*" (p. 94, italics mine).

The practice of vocal turn taking lays the groundwork for conversations, in which speakers also alternately take and yield the floor. Ironically, this seemingly advanced application of linguistic knowledge is in actuality an early precondition to the acquisition of language. Later, I will ask more specifically how turn taking facilitates vocal learning. In the meantime, let us look at the circumstances in which turn taking begins.

A BIOLOGICAL CONTEXT FOR TAKING TURNS   To fully understand the origins of turn taking we must begin with several larger questions pertaining to the biological dependencies of the human infant. Studies throughout the animal world suggest that the potential for complex social interaction between mothers and their infants (Bekoff, 1972; Hebb, 1949; Tobach and Schneirla, 1968) is associated with neoteny, the persistence of neonatal or, more properly, juvenile characteristics in the offspring. Neoteny tends to increase as one ascends the phylogenetic tree, with notable exceptions. My impression is that with increases in the duration of neoteny there may be

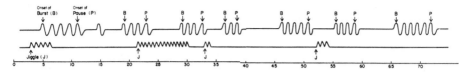

Figure 3.3. Seventy-five seconds in the bottle feeding of a two-week-old infant. The baby's sucking bursts are revealed in the upper tracing, it's mother's jiggling patterns in the lower one.

a longer period of autonomic control and that autonomically controlled behavior tends to be fairly regular. If so, neotenous infants may be more predictable, permitting more opportunities for coordinated interactions than would otherwise exist (Kaye, 1977).

Systematic interplay between mammalian mothers and babies begins during sucking (Newman, 1985). As human mothers discover almost immediately, babies suck in bursts separated by pauses.[3] Most mothers develop the impression that when babies pause, their sucking needs to be restarted, and they attempt to accomplish this by jiggling the baby (if breast feeding) or by jiggling the bottle. Figure 3.3 contains a sample tracing showing a baby's sucking and its mother's jiggling patterns. As the figure reveals, the mother in this particular episode jiggles her infant mainly during intervals when the infant is not sucking.

Though this is typical maternal behavior, jiggling unfortunately has the opposite effect: it forestalls sucking. As is revealed in Figure 3.4, there is a greater probability that a sucking burst will follow the cessation of jiggling (a "jiggle-stop") than that it will occur during the act of jiggling. Observant mothers soon notice that jiggling delays the resumption of sucking, and over the first few weeks they shorten their jiggling responses. In one study, the median duration of jiggles at two days was 3.2 secs; by two weeks mothers had reduced it to 1.8 secs (Kaye and Wells, 1980). According to the picture that is emerging, then, the neonate produces oral motor activity according to an internal schedule. Detecting this, and playing her own behavior off that of her baby, the nurturant and watch-

3. Newborns produce rhythmic and discontinuous mouthing even when they are asleep (Korner, Chuck, and Dontchos, 1968; Korner, 1969; Korner, 1973). In these mouthings, sucking bursts occur at a rate of about two sucks per second, separated by intervals of total inactivity.

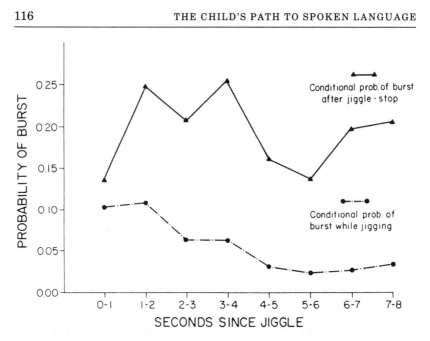

Figure 3.4. Probability of the resumption of sucking as a function of time since the onset of jiggling, depending on whether the jiggling was continued (lower graph) or stopped (upper graph).

ful mother creates a measure of harmony by filling in the gaps left by her suckling child.

DEVELOPMENT OF VOCAL TURN TAKING   We know that from their earliest postnatal days, babies will work hard to get a sample of their mother's voice. At about eighteen weeks of age, infants begin to vocalize less when their mother is in the room and is talking than when they are alone (Delack, 1976) or the mother is silent (Berger and Cunningham, 1983). And presumably to make their voice even more interesting than it would otherwise be, mothers systematically exaggerate normal variations of prosody (Fernald and Kuhl, 1987; Fernald et al., 1989).

Several investigators have found a marked increase in vocal turn taking between three and four months of age, and some of the credit is due to the infant. Ginsburg and Kilbourne (1988) followed several children from one to forty-two weeks or from thirteen to fifty-four weeks of age. Vocal clashing peaked between seven and thirteen weeks, and turn taking began in earnest between twelve and eighteen weeks. During this latter interval, infants are less likely to begin vocalizing while their mothers are speaking than when they are silent (Moran et al., 1987). Apparently, the tendency to take turns continues to increase steadily until at least five months of age (Papousek and Papousek, 1989) and there is no reason to assume that it tapers off then. In a study of nine-month-old infants and their mothers, Jasnow and Feldstein (1986) found that for the infants there were nearly sixteen noncompeting vocalizations to every interruptive utterance; for their mothers the ratio was twenty-eight to one.

In vocal turn taking as in sucking, the mother is largely responsible for the coordinate structure of the infant's earliest conversations. There are several reasons for this. First, the infant initially lacks the central capability to make the rapid adjustments required for volitional turn taking (Elias and Broerse, 1989). Second, in vocalization as well as sucking, the infant "periodically emits bursts" (Schaffer, Collis, and Parsons, 1977, p. 306) of vocal action. Between these bursts the "mother may skillfully insert her own copy of that action . . . and hence create a simulation of a deliberate act of imitation on the infant's part" (Pawlby, 1977, p. 220).

As they develop, infants increasingly play a role in interpersonal vocal coordinations. In Murray and Trevarthen (1986), mothers talked to their infants over a video system in two different situations. In the live situation, both the mother and the infant could see each other on a video monitor and respond to each other. In the taped situation, the mother was shown a videotape of her infant from one of the earlier live sessions but was not told it was a tape (and presumably thought the action was live). Murray and Trevarthen reasoned that if mothers merely inserted themselves into their infants' pauses, as has been suggested by child-dominated models (for example, Kaye, 1982), the mothers' utterances would be of similar nature and distribution in the two cases. However, if infants played their own behaviors off those of their mother more actively, this would be "read" by the mothers and, as a consequence, there would be systematic maternal variation in the two video situations.

In the live situation, Murray and Trevarthen found a higher incidence of maternal utterances that were oriented to the child's behavior (genuine questions, expansions, and extensions) than of utterances that were mother-centered (for example, directives, prompt questions, calls for attention, utterances about the mother herself, or corrections). In the taped situation, there was an opposite trend—mothers were more self-oriented. In addition, in the taped situation mothers commented negatively on their infants' behavior ("You're not interested in mummy, eh? You're ignoring me again then, aren't you?"). Because mothers were influenced in this way by the perceived unresponsiveness of their infants, Murray and Trevarthen took their results as "evidence for the infant's active role in contributing to the nature of interactions with adults" (p. 15).

CONTRIBUTION OF TURN TAKING TO VOCAL LEARNING   The vocal exchanges of infants and mothers contain the seeds of expressive vocal learning. Pawlby (1977) studied eight mother-infant dyads in which the infants were seventeen to forty-three weeks of age, looking at the incidence of mother-to-infant and infant-to-mother imitations in five categories: facial, manual, speech, nonspeech, and object manipulation. Pawlby's data reveal that imitation of facial movement by both infants and their mothers declined over the age range of her subjects, while infants' imitation of mothers' speech sounds increased. By my calculations, there was an 83 percent *increase* in mothers' imitation of speech sounds from the second to the third age interval, during which period there was a 59 percent *decrease* in mothers' imitation of infants' nonspeech sounds (the infants show a weaker version of the same pattern). This could be because infants make relatively fewer nonspeech sounds, since this period is associated with variegated babbling, in which infants may produce a wider variety of speechlike sounds (Oller, 1980). It could also be because of preferential reproduction of speech sounds by mothers, who recognize that words are just around the corner. My guess is that it is both.

In this research, Pawlby found that imitation of either partner by the other occurred in *imitative sequences*. To her, "an imitative act may not only be a response to the preceding gesture but it may also be a signal eliciting a further response which may in turn be imitative" (p. 216). She also says that "the ability to imitate actions . . . emerges only gradually in the context of the reciprocal pattern of social interplay between mother and child as a result of the mother's intention to communicate . . . almost from the time of birth there seems to be a marked tendency for mothers to reflect back to their infants certain gestures which occur spontaneously within their baby's natural repertoire of activities. She appears, however, to select actions which she can endow with communicative significance, especially vocalizations" (pp. 219–220).

There is empirical confirmation that maternal responding of the type Pawlby observed makes a positive phonetic difference, frequently inducing the production of wordlike forms. I will review this evidence in Chapter 4.

If vocal turn taking facilitates language development, one might expect a later onset or reduced occurrence in children with delayed language. In this regard, it is interesting that two studies have found that Down syndrome infants are slow to engage in vocal turn taking. Berger and Cunningham (1982) placed normally developing and Down syndrome infants with their mothers in two situations. In the silent condition, the mother was to sit silently with her infant. In the talking condition, the mother was to talk as she normally would. Figure 3.5 indicates that when the mother was silent (right panel), both groups vocalized with increasing frequency over age. When the mother talked (left panel), normally developing infants vocalized with increasing frequency up to the age of thirteen to sixteen weeks, when their vocal frequencies declined, but the retarded infants continued to vocalize past that age. The authors thought this difference might be due to a reduced interest in the mother's speech by infants with Down syndrome.

Jones (1977) also studied Down syndrome and normally developing infants. Her subjects were eight to nineteen months old at the beginning of the study. In her coding scheme, maternal and infant vocalizations were considered "clashes" if separated by less than a second. She found that the Down syndrome infants were involved in more of these vocal clashes with their mothers than the normally developing infants. Because most of the clashes occurred after the mother had begun speaking, it appeared to Jones that the majority were the "child's fault."

In Brooks-Gunn and Lewis (1982), normally developing infants were compared to a "handicapped" sample that included both cognitively delayed and physically impaired infants. Vocal initiatives were differentiated from vocal responses. It was found that among the handicapped population, there were fewer infant and more ma-

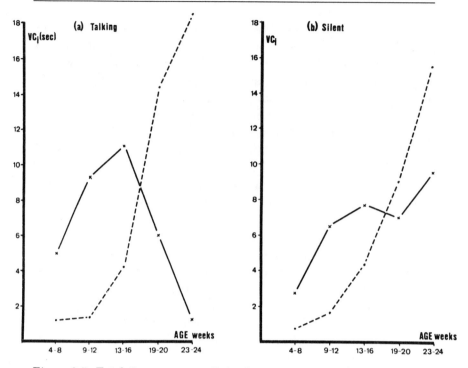

Figure 3.5. Total time spent vocalizing by normally developing (solid line) and Down syndrome (broken line) infants during sessions when the mother talked or was silent.

ternal responses than there were among the normally developing controls. While the vocal responses by the mothers in the handicapped sample remained steady or decreased from three to twenty-eight months, the vocal responses among the mothers of normally developing infants increased dramatically during this same period. As the handicapped subjects would have been at risk for language disorder, one senses that early interactional analyses of this sort may have predictive possibilities.

It is of more than passing interest that the cognitively and physically impaired infants *cried more* and *smiled less* than the normal infants. Because crying was eliminated from analyses of vocal behavior, it could be said that crying penalized handicapped infants by making them seem less vocally responsive. But I would submit that this is no statistical artifact. Crying infants are not ideally positioned to learn language. They cannot effectively attend to the vocal behavior of others or themselves, and they miss opportunities to play with sound as infants do when they babble.

If vocal turn taking promotes phonetic learning, we should expect the "situational variables" that favor or facilitate effective mother-infant interaction to act like the "factors" that promote language development. For example, the literature contains evidence of parallel sex effects: mothers of girls vocalize significantly more to their infants than do mothers of boys (Lewis and Freedle, 1973), and it is widely known that in the early years female infants develop language at a faster rate than males.

There are other correlations. When Roe (1975) gave the Gesell Developmental Schedules to infants from three to nine months of age, she found that infants who scored high on this measure had an earlier peak (three months) in their cooing and babbling during maternal interactions than infants who scored low on these tests (seven months). She also found that at three months, infants who were more vocally responsive to their mother than to a stranger scored higher on a standardized intelligence test at three years and a traditional language measure at five years than infants who were less vocally responsive (Roe, 1978). In these same research subjects, Roe and her colleagues (Roe, McClure, and Roe, 1982) also found a significant correlation between vocal responsiveness at three months and several verbal processing and comprehension measures as well as tests of reading and arithmetic at twelve years.

If coordinated interactions promote vocal learning, what kinds of dyadic exchanges occur in nonhuman primates, whose capacity for vocal learning is limited? Plooij (1979) noted some incidence of maternal-infant turn taking during the act of feeding, but this occurred at the level of gross acts such as tickling and biting, and was distributed with less regularity than the sucking of human infants. Mature nonhuman primates are not without the capacity to coordinate their vocalizations with those of a conspecific. In gibbons, the vocal duetting of mated males and females occurs in strict alternation, facilitated by special signals (Deputte, 1982). These special signals comprise a series of short monotonous notes sung by the female. "When she begins her full song," according to Marler and Tenaza (1977), "the male normally stops singing until she has completed it, whereupon he adds a short coda, then pauses for several seconds before starting to sing again" (p. 1007). I would note, however, that this turn taking occurs between mated adults, not mother-infant dyads.

There is evidence that nonhuman primates produce a vocal effect which could be used in turn taking, much as it is used by humans. I am referring to the so-called declination effect, the lowering of fundamental frequency at the end of a vocalization. This effect seems to occur universally in humans (Ohala, 1978). Hauser (Hauser, 1992c; Hauser and Fowler, 1992) has found that it also occurs in vervet and rhesus monkeys. Moreover, his analyses suggest that call sequences that lack declination may be interrupted by other monkeys' calls more frequently than those having the usual frequency lowering.

According to Terrace and his colleagues (Terrace et al., 1979), the chimpanzee they instructed in sign language, Nim Chimpsky, had frequent *manual clashes* with others. They commented that "Nim imitated and interrupted his teachers' utterances to a much larger extent than a child imitates and interrupts an adult's speech . . . he had not learned the give-and-take aspect of conversation that is evident in a child's early use of language" (p. 900).[4]

LOOKING AND LABELING   While waiting to take and relinquish the floor, mothers and their infants keep careful track of one another's glances.

Mother's Eyes. Babies spend a great deal of time looking at their mother, seemingly attempting to find out what she is thinking about. As early as two to four months, but rising sharply by eight to ten months, infants will follow an adult's line of regard (Scaife and Bruner, 1975). This would not be particularly helpful if they were unable to appreciate a vital concept: the object of a mother's attention while vocalizing is probably the subject of her reference. Though rarely mentioned, this may be one of the more important conceptual precursors to lexical acquisition.

Jones (1977) noted the incidence of "referential looking" in normally developing and Down syndrome infants. Referential looking

4. Terrace et al. may not have known that there is typically more interrupting in sign than in speech (Baker, 1977), probably because interrupting in sign is less disruptive of intelligibility.

was said to occur when the infant's visual gaze shifted from the object of its attention to the mother's face and then back to the object again. According to this definition, in a free play situation 77 percent of the total gazes of normally developing infants were referential compared to just 21 percent in the Down infants. In the Down infants there was also far more isolated vocalization, relative to vocal dialogue with the mother, than in the normally developing controls.

Baby's Eyes. As we will see below, mothers keep track of their infant's viewing habits. Indeed, it looks as if much lexical learning depends on mothers' seeing what it is their child is looking at. But they also seek to influence their child's viewing behavior: "If we will observe how children learn languages, we shall find that, to make them understand what the names of simple ideas or substances stand for, people ordinarily show them the thing whereof they would have them have the idea; and then repeat to them the name that stands for it" (Locke, 1690). Bornstein (1985) reported a relationship between mothers' tendency to "encourage their infants' attention" to properties, objects, and events in the environment and measures of expressive vocabulary at one year and of intelligence at four years. In their tutorial ways, mothers generally encourage their infants to focus on those aspects of the immediate environment about which knowledge will be needed (Tamis-Lemonda and Bornstein, 1989). Evidently these practices are helpful. Collis and Schaffer (1975) report that maternal encouragement of infant attention at five months predicts language comprehension and representational competence at thirteen months.

If an infant points or gazes at an object while vocalizing, this often causes its mother to infer that the object is central to the child's attention. This is a valid inference; Golinkoff et al. (1987) found that sixteen-month-olds tend to look longer at objects and actions that have just been named for them. Following a simultaneous gaze and vocalization, mothers also tend to name or talk about the object of their infant's attention, impute referential intent to their infant, and expand upon incomplete utterances that accompany these nonverbal gestures. Collis (1977) studied the eye gaze and labeling behavior of nine mothers during interactions with their forty-three-week-old infants in a room with four toys. He found that mothers named the toys at precisely those moments when they could see that their children were looking at the toys. Of a total of 102 times toy names were used, exactly half occurred when the infant was looking at the toy the mother then identified. In 98 percent of the cases in which mothers uttered a name while looking at a toy, the mothers were looking at the same toy they named. Head and eye movements are highly correlated with labels and, thus, serve as reliable referential cues.

Joint Attention. Tomasello and his colleagues (Tomasello, Mannle, and Kruger, 1986; Tomasello and Farrar, 1986) have studied vocabulary development in children from whom they also obtained a measure of joint attention, defined as the amount of time spent by mother and infant in focusing upon the same object or event. They obtained a positive correlation between the amount of time spent in joint attention episodes at fifteen months and expressive vocabulary at twenty-one months. They also found that "words referring to objects on which the child's attention was already focused were learned better than words presented in an attempt to redirect the child's attentional focus" (Tomasello and Farrar, 1986).

It appears that at least one other primate rather freely engages in joint visual attention and uses head turning and eye gaze to manipulate the perspectives of others. Recently, Gomez (1990) described a number of circumstances in which a young lowland gorilla displayed behaviors for instrumental, communicative ends. In all, there were 352 cases of what appeared to be intentional problem-solving attempts in this animal. One human was always within reach of the gorilla. Gomez classified each attempt to solve a problem as a solution involving objects (inanimate objects) or a solution involving humans (animate objects). A large number of all attempted solutions involved solicitations for human assistance, as in this one (Note: G = gorilla, H = human observer):

G approaches H, takes him by the hand, and pulls him toward the door, which is about 4 m away. The initial pull is moderately strong; then it is weakened and becomes very soft, even nonexistent, despite the manual contact between G and H. During the walk to the door, G looks alternately at the door and at H's eyes. (p. 343)

Gomez described a number of similar interactions in which the gorilla may or may not have led the human to an advantageous location, but in any case looked alternately at a desired object and the eyes of the human. Gomez commented that "when an organism produces a behavior with the intention that another organism perceive it and, as a consequence, carry out a certain action, it is engaging in *intentional communication* in its most basic form" (p. 345, italics his). This would not seem to be very different from the situation in which a human speaker uses the word "this" while looking at one of a number of objects, knowing that the listener-observer will follow his line of sight to the particular object the speaker has in mind.

POINTING   When infants noticeably look at something, their ocular behavior isolates that thing from local alternatives. Pointing has the same effect. The context in which pointing occurs helps observers to surmise the infant's reasons for isolating a particular object or action as it has.

Andrew Lock (1980) believes that pointing may initially grow out of unsuccessful attempts to reach for or grasp an object that at some point becomes intentional. Intentionality is difficult to prove, of course, but Lock's case studies are suggestive. In one, the mother of a boy named Paul, a fourteen-month-old infant, "has just left the room leaving her cup of tea on the mantelpiece. Paul crawls directly to me, pulls himself up, turns to look at the mantelpiece and points towards the cup. He turns back to look at me but continues to point to the cup" (p. 61).

Prior to the intentional use of pointing, there may be an interval of a month or more in which infants point but do not yet comprehend or follow the pointings of others (Murphy and Messer, 1977). In this sense, it can be said that meaningful pointing—a precursor to speech—has its own precursors in the eye movements, reaching, and grasping that precede it.

Practically every instance of pointing is accompanied by vocalization, a glance at the mother, or both (Leung and Rheingold, 1981). Accompanying vocalizations act as intensifiers: the infant is *delighted* by the girl doing cartwheels on the lawn; it *really* wants the doll. When a baby performs this sort of coordinated action predicated on the assumption that observers will thereby acquire information about its thoughts, it is behaving in a richly communicative fashion. Indeed, no information would be added were the infant to name the object at which it is pointing. However, if the infant were to say "big" while pointing at a ball, the totality of its actions would coalesce into a complete comment: "The ball is big." Or if the infant said "ball" while pointing to a grapefruit, parents would discover something about their child's progress in lexical semantics.

It appears that communicative pointing usually begins between nine and twelve months and that vocal coordination comes in a few months later (Leung and Rheingold, 1981; Murphy, 1978). At this time speech perception and vocal-motor control are adequate for the production of isolated words, so it is not surprising that speech is usually just around the corner.

In the socially normal child, communication is a precursor to language. Gestural activity that subserves social communication, especially pointing, appears to be a harbinger of communicative and linguistic things to come. This raises questions about clinical populations whose risk for language disorder derives at least partly from deficits in social cognition. Though the retarded have problems on many levels, there is evidence of reduced affect in situations associated with humor and attachment. Autistic children have a very different assembly of emotional and cognitive resources available to them, but their social-affective deficits make them susceptible to language deficits. What, then, do we know about the pointing of retarded and autistic children? As might be expected, there is evidence of delays and reductions among autistic children; the evidence on Down syndrome is less clear. Autistic children also reveal reduced "indicating behaviors," such as showing and pointing, and less than a normal amount of referential looking (Mundy and Sigman, 1989).

If pointing has a natural emergence, what about the manual gestural behavior of nonhuman primates? Pointing would seem to enhance their ability to communicate with one another about the location of various items of interest, such as a baby that has become separated from its mother. Moreover, training studies reveal that chimps can be made aware of meaning-gesture associations and are able to produce a variety of manual gestures. It is somewhat surprising, then, that a literature review by Hewes (1981) came up with less than compelling evidence of pointing among nonhuman primates. Although he was able to locate some reports of spontaneous pointing in captive pygmy chimpanzees, there was little evidence of pointing in Old World monkeys, which make extensive use of facial expressions, or in wild-reared chimpanzees.

DEVELOPMENT OF SOCIALIZATION   Theorists occasionally debate the question of whether there is a critical or even a sensitive period for the development of language in human children. Usually the focus is on languages other than the first, or native language, especially since complete linguistic deprivation is typically associated with social and other forms of abuse and we have few well-documented cases. But there is some suggestion that the social relationships within which language develops may also have a sensitive period. Much of the evidence comes from animals (see Hahn, 1990), although there also is evidence from humans, particularly in relation to attachment.

In a review, Kennell, Trause, and Klaus (1975) compared the developmental course of premature infants who were given early contact with their mother or separated from her at birth. In one study, differences in maternal behavior were found at one month and one year; early contact mothers offered more comfort to their babies on each occasion and used different language patterns in interactions with their infants at two years. In another study, there were IQ differences in the predicted direction at forty-two months. The investigators hypothesized that there is a *maternally sensitive period* soon after delivery "which is the optimal time for an affectional bond to develop between the mother and her infant" (p. 94). A maternally sensitive period might properly be regarded as a constituent of a larger sensitive period for spoken language, which I suppose to be linked to the social relationships that breed vocal imitation and to the state of the neural machinery that phylogeny has provided for phonological processing.

It is interesting that in songbirds the early claims for a sharply delineated period for song learning have now been revised in recognition of the value of *social factors*. In his experiments with the white-crowned sparrow, Marler (1970) raised birds in cages with little or no social stimulation. Model songs were conveyed by audio recordings. To be learned under these circumstances, song had to be heard before the fiftieth day of life. However, Baptista and Petrinovich (1984, 1986) found that when sparrows were exposed to live tutors—that is, raised socially—they continued to modify old songs and learn new ones well beyond the fifty-day outer limit that was observed with taped tutors. These effects have been attributed to the influence of social interaction, and in these engagements the identity of the prospective tutor may be very important. Marler (1987) commented that "interactions between tutor and pupil may exert an influence on learning preferences, as when young males learn from the father in preference to other males within earshot, or favor as tutors males with high rank in the local community" (pp. 105–106).

In a study of monozygotic and dizygotic twins, Plomin and Rowe (1979) found that social behaviors toward strangers were heritable across several situations. In a five-minute warm-up session, monozygotic twins were significantly more likely than dizygotics to share a tendency to look at and approach strangers; in a two-minute play situation, monozygotic twins were more concordant in their tendency to vocalize positively and smile at strangers.

Research by Jerome Kagan and his colleagues (Kagan, Reznick, and Snidman, 1988) suggests that before children reach their second birthday they are already separable into those who are consistently shy, quiet, and timid in unfamiliar situations and those who are affectively spontaneous in such circumstances. This by itself might suggest the early operation or interaction of endogenous factors with environmental ones. In longitudinal analyses, Kagan et al. found that the inhibited children continued to appear socially avoidant at age seven relative to the highly spontaneous children, who were more talkative and interactive at age seven. Because the groups differed on peripheral physiological measures (such as mean heart rate and variability), the authors suggest that shy children may be predisposed to physical differences and that their tendency to shyness may be inherited. To the degree that reticent and sociable children also differ in their linguistic abilities, these studies may have incidentally happened upon a (minor) genetic influence on language development.

INFANTS INFLUENCE THEIR PHONETIC STIMULATION   Social interactions expose infants to linguistically behaving people, and thus to the sounds and other behaviors their family members choose to display. But to a considerable degree, infants also configure their own stimulation. In subtle ways, reactions to infants' speech do influence parental utterances and thus the phonetic sample from which infants will glean their knowledge of linguistic structure.

From the earliest postnatal moments, infants turn toward the source of sounds. Long before they can walk, infants induce talkers to come closer through various facial expressions, especially smiling. When locomotion becomes possible, of course, they alter their linguistic environment by approaching or distancing themselves from individuals who are speaking directly to them or in their presence. Merely by vocalizing, infants induce a backflow of similar sounds from contingently responding adults. Infants also have a say in the quality of the sounds other people make. They create their own phonetic environment by producing sounds that bias and constrain the speech of nurturant mothers. They solicit vocal stimulation and thus control the quantity of phonetic experience they receive.

These effects happen so naturally and easily that we may have difficulty appreciating their significance. But compare the naturalistic circumstance with the structure of most training experiments. The investigator preselects the stimuli to be used and decides on the amount of stimulation and the intervals between trials. Frequently the stimulation is presented regardless of the learner's response on previous trials. Unlike rigid experimenters, most mothers naturally do all the right things. They study their infant's sounds, try to think of the closest lexical equivalents in the language, puzzle out what the child might be attempting to say, and encourage repetitions of wordlike productions.

The infant's own vocal productions cause it to value perceptual experience involving similar sounds as produced by others, perhaps to listen more closely to those vocal selections, and to notice similarities and differences between the sounds of others and its own utterances. In Figure 3.6, I have attempted to depict in a simple way the collaboration of supporting resources. Parental genes are passed along to the child and, through the structures and functions they helped to construct, they also continue to influence the parents' own behaviors, which are the larger or more salient part of their infant's exogenous stimulation. The parents' own behaviors are indirectly returned to them by way of their child's own genetically and socially influenced behaviors. The parents alter their behavior toward their infant, based on the infant's responses to them. It is

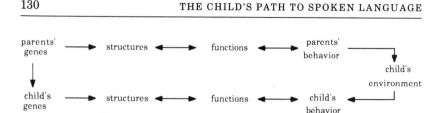

Figure 3.6. Model depicting genetic and environmental contributions to the infant's perceptual development. In principle, the infant's control and processing mechanisms resemble those of its parents, and its vocal behavior—through parental responses this behavior sets in motion—influences the phonetic stimulation that is available to the infant.

all delightfully tangled up, and this is precisely why language works so well, why language robustly withstands the vicissitudes of environmental slights and physical disadvantages.

There may be little theoretical advantage in trying to puzzle out further who does what to whom—in the end it is indivisibly interactive. If researchers want to isolate genes, or gauge the joint effect of genes and behavior, there are paradigms, such as the adoptive twin design (Hardy-Brown, Plomin, and DeFries, 1981) available, but I am not sure the yield will justify the effort.

It is often said that language develops in a social context, and social contexts are defined by physical cues, particularly those given off by the faces and voices of individuals who speak. Movements of the eyes are particularly important here: if others seem to be looking at us we generally surmise that they are aware of our existence and may be thinking about us and prepared for an interaction. As we will see in Chapter 6, behavioral and neurophysiological experiments reveal that other primates have an acute awareness of ocular patterns and process face movements with a dedicated set of "face neurons." There are indications that human primates are similarly specialized. There would appear to be a similar preadaptation to conspecific voice, though this has been studied less than face processing and therefore currently remains a matter for speculation.

Because the human infant is born helpless and is very much dependent upon its mother, I believe the proximate value of faces and voices is attachment. As a general rule, attached infants feel more secure when their mother is around, and they can know if she is nearby by processing vocally self-identifying information. By tracking the movements of the face and voice, the infant also can infer the emotional state of the mother, including any desire she might have to be loving and nurturant. For reasons closely related to survival, the human infant pays especial attention to that complex of cues that happens to contain all the information a parent can supply about spoken language.

Infants fall into rhythmic interactions with their mother at an early age thanks to her tendency to inhibit and emit behaviors during "on" and "off" intervals in her infant's behavior. These turn takings include the use of voice. After several months, infants usually begin to do their share to promote vocal rhythmicity. On logical grounds this practice would appear to favor language learning, and there is evidence that it does.

Mothers and their infants spend long periods gazing into each other's eyes, but they also tend to look at whatever the other seems to be focused on. This practice is indispensable to the creation of an initial lexicon, since mothers tend to name whatever their infant appears to be looking at, and infants implicitly understand that the utterance is the name of the object. Moreover, whatever behaviors can be transferred from mother to infant seem more likely to get through when mutual regard is in progress.

In our species, the standard currency of social interaction includes the exchange of vocal messages of one kind or another. This practice increases during a period of great plasticity in which the brain and vocal tract develop and the potential for more complex utterances increases. In their own vocalizing, infants are inclined to accommodate to the vocal patterns of others, presumably to the speaking behaviors of their mother first, then those of other family members. They therefore become increasingly inclined and able to imitate wordlike forms.

4

VOCAL COMMUNICATION
AND VOCAL LEARNING

As we all know, humans do not go through a protracted period before they begin to communicate with their voice, nor do other primates. Indeed, not a minute of postnatal life goes by before the larynx makes its first phonatory report. Here and in the following chapter, I will trace the growth and differentiation of the child's vocal and articulatory capacities asking specifically how the newly formed syllabic potential might converge with affective vocalization to produce speech.

In Chapter 2, we saw that the infant's first exposure to the voices of others occurs not at birth, as has been traditionally supposed, but several months before it. Correspondingly, it is widely believed that the well-known "birth cry" is the infant's first exposure to its own voice, and while this is true, it may not always be so. Once, in the middle of a delivery, a Scottish obstetrician named Robert Blair thought he heard the cries of a baby. "The cries," he later recalled, "were heard by two doctors, three midwives, and the patient. All were startled, and the operator looked about the labour room in his incredulity to make sure that a nurse had not carried in a baby" (Blair, 1965, p. 1165). The source of the cries, as Blair was soon to discover, was the still encapsulated fetus!

Intrauterine crying is more common than one might believe. Other documentations of this behavior, termed *vagitus uterinus*, are scattered throughout the obstetrics literature—over 120 cases were located by Ryder (1943)—going back over seventy years. Fetal vocalization is thought to occur under restricted circumstances, as when the fetus is stimulated by some operative manipulation or asphyxia, or when the membranes rupture and air enters the birth canal (Kitzmiller and Mitchell, 1942). Since intrauterine crying occurs only sporadically, I raise it here not for its developmental significance but simply to reinforce the point that vocal experience may begin somewhat before "common sense" would have us believe.

The Early Vocalizations

We can say little about the development of vocal affect, since the newborn's feelings are conveyed in the first few milliseconds of its premier vocalization. Sense impressions tell us that vocal behavior begins on a negative note. Crying is one of the first things babies do when they encounter the "outside world," apparently because of the abrupt switch-over to a completely new kind of oxygenation system as well as various other sources of acute distress. Although crying is audible, it also is displayed visibly in the form of a "cry face," which even aphonic infants display.

The neonate's crying is an involuntary response to unpleasant somatic and emotional states and may not be repressible or particularly modifiable by its immature vocal control mechanisms. But if the neonate cannot intentionally or even knowingly transmit vocal messages, information is nonetheless received and interpreted by listeners. To assess the developmental significance of crying, it may be helpful to ask if infants are grossly aware of the audibility and, more to the point, the quality of their voice while crying. If they are, infants in nurturant environments may begin to sense the instrumental implications of this earliest form of vocalization and discover early on some of the possibilities for affective vocal communication.

AWARENESS OF SELF-VOCALIZATION
Gilbert Gottlieb's research (1975, 1978) suggests that newly hatched ducklings are attracted to the call of adult female conspecifics because this sound resembles a voice heard prior to hatching— their own! His experiments reveal that chicks vocalize in the shell, can hear this sound, and prefer conspecific calls only if they have

had this *in ovo* vocal experience. In humans, conversely, one might speculate that the infant is attracted to the sound of its own voice partly because it resembles stimulation received in the uterus from its mother's voice.

Within the first day of life, neonates apparently have their own vocal signature and can recognize it themselves. As indicated earlier, one study has shown that sixteen-hour-olds respond differently to audio recordings of their own vocalizations—made just a few hours earlier—than to the taped voices of other newborns (Martin and Clark, 1982). Infants were more likely to begin crying at the sound of other infants' crying; if already crying, neonates were more likely to cease doing so to the sound of their own crying voice. This result suggests a strong native affinity for vocal learning and vocal self-awareness.

In a very different paradigm, there is evidence that babies are aware of their own voice at one week. When neonates of that age experience electronically delayed auditory feedback (DAF), their cries are significantly shortened compared to measurements made during synchronous feedback (Cullen et al., 1968), a curious reversal of the syllable prolongation effect that typifies the adult reaction to delayed feedback. Later—at six to ten months, when vocal self-awareness will soon be enlisted for lexical and phonological learning—infants do show the adult lengthening effect (Belmore et al., 1973). In fact, at that age there may even be a weak relationship between degree of vocal self-awareness, as manifested in response to DAF, and phonetic sophistication.

SOCIAL CONDITIONS FAVORING PLAYFUL VOCALIZATION

Infants produce much of their vocalization in order to join in with people who are talking. There is very little evidence for vocal imitation of heterospecific voices (but see Sweeney, 1973) or nonvocal sounds (though in autism there is reputedly some imitation of "mechanical" sounds). Vocalization may be prompted among normally developing (Jones and Moss, 1971; Ramey and Ourth, 1971) as well as Down syndrome infants (Poulson, 1988) by social reinforcement consisting of speaking and touching.

The quantity, and perhaps quality, of infant vocalizations appears to be affected by the identity of those nearby. Tulkin (1973) found that infants vocalized more following exposure to their mother's

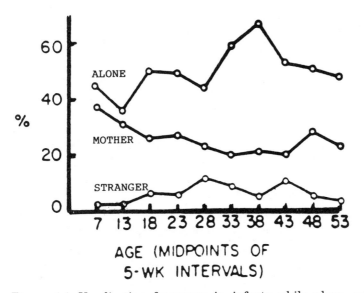

Figure 4.1. Vocalization frequency in infants while alone, with their mother, or with a stranger.

voice than the voice of a strange woman.[1] It also appears that babies are more likely to vocalize playfully in the presence of their mother than in the presence of a stranger (Delack, 1976; Camp et al., 1987).[2] Figure 4.1 shows the results of Delack's analysis of normally developing infants' vocalization frequency as a function of social context. The figure indicates that maternal effects are maximally evident at seven weeks but never disappear. Infants vocalize the most when they are alone, especially at thirty-eight weeks, when at least 90 percent would have begun to babble (see Figure 5.1 in the next chapter).

In ways not currently understood, there may be a relationship between vocal self-awareness and frequency of vocalization. Historically, there has been interest in and no absence of speculation about why infants vocalize. Various observers have said they believe babies initiate vocal activity for the pleasure of its sound and

1. For some reason, this was true only for infants of middle-class mothers.

2. Babies do not merely vocalize to the sound of their mother's voice. Lewis and Freedle (1973) found that in the case of female infants, at least, there was more vocalization when the mother was directly addressing the infant than when she was speaking to another person in the infant's presence.

babble to obtain that enjoyable sensation. And, indeed, infants seem to do more vocalizing when alone than when accompanied by others who are speaking.

Why do babies in no evident distress spend so much of their time vocalizing? Little monkeys and apes do not wile away the hours in idle vocalization; quite the contrary. Comparative psychologists (Gardner, Gardner, and Drumm, 1989) have observed that humans "are noisy animals. There is a hubub of voices at almost every social gathering; a great din at the most peaceful cocktail party or restaurant dining room. It is a mark of discipline and respect when an audience settles down in silence to listen to a single speaker" (p. 29). However, these authors continue, "in the rest of the animal kingdom there are very few creatures, perhaps only some of the birds, whales, and dolphins, that make nearly so much vocal racket when they are otherwise undisturbed. Chimpanzees are silent animals most of the time. A group of ten wild chimpanzees of assorted ages and sexes feeding peacefully in a fig tree at Gombe may make so little sound that an inexperienced observer passing below can altogether fail to detect them" (p. 29).

Note that our concern here is not about differences in the quality or complexity of vocal behavior between human and nonhuman primates but about the tendency to use the voice at all. Conditionally, chimps seem more likely to vocalize when they are emotionally aroused in some fashion (Gardner et al., 1989), and while this may also be true of the human neonate, at some point we must assume that the infants of our species vocalize for a variety of reasons. Little is known about these reasons, but I think there may be clues in the conditions favoring initiation and termination of playful vocalization. Investigators studying cooing or babbling have happened upon a variety of techniques for encouraging the behaviors they seek to observe. First, sessions are typically held when the infant is in good general health and is expected to be rested, physically comfortable (not hungry), and in good spirits. These conditions favor *play behavior* in a variety of young animals (a subject I will deal with later). In addition, during recording sessions investigators may lightly touch the baby's abdomen and address the baby in a soft voice but otherwise remain still. It is plain that researchers believe that the route to playful vocalization is through the baby's mood in quiet social interaction.

Recently, some direct evidence has been supplied by a group at Miami (Lewedag et al., 1991) that analyzed vocalizations collected in two very different settings. Some were collected at home by infants' mothers, who typically chose to record when their baby was "in a good mood," others during prearranged laboratory visits when strangers were around. Infants vocalized more frequently in the home sessions and also produced higher quality (more speechlike) utterances in that setting. The investigators attributed these differences to several factors, including variations in the infants' familiarity with the observer and the emotional atmosphere.

If mood matters and self-hearing is pleasurable, then what about children who are healthy and happy but cannot hear themselves vocalize? Lenneberg, Rebelsky, and Nichols (1965) followed two small groups of infants over the first three months of life. The control group consisted of ten normally hearing infants being reared by their hearing parents. The other group contained children whose parents were deaf. One of these children was himself deaf. Did he vocalize less than the hearing children of deaf parents? Inspecting their frequency data, Lenneberg et al. commented that the cooing of this child, "unheard by his parents, *as well as* by himself, shows an emergence pattern similar to the rest of the children" (p. 31). Did the child initiate cooing bouts as often as the hearing infants but pursue them for less time? This would fit my own hunches about the role of mood and self-hearing, but the data unfortunately do not speak to this point.

It is a little surprising that a deaf infant would vocalize with the same frequency as its hearing peers, but this was the case in Lenneberg et al., and the same finding has emerged in other research. In one report, it appeared that a congenitally deaf infant may have vocalized more freely than eleven hearing infants. At just over seven months, the hearing infants produced from 33 to 68 utterances per half-hour session; in contrast, at just over eight months, the deaf infant produced 76, 62, 75, and 90 utterances in four half-hour sessions. The authors remarked that they "found no difficulty in obtaining a full sample from the deaf baby on each [occasion]" (Oller et al., 1985, p. 62).

I think Lenneberg et al. may have quit too soon. At three months, their subjects were still several months away from the more interesting phonetic behaviors. Consider, for example, the studies of vocalization by deaf children who, but for their deafness, were old enough to be talking (see Locke, 1983). To ensure an adequate vocal sample among their subjects, investigators tried to create appropriate conditions. In a study of five-year-old deaf children, one investigator noted that "at least three children were necessary to the group play to insure vocalization. When there were fewer subjects present, there often was a tendency for the children to play individually, without vocalization" (Carr, 1953, p. 24). Nevertheless, with these social circumstances a suitable sample of sounds was obtained. But hold on a moment. Isn't hearing critical to interpersonal vocalization? Possibly not. Sykes (1940) studied the vocal behavior of three- to six-year-olds with a range of hearing losses. She found that children with moderate losses vocalized no more often than profoundly impaired children. Hearing aside, Sykes thought personality and intelligence might be more closely related to frequency of vocalization, a view supported by evidence I present elsewhere.

Sykes also conducted an inquiry into variations in the children's use of spontaneous gesture and the combined use of gesture and vocalization as a function of three "pragmatic" situations. She classified each child-initiated communication as an inquiry or question, a desire or wish, or an explanation. Their occurrence broke down as follows (in percentages):

	Gesture alone	Gesture + vocalization
Question and inquiry	63	37
Desire or wish	35	65
Explanation	49	51

Probably none of these children would have been able to hear much or to produce words, given the inadequacy of diagnosis and amplification devices in the late 1930s, or to communicate by sign, given attitudes and practices in regard to manual communication at the time. It is, therefore, of considerable interest that vocalization varied across these pragmatic categories. In her effort to explain the variations, Sykes appealed to possible differences in "urgency" and general level of "tension" in addition to the utility of pointing. This observation seems congruent with other research suggesting that hypotonicity in children with Down syndrome may contribute to that population's generally attenuated responses to emotional experience.

These findings on vocal and gestural pragmatics relate to several general factors associated with vocalization—socialization, mood, and level of arousal. But we should ask if there are specific sensory experiences that motivate bouts of spontaneous, playful vocalization. If infants vocalize for the sound of it, we would expect profoundly hearing impaired infants to be silent most of the time, yet they vocalize frequently. In the mildly hearing impaired one might expect vocal activity to be less frequent than normal, or generated at greater intensity levels, but there seems to be no relevant research on this.[3] If infants babble for the "orality" of it, why do deaf babies do it out loud? Do aphonic infants, who likewise cannot hear themselves, go through all the same articulatory motions as phonating babies?

VOCAL SATIETY

We could perhaps come at these questions from a different direction. Do we know what terminates vocal behavior, what causes individual bouts of vocalization to stop? Recently, there has been a rebirth of interest in "satiety," the circumstances under which animals discontinue consummatory activities. Psychologists are asking if animals quit eating because they are no longer hungry, that is, have satisfied gustatory drives, or feel pressure in their stomachs.

Perhaps we can get some clues about what triggers or sustains vocal activity by studying *vocal* satiety—the conditions under which vocalization is turned off. Casual observations suggest that infants often stop babbling when speakers enter the room, just as "talking birds" vocalize less when their trainers enter the room (Mowrer, 1960). The observation that infants of babbling age vocalize more when alone than when in the company of another person offers some support for this notion.

We are flooded with questions. Are infants' bouts of vocalization

---

3. If they seek auditory feedback, one might expect hearing impaired infants to vocalize more intensely in the presence of background noise, as occurs experimentally in the Lombard effect.

terminated by oral or laryngeal fatigue or by satisfaction of a basic human desire for kinesthetic stimulation? Is some fundamental "appetite" for one's own vocalizations satisfied by high-saturation bouts of vocal activity? Are neural developments (and phonetically relevant cognitive operations) fostered by this activity, as seems to be the case among animals who seek out stimulation during critical periods of brain development? If so, is the frequency of infants' vocalization controlled by time-locked neural growth mechanisms similar to those that impel other animals into self-stimulatory activity? Would that we were also flooded with answers!

Studies of auditory function in primates suggest that "the joy of hearing" is specifically built around aural reception of certain types of auditory patterns. Human and nonhuman primates generally seem to prefer sudden or extended frequency sweeps, a fundamental fact underlying the interest in prosody shared by human infants and their mothers (Fernald, 1991; Fernald and Kuhl, 1987). This fact may be behind squealing, a behavior that occurs commonly among normally developing infants, who may occasionally raise their fundamental frequency by an octave within utterances (Oller, 1986). Extant data do not indicate whether deaf infants are less inclined to squeal than their hearing peers.

There is another type of vocalization that contains frequency sweeps—*human speech*. I am referring to formant transitions between consonants and vowels. We know that these formant shifts are very salient to the mammalian auditory system—whether that of the human, chinchilla, nonhuman primate (Kuhl and Miller, 1975), or bird (Kluender, 1991). Now, many human infants who are "deaf" can still hear low frequency sounds, which may include the lower frequencies of their own voice, but are unable to hear the higher frequencies, which include the "sweepier" transitions from consonantal bursts to the second and third formants (where nearly a thousand Hertz may be traversed in just 30 or 40 msec). These differential auditory sensitivities, operating on infants' own vocal activity, would be predicted to cause deaf babies to *vocalize as frequently* as their normally hearing peers, but to *babble less frequently*. As we will see in the next chapter, this is precisely what happens.

Studies reveal that it is not just the sound of speech that sets infants to vocalizing or reinforces them for doing so: the person

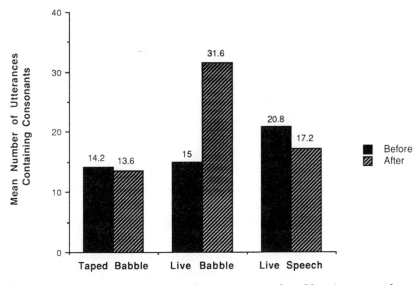

Figure 4.2. Number of consonantal utterances produced by nine- to twelve-month-olds before and after three stimulus conditions.

doing the speaking must be physically present (Todd and Palmer, 1968) and it may help if the speaker is visibly looking at the child (Bloom, 1974). A study by Dodd (1972) suggests that vocal imitation may occur more commonly when the baby can see the person who is talking or see a person *while there is talking*. In her study, nine- to twelve-month-old infants were presented with babblelike strings of CV syllables (such as [daedaedaedae]) in different settings. In an audio only condition ("taped babble"), the subjects heard a prerecorded tape of these sounds while in a playpen. In a social-vocal setting ("live babble"), the infants heard these same sounds live, while seated on the experimenter's lap. Finally, in a social only setting ("live speech"), the subjects heard the experimenter's normal speech while sitting on her lap. Figure 4.2 shows the results. Analyses of pre- and poststimulatory vocalization by the infants revealed an increase in the number and length of consonantal utterances only in the social-vocal condition; audio only and social only conditions had no such effects.

This finding reinforces my earlier statement that faces are an important stimulus to speech. But moving faces alone will not do much of anything. Kuhl and Meltzoff (1988) found that a face with moving articulators was less likely to elicit vocalization when paired with pure tones than when paired with vocalization. Forty of sixty-four subjects produced speechlike vocalizations in response to speech, but only five of seventy-two infants produced speechlike vocalizations in response to pure tones. The face, by itself, is apparently a poor cue to vocalization. The authors concluded that "infants talk to faces that are talking to them" (p. 259).

Infants vocalize increasingly with age, at least until the end of the first year (Camp, Burgess, Morgan et al., 1987). In this connection, Katherine Nelson (1973) has reported an interesting finding from her studies: the sheer *number* of utterances recorded in a session held when the children were twenty months old was positively related to the age at which they later attained a fifty-word expressive vocabulary. Number of utterances also was correlated with the age of children at their tenth phrase, and with their rate of lexical acquisition and mean length of utterances (MLU).[4]

During the interval in which frequency of vocalization increases, the proportion of crying decreases (Lewis, 1969). The scanty chronological evidence that is available suggests that speechlike utterances begin to pull away from cries and other nonspeech sounds at about five months. At that point, there is an increase in the ratio of speechlike to nonspeech sounds in infants who hear normally, a ratio that holds steady or drops in hearing-impaired infants (Maskarinec, Cairns, Butterfield et al., 1981).

The path to spoken language is paved with the processes of social cognition from which infants derive their intense interest in interactive vocalization. This interest is primed and nurtured by faces that smile and eyes that attend. Let us take a look at the evidence.

ELICITATION OF VOCAL PLAY

We saw earlier that in song birds, the physical appearance of the tutor is important to vocal learning. Physical appearance is impor-

---

4. Since a stranger was present during observation, there may be a connection between shyness and rate of lexical learning. Although this remains to be demonstrated, it seems entirely reasonable. Landon and Sommers (1979) observed that loquacious children score higher on a number of developmental language measures than children judged to be taciturn.

tant in humans, too, but what goes into "appearance"? Is the entire body important or is it mainly the face? According to Sherrod (1981), "in addition to being social behavers, caregivers, and attachment figures, *people are also physical stimuli* composed of parameters such as contour density and color" (p. 11, my emphasis).

Studies have found that infants typically vocalize more frequently when with their mother than when alone or with a stranger (Delack, 1976). They also vocalize more frequently when they are looking attentively at their mother (Kaye and Fogel, 1980), at least if she looks back and facially responds.

It appears, other circumstances being favorable, that vocalization is encouraged by a face that is smiling and by eyes that are looking toward the infant and possibly into its own eyes. How do the eyes contribute to vocal behavior? In an interesting study by Bloom (1974), an attempt was made to get infants to vocalize by smiling at them, touching their abdomens, and uttering "Hi, Baby." This stimulation increased infant vocalization relative to a control condition in which the experimenter also smiled, touched abdomens, and said "tsk tsk" *if the experimenter's eyes could be seen.* Vocalization had no facilitative effect if the experimenter wore skin-toned opaque glasses. A visual effect of this sort may have occurred in Dodd (1972), described above.

EARLY VOCAL IMITATION

As for the mouth, although there has been a lot of disagreement as to whether Meltzoff's research (for example, Meltzoff and Moore, 1977) reveals imitation or something less sophisticated,[5] few scholars dispute a central finding of his research: *newborns know when other people protrude their lips, open their mouth, and stick out their tongue.*

A face with attentive eyes and a mouth that moves in synchrony with vocal sounds may elicit vocal imitation. Earlier, I described a study by Kuhl and Meltzoff (1982) in which eighteen to twenty-week-old infants saw a film of a woman rhythmically articulating [i], which involves lip spreading, and [a], which involves jaw lowering. A subset of the subjects vocalized in time with the film,

5. An excellent treatment of the distinction between imitation and several forms of social contagion is available in Brothers (in submission).

seeming to use a similar intonation pattern. It is significant that
in a later study, Kuhl and Meltzoff (1988) replicated the original
result with the original stimuli as well as with [i] and [u], and also
looked for any vocal imitation that might have occurred in both the
original and the replication studies.

Forty of the sixty-four subjects had produced speechlike vocalizations to the vocalic stimuli. Kuhl and Meltzoff played these vowellike sounds to adult listeners for perceptual classification. Although procedural details were not reported, listeners apparently
were to decide whether individual vowels were more like /a/ or more
like /i/. (The number of vowels heard and classified was not specified.) Kuhl and Meltzoff reported that in 90 percent of infants' vocal
responses to stimuli the target vowels were recoverable perceptually, that is, they could be identified in a forced choice format.
This suggests that for infants at four and five months, awareness
of visible articulation, audible structure, or both are linked to vocal
imitation. This has been confirmed in a similar study by Legerstee
(1990) in which three- and four-month-olds imitated [a] and [u], but
only when the articulatory and auditory signals matched.

If the appearance of the experimenter's face and facial activity
encouraged vocal imitation, what do we know of infants exposed
only to audio recordings? I am unaware of any vocal imitation under
these circumstances, and there is one case, perversely, in which a
suppression effect was obtained. Webster (1969) played a tape of
isolated vowels or of CV syllables to four six-month-olds. Recordings
of the infants' vocalization before, during, and after this stimulation
showed a net reduction of vowels following vowel stimulation and
a net reduction of consonants following the presentation of syllables.

As Figure 4.2 revealed, in Dodd's study of nine- to twelve-month-
olds live babble (such as dadadada) was more likely than live speech
to elicit vocalizations that included consonants, which implies that
a mother may have to key into her child's segmental repertoire to
get it to do much vocalizing, and of course mothers do so regularly
with baby talk. This is seen in other work by Ricks (1979), who
with six normally developing one-year-olds played audiotapes of
their own babbling as well as the pseudobabbling of their parents
and an unrelated adult. Of interest here are the infants' responses
to the tape of their own vocalizations. Overall, it was found that
babies were disinclined to reproduce vocalizations presented in this

fashion. However, Ricks's data (in his Table 2a) indicate that the infants were far more likely to reproduce consonant-vowel reduplications such as "dada" and "mama" than other sounds of their own making.

Though visual cues facilitate vocal learning in song birds, they may not be strictly necessary to the "talking birds" who imitate human speech. One book on the subject proclaims that "the easiest way to teach a bird to talk is to buy a bird training record and use it on an automatic record-changing phonograph" (Bates and Busenbark, 1969, p. 56). However, Pepperberg (1990) has shown that when social interactions are modeled for the African Gray Parrot, a great deal of vastly more complex behavior is possible.

What of the infant who cannot see? Certainly, it would seem that blind infants must be in a very different situation, and indeed, Fraiberg (1979) observed the absence of visual effects in the blind. She commented that the lack of visual-social reinforcement by the blind infant seems to cause adults to discontinue their own smiles and other facial bids for attention.

Congenitally blind children with no other risk factors do not necessarily experience a slower development of spoken language (Landau and Gleitman, 1985; Mulford, 1988). This is surprising, since Fraiberg (1979) observed that blind infants are less likely to vocalize than sighted babies: "throughout the first year, it seemed to us that the spontaneous vocalizations of our blind babies were sparse . . . vocalization for self-entertainment was infrequent and scant . . . vocalizations to greet were rarely recorded . . . initiation of a 'dialogue' with mother or other partners was rarely observed" (p. 166).

Nevertheless, we are left with the impression that visual cues are needed only by the children who can use them—the normally sighted. Infants lacking access to sight evidently allocate differently the resources that are available to them. Of course, problems at higher levels can still occur. Randa Mulford (1983) has pointed out that blind children have particular difficulty in knowing what other people are paying attention to and what they might be thinking about. Unless some adjustment is made, they may be unable to infer which of the things seen by speakers are identified by words like *this*, *then*, or *that one*.

The infant's capacity for vocal learning is demonstrated early in life, but the processes of vocal learning become more complex as the infant progresses down the path to spoken language. It must have reasons for staying in the vocal imitation business; presumably, the infant sees significant value in learning to sound like others. It makes sense, then, to ask how vocal learning serves the infant's social and communicative ends. What are the first uses to which infants put their voices?

ONTOGENY OF VOCAL SIGNALING

Let us look at the infant's initial use of vocalizations that convey information, whether or not they are launched with the utilitarian objective of imparting thoughts or feelings. Most primates communicate affective states by voice, often in conjunction with movements of the face and other parts of the body. This is readily achievable because the mechanisms that control the expression of vocal affect are capable of doing so by degrees, so that humans and some nonhuman primates are able to signal degrees of feeling vocally (Green, 1975; Malatesta, 1981; Moynihan, 1964). This provides primates with a vocal mechanism that can be used to convey degrees of meaning or to intensify messages whose referential content is carried by discrete vocal signals or by nonvocal cues.

In human infants, the affect conveyed by vocalization is grossly discriminable and separately classifiable from the start. Babies in pain sound different from angry infants (Wolff, 1969), a distinction reflecting differences in frequency and duration as well as a variety of other vocal parameters (Thoden and Koivisto, 1980; Zeskind and Collins, 1987). Initial distinction of this sort also appears to be possible in nonhuman primates (Malatesta, 1981; Newman, 1985).

We may assume that initially, distinctive vocal signaling occurs without communicative intent, presumably as a form of irrepressible "leakage" analogous to the unconscious facial display of one's true feelings (Ekman and Friesen, 1969). Some infants may begin to use their voice at some point before the middle of their first year. D'Odorico (1984) followed four Italian infants from the age of four months to the age of eight months. Recordings were made in four naturalistic circumstances in which the mother or the experimenter played with the infant in a normal fashion, with or without a toy, or the infant was observed alone with a toy. D'Odorico analyzed her recordings for instances of different types of vocalizations. She found that *discomfort sounds,* which included cries, whimpers, and moans, occurred mainly when the infant was bored, having lost interest in a toy. *Call sounds* occurred when the infant, left alone, was no longer interested in a toy and began to look for its mother. *Request sounds,* the third type of call, included noncry vocalizations that in other respects resembled discomfort sounds but lacked the facial expressions associated with crying. Both discomfort and request sounds ceased when the mother entered the room. There was, then, some vocal differentiation according to pragmatic context. In addition, D'Odorico found that within infants there was some internal consistency in the "call structure" of her subjects according to acoustic analyses of fundamental frequency, melodic contour and duration, and perceptual analyses of phonetic length. This finding was reinforced recently in a study by Hubbard and Asp (1991) showing that several acoustic parameters varied with separation and with circumstances associated with anger, fear, joy, and elation.

It is my understanding that we have discovered few infant vocal patterns that are consistently associated with particular emotional states and thus could serve as reliable signals for those states. But this does not mean that such associations do not exist. Optimism is justified, I think, by recorded variations in vocal prosody that correspond to variations in the pragmatic circumstance or context in which the vocalizer finds him or herself. A few such cases have been documented in nonhuman primates (Green, 1975) and in mothers addressing their babies (Fernald, 1989).

Among older infants, there is better evidence for the intentional use of the voice in order to communicate. For example, in experimentally induced "frustration" episodes, Harding and Golinkoff (1979) found that some 60 to 70 percent of the infants who had demonstrated an appreciation of causality used their voice intentionally to communicate with their mother in an experimental setting. These subjects were, on average, just over eleven months old. In contrast, infants who had not yet demonstrated an appreciation of causality (just over nine months in age) produced no intentional vocalizations during the frustration episodes.

Malatesta (1981) saw maternal contingent responding as the experiential means by which "raw affect expression" is modulated into adultlike forms. More recently, Papousek and Papousek (in press) have suggested that "when parents respond only to crying and discomfort sounds, the infant develops instrumental crying as the only effective means to attract parental attention" (p. 18). Presumably, contingent responding stabilizes some species-specific patterns of affective expression and nudges other patterns into conformity with culturally defined standards.

Children intercepted at this point are proceeding along a path that leads to spoken language. Affective signaling with the voice is related to later success in linguistic communication. Some studies have found relationships between quantity or quality of vocalization in infancy and later measures of intelligence. For example, one investigator found that the amount of vocalization by four-month-old females (but not by males) to facial stimuli was correlated with verbal intelligence at two-and-a-half years (Kagan, 1971). In another study, perhaps the longest running longitudinal study of infant vocalization in history, it was found that for female (but not for male) infants, there were significant positive correlations between vocalization measures on the California First Year Mental Scale[6] in the first year of life and verbal IQ scores at six to twenty-six years of age (Cameron, Livson, and Bayley, 1967).

If infants in pain sound different from angry babies, what of the early vocal sounds of infants who are considered "at risk" for delays or disorders of spoken language? There are several reasons why their crying might differ from that of typically developing babies. For one thing, the emotional distress associated with any physical ailments that might exist could interfere with normal phonatory operations. Second, since vocalization is a function of respiratory and laryngeal operations, and their neural control centers, any disease or malformation that affects these systems may be reflected in the control and quality of cry.

Since 1960, Ole Wasz-Hockert and his colleagues have conducted a number of spectrographic studies of crying among variously impaired neonatal populations in Finland. According to a review (Michelsson, 1986), this research has identified acoustic differences between healthy babies and those with low birthweight, metabolic disorders such as hyperbilirubinemia, chromosomal abnormalities

---

6. These included vocalizing eagerness and displeasure; using vocal interjections; saying "da-da" or some equivalent; saying two words; and using expressive jargon.

such as Down syndrome, endocrine disturbances such as hypothyroidism, and brain damage associated with asphyxia, bacterial meningitis, and herpes virus encephalitis.

These investigators were not the only ones to observe cry differences in unhealthy infants. Prechtl and his colleagues (Prechtl et al., 1969) studied the vocalizations of three groups of newborns. One group was neurologically normal, the second group had transitory signs of neural abnormalities, and the third group had abnormal neurological findings. Although no vocal "marker" was found, both clinical groups had much more variable durations of cry than did the normal infants.

Later I will be looking at the phonetic content of otherwise healthy babies who appear to be at risk for language delay or disorder. But for now, let us return our attention to the process by which infants normally gravitate from their native vocal patterns to those of their environment.

Vocal Accommodation

In Chapter 2 we saw that newborns orient to faces and voices in the first hours of postnatal life, with demonstrable learning effects surfacing just several days later. We learned that the capacity for facial mimicry may be exercised within an hour of birth. In Chapter 3 we saw that infants do their fair share to eliminate asynchronies between their caregivers and themselves. I should like to suggest here that infants accommodate to ambient vocal patterns as well as they can, consistent with their perceptual biases and motoric constraints, and that—developmentally played out over the first several years of life—this process leads to the incorporation of behaviors that linguistically sophisticated listeners hear as German, Latvian, or whatever the community's language happens to be.

By using the term *vocal accommodation* I am invoking a concept that has a small but growing literature under the name "speech accommodation." Most of the research on speech accommodation has been performed on adult subjects, and much of that was reported by Cappella (for example, Cappella and Greene, 1982) and by Giles and his colleagues (Giles, 1984; Giles et al., 1987),[7] who define

7. I am indebted to James Flege for telling me about the existence of this research.

speech accommodation as the adjustment of one's speech and other communicative behaviors into closer conformity with those of the person with whom one is interacting. Among adult speakers, the subtlety of vocal convergence is revealed in a variety of studies. For example, in an experiment by Natale (1975), an interviewer's voice was experimentally adjusted to fall within three distinct intensity ranges: 80–83, 86–89, and 92–95 dB. The average intensity of interviewees' responses varied reliably over the three signal levels, the means falling at approximately 80, 82, and 84 dB, respectively.

The motivation for speech accommodation, according to Giles, relates to a speaker's often unconscious need for social integration or identification with another person. By increasing similarity (or reducing dissimilarity) of speech and speaking behaviors, the accommodating individual apparently believes, on some level, that he can increase his perceived attractiveness to the listener. The speaker may also accommodate in order to increase his level of interpersonal involvement with the listener and to become more intelligible.

Forty years ago, the learning psychologist O. Howbart Mowrer (1952) brought up a similar idea in his discussion of what motivates talking birds to reproduce the sounds of speech. He said that the bird, as a result of a bond with or affection for its caretaker, "identifies with and tries to *be like* that person. Birds cannot do much by way of making themselves *look like* human beings . . . but they can make themselves *sound like* human beings, and this they do . . . Once . . . perfected . . . these same responses can, of course, be employed socially or communicatively . . . So far as can be determined at present, essentially the same account holds, at least up to a point, for acquisition of speech by human infants" (p. 264, italics his).

According to Street (1982), individuals accommodate mainly for two reasons: enhancement of mutual intelligibility and a more favorable social response from listeners. Street's own study dealt mainly with speech rate. In practice, accommodation studies frequently address vocal and nonvocal behaviors (Gallois and Callan, 1988) as well as speech content. And accommodation research is undertaken in relation to a variety of domains, including second language acquisition, dialect change, and language maintenance and shift, and in several different interactive settings, including efforts to gain compliance of various sorts, courtroom interactions, diplomacy, and radio news reporting.

Why do I suspect that infants accommodate vocally? First, though theories of speech accommodation have grown up around the behavior of adult humans, vocal convergence also occurs in nonhuman primates and signals the emotional union or attachment between human mothers and their offspring. Second, such a tendency would be consistent with a larger category of behavior known to characterize all members of our species. This behavior, *motor mimicry,* has been defined as "overt action by an observer that is appropriate to or mimetic of the situation of the other person, rather than one's own" (Bavelas et al., 1987, p. 14). In their review, Bavelas et al. describe a history of interest in motor mimicry going back at least two hundred years. Examples of motor mimicry include an observer's facial reproduction of smiling or reactions to a painful experience, bodily reproduction of reaching or leaning, and certain speech mannerisms. As mimicry is evidently somewhat more likely when the observer is himself able to be observed, Bavelas et al. treat mimicry as a form of communication that reveals to the person observed a bond or other special relationship sought by the observer.

Another reason to expect vocal accommodation in human infants is that motor mimicry is not unique to our species; vocal accommodation also occurs in some nonhuman primates (Maurus et al., 1985, 1987; Maurus et al., 1986). For example, when a squirrel monkey engages in "dialogue" with a conspecific cagemate, the frequency and morphology of its vocalizations may be influenced by the immediately preceding vocal behaviors of the other animal (Maurus et al., 1987). Of importance to theories of linguistic evolution, some of the vocal parameters on which there is evidence of accommodation in nonhuman primates have been appropriated by humans for use in spoken languages, for example, fundamental frequency modulations as tonal contrasts (Maurus, Barclay, and Streit, 1988).

The most interesting case of suggestive vocal accommodation with which I am familiar is the recent study by Marc Hauser (1992a) of the coo calls of free-living rhesus monkeys. By keeping careful track of which animals were vocalizing, and their genetic relationship to other animals, Hauser was able to discover something quite remarkable. His spectrographic analyses revealed that coo calls from the members of one matriline differed systematically from the coos of other matrilines. The acoustic basis for differences lay in the spectral prominences above the second harmonic, the proportion of missing harmonics, the intensity of the fundamental frequency and second harmonic, and the energy between harmonics. The net effect of these variations was that, to the human listener, one matriline sounded "nasal" and the others did not. Though Hauser could not absolutely rule out an organic explanation such as a heritable palatal deficiency, these effects may well have been the result of infants' accommodations to their mother's nasal quality.

A developmental version of vocal accommodation theory, as I imagine it, would predict that the children of parents having a salient vocal characteristic will be inclined to incorporate that feature into their own speech whether it is linguistically significant or not. For example, one would predict that vocally accommodating children raised by highly loquacious or quiescent parents will be similarly loquacious or quiescent. This particular prediction is realized in data from a large-scale investigation by Kagan and his colleagues (Kagan, Kearsley, and Zelazo, 1978), who reported that working-class Chinese parents living in Boston were less likely than Caucasian counterparts to talk and to interact with their infant in an affectively excited way. At various intervals between seven and twenty-nine months of age, their children were observed to be considerably less vocal when engaged in spontaneous play, presented with visual and auditory stimuli in a laboratory, and responding to relevant items on the Bayley Scale.

Beyond frequency of occurrence of vocalization, one would expect accommodating infants to pick up qualitative aspects of voice. These would include the pitch, rhythm, voice quality, and other cues that characterize the speech and delivery of their parents. There has unfortunately been remarkably little research on this, presumably because we have assumed that children target primarily for linguistic units or that phonemically encoded material is all that ultimately counts.

Earlier, I discussed the development of turn-taking. Although initially it is the mother who falls in step with her infant, this is followed by the infant's own efforts to conform to the maternal pattern. In the minuscule literature on voice imitation, one finds minor accomplishments among infants in their first year. Jones

(1965) studied the fundamental frequency of deaf and hearing infants' spontaneous vocalizations from early infancy to the age of four years. Data were broken down into six-month intervals. Though the sample sizes were small and the data were not analyzed statistically, measurements revealed that in the first interval in which comparisons were possible (seven to twelve months), deaf infants already had slightly higher mean fundamental frequencies at the beginning and end of utterances, and higher utterance-internal frequency shifts. Because in all cases the control subjects measurements were closer to adult standards, these data suggest that even in their prelexical utterances hearing infants may accommodate to the acoustical frequency norms of their environment.

Lieberman (1967) reported that two children produced different average fundamental frequencies when alone with their father and mother. A ten-month-old boy's fundamental frequency was 340 Hz when with his father and 390 Hz when with his mother; a thirteen-month-old girl's fundamental frequency was 290 Hz and 390 Hz when in the company of her father and then her mother. His report contained no information about the number of utterances analyzed, but in a well-documented study of twelve infants at nine to twelve months, Gerald Siegel and his colleagues (Siegel et al., 1990) were unable to replicate Lieberman's findings. In their study, as in Lieberman's, individual infants interacted with just their mother or their father. But the data failed to support imitation of parental pitch, even for vocalizations occurring within two seconds of parental utterances, and there likewise was no apparent mimicry of frequency contour, amplitude, or intensity values.

Infants even younger than those studied by Jones may have a talent for matching absolute pitch. Kessen, Levine, and Wendrich (1979) asked a "tutor" to sing "ah" with a pitch of D, F, or A above middle C. At the time of test, infants were five to six months old. The tutor was to use a pitchpipe as a guide or, if the baby seemed to prefer pitchpipe tones, to present those instead of his or her voice. Musically trained judges evaluated all pairs of mother-infant notes using a matrix in which the three notes were the possible stimuli and the possible responses, the latter accommodating all vocalizations falling within a quarter-note of the three experimental notes. The proportion of correct matches significantly exceeded chance, and the authors commented that "the babies worked hard at their

assignment. They watched the experimenter closely and they vocalized to her often and energetically" (p. 96).

This experiment is intriguing but it also is troubling. To my
knowledge a replication has not been attempted, but one certainly
should be. For reasons not explained, pitches were analyzed by
listeners instead of acoustical equipment, and listeners were exposed to pairs of notes instead of isolated excerpts. Kessen et al.
found no social effects—they observed no greater matching when
the presenter was a parent (either father or mother) than when it
was another adult. Finally, whether they could have obtained such
effects in the absence of, or lacking visual contact with the speaker
is unknown. Inexplicably, the investigators offered no comment on
an important comparison that would have been possible, whether
there was more pitch matching to voices than to tones.

Actually, the best evidence may not come from experiments but
from naturalistic situations. Masataka (1992) observed six Japanese infants at three to four months, tabulating the joint occurrence
of four intonation patterns in the utterances of mothers and their
infants. She found that when the mothers produced more than two
utterances before their infants responded, there was a significant
level of accommodation by the infants to all four vocal contours.

Other examples of speech accommodation include the phonetic
shifts that occur in individuals casually exposed to but not formally
trained in a second language. Flege (1991) studied the voice-onset
times of American English stops produced by speakers whose native
language was Spanish. Voice-onset time (VOT) is an important
feature that distinguishes voiced stop consonants from voiceless
stops. For example, in the production of [d], which is voiced, laryngeal pulsing occurs as or soon after the tongue breaks contact
with the alveolar area of the palate. In the production of voiceless
sounds like [t], laryngeal pulsing typically begins with the following
vowel. In the first experiment in his report, there were two groups
of adults. One group of subjects had learned English as five- to six-
year-old children and received an average of thirteen years of formal instruction. The second group was first exposed to English in
adulthood. They had received a mean of six years of instruction,
but the group included several individuals with no history of language training, even though they had resided in the United States
for some years. Flege found that these adult learners tended to
produce English /t/ with "compromise" properties that fall between

the short-lag values associated with monolingual Spanish and the long-lag values observed in English monolinguals. These learners had partially accommodated to but not fully achieved the native VOT values attained by the adults who were younger at the time of learning.

One could well ask, if these VOT shifts were achieved by the process of accommodation, how in principle does this differ from the acquisition of compromise VOT values by children partway through the learning of their native language? Macken and Barton (1980) found that at one point in the acquisition of American English (at age twenty to twenty-four months), the VOT of infants' voiceless stops fell somewhere between those associated with adult usage and the infants' own "natural" (that is, nonlinguistic) productions. A distinction between these cases—the compromise values of children acquiring their first language and those of uninstructed second-language learners—is that for the children the native values are truly *native,* and of course we expect them to move on with additional experience and maturation. But this is not to say that infants' motivation to learn speech is linguistic or even oriented exclusively toward lexical communication. Lacking such motivation, infants may initially engage in the act of speaking but not necessarily seek to convey lexical meaning.

WILLIAMS SYNDROME: GOOD FACIAL PROCESSING, GOOD SPEECH

The plausibility of the suggestion that infants are initially drawn into speaking by extracommunicative motives is dramatized by "cocktail party speech," as may occur in cases of Williams syndrome. By definition, affected individuals are mentally retarded, yet their speech often passes for normal. More careful analyses reveal, however, that many of the utterances of the victims of Williams syndrome are vacuous formulas that have been overheard in the speech of others, including clichés and idioms, social phrases and fillers (Udwin and Yule, 1990). Williams individuals are also known to fabricate many of the things they say. This is exactly what one would expect if the preeminent desire is social convergence in the absence of communicable experience.

Children with Down syndrome typically appear to be more impaired linguistically than Williams individuals with similar levels of measured intelligence. What accounts for the difference? So little is known about both syndromes that it seems risky to speculate. But along with all the other possibilities we might consider, a logical one in the present context is that the greater impairment manifested by individuals with Down syndrome is somehow related to a reduced desire to imitate speech or to phonetically accommodate. Rather than interpreting Williams syndrome as evidence for a "language module"—treating it as a proof that language can develop in the absence of putative cognitive substrates—I think this interesting case may be telling us something quite different; that speech can develop without language if the child is sufficiently accommodative vocally. For we must assume that if parrots can do it, humans lacking deep linguistic knowledge can also achieve a quantity of properly ordered language sounds. This may enable a measure of success in language communication, pushing the child farther along on the linguistic path that leads to substantive increases in linguistic competence and greater levels of performance.

What causes Williams infants, not measurably more intelligent than Down infants, to move farther along on the path to spoken language? If Williams infants are found to be less deficient in neurotransmitters such as noradrenaline, this could well be a factor (see Chapter 8). However, research has identified an interesting difference between Down and Williams infants that may be related to their uneven propensities for social communication. In neuropsychological studies (Bellugi et al., 1990), it was found that both Williams and Down adolescents performed poorly on a visuospatial task, but that those with Williams syndrome had an essentially normal ability to discriminate unfamiliar faces. Down adolescents, by contrast, showed marked deficits in face processing. These same investigators reported a high incidence of left-handedness in the Williams group but not in the Down subjects. Thus some of the manifest differences between these syndromes may relate to differential efficiency in the interpretation of social information.

In cocktail party chatter, linguistically acceptable utterances are fluently (re)produced in appropriate social contexts by an individual with neither full comprehension of the meaning nor awareness of the structure of his own speech. Listeners may at first be tricked by this, but linguistic formulas are not tricks and formulaic speakers are not tricksters. Thus, while I agree with MacKain (1982) that analysis of the sound system requires a series of complex operations, I am unconvinced that the infant's initial word forms require such analysis or are forged by pressures associated with lexical communication. It follows from my argument that some of the best young talkers are those who particularly seek social concordance and approval.

"REFERENTIAL" AND "EXPRESSIVE" CHILDREN

Katherine Nelson (1973, 1981) has written at some length about two interesting subgroups of children whose linguistic differences are evident as early as the first fifty words. The initial lexicon of conspicuously *referential* children contains a large number of object-oriented words. In contrast, *expressive* children's initial lexicon is more self-oriented, and consists of relatively few object-oriented words. Of interest here is the fact that in place of object words in the lexicons of expressive children is an appreciable supply of personal-social terms for expressing feelings, needs, and social forms. Nelson (1973) commented that even at this very early stage of acquisition, the function of language conspicuously influences its form. Interestingly, these expressive children are heavily formulaic; at an early age they appear to produce phrases and sentences as gestalts, and their speech contains functors and pronouns as well as nouns. According to Nelson (1981), these gestalts "have the characteristic of being wholistically produced without pauses between words, with reduced phonemic articulation, and with the effect of slurred or mumbled speech *but with a clear intonation pattern*" (p. 174, my italics).

Even the object names in the initial lexicons of children bespeak a highly personal and active orientation to speech. Nelson (1973) observed that there are relatively few words that cannot be acted on—words such as *sofa, table, stove, windows,* and *vase:* "children learn the names of the things they can act on, whether they are toys, shoes, scissors, money, keys, blankets, or bottles as well as things that act themselves such as dogs and cars. They do not learn the names of things in the house or outside that are simply 'there' whether these are tables, plates, towels, grass, or stores. With very few exceptions all the words listed are terms applying to manipulable or movable objects" (p. 31). This is of some interest in relation to the argument presented in Chapter 8 that children's cognition and language are fostered by a strong effectance motivation, a desire to act upon the people and objects in their environment.

Others (such as Bloom, 1973; Lieven, Pine, and Dresner Barnes, 1992; Peters, 1977) have noted the existence of expressive children. One group of observers has claimed that expressive children are more imitative (Bloom, Lightbown, and Hood, 1975). Lily Wong Fillmore (1977, Table 10.1, p. 209) has suggested a number of social strategies for children who want to learn a second language. I believe these strategies are what all infants do when they acquire their native language:

- Join a group and act as if you understand what's going on, even if you don't.
- Give the impression—with a few well-chosen words—that you can speak the language.
- Count on your friends for help.

Fillmore also recommended some *cognitive* strategies for learning a second language. These overlap somewhat with some of her social recommendations, and they also seem to describe the approach taken by infants to social communication in pursuit of a native language:

- Assume that what people are saying is directly relevant to the situation at hand or to what they or you are experiencing.
- Get some expressions you understand and start talking.
- Look for recurring parts in the formulas you know.
- Make the most of what you've got.
- Work on big things first; save the details for later.

As Nelson (1981) was careful to point out, more formulaic or expressive children are probably not different from other children in anything but degree. They merely operate more conspicuously on social motivations and their initial progress more dramatically reflects accommodative processes.

If I am right, it should be possible to catch children parroting back, with less than full comprehension, the sounds they hear others use. Anyone who has read the research of Warren Fay knows how common this practice is. In his observations of hundreds of normally developing children, Fay documented a high rate of echoic responding at thirty-six months, when nearly half echoed at least once in a brief test session; rates in younger children are unknown but presumed higher (Zipf, 1949).

Fay found that echoic responding occurs more frequently following an utterance that is difficult to comprehend than an utterance that is more easily understood (Fay and Butler, 1971). He also found that three-year-olds who are unusually echoic performed significantly less well on tests of verbal comprehension, verbal expression, and object naming than nonechoic children. However, the two groups had equivalent speech articulation scores (Fay and Butler, 1968). In other words, the echoers had superior phonetic scores, relative to other levels of language, than nonechoic children.

These findings suggest that vocal accommodation is closely tied to the phonetic level of spoken language, an idea that was reinforced in other studies in which Fay tried out some nonsensical utterances that were normally intoned. When Fay *stated* "El camino real" to monolingual-English three-year-olds, 24 percent responded in the affirmative. But when he *asked* "El camino real?" with the rising intonation associated with American English questions, the frequency of affirmative responses rose to 62 percent (Fay, 1975). Clearly, these normally developing children were under prosodic control![8]

When young children accommodate to connected speech, they may form internal representations that correspond prosodically, but not lexically, to commonly heard utterances. Waterson (1971) built a theory of phonological development around the need to explain children's reproduction of words that seemingly are apprehended and stored prosodically. Peters (1983) has written extensively about this practice, in which phrase-length stretches of speech are mistaken for single words or, in Peters's linguistically neutral terminology, "long units." In the small repertoire of a young child, these emblematic behaviors are not terribly different from vocal displays. I will say more about these prosodic emblems in Chapter 10.

If infants are readily inclined toward vocal accommodation, immediate responses may be more like model utterances than those

---

8. As is well known, the rate of echoic responding among autistic children is high, but prosody is typically not preserved even when lexical content is faithfully reproduced (Fay, 1969; Fay and Schuler, 1980). Among nonautistic children, we would expect phonetic values to be more adultlike in echo than in self-inspired, independently generated utterances.

that are delayed. Investigators are usually aware of this and may ask mothers and experimenters to speak no more than necessary "in order to avoid possible imitation" (Boysson-Bardies et al., 1989, p. 6). And well they might; even children with attested difficulties in the acquisition of phonology speak more accurately when they are exposed to an adult model than when they speak spontaneously, a phenomenon so frequently observed that speech clinicians have given it a name: "stimulability."

Some sounds continue to develop until children are nearly eight years of age (Templin, 1957), yet most children speak intelligibly after the age of three or four. To explain phonological acquisition, then, we must explain why it is that children's speech continues to move toward adult models long after intelligibility has peaked. We could assign the late refinements to delayed maturation, a notion that always comes in handy. But while not wishing to reject such effects out of hand, I believe the "functional" value of continued improvement has less to do with this than social factors, for example, behaving "in talk," as in all other matters, like the individuals the child wishes to resemble.

Animal behaviorists have had similar suspicions. In one paper, Meredith West and her colleagues (West, King, and Duff, 1990) asked, "If cowbirds can produce effective songs at six months of age, why do wild birds continue to change their songs for several months thereafter?" (p. 588). To explore this question, West conducted several experiments on the singing of naive males kept with conspecific females or with heterospecific birds. She found that even though females are largely silent, they do influence the song of males through subtle (to the human observer) nonvocal responses, such as movements of their wings or "wing strokes" (West and King, 1988a). In a playback experiment, West and King (1988b) found that song excerpts that had elicited wing strokes in previous observations were more likely than adjacent songs to release copulatory postures in male-deprived females. In a longitudinal study of males housed with females from different geographic regions, it was found that significant vocal differences emerged early in development, even though the birds' associates were silent (King and West, 1988). Song development in the cowbird, then, appears to unfold according to some sort of maturational schedule and to respond to external social factors.

Those who test "speech accommodation theory" in adults see

areas here where study is needed. "What," they ask, "is the precise relationship between momentary interpersonal accommodative shifts and longer-term idiolectal, dialectal, or language-shifts? What further mechanisms and processes, if any, need to be given theoretical recognition before long-term accommodation can be modelled" (Coupland and Giles, 1988, p. 180). In the case of infants, all accommodations are momentary but potentially able to structure or reorganize an evolving system. I see no reason, then, to assume that affectively driven learning is a strictly transitory matter with no possibility of lasting effects. Material that goes into semantic memory first passes through episodic memory. The contents of a person's long-term memory were, at one time, perceptions. Exposure to people speaking casually is evidently behind the acquisition of casual speech registers, those dialectal variants having implicit moods. Irvine (1990) regards registers as "a convenient way to look at the verbal aspects of affective display" (p. 127) and has argued that "the communication of feeling is not merely a property of the individual, or a function of transient irrational impulses, or an unruly force operating outside the realm of linguistic form. Instead, it is socially, culturally, and linguistically structured, and we cannot adequately interpret individuals' behavior as emotional expression until we understand some of that framework" (p. 128).

Irvine analyzed two affective registers in Wolof, a language spoken in Senegal. One register is associated with high-ranking nobles, known for their restraint and lethargy, and the other with members of a low-ranking caste called "griots," known for their volatility and high affectivity. In actuality, both registers are used by all speakers of Wolof. The registers differ in their prosody, phonology, morphology and syntax, lexicon, and discourse management and interactional devices. Differences in the way emotionality is handled by individuals in the two castes, then, are built directly into their linguistic registers.

I introduce this material on affective registers as partial support of my hypothesis that emotional communion entices infants into accommodative behaviors that, in time, become symbolic. Though launched as an instrument of socialization, vocal accommodation gradually leads to phonetic learning. Behaviors incorporated through these processes are subsequently reanalyzed and become internal phonetic representations as needed for speech, in parallel with the internalization of other displays in ontogeny. Vocal accommodation emerges, then, as a legitimate stage in a process that leads to speech when analytical skills are refined and referential capabilities expanded, laying the groundwork for the shift from exclusively affective vocalization to lexically encoded reference.

If the signs directing infants to spoken language are, in part, prosodic, we should expect ontogenetic correlations between measures of performance in language and prosody. We might expect that children who are attentive to voices and vocal variations will be in an advantaged position when it comes to words, other things being equal. Dimitrovsky (1964) studied children's ability to interpret various emotions conveyed by the voice. She found that five-year-olds were fairly good at it, and that girls were consistently superior to boys in differentiating happy, sad, loving, and angry emotions. This, she noticed, "fits in well with findings concerning the superiority of girls in general language development" (p. 83). In Chapter 7, I will discuss the linguistic deficits of autistic children, whose developmental disorders are closely associated with relative indifference to facial and vocal displays of emotion. Later I will revisit selected aspects of accommodation, treating it as an expression of children's social need to seem competent and to exert a demonstrable effect upon their social environment (Chapter 8).

We have seen that the infant's interest in facial-vocal communication is great and that infants are inclined to reproduce the behaviors of their caregivers, to increasingly harmonize with the nurturant others in their life, and to achieve and then share with them their newfound social competence. In the following sections I will take a look at how infant vocal behavior is influenced by sensory stimulation and social experience. In doing so, I will be examining the preliminaries to phonetic and phonological learning.

Induction of Vocal Content

Though the term "vocal learning" is widely used, it is rarely defined. As one goes through the literature on vocal learning, however, one encounters a number of different types. I will briefly describe a demonstration study to illustrate each of the several different types and levels of vocal learning that have been documented in the human infant.

VOCAL CONTAGION

Infants' earliest vocal reproductions could well be classified under the term *vocal contagion*. This term was used by Piaget (1962), who observed reproduction of specific sounds in one- and two-month-olds. He defined two types of vocal contagion and distinguished these from other kinds of vocal reproductions that occur early in life.

SELECTIVE REINFORCEMENT

Since the infant has a native repertoire, vocalization can be altered without imitation of novel material. In several studies, it has been demonstrated that sounds or syllables produced by the infant can be increased in frequency via *selective reinforcement*. Routh (1967) recorded the sound production of two- to seven-month-old infants over a two-day period. Then he selectively reinforced vowel- or consonantlike productions for the succeeding three days. Routh observed an increase in consonantlike sounds when consonants were selectively reinforced and an increase in vowellike sounds when vowels were reinforced. He thus found changes in vocal output—technically, vocal learning—as a function of environmental response. But in this research the environment supplied no phonetic targets and the infant performed no imitation.

There is also evidence for negative reinforcement. Wahler (1969) studied a single male infant from three weeks of age to about one year. The mother was instructed to attend to her son as she normally would, but to selectively "freeze" whenever he produced certain categories of vocalization. For example, beginning at about ten weeks of age, the mother froze whenever her son babbled or cooed. This produced a diminution of babbling and cooing, which recovered after the freezing was discontinued. The child's first word rarely occurs before eleven months of age, so two to three months is a young age for vocal learning to occur. But we must keep in mind that the infants in this research did not emit novel responses, they just changed the frequency with which they uttered sounds that had been produced before the selective reinforcement began.

ECHOIC RESPONDING

Several studies suggest that ambient vocalizations may be *echoed* at a fairly early age if eliciting conditions are right. We might recall that in Kuhl and Meltzoff (1982), four- and five-month-olds were exposed to video-audio tapes of a woman saying [i] or [a] at regular intervals and that many of the infants responded by vocalizing in time with the woman. Subsequent analyses (Kuhl and Meltzoff, 1988) suggested that about half the subjects echoed either or both of the vowels.

The analysis by Kuhl and Meltzoff leaves unclear which aspects of the stimuli were targeted in the infants' reproductions. The stimuli had visible lip movements, and it is known that infants imitate silent mouth openings (Meltzoff and Moore, 1977). The infants may have imitated the sound, but it is conceivable that they merely vocalized in time with the rhythmic stimuli they heard while imitating the oral movements or configurations they saw.

Such an interpretation is not possible for the study of pitch imitation reported by Kessen et al. (1979). As we saw in that study, the mother or father of four- to seven-month-old American infants sang an [a] vowel on the pitch of D, F, or A above middle C. Perceptual analyses by trained musicians revealed significant levels of pitch matching. However, it should be noted that pitch manipulations differ from spectral contrasts acoustically and in the neurophysiology of their perception. Moreover, pitch contrasts are less common in the languages of the world, only about a fourth of which have tones (Ruhlen, 1976), while all languages have vocalic contrasts.

If echo occurs reflexively, with little in the way of higher order signal analysis and motor planning, then echoic responding may require relatively little neural support. This assumption is supported by a case report (Geschwind, Quadfasel, and Segarra, 1968) of an adult woman who had sustained diffuse brain damage and lived as a chronic echoer. Postmortem analyses revealed a reasonably intact speech perception and production system—Broca's area, Wernicke's area, and the arcuate fasciculus appeared to have been spared—but almost every other area of the brain was severely damaged.

CONTINGENT RESPONSE LEARNING

How does a mother's behavior facilitate the vocal learning of her infant? Typically, she responds in kind. In contingent responding of this sort, the mother frequently follows up her infant's vocalization with one of her own, usually a direct imitation or a form of similar phonetic shape and semantic content. Papousek and Papousek (1989) have said that "the majority of mothers seem to act as if the baby had the capacity to imitate" (p. 149) and that "maternal matching and modelling in dialogues with precanonical infants may well indicate a species-specific social support to the infant's development of imitative abilities, vocal production, and communication" (p. 154). Elsewhere (Papousek and Papousek, 1991) they refer to parents' efforts to model and reinforce phonetic behaviors as "didactic parenting."

Earlier, I described Pawlby's (1977) study of the interactions between eight mother-infant dyads, which found that of all the phonetic imitation that occurred, over 90 percent involved the mother imitating the child! The imitation of infants by their mothers also takes in facial and manual activity, though in conjunction with vocal behavior. Uzgiris et al. (1989) studied imitation of a variety of motor activities by eighty mother-infant dyads in a nine- to twelve-minute face-to-face interaction. Like Pawlby, Uzgiris et al. found that at all ages maternal imitation of the infant exceeded the infant's imitation of the mother. At 8.5 months, however, there was a significant increase in the mean number of episodes in which the infant's act was matched by the mother, and an increase in the ratio of infant matching to maternal matching:

Age	A Infant's act matched by mother	B Mother's act matched by infant	A/B ratio
2.5	4.85	0.90	5.4
5.5	5.20	0.60	8.7
8.5	8.20	2.45	3.4
11.5	11.70	3.50	3.3

As it turned out, every imitative act involved the voice. In about a third of the instances of matching, the voice was the only behavior reproduced. The remaining cases involved the voice and the face or the voice and the hands.

What does this accomplish besides giving mothers the false impression that their infants, who are merely repeating their own original behaviors, are imitating her? Well, for one thing, this phonetically contingent responding may increase infants' receptivity or attention to adult speech (Papousek and Papousek, 1975, p. 249). Indeed, Pawlby (1977) herself interpreted the effects of phonetically contingent responding in a similar way. She commented that "babies do pay special attention (in that they laugh and smile and appear to be pleased) when the mothers themselves imitate an action which the child has just performed. The infant's action is thus 'highlighted' or 'marked out' as something special" (p. 220). She also thought that "in kind" maternal responses "may be what leads to the infant's more deliberate production of the action. Because the mother has repeatedly reflected back an event which he himself has just performed and since he finds this pleasing and attractive, the same action is produced by the child on a different occasion *in order that* his mother does likewise" (p. 220).

Veneziano (1988) found that contingent responding, in which mothers echo their infants' prelexical forms, encourages the baby to reproduce the original utterance and, in some cases, to accommodate to the mother's pronunciation. Hardy-Brown et al. (1981) found a significant correlation between mothers' frequency of contingent responding and the communicative development of their infant at one year. If contingent responding has these beneficial effects, it is conceivable that reduced contingent responding would retard the rate of (early) language development. Some evidence suggests that this is, in fact, the case (Tomasello, Mannle, and Kruger, 1986).

For a species in which vocal learning is so robust, one would think that evidence for vocal learning in humans abounds, but there is less documentation of infants' vocal learning than one might expect. It may be that since we have not required proof of vocal learning we have made few serious efforts to document it. This attitude may have been reinforced in the minds of all those who have heard their own nine- and ten-month-old infants "talking up a storm" and naturally concluded that these utterances—which resembles the parents' own—were learned. But as far as we know, the normal infant's "choice" of sounds is not an automatic translation of what it has heard. Because the similarity of infant and adult sounds can be independently explained on neuromuscular and anatomical grounds (Locke, 1983), there must be hard evidence that infants have heard and specifically targeted certain sounds for reproduction.

There is another reason for the relatively scanty evidence on children's vocal learning. The developmental literature of the last twenty years is replete with failures to demonstrate vocal learning in the human infant (Atkinson, MacWhinney, and Stoel, 1968; Eady, 1980; Enstrom, 1982; Huber, 1970; Oller and Eilers, 1982; Olney and Scholnick, 1976; Preston, Yeni-Komshian, Stark et al., 1969; Thevenin, Eilers, Oller et al., 1985). Just recently we registered yet another failure: in a perfectly respectable study by Gerald Siegel and his colleagues (Siegel et al., 1990) described earlier, no evidence could be obtained that nine- to twelve-month-old American infants imitate the fundamental frequency, frequency contour, amplitude, or intensity values of their parents.

In the vocal learning of infants, what is the role of the "tutor"? First, when mothers initiate stimulation or seek specifically to induce imitation, they tend (with exceptions) to choose vocal material that falls within the apparent productive capabilities of their infant. In the usual case, they present for imitation sounds they have heard at some previous time or—more commonly—have just heard. This takes the form of baby words such as *daedae, mama, bye-bye* and the like. Usually, they do this unwittingly, so that when the baby repeats its original behavior, the mothers believe that it has imitated them rather than the converse.

What do mothers do when it is the baby that initiates vocalization? The evidence on this is fairly clear. When infants initiate vocalization, mothers tend to respond contingently. That is, they reproduce or in some cases expand upon the child's own utterance. Veneziano (1988) has reported evidence that this sort of phonetically contingent responding causes infants to repeat their original behavior. Vocal learning that is responded to contingently represents a type of phonetic learning that is perhaps one step up from selective reinforcement, since utterances rather than some completely nonvocal behavior accomplish the reinforcement and the original utterance is expanded in the direction of the maternal form. Continuation of this behavior ought to produce environmental effects, and indeed, there is evidence that contingent responding increases the frequency of vocalization (Jones and Moss, 1971; Ramey and Ourth, 1971) and the "speechiness" of infant utterances (Bloom, Russell, and Wassenberg, 1987; Veneziano, 1988). In addition, it has been speculated that contingent responding increases infants' receptivity or attention to adult speech (Tomasello and Todd, 1983) and may cause infants to discover their capacity to alter the behavior of others (Papousek and Papousek, in press).

VOCAL IMITATION

Schwartz and Leonard (1982) performed an experiment with children whose ages, at the outset, were thirteen to fifteen months. None of the children had produced more than five different words prior to the experiment. Phonetic analyses were performed to determine each child's phonetic repertoire. Then, on an individual basis, eight contrived or "nonce" words were constructed of the sounds heard in a child's speech (IN words) and an equal number of nonce words were created from the sounds not previously heard in a child's speech (OUT words). These sixteen items were then randomly assigned to sixteen novel objects or actions and demonstrated for the children, who were then queried as to the names of the objects and actions. If the child responded, social reinforcement was presumably administered in some form. Analysis of all cases of both immediate and delayed imitation revealed that IN words were mastered in fewer sessions and produced more frequently than OUT words.

As this experiment shows, infants at just over a year were able to acquire a handful of wholly new words and referents in several short sessions. The source of the phonetic behavior was someone other than the child and the result was an approximate phonetic copy. Sounds that the child was producing in advance of the experiment were now said even more frequently.

TOPOGRAPHICAL LEARNING

As developmentally significant as the first act of vocal reference is, the child still may have done nothing new at the vocal level. Infants typically say [dada] before they know "dada" refers to their father (Locke, 1985, 1990b). So the infant may now be receiving credit for vocal reference—for "talking" as it were—but still may not have demonstrated *topographical learning*. By this term I mean the reproduction of surface physical features that were not previously a part of the child's output repertoire, and which therefore shift the vocal contour or constituent parts of utterances in the direction of ambient stimulation. Topographical learning requires that the infant perceive differences between ambient sounds and the sounds of its current repertoire and possess whatever articulatory control is needed to achieve adultlike patterns.

In view of the fact that all natural languages are spoken, one is normally disinclined to question the human capacity for vocal learning. And we have already seen some reasons why. Children who wish to speak will naturally pay attention to and reproduce a number of phonetic nuances. But if infants merely want to sound like adults, they need not wade as deeply into the phonetic stream as they do during the second and third years of life. What is the evidence for this sort of topographical learning in the human infant?

For some reason, until recently there has been little interest in the question of when the children of one linguistic community can be discerned from those of a different community strictly on the basis of vocal topography. At some point French children nasalize vowels more than English children do, and Spanish children trill their [r]s while their German peers do not. Some of this differentiation may commence long after talking has begun, and when language acquisition is obviously under way many researchers shift their attention from phonetics to semantics and syntax.

Left to operate, contingent responding should produce topographical learning in which the utterances of infants come to resemble the sound patterns they have heard solely because of perceptual experience. And there is recent evidence that before the child's first words, some shift in phonetic, that is, prephonological values, may occur. If vocal accommodation is affectively guided, we might expect the first evidence of segmental learning to involve the bearers of emotion, sex, age, and personal identity—the vowels. At ten months, Boysson-Bardies and her colleagues in Paris (Boysson-Bardies et al., 1989; Boysson-Bardies et al., 1992) have found vocalic differences between infants reared in different linguistic environments. In one study, they examined the fundamental frequencies of ten-month-old infants living in monolingual English, French, Arabic, and Cantonese environments. They found systematic differences in fundamental frequency, which gravitated in the direction of the presumed frequency values in the ambient languages.

In a second study, Boysson-Bardies et al. (1992) reported differences in the relative frequency of consonantlike sounds in babbling. However, these were not traced to the ambient language per se but to differences between the infants at older ages. There were nine- to thirteen-month-olds (at initial observation), five each from monolingual French, American English, Japanese, and Swedish homes. These infants were recorded in several sessions, beginning when they had no words and continuing until they were using four, fifteen, and twenty-five words, the last interval falling at about sixteen to seventeen months. In an interesting approach, the investigators began their analysis by examining the relative frequency of consonantal elements in words produced at the older ages. When the phonetic patterns that differentiated the groups at these intervals were identified, the investigators then asked at how young an age (and constricted a lexical system) the infant groups could be differentiated along similar phonetic lines. The analysis focused on the relative frequency of articulatory place, manner, and voicing patterns.

Boysson-Bardies et al. found that the groups could be distinguished with surprising accuracy as early as the first (zero-word) session when the infants were just nine to thirteen months old. In their effort to account for this early differentiation, the authors noted that at similar ages some lexical comprehension has been observed in other work. It was therefore plausible, they reasoned, that prelexical infants at that age attend to and in some sense know about ambient phonetic forms. This would perceptually pave the way for the infants to reproduce such forms in their own phonetic activity.

In addition to vocalic frequency and consonantal patterns, Halle, Boysson-Bardies, and Vihman (1991) have recently reported an early expression of distinctive phonological experience in Japanese and French infants. Infants in this study had already acquired the disyllabic stress patterns associated with the ambient language at the twenty-five-word stage. Astonishingly, though speech development has been studied in earnest for several decades, to my knowledge Boysson-Bardies' reports are the first to document the age at which children reared in different linguistic environments diverge in terms of their own prelexical sound productions. The only other attempts with which I am familiar involved infants of similar ages but with uniformly negative results for tonal variations, inventory of consonantlike and vocalic segments, consonantal features, voice-onset times for stops or whatever perceptual cues could be used to discriminate languages in listening experiments.

Why did Boysson-Bardies and her colleagues obtain positive findings when all the other studies yielded negative results? In some cases, I suspect the features or contrasts under study conveyed so little information about the identity, attitude, or mood of speakers that infants ignored them. In other cases, I suspect the segmental features tested were motorically irreproducible by nine- to twelve-month-olds. Moreover, Boysson-Bardies and her associates were among the few investigators to collect vocal samples in the home in the presence of the infant's mother and to submit selected utterances either to acoustic analysis (vowels) or to within-subject developmental analyses (consonants).

A second source of surprise in the work of Boysson-Bardies and her colleagues is the finding of ambient phonetic differentiation among infants who, by reference to the literature on lexical development, are too young to talk. There is little reason, according to word-driven models of phonetic development, to expect such systematicity in utterances having no morphemic units or lexical targets. But as I have said, the process by which they got uttered by the infant may not be referentially driven.

These studies provide evidence that as infants approach the end of their first year, contingent responding or vocal imitation alters the frequency of certain of their spontaneous phonetic behaviors, causing them to sound more like the mature speakers in their culture. This research furnishes no evidence of changes in the context or the manner in which vocal behaviors are normally deployed and no evidence of vocal reference.

For other examples of topographical learning, I would point to a study of Mexican Spanish (Macken and Barton, 1980), which found that two-year-olds commonly expressed word-initial stop consonants (such as [d]) as fricatives (such as [z]). I consider this an example of topographical learning for several reasons: in Mexican Spanish, the children's environmental model, utterance-initial voiced stops are frequently expressed as fricatives; the conversion of stops to fricatives is not arguably a maturational effect, since voiced fricatives are virtually nonexistent in the spontaneous vocalizations of two-year-old deaf children; and word-initial voiced stops are rarely expressed as fricatives by two-year-old hearing children who are exposed exclusively to English (Locke, 1983).

REFERENTIAL LEARNING

In referential learning, the child associates an existing vocal form with an external referent, a process that appears to be correlated with the development of causal relations (Harding and Golinkoff, 1979) and may be preceded by the child's discovery that one can mean things with sound. At a simple level, such a discovery could begin as early as the differentiation between cry and noncry, or pain cry and fear cry, to which adults may respond differently. Such vocal differentiation may occur unintentionally, as a form of vocal "leakage." I think this is what occurred in D'Odorico (1984), whose four- to nine-month-old infants' fundamental frequency and intonation contour seemed to vary in discomfort, calling, and requesting situations. Unintentional or not, it seems likely that when infants observe adults responding differentially to their vocalizations, they discover the possibilities for vocal reference.

Ironically, reference frequently emerges with the child's first use of *invented* words, in which the infant uses a sound pattern that is apparently of its own making to refer to some particular thing or action (for examples, see Leopold, 1949). In the case of invented words, vocal reference precedes vocal learning; the acquisition, if there is any, is not of the phonetic form but of the concept of vocal reference or the child's assumption of an active speaking role. Frequently, the attentive family discovers the sound-meaning relationship devised by the infant and begins to use this form themselves, but only when addressing the child.

Some of the delayed imitations in Schwartz and Leonard (1982) may have been referential. In naturalistic circumstances, truly acquired forms may be expressed as early as eleven or twelve months, or they may not appear until several months later. A number of studies document children's first words (see reviews in Bretherton, 1988; Meier and Newport, 1990). In Benedict (1979), nine- to ten-month-old American infants were followed for six months. Using parental report and direct observation, it was determined that children comprehended twenty different words by nine to twelve months and produced twenty different words by eleven to twenty months.

SYSTEMIC LEARNING

In systemic learning, the child develops knowledge—through inference or deduction of linguistic structure—of "rules" governing the distribution and combinatorial privileges of sound segments. For example, English-learning infants discover that /m/ can precede /p/ but not follow it within syllables, and that the /mp/ sequence can end words (such as *lamp, jump*) but not begin them. There is, then, a syntax of phonemes in each language that children must learn. Systemic learning involves the physical level of spoken language but exists above this level.

Because they know the system, three-year-old children can distinguish possible English words from phonetic sequences that cannot occur in English (Messer, 1967). Because of systemic learning, children's speech errors generally fall within constraints that are not purely motoric but respect the structure of the sound system they have learned. This is suggested by cross-linguistic analyses, which reveal that children in different linguistic systems make different errors (Bortolini and Leonard, 1990; Locke, 1983).

There is no time in the life of a human infant when it is without voice or fails to exercise vocal potential with some regularity. The infant conveys physical and emotional states by voice and they are reliably interpreted by the observing family. All parties are aware of one another's voices, and the infant is aware of its own voice from birth. The human infant does not merely vocalize to pain and discomfort and when favorably disposed, it uses its voice playfully. Nevertheless, it is not altogether clear that the motivation to vocalize is entirely an auditory matter, for the congenitally deaf also indulge in this behavior with some frequency.

Those most inclined to vocalize playfully, other things being equal, seem to be headed for bigger and better things down the linguistic road. Initially, the infant accommodates to the vocal patterns of its home, probably unconsciously and perhaps contagiously.

The act of vocal accommodation represents a subset of the larger constellation of verbal and motor activities that are observed by the infant and incorporated into its repertoire. Vocal accommodation is a broad net, and it brings in a number of linguistically irrelevant vocal behaviors along with real language material. As a consequence, infants' speaking behaviors probably resemble those of their parents in matters of rate, tone, and style, as well as lexical substance. For this reason, some of the infant's early words and phrases will later be revised under the terms of a linguistic regime.

There are many ways that infants can reveal in their own utterances their growing knowledge of ambient vocal and linguistic patterns. Some forms of learning involve very little reaching or compromise; for example, in selective reinforcement, the infant merely makes more or less of something it was doing naturally. In other forms of vocal learning, the infant reaches beyond its prelinguistic phonetic repertoire and in the direction of heard sounds. How well the infant is able to capture its parents' level of vocal complexity is influenced by perceptual factors, of course, but in large measure success is dependent upon oral-motor control. Vocal complexity takes a huge step forward during the babbling period.

5

THE INFANT
BECOMES ARTICULATE

[T]he most powerful tool in the ethologist's armory is the description of specific motor patterns . . . it must be known what behavior there is to be modified . . . and also the normal range of individual differences within a given species . . . the unit of analysis should involve discrete motor action patterns . . . that are relatively simple, observable, and measurable . . . In this way, the time of first appearance of specific actions (and sequences) may be noted, and changes over time (in frequency, amplitude, or motivational context) may be observed.

M. Bekoff, "The Development of Social Interaction,
Play, and Metacommunication in Mammals"

An inclination to imitate and all the good communicative intentions in the world are insufficient for being a speaker of language. One needs to develop motoric abilities and the capability to use these skills to express phonetic representations. Let us look at the emergence of the tendency and the ability to perform articulate movements while phonating.

Early Forms of Playful Vocalization

Several investigators have described early vocal behaviors and the time frame for stages of vocal development through which infants normally pass (Oller, 1980; Stark, 1980). Oller has roughed out these stages approximately as follows:

Phonation Stage (0–1 month): Nondistress sounds at this stage are those associated with an open vocal tract, with little in the way of oral closures and limited lingual and mandibular movement.

GOO Stage (2–3 months): The GOO stage marks the appearance of crude syllables initiated by closures that perceptibly resemble voiced velar stops (such as [g]). When produced repetitively, these syllabic forms are distributed irregularly. Some tongue contact with the velar area may occur purely because the infant's tongue tends to overly fill the small mouth available to it at that point in its anatomical development (Kent, 1981).

Expansion Stage (4–6 months): As the name implies, vocal behavior diversifies as infants approach the end of their first six months of life. New forms include more substantial vowel-like sounds, as well as a variety of less "speechy" sounds such as bilabial trills ("raspberries"), squealing, and growling. Significantly, at this stage there may be some marginal babbling in which vocal tract closures are imprecisely and irregularly alternated with vowel-like elements.

Reduplicated Babbling Stage (7–10 months): This stage refers to the onset of well-formed syllables. Babbling is the most dramatic stage in the infant's vocal development because it usually starts suddenly, it is very different from what comes before, and it is remarkably similar to what parents hope will happen next—speech! Babbled syllables typically involve closures that are released into an open vocal tract, giving the impression of a consonant-vowel syllable (such as [da]) that may be produced repetitively ([dada-dada]).

Variegated Babbling Stage (11–12 months): In this stage, infants display sounds having several different points of articulatory closure within multisyllabic strings (such as [daba]). Recent research suggests that reduplicated and variegated stages are likely to be greatly overlapped and may even constitute a single stage (Smith, Brown-Sweeney, and Stoel-Gammon, 1989).

By the age of six months, the baby is an old hand at vocal communication and "conversation," but the content has not sounded all that much like speech. It is inarticulate. This changes when babbling begins and babies begin to partition their voice into syllable-sized elements. I believe the developmental linguistic significance of babbling goes way beyond what is envisioned in current theories of language development.

BABBLING

Unlike the sounds of crying, shrieking, cooing, yelling, and fussing, babbling is characterized by the production of well-formed or *can-*

onical syllables that have the acoustic characteristics of adult speech. Canonical syllables are defined in specific physical terms relating to duration, and to changes in their frequency and amplitude (Oller, 1986). These syllables are the product of infants' natural tendency to alternately elevate and depress the mandible (Lindblom and Engstrand, 1989; MacNeilage and Davis, 1990a). The elevation of the mandible, along with labial or lingual action, narrows and obstructs the vocal tract. This yields closants, which resemble consonant sounds. The depression of the mandible, with collateral oral adjustments, yields vocants, which sound like vowels (Kent and Bauer, 1985).

The evidence suggests that babbling typically begins abruptly at some time after the age of six months, regardless of whether the ambient language is American English (Oller and Eilers, 1988; Ramsay, 1984), Dutch (van der Stelt and Koopmans-van Beinum, 1986), Russian (Bel'tyukov and Salakhova, 1973) or Swedish (Holmgren, Lindblom, Aurelius et al., 1986). Oller and Eilers (1988) place the onset at six to ten months, since it is between these ages that the ratio of canonical syllables per utterance first exceeds a level unsurpassed in the deaf until some time later. Figure 5.1 shows cumulative data on the onset of babbling by maternal report, in fifty-one Dutch infants. As the figure reveals, the majority of infants begin to babble by just over seven months.

Perceptual and instrumental evidence indicates that babbling is rhythmic (Bickley, Lindblom, and Roug, 1986). In the reduplicated strings of thirteen-month-olds, syllables tend to repeat every 200 msec (Kent and Bauer, 1985), which approximates the rate of adult conversational speech. MacNeilage and Davis (1990a) have suggested that reduplicated babbling is responsible for the formation of phonological "frames" into which speech segments, when available, will be inserted.

Authoritative pronouncement (for example, Jakobson, 1968) notwithstanding, empirical evidence suggests that the phonetic segments of babbling are highly restricted. Typically, consonantlike segments are featurally limited to a small set of oral and glottal stops, nasals, and approximants. Babbling has an extremely low occurrence of other sounds, including those classified as liquids, affricates, and supraglottal fricatives. Among vocalic sounds, low

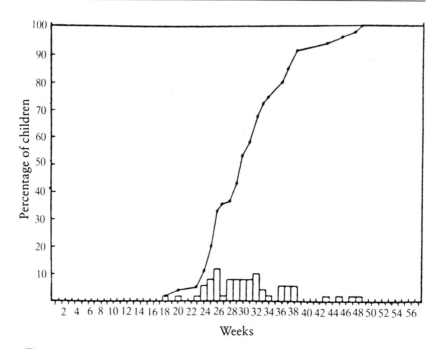

Figure 5.1. Onset of babbling in fifty-one Dutch infants by parental report.

central and low front vowels predominate (Kent and Bauer, 1985). Syllable-final obstruents occur rarely in babbling, and consonant clusters are virtually nonexistent (Locke, 1983).

THE PHONETIC REPERTOIRE OF BABBLING   Thus infants produce a characteristic repertoire of oral movements that listeners hear as speech sounds. At about one year of age, [h d b m t g w n k] account for over 80 percent of all consonantlike segments in the babbling of infants reared in American English homes (Locke, 1983, 1990a). Infants reared in non-English linguistic environments produce a similar repertoire of consonantlike segments. The rather extensive evidence for this, which is reviewed elsewhere (Locke, 1983), includes the highly similar phonetic diaries of infants reared in diverse linguistic environments.

Analyses reveal that the sounds most favored by infants in their babbling are also produced most accurately by children and occur with very high frequency in the languages of the world (Locke, 1983). Considering such relationships, one develops the impression of an irrepressible biological substrate that is revealed every time we open our mouths to speak. What is this substrate? Where does the phonetic substance of babble come from?

If the infant sounds that we perceive seem pretty much the same from one linguistic environment to the next, the inspiration for sound-making movements may come mostly from within, that is, they may be motivated by *phonetic* (for example, anatomical, physiological, aerodynamic) factors. First, several of the more prominent sound patterns of babbling can be independently motivated by phonetic models of sound production, making unnecessary any appeal to specific environmental stimulation (Kent, 1981; Locke, 1986a). Second, the initial period of babbling is relatively the same across cultures; cross-linguistic studies typically have found few differences in sound production that could be differentiated perceptually or acoustically (Locke, 1983). Moreover, if the infant's repertoire were due to exposure, how would one explain the fact that the nine sounds so popular at one year approach 90 percent of the infant's inventory of consonantlike sounds at five to ten months (Irwin, 1947)?

Phonetic Action Patterns   These findings on the phonetic content of babbling suggest that for most of the first year, infants' sound-making movements are relatively unaffected by potentially distinguishing ambient experience. Rather, as "primitive actions of the vocal tract articulators," these gestures are carried over into speech with no more than minimal readjustment, ultimately becoming the contrastive units of language (Browman and Goldstein, 1989), which is why many of the sounds that appear frequently in babbling resemble phonemes that occur in the majority of the world's languages (Locke and Pearson, 1992).

The gestures of babbling are so robust they survive retardation, neonatal brain damage, and congenital deafness. In a study of the babbling of Down syndrome infants, the relative frequency of sounds with a labial, apical, or velar point of articulation was not different from the featural profiles of normally developing infants (Smith and Oller, 1981). Marchman et al. (1991) analyzed the phonetic patterns of ten neurologically normal infants and five infants with unilateral focal lesions. They observed that in both the control and the focal lesion groups, stops were more frequent than other manners of consonant production. Labials and dentals were also more frequent than velars in both groups, and both groups were unlikely to produce final consonants or consonant clusters.

Brain damage did not let these infants off scot-free, however. It appears that control subjects produced a higher proportion of "true" consonants, a category of very speechlike sounds that excludes stops of glottal origin and glides. However, since the vocalizations of these normal subjects were transcribed by a different team of researchers, it is not obvious that these intergroup variations were "true" differences.

Studies of hearing-impaired infants (Carr, 1953; Smith and Oller, 1981; Stoel-Gammon, 1988; Stoel-Gammon and Otomo, 1986; Sykes, 1940) reveal place, manner, and syllabic patterns that parallel trends observed in hearing infants. Sykes (1940) studied three- to six-year-old hearing-impaired children who would not have been detected early in life and fitted with effective amplification given the state of the diagnostic art over fifty years ago. Nevertheless, most or all had begun to babble by the time of the study, and their syllabic and segmental patterning broadly resembled that of hearing infants and children in many ways: consonant-vowel syllables exceeded vowel-consonant syllables by nearly fourteen to one and singletons predominated over clusters by a wide margin. Just as in hearing infants, stops, glides, and nasals surpassed 90 percent, greatly exceeding fricatives, affricates, and liquids, which amounted to less than 10 percent of the sounds perceived and transcribed.

These findings suggest that the more predominant vocal tract shapes commanded by the human infant are like the movement patterns of animals who are relatively unaffected by sensory experience. These patterns of activity seem to require little more than appropriate "releasing stimuli" (Fox, 1971). Indeed, if there are natural categories of vocal activity that are strong enough to survive deafness and brain damage, their induction or stabilization may require little from the recognized mechanisms of learning. Accordingly, we would expect certain phonetic movement patterns to "behave" somewhat like the modal action patterns of animals in whom the role of postnatal learning remains to be demonstrated

(Barlow, 1977). This would exist apart from any tendency to produce the movements as stereotypes, that is, chainlike recurrences of particular articulatory movements.

The sound-making movements that emerge first may be less susceptible to environmental influence than the less frequent vocal movement patterns. Acknowledging Mayr's (1976) distinction between open and closed behavior programs, Tooby and Cosmides (1988) have suggested that "the more universal preferences are the product of more closed behavior programs, whereas the more variable are the expression of more open behavior programs" (p. 37). This relationship, they say, has evolved because open behavior programs are "open to environmental inputs, and hence variable in expression, versus those that are closed to environmental input, and consequently uniform in expression" (p. 36).

If the more frequently operationalized *phonetic action patterns* are the product of relatively closed behavior programs, we might expect that "universal" phonemes would assume fewer different forms of expression than "nonuniversal" phonemes. According to the *UCLA Phonological Segment Inventory Database* (1981), the /m/ in American English is the most "popular" phoneme in the world, occurring in 97 percent of the languages in the archive. On the other hand, the /r/ in American English is the least frequent of the phonemes, popping up in fewer than 5 percent of the languages. On purely statistical grounds, we should expect the more universal /m/ to have about twenty times as many variants as the less frequent /r/. On strictly biological grounds, we should expect universal phonemes to be more closed—and therefore to reveal fewer variants within and across languages—than the less widely distributed and more open ones. And sure enough, the *Handbook of Phonological Data from a Sample of the World's Languages* (1979) reveals only half as many types of bilabial nasals as /r/-like liquids.

Whether one looks at babies, native speakers, or languages, one finds the threads of biology everywhere, woven through the fabric of phonetic behavior and phonological structure. This is illustrated in Table 5.1, using the phonetic categories *m* and *r*. Sounds that are frequent in languages, like /m/, are generally well represented in babbling and also tend not to assume as many forms as the less restricted phonemes, either across languages or within them as dialectal variations. These same, "unmarked" sounds appear to

Table 5.1 Some attributes and distributional characteristics of two
phonetic gestures (from Locke and Pearson, 1992).

Attribute	*m*	*r*
Prominence in babbling	prominent	restricted
Breadth of linguistic distribution	"universal"	restricted
Variation across dialects	narrow	wide
Patency of behavior program	closed	open
Role of linguistic stimulation	limited	moderate
Developmental "schedule"	early	late
Probability of disorder	low	high

have relatively more closed behavior programs and to require fewer
exemplars in order to be mastered. Finally, /m/ is inclined to develop
early and is less likely than /r/ to be disordered.

THE PLACE OF BABBLING IN NEUROMOTOR DEVELOPMENT Figure
5.2 shows the onset of a number of motor behaviors, including
babbling, from the same Dutch population described earlier (Koopmans-van Beinum and van der Stelt, 1986). Because infants do not
smile, roll, crawl, sit, and pull up to a standing position because
they enjoy the "sound" made by these activities, we should perhaps
suspect at the outset that the motivation for babbling initially has
a large motoric factor.

Figure 5.3 is from Esther Thelen's (1981) studies of rhythmic
motor behaviors in normally developing infants, broken down anatomically. The display at the bottom of the figure shows the very
sharp increase in rhythmic hand movements at twenty-six or
twenty-seven weeks. This is chronologically, and perhaps functionally, related to the finding by Ramsay (1984) that both right-handed
reaching and reduplicated babbling begin at 6.7 months. Figure 5.4
displays Ramsay's reaching data. The preference for unimanual
reaching came and then unceremoniously left a few weeks after-
wards, only to return a short time later. This sort of momentary
reversal typically concerns psychologists, who are inclined to consider such phenomena as unwelcome statistical "noise" or inex-

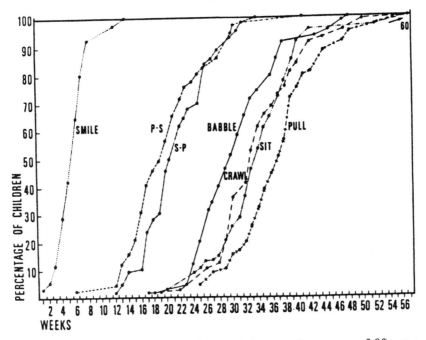

Figure 5.2. Onset of a number of motor behaviors in a group of fifty-one Dutch infants. Activities include smiling, rolling from prone to supine, rolling from supine to prone, babbling, sitting without support, crawling, and pulling to a standing position.

plicable developmental regression. And yet, such variations offer excellent opportunities for establishing functional linkages in development. For all we currently know, babbling activity also briefly subsides just after its onset. If unimanual reaching and babbling were to wax and wane *together,* or if vocal behavior were to mutate further when bimanual coordination began, I should think this would merely increase our confidence in the relationship between hand and vocal activity.

These studies converge to suggest that mechanisms in the left cerebral hemisphere may control the infant's speechlike activity. This is an exceedingly important point. Since it is the left hemisphere that appears to be primarily responsible for the phonetic substance of speech, that is, segmental speech sounds, there is the possibility that babbling marks the beginning of the neural preconditions for the development of spoken language.

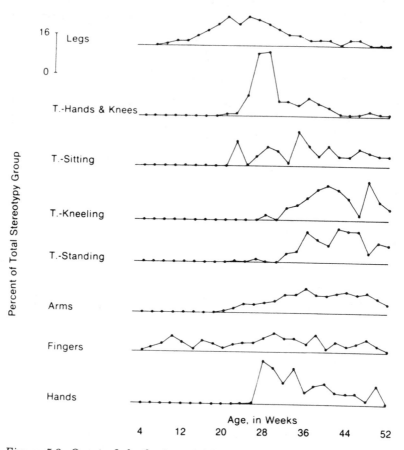

Figure 5.3. Onset of rhythmic activities (T = torso). Lower panel shows the sharp onset of rhythmic hand movement.

What about infants who are motorically delayed? Infants with Down syndrome characteristically are delayed in the expression of various gross motor "milestones" such as crawling and walking (Kravitz and Boehm, 1971) as well as some motorically finer gestures; it is not clear whether this includes pointing. Neuroanatomically, Down infants also appear to be less developed in the posterior cerebral areas responsible for motor function (Jernigan and Bellugi, 1990). Is the onset of their babbling delayed? The answer would seem to be "yes." Studies by Kim Oller's group at the University of Miami suggest that Down infants' babbling, as far as can be judged

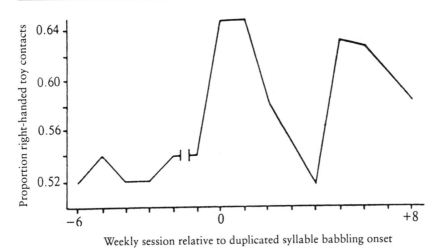

Figure 5.4. Incidence of right-handed reaching before and after the onset of babbling.

from parental report and follow-up visits to the lab, begins on average at about thirty-eight weeks of age, some eleven weeks later than normal (Levine et al., 1991). Apparently their hand banging is also delayed, beginning at thirty-six instead of twenty-five weeks, the reported age at which it begins in normally developing infants.

THE CONTROL OF BABBLING   The topographical similarity between phonetic material in babbling and in speaking implies common control mechanisms. We saw a hint of this in the data of Thelen and Ramsay, but what more can be said about these mechanisms? One strategy for explicating the relationship of babbling to speaking is to look for neuropsychological factors that might be shared by these activities. Studies of vocal-manual relationships in older children (Fogel and Hannan, 1985; Hiscock and Kinsbourne, 1978; Kinsbourne and McMurray, 1975) suggest that speech and hand activity are under the gross control of neural mechanisms that are located in the same cerebral hemisphere. Recently, this relationship was dramatized in studies of epileptic patients in which vocalization and right arm activity were provoked by electrical stimulation to adjacent areas in the left hemisphere (Fried et al., 1991). If it is dependent on similarly lateralized control mechanisms in the brain, babbling should have a relationship to right hand activity (that is, left hemisphere motor control centers) that it does not share with left hand activity.

A related question is whether babbling, like speaking, is "special" in the sense that it relies on mechanisms that have evolved or have been usurped specifically for this activity. Is babbling motivated and shaped by factors that are associated only with the act of phonation, or is babbling a species-characteristic manifestation of an underlying tendency to produce repetitive movements with audible consequence?

It has been observed that babies from all cultures are attracted to the use of noisemakers of one kind or another (Gesell and Thompson, 1934). In his experiments, McCall (1974) found that 7.5- to 11.5-month-olds prefer noisy toys to silent ones (with no age effect over this range). In a review of studies reporting infants' manipulation of sound-making objects, Lockman and McHale (1989) concluded that "by 8 months, possibly by 6 months, infants engage in greater manipulation of sound-producing objects" (p. 156). In their own studies, infants at six, eight, and ten months were observed playing with various objects, which included "sounding" objects that contained either a bell or grains of rice. Although no data were reported, the authors noted that "for the sounding objects, infants showed more shaking and banging. Here, however, age differences emerged. Six-month-olds did not display appropriate behaviors with the sounding objects. In contrast, 8- and 10-month-olds did show appropriate but different patterns of behaviors with these objects. Ten-month-olds shook the sounding object most frequently, whereas 8-month-olds engaged in more object-appropriate shaking than 6-month-olds. In contrast, 8-month-olds banged the sounding object more frequently than either of the other age groups or objects" (p. 159).

There are also indications in the literature that repetitive hand activity, with some degree of frequency, may occur in the service of audibility. One clue comes from analyses (Uzgiris et al., 1989) of the imitative or "matching" behaviors seen in face-to-face interactions between mother-infant dyads: "For the youngest age group [2.5 months], the most frequently matched acts were various vocalizations and mouth movements, especially opening the mouth wide. For the 5.5-month-olds, following of the partner's gaze was added to vocalizations and mouth openings as a frequently matched act. In most cases, it was the mother who matched one of these acts of her infant. In the 8.5-month group, vocalizations and motoric acts such as following of the partners' gaze and hand banging constituted the frequently matched acts" (p. 113). My guess is that most of the hand banging was initiated by the infant and imitated by the mother, especially since at 8.5 months the mother imitated the infant nearly four times more often than it imitated her.

When an infant recurrently uses its right hand to bang an object against a hard surface, its left hemisphere is engaged in the control of repetitive activity with auditory result, very likely—one might suppose—with auditory intentions. If the production of canonical syllables in babbling and speaking have a common control mechanism, as seems reasonable, when an infant babbles its left hemisphere is also engaged in the control of audible, rhythmic activity. Do both activities express the same underlying motives and satisfy the same underlying drives? Do babies babble less while banging and vice versa? There are indications that babies of babbling age vocalize less when playing with toys that make a sound than they do with nonauditory toys (Delack, 1976). Does babbling satisfy some general, nonlinguistic appetite for activity and stimulation?

A recent study in my own laboratory (Locke et al., 1991) tested the hypothesis that the onset of babbling coincides with the onset of left hemisphere control over vocal tract activity, which appears necessary for speech. Our experiment was premised on the following observations: Electrical stimulation studies suggest that there may be a common mechanism in the left perisylvian cortex that controls precisely timed movements of the hand and the vocal tract (Ojemann, 1984). At five to six months postnatally, there is evidence of greater dendritic branching in manual and vocal-motor areas of the left hemisphere than in homologous areas in the right hemisphere (Simonds and Scheibel, 1989). There is evidence of longer right hand grasping when toys are placed equally often in right and left hands at approximately the same age (Caplan and Kinsbourne, 1976; Hawn and Harris, 1983). As we saw above, at the onset of babbling there is often an increase in right-handed reaching and toy contacts; at about the same age, there is typically an increase in infants' rhythmic manual activity and preference for toys that make a sound.

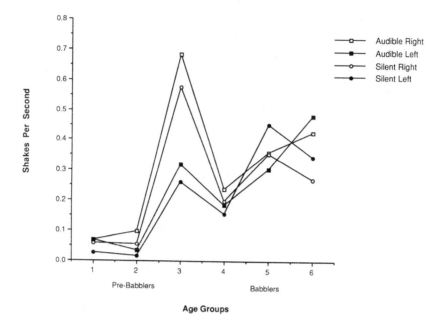

Figure 5.5. Manual laterality and audibility effects upon rattling behavior in infants who had not yet begun to babble and those who had been babbling for various lengths of time.

For the experiment, we observed two groups (Groups 1 and 2) of normally developing prebabblers (ages four and five months) and four groups (Groups 3–6) of infants who were already babbling (ages six to nine months). An audible and a silent rattle were placed in the right or left hand of each infant according to a predetermined schedule. Grasp time, number of shakes, and shakes per second were assessed. The analyses reported below were based on shakes per second.

Because babbling is a precisely timed motor behavior, we predicted that there would be a selective increase in repetitive right hand activity commencing with the onset of babbling. Because babbling is an audible behavior, we expected to observe an auditory enhancement of repetitive right hand activity commencing with the onset of babbling. In the analysis, we found a significant increase in shakes per second from the prebabbling to the babbling period. This may be seen in Figure 5.5, which shows laterality patterns and audibility effects. Follow-up tests revealed that Groups 1 and 2 differed from Groups 3, 5, and 6. We also found that right-handed shaking significantly exceeded left-handed shaking overall and that there was a significant interaction, which was due primarily to the greater amount of right than of left hand shaking in Group 3, the infants who had most recently begun to babble. The audibility effect was only marginally significant, and there was no tendency for one of the groups or one of the hands to favor the audible rattle over the silent one.

We drew several conclusions from this simulation task. First, our findings are consistent with the view that in the second six months of postnatal development, the left hemisphere assumes control of speechlike activity. Second, babbling seems to represent the functional convergence of motor control and sensory feedback systems. Finally, the very slight audibility effect seems consistent with the observation that congenitally deaf infants babble but do not begin to do so until their second year of life.

A "SOUND" MOTIVATION: MORE ON THE ROLE OF AUDITION
Whether babies babble because they like the sound, as scholars have speculated, should be answerable by direct observation and experimentation. As I mentioned earlier, a number of studies reveal preferences for toys that can be made to produce a sound over toys that remain silent, despite the infant's best efforts. I also mentioned block or hand banging, which appears to begin just before babbling, and rattle shaking, which seems to begin in earnest with the onset of babbling. If this preference for self-produced sound extends to recurrent oral movements, we might expect deaf infants not to babble—even if they have vocalized previously—and the failure of any infant to do so might alert us to the possibility that its hearing is impaired.

STUDIES OF HEARING-IMPAIRED INFANTS   Research indicates that congenitally hearing-impaired infants, even those who receive amplification, are usually late to begin babbling. Oller and Eilers (1988) studied seven severely to profoundly hearing-impaired infants (all of whom wore hearing aids) at eleven to fourteen months of age. They found that the ratio of canonical syllables to utterances was greatly reduced in the deaf, relative to hearing controls. Figure

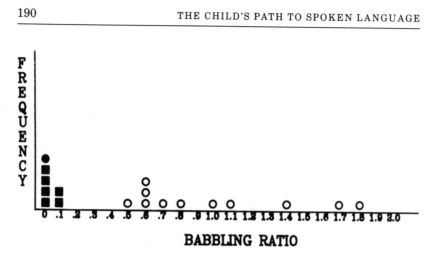

BABBLING RATIO

Figure 5.6. Ratio of canonical syllables to utterances in seven hearing-impaired (filled symbols) and eleven normally hearing (open symbols) infants.

5.6 is a frequency distribution of these babbling ratios. Note that the two populations are completely separate; no deaf infant's ratio exceeded 0.1 and no hearing infant's ratio fell below 0.5. According to onset criteria derived from the utterances of hearing infants (five canonical syllables per hundred utterances), the babbling stage was delayed in all cases. Where all twenty-one hearing infants had begun to babble by ten months, none of the nine deaf infants started until eleven to twenty-five months. Figure 5.7 shows the distribution. When they do finally begin to babble, deaf children appear to have reduced repertoires of consonantlike segments. Stoel-Gammon and Otomo (1986) found that eleven hearing-impaired infants had just a fraction of the sounds of normally hearing infants, and their smaller repertoires shrank still further over time.

One assumes that the deaf children were delayed because of their inability to hear and not because of concomitant motoric or other delays. But why does severe hearing impairment delay babbling but not eliminate it altogether? Oller and Eiler's answer is that hearing-impaired subjects perceive some speech visually and through residual (amplified) hearing. This leaves open the question of whether the observed delay is due to deaf children's inability to hear other people, reduced sensitivity to their own ("autogenous") vocalizations, or lessened awareness of both others and themselves.

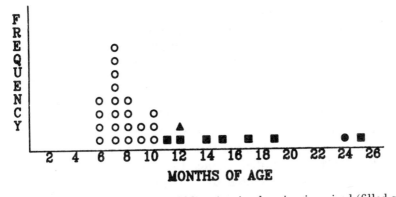

Figure 5.7. Age of onset of babbling in nine hearing-impaired (filled symbols) and twenty-one normally hearing (open symbols) infants.

There is little evidence on the subject of which voices contribute most to human vocal development, mainly because hearing children are typically exposed to others and themselves, and hearing-impaired children receive relatively little information about all sources of speech. But two cases merit some attention. One involves hearing children reared by deaf parents who sign and do not speak, or do not speak often. These children can hear themselves but not their parents. Several investigators have reported on normally hearing children who were being reared by nonverbal deaf parents, but the children currently documented have been in their second year or more when first reported (Sachs et al., 1981; Schiff, 1979). These accounts therefore provide little or no information about the infants' vocal behavior over the first eighteen months of life. The other evidence involves the vocal behavior and development of infants who are tracheostomized (and aphonic) through much of their infancy. They can hear others but not themselves. I will also look at the vocal learning patterns of songbirds reared under a variety of circumstances.

THE DENNIS CASE   In the 1930s, a psychology professor named Wayne Dennis took into his home a set of thirty-six-day-old fraternal twin girls and observed them until they were about fourteen months old. Because he wished to learn the effects of experience on

development, Dennis and his wife did something quite inappropriate—they systematically underexposed the girls to normal social
routines. Incredibly, one of the things they rarely did in the immediate presence of the girls was talk or, for that matter, vocalize
in any other way. It was not until the thirteenth month, some four
to six months later than usual, that the children began to babble.
During that month, according to Dennis, "vocalization was frequent, and consisted very largely of duplicated syllables. Among
the sounds made by one or both infants in this month were baba,
dada, lala, and byby" (1941, pp. 166–167). Because the twins were
evidently healthy and quite sociable, it is conceivable that the lack
of ambient speech contributed to the delayed onset of babbling.
However, a variety of other factors could well have been operating.

Aphonia during the Babbling Stage   What of the reverse
case—infants who can hear others but not themselves? How might
aphonia during the ages normally associated with babbling influence later utterances? The few reports available seem to suggest
that infants who are temporarily tracheostomized may experience
speech or language delay later on. In one study (Simon, Fowler, and
Handler, 1983), speech and language evaluations were performed
on several dozen decannulated children who had previously been
tracheostomized for periods ranging from six months to nearly
seven years. Children who were aphonic from birth and decannulated "prelinguistically" (according to cognitive age) seemed eventually to develop speech and language appropriate to their cognitive
capabilities, while children who were decannulated during or after
the time when first words normally emerge showed poor language
development later.

In Simon et al. (1983) and most other direct accounts of tracheostomized infants, aphonia and developmental delay have been
confounded, and vocal behavior following decannulation has not
been analyzed acoustically or described in detail. However, a few
years ago Dawn Pearson and I reported on a relatively "clean" case
of intermittent aphonia (Locke and Pearson, 1990), and another
report has since appeared (Kamen and Watson, 1991).

Jenny was born with various respiratory abnormalities and was
intermittently intubated during the first few months of life and
tracheostomized at five months. When we first began to observe

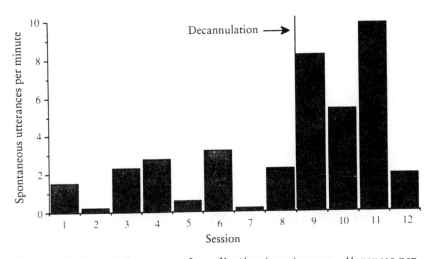

Figure 5.8. Jenny's frequency of vocalization (spontaneous utterances per minute) over the eight sessions before and four sessions following decannulation.

Jenny systematically at seventeen months, she was able to vocalize for brief intervals, and on rare occasions did so. This capability was undoubtedly made possible by the growth of her trachea. When Jenny did vocalize, it was usually a single vocalic sound of approximately syllabic length that resembled [aɪ] or [haɪ]. We video- and audiotaped Jenny eight times during the period of Jenny's tracheostomy and in four sessions during the month following decannulation. Luckily, we were able to record her just six days before and two days after decannulation.

Figure 5.8 shows the number of spontaneous utterances per minute for each session. It reveals a marked increase in frequency of vocalization following decannulation. The figure also shows the number of canonical syllables per utterance using Oller's measurement criteria. In all sessions before and after decannulation, the incidence of canonical syllable production approached zero. Even by the end of her twenty-first month, Jenny's ratio of canonical syllables to utterances still had not reached 0.2, the criterion for the onset of the canonical babbling stage.

In the next two analyses we compared Jenny's phonetic output to that of the deaf and normally developing infants in the studies described above. Figure 5.9 shows the average number of canonical

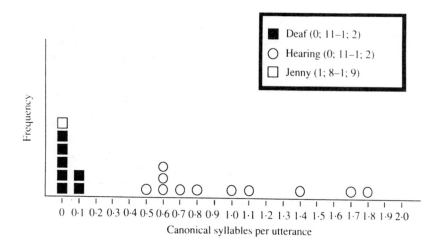

Figure 5.9. Ratio of canonical syllables per utterance in eleven- to fourteen-month-old deaf and hearing infants studied by Oller and Eilers (1988); comparable data from Jenny at twenty to twenty-one months may be seen in the extreme left-hand corner. A cut-off of 0.20 effectively distinguished the hearing from the deaf infants.

syllables produced per utterance of eleven- to fourteen-month-old deaf and normally hearing infants (Oller and Eilers, 1988) and the average of Jenny's four postdecannulatory sessions at twenty to twenty-one months. Jenny's average rate of canonical syllable production was only 0.02, a tenth of the rate of normally developing infants who are approximately six to nine months younger. Jenny's rate resembles that of the hearing-impaired infants reported in Oller and Eilers, whose oral-motor activity would also have been mostly inaudible to them, although of course for a different reason.

In a second analysis, we calculated the number of consonantlike segments in Jenny's vocal output and compared her inventory to that of normally hearing and deaf children. In the four postdecannulatory sessions at twenty to twenty-one months, Jenny averaged fewer than five different consonantlike sounds. This approximates the output of congenitally deaf infants of nearly the same age (Stoel-Gammon and Otomo, 1986). In contrast, the inventories of normally hearing infants expanded from eleven or twelve segments at five months to nearly thirty segments at a year and a half. A tally of the consonantlike sounds in Jenny's canonical syllables revealed just one such consonantal phone per session.

Jenny's segmental output at twenty to twenty-one months approximated that of normally developing infants at six months or less in terms of rate of canonical syllable production and size of consonant inventory. But she had the bilabial preferences of prelexical (hearing-impaired) children of her own age. In all ways, then, Jenny's sound production patterns resembled those of infants of the same chronological age who had also been denied access to self-produced vocal activity. Other evidence that temporary aphonia in infancy can produce long-term effects is available in a study published recently, which showed that even a year or more after decannulation, formerly tracheostomized children produce vowels within a restricted acoustic space (Kamen and Watson, 1991).

Far more research is needed, but from present evidence it appears that vocal self-stimulation may promote babbling. The ability to hear one's own voice, including the rapid formant sweeps associated with articulatory closures, may be a condition that favors babbling (even though babbling normally starts up in concert with inaudible motoric behaviors). Remarkably, self-audition seems to play a similar role in songbirds.

AVIAN AUDITION   In various studies of song learning, many of them conducted by Peter Marler and his associates (Marler, 1975), sparrows or canaries have been reared in social isolation and exposed either to no song or to audiotapes of live birds producing conspecific (or heterospecific) song. In each of these cases the birds could hear their own vocalizations. The results indicate that while exposure to conspecific song resulted in well-formed syllables and organized melodies, lack of exposure resulted in small repertoires and anomalies (but still a very adultlike song).

In Marler and Waser (1977), birds were denied access to their own vocal output, as well as to that of taped tutors, either temporarily (through intense masking noise) or permanently (through surgical deafening). Birds that received masking noise were subsequently exposed to taped songs but heard them at a reduced level (because of permanent threshold shifts resulting from their earlier exposure to the masking noise). Birds receiving forty days of continuous masking experienced threshold shifts of approximately 20 dB; two hundred days of noise shifted thresholds between 50 and 60 dB. It is relevant to the work on deaf human infants that the birds in this latter group still "had sufficient auditory feedback from their song to increase its complexity quite significantly. Whereas in the first season the syllable repertoire was not significantly different from that of deaf birds, in the second season it came close to matching the repertoire of birds reared in noise until weaning and then isolated from adult song . . . It is intriguing that the *improvement was delayed until the second season.* The explanation for this is unclear" (Marler and Waser, 1977, p. 14, italics mine). The surgically deafened birds produced very crudely formed song. Collectively, it appears that bird song—like child babble—is facilitated by self-hearing, for there is a better quality result when the learner can hear himself than when he can hear no one.

Do Other Animals "Babble"?   Other animals engage in behavior that is repetitious and regular. Do other primates perform any motor activities that might be likened to babbling? Do chimps not learn to speak because they lack a "prelinguistic behavior" or "prepertoire" (West, King, and Duff, 1990) that parallels babbling?

Infant monkeys characteristically exhibit a behavior whose outward characteristics have certain of the properties of babbling. It is called *lipsmacking,* even though the sound seems not to be made by the lips but, as far as the ear can tell, by the tongue breaking contact with the palate (Anthoney, 1968; Redican, 1975) at an estimated rate of about six to seven times per second. The larynx is apparently not involved, and the behavior does not closely resemble babbling.

According to Redican (1975), lipsmacking occurs in many different social circumstances, including grooming, greeting, confronting, and copulating, and is usually offered as a gesture of pacification, affiliation, or appeasement. It has been speculated that lipsmacking originated in the oral movements associated with nursing (Redican, 1975) or the ingestion of ectoparasites and other foreign particles removed during grooming (Marler and Tenaza, 1977). Kenney, Mason, and Hill (1979) studied the development of lipsmacking in rhesus monkeys reared individually under various social conditions. They also recorded the incidence of grimacing, a response to fear in which the lips are drawn back to reveal the teeth. Their data indicate that grimacing was present at birth and increased sharply for at least 117 days, when their observations were discontinued. Lipsmacking was likewise present at birth and increased subsequently. At about thirty-five days, however, lipsmacking began to decline in frequency, a trend that continued until the end of the study. Yet nonhuman primates do not lose the ability to do lipsmacking. Rather, with maturation they may simply limit lipsmacking to certain contexts.

Why, independent of a social context, is this behavior not sufficiently enjoyable to sustain itself or to increase? Is it because the repetitive tongue movements of lipsmacking are not coupled with phonation in the way babbling is? There is plenty of evidence that primates seem to enjoy repetitive motor acts that make noise. Like human infants who vocalize more when alone and without toys (Delack, 1976), cage-dwelling chimpanzees are more likely to perform repetitive, stereotyped movements when they are alone and when they have no objects or toys to play with (Berkson and Mason, 1964; Berkson, Mason, and Saxon, 1963; Menzel, 1963).

Primatologists do not seem to regard lipsmacking as the monkey's or chimpanzee's version of babbling. Marler (1977) has said that "primate young are not known to 'babble'" (p. 64), and other careful observers such as Jane van Lawick-Goodall (1967) have denied the existence of babbling in the chimpanzee. According to Susanne Langer (1942), the chimp "is conceptually not far from the supreme human achievement, yet never crosses the line. What has placed this absolute barrier between his race and ours? Chiefly, I think, one difference of natural proclivities. *The ape has no instinctive desire to babble in babyhood.* He does not play with his mouth and his breath as infants do" (p. 116, italics mine).

If the behavior of lipsmacking were persistently available, and readily producible in coordination with phonation, would monkeys use similar articulations in social communication? This requires consideration of the neural control systems of nonhuman primates, a subject I take up in Chapter 6.

The Transition to Speech

Before the infant can advance from babbling to the motor demands of spoken language, a good deal of brain development must occur. There must also be an urge to use vocal behavior instrumentally for the accomplishment of referential communication, and a richer appreciation of lexical reference. But given the perceptual, social, and vocal development achieved up to this point, it appears that by eight or nine months, many infants could perform enough audible mouth movements to launch a few words.

To many parents, babbling *is* speech. This is partly to the infant's credit and partly to our own. Babies cannot keep from saying [dada] and our American English ancestors apparently could not keep from calling the infant's father "daddy" or—giving the baby every chance to stumble into speech—"dada" (Locke, 1985, 1990c). Under such circumstances, the question is less one of how infants learn to speak and more one of what they would have to do to avoid saying an English word! Indeed, in studies of emergent vocabulary, investigators, *to be on the safe side,* sometimes eliminate "daddy" and "mama" from the tally of prospective words (Gesell and Thompson, 1934; Capute et al., 1986). I would contend that this overlap between babble and speech is why, from an ontogenetic perspective, phonological language is on the safe side for humans.

To many mothers, babbling is enough like speech that with a small investment of energy it can be taken the rest of the way. Harding (1983) asked mothers which of their infants' behaviors they took to be communicative. Many "mentioned the first 'da da' or other word at about 7 months and indicated that they did not think it was used as a label at the time. They did describe, however, how they began to teach their infant its meaning; by repeating the sound consistently in context such as when the father was in the room or by taking the baby to 'daddy' when the sound 'da da' was made" (p. 101).

There are several studies that suggest continuity between babbling and language development. In the transition from spontaneous to instrumental phonetic behavior, the infant's babbling repertoire is typically preserved and, indeed, forms the inventory of sound segments used to express the child's first words. The consonants in the first fifty words that children use are typically built with sounds that figure prominently in the babbling repertoire of infants. With one exception, all the consonants produced by at least half of the two-year-olds seen by Stoel-Gammon (1985) are among the sounds most frequently babbled. In several studies, Marilyn Vihman and her associates (Vihman, 1986; Vihman et al., 1985; Vihman and Miller, 1988) have observed a significant degree of continuity between the consonants of babbling and the sounds of speech.[1]

---

1. One finding from the Davis and MacNeilage (1990) study reported earlier is

The similarity between babbling and speech is not limited just to the selection of segmental gestures. Syllabic shapes are also similar, and the consonant-vowel syllable predominates in both by a large margin. Oller et al. (1976) found that initial consonants greatly exceeded final ones in infant vocalization at six to eight and twelve to thirteen months. More recently, Stoel-Gammon (1985) found that word-initial consonants were nearly six times as plentiful as word-final ones in the spontaneous word use of fifteen-month-olds.

A few case studies suggest continuity on a more individual level. Speidel (1989) anecdotally described two children, Sally and Mark. In her words, Sally "began with repetitive babbling around 7 months and began to speak in words when she was a little over 1 year old. From the beginning her speech was fairly intelligible. Mark, on the other hand, showed no repetitive babbling and spoke nearly unintelligibly until he was over 2 years old" (p. 202). In a more systematic investigation, Stoel-Gammon (1989) found that nested in a larger sample of thirty-four children were two whose early phonetic development was atypical. One child produced few canonical babbles from nine to twenty-one months. The other had an unusual pattern of sound preferences in its babbling. At twenty-four months, both subjects produced words with a more limited phonetic repertoire and with simpler syllable shapes than their peers. Compared to those of their peers, the words of both subjects at twenty-four months were produced with a more limited phonetic repertoire and with simpler syllable shapes. With a somewhat different population and mode of analysis, congruent findings were provided by Whitehurst et al. (1991), who found that the ratio of

---

relevant to the relationship between babbling and speech. Though the authors first recorded their subject after the "prelinguistic period" was over, her babbling—like that of other infants—did not cease when speaking began. In the report they commented that the girl's sound productions in concurrent babbling and word production were closely related, which agrees with other observations reviewed here. This finding broadens empirical support for the argument that children assemble the segmental constituents of early words from their prelinguistic phonetic repertoire. Davis and MacNeilage observed a marked discrepancy between grouped prelinguistic data on the vowels in other studies and the vowels in their subject's words. Because consonantal development is generally considered to be continuous, it is conceivable that babbling and speech bear a different relationship vocally than consonantally. On practical grounds, this intriguing prospect would not be all that difficult to accept, since Davis and MacNeilage's data (along with other findings) suggest that vowels and consonants often, perhaps even usually, develop at different rates.

consonants to vowels was the single strongest predictor of subsequent language development.

Jensen and his colleagues in Denmark (Jensen et al., 1988) longitudinally followed a number of infants who were, or were not at risk for developmental delay (based on Apgar scores, birthweight, and presence or absence of neonatal cerebral symptoms). During the first year, subjects who were judged to be at risk produced significantly fewer consonantlike sounds and reduplicated syllables than normal children. In addition, some five years later, a much higher proportion of the at risk children also scored below age level on a language test.

We need far more definitive studies on the relationship between babble and speech. If there is a connection, what precisely is it? Certainly some imitative ability is present long before infants have much vocal self-experience.

THE FUNCTION OF BABBLING

What does babbling accomplish for the baby? Does it accelerate the development of spoken language? Does babbling index some behavioral state that is itself correlated with phonetic learning? We may begin by taking a look at what infants can do before vocalization becomes articulate.

EXPERIENCE-EXPECTANT SYSTEM   Infants are aware of auditory-motor equivalences well before the babbling stage. This knowledge appears to be traceable to a preadapted, "expectant" neural capability, which is activated by no more than token exposure to ambient stimulation. I have called this source of information about articulatory-auditory correlations "experience-expectant" after Greenough, Black, and Wallace (1987), who used the term to characterize information storage systems that develop early in the life of the organism and require little or no specific environmental stimulation. These systems are "expectant" in that they anticipate, rather than develop in response to, experience that the organism is likely to have. An experience-expectant information system would enable infants to imitate the speech articulations they see and hear without a great deal of articulatory practice.

Some of the evidence for such an experience-expectant system comes from studies indicating that infants are able to imitate static and dynamic oral configurations at less than one month of age (Meltzoff and Moore, 1977, 1983). Evidence of facial imitation at less than one hour (Meltzoff, 1986), when infants have not yet seen their own face, suggests that they are born with whatever knowledge of visual-motor equivalences is required for such intermodal imitations and that visual and motoric experience play no more than a minor role in the induction of this capability.

The imitated acts include protrusion of the lips and tongue, and mouth opening. Since these visual motor movements are exaggerations of oral gestures used in speech, one wonders about infants' knowledge of auditory-motor equivalences of the type associated with speech articulation. And the wondering would be right: prior to the onset of babbling, infants demonstrate awareness of the relationship between heard auditory patterns and seen motor configurations (Dodd, 1979; Kuhl and Meltzoff, 1982; MacKain et al., 1983). In Kuhl and Meltzoff (1982), two groups of eighteen- to twenty-week-old infants watched a film of a woman repetitively articulating [i] and [a], which involves lip spreading and mouth opening. While the film played, one group of infants heard the same vowel the woman visibly articulated in the film or a different vowel. The other group of infants heard control stimuli that contained no formants but did have similar durations and amplitude contours. Infants who heard the intact vowels looked significantly longer at the face whose visible articulation matched the vowel heard than the face whose articulation differed from the vowel heard. No such effect occurred for control stimuli.

It is significant that in a later study of these and additional subjects of similar age, Kuhl and Meltzoff (1988) found that in 90 percent of infants' vocal responses to stimuli, the target vowels were imitated well enough to be identified by listeners. This suggests that the awareness of visible articulation, audible structure, or both are linked to the capacity for vocal imitation prior to the production of canonical syllables in babbling.

In a similar study (MacKain et al., 1983), five- and six-month-olds watched a videotape of a woman silently articulating two different CVCV constructions (drawn from [mama lulu], [bebi zuzi], and [vava zuzu]). On each trial, a pair of disyllables appeared on one screen and a different pair on an adjacent screen. Infants heard a synchronous sound pattern that corresponded with one pair and contrasted with the other. Infants looked significantly longer at the face whose movements corresponded to what was heard, but only when these corresponding trials were displayed on the screen to the right, suggesting that infants intermodal matching capability is performed by the same cerebral hemisphere that is responsible for speech processing.

ACTIVITY-DEPENDENT VOCAL GUIDANCE SYSTEM   Because infants typically have little experience with consonantlike articulation prior to babbling, these studies implicate other than articulatory factors in the development of intermodal matching ability. To become fully operational, however, the system may need to engage in certain kinds of activity. Campos and Bertenthal and their colleagues have done some interesting research on the developmental effects of an emergent motor capacity. Although their studies have addressed self-locomotion, I hope to demonstrate that this research is relevant to vocal behavior and to my hypothesis that babbling helps tune the infant's species-characteristic vocal guidance system.

When infants begin to crawl they also become better able to negotiate precarious situations, such as the visual cliff task. In this task, the mother encourages her infant to crawl to her across a Plexiglas platform under which is a shallow side and a deep side (Bertenthal et al., 1984). Fearful infants generally avoid the deep side, and it is thought that fear is acquired through the experience of crawling. In one study of 6.5- to 9.5-month-olds (Barrett and Campos, 1983), the infants tested on this apparatus had naturally accrued different amounts of locomotor experience. Those who had begun crawling early had been doing so for an average of forty-one days at the time of test; infants who had begun to crawl later had just eleven days of crawling experience.

The results of this research indicate that, independent of chronological age, the more crawling experience an infant has had (up to a point) the more likely it is to fear and to avoid the deep side. Figure 5.10 shows the percentage of babies who avoided the deep side of the cliff as a function of both locomotor experience and age of testing. It is obvious that babies with greater locomotor experience were more afraid of falling, whatever their age. This result is directly analogous to some of Held's findings with kittens (see below), which were adept at walking the fine line between the shallow

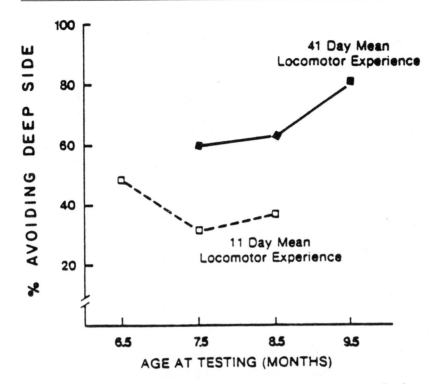

Figure 5.10. Percentage of infants who avoided any descent into the deep side of the cliff as a function of locomotor experience and age of testing.

and deep sides but only if they had previously walked while watching their feet.

In other research (Telzrow et al., 1987), children with myelodysplasia were studied. In this disorder, congenital spinal lesions typically delay the onset of self-produced locomotion for a little over three months. The investigators placed each child in a high chair mounted on wheels. Subjects were then presented with a task in which they were to retrieve a partially hidden object from one of two "wells." After the child found it once, the object would be put back in the same well and the child would be turned around 180 degrees. Figure 5.11 shows the number of successes in finding the objects during the two months preceding self-produced locomotion (the prelocomotion period) and the two months following the development of self-produced locomotion (the postlocomotion period).

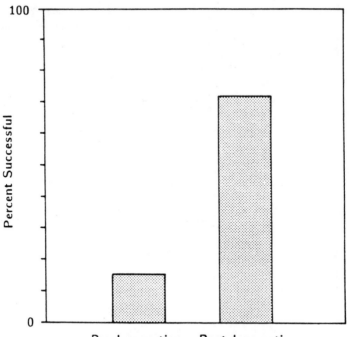

Figure 5.11. Success rate in mastering a spatial cognition task (uncovering a hidden object) as a function of locomotor status.

With crawling experience, accuracy went from 15 percent to 72 percent.

These studies of locomotion suggest that the salience of environmental cues (such as distance and heights) is increased once they become relevant to the infant, which is what happens when a baby begins to crawl. Analogously, when babbling begins the infant becomes a major player in the sound-making game, and articulated sound patterns should become more salient than they ever were before and ever would be otherwise. On this level alone I would expect that babbling faciliates development of the vocal guidance system used for speech.

There is subtle support for this prediction in some data from

Belmore et al. (1973). They studied the effects of delayed auditory feedback on several vocal parameters in an effort to estimate how closely infants auditorily monitored their voices. Preverbal infants in the sample, who were six to ten months of age, were assigned to one of two categories according to their degree of vocal sophistication. In eight subjects, fewer than a fourth of the spontaneous utterances included CV sequences made of true consonants. In three subjects, 34 to 60 percent of the utterances included CV syllables with these supraglottal characteristics. It is of interest to note that delayed feedback significantly altered utterance duration in only one of the eight less vocally sophisticated subjects but did so in all three of the more vocally advanced infants. Although the number of subjects was small, these results support a link between vocal monitoring and phonetic complexity.

An animal model can be found in the work of Richard Held and his associates (Hein and Held, 1967; Hein, Held, and Gower, 1970; Held, 1961; Held and Bauer, 1967; Held and Bossom, 1961; Held and Hein, 1963), which suggests that self-initiated activity in infancy produces more accurate guidance of motor behavior in various species of animals. In the Held studies, it was found that denying animals access to sensory feedback from their motor activity reduces their ability to use such information in guiding movement, and by inference, prevents the establishment of long-term storage of motor-sensory correlations. In one experiment (Held and Hein, 1963), pairs of kittens were dark-reared for a period and then placed in a gondola situated at the center of a circular room with striped walls. By walking, the experimental or active kitten was able to rotate the gondola and thus to "produce" visual stimulation by dint of its leg movements. The control kitten was passively transported through the same space; this passive animal therefore received access to exactly the same visual stimulation but without the corresponding motor activity. Motor coordination tests subsequently indicated that the active kittens were considerably more likely to predicate their movements upon available visual information than were the passive kittens.

In later experiments, fundamentally the same result was observed in other neonatally deprived kittens (Hein and Held, 1967) and in monkeys (Held and Bauer, 1967), as well as in adult humans participating in a variety of "rearrangement" experiments, where,

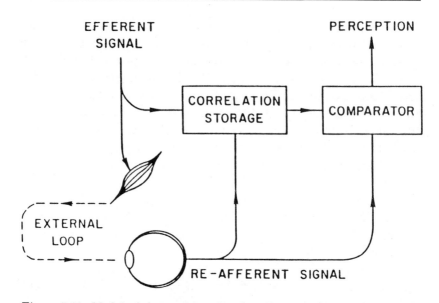

Figure 5.12. Model of the process whereby efferent sensations are coordinated with self-produced afferent feedback in sensory motor learning. The model uses vision for illustrative purposes, hence the inclusion of the eyeball along with the muscle spindle.

for example, prisms would be used to alter visual-motor relations (Held and Bossom, 1961). In an attempt to account for such findings, Held (1961) offered a unified model. Picking up on some distinctions offered earlier by von Holst (1954), the model recognized the distinct contributions to motor activity of reafference, stimulation that varies with the natural movements of the organism, and exafference, stimulation that is independent of such movements.

According to Held's model, reproduced in Figure 5.12, efferent signals associated with motor activity and afferent feedback from the visual (or other) sensations associated with that activity are both referred to Correlation Storage, which "retains traces of previous combinations of concurrent efferent and re-afferent signals. The currently monitored efferent signal is presumed to select the trace combination containing the identical efferent part and to activate the re-afferent trace combined with it. The resulting revived re-afferent signal is sent to the Comparator for comparison with the current re-afferent signal" (Held, 1961, p. 30). I think vocalization may work approximately like other forms of self-produced stimulation, and I am suggesting that babbling—among other effects (Locke, 1986a)—supplies the human infant with a phonetic guidance system that aids sound learning and facilitates the development of spoken language.

Infants, like Held's kittens and nonhuman primates, are similarly affected by the stimulation provided by their own activities. Finkelstein and Ramey (1977), noting infants' evident "delight in making events occur" (p. 806), put nine-month-olds in a task in which the stimulation they received was either contingent upon their own actions or noncontingent. Infants assigned to the contingent group received two seconds of music and a photograph of an unfamiliar adult female face whenever they moved one of their arms. Infants in the other group were given the same type and amount of stimulation noncontingently. Analyses revealed that contingently trained subjects were better able to learn a subsequent task in which they were to press a panel to control presentation of colored lights. In a second experiment, a group of six-month-old infants were given audiovisual stimulation whenever they vocalized. During the course of the experiment, this group learned to vocalize in order to control stimulation. Infants "who received prior experience learning to control stimulation," wrote Finkelstein and Ramey, "were subsequently better able to determine the relation between their behaviors and environmental events" (p. 818).

When the infant gains control over the range of articulatory closures used in babbling, it can add to its capability for continuous or graded vocalizations a repertoire of discrete vocal patterns capable of generating words. And here, at the level of Vocal Morphology, the human infant takes a distinct step forward. It is a step nonhuman primates never take.

What I am hypothesizing is that our speech monitoring system is activated and fully empowered through the action of two mechanisms. One mechanism is experience-expectant and requires very little articulatory experience. The other is activity-dependent, and that activity is babbling, which helps establish the auditory feedback loop linking tactual and kinesthetic impressions with the auditory sensations arising from the infant's own utterances. Babbling, to paraphrase Michael Studdert-Kennedy, helps get sound into the muscle. From these intermodal associations, auditory-articulatory mapping rules are constructed, enabling the infant to match ambient (and internal) phonetic targets. A working vocal guidance system is thus refined in which the ear monitors vocal tract activity and informs speech-motor control systems about targets and adjustments needed for mimicry of ambient speech. Babbling further endows infants with a repertoire of speechlike syllables and segments that it elaborates prior to and during the development of an expressive lexicon.

BABBLING AS PLAY

Speech learning may be facilitated by babbling, but what motivates this babbling? The feel and sound of babbling may influence its frequency and form, as I discussed earlier, but is sensory stimulation the whole story? Can more be said about higher level incentives for producing repetitive movements? I believe it can when we view babbling as play.

Several scholars have seen babbling as play, and play as practice for behaviors that arise later. Perhaps the first was Karl Groos, a philosophy professor at the University of Basel. In *The Play of Man,* Groos wrote of babbling that "without this playful practice [the infant] could not become master of his voice, and the imperative impulse to imitation which is developed later would lack its most essential foundation" (1901, p. 32). M. M. Lewis (1936) also attributed the motivation for babbling to play. When "in a state of comfort [and] full of energy," Lewis wrote, "[the child] will make various movements—including sounds—for the mere sake of making them" (p. 60). More recently, Philip Lieberman (1984) has said that "babbling constitutes a necessary, innately determined type of play behavior that establishes the neuromotor skills necessary for human speech" (p. 201).

These conceptions aggregate around the idea that babbling is enjoyable play that serves as practice for speech. That play can have a preparatory function has been addressed by Bekoff (1972), who commented that play "allows the developing organism to realize behavioral potentialities essential for normal behavioral development and adult life" and encourages "the channeling of innate motor action patterns into adaptive sequences of behavior" (p. 424).

How do we know that babbling is a form of play? There are many definitions of play, perhaps none satisfactory, but some key characteristics can be identified, and babbling seems to have these characteristics. First, in primates (Loizos, 1967) no immediate function appears to be served by play activity. Second, play occurs mainly in the young and particularly in neotenous species having fairly open developmental programs. Third, the play of nonhuman primates frequently involves repetition, and acts of stereotypy tend to increase when external stimulation is reduced, as we saw earlier. Although play behaviors are frequently performed interactively, many are performed alone and are considered "self-rewarding" (Loizos, 1967).

I will look now at supramechanical reasons—nested in the more global conditions for play—why babbling might be correlated with the acquisition of spoken language. I will examine the premise that healthy individuals tend to babble frequently *and* to learn language apace because both the activity of babbling and the process of language learning are facilitated by comfort and good health.

PLAYING CONDITIONS   It has been pointed out that play is a labile behavior (Martin and Caro, 1985) that is influenced by the conditions in which animals find themselves, which produces differences in the tendency to play both between and within species. Intraspecifically, a condition that greatly curtails the frequency of play is illness. In fact, reduction in play can be "the first and most obvious sign of illness in an animal that may otherwise appear very healthy" (Fagen, 1981, p. 361). Hunger and fear also cause reductions in behaviors that can be classified as play (Baldwin and Baldwin, 1976; Farentinos, 1971; Hafez, Schein, and Ewbank, 1969).

Because of an accidental turn of events, James Loy (1970) found himself in a perfect position to observe the effects of hunger on play. He was on Cayo Santiago, a small island off the coast of Puerto Rico, to study various behaviors of rhesus monkeys living there. Because Cayo Santiago cannot naturally sustain primate life, the animals were regularly being fed monkey chow. In June of 1967, Loy had been studying play behavior for eleven months, and had plans to continue his studies for a time. But in July there was a delayed shipment of chow, and except for sporadic distribution of occasional mangoes or corn the monkeys had very little to eat for a seventeen-day period. Fortunately, the food shortage did nothing to stop Loy from recording instances of play. Figure 5.13 shows

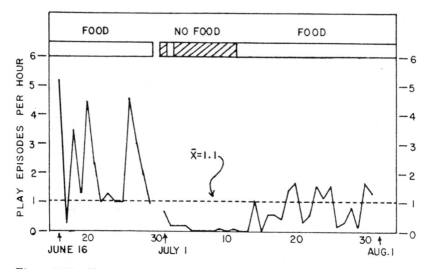

Figure 5.13. Changes in frequency of play in rhesus monkeys as a function of availability of food.

reductions in play at the beginning of food deprivation and re-sumption of play following reinstatement of a normal food supply.

Inadequate diet also affects the play behavior of human children. Chavez, Martinez, and Yaschine (1975) studied two groups of mother-infant dyads in a poor rural community in Mexico. In the control group, mothers ate whatever (nonnutritious) food they chose during pregnancy and fed their infants little more than breast milk for nearly two years, as was customary in the community. Not surprisingly, these infants were malnourished. In the experimental group, mothers were provided with a supplemented diet during pregnancy and their infants were given milk and baby food during the twelfth and sixteenth weeks of age. Systematic observations were then made of the mothers and infants in their homes.

Chavez et al. found that at twenty-four weeks the supplemented infants spent nearly 50 percent of their outdoor time in play activ-ities as compared to a 10 percent rate of play in the control group. Using different measures of play, this intergroup margin narrowed some but was still sizable at eighteen months. Significantly, die-tarily supplemented infants also spent less time crying and more time talking than the control infants, ultimately performing better on the "language" items of the Gesell test of mental development at eighteen months.[2]

Whether they also babbled more we do not know. But if sick animals play less than healthy ones, and babbling is a form of play, then unhealthy babies may babble less than healthy ones. Their brain may also develop more slowly, causing delays in babbling, as well as a variety of capabilities that are unrelated to language (a contingency imagined in Chapter 10). And if the learning required for language acquisition is jeopardized by the stress of illness, then we should expect delayed babbling to be associated with delayed language for this reason alone, quite independent of any practice effects associated with the activity of babbling.

What, then, are the phonological consequences of vocal play? It may be instructive to examine Martin and Caro's (1985) model of the developmental effects of play behavior generally, reproduced here in Figure 5.14. In the figure, "outcome variable" refers to any functional behavior that is facilitated by play. The upper panel (a) depicts "play as practice," as I discussed earlier. On measures of functional behavior, the animal that plays (dotted lines) comes out better than the one that does not play but is otherwise similar. This advantage first becomes evident at point 3, when the relevant adult behavior manifestly develops. The middle panel (b) depicts an effect of play that is transient and without lasting developmental effects. Martin and Caro thought this category might include changes in children's creativity while in a play-induced mood. The lower panel (c) represents a third hypothesis regarding the developmental consequences of play, specifically that play accelerates development of adult capabilities but is neither necessary for such development to occur nor associated with higher levels of performance because play took place. With (c), during or immediately following the relevant play behavior there is a short-term effect that subsequently dissipates.

It might be instructive to treat babbling as play behavior and consult Martin and Caro's model to see what could be expected for speech. If babbling serves an important practice function, the result

---

2. Since mothers and fathers also spoke more to supplemented infants, presumably in response to the greater amount of talking done by these infants, social as well as nutritional and play hypotheses could explain this outcome.

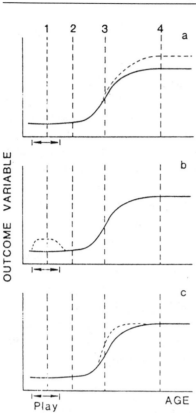

Figure 5.14. Hypothesized differences in a behavior that is expected to develop ("behavioral outcome variable") in playing (dotted line) and non-playing (continuous line) subjects, as a function of age. The upper panel (a) depicts a lasting practice effect; the middle panel (b) depicts immediate benefits only; and the lower panel (c) refers to an acceleration of normal development over the short term.

depicted in the upper panel (a) will occur and the babbling infant, other things being equal, will go on to become a speaking child. On the other hand, even if the activity of babbling does little or nothing to benefit the infant directly, if it has the developmental support of a nurturant family it is likely to incite parents into thinking that their baby is "talking" or about to start doing so. This assumption characteristically unleashes a variety of potentially helpful behaviors (Locke, 1986), as parents approach their baby, responding in kind at the strictly phonetic level (for example, [dadada]) if not the lexical level (for example, "daddy"). Contingent responding, as we know, encourages lexical development, so the depiction in the upper panel applies here too.

On the other hand, what if babbling has only transient effects, amusing the infant, say, during times of reduced ambient stimulation? This seems entirely possible, and if it ended here we would have to relegate babbling to the middle panel. But even if we limit our attention to the sensorimotor aspects of babbling, there is the possibility that babbling will "fine tune" (Bekoff, 1984; also the Held effects discussed earlier) a species-characteristic ability to perform cross-modal matches. To represent fine tuning we would need panel (c) of Martin and Caro's model, panel (a) being sufficient to account for a grosser level of calibration.

The developmental force of "babbling as tuning" certainly applies phonologically and perhaps at all other levels of language that depend on efficient phonetic implementation. But speechlike behaviors are also apt to reassure the infant of his capacity to behave like adults, to enter into family activities, and to be one of the domestic group. This consequence would surely not be a trivial one over the long term, and indeed would seem to be captured only in the upper panel of Figure 5.14.

The persistently sick or hungry child is thus unlikely to babble often or profitably and will ultimately find itself in linguistic trouble for the reasons I have suggested. I would also guess that prelinguistic vocal behavior, all things considered, is likely to produce the effect imagined in the lower panel. The reason has to do with the "robustness" of spoken language, or what Martin and Caro refer to as *equifinality,*

> which asserts that in an open system (such as a living organism) the same steady state in development can be reached from different initial conditions and in different ways . . . Thus, the same state in behavioral development . . . could be achieved via a variety of different developmental histories. In other words, different developmental routes involving different amounts and types of play, or perhaps none at all, might converge on the same developmental end point, and playing when young might be only one way of achieving . . . competence. Thus, an alternative to the suggestion that play has no major benefits is that play does have important benefits under some circumstances, but these benefits can also be obtained in other ways. (p. 88)

I have spoken of the animal's natural disposition to play as an epiphenomenon that is correlated with other factors (health and comfort) that by themselves can regulate acquisition of language. But what about play per se? What happens to learning if the animal is healthy, rested, and so on, and seeks to play but for some reason is prevented from doing so? The only documented case of this with which I am personally familiar is the aphonic girl discussed earlier. When phonatory capacity was fully instated at twenty-one months, the girl was behind the species-typical vocal maturation schedule by a good fifteen or sixteen months. Subsequently, however, she made up for lost time. By four years, four months her combined receptive and expressive language age was three months ahead of chronological age. In the face of normal cognitive and social development, the girl's vocal deficit apparently had been overcome by the sheer, single-minded force of the biological imperative to communicate by way of spoken language.

This late rally takes nothing from the developmental significance of the infant's experience of its own babbling. We can argue by analogy. In early childhood, damage to linguistic areas of the left hemisphere usually stops language development in its tracks, but in the subsequent recovery period there is often a restorative surge that takes the child to, or close to, age-appropriate levels of linguistic performance (Aram, Ekelman, and Whitaker, 1986, 1987; Dennis and Kohn, 1975). But no one doubts that the left hemisphere is important for language, and on occasion we will hear about a child who did not babble but certainly did learn to speak without complications.

FROM VOCAL IMITATION TO SPOKEN WORDS   Much that I have said about vocal imitation assumes that this capability underlies many of the linguistic accomplishments to come. Research by my colleague at Harvard, Catherine Snow (1989), suggests that this is indeed the case. Using structured elicitation tasks, she observed the frequency of vocal and verbal, gestural, and object-mediated imitation in a hundred normally developing infants at fourteen months and at twenty months. Snow found that at the earlier interval vocal imitativeness varied from child to child but was not correlated with gestural or object-mediated imitativeness. This and other comparable findings suggested to Snow that vocal imitation is "domain specific." This is an interesting possibility in light of the fact that spoken language, the capability to which vocal imitation contributes, has been characterized with precisely the same words (see Chapter 9).

It is of interest that vocal imitation at fourteen months was moderately correlated with verbal imitation at twenty months. Vocal imitativeness at fourteen months also correlated significantly with the number of nouns and the number of verbs produced, the total productive vocabulary, and the ratio of words produced to words comprehended at twenty months. These correlations were specific to vocal imitativeness; no correlations of similar direction or magnitude were found for gestural and object-mediated imitation. When the infant's vocal monitoring system gets cranked up, it would appear that good things start to happen linguistically.

Infants begin to sound like talkers when they start producing the well-formed syllables that occur in babbling; to a degree, they do sound articulate. The specific sounds—actually, the particular movement patterns that produce the sounds—are not obviously inspired by listening to others talk, although the readiness to indulge in this infant version of speech may be. Rather, the inclination to make certain vocal movements seems to come from within, and in terms of phonetic features tends to be largely the same from one infant to the next. Since a number of perfectly soundless motor functions are instated at about the same time as babbling, the coordinative aspects of reduplicative syllabic activity may be due more to motoric than to auditory factors. Nevertheless, this activity is presumably not kinesthetically so enjoyable that it will be done with the same frequency by infants who are aphonic or deaf, at least over the first year of life.

There are several reasons why babbling bodes well for speech. First, the timely onset of this behavior probably means that the brain is maturing and specializing in ways that will benefit speaking. Second, infants who babble tend to get back from their parents a level of reaction that is developmentally helpful. This reaction typically includes contingent responding, in which parents tend to respond in kind, and other efforts designed to lure the infant ever farther into speechhood. Finally, the baby who babbles freely may be playing and as a major player is likely to be free of illness, discomfort, fatigue, or fear—conditions, one supposes, that threaten the learning of languages.

No other animal does anything quite like babbling. The lip-smacking of monkeys is not really close, since the sounds are seemingly produced without laryngeal support, and the activity tends to occur only as a display in certain social contexts. Nonhuman primates also give little evidence of vocal control in experiments or seminaturalistic observation and, indeed, are far less inclined than humans to vocalize at all, which reflects a major difference between human and nonhuman primates.

Even prior to the onset of babbling, infants reveal an awareness of visual-motor and auditory correspondences associated with the act of speaking. This suggests that elements of the monitoring system that will be used to learn speech are already in place before there is a great deal of articulatory self-production. With babbling experience, it is hypothesized from animal models of skill acquisition that the infant's vocal monitoring system elaborates and becomes more effective. Infants who do not babble may be in double jeopardy, then, because of the reason why they are not so inclined, whatever that is, and the beneficial effects of articulatory-auditory experience.

Clearly, a vocally accommodating infant who is aware of referential eye movements and possesses a degree of motor control is in good shape as it approaches the age at which speaking would be expected. But there are other advances that will be necessary, some in the cognitive area, and in any case all steps forward will require neural support. The brain and brain development are the subjects of the next two chapters.

6

THE NEURAL
SPECIALIZATION FOR
LINGUISTIC COMMUNICATION

Anyone who takes [linguistic innateness] arguments seriously should also take seriously the search for innate neurological mechanisms corresponding to the unlearned principles.

G. A. Miller, "The Place of Language in a Scientific Psychology"

Normally, a biologically oriented book about language will have a chapter on the brain. The brain that is considered is the adult brain. The language behaviors that are to be explained neurologically tend to be those that are evaluated in tests of aphasia, such as object naming, word retrieval, and sentence comprehension. This is a legitimate approach, but it is not an ontogenetic one. If it were ontogenetically oriented, it would treat language as a medium for social and emotional interaction, which it is, as well as the abstract code for storing and transmitting information, which it also is. This chapter, in anticipation of various neurodevelopmental issues that need to be addressed, focuses heavily on the neural implications of interpersonal communication by way of face, voice, and linguistic expression. If we are to look at neural capacities that allow spoken language to develop, we must ask what the brain does when people convey information about their identity, emotionality, and social intentions while simultaneously expressing their thoughts verbally. We must ask about the neurology of babbling, intentional pointing, and other behaviors that lead to spoken language. The next chapter then asks how children with emerging neural capabilities move along the path of cues and interactions that leads to the mastery of spoken language.

How does the brain develop the networks of interconnecting cells that enable the human child to perceive, process, store, and express linguistic knowledge? It is a question that must be answered if we are to lay claim to an understanding of the child's acquisition of language. But if properly ontogenetic in our orientation, we must first ask about the neurology of affective and social communication by way of the vocal-facial complex, and then about the neurology of the transition to linguistic expression.

Most neurolinguistic studies have focused on the adult brain in connection with fully developed language. These studies are of limited relevance to my interest in the neurology of social interactions that lead to language. Therefore, I have had to examine physiological studies of nonhuman primates and pathological studies of human patients with communicative, but not necessarily linguistic disorders.

In Chapter 7, I will examine the development of the neural capabilities for affective communication. Where possible, I will identify converging brain developments that, when joined with affective capabilities, enable linguistic processing. I will ask how the infant's brain comes to possess the wherewithal for competent levels of performance in phonological language. But I will launch our inquiry into neurolinguistic capacity here, first by looking at the anatomical context within which language mechanisms are sited, then by assessing the neurology of social communication.

It is often presumed that brain size is correlated with intelligence. The anthropoid primates, especially *Homo sapiens,* have a very large brain not only in relation to body size but also in absolute terms. Figure 6.1, taken from Sacher and Staffeldt (1974), depicts brain weight data as a function of gestation time. This display reveals that species with large brains also have a long gestation time, and they also tend to have small litters.

In mammals, the brain is the slowest growing organ, and it paces the growth of other bodily tissues. Brain development consumes 87 percent of the basal metabolic rate of neonates; at two years the expenditure drops to 64 percent and declines further to 23 percent of the basal metabolic rate of adults (data from Lancaster, 1986, cited by Parker, 1990). Because of the competition between the brain and other organ systems, species with large brains tend to grow more slowly and enjoy a longer lifespan than species with small brains. Longer life is also associated with a greater repro-

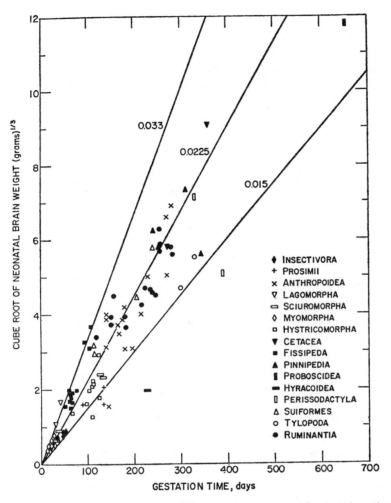

Figure 6.1. Neonatal brain weight (cube root) and gestation time for mammals. Human neonates are represented by the uppermost x.

ductive span, which offsets the decreased reproductive rate brought about by the larger brain.

What causes the mature human brain to be so much larger than that of other primates? If one were to isolate one evolutionary force that has worked disproportionately to expand intelligence in the human, "intense social behavior" would be the most likely candidate according to Lovejoy (1981), although undoubtedly many factors were involved. In humans this social behavior is manifested in many ways, beginning with a nuclear family structure. In most nonhuman primate species, family structure is less developed than it is in humans and comprises maternal and sibling relationships primarily.

A Neural Specialization for Language

This chapter began with a challenge to those who would create biologically responsible theories of language: explain the brain mechanisms that underlie linguistic capacity. In the work from which that quotation is excerpted, Miller (1990) offered some clues to get us started. Here are Miller's four arguments for an "innate" capacity for human language (p. 10):

1. The acquisition of language unfolds in much the same way in all normal children.
2. Language is species-specific—even the most isolated human groups have language, yet extremely intelligent apes do not.
3. The basic design features of human languages are universal.
4. Specialized neurological structures devoted to the production and perception of speech have been identified.

With specific reference to *spoken* language, Miller added that "no one has ever seriously challenged the assumption that the ability to make and recognize the sounds of natural language is innate and species-specific. The nature of those sounds depends intimately on the neurophysiological structure of the speech organs, and that structure is a part of our genetic inheritance" (p. 10). Of course, the features listed by Miller do not preclude environmental influence. No behavior that is species-specific arises without an experiential context, even those that seem only to be "triggered" by stimulation. It is in this sense that the phrase "true of all members of a species" says very little about the *mode of transmission* of the mechanism whose phenotype is invariant.

There are several arguments for an experiential view of this sort. First, except for cases of extreme neglect, all human infants receive the minimal exposure needed for language. It is therefore unlikely that one will see gross variations in rate of acquisition that are correlated with environmental variations. Behavioral geneticists find very small environmental effects when analysis is limited to the factors that are shared by children's environments (Plomin and Daniels, 1987). Second, infants shape the social structure of their environment. They can—and there is evidence that they do—"solicit for" appropriate levels and types of linguistic stimulation on their own, naturally confounding genetic and environmental contributions.

It is also the case that genetic factors can influence developmental processes at many points and levels. Some young animals living in the wild are taught to hunt by their mother or father. In her observations at the Gombe Stream National Park in Tanzania, Goodall (1965) noted that when infant chimpanzees climbed too high, their mothers tapped on the tree trunks, causing the infants to come down immediately. These might seem to represent environmental effects, but nurturance and parental instruction can also be species-specific behaviors, subject to hormonal and other internal influences (Rosenblatt, 1975). When infants are exposed to their mother's species-specific behaviors, there is automatic interplay between genetic and environmental factors at multiple levels.

Whenever the development of behavior among the individual members of a species proceeds along a common path with relatively few individual variations, biological mechanisms are operating to hold organisms on some sort of central ontogenetic program or plan. There are two processes that act to limit the range of variation that occurs during development (Scarr, 1983). One process is *canalization,* a concept put before us over fifty years ago by Waddington (1940) and subsequently defined as "the capacity to produce a particular definite end-result in spite of a certain variability both in the initial situation from which development starts and in the conditions met with during its course" (Waddington, 1975, p. 99). Canalization provides animals with an internally regulated growth path, called a *chreod.* Although genetically preadapted, chreods require a supportive environment of the type that is available to all members of the species. It is therefore very difficult to deflect the general direction of a chreod.

Although defined many years ago, canalization is completely harmonious (if not synonymous) with the conceptual centerpiece of a current approach to motor development—dynamical systems theory

(Thelen, 1991). Central to dynamical systems theory is the *attractor state,* a condition of developmental stability or homeostasis to which organisms adhere as long as environmental circumstances are supportive, and to which organisms return if mild perturbations temporarily provoke deviations.

Canalization does not imply lack of variation. Quite the contrary, since variation is crucial to evolution, canalization refers only to general mechanisms that delimit the *range* of structural or functional variation displayed by individuals. Elsewhere I have discussed the monomorphic design of the human cognitive and vocal production systems that provide central tendencies in the development of phonetic behavior, the deployment of well-formed utterances, and the structure of standard phonological systems (Locke and Pearson, 1992).

A second process that limits the range of phenotypes is *developmental adaptation.* In the case of weakly canalized behaviors, there is more room for individual response to environmental variation. Variation in individual responses is allowed by the genome, but the range of variations is kept small by the adaptability of organisms that are seeking to accommodate to the same set of environmental factors.

Canalization is revealed in very concrete terms in the form of perceptual and attentional biases that operate under affective control. This has been argued for mammals (Seligman, 1970) and I pointed earlier to perceptual biases in birds. One reason we know relatively little about the perceptual biases of human infants, and have made less of them than we should, is that these biases support learning that occurs early or "automatically." These behaviors may run their ontogenetic course so rapidly that we miss it and incorrectly (and inappropriately) surmise that the behaviors must be "innate."

The Linguistic Canal

If a fully canalized phenotype receives less than normal levels of assistance, either from the animal's own biologic systems or from the environment, there should be momentary disruption that is relieved once needed supports are restored. A normal linguistic outcome in spite of severe neonatal brain damage suggests that spoken language has those qualities that apply to other canalized behaviors. This is why so many psycholinguists have grown fond of saying that language development is "robust." If we were to follow Scarr's (1983) advice, the better question for language theorists would be not what happens to linguistic capacity under conditions of extreme deprivation but how much or what kinds of stimulation are necessary for optimal development to take place.

With reference to behavior in general, Scarr commented that "if infant development is highly canalized at a species level, one might expect to find universal patterns and rates of infant behavioral development, in spite of differences in child-rearing practices" (p. 217). The linguistic variant of this general hypothesis is that children's speech should develop along similar lines regardless of their parents' language, and there is ample evidence that this is true (Locke, 1983).

Spoken language is surely one of our species' more magnificent canalizations. Basic linguistic properties such as those listed by Miller leave little doubt about this.[1] Normally developing infants from disparate cultures take the same general path to increasing mastery of phonological language (Locke, 1983). Even deafness and brain damage may lack sufficient force to knock infants off the path to spoken language, off their *vocal chreod*. This particular chreod is buffered against a variety of negative external effects. Because the linguistic canal is a feature of our species, all human infants have the neural capacity to acquire language despite natural variations in structure, maturational course, and environmental circumstances.

The greatest threat to the development of spoken language is thus posed by weak canalization paired with a linguistically unsupportive environment. Research in the past few years suggests that weakly canalized children exist, and each year a considerable number reach linguistic age without having achieved a commensurate amount of linguistic knowledge. I will review the growing evidence of neurogenetic effects in language development in Chapter 10.

___

1. Evidence in support of each of the listed properties appears in various places. For the time being, I will assume that the general premise is accepted, although I will revisit this issue in Chapter 9.

We can put a sharper point on our explanatory responsibilities with respect to the brain. What neurodevelopmental theories need to explain is the canalization of spoken language. In the pages ahead, I ask what is known about any specialized structures that may have evolved for, or that now subserve this canalization, regardless of their evolutionary history. (In the following chapter, I will then attempt to trace neural developments eventuating in linguistic capacity.)

Neurology of Face Processing

There is theoretical value in asking which mechanisms of the adult brain process affect and personally identifying information. If they can be localized, the ontogenetic question will be: Do these mechanisms develop before or, in effect, join or become the neural systems responsible for speech, if indeed they are altogether different mechanisms?

FACE RECOGNITION

If human brains are designed to recognize faces, this specialization presumably underlies our biological need to socialize and reproduce. If so, our recognition mechanisms should be activated only by human faces. And indeed, there is evidence that human subjects who are lateralized for human faces are not lateralized for monkeys. Overman and Doty (1982) presented macaques and human adults with photographs of expressionless conspecific or heterospecific faces. On each trial they saw an unaltered photo followed by two chimeric photographs that were duplicates of the left and right hemiface. Subjects were to indicate which of the two chimeras most resembled the original photo by pressing the appropriate panel.

Figure 6.2 shows the results. Monkeys gave no evidence of asymmetry, revealing a left visual field bias for 52 percent of the monkey faces and 53 percent of the human faces. The left visual field bias of human subjects, on the other hand, differed significantly for monkey faces (54 percent) and human faces (68 percent). The bias for human faces was almost exactly that found in other research that had used the same procedure. Morphometric analysis showed that key facial features were equally asymmetrical in the monkey and human faces that were used as stimuli. Overman and Doty

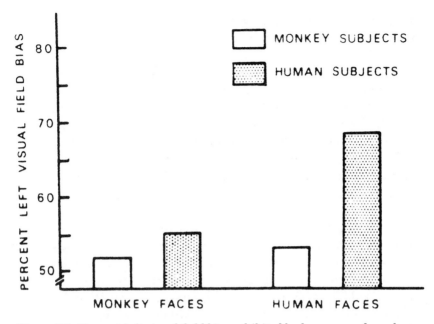

Figure 6.2. Percent left visual field bias exhibited by humans and monkeys when viewing the same slides of human and monkey faces.

concluded, therefore, that the lack of a visual field bias for macaques occurred not because their faces are more symmetrical but because the monkeys have no lateralized face processing mechanism, and that the lateralized mechanism of humans works only for that species.

Later research in the split-brain paradigm (Hamilton and Vermeire, 1988a) did reveal a right-hemisphere advantage for conspecific facial features and expressions in macaques having a left-hemisphere advantage for visuospatial patterns.[2] But to my knowledge, no research has disconfirmed Overman and Doty's finding that humans are lateralized for conspecific faces and not heterospecific ones, or their finding that monkeys are not lateralized for human faces.

Overman and Doty's findings may contain hints about our hemispheric specializations. One assumes that hominids, like nonhuman

2. These findings were obtained in monkeys giving little or no indication of lateralized hand preferences (Hamilton and Vermeire, 1988b).

primates, were bilaterally wired-up for affective communication. When the left hemisphere took on fine motor coordination, language followed in line, crowding out affective communication and leaving it to the hemisphere that was already engaged in this activity.

Behavioral studies in nonhuman primates reveal very selective responses to faces. In one study, it was found that rhesus, pigtail, and stumptail macaque monkeys preferred photographs of a conspecific to those of a heterospecific adult female (Sackett, Suomi, and Grady, 1970). In a second study by the same investigators, rhesus monkeys that had been separated from their mother at birth and cage-reared were tested. Like the other animals, these monkeys preferred the sight of conspecific over heterospecific females. If such effects were the result of experience, the authors reasoned that they could only have been due to the sight of conspecific agemates, since these were the only rhesus monkeys that had been previously seen.

In a third study (Suomi, Sackett, and Harlow, 1970), it was found that in wild-born rhesus monkeys, one- to ten-month-old infants preferred to look at an adult female rather than an adult male of their species. The investigators were unable to explain this preference for females, although it does not seem surprising that infant monkeys, like infant humans, would prefer to view animals that resemble their mother.

In neurophysiological research, single unit recordings from the temporal cortex show that in nonhuman primates there are cells that respond differentially to faces. Microelectrodes placed in visual and polysensory regions of the temporal cortex, and in the amygdala, reveal neuronal responses to the faces of other primates, whether conspecific or heterospecific; to specific faces that are familiar; to particular viewing angles; and to a variety of facial expressions (Baylis, Rolls, and Leonard, 1985; Desimone et al., 1984; Perrett, Mistline, and Chitty, 1987; Perrett, Rolls, and Caan, 1982; Perrett et al., 1984, 1985). Findings of a similar nature have also been obtained in sheep (Kendrick and Baldwin, 1987a), and there is some evidence for facial expression cells in humans (Holmes et al., 1991).

In Yamane, Kaji, and Kawano (1988), a single monkey was trained to discriminate three target faces from a large number of alternative faces. All faces were those of adult male humans and were presented in natural color. Microelectrodes were situated in the monkey's inferotemporal cortex. Of 446 neurons reporting, there were 86 that responded to faces or to control stimuli, and 21 that responded only to faces; 18 of these neurons were near the gyrus of the inferotemporal cortex. The investigators found that certain neurons were more responsive to particular facial relationships, including the displacement of the eyes, the distance between the eyes and the mouth, and the nature of the hairline. Yamane et al. noted that these relationships account for much of the variance in facial memory among humans.

How do we decide whether we have seen a particular face before? We scan it for distinctive features, and in doing so our eyes move over the face in characteristic *scanpaths*. Walker-Smith, Gale, and Findlay (1977) described the scanpaths of three young adults when presented with black-and-white photographs of other adult faces for recognition. Using a videocamera to record eye fixations, they found that eye movements were directed to a very limited portion of the total face, and that scanning strategies were consistent within, but differed across each of the three subjects. For example, Subject A looked selectively at the right eye and nose, while Subject B preferred the nose and mouth and Subject C looked mainly at the left eye. Other facial features, such as the chin, cheeks, ears, and hairline, were not included in the scanpaths and may have been ignored.

PROSOPAGNOSIA, A DISORDER OF FACE RECOGNITION
In the clinical syndrome called prosopagnosia, patients are unable to recognize the faces of people who were previously familiar (Damasio, 1989; Ellis and Young, 1988). Typically, such patients continue to process most (but not all) other visual stimuli normally, which fits with experimental findings in normal subjects of a right hemisphere specialization for visual encoding that includes faces and little else, that is, extends beyond the right hemisphere's specialization for visual configurations in general (Carey, 1981). In a typical case of prosopagnosia, the unrecognizable faces include those of individuals as familiar as family members and may even include the patient's own face. The patient characteristically does not have a feeling of knowing the people that cannot be recognized.

There is no reason to suspect that prosopagnosic patients have somehow forgotten how to tell if a face is familiar. One eye movement study found that normal adults did not exhibit different facial scanpaths than prosopagnosics (Rizzo, Hurtig, and Damasio, 1987). In addition, autonomic measures disagree with the conscious experience of prosopagnosic patients. Even when patients fail to recognize a familiar face, skin conductance data typically are consistent with recognition (Tranel and Damasio, 1985, 1988).

There is an interesting selectivity in prosopagnosia. Even where overt face recognition is completely wiped out, the patient usually remains fully able to recognize the facial signs of age and sex, and to interpret facial expressions (Etcoff, 1984a, b; Tranel, Damasio, and Damasio, 1988). Based on such dissociations, Etcoff argued that there are independent processing mechanisms for facial identity and facial affect, which is congruent with experimental findings on intact nonhuman primates.

Much of this processing occurs in the right hemisphere, but the locus of damage in prosopagnosia is typically bilateral, usually involving a focal lesion near the inferior margins of occipitotemporal cortex (Meadows, 1974; Whiteley and Warrington, 1977). Learning new faces may require connections from this area to more anterior temporal cortex and medial limbic structures (Meadows, 1974). There have also been several reports of unilateral right hemisphere damage (Campbell, Landis, and Regard, 1986; Hecaen and Angelergues, 1962), including a right hemispherectomy (Sergent and Villemure, 1989).

LIPREADING AND MOUTH WATCHING
The independence of these visuofacial operations was reinforced and extended by an interesting study of lipreading in two women with unilateral infarctions of the posterior cerebral artery (Campbell, Landis, and Regard, 1986). The infarct was on the right side in Patient D, age sixty-one, who was severely prosopagnosic. She performed poorly on a recognition test for famous people and also was unable to match facial profiles to schematic faces on the basis of facial expression. The infarct was on the left side in Patient T, age sixty-five, who had no difficulty recognizing faces but was alexic (without agraphia). Both patients were able to imitate buccofacial actions and had no difficulty speaking or perceiving speech.

The patients were given several tests of lipreading ability. In one test, the patients were to repeat single- and double-digit numbers, isolated vowels, and isolated (continuant) consonants that were produced live but without voice. In a second test, photographs of static articulatory gestures were to be identified by phonemic class (for example, for visibly sealed lips, any bilabial phoneme was accepted). In a third measure, the patients saw and heard a videotape of a woman producing CVC or CV syllables composed of stop consonants. The video and audio portions of the syllables were either normally congruent or were noncongruent in that the patients saw one syllable (such as [ga]) and heard a different one (such as [ba]). In normal subjects, these noncongruent cases produce a blended perception (such as [da]), the so-called McGurk effect, on the majority of trials. The audio and video tracks of the tape were played separately and also together. In the visual condition, homophenous responses (for example, the confusion of [da] and [ta], which look alike) were considered correct.

Campbell et al. found that Patient D—the prosopagnosic with right but not left hemisphere damage—performed normally on all lipreading tasks. She achieved a perfect score on all measures, and on the McGurk task experienced perceptual blends on 71 percent of the noncongruent trials (approximating the performance of normal controls). In contrast, Patient T—who had left but not right hemisphere damage—gave a rather different result. Like D, she was able to repeat silently produced numbers and vowels, could name static vowel articulations, and scored at or near 100 percent on the audio and video portions of the spoken syllable test. However, T had difficulty naming static consonantal configurations and repeating spoken consonants, and on the McGurk task she reported no blends (instead reporting the sounds that were *heard*).

Consistent with these results, the authors concluded that "face identification and the extraction of speech information from faces do not call on the same cortical processing mechanisms" (p. 517). And here we have a comparison of mouth processing when it is linguistically critical and when it is not. For the prosopagnosic patient (D) scored perfectly on a task that required sorting of static speech configurations, but 45 percent correct on a task that required sorting of nonspeech oral configurations; the other patient (T) was exactly reversed on these measures.

From this and other evidence it can be said that left hemisphere lesions impair comprehension of spoken language auditorily (the sounds of speech) and visually (the movements of speech) but generally leave intact comprehension of prosody and face recognition. For face recognition to be impaired, there generally must be a lesion in at least the right hemisphere, where infarcts frequently impair prosody but spare speech and lipreading. The movements of "speech organs" that convey words are submitted to altogether different perceptual processing than movements of the same organs when they convey emotionality.

NEUROPSYCHOLOGY OF FACE RECOGNITION

It has long been known that patients with unilateral right hemisphere damage have difficulty with a variety of visuospatial tasks (Levine, 1985). If the right hemisphere is more useful or reliable on spatial tasks per se, and is also more involved in the processing of affect regardless of modality, then we might expect right hemisphere mechanisms in humans to perform many of the operations pertaining to the face, from recognition of the individual to interpretation of emotional displays. Levine (1985) used tachistoscopic tests to determine the presence of visual field effects in eight- to fourteen-year-olds. She obtained a left visual field advantage when subjects were asked to signal their recognition of faces that were unfamiliar, beginning at nine years. Other research indicates that this left visual field (right hemisphere) advantage continues into adulthood both for familiar and unfamiliar faces (Leehey and Cahn, 1979).

Neurology of Voice Processing

We have seen that face recognition is somewhat localizable, although the specific structures in charge of this capability have yet to be defined. What does behavioral evidence tell us about the brain's recognition of voices? There is far less information on this important question. Some years ago, Doehring and Bartholomeus (1971) attempted an experiment on the recognition of voices. On each trial, subjects heard a sample voice followed by a dichotic presentation of material said by the same speaker or by a different speaker. Doehring and Bartholomeus generally obtained a right-ear advantage. Superior right ear (left hemisphere) performance for consonants has been found in tasks requiring phonemic processing, but commonly this bias disappears or even reverses when the listeners are to process the same stimuli but in reference to some other attribute, such as the pitch of the syllable initiated by the consonant (Wood, Goff, and Day, 1971). The results are thus difficult to understand unless there is a natural preemption of voice by speech. As we will see in our discussion of duplex perception in Chapter 9, this sort of thing does happen.

PHONAGNOSIA, A DISTURBANCE OF VOICE RECOGNITION

As we have seen, there are acquired disorders of face recognition. As we will see later, there are also acquired disorders of vocal expression. If nature is symmetrical, we may expect to find an acquired disorder of vocal recognition.

It would be logical to begin by asking if prosopagnosic patients have any unusual difficulty recognizing the voices of their friends. However, it has been reported that prosopagnosic patients *compensate* for their visual difficulty in recognizing family members and associates by paying special attention to their speech or voice (Beyn and Knyazeva, 1962; Bornstein and Kidron, 1959; Bornstein, Sroka, and Munitz, 1969; Campbell, Landis, and Regard, 1986; Hecaen and Angelergues, 1962). In the prosopagnosic patient described by Beyn and Knyazeva, "identification of individuals by voice was fully intact and was indeed employed as a basic method of compensation" (1962, p. 158). The patient described by Bornstein and Kidron told his physicians "as soon as I hear your voice I know who you are and can tell you apart from your colleagues" (1959, p. 125). I find this interesting, for if the lesions causing prosopagnosia involve the temporal cortex bilaterally, I would expect some reduction in sensitivity to the subtleties that differentiate one speech pattern or voice from another.

Van Lancker and her colleagues (Van Lancker et al., 1988) administered tests of voice recognition and vocal discrimination to six patients with unilateral or bilateral lesions in various parts of the brain. The voice recognition task required patients to listen to an excerpt of speech material produced by famous individuals. Patients were to identify the speaker by pointing to the appropriate picture in a plate of four photographs. To make sure patients understood who each of the pictures represented, the name of the individual was printed below the photo and was also said by the examiner. Healthy control subjects scored over 80 percent correct on this task, well above chance. Three of the patients achieved a similar level of accuracy, but the other three scored no better than 50 percent, exhibiting what the authors chose to call *phonagnosia*.

The same patients and control subjects also participated in a discrimination task for sentences spoken by the same unfamiliar individual or by two different unfamiliar individuals. On average, control subjects were 85 percent correct on this binary task, and four of the six patients did not significantly exceed chance levels of performance. It is interesting that three of these four patients were better than the normals on the voice recognition task. In other words, there was a dissociation, with vocal recognition exceeding discrimination. The two remaining patients were dissociated in the opposite direction; they scored above chance on the discrimination task but performed poorly on the recognition task. These patients were like *vocal prosopagnosics,* aware of voice "movements" but unable to recognize voices.

Van Lancker et al. concluded that "recognition of familiar voices and discrimination of unfamiliar voices are separable neuropsychological abilities, can be differentially affected by cerebral injuries, and may be mediated by different anatomic structures" (p. 204). According to CT scans, damage to patients with discrimination deficits was located in the temporal lobe of either hemisphere. In contrast, all three patients with recognition deficits had lesions in the inferior parietal area of the right hemisphere. Because in prosopagnosia lesions are usually more mesial and ventral than this (Leslie Brothers, personal communication), one should not be surprised that the patients' histories included no mention of any special difficulty in recognizing familiar faces.

Actually, an earlier pilot study by Van Lancker (Van Lancker and Canter, 1982) contained more direct comparisons of voice and face recognition in brain-damaged patients. In that study, recognition of famous voices was tested in left hemisphere–damaged aphasic patients and right hemisphere–damaged nonaphasic patients. Voice recognition was generally impaired in the right hemisphere–damaged patients, but it was normal in all but one of the aphasics, including five severely global aphasics with "virtually no functional expressive or receptive language."

The performance of left hemisphere patients was sufficiently high that Van Lancker and Canter were unable to observe a relationship between voice- and face-processing disturbances in that group. However, of the four right hemisphere patients with face recognition abnormalities three were abnormal in voice recognition and three of the four patients with poor voice recognition also were impaired in face recognition.

Facial and Vocal Processing

If the cortex contains voice cells that function in a way analogous to face neurons, then voice identification and the processing of vocal affect must be independent functions, for as we saw earlier, some face cells respond during efforts to identify faces, and others respond to facial expressions.

In adults, whether a stimulus is or is not a human face is a decision that rests upon analyses performed in the right cerebral hemisphere. Parkin and Williamson (1986) presented to the right or left visual field of normal adults stimuli that differed in the degree to which they resembled a human face. Subjects were to indicate whether the stimulus was or was not a face. Response times to face stimuli were significantly shorter when they appeared in the left visual field, that is, were processed by the right hemisphere. Similar results were reported by Small (1986), who obtained maximal responses to faces in the right occipito-temporal cortex using evoked potentials. Right hemisphere–damaged patients are also more impaired in perceiving facial emotions than patients whose damage is in the left hemisphere (Etcoff, 1984a, 1984b).

MULTIMODAL CELLS AND NEURONAL INTERACTIONS

Recording from the superior temporal sulcus in macaques, Bruce, Desimone, and Gross (1981) found that while 41 percent of the cells in their sample were exclusively visual, 21 percent responded to visual and auditory stimuli, 17 percent were responsive to visual and somesthetic stimulation, and an equal percentage were responsive to stimulation in all three modalities. Although certain units responded selectively to human and monkey faces, the report does not say whether there were any auditory-visual interactions involving these cells; what happens, for example, if a monkey hears a conspecific voice while viewing a conspecific or heterospecific face?

Are there face cells that turn on "voice cells" or vice versa? Some researchers have identified neurons that react to auditory stimulation, visual stimulation, or stimulation in both modalities. Benevento et al. (1977) recorded from the superior temporal sulcus and orbital cortex of macaques while presenting the animals with auditory (tones and clicks) and/or visual (white light) stimulation. The investigators found that fewer than a third of the cortical units responded to stimulation in just one of the modalities. Most units seemed to respond indiscriminately to auditory or visual stimulation, or to both auditory *and* visual stimulation. Although inhibitory interactions were obtained in both recording areas, in the orbital cortex sounds frequently facilitated responses to visual stimuli.

Meredith and Stein (1986) obtained evidence for sensory interactions in the deep laminae of the superior colliculus in cats using visual, somatosensory, and auditory stimulation in combination and in isolation. Nearly half of the cells in the deep laminae were multisensory. The majority of the interactions between modalities involved response enhancement, expressed as an increase in the number of discharges from a neuron when activated by stimuli in two or more different modalities. Less frequently, interactions involved response depression, characterized by a decrease in the number of neuronal discharges elicited by a stimulus when co-presented with a second stimulus in a different modality. The activity of some cells was enhanced by a second stimulus in one modality but depressed by a second stimulus in a different modality.

The response of neurons exhibiting multisensory interactions tended to be multiplicative rather than additive, especially when the cells were naturally inclined to respond weakly with unisensory stimulation. In some cases, the multisensory property of a cell became evident only when it was presented with combined stimulation. For example, cells not responding to auditory stimulation alone reacted to light in an exaggerated fashion when an auditory stimulus was also present.

VOICE CELLS?

In Meredith and Stein's (1986) studies of the cat, visual stimulation included flashes or moving slits or spots of light; auditory stimulation consisted of claps, hisses, whistles, and broad-band noise bursts. But if reproducible in humans with conspecific faces and voices, the sight of a vocalizing face might alter the threshold of *voice cells,* causing them to fire more or less vigorously when they are then presented with conspecific vocal stimulation. This would neurophysiologically define the linguistic face. And if the speculation were confirmed, we would wish to ask similar questions about clinical populations that currently are not well understood. For example, when autistic children avoid the sight of a face, does this prevent them from experiencing facial facilitation effects in voice processing? Or does avoidance of the face function adaptively to preserve inactivity in facial neurons that would otherwise depress the activity of voice cells?

Since neurophysiologists have located some auditory cells in the primate brain, it also would be interesting to know if some cells fire to voices but not to other auditory patterns, in a way analogous to face cells that fire to intact facial configurations but not to other complex visual patterns. Ploog (1979) reported that in the squirrel monkey there are cortical cells that respond to tape recordings of self-produced calls.

Display and Interpretation of Affect

Evolutionary linkage of vocal and facial activity seems to have produced a common neural substrate for the execution and interpretation of affective displays, which is revealed ontogenetically, functionally, and pathologically. Evidence from these domains collectively argues for a dedicated neurobiology of social cognition that carries out vocal learning and, in conjunction with a linguistically analytical specialization, enables development of spoken language.

EVOLUTION OF THE RELATIONSHIP BETWEEN FACE AND VOICE

In affective displays, characteristic facial movements commonly co-occur with characteristic vocal sounds.[3] The movements and sounds of laughing and the facial and vocal activity of crying are ubiquitous

---

3. In Goodall's (1971) description of free-ranging chimpanzees, "Facial Expressions and Calls" (her Appendix B) constitutes one more or less undifferentiated category of behavior.

examples. How did these gestures of the face and vocal tract become joined and integrated into a single, larger pattern of expression?

Phylogenetically, the capability for visuofacial communication may have been preceded by olfactory communication in nocturnal or crepuscular primates who could not easily see each other (Allman, 1977). It seems logical that vocal communication may also have played some role during this period of minimal visual contact; nocturnal primates can be prolific vocalizers, as studies of "night monkeys" have revealed (Moynihan, 1964). When primates became diurnal, one might speculate, brain centers controlling vocal communication retained their sound making function while adaptively taking on a capability for visuofacial transmission. For example, in a variety of primate species, contraction of the orbicularis oris occurs during many different types of vocalization. However, contraction of this muscle by itself has come to function as a visual signal (Andrew, 1963b).

Perhaps as a consequence of this shift from a heavy reliance on olfactory and auditory communication to auditory and visual communication, some facial configurations occur in modern apes only with particular vocalizations, while others may either be accompanied by vocalizations or are able to convey information about what the animal is likely to do next even when they are displayed silently (Marler and Tenaza, 1977).

In nearly all primates, startle reflexes are manifested in mouth-corner retraction and glottal closure (Andrew, 1964). When threatened, primates emit a reflex grin and a vocalization or—significantly—just a grin. This visible smile survives as an "intention movement" (Fridlund, 1991), a component of the larger act that it may precede and therefore predict—a joint communique between face and voice, a message of appeasement.

Because "vocalization and facial expression are inextricably associated in their evolution" (Andrew, 1964, p. 284), these logically separable signal systems now function with some degree of interchangeability, even in humans. For example, although one thinks of smiling as a strictly visible expression, we can tell that a person we are talking to on the telephone is smiling. In Tartter (1980), speakers were instructed to read while smiling and while straight-faced. Listeners associated smiled vocalizations with the act of smiling, or considered these utterances to be happier sounds, than unsmiled vocalizations. Acoustic analyses revealed that smiling raised the fundamental frequency and the first three formant frequencies in most of the speakers. In some of the speakers, amplitude and duration were also increased by smiling.

John Ohala (1980) has suggested that phylogeny could have given us the smile for acoustic reasons. Primate infants have short vocal tracts relative to adults and vocalize with higher formant frequencies. They are also relatively unthreatening.[4] Using a physical model of the vocal tract, Ohala demonstrated that mouth-corner retraction, which is associated with smiling, shortens the tract. This should slightly raise the frequency of the first formant and the perceptible pitch of the speaker's voice. Ohala has also suggested that lip retraction may have facilitated pitch elevation in animals that wished to appear submissive, pointing to observations (Andrew, 1963a) that in nonhuman primates smiling and high-pitched vocalization co-occur. Ohala speculated that in phylogeny, natural selection favored animals that uttered high-pitched vocalizations while retracting their lips (that is, "smiling"). Ultimately, these animals merely "smiled" when threatened by animals who also happened to respond sympathetically to infants in distress. In the course of time, according to Ohala, this behavior became ritualized into "social smiling."

All primates possess the neural capacity to identify faces and to process facial affect. This potential implies the existence of a neural specialization for social cognition (Brothers, 1990), which underlies intraspecific communication, and therefore a significant portion of what is needed for language. One might speculate that because they co-evolved, the neural control of facial gestures is now linked to the command system for vocal activity. And indeed, electrical stimulation studies with epileptic patients reveal inhibition of vocalization and speech when the adjacent supplementary motor representation of the face is stimulated (Fried et al., 1991).

Greenfield (1991) has defined phylogenetic homology as "descent from a common antecedent structure within an ancestral species,"

4. Morton (1977) has suggested a direct relationship the species-characteristic size of animals and their vocal frequency. In general, he reports, "the larger the animal, the lower the sound frequency it *can* produce" (p. 861). Though Morton regards high frequency sounds as cues to submissiveness, he predicts that low frequency vocalizations will generally be favored in hostile encounters.

and ontogenetic homology as "descent from a common antecedent structure within the same organism" (p. 533). I believe that by these definitions, the vocal-facial signaling system qualifies as a *double homology,* with common antecedents in both phylogeny and ontogeny.

INTERPRETATION AND DISPLAY OF FACIAL AFFECT

Hasselmo, Rolls, and Baylis (1989) found that facial expression and facial identity are encoded independently by cortical neurons. In this research, three macaque monkeys viewed photographs of an equal number of conspecifics, each wearing three different expressions: a calm expression, a slightly open-mouth threat expression, and a full open-mouth threat expression. While the test animals viewed the photos, the responses of forty-five neurons were recorded. Of these neurons, fifteen responded to different identities but not expressions; they were located mainly in the inferior temporal gyrus, as reported in Yamane et al. (1988). Nine neurons responded to different expressions but not faces; these cells were located primarily in superior temporal sulcus. Of the neurons responding to expressions, several were more responsive to calm faces and others were more responsive to faces with threatening gestures.

This study suggests that in the macaque, different neural tissue is dedicated to face identity and face expressions, which is consistent with certain of the pathological findings in humans, for example, the observation that in human prosopagnosia, loss of the ability to recognize familiar faces does coexist with preserved appreciation of facial expressions. In autism, levels of performance on facial recognition tasks may be normal (although as we will see later, strategies may differ from those of affectively normal children; Langdell, 1978) in spite of disturbance in the ability to interpret facial affect.

Perception of Vocal Variations

In nonhuman primates, cortical ablation studies suggest that auditory-visual associations are processed or stored mainly in the left hemisphere (Dewson, 1977). Behavioral experiments also suggest that the left hemisphere is disproportionately involved in the processing of conspecific vocal patterns.

Green (1975) has described acoustic variation in the coo calls of Japanese macaques. From his studies, it is obvious that these monkeys produce a substantial number of different coos, perhaps as many as ten, which correlate with the circumstance in which the monkey finds itself. This raises questions about the responses of conspecifics to these calls, and the perceptual capacity of macaques to recognize variations in the coo call. To investigate such questions, Petersen et al. (1978) trained five Japanese macaques and five other Old World monkeys, including other closely related macaque species, to discriminate macaque vocalizations. In one task the stimulus to be discriminated was the difference between the early and late components of the peak frequency in coo calls, a feature that is communicatively relevant to macaques. Late peak coos are produced mainly by estrous females who are soliciting male consorts; early peak coos are produced by all macaques in a variety of circumstances associated with socialization. Using a dichotic listening task, the researchers delivered early and late peak calls to each ear simultaneously. If nonhuman primates are lateralized like humans, it was expected that these stimuli would produce a right-ear advantage in those animals for whom such peaks are acoustically relevant (the Japanese macaques), but not in the other Old World monkeys.

In a second task using the same stimuli, animals were trained to discriminate calls on the basis of their fundamental frequency (above or below 600 Hz). Such pitch distinctions are not necessarily irrelevant to the macaque; they may convey indexical information about the identity, age, or sex of the vocalizer. If so, one would expect this contrast to produce a left-ear advantage or an attenuated right-ear advantage for the Japanese macaques but not necessarily any change, in terms of the early-late distinction, in the other Old World monkeys.

Both predictions were, in fact, realized in the data. The macaques displayed a right-ear advantage for the peak contrasts but not for pitch contrasts; the other Old World monkeys showed no right-ear advantage for either type of contrast. Accordingly, the authors concluded that Japanese macaques are neurologically specialized for these different categories of stimuli, which they subject to different types of auditory analysis.

Later research by these investigators and their associates (Petersen et al., 1984) confirmed these findings and also demonstrated that the Japanese macaques' right-ear advantage for coo calls was due not to the acoustic structure of the late and early peaks but to the biological significance of this contrast. As in the earlier study, control monkeys performed just as well on the inter-peak discrimination task as the Japanese macaques but did so without lateralization effects. On a generalization task, both groups revealed an awareness, on some level, of the inter-peak contrast. The researchers concluded, therefore, that it was the contrast in peak location that was processed in the left hemisphere, and that "Japanese macaques engage a neurally lateralized system when selectively attending to a communicatively significant feature of their vocal signals" (p. 786).

Heffner and Heffner (1984) confirmed the neuroanatomy of these behavioral findings. First, they trained adolescent male macaques to discriminate the early-late contrast. Then they performed unilateral or bilateral ablations either of the superior temporal gyrus, including auditory cortex, or of adjacent areas, sparing auditory cortex. The investigators found that ablation of the left superior temporal gyrus produced an initial deficit in call discrimination, after which spontaneous recovery occurred. The same surgery on the opposite side had no effect. Bilateral lesions completely eliminated reliable performance, but lesions that spared the auditory cortex had no effect on call discrimination. Heffner and Heffner ascribed a key role to the left temporal lobe and concluded that "the perception of species-specific vocalizations by Japanese macaques is mediated in the superior temporal gyrus" (p. 76), an area they likened to Wernicke's area in the human brain.

Other investigators have found cardiac accelerations to conspecific threat calls in neonatal chimpanzees that were not found for other conspecific calls and noises and not obtained in orangutans (Berntson and Boysen, 1989). At three and four months, isolation-reared chimpanzees showed different cardiac responses to conspecific screams and laughter, suggesting specialized perceptual processing mechanisms in these species (Berntson et al., 1990). If the primate brain is specialized for processing conspecific vocalizations, we should expect to find that certain cells or cell ensembles are dedicated to such processing just as they are to the recognition of faces and facial expressions.

Recently, research with humans has shown a similar degree of specificity for the perception of speech. Creutzfeldt, Ojemann, and Lettich (1989a, 1989b) recorded single-unit neuronal activity from the temporal cortex in epileptic patients during brain surgery. Recordings were made only from areas to be surgically resected. All neurons in the superior temporal gyrus were responsive to phonetic (but not semantic) characteristics of the speech presented to these conscious subjects. Interestingly, some neurons or populations of cells responded only if the patient was attending specifically to the message or was himself speaking.[5]

NEURAL SPECIALIZATION FOR INTERPRETATION OF VOCAL EMOTION

A few studies have approached the processing of vocal prosody and affect experimentally. When studies of dichotic listening were first initiated, Haggard and Parkinson (1971) conducted a study in which listeners heard sentences that varied in emotional tone (angry, bored, happy, distressed) in one ear and masking noise in the other ear. On each trial, listeners were to identify the tone and the sentence. Interestingly, sentence identification was not better in one ear than the other, but emotional tone was significantly better when the sentence was presented to the left ear.

A year later, King and Kimura (1972) reported a study of ear advantages for vocal material that had no verbal content, such as hummed melodic patterns, laughing, crying, moaning, and sighing. Subjects were significantly more accurate in reporting vocal sounds that had been presented to the *left* ear. A similar finding was reported for comparable stimuli by Carmon and Nachson (1973). Dichotic tasks have also shown that linguistic prosody typically is processed preferentially by the right hemisphere (Zurif and Mendelsohn, 1972; Zurif, 1974).

---

5. This may be analogous to certain findings in songbirds. Margoliash (1987) reports that in the white-crowned sparrow, some auditory neurons in the HVc region respond maximally to the bird's own ("autogenous") song relative to similar songs produced by other birds with the same dialect.

An interesting demonstration of our hemispheric specialization for verbal content and vocal affect was provided by Safer and Leventhal (1977). They presented adult listeners with sentences that were positive, negative, or neutral either in their content or in the emotional tone with which they were read during the taping session. Subjects heard the sentences monaurally, in either the left ear or right ear, and were to classify them as positive, negative, or neutral. Analysis of overall performance showed that subjects were equally accurate in judging content and tone. Analysis of performance by ear showed that listeners who had heard the sentences in the left ear were significantly more likely to base their judgment on emotional tone; subjects who had heard the sentences in the right ear were significantly more likely to base their judgments on content. Using a dichotic task, Saxby and Bryden (1984) obtained a similar finding in children ranging from five to fourteen years of age.

How are we to make sense of these findings psycholinguistically? How are we to regard a right hemisphere preference for voices that contain no speech, voices that contain emotional messages? We know that voices tell listeners about the identity and intentions of their associates. The literature suggests that if English listeners are to process vowels for their pitch or some other supposedly "linguistically irrelevant" attribute, they rely heavily upon their right hemisphere to do so. How did our two cerebral hemispheres come to divide up language as they do?

Some nonhuman primates process species-identifying vocal information on both sides of the brain (Petersen et al., 1978), and my guess is that in their efforts to identify their fellow hominid, and to infer his motives, our prehistoric ancestors also relied on both hemispheres. We might speculate that in evolution, both hemispheres processed vocal information of all types, probably before there was any such thing as spoken language. It is presumed that when hominids developed precise control over manual activities such as throwing or grasping, their brain assumed a specialization that also allowed for rapid articulatory movements (Calvin, 1983; MacNeilage, 1986; Ojemann, 1984). Analyses of the grasping patterns of nonhuman primates suggest that this specialization may well have been lateralized to the left hemisphere (MacNeilage,

1991; MacNeilage and Davis, 1990a; MacNeilage, Studdert-Kennedy and Lindblom, 1984, 1987).

The consequence of articulated phonation for social communication can hardly be overstated. This capability allowed our ancestors to "particulate" their vocal repertoire into segmental constituents that could be combined and sequenced without losing their indentity, a characteristic that describes all particulated systems (Abler, 1989). These rapid movement sequences with little affective or indexical value apart from the voice they modified naturally were sent to the left hemisphere, which was better at precise motor coordination. The consequent "overcrowding" drove out vocal affect, leaving the right hemisphere to control this important communicative function. I will argue in the next chapter that in ontogeny, correspondingly, the right hemisphere specialization for vocal affect develops before the left hemisphere takes on the responsibility for consonants.

The perception and control of phonation appears to involve disproportionate activity of the right hemisphere. This is supported by dichotic listening experiments in normal adults and by selective loss in right-hemisphere patients of the ability to perceive and produce vocal prosody while maintaining otherwise normal levels of linguistic comprehension and expression (Ross, 1981). It is not known whether these dysprosodic patients also have any particular difficulty recognizing familiar individuals from their voice.

There are two types of evidence for the involvement of the right hemisphere in voice recognition. Lesion data reveal that the right hemisphere is typically the damaged one in unilateral phonagnosia, and experiments indicate that the vocal resonance cues that primarily account for voice identification are among those processed preferentially by the right hemisphere. We might recall that in Doehring and Bartholomeus (1971), "voice" identification by children and their teachers was only moderately impaired when speech was played backwards, suggesting that articulatory cues contribute less to voice identification than laryngeal cues.

Independent of speaker identification, both vocal and facial processing may be impaired in the dysprosodias. In testing dysprosodic patients, Ross (1981) noted the common co-occurrence of prosodic deficits and impaired comprehension or expression of facial gesture.

The ability to express facial gesture was estimated by asking patients to discuss emotionally laden topics. Comprehension was tested by pantomiming an affective state such as surprise, anger, lack of interest, sadness, or elation and asking the patient to identify the emotion by name or description, although how these behaviors were scored was not described. Ross indicated that comprehension of both prosody and emotional gesturing was impaired in sensory, global, transcortical sensory, and the mixed transcortical dysprosodias; both functions were spared in motor and transcortical motor dysprosodia (as they were in a later study [Gorelick and Ross, 1987] of two cases of conduction aprosodia and a case of pure affective deafness). In other words, in no attested category of dysprosodia was there good performance in one area and poor performance in the other.[6]

The expression of prosody and facial gesture are a different matter. It is impossible to know if patients were ever impaired in one area and spared in the other because Ross put these behaviors in a single category—"spontaneous prosody and gesturing." Fortunately, in other research these behaviors have been kept separate. Borod et al. (1985) tested right-handed men with right- or left-hemisphere damage, as well as normal controls. Subjects were shown slides designed to elicit spontaneous feelings, hence displays of positive or negative emotion. After each slide, subjects were to describe their feelings about the content. Observers rated the degree of activity and the appropriateness of messages in three categories: facial expression, intonation (vocal affect), and speech. Even where a left hemisphere–damaged aphasic patient might be assigned a zero for speech, in principle he still could receive a higher rating for vocal affect or facial expression.

An important finding of this research is that across all subject groups *facial expressivity and vocal affect were significantly correlated* (r = .71), and this correlation was also significant within each of the three groups. As for the specific effects of brain damage, analysis revealed that the right-hemisphere patients were impaired

6. In parallel with the aphasias, Ross postulated two additional forms of dysprosodia, conduction and anomic. If these two forms exist, in conduction dysprosodia there would be no comprehension impairment either for prosody or facial gesture, and in anomic dysprosodia, prosodic comprehension would be spared but interpretation of facial gesture would be impaired.

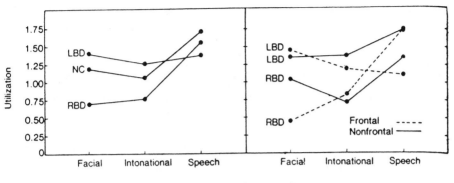

Figure 6.3. Communication of emotion as a function of group and mode. LBD indicates left brain-damaged patients, RBD stands for right brain-damaged, and NC represents normal controls.

in facial expression and vocal affect relative to the left-hemisphere patients and controls. The data are displayed in Figure 6.3, along with the results of an additional site of lesion analysis. In this second analysis (right panel), it was found that when the lesion was in the right hemisphere, damage to both frontal and nonfrontal lobes impaired vocal affect, whereas damage to the frontal area impaired facial expression disproportionately.[7]

If one ignores the frontal-nonfrontal distinction, it appears that Ross (1981) may have been justified in lumping facial gesture together with prosody. But within Borod et al.'s right hemisphere group, it is clear that frontal lobe damage impaired facial expression more than vocal affect, and nonfrontal damage impaired vocal affect more than facial expression. Overall, then, facial and vocal expressivity are correlated "in nature" but the location of lesions within the responsible hemisphere can pull them apart.

Dordain, Degos, and Dordain (1971) found voice alterations in right-handed patients with right-hemisphere lesions. The patients' vocal disorders suggested the presence of dysprosodia, since some

---

7. Since the left hemisphere patients also performed significantly worse than controls on affective prosody, it is possible that the left hemisphere helps to process this kind of material. However, the authors thought this impairment could also reflect a "generalized effect of brain damage."

spoke with a monotonous voice while others had difficulty controlling pitch and volume. In motor dysprosodia, the site of lesion is generally limited to the area of the right posterior frontal and parietal lobes in a supra-Sylvian distribution in both children (Bell et al., 1990) and adults (Ross, 1981; Ross and Mesulam, 1979).

Other studies confirm that right-hemisphere lesions are disproportionately associated with impaired comprehension of prosody. But broadly speaking, there are two different categories of prosody: linguistic and affective. In linguistic prosody, stress variations make a linguistic difference, distinguishing noun and verb forms of two-syllable words (*conflict, conflict*), and differentiating lexical compounds from adjective-noun combinations (*green*house, green *house*). Is this type of prosody equally affected by damage to the right hemisphere? Heilman et al. (1984) tested for this by playing differently intoned material to patients with damage to the right or to the left hemisphere, and to normal control subjects. Linguistic prosody was contrasted in declarative, interrogative, and imperative sentences. Following each sentence, listeners were to point to a punctuation mark (? ! .) that corresponded to the prosodic pattern heard. Affective prosody was contrasted in sentences that were spoken with a happy, sad, or angry tone of voice. These "tones" were identified by pointing to one of three faces whose expression implied the corresponding emotion. All sentences were heard with low-pass filtering, which destroyed intelligibility but preserved the intended intonation pattern. The following pattern of performance was observed (numbers represent percent correct):

	Affective prosody	Linguistic prosody
Right hemisphere–damaged	52.5	60.3
Left hemisphere–damaged	78.9	59.8
Control	88.2	88.8

Heilman et al. found that, relative to the controls, the right-hemisphere patients had reduced comprehension of affective and linguistic prosody. Moreover, they were less able to comprehend affective prosody than were the left-hemisphere patients. On linguistic prosody, the patient groups performed worse than normal controls but did not differ from each other. To the authors, these results suggested that "the two hemispheres mediate prosodic information differently" (p. 920). In addition, these findings suggest that both cerebral hemispheres contribute to the processing of linguistic prosody, whereas affective prosody is mainly the responsibility of the right hemisphere, particularly the basal ganglia (Cancelliere and Kertesz, 1990).[8]

To summarize, the identification of spoken and written words is typically conducted in the left cerebral hemisphere and the interpretation of linguistic prosody is carried out in both hemispheres. Consequently, a patient who cannot understand or express linguistic messages is likely to have a disturbance of the left hemisphere, while a patient who speaks in a monotone or with a lifeless facial expression, or who misses the emotional force of a message, may have a lesion in the right hemisphere.

In future research, we might consider these words of Desimone et al. (1984), whose own work has concentrated on the neural bases of social response in nonhuman primates:

> There are at least two examples of specialized neural mechanisms that have evolved to facilitate social communication in other species. One is the specialized structures that mediate the perception and generation of song in birds . . . another is the cortex specialized for language in man. In each case, specialized perceptual mechanisms have evolved that are separate from those of audition in general. In man, the supramodal language cortex of the temporal lobe is located within the second temporal convolution, adjacent to the auditory association cortex . . . this appears to be the location of the superior temporal sulcus in the monkey, which contains both face-selective and polysensory cells. Thus, this portion of the primate brain may be a fertile zone for the development of supramodal mechanisms for communication. (p. 2062)

The ontogenetic scenario would go something like this. The human infant has mechanisms on both sides of the brain that participate in affective communication. The left hemisphere takes on motor (and perceptual) control of activity of the type associated with language. The neural machinery needed for spoken language is active from the start and only later becomes linguistic. It is not linguistic from the start, waiting to become active.

---

8. Shapiro and Danly (1985) also found that damage to the anterior (and central) area of the right hemisphere reduced vocal affect and speech prosody but that posterior damage had no more effect than left hemisphere damage.

DISPLAY OF EMOTION VOCALLY AND FACIALLY

Affect is conveyed by both facial and vocal means, usually concurrently, and these channels appear to be functionally correlated. It would be extremely unusual to encounter a speaker whose voice was a dreary monotone but whose face lit up whenever she spoke, or to meet up with a poker-faced person whose intonation patterns were marked by great frequency sweeps. Attempts to simulate these conditions seem to require conscious suppression of one system or the other, which can be difficult to do persuasively. I can recall films of the production of early radio programs in which studio actors seemed to use a full range of supporting facial gestures, even though their expressions went unseen by the listeners. As we learned earlier, Ross's typology of dysprosodias (Gorelick and Ross, 1987; Ross, 1981) suggests that when the capacity for facial expression is knocked out by brain damage, so is vocal prosody.

NEUROLOGY OF LEARNED AND SPONTANEOUS VOCALIZATION

In a carefully controlled cross-fostering study recently conducted by Michael Owren and his colleagues (Owren et al., 1990) no evidence was obtained that young rhesus and Japanese macaques were able to learn each other's food call. I find it difficult to interpret this finding. Since monkeys are vocally communicative and sociable,[9] one expects them to be capable of learning the vocal patterns of a related species, especially if reared by nurturant foster parents from an early age. On the other hand, one might suppose that food calls are biologically imperative, and that their instatement in the infant would not, therefore, be left to a possibly unreliable process like learning. What if the environmental conditions are somehow not optimal for learning food calls? If this distinction between imperative and optional vocal behavior is an appropriate one, we might expect better results where infants are exposed to biologically optional vocalizations. But even here one has some level of doubt, for there is little evidence that monkeys acquire novel behaviors through the process of imitation (Visalberghi and Fragaszy, 1990).[10]

9. Since there is a great deal of acoustic overlap between the calls of the rhesus and Japanese adult females, and considerable acoustic variability in the vocalizations of the young, the door to vocal learning in nonhuman primates is still slightly ajar.

10. But see Tomasello et al. (1987).

Do nonhuman primates have the requisite flexibility and control to express any sounds they might notice which fall outside their species-specific endowment? Can they vocally mimic? Savage-Rumbaugh's (1990) experiences with Kanzi, a bonobo chimp, are informative. At this writing, Kanzi has a receptive vocabulary of some size and follows a number of fairly complex sentential commands. However, Savage-Rumbaugh reports that "despite significant efforts on his part, it was not possible to reliably associate English words with the sounds Kanzi made" (p. 612). Kanzi, in her judgment, "could not produce English as he heard it, due to differences between his vocal mechanism and our own, though he did often attempt to do so" (p. 611).

One possibility we will have to entertain is that the nonhuman primate's vocal control centers are set in motion only by affective states. Myers (1976) suggested that in nonhuman primates, facial and vocal displays are closely linked, but only at an involuntary, emotional level; neither type of activity, in his view, can be voluntarily controlled. In support of this contention he pointed to a number of studies in which caged monkeys readily used their hands to effect bar-pressing responses for food but were unable to produce a vocal response for the same rewards. In Myers's own experiment with six rhesus monkeys, three animals were conditioned to press a bar whenever a lamp went on and three were trained to vocalize. Bar-pressers learned to effect the desired response within one thirty-minute session. Moreover, when the reward-punishment values of the two conditions were reversed, these monkeys very neatly reversed the conditions under which they pressed the bar. In contrast, over the course of fifty sessions the other animals never learned to vocalize on cue.

Other experiments give one a somewhat different impression of the nonhuman primate's ability to control vocalization. When reinforcement is offered on a different basis, conditioning studies suggest that nonhuman primates are able to learn when to vocalize and with what duration. For example, Sutton and his colleagues (Sutton et al., 1973) delivered applesauce through a feeder tube whenever the vocalizations of three juvenile rhesus monkeys that fell within a certain intensity range also matched individually preset durational criteria (485, 644, and 770 msec). Each of the three monkeys learned to produce vocalizations of a duration different from that of the other two subjects.

In a later experiment, Sutton and his colleagues did something even more interesting (Sutton, Samson, and Lindeman, 1978). They were able to train monkeys to emit a coo to a red light and a bark to a green light. This result implies the neural capacity for associative vocal responding, whether it is ever manifested naturally or not. And except for the mode of reinforcement, at the behavioral level this differential vocal learning is not different from some human findings. For example, Wahler (1969) asked the mother of a baby boy, three weeks old at the beginning of the experiment, to be normally attentive or to "freeze" whenever her son produced vocal types that belonged in certain predesignated categories. Over a year's time, as certain vocal behaviors naturally emerged, the mother was to respond normally whenever her son displayed the targeted behavior and to freeze to all other vocalizations. Then, after several sessions of this, the mother was to reverse the situation and to respond normally to the contrasting behavior and freeze otherwise. This seemed to affect the frequency of glottal sounds differentially in contrast to those that were babbled or cooed; squealing as opposed to coughing or gasping; and one type of consonantlike sound versus another.

We can see, then, that in nonhuman primates and human infants alike the frequency of extant, species-typical behaviors can be influenced by external response, though in these populations the response was food and social behavior, respectively. But even here, monkeys were not trained to alter their natural vocal quality or morphology in response to feedback or reinforcement. Something is obviously different about the vocal control centers of nonhuman primates. It is not related to the size of their brain; monkeys have enough cortex to conduct a variety of cognitive operations (Passingham, 1979), but they seem to lack the capability and therefore, we might suppose, the equipment for vocal mimicry or instrumental modification of vocalization.

Nottebohm (1975) and Ploog (1988) have raised the possibility that nonhuman primates do not vocally imitate because they lack the neurological connections for a vocal feedback loop. However, there is some indication that monkeys do respond in ways similar to humans in certain feedback situations. Sinnott, Stebbins, and Moody (1975) found that in Old World monkeys, low frequency noise (corresponding to the monkey's fundamental frequency range) increased vocal amplitude by about 2 dB for every 10 dB of masking noise, a magnitude that approximates the Lombard effect observed in humans.

One might suppose that this will be a simple matter to resolve. We dissect the brain of humans and monkeys, look for differences, and thereby find out why we can imitate the sounds of others very readily and they cannot. Perhaps we find that nonhuman primates do not speak or have a wide range of vocal behaviors because they lack something like Broca's area or connections to their analogue of Wernicke's area. But as Hayes (1962) has warned us, it would be futile to look for a hole in that part of the nonhuman primate's brain "where Broca's area should be." Nonhuman primates have a different brain, not a deficient human brain.

Nevertheless, when efforts have been made to condition vocal behavior and then to bilaterally lesion portions of the neocortex that are possibly homologous to Broca's area in anterior cortex and Wernicke's area in parietal cortex, no change occurred in either the number or the duration of learned (or spontaneous) vocalizations (Sutton, Larson, and Lindeman, 1974). These kinds of changes occurred only when lesions were made in the area of the anterior cingulate gyrus (Sutton, Trachy, and Lindeman, 1981; Trachy, Sutton, and Lindeman, 1981), a structure associated with the initiation of vocalization and speech in humans (Brown, 1988). This reinforced the notion of a control system with separate mechanisms for the production of learned and unlearned vocalizations. If neocortex plays little or no role in conditional vocalization, as the work of Sutton and his colleagues suggests, it seems unlikely that nonhuman primates would be capable of complex vocal learning.

But there are other factors that complicate inquiry into this question. We do not know enough about our own brain, including those components that are responsible for vocal control, to effectively compare it to the nonhuman primate's brain. What we have learned indicates that linguistic capability is very widely distributed throughout cerebral cortex and subcortical areas, fanning out in complex networks of nerves and their interconnections (Mesulam, 1990). It is therefore unlikely that we will soon be finding the critical difference that accounts for grammatical language.

Neuroanatomically, one expects nonhuman primates to be hooked up quite differently than humans, and indications are that the left

Sylvian fissure of monkeys is not significantly longer than the right (Yeni-Komshian and Benson, 1976), although it is longer in humans. Unfortunately, the left fissure may be longer than the right in great apes (LeMay and Geschwind, 1975) and Old World monkeys (Falk, 1978), so just how to interpret our own asymmetries is unclear.[11]

How, then, do nonhuman primates initiate the vocal activity that is ethologically natural for them, the vocalizations that were not conditioned to applesauce in laboratory experiments? Research by Jurgens and Pratt (1979) and more recently by Charles Larson (Larson, 1985, 1988; Larson and Kistler, 1984, 1986) suggests that much of monkeys' spontaneous phonatory activity is set in motion by activity in an area, the midbrain periaqueductal gray, which receives projections from the limbic system, although other sites may be involved. The limbic system, in fact, sends fibers to several areas of monkey brain that are homologous to language areas in the human brain, including Broca's area, Wernicke's area, and the supplementary motor area (Muller-Preuss, 1988). Limbic control of vocalization in nonhuman primates accords well with the observation by some comparative psychologists that chimpanzees vocalize primarily under conditions of emotional arousal. Pointing to what they see as "the obligatory attachment of vocal behavior to emotional state" (p. 49), Gardner et al. (1989) comment that "when chimpanzees use their voices they are usually too excited to engage in casual conversation" (p. 29).

Before we set this matter aside, I would like to suggest some ways we might think about the neural control of vocal communication more productively, both in phylogenetic and in ontogenetic terms. Why not ask what behavioral functions monkeys do control with those parts of their brain that are anatomically the most analogous to human language mechanisms? If, according to Desimone (1991), one looks in the brain of monkeys for a structure analogous to the supramodal language cortex of the human temporal lobe, one is likely to come up with superior temporal sulcus, an area that con-

11. In light of psycholinguistic research suggesting that retarded individuals may use their *right* hemisphere to control speech (Elliott and Weeks, 1990), it would be interesting to know if the retarded are less likely than normally intelligent individuals to have larger *plana temporale* on the left, or if, like the great apes and Old World monkeys, they are likely to have larger structures in the right hemisphere.

tains face-selective cells and polysensory cells. He believes, as I quoted earlier, that this region "could be a fertile zone for the development of supramodal mechanisms for communication" (p. 6). Lacking a language area, this region could be the monkey's communication center, and one might speculate that this area was a phylogenetic precursor to the human mechanisms responsible for language.

We have looked at research on phonatory control in the nonhuman primate. These studies are important, and yet, ontogenetically, they seem to miss the mark. When one searches the monkey's brain for a volitional voice control center, one hopes to find the seat of a signaling system that adults could use to communicate vocally. But we have no evidence that human infants can make instrumental use of *their* voice, although human neonates routinely send and receive affective signals through that channel. For these reasons, perhaps we should compare the functional neuroanatomy of the juvenile (or adult) monkey and the infant human. Both appear to control vocal behavior with subcortical mechanisms, and these areas are therefore relevant to communication by way of unlearned vocalizations.

The facial cortex of monkeys, and the interconnections between facial and vocal areas, may be relevant to our capacity for spoken language. Analogous areas in the brain of the human infant may control his vocal communications, motivating their use, determining their mode of deployment, governing their frequency, and configuring their surface topography. This modified focus will cause us to ask questions about the neurology of interconnections between coldly cognitive and warmly emotional areas of the brain. Studies to date underscore the importance of separate but interacting neural systems involving cortical and limbic systems, which attach emotional value to stimuli that are processed in the cortex (Kling and Brothers, 1992; LeDoux, 1986; 1989).

Anticipating ontogenetic concerns, we have looked at the neurology of affective and social communication by way of the vocal-facial complex, which precedes a different neurology, that of the transition to words, morphology, phonology, and syntax. Since spoken language is a highly specialized behavior with its own brain mechanisms, it is not surprising that there would be a species-typical developmental path leading to the empowerment of linguistic capacities. Whenever the development of behavior among the individual members of a species proceeds along a common path, with a relatively small number of individual variations, biological mechanisms are operating to hold organisms on a central ontogenetic program or plan. One mechanism limiting the range of variation that occurs during development is canalization, a concept introduced by Waddington (1940). Canalization provides animals with an internally regulated growth path, which can be adhered to as long as they have access to a supportive environment of the type that is available to all members of the species.

Normally developing infants from disparate human cultures take the same general path to increasing mastery of linguistic expression. Even severe sensory and neurological disorders may lack the force needed to deflect them from the path to spoken language. This canalization for language is buffered against a variety of negative external effects. Because linguistic canalization is a defining feature of our species, all normally constituted human infants have the neural capacity to acquire language despite natural variations in their brain and social environment.

It is important to know which mechanisms of the adult brain process affect and personally identifying information. If they can be localized, we can then ask if these mechanisms develop before, or in effect join or become the neural systems responsible for speech, if indeed they are altogether different mechanisms. This approach requires that we consider the neurology of personal recognition and emotional interpretation by way of facial and vocal cues.

Neurophysiological studies have found cells throughout the inferotemporal cortex of monkeys that respond only or primarily to faces. These cells are additionally specialized in that some respond only to the appearance of a face and other neurons fire only in response to the sight of facial activity. Pathological studies have identified a face processing specialization in humans as well, and there is some electrophysiological evidence that humans also have face cells. Unilateral damage to the right hemisphere tends to impair both facial and vocal affect, expressively and receptively. These findings support the existence of a facial-vocal complex, as I hypothesized on the basis of other kinds of evidence.

These findings also suggest that humans may have cells that fire selectively in response to vocal stimulation, and they imply that any such cells are in communication with face neurons. Recent work with animals suggests the reasonableness of this supposition. Some multimodal cells exist, they can be activated either by vision or audition, and they fire more vigorously when both modalities report.

How did our two cerebral hemispheres come to divide up language as they do? Macaques process indexical vocal information on both sides of the brain, and it is speculated that in their efforts to identify their fellow hominid and infer his motives, our prehistoric ancestors also relied on both hemispheres. In hominids, both hemispheres may have processed vocal information of all types before there was anything as complex as present-day spoken language. When our ancestors began to interrupt the voice with their articulators, their vocal repertoire took on a segmental content whose mode of production required precise timing and coordination. These unfamiliar, transient patterns with little affective or indexical value were naturally sent to a hemisphere, the left, which was better able to coordinate precise movements in any reproductions, and ultimately became coldly analytical. The competition drove out vocal affect, leaving the right hemisphere to control this important communicative function. In ontogeny, correspondingly, our expectation is that this right hemisphere specialization for vocal affect would develop before the left hemisphere takes on the responsibility for consonants.

The ontogenetic sequence does not seem to be dissimilar. The young infant has mechanisms on both sides of the brain that participate in affective communication. The left hemisphere assumes motor and perceptual control of activity of the type associated with grammatical language. The neural machinery needed to process information that carries spoken language is active from the start and later becomes linguistic. It remains to be seen if there are other systems of the brain that are linguistic from the start, merely waiting to become active.

7

DEVELOPMENT OF THE NEURAL CAPACITY FOR LINGUISTIC COMMUNICATION

One might suppose that questions about the development of the brain's capacity for linguistic communication are fairly straightforward. First one pins down the relevant structures, most of which would already be well known from studies of brain lesions in adults. Then, in the immature brain, one estimates the myelination of these structures, counts synapses in the immediate vicinity, and documents any morphometric changes that occur over the first several years of life. In parallel, one looks for increases in the demonstrated capacity for language, that is, in receptive and expressive language, which one would expect from the brain studies.

This scenario is tidy and perhaps manageable, but it will not do. Our requirements are different. We are not asking about the development of the neural mechanisms responsible for language, nor are we questioning ontogenetic changes in the brain's capacity for language. Rather, we are seeking to understand the *neurology of development*, specifically the neural bases of the growth path extending from affective communication to spoken language.

To ask the questions most relevant to language development we must inquire into the neurobiological bases of social communication. Everything we have seen to this point suggests that the activation of neural operations associated with facial and vocal affect is the premiere biocommunicative development, in effect, the awakening of the systems that impel the infant toward spoken language.

Activation of certain lateralized vocal-motor and perceptual functions completes an ontogenetic triangle—very possibly recreating a step taken long ago in human evolution—and the brain's capacity for social communication is now indexical, affective, and phonological.

Since the capacities we are inquiring about are possessed by all normally constituted humans, it is important to ask some basic questions about how appropriately empowered and informed brain systems come into being.

Development of Information Storage Systems

Several theorists (Bekoff and Fox, 1972; Carmichael, 1970; Greenough, Black, and Wallace, 1987) have proposed that mammalian brain development relies upon two grossly different systems for the storage of environmental information, which are based on the types of information stored and the brain mechanisms doing the storing. In both systems, the sensory environment plays an important role, either by maintaining or inducing neural capacity or in some cases by not doing so. The specific modulations that occur in brain development include induction, stabilization, and atrophy (see Changeux and Danchin, 1976; Cowan et al., 1984).

EXPERIENCE-EXPECTANT SYSTEMS

Experience-expectant information systems, which develop early in the life of organisms, include the activation of auditory and visual mechanisms. Such systems represent a preadaptation that was initially fabricated at a far earlier time in evolutionary history. These systems are triggered by ambient stimulation, but this is not to say that nothing happens until the triggering occurs. As Susanne Langer (1988) has said, "No living mechanism is ever doing absolutely nothing. If its normal and special action is inhibited, something is covertly going on, there are changes with the maturing, proliferating or perhaps aging processes of the surrounding tissues; the inhibited complex is waiting, and waiting is a physiological activity" (p. 175).

When appropriately activated, experience-expectant systems store environmental information of a kind that is available to all individuals. During the development of these expectant systems, synaptic connections—prescribed by the genes—are overproduced. If appropriate stimulation is lacking, these connections atrophy. In their classic study, Wiesel and Hubel (1963) found that in kittens whose right eyelid had been sutured shut before the time of normal eye opening, there was "profound atrophy" in cell layers along the visual pathway receiving input from the covered eye. Anatomical changes within those areas of the brain also included a reduction in the size of cell bodies and nuclei. The direct effect of visual experience on brain growth in young cats is demonstrated further by the finding that monocular lid closure after about two months of visual experience produced less severe atrophy than deprivation from the date of birth. In mature cats, closing the right eye for three months produced no abnormal changes in the layers receiving input from the closed eye. More recently completed studies suggest that the brain of nonhuman primates is also fairly well developed at birth. In fact, intracortical association areas have an adultlike organization at least a month before birth (Schwartz and Goldman-Rakic, 1990).

EXPERIENCE-DEPENDENT SYSTEMS

In most animals, brain development falls heavily into the experience-expectant category. But it is now clear that the number of genes that contribute to the construction of the mammalian brain is simply insufficient to specify the total number of neuronal interconnections. It is therefore necessary, on strictly statistical grounds, that the genome collaborate with the environment to produce all those cells the brain will ultimately contain (Benno, 1990). There are also cases in which cellular structure that is absent at birth develops in response to appropriate stimulation, presumably as an adaptation to specific circumstances.

According to Greenough, Black, and Wallace (1987), experience-dependent systems are less sensitive to the age of developing organisms and involve the storage of information that is unique to particular individuals. In the storage process, experience stimulates changes in synaptic efficacy or dendritic morphology as well as the growth of new connections in regions receiving input from the stimulating experiences (Knudsen, 1985).

The capacity of organisms to move about in their environment also has a profound effect on the development of motor control, a phenomenon of interest at least since the classic experiments by Harrison (1904) and Carmichael (1926, 1927). Carmichael temporarily anesthetized frogs and salamanders that were in an early stage of development. Later, when the anesthetic had worn off, the amphibians were slightly delayed in the development of swimming. This suggested to Carmichael that motor development was not entirely maturational, and that "the excitation and response of the elements of the neuromuscular system is itself a part of the growth process" (1926, p. 56). Much more recently, Changeux (1985) has summarized experiments in which chick embryos were peripherally paralyzed for a short time. These chicks later revealed a decreased number of motoneurons in the spinal cord.

There are similar findings in mammals. Greenough, Larson, and Withers (1985) trained rats to use one paw or both paws to reach for food. Postmortem brain studies revealed that dendrites were more highly branched in "both paw" animals; ipsilateral branching was less than contralateral branching in "one paw" animals. Johnson et al. (1972) found that if one leg of a baby opossum is amputated when the baby has just entered its mother's pouch, neural columns in the cortex that are designed to control the digits on the amputated limb fail to develop.

These studies suggest that rudimentary levels of physical activity foster enhanced capacity for more complex forms of motor behavior. However, it now is evident that these effects are not limited to developing animals. Recent work by Merzenich, Jenkins, and their colleagues reveals that in adult owl monkeys the brain is dramatically reorganized after fairly brief periods of reduced sensory experience. In these experiments (Jenkins, Merzenich, and Recanzone, 1990), multiple microelectrode maps are made of the sensory areas of the brain responding to manual stimulation, which show that the processing of sensation from adjacent digits is handled by areas of the brain that are themselves adjacent. Then one or more digits are excised and, following excision, responsivity to tactile stimulation is tested, revealing a reallocation of processing responsibilities within two months of the surgery (Merzenich et al., 1984). Areas of the brain responsible for newly adjacent digits expand into the area that previously responded to stimulation from the excised digit. The conclusion Jenkins et al. (1990) draw from these experiments is that "receptive fields of cortical neurons can be altered and the representational topographies of cortical fields modified by use throughout life" (p. 100) and, moreover, that "the strikingly individual representational details of hand representations in different adult monkeys . . . have been shaped by each monkey's unique experiential history" (p. 101).

The Merzenich-Jenkins work is nothing less than stunning, given the amount of cortical reorganization that occurred in mature animals after just two months of deafferentation. But what if the period of sensory deprivation is longer? Work very recently reported suggests that if the period of deafferentation is fairly long, the amount of cortical reorganization may be essentially complete. Pons et al. (1991) conducted electrophysiological recordings on four monkeys who had participated in a deafferentation experiment twelve years earlier.[1] In that experiment, unilateral or bilateral deafferentation was performed on upper limbs. In the cortex, upper limb areas normally are bounded by the trunk medially and the face laterally. Therefore, Pons et al. were expecting that trunk and facial stimulation would be registered in the area where limb stimulation was processed presurgically. In fact, they found that trunk stimulation was still confined to the trunk area of the cortex, but that face stimulation activated all 320 test sites in the deafferented zones of the four animals as well as the normal facial area. Facial stimulation had greedily and completely colonized the area normally responsible for registration of limb sensation!

Analyses further revealed that only a restricted portion of the face participated in this massive reorganization of the cortex. The area from the chin to the inferior surface of the lower jaw was responsible for the complete occupation of the old limb area. Because old chin and jaw areas were not abandoned, the area of the brain to which they reported was found to have stretched laterally to a zone many times longer than its normal size.

Where neural atrophy is concerned, it appears that some early connections will be lost even if appropriate experience is available. In the case of transient neural connections, however, experience can slow the rate of atrophy or even permanently stabilize these connections, which otherwise would be completely eliminated (Frost,

1. This work, by Taub, Goldberg, and Taub (1975), was performed when the monkeys were already three to four years old. The original experiment was interesting in its own right, for it suggested that monkeys lacking somatosensory feedback are able to learn to point, a behavior not necessarily natural to nonhuman primates.

1989). Frost and Innocenti (1986) investigated the role of early postnatal visual experience in the development of visual callosal connections. They found that in cats, "binocular visual deprivation . . . accentuates the normally occurring loss of juvenile callosal axons" (p. 260). Frost and Innocenti concluded that normal visual experience has a stabilizing influence on certain axons crossing at the corpus callosum. That is, the visual cortex undergoes a postnatal reshaping whereby certain callosal connections that are present at birth are eliminated. The redistribution of axonal connections as the kitten matures appears to be based in part on visual experience. An excellent review of these and other experiential effects appears in Greenough and Chang (1985).

The studies reviewed here indicate that exposure to sensory stimulation enhances and stabilizes neural functions that are genetically dedicated to signal processing, and they suggest that physical activity helps to expand an organism's capacity for the control of movement. It therefore seems likely that appropriately timed exposure to speech and opportunities to engage in articulatory activity enhance the human infant's capacity to process and control phonetic material. As we saw earlier, we vocalize far more frequently than nonhuman primates, and we may thus assume that our infants vocalize playfully far more often than theirs. Perhaps this difference in some measure contributes to our differing neural capabilities for vocal control.

Neural Factors Favoring
Acquisition of Complex Behaviors

If we are to consider the development of the capacity for human language adequately, it may be necessary to contemplate the development of complex behaviors in general. Correlations between brain weight and evolutionary advancement suggest that brain size is important to the development of complex behaviors. But from an ontogenetic viewpoint, the ultimate size of the brain may be less important than when the brain does its developing and how prepared it is to respond to, and to be reshaped by, early experience.

Skeletal evidence suggests that when early hominids began to stand erect and to walk, pressures on the hip and pelvis were altered (LeBarre, 1954, 1973; McHenry, 1975). Since body weight is transmitted downwards through the sacroiliac joint, and ground reaction

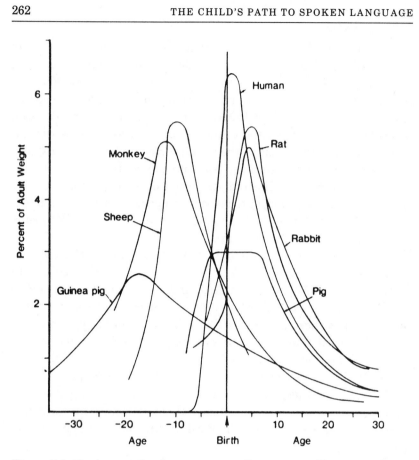

Figure 7.1. Brain growth of seven mammalian species. The units of time on the abscissa are guinea pig = 1 day; rhesus monkey = 4 days; sheep = 5 days; pig = 1 week; human = 1 month; rabbit = 2 days; rat = 1 day.

is transmitted upwards through the hip joint, torques are produced at these pressure points. Having the entire weight of the body on the hind limbs caused a ventral tilt of the pelvis and eventually shortened the distance between sacroiliac and hip joints (Leutenegger, 1974, 1980). While this made for more efficient bipedal locomotion, it created an "obstetrical dilemma" in Washburn's (1960) words, because of the rapid enlargement of the fetus's head. Figure 7.1, which depicts the brain growth of seven mammalian species (Dobbing and Sands, 1979), shows the sharp increase in human brain growth just before birth.

Figure 7.1 also reveals that the monkey's brain does more of its

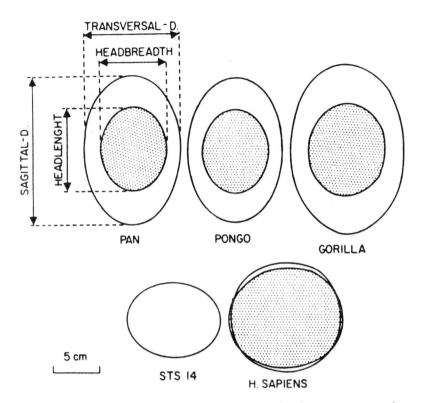

Figure 7.2. Schematic depiction of the relationship between neonatal cranial size and size of female pelvic inlet in pongids, *Australopithecus africanus* (STS 14), and humans.

growing relatively sooner than ours. By birth, the rhesus monkey has already achieved 68 percent of its ultimate brain weight, whereas the human newborn's brain is only about 26 percent of what it will weigh in maturity (Harvey and Clutton-Brock, 1985; Lindburg, 1982). Nevertheless, the human newborn's head is relatively large, a direct reflection of the fact that its body is large (Leutenegger, 1974; Sacher, 1980).

   Put these two facts together—the increased narrowing of the birth canal and expansions in the human brain, and therefore the newborn's head—and it makes for a conflict: relative to most other primates, the pelvic area in humans is narrow in relation to the size of the neonatal head. Figure 7.2 depicts differences in cephalo-pelvic relationships among several nonhuman primates, early hominids *(australoapithecus)*, and modern humans. In humans, there is incompatibility of both head size and shape.

In phylogeny, this pelvic narrowing, taken with later increases in head size, produced some interesting consequences. If the fetus was not delivered during a time when the cephalo-pelvic relationship was favorable, birth complications were certain to occur. Indeed, even with our relatively short gestation period, birth is more difficult in humans than in other primates, and I believe it is the case that we have more stillbirths and spontaneous abortions than other members of our class.

The ontogenetic significance of this is clear. The solution to the obstetrical dilemma is premature birth—to be born at all, the infant must be delivered early in the gestational game. The human infant, according to Stephen Jay Gould (1977b), is born nine months too soon. This is why less of our species' brain growth takes place prior to birth, and more of it occurs "on the outside." The human infant's brain does most of its forming, then, during a protracted interval of intense social stimulation. One can hardly think of a developmental circumstance that would more favorably affect acquisition of complex behavior.

Though the human neonate is sensorily precocial, that is, it can sense stimulation long before gestation runs its course, the opposite is true where the control of movement is concerned. Human infants are motorically altricial; they cannot walk, hunt, or forage, as many other animals are perfectly equipped to do. It is in this sense that human offspring may be said, in a word, to be *neotenous*—they retain their juvenile characteristics even while becoming sexually mature (de Beer, 1958). In anything but a protective family environment neoteny would be risky, but as we have seen, there are huge advantages to this state. The central nervous system of altricial animals is in a highly malleable and absorptive state during exposure to a variety of experiences.[2] Because they remain better at sensing than doing over a fairly long period of time, human neonates are able to take in a great deal of information before they can competently act on it. I suspect the protracted discrepancy in

2. This plasticity may be due to protein molecules such as MAP2 (Aoki and Siekevitz, 1988) and GAP-43 (Benowitz and Routtenberg, 1987; Fishman, in press), whose concentrations are greater during neural development and axonal regeneration.

early childhood between the ability to sense and the ability to do contributes a great deal to the adult human's capacity to plan and execute complex behaviors.

Though the rate of human head growth peaks a month or so after birth, it continues at a reasonably brisk pace over the next several months, and, although it is not shown in Figure 7.1, brain weight and head circumference keep growing yearly until the late teens. The average age of the final growth spurt in adolescence comes at eleven to twelve years for females and fourteen to fifteen years for males (Eichorn and Bayley, 1962).

Before leaving this discussion, I should point out that the relationship between brain size and cognition does not manifest itself only in phylogeny. A clear relationship has been found between head circumference and cognitive development in infants of very low birthweight. In one study (Eckerman, Sturm, and Gross, 1985), the gestational age of subjects varied from twenty-five to thirty-six weeks; birthweight ranged from 660 g to 1500 g. There were two categories of head circumference: (1) microcephalic at birth (below the tenth percentile in head circumference according to normative data); and (2) normocephalic at birth (above the tenth percentile). There were also two categories of head growth: (1) large increases in head circumference (3.5 cm or more between birth and 6 weeks); and (2) small amounts of increase (less than 3.5 cm.). All subjects were given the Bayley Mental Development Index and the Bayley Psychomotor Development Index. The following table shows the percentage of subjects in each group that had no mental or psychomotor delay in relation to a full-term control group of normal birthweight:

Size	Growth	Mental	Psychomotor
Microcephalic	less	0	0
Microcephalic	more	36	64
Normocephalic	less	25	46
Normocephalic	more	62	89
Controls		70	93

It is apparent from these data that both the absolute size of the head at birth and the amount of increase in head circumference following birth are important. The message to the fetus seems clear:

if you are going to come out too soon, bring a large head with you. If you do not, get one as soon as possible!

Maturation and Experience in Language Development

At an abstract level, most of us would accept that language develops in response to maturation and experience, but the meaning of these terms is not particularly clear. If "linguistic experience" is to be a scientifically useful construct, it will have to mean far more than growing up in a place where language is spoken; "experience" will need to denote a great deal more than mere exposure to individuals who are talking. But in actuality—though the word is bandied about quite freely by psycholinguists—experience is rarely defined. In effect, we are asked to assume that any three-year-old child reared in a normally stimulating environment has had three years of linguistic experience. Since in most plots of brain development chronological age is usually on the abscissa, we are asked to assume that the same child has also had three years of neural maturation. How then do we evaluate the relative contributions of experience and maturation?

THE EFFECTS OF MATURATION ON EXPERIENCE

A decade ago, Kristine MacKain (1982) wrote an intriguing essay on the nature of experience at the phonological level. For her, experience is more than exposure to ambient stimulation. In fact, learners must be perceptually selective if they are to convert raw exposure into useful experience. To have directly benefited from linguistic exposure, MacKain said, infants would have to have:

> (1) segmented the speech stream into discrete units, (2) recognized that the sounds to be contrasted vary along some underlying perceptual continuum(s); (3) ignored covarying redundant information; (4) identified variations along certain continuum(s) as perceptually equivalent (perceptual constancy); (5) recognized that these instances along the continuum(s) separate into contrasting categories; (6) recognized that these instances have occurred before (such that current experience is identified with previous experience); and (7) accounted for the frequency with which such instances have occurred. (1982, pp. 534–535)

This intensely analytical scenario is necessarily a heavily maturational one, for the child cannot get much useful experience in advance of the maturation that enables those cognitive functions that permit "experience." On the other hand, it would be unwise to suppose that all linguistically relevant cognitive functions develop prior to vocal imitation. As Studdert-Kennedy (1991) reminds us, complex linguistic structures—and, we must assume, complex linguistic operations—typically differentiate from simpler ones.

MacKain also argued convincingly that one cannot establish which sound patterns strike the child's eardrums simply by knowing which language the child is exposed to. In fact, a number of investigators have committed serious blunders merely by trusting formal analyses of established languages. These grammars frequently contain descriptions not of what real people say when they talk to each other but, in the interests of parsimony, the minimum behaviors that linguists must know about to understand the functional units and rules of phonology (Locke, 1983, Chapter 7).

There is a third, rather humbling aspect to the concept of experience. If Atkinson (1982) is correct in his assertion that infant attention is variable, how grammatical are the utterances that get registered in the infant's brain? With wavering attention, would not many utterances in effect be poorly formed? Lacking a good answer to this question, how are we to estimate the child's access to the expressed grammar of the ambient language? Scarr and McCartney (1983) have made a related point. The environment, they say, is in the first instance a psychological construct. Which constituents of the environment exist for the infant is heavily influenced by which stimuli it selectively attends to and which activities it chooses to initiate.

THE EFFECTS OF BRAIN DEVELOPMENT ON BEHAVIOR

"Every day," as the saying goes, "I am getting better and better," and every day in the infant's life multiple structures grow larger and numerous operations become more efficient. Some of this enhanced capability is undoubtedly due to "growth" and "maturation," but these concepts carry some unfortunate baggage. They imply that behavioral systems are preformed, and that the infant merely needs to await the unfolding of its genetic plan; environmental stimulation would be unnecessary. These concepts also fail to capture the processes of transformation and differentiation by which organisms develop behavioral capacity, and yet, as Karl Ernst von

Baer declared many decades ago, "All is transformation, nothing is development *de novo*" (in Gottlieb, 1992, p. 8).

Regardless of the overall quality of environmental stimulation, the brain grows larger and heavier in the first year of life, myelin forms, dendrites branch, synapses disappear. So we can, in fact, speak of the maturation of the brain. But how are we to decide which of the individual "maturations" are responsible for language? Fortunately, there are some specific "milestones" on which to orient our exploration of this issue. As we saw in Chapter 5, several motoric developments occur, more or less simultaneously, at about six to seven months—babbling, one-handed reaching, and rhythmic hand activity. Is there a neural spurt at this age that might account for these co-occurrences? Goldman-Rakic (1987) has found peaks of brain growth in monkeys that coincide with cognitive developments, so is it not reasonable to suppose that human infant brains also experience growth spurts coinciding with behavioral changes of a motoric or symbolic nature?

As I mentioned earlier, brain growth begins to decline in magnitude at about six months. Conel (1939–1967) reported cortical thickness data on humans from birth to eighty months of age. His data show sharp increases in the thickness of the temporal cortex throughout the first year of life, paired with a distinct peak in the growth of the motor cortex at approximately six months. Other data (Lecours, 1975; Yakovlev and Lecours, 1967) suggest that intra- and interhemispheric cortical association bundles begin to myelinate at about five to six months postnatally.

Myelin, as insulation of peripheral and central nerve fibers, is an "energy-efficient adaptation that provides for rapid impulse conduction" (Konner, 1991, p. 186), and yet myelin is not strictly necessary for function (Gibson, 1991). Motor neurons can fire without it. Its theoretical value derives from correlations with dendritic branching (Gibson, 1990, p. 115), and possibly cognitive development (van der Knaap et al., 1991).

In more specific, histological studies, Simonds and Scheibel (1989) counted and measured the length of dendrites in the left and right speech-motor areas (pars opercularis and triangularis) and motor areas (the foot of the precentral gyrus and the orofacial zone of the primary motor area) bilaterally in seventeen children from three to seventy-two months old. Dendrite location was categorized, along the dendritic spine, as proximal (the three dendrites closest to the soma) and distal (the three dendrites beyond the proximal ones). The investigators found that at three months there were no differences in the number of left or right dendrites in speech-motor and motor areas. However, at five to six months there were more distal dendrites in the left hemisphere in both speech-motor and motor areas. In length analyses, this trend toward left hemisphere superiority was first evident at twelve to fifteen months.

The brain, then, has given up a few of its secrets, and we can see some correlation between neural expansion and elaboration on the one hand, and prelinguistic advances in vocal-motor development on the other. One hopes that with the neuroimaging techniques now available there will soon be more detailed structure-function data at hand.

Although I have spoken as though maturation and experience were factors unto themselves, the two are interconnected. Several of their interconnections will become clear as I discuss some effects of experience on maturation, concentrating particularly on stimulation arising out of the infant's own activity.

The Infant as Neural Architect

Traditionally, scholars have believed that "the major function of the environment was to 'support' the developing organism by maintaining a milieu which would permit the natural unfolding of the organism's genetic potential" (Dennenberg, 1969, p. 95). If scholars believed in a passive environment, it was also necessary to accept "a unidirectional relationship between structure and function, wherein there is no reciprocity or regulative feedback during the maturational process (structure → function)" (Gottlieb, 1971a, p. 111). In actual fact, according to Gottlieb, "during the maturation of a system there is a bidirectional or reciprocal relationship between structure and function, whereby each affects the other" (p. 111) because the brain develops in response to stimulation, much of which is provided by the infant itself. On statistical grounds, Benno (1990) has claimed that it could not be otherwise; the brain could not develop in other than an epigenetic fashion because there simply are not enough genes to specify all the neuronal interconnections that exist in the mammalian nervous system. The correct sequence, then, according to Gottlieb (1971b), is:

Genes → Structural Maturation ↔ Function ↔ Behavior

Stimulation ranges from presensory or nonsensory mechanical agitation to interoceptive, proprioceptive, exteroceptive, and neurochemical stimulation, and may include the musculoskeletal effects of use.[3] Gottlieb cites a number of avian experimental findings that support bidirectionality, such as anomalous development of structure in cases of prenatal paralysis and enhanced optic function in cases of prenatal stimulation. In the several decades since Gottlieb's paper, findings on chicks and other animals have continued to support the bidirectional development of structure and function. Experimental deprivation and enrichment studies (Diamond, 1988) make it clear that experience affects the rate and ultimate degree of brain development.

The development of patterns of cell connectivity is so heavily influenced by a variety of unforseeable endogenous and exogenous factors—including competitive interactions between cells that are set in motion by the trophic demands of early experience—that it is termed "reactive synaptogenesis" (Rakic, 1989). Wimer (1990) has conceptualized the process by which genes interact with environmental stimulation to produce morphological variation and behavioral variability. Figure 7.3 depicts Wimer's conception. What is important to keep in mind about these interactions is that they do not occur in a rigid left-to-right sequence from genes → genes + experience → variability. Both elements are always present in varying degrees, and I know of no reason why gene action could not be "bled" or coopted by prior responses of the organism to environmental stimulation. Indeed, the relatively new field of developmental behavior genetics is built around the proposition that "gene action changes during development" (Arnold, 1990).

Rakic (1989) views the competition between neurons as "an additional cellular mechanism that has emerged and been elaborated during the course of evolution" (p. 455). Figure 7.4 depicts the

3. The influence of stimulation upon structure also works indirectly by altering gene activity. The link between genes and environmental factors is hormonal, since DNA elements are turned on or off by steroids. These steroid hormones can act alone or in collaboration with other neurotransmitters and hormones (McEwan, 1989).

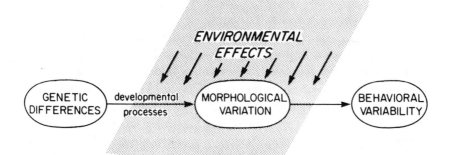

Figure 7.3. A model of the process by which genetic instructions interact with environmental stimulation to produce neural structure and capacity.

manner in which a variety of epigenetic factors are thought to affect the expression of genetic commands (left column) at different levels of analysis. As the figure indicates, genes exert an influence on structure at each of several levels, but nongenetic factors exert an influence on every level of structure and function. This makes it

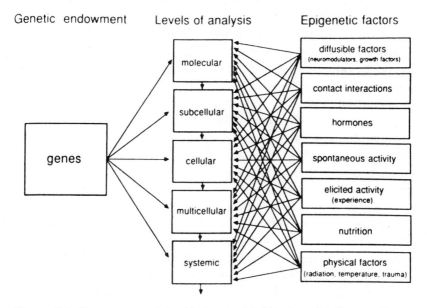

Figure 7.4. Some ways epigenetic factors (right column) influence the action of genes (left column) to produce various levels of analysis.

difficult to trace the cause of cortical dysfunction in cases where no cellular abnormalities can be found.

The picture that emerges from embryological research is one in which experience and maturation enable behavior that in turn encourages brain development. Findings in behavioral genetics also speak to the role of behavior in producing behavioral capacity. In the twin adoption design, investigators attempt to locate identical or monozygotic twins who have been separated soon after birth and raised in separate homes. These siblings are compared to fraternal or dizygotic twins who were also separated soon after birth and raised by different families. The design takes advantage of the fact that monozygotic twins share all their genes and dizygotic twins only about half of theirs, and it assumes that any surplus of behavioral similarities found between identical twins reflect genetic factors (Plomin and Daniels, 1987).

Investigations using this design reveal greater similarities between monozygotic than between dizygotic twins on a variety of psychological measures including, curiously, attitudes toward religion and politics (Bouchard et al., 1990; Martin et al., 1986; Waller et al., 1990). In one study, for example, attitudes on the death penalty, fluoridation, mixed marriage, censorship, disarmament, and a variety of other subjects were more concordant between pairs of monozygotic than dizygotic twins (Martin et al., 1986). In another study, the religious and social attitudes of monozygotic twins reared together were no more concordant than the attitudes of monozygotic twins reared separately (Bouchard et al., 1990).

Viewed against the current knowledge base in neuropsychology, these findings present serious difficulties for a strict left to right structure → function view because, according to present conceptions, one cannot inherit attitudes and behaviors. But as mechanisms that produce behavior, brain structures are set up by genes, so there is a theoretical choice to be made here. According to a *direct structural* hypothesis, parts of the brain are preconfigured and functionally responsible for patterns of voting and church attendance. Although there is some evidence of a genetic influence on brain function (Stassen, Lykken, and Bomben, 1988), at this time the collected neurogenetic research contains no support for such an influence on behavior, and I think it unlikely that this type of information would be genetically specified.

THE INFANT PICKS ITS NICHE

If the direct structural hypothesis is unlikely, there fortunately appears to be room for an *indirect environmental* hypothesis. According to this notion, genes specify neural structures that impel the infant toward certain kinds of sensory stimulation and motor action. Evidence has recently emerged to support a genetic basis for infants' level of spontaneous motor activity (Saudino and Eaton, 1991). The infant seeks out such stimulation and activities and in the process constructs its own environment. This is possible because genes lay down enough structure to prod the infant into motion: to actively seek out and attend to particular patterns of stimulation, a form of "niche picking" according to Scarr and McCartney (1983). Sights, sounds, and other sensations from this activity flow back to influence the infant in a variety of ways. The infant's self-styled environment then functions as environments do, influencing the infant's behavior and ultimately many of its attitudes and beliefs.

I suspect that behavioral geneticists are relieved by such a conception of the child, for on the present evidence how else could their findings be explained? And indeed, Martin et al. (1986) have pointed out that humans are "exploring organisms whose innate abilities and predispositions help them select what is relevant and adaptive from the range of opportunities and stimuli presented by the environment" (p. 4368). Bouchard et al. (1990) argued that monozygotic twins raised apart "tend to elicit, select, seek out, or create very similar effective environments and, to that extent, the impact of these experiences is *counted as a genetic influence*" (p. 228, italics mine).

After finding a significant genetic influence (apart from IQ and temperament) on children's television viewing habits, Plomin et al. (1990) observed that "whether or not one watches television seems to be completely a matter of free will. We can click the set on or off as we please, so how can genes affect it? It is critical to recognize that genetic effects on behavior are not deterministic in the sense of a puppeteer pulling strings. Genetic influences imply probabilistic propensities rather than hard-wired patterns of behavior. We can turn the television on or off as we please, but turning it off or leaving it on pleases individuals differently, in part due to genetic factors" (p. 376, italics mine).

An extreme form of this hypothesis was recently supported by analyses of the extensive data compiled by the Minnesota Twin Family Registry and the Finnish Twin Registry. In these studies, it was found that monozygotic twins who spend a great deal of time together tend to be more similar in their perceived or actual behavior than monozygotic twins who spend less time together (Lykken et al., 1990; Rose et al., 1988). Although it is tempting to take such an association as proof that togetherness fosters similarity, it turns out that the causality may actually run in the opposite direction. First, Lykken et al. (1990) found that even among monozygotic twins living at home there were differences in aptitude, personality, or interests that were associated with different stopping points in their educational careers. Second, they found no evidence that similarity grew with increased contact. The investigators concluded that monozygotic twins "especially enjoy each other's company because they are so similar in personality, interests, and attitudes" (p. 560).

I will take up the linguistic similarity of monozygotic and dizygotic twins in Chapter 10, but here I should note that of twins living (but not raised) apart, monozygotics speak with each other more frequently than dizygotics. In the data of Lykken et al. (1990), 29 percent of monozygotic females and 23 percent of monozygotic males speak once a day, compared to 15 and 8 percent of dizygotic females and males. If such consortative tendencies are true of adults, they will complicate exclusively organic explanations of the greater linguistic similarity associated with monozygosity.

The active hypothesis I discussed above was also embraced by Plomin, DeFries, and Loehlin (1977), who imagined three distinct types of genotype-environment correlations. In the *passive* type, parents provide their children with genes and an environment conducive to the development of a particular trait. Highly literate parents, for example, may provide alleles that favor development of verbal abilities and a home in which speaking and reading are valued. In *reactive* correlations, adjustments to a child by other people produce an environment that reinforces endogenous tendencies. Such cases may include the artistically or musically gifted child who is provided with formal training in these areas.

Plomin et al. discussed a third type of genotype-environment correlation that is relevant to the child's active role. In the *active* type of correlation, the child participates in the structuring of its own environment and may seek out behaviors that are genetically harmonious with it. An active child, they suggest, "can create mayhem in the most placid environment, and a sociable child will seek out others and perhaps create imaginary playmates if real ones are not at hand" (p. 310).

Precisely this type of active notion was identified by Hayes (1962) in an intriguing paper on the inheritance of drives. Hayes argued that drives could be inherited and, once in full bloom, could in turn influence the child's capacity for intelligent behavior. In support of his view, Hayes reviewed evidence in the animal literature that (1) genetically controlled differences in motivation occur across a variety of species, (2) differences in motivation lead to variations in experience, and (3) differing experiences produce differences in cognitive capacity. Hayes called these effects "experience-producing drives" (or EPDs), and they consist of genetically controlled preferences for certain activities conducive to the "acquisition of corresponding skills and information." This was picked up by McGue and Bouchard (1989), who suggested that individuals who seem to inherit a high IQ in fact inherit "a propensity to seek out intellectually stimulating environments" (p. 8).

Hayes (1962) attributed the presence of language in humans to the existence of specific EPDs for language, drives that humans have and nonhuman primates lack. Ontogenetically, he supposed that variations in EPDs for language might also occur between individuals. Hayes suggested that genetic differences could, in principle, cause individuals to differ

> with respect to their *tendencies to engage in certain kinds of intrinsically-motivated activities*. Specifically, twin A displays a strong preference for linguistic activity. At the age of 2 years he is unusually talkative, and at 8 years he does an unusual amount of reading. Twin B, on the other hand, shows an equally strong preference for athletic activity. The twins' brains do not differ appreciably in size, or biochemistry, or capacity to form associations or develop complex neural circuits. In the course of time, A acquires a larger vocabulary than B, as well as a larger store of linguistically transmitted information—simply because he *devotes more time to relevant activities*. (pp. 301–302, italics mine)

But what of the "stuff" in the environment that is not of the infant's own making? Is this not responsible for "nongenetic" contributions to behavior? To respond in an unqualified affirmative would be to ignore a fundamental fact: the behavior of parents expresses the phenotype of their own genes, which the parents share with their biological child. Peter Wolff (1971) has observed that the behavior that newly born infants assimilate includes "the species-specific characteristics of the parent" (p. 81). So even when the assimilated behavior is the parents', genes are not completely off the hook.

Estimates of the genetic contribution to development would be even greater if we knew more about the role of genes in adult behavior. Tooby and Cosmides (1988) have written that "the environment of an animal—in the sense of which features of the world it depends on or uses as inputs—is just as much the creation of the evolutionary process as the genes are. Thus, the evolutionary process can be said to store information necessary for development in both the environment and the genes. Both are 'biologically determined,' if such a phrase has any meaning" (pp. 5–6).

In mother-child interactions, it could be said that the dyad is genetic in the sense that the behavior of both parties is influenced by their genes. As Figure 3.6 revealed, the child is influenced by its own genes on the one hand and by maternal behavior that is structured by similar sets of genes on the other. The relationship between the child's behavior and its environment is a bidirectional one: nurturant parents observe their infant closely and alter their own conduct based on what they see and hear. Children receive genes from the same people whose phenotypic behavior provides much of their stimulation. It would be difficult to segregate the individual effects of these cascading forces. Their inseparability may be why spoken language "works" so well for our species.

Ironically, the genetics that do vary from one person to the next may be at the heart of developmentally influential environmental variations. Indeed, according to Scarr and McCartney (1983), "phenotypic variation among individuals relies on experiential differences that are determined by genetic differences" (p. 429). The inexorability of the path to spoken language is assured by similar collaborations.

Though much research asks what factors distinguish two children who are genetically related or raised in the same home, in the end the factors that are most important in development are those that could not possibly differentiate any two children. Ontogenetically, the critical genetic influences and environmental effects are the ones available to all members of a species. This arrangement takes much of the risk out of human evolution, but it also presents scientists with a dilemma: "there is almost no way to assess the heritability of a species-general developmental function because there are no individual differences by definition" (McCall, 1981b, p. 4).[4]

I have discussed genetic factors that set the phenotype of the child and shape the behavioral repertoire of the adults to whom children are exposed. But even the process of parenting itself is under genetic control in mammals, since the internal changes associated with pregnancy and child bearing evidently trip off a variety of nurturant behaviors (see Krasnegor and Bridges, 1990). This should not be misconstrued to mean that the content of parenting is completely fixed. What parents do and when they do it is influenced by the external sensory and internal chemical cues that happen to be available at the time. What is species-specific more than anything else is the mother's initial diversion of her attention to the needs of her newborn child. This leaves the content and subsequent time course of parenting to some significant degree open; for "once initiated, the maintenance of parenting requires continuing stimulation of the parents by their offspring . . . *the persistence of parenting is a function of the stimulation provided by the young,* rather than a programmed sequence determined by hormones" (Eisenberg, 1990, p. 16, italics mine).

Stimulus-seeking Behavior and Its Neural Consequences

Maneuvering themselves into stimulating social circumstances is not all infants do to get the experiences they enjoy. They also expend energy in order to get desired stimulation, as we saw in Chapter 2. At one time, models of motivation assumed that animals mainly needed to reduce excessive stimulation not to seek additional stimulation different from what was already available (Ulvund, 1980).

4. The same can be said for linguistic universals, as I will discuss further in Chapter 8.

But recent evidence suggests that animals are excellent diagnosticians; they know the kinds of stimulation they (and their brains) need and they go after it. If possible, they make it happen. There is every reason to believe that the infant's episodes of active stimulus-seeking during sensitive periods of development influence the behavioral capacity of its brain.

NEURAL EFFECTS OF SELF-PRODUCED STIMULATION

Evidence from a variety of research populations and domains suggests that neonates' early sensory and motor experience challenges the brain to develop its capacity for more complex behavior. In research by a Canadian group (Dodwell, Timney, and Emerson, 1976; Timney, Emerson, and Dodwell, 1979), kittens were reared in total darkness until the end of their third month. For an hour each day, the animals were placed in an apparatus where visual stimulation (vertical stripes) was made available at the press of a bar. The authors found that at about the end of the second month (during the critical period for visual development), kittens began to press the bar frequently, and continued to do so until the end of the experiment at one hundred days. Figure 7.5 reveals that normally reared kittens did not press the bar to illuminate the visual pattern, but dark-reared kittens did.

In a second experiment, kittens were normally light reared for a period and light deprived thereafter. As before, they were given an opportunity each day to press the bar for visual stimulation. It was found that these kittens began bar pressing at about the same age as kittens in the first experiment. The stimulus seeking effect, then, was age-dependent in these studies. It was due not to previous deprivation but to the animal's maturational state and sensory experience at the time of test. In an additional experiment in which stimulation involved either the visual display or several different types of tones, dark-reared kittens pressed the bar selectively to obtain visual but not auditory stimulation. As is revealed in Figure 7.6, the kittens rarely pressed the bar for tones, and since they had not been deprived of sound, their brain would not have needed any additional auditory stimulation. On some level, the kittens "seem to know" what kinds of excitation their brain needs in order to develop; they worked only for the stimulation their brain required to reach its capacity.

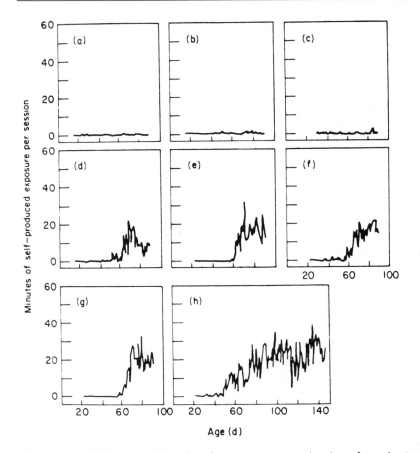

Figure 7.5. Minutes of self-produced exposure per session (equal to minutes of bar pressing) by the normal (a–c) and dark-reared (d–h) kittens, as a function of age in days.

Do human infants work for stimulation in order to "feed" developing areas of the brain? Do babies "know" what sensory nourishment their brain requires to develop fully the capacity for behavior that evolutionary changes have provided for? If there is a human auditory parallel to the kitten's need of visual stimulation, we should expect sound deprived infants to work for auditory stimulation. If they do, we might speculate that in vocalizing, infants foster the cerebral capacity to process auditory patterns; and that in babbling, infants develop the capacity of their brain to match

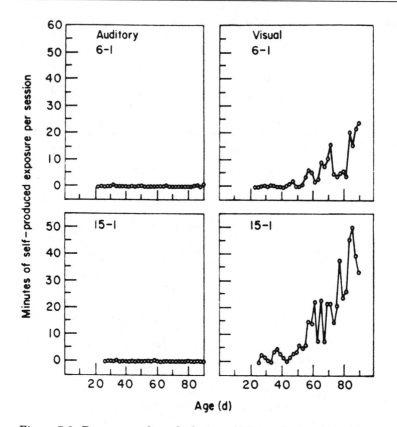

Figure 7.6. Responses of two dark-reared kittens (6-1 and 15-1) for auditory (left panels) and visual (right panels) stimulation. Although the plots appear continuous, days on which visual input could be obtained alternated with "auditory" days.

ambient auditory patterns with those of their vocal tract. According to this speculation, infants on their own initiative would build their neural capacity for spoken language on the back of their own behavior.

One might guess that sound-deprived infants would vocalize less than hearing infants, but this does not seem to be the case. Lenneberg et al. (1965) tape-recorded two groups of infants over the first three months of life. One group consisted of ten normally hearing infants being reared by their hearing parents. The other group contained six children whose parents were deaf; five of these children were hearing and one was deaf. Two of the hearing children had an older hearing sibling. Thus, this second group contained three hearing children who were exposed mainly to their deaf (and essentially nonoral) parents, and their access to phonetic stimulation was documentably less than that of the children of hearing and speaking parents. Lenneberg et al. reported that the infants who were hearing impaired or otherwise auditorily deprived cried, fussed, and cooed just as frequently as the children who were freely exposed to speech.

If infants vocalize in order to supply their brain with needed stimulation, we might expect increases in the vocalization of hearing infants during times when environmental stimulation is merely less. In Jones and Moss (1971), two-week-old infants vocalized more frequently when alone than when an observer was present (even after "protest" vocalizations had been eliminated). Delack (1976) found that infants vocalized more frequently when they were alone than when other "speakers" were in the room. This pattern was evident from the first observations at seven weeks, rose sharply at eight months, and reached a peak at nine months, when over 90 percent would have begun to babble, an activity that may well be supported by self-stimulatory intentions.

FUNCTIONAL EFFECTS OF SELF-PRODUCED STIMULATION

How do animals benefit "down the road" from the sights and sounds of their early motor activities? What harm is done when developing animals are denied the opportunity to hear both their own and other people's vocalizations? Several studies have deprived animals of self-hearing in an effort to investigate its role in vocal control or vocal learning.

Both animals and neonatal humans react when their vocal feedback is tampered with. Buchwald and Shipley (1985) found that kittens deafened at the age of four weeks vocalized much more loudly than their hearing littermates. They also observed that 80 dB of white noise caused a 10 dB increase in the vocal intensity of kittens' vocalizations. As we saw earlier, Sinnott et al. (1975) obtained similar results in macaque monkeys.

There is now a great deal of evidence that infants of all ages are willing to work hard to get certain kinds of sensory stimulation (including their mother's voice) whether they must press their tongue against an artificial nipple, push their head against a pillow, or exert manual pressure against a knob. Whether stimulation provided by an animal's *own* activity is processed differently and affects the brain differently than externally-presented stimulation is difficult to say on the basis of present evidence. Ploog (1979) reported that in the squirrel monkey there are some auditory cortical cells that do not respond to self-produced calls (even those that are artificially elicited by electrical stimulation) but do respond to externally presented tape recordings of the same sounds. This finding is congruent with Perrett et al.'s (1990) discovery of tactile cells that do not respond to touch if the movement producing contact is the animal's own. It would be interesting to know if there are some afferent cells that respond only to the primate's own vocal activity. This is apparently the case in white-crowned sparrows (Margoliash, 1987), and it may be in humans as well (Creutzfeldt et al., 1989a, 1989b).

Developmental Neurophysiology of Affect

Lamendella (1977) has written that the limbic system plays a large role in the neonate's processing of facial and vocal stimulation. In particular, he sees the anterior affective subsystem as

> the means by which the infant is assimilated into a network of social relationships; that is, it controls a variety of instinctual interactions of the infant such as the establishment of the primary attachment with its mother and the special attention the infant pays to the human face and voice. This subsystem produces an abundance of sign behavior that communicates information about the affective state of the infant from which people may make more specific inferences. This level of limbic activity controls many involuntary oro-facial behavior sequences, facial expressions, agonistic vocalizations, and the standard set of primordial cries of our species. (p. 193)

LeDoux (1992) seems less certain. He has observed that there are no objective criteria that clearly define the limbic system anatomically and that most limbic areas are unnecessary for the emotional processes studied thus far. However, one specific limbic structure—the amygdala—does seem to play an important role in emotion, and LeDoux calls for more research on the brain's role in emotional behavior, including the functions of the limbic system.

One thing is clear. If the limbic system is responsible for much of our emotional experience, it will be difficult to deal adequately with the developmental neurology of the developmental growth path leading from affective communication to spoken language because limbic activities are inaccessible to surface electrophysiological recordings. For this and other reasons, most of our imputations regarding the role of the brain in the development of affective control involve the more accessible cortex. A review of this more cortically oriented literature suggests that the right hemisphere controls facial displays of emotion in infants and adults more than the left. However, Fox and Davidson (1986) found that lateralization patterns can differ for positive and negative emotions. In an interesting study of two- and three-day-old neonates, they took EEG recordings from frontal and parietal areas bilaterally while orally administering several solutions including sucrose, which was to be an experimental condition, and distilled water, which was to serve as a control. Consistent with expectations based on previous research, there was greater activation of the right hemisphere than the left at both sites during the administration of sucrose.

In the end, water turned out not to be a control condition, or at least the kind of control condition that Fox and Davidson had in mind, since the newborns had an unexpected aversion to distilled water, which they conveyed with facial expressions the researchers interpreted as disgust. And instead of finding no interhemispheric differences during the administration of water, Fox and Davidson observed greater activation of the left hemisphere than the right at both recording sites. They concluded that both positive and negative emotions were lateralized in neonates, and in opposite directions.[5]

Investigators without access to EEG may be pleased to know that the hemisphericity of affect is not merely revealed in exotic electrophysiological studies. It also is exposed to the naked eye! As in handedness, one side of the face is used more than the other. In adults and older children, the left side of the face reveals more emotion than the right. This is consistent with the fact that the right cerebral hemisphere, which activates the left side of the face,

5. This finding of negative affect in the left hemisphere and positive affect in the right hemisphere has also been found in adults using sodium amobarbital injections (Lee et al., 1990).

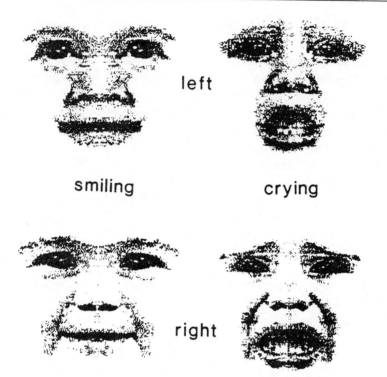

left

smiling   crying

right

Figure 7.7. Chimeric photos used to test laterality effects in infants' face-scanning behavior.

is more involved in the emotions. But the story is very different for infants.

Working from photographs of seven- to thirteen-month-olds who were caught in the act of smiling or crying, Best and Queen (1989) made mirror-image reproductions of the left or right half of the face. Figure 7.7 shows some of these "chimeric" stimuli. Photos like these were shown to adults, who were asked to judge their emotionality. It was found that among these infants, the right side of the face carried more information about emotional expressions than the left. A second study showed that, beginning at about seven months, there again was a stronger rightward bias, which derived more from the mouth region than from the eyes and eyebrows.

Best and Queen explained their findings in the following way. Brain research suggests that as the neocortex begins to mature, its initial influence is to inhibit lower neural centers, hence the disappearance of neonatal reflexive and spontaneous behavior patterns. Therefore, the right hemiface bias they observed could reflect the inhibition of subcortically mediated influences on the left hemiface. Later, with additional maturation, the cortex would develop sufficiently to do what genes ultimately intend—to actively guide and control voluntary behavior—and at that point the right hemisphere would be more fully in charge of expressing emotion.

That the left side of the face carries more emotion than the right in adults and children is consistent with the fact that the right cerebral hemisphere is more involved in affective expression than the left. The right hemisphere is also more active than the left in the processing of facial emotion from a fairly early age (Levine et al., 1987). In addition, there is evidence to suggest that face recognition in infants and children is the result of activity occurring mainly in the right cerebral hemisphere (deSchonen, Gil de Diaz, and Mathivet, 1986; Levine, 1985; Young and Ellis, 1976; Young and Bion, 1980).

CEREBRAL LATERALITY AND LANGUAGE DEVELOPMENT

Facial and vocal affective communication may be controlled bilaterally or through a greater involvement of the right than the left hemisphere, but the coordination of manual- and speech-motor activity is sited principally in the left hemisphere in most individuals. In phylogeny, it may have been this asymmetry of fine motor control that coaxed linguistic communication into the left hemisphere in the first place (Ojemann, 1984; MacNeilage, 1986), with perception—for reasons of efficiency—taking an adjacent location.

There are ontogenetic parallels. On logical grounds, the child's discovery of the phoneme and attendant analyses of words into their component segments increases the coordinative responsibilities associated with lexical expression. What had been or were destined to be holistic, "logophonic" patterns are henceforth conceptualized pluralistically as concatenations of individual elements. One assumes that spoken vocabulary cannot increase beyond certain limits without a neural mechanism to control the oral-motor activities needed for deployment of linguistic segments. To understand the emergence of linguistic capacity, then, it becomes necessary to trace the development of the lateralized motor functions associated with communication and to ask about their own natural history independent of any association with language.

EARLY EXPRESSIONS OF CEREBRAL LATERALIZATION

The earliest documented expressions of physically lateralized behavior in the human infant are cephalic and manual; later in development, lateralization will be expressed ocularly and, of course, vocally. Because certain structures are larger in the left hemisphere of the fetal brain, it would not be surprising to find disproportionate movement of, or orientation to the right side of the body. And, indeed, there seems to be some evidence that lying in the birth canal, the fetus's head is more likely to be turned to the right than to the left. This is at least the prevailing direction of head orientation at birth (Michel and Goodwin, 1979), and it is the predominant head orientation in the first few weeks of life (Hopkins et al., 1987; Liederman and Kinsbourne, 1980a, 1980b; Turkewitz and Creighton, 1974).

The earliest lateralizations of manual behavior are also primarily dextral (Butterworth and Hopkins, 1988; Cobb, Goodwin, and Saelens, 1966; Hawn and Harris, 1983; Mebert, 1983; Petrie and Peters, 1980; Provins, Dalziel, and Higginbottom, 1987), although these indications are task- and measure-sensitive and may (or may seem to) wax and wane for some months before stabilizing. Indeed, many children who seem to start out with a left hand preference may shift at some point to a right hand preference. A shift from the predominant use of the left hand to the right hand in infancy could index other changes, such as a shift from exclusive reliance upon right hemisphere–controlled affective communication to a dual system that now includes left hemisphere–controlled phonological language. In this sense, transitory left handedness might be an indirect clue that the infant is treading the vocal-facial path that extends from affective communication to spoken language. Increasing reliance upon the right hand may be an indication that the infant has progressed past the first motoric turn in the path.

Manual laterality preferences may have a hereditary factor. Children are less likely to be right-handed if they come from families in which one or both parents is left-handed (Hawn and Harris, 1983; Liederman and Kinsbourne, 1980a, 1980b). Research on adults (Bever et al., 1989) shows that right-handers with left handedness in their family behave very differently on a variety of language tasks than right-handers from nonleft-handed families.

MANUAL LATERALITY AND SPEECH

To my knowledge, the earliest evidence of speech lateralization—which, as it turns out, was motorically expressed—was obtained by Segalowitz and Chapman (1980). Their subjects had an average conceptional age of thirty-six weeks at the time of observation but, because they were delivered prematurely, were tested *ex utero*. The investigators recorded the infants' limb activity following a period of exposure to either a woman's speech or classical music. They found that tremors of the right arm more than those of the left were selectively quieted by speech but not by music. Although the mediating mechanism was unclear, this research established a very early link between the sound of speech and motor control functions of the left hemisphere.

The next earliest evidence of speech lateralization with which I am familiar was obtained in the first week of life. At this age, binaurally presented speech (but not other sounds) evoked more left than right hemisphere activity in an infant studied by Molfese et al. (1975). This hemisphere appears to be unusually sensitive to consonantal contrasts at as early as four days of age (Bertoncini et al., 1989). It appears that the left hemisphere is where infants *want* speech. Prescott and DeCasper (in submission) found that newborns will suck harder to get maternal voice into the right ear (mainly left hemisphere), but will suck harder to get nonvocal sounds into the left ear.

Other evidence of cerebral lateralization for speech was obtained by Best, Hoffman, and Glanville (1982), who tested for ear asymmetries using a dichotic method of presentation and a measure of cardiac activity. Two-month-olds showed a left ear (right hemisphere) advantage for music but no advantage for speech; three- and four-month-old subjects showed both effects. (Other such studies are described and interpreted in an excellent review by Best, 1988.)

Early manual behavior seems to tell us something about a child's cerebral lateralization for speech. Fogel and Hannan (1985) caught an early glimpse of this relationship when they looked at the emergence of manual, facial, and vocal behavior in infants between nine and fifteen weeks of age. When pointing followed silent mouth movements, it was significantly more likely to be right- than left-handed. However, when pointing followed vocalization, which at the ages in question would be affective and not syllabic, it was significantly more likely to be left-handed. These behaviors seem to anticipate cerebral relationships that will stabilize in early childhood as a right hemisphere priority for vocal affect and a left hemisphere priority for articulate speech.

A NOTE ON "LAB SPEECH"

I want to note a complication that arises in laboratory studies that use synthetic speech. When adults speak, infants get needed information about their voices. But the speech elements that carry the most vocal information are *vowels* to those who utter them. They are also vowels to developmental psycholinguists, which is why we have not recognized this disparity or seen it as a problem. As a result, one finds laboratory studies of infants' perception in which the stimulus (for example, [a]) is referred to as a vowel instead of a piece of voice. This extravocalic orientation is why synthetic speech is usually endowed with only the critical segmental cues and the minimal amount of other information needed for the stimulus to sound somewhat "natural." It is the phonetic equivalent of a black-on-white line drawing. Thus, the customary stimulus in experimental phonetics is a deprived stimulus, completely devoid of either personal identity or emotionality—an impersonal poker voice.[6]

Under such circumstances, it would not be surprising to find that the right hemisphere was less active than the left, not because the sound was "heard as speech" and processed in the left hemisphere, but simply because it lacked emotionally salient properties and was therefore of little interest to the right hemisphere. In time, infants

6. Van Lancker (1991) has marshalled a large amount of evidence in support of her argument that the right hemisphere is not just partial to facial and vocal displays of emotion but is, in effect, predisposed to handle all information—whatever the modality—that is intensely *personal*. She has proposed that individuals assign personally relevant information a high emotional value and suggested that personal familiarity is properly regarded as an affective state. In principle, it is possible that the hemispheric resources used to analyze speech are influenced by the degree of familiarity and personal relevance that speech holds for the listener.

develop the cognitive sophistication to discover that voices are also vowels. At that point, the vowel is understood to contain information not just about the identity and social intentions of the speaker but about the vowel itself and any adjacent consonants. One might speculate that as a depersonalized element, the vowel has a greater chance of being processed in both hemispheres.

RELATIONSHIP BETWEEN SPEAKING AND HAND MOVEMENTS

"It is common knowledge that people move their hands while speaking," declared Doreen Kimura twenty years ago. But until her own studies, few had explored the relationship between manual gesture and speech. In a classic experiment (Kimura, 1973a), she observed manual activity while right-handed adults spoke on various topics, silently read limericks, or visually attempted to locate geometric figures embedded in a larger display. Kimura classified all hand movements as either "self-touching" (such as grooming) or "free." She discovered significantly more free movements in the speaking exercise than in the two silent conditions and significantly more right- than left-hand free movements during speech. One might suppose that this lateral bias merely reflects the fact that subjects were preselected to be right-handed. However, where self-touching movements were concerned, the left hand was involved as much as or more frequently than the right hand. In a second study, free right-hand movements again predominated during speaking but not during a nonverbal vocal exercise (humming).

What does this have to do with the locus of speech control? Of the sixty-five subjects whose hand movements were recorded in the studies above, it turned out that seven made more free movements of the left hand than of the right, and six of these subjects were among thirty-four who were available for further service in a dichotic listening experiment. Analysis of ear effects from that task indicated that four of the six left-hand–dominant subjects had a left-ear advantage on the dichotic task. This differed reliably from the performance of the right-hand dominant subjects, most of whom displayed a right-ear superiority on the dichotic task. Kimura speculated that "there is some system common to control of both free movements and speaking . . . this system, for most people, is based primarily in the left hemisphere" (p. 49).

In a companion experiment (Kimura, 1973b), the hand movements and ear preferences of subjects who were right-handed were compared to those who were left-handed or ambidextrous. In the free movement analysis, Kimura found, as expected, that right-handed subjects with the species-typical dichotic right-ear advantage made significantly more right-hand than left-hand movements during speaking. Next, she found that left-handed or ambidextrous subjects with a dichotic right-ear advantage, that is, individuals whose speech and hand control centers were based in *different hemispheres,* made about the same number of left-hand and right-hand movements while talking. Finally, left-handed subjects with a dichotic left-ear advantage were far more likely to use the left hand during speaking. We can conclude from these findings that free hand activity during speech permits us to infer which side of the brain is dominant for spoken language and can support estimates of the degree of asymmetry between hemispheres.

"TAPPING" THE SPEECH CONTROL MECHANISM

These links between vocalization and hand movement are the basis for a "tapping" (or "competition") paradigm that has been used with a variety of populations. In this paradigm, the individual talks or otherwise vocalizes while tapping a telegraph or computer key as fast as possible with the left or right hand. Since one hand is controlled by the hemisphere that is primarily responsible for spoken language, we can infer the hemispheric locus of speech by finding out which hand provides the greater interference with speech but not with vocalization.

Marcel Kinsbourne may have been the first to exploit the competition paradigm. In an early study (Kinsbourne and McMurray, 1975), five-year-olds tapped first in a nonspeaking control condition and then in two speech tasks in which they concurrently recited a nursery rhyme or repeated the names of four familiar animals. In the control condition, it was found that right-hand tapping was significantly faster than left-hand tapping. Both speaking conditions significantly slowed tapping with right and left hands but seemed to exert a disproportionate effect on the right hand.

In a more elaborate study, Piazza (1977) presented a large number of three- to five-year-old right-handers with both a dichotic listening task and a tapping task. Overall, she obtained a right-ear advantage for verbal material and a left-ear advantage for nonverbal material on the dichotic task. These effects varied somewhat with gender and generally seemed to increase with age. In the tapping task, Piazza asked a different group of three- to five-year-old right-handers to tap with left or right hands while quiet, reciting a familiar rhyme, or humming. As had been expected, speaking slowed the right hand more than the left and humming slowed the left hand more than the right. These findings were replicated and slightly extended in a later study by White and Kinsbourne (1980).

Taken together, these naturalistic and experimental studies of spontaneous hand activity during speech lay the groundwork for developmental and clinical questions about cerebral organization and the allocation of hemispheric processing resources for spoken language. To a degree, they also validate the use of certain hand-edness and hand activity tasks as indices of cerebral organization. These tasks can be used to investigate the manual activity and hand preferences of individuals with variations in linguistic experience and developmental linguistic success.

HAND PREFERENCE IN THE DEAF

In 1974, I conducted a study in a so-called "oral" school for the deaf. My adolescent subjects were first asked to look at letters that were presented one-by-one on a slide screen and then to write down, in order, those they recalled. Much to my astonishment, the first seven subjects wrote with their left hand. I continued to take note of the writing handedness of all subsequent subjects and found that about 30 percent were left-handed. Raising these statistics with teachers at the school, I found that they had long known about deaf children's greater than expected sinistrality. One teacher thought it might be ushered in by the damage that occurs to the brain in children with acquired deafness. My own guess was very different, having just read that Genie, a socially deprived girl exposed to very little speech from the age of twenty months to about thirteen years, was adjudged from dichotic listening tests to be right-hemisphere dominant for speech (Fromkin et al., 1974). On the assumption that exposure to speech trips off neural reactions capable of altering cerebral organization (as expressed in hand preferences), I conjectured that those who had never heard would be more likely to be left-handed because they would not have had the left-hemisphere experiences that are associated with speech.

A check of the files on my subjects was disappointing. In most cases, either the cause or the probable age of deafness was uncertain. Fortunately, however, we now have a few empirical reports on the manual lateralization of deaf subjects, and they are theoretically enlightening. In the early eighties, John Bonvillian and his colleagues at the University of Virginia (Bonvillian, Orlansky, and Garland, 1982) administered a hand preference questionnaire to several hundred deaf and normally hearing young adults. Though both groups were predominantly right-handed, there were significantly more left-handers among the deaf subjects. Bonvillian et al. then looked more closely at thirty-three deaf subjects who were left-handed in nearly all activities queried, including writing. These left-handers were far less likely to have deaf relatives than the group as a whole.

Why do strongly left-handed deaf individuals have a lower incidence of hearing-impaired relatives than other deaf individuals? Or, said differently, why are deaf individuals from hearing homes less likely to be strongly left-handed? The reason, Bonvillian et al. speculated, was that these individuals would have received less exposure to manual language, which tends to be processed in the left hemisphere. But there are other sources of variation among deaf individuals with no family history of hearing impairment. For one thing, since their own deafness was evidently not hereditary, the incidence of acquired deafness may have been higher among the left-handers. With acquired deafness, of course, one might expect a higher incidence of damage to, and reorganization of, the brain beyond the sensory loss associated with deafness.[7]

Gibson and Bryden (1984) administered a dichaptic task to deaf and hearing preadolescents in which these subjects were to feel a palpable letter or shape with each hand and then to point out both stimuli in a larger display. The task was a tactile analogue to dichotic listening, without oral report. With the letters, the deaf had a significant left-hand advantage and the hearing revealed a significant right-hand advantage. As for the shapes, the deaf showed no difference between right and left hands; the hearing

---

7. Conrad (1979) offered this same explanation for a set of similar data obtained on deaf adolescents in Great Britain.

showed a left-hand advantage. Several possible explanations were advanced to account for these disparate findings, including the obvious one, that the hearing children used a phonetic strategy for the letters and a spatial strategy for the shapes, while the deaf subjects used a spatial processing scheme for both types of stimuli.

Earlier, we looked at the yield of the tapping paradigm with hearing children who rapidly pressed a telegraph key while speaking. Marcotte and LaBarba (1987) were able to use this paradigm with two groups of deaf adolescents (and hearing controls). One group was born deaf, mainly because of maternal rubella or hereditary factors; the other group had lost hearing between two and thirty-six months after birth. All were right-handed and attended a school that encouraged communication by speech and signs. In the experimental task, subjects tapped without verbalizing or while uttering syllables ("ba-ba"), words ("cat-dog-horse"), or a phrase ("How are you?"). Consistent with the findings of other investigators, the hearing subjects showed a significant suppression of right-hand but not left-hand tapping under all three speaking conditions, relative to baseline measurements. However, in both deaf groups, speaking suppressed left- and right-hand tapping about equally, causing the authors to conclude that deaf individuals have an "anomalous (bilateral) brain organization for speech production" (p. 286).

Marcotte and LaBarba also analyzed tapping suppression patterns in relation to the age of the onset of deafness in the group with acquired hearing losses. This analysis revealed a strong association between deafness acquired between birth and eighteen months and atypical brain organization for speech production. However, in two subgroups—one whose deafness began between twenty-two and thirty-six months of age, and a second whose deafness began between thirty and thirty-six months—there was significant and equal suppression of right-hand tapping on all three speech tasks. Left-hand tapping was not affected by two of the three speech tasks but was reduced by the third ("cat-dog-horse"). These results suggest that when deafness begins between two and three years of age, cerebral dominance for speech is likely to be mixed.

In a final analysis, Marcotte and LaBarba used difference scores to set up a system for classifying the hemispheric dominance of individual subjects. This produced the following distribution of scores:

	Dominant hemisphere for speech production		
	Left	Bilateral	Right
Congenitally deaf (N = 16)	19	43	38
Acquired 2–18 mos. (N = 13)	38	39	23
Acquired 22–36 mos. (N = 9)	44	34	22
Hearing (N = 16)	88	12	0

As this tabulation makes clear, left-hemisphericity for speech production increases and bilaterality and right-hemisphericity decreases with amount of "hearing time" over the first three years of life. One assumes that period of hearing effectively translates into degree of exposure to sounds that tend to be processed in the left hemisphere—for all intents and purposes, speech—although the critical variable could be the children's own production experience. In this regard, the hearing subjects had something in common with those who lost their hearing between twenty-two and thirty-six months: all subjects in both groups would probably have begun babbling between six and ten months and, thus, would have had ample time to achieve and use expressive vocabulary. This would be true of a few subjects in the two- to eighteen-month-old group, and of course the congenitally deaf would be expected to begin babbling late and perhaps do less of it.

Under normal conditions, the age of babbling onset is probably influenced by neuromotor maturation of the supplementary motor area (MacNeilage and Davis, 1990b) as well as auditory experience, since there is a four- to five-month range of onset in hearing infants. If development of vocal control encourages growth of manual control capabilities, one might speculate that infants who begin to babble early will be more likely to end up right-handed than late babblers. Where hearing is normal, we may suppose that late onset of babbling points to maturational delays in neuromotor development. These neuromotor delays, independently or in collaboration with reduced babbling experience, may further forestall the cortical differentiation which normally leads to manual (among other) asymmetries.

Congenitally deaf babies participate in (right hemisphere) affective facial communication without receiving concurrent phonetic stimulation. This might be expected to encourage development of the right more than the left hemisphere and should lead to left-handedness and babbling that is delayed and possibly poorly formed. It would be "right-hemisphere babbling" and perhaps for that reason less precisely coordinated, less variegated. In the normally hearing infant, there is (right hemisphere) affective facial stimulation, but it is almost invariably paired with auditory phonetic experience and, when babbling begins, motor-phonetic experience. The left hemisphere of the hearing infant therefore receives more phonetic stimulation, and presumably responds to this experience by generating additional myelin and additional dendritic branches. The auditory cortex develops more quickly than it otherwise would, as does dominance of the left hemisphere over the right. According to this conjecture, parallel development of vocal-motor centers as well as those involved in perceptual processing cause babbling to begin and to elaborate earlier in hearing than in deaf infants.

HAND PREFERENCE IN THE RETARDED

Neuropsychological studies (Bellugi et al., 1990) reveal that individuals with Williams syndrome, although they characteristically perform poorly on visuospatial tasks, tend to have an essentially normal ability to discriminate unfamiliar faces and are more likely to be left-handed (Trauner, Bellugi, and Chase, 1989). Adolescents with Down syndrome, by contrast, show marked deficits in face processing and tend to be right-handed. We might suppose that those with Williams syndrome have a higher functioning right hemisphere than left, and this would fit with their characteristic use of empty phrases, which studies of aphasia suggest the (intact) right hemisphere is all too happy to accommodate.

LATERALIZED GAZE

The direction of eye gaze can tell us something about an individual's cerebral laterality and possibly even the type of cognitive processing that individual is undertaking. In MacKain et al. (1983), as we saw earlier, a woman silently articulated two different CVCV constructions on each of two videoscreens while infants heard a synchronous sound pattern that matched the activity on one of the screens.

Infants looked longer at the face whose movements corresponded to what they heard but only when these congruent trials were displayed on the right screen, which suggests that infants' intermodal matching capability is performed by the hemisphere that is responsible for speech processing. In a subsequent post hoc inquiry (MacKain et al., 1983), the authors found that all infants who failed to show the right lateralization effect were from families having one or more left-handed members.

Additional observations on infants' lateralized visual behavior at somewhat later periods in development are available. One group of investigators (Mount et al., 1989) found evidence of lateralized looking behavior among the infants who had served in a previous, unrelated experiment on object categorization. At monthly intervals, each subject in the categorization task also produced a spontaneous language sample from which the investigators computed mean length of utterance (MLU). Analyzing only the control trials, in which pairs of identical pictures had been presented, Mount et al. observed a significant rightward eye gaze beginning at about fourteen months and increasing monotonically over the eight remaining months of the study. They then computed month by month correlations between rightward looking bias and MLU. The correlations were low and nonsignificant at the younger intervals, but attained significance at 20 and 21 months, with r values of .90 and .74, respectively. The authors concluded that "the acceleration of vocabulary and maturational changes in the central nervous system that occur between 16 and 22 months are associated with a special excitatory state in the temporal cortex of the left hemisphere" (p. 406).

Sensitive Period for Language

Many psychologists and linguists have asked about the possible existence of a critical or sensitive period for the acquisition of spoken language. Their inquiry was set in motion by Eric Lenneberg (1967), who claimed that "most individuals of average intelligence are able to learn a second language after the beginning of their second decade, although the incidence of 'language-learning-blocks' rapidly increases after puberty. Also automatic acquisition from mere exposure to a given language seems to disappear after this age, and foreign languages have to be taught and learned through a conscious and labored effort. Foreign accents cannot be overcome easily after puberty" (p. 176).

Lenneberg knew there were critical periods in animals, but he also understood the hazards of generalizing from animal learning to human learning and language acquisition. In fact, some of the research that sparked consideration of a critical period for language was reported after the publication of Lenneberg's book, *Biological Foundations of Language*. For example, research on sparrows conducted in the early eighties, much of it by Peter Marler and his associates (Marler and Peters, 1982a, 1982b, 1982c; Marler and Sherman, 1983), described a sharply demarcated interval within which exposure to conspecific song is "critical" and outside of which song stimulation has demonstrably little value. These studies were typically conducted with cage-reared birds exposed only to recorded songs. Subsequent research revealed that birds reared socially—in the wild—continue to learn and improvise song for considerably longer periods of time (Baptista and Petrinovich, 1984, 1986). Partly as a consequence of such findings,[8] the term "critical" period has been softened to "sensitive" period, both in the nonhuman animal literature and in writings on human language (Oyama, 1976). The distinction may still have some theoretical utility, however. Knudsen and Knudsen (1990) make a neurological distinction between critical and sensitive periods: critical periods are characterized by the stabilization of synaptic gain, sensitive periods by the potential for anatomical modification.

Bateson (1979) envisioned several different types of sensitive periods, which are represented by the "developmental trains" in Figure 7.8. Bateson felt that his train window analogy worked if we pretend that the windows are opaque and that the passengers can take in no information unless the windows are opened. In Stage 1, the windows in each of the developmental trains are closed. This changes in Stage 2. In the top panel, all the windows in the train remain closed until the second stage, when each opens briefly and then completely closes down. Bateson considered this scenario an

---

8. Hinde (1970) also advocated the term "sensitive period" because it reflects the more nearly gradual nature of the offset, a preference with which Lenneberg is said to have concurred (Oyama, 1976).

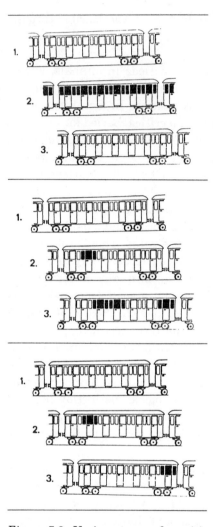

Figure 7.8. Various types of sensitive periods as illustrated by Bateson's passenger trains. Spoken language most closely resembles the cars in the bottom panel, although still imperfectly (see text).

extreme view. In the middle panel, windows open at different times but each remains open for the rest of the journey. In the bottom panel, certain windows open at a particular stage in the developmental journey and then shut during a later stage when other windows open up.

Where is spoken language in all this? On one level we must assume that none of these depictions is exactly right, since the sensory windows to attachment and vocal affect typically are open before or within the first few days of birth. But with this one qualification, I am inclined to put my money on the bottom panel, or a cross between that depiction and the one above it. I see a need to open the windows of prosody in Stage 1 and keep them open in Stage 2. After that I would lower them most of the way (not an alternative Bateson gives us) in Stage 3 and throw open the windows to linguistic grammars.

What do our young derive from all this? When the window to vocal resonance and prosody is open, the infant has an opportunity to learn the voices of its mother and other caregivers and family members. To guard against potentially risky false positives, it is perhaps best that the window be open only briefly; in any case, an early closing poses no problems because the needed stimulation naturally occurs in an interval that is early and short. Beyond such a safeguard, what benefits accrue when a window is closed, when the infant is prevented from taking in additional information? In principle, the infant's special relationship with its mother could suffer if its ability to respond differentially to her voice were thrown off or its ability to interpret maternal prosody and resonance patterns were modified by subsequent input.

Babies encounter their family members at an early age and learn to interact with them over a restricted period. There seems to be no reason to keep intake systems wide open after this has been accomplished. If we are to respect family structure there may also be reasons to begin shutting down such systems after infants become safely socialized with their parents and siblings. For these reasons, too, a sensitive period for person-identifying vocal resonance and prosody is beneficial. Ontogenetically, the mechanisms of social cognition responsible for infants' entrée to spoken language may seize upon this primary fact and use it in much the same way that Gould and Lewontin (1984) imagine Italian cathedral painters once appropriated the spandrel for their art.

The fact that learning systems remain somewhat open after the initial period of greatest sensitivity takes nothing away from the biological significance of the original period. As Bateson observed, "the fact that in some circumstances the effects of experience can be over-ridden by subsequent events, does not alter the adaptive significance of either the timing or the mechanisms that normally protect preferences from subsequent disruption" (p. 483). He added that even after the closing of windows, there is still the possibility of continued learning under specialized conditions: "the occupants can, under certain circumstances, be persuaded to study strange things outside the train later in the journey" (p. 475). Linguistic examples might include the language course needed for college graduation or communicative proficiency required for employment abroad.

To be accurate, we probably should speak in the plural of sensitive *periods* for language, as several animal ethologists recently advised (Rauschecker and Marler, 1987), because if language depends on a number of sensory and motoric functions, as it surely must, then aspects of language could each have their own period of maximal sensitivity. One can well imagine that prosody, segmental phonetics and phonology, and morphology and semantics are governed by neural systems that differ in this respect.

If the brain is unusually receptive to or influenced by linguistic stimulation at particular stages in its development, what accounts for this unusual responsivity? Why does this receptivity seemingly dissipate in children but linger in some adults? At this point, one can only speculate that answers at the neural level lie in our changing neurochemistry. While noting the existence of literature on both sides of the question, Rauschecker (1987) concluded a recent review of nonhuman animal research with the observation that "the current trend seems to attribute at least partial responsibility for the existence of critical period plasticity to norepinephrine" (p. 203). One might suppose that in humans—as in songbirds—variations in the levels of particular hormones and neurotransmitters may somehow be linked to vocal learning, although this has yet to be demonstrated.

Was Lenneberg right in his assertion that "automatic acquisition from mere exposure" declines with age and that speech accents are particularly difficult to overcome? I have a pragmatic reason for revisiting these claims: if we knew what determines the offset or controls the length of a sensitive period for languages learned after infancy, we might be a step ahead in our efforts to explain the development of *native language*. Something in the brain must change to lower or close developmental windows. Bateson (1979) has said that "the timing of the ending of the sensitive period is also dependent on the internal processes responsible for opening the window in the first place" (p. 475). I do not know what the brain changes are, but the biological need for them is satisfied, as I have said, by a thriving social and emotional relationship between the infant and caregivers, both real and prospective.

At present, we understand too little about the action and inter-action of hormonal, neural, cognitive, social, and a variety of other factors in children's acquisition of their first language. Most of us are confident that these factors play important roles, but we know little about how their influence is exerted. Consequently, there are currently no adequate scientific responses to the most elementary ontogenetic questions, such as what brain signals cause infants to attend to, store, and imitate speech. But if we could find out which factors declined with the ability to learn spoken language after infancy, we would then be in a good position to ask if those factors contribute to emergence of the mother tongue.

A reading of the relevant research suggests, as does the concept of a sensitive period, that the capacity to learn and to produce spoken language is not, in fact, stable over the early lifetime of humans, especially if one's attention is limited to accent or other phonetic factors. Later, I will look at a neural precondition for the special effects of early experience—cerebral plasticity—and briefly review some of the language research, paying especial attention to two points: (1) evidence of phonetic or phonological selectivity and (2) age of decline of phonetic sensitivity.

CEREBRAL PLASTICITY

Animals with a large brain and relatively short gestation period must have the capacity to respond readily to experience. Yet this capacity does not exist merely to subserve language. Anatomical changes in sensory and motor systems also require cerebral adjust-ments. Consider the problems presented by expanding head circum-ference. In apes and most other mammals, the sutures of the skull fuse fairly soon after birth, but in humans skull fusion does not occur until adulthood, so there is room for the brain to expand and, therefore, for neural structures to develop in response to experience. But increases in head circumference do not merely accommodate a growing brain whose composition responds to experience, they also *require* cerebral plasticity. Although newborns can localize sound, increases in head circumference affect auditory localization by increasing inter-aural distance, throwing off calculations based on previous structural arrangements (Clifton et al., 1988). This change requires neural adaptations (Knudsen, 1985; Beggs and Foreman, 1980). Neural adaptations are also required by architectural changes in the vocal tract, especially over the first four to five months and probably over the first year of life. The internal representations for any vocal targets requiring precise positioning of the articulators have to be modified as the size of the tongue changes in relation to the available space in the oral cavity.

COMPETITION

In humans, it is possible to study the effects of sensory deprivation upon brain development indirectly. Neville, Schmidt, and Kutas (1983) found that on the surface of temporal cortex, a region normally associated with auditory processing, visual peripheral stimulation evoked larger brain responses in congenitally deaf subjects than in hearing subjects. Using resting EEG with a similar population, Wolff and Thatcher (1990) observed decreased cerebral differentiation, especially in the left fronto-temporal area, and increased differentiation in the right hemisphere relative to hearing controls. These studies suggest that auditory deprivation does not prevent development of auditory cortex because visual (and probably other) stimulation—without competing audition—usurps that region of the brain for itself. Studies reveal that sensorily dedicated brain regions, such as auditory cortex, visual cortex, and so on are hooked up normally to handle auditory or visual stimulation but are "up for grabs" should Nature or an experimental neurophysiologist (Frost, 1989; Roe et al., 1990) link things up differently.

As Rakic (1989) has suggested, synaptogenesis is heavily influenced by multiple sources of stimulation, all competing for neural capacity more or less simultaneously. Following unimodal sensory deprivation, there are two types of change: "compensatory hypertrophy," increased growth and activity of remaining sensory systems that do not have to compete with the "undernourished" system, and early growth (experience-expectant, in Greenough's terms) in the "disconnected" area that is maintained by sensory functions

normally handled in adjacent brain regions. Among the congenitally deaf, according to Neville (in press), both the anterior expansion into areas normally used for auditory processing and the increased activity in posterior areas could be accounted for by early
visual afferents that are stabilized by visual experience when there
is no competing input from the auditory modality.

LANGUAGE DATA

In an excellent review, Snow (1987) identified a number of studies
that produced evidence of language learning outside the sensitive
period as it is normally construed. Some of this research reported
trials in which languages were learned faster by adults than by
children. They did not necessarily end up at the same point as the
children, however, and Snow cited several cases in which the adults
were less competent after equivalent amounts of exposure or training.

Newport (1991) administered a grammaticality judgment test to
Chinese- and Korean-speaking immigrants to the United States
and analyzed responses in relation to age of initial exposure to
English. The test contained twelve types of rules of English morphology and syntax. Newport found that accuracy of judgment,
viewed against native performance, declined significantly following
the youngest age of initial exposure, at three to seven years (see
Figure 7.9). Multiple regression analyses revealed that judgment
accuracy was independent of many factors that normally would be
considered important, including formal instruction and length of
experience in English, amount of initial exposure to English, and
reported motivation to learn the language, as well as several other
factors.

What of phonetic effects? Snow's (1987) review implied that differences at this level may be our best (if not only) evidence of a
sensitive period for language. "Assessments of accent," she wrote,
"typically find that correctness of accent is negatively related to
age at first exposure to the second language, suggesting that
younger learners are more likely eventually to lose their accents
than older learners" (pp. 194–195). In earlier work, Snow and Hoef-
nagel-Hohle (1978) measured discrimination of Dutch speech by
two groups of English-speaking subjects. The "Beginners" were just
beginning to learn Dutch, while subjects in the "Advanced" group

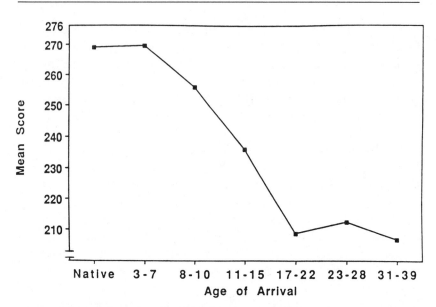

Figure 7.9. Total score on a test of English grammar in relation to age of arrival in the United States.

had been living in Holland and speaking Dutch for at least eighteen months at the time of test. Beginners were tested three times during their first year in Holland. As Figure 7.10 reveals, there was a steady improvement in discrimination performance until adolescence, after which discrimination errors increased.

Oyama (1976) found a strong negative relationship between degree of accent and age of learning English. This effect was independent of the learner's length of stay in the United States. Wondering if accent was a motoric or a perceptual phenomenon, she then looked at comprehension of English sentences heard against white noise by native English speakers and by Italian immigrants who had come to the States at different ages (Oyama, 1978). About a third of the subjects had immigrated between the ages of six and ten, and another third between the ages of eleven and fifteen; the remainder had been in the United States since the age of sixteen to twenty years. Oyama found a highly significant (negative) correlation between age of entry and comprehension, even when length of residence was statistically controlled. Using the performance of native speakers as a benchmark, I calculated that in descending order of

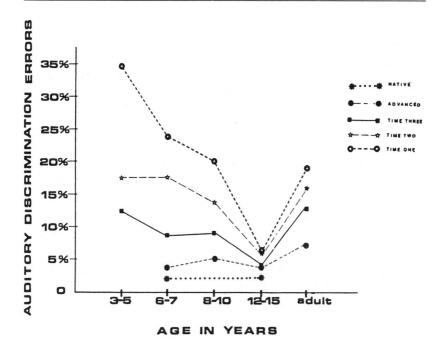

Figure 7.10. Discrimination of Dutch speech by advanced and beginning groups of native-English speakers and by a reference group of native-Dutch speakers.

exposure to English, Oyama's subjects achieved comprehension scores of 92.8 percent, 75.7 percent, and 70.5 percent. Oyama concluded that accent "is not exclusively a matter of getting the articulatory apparatus to do the right things" (p. 9).

In a similar vein, Snow and Hoefnagal-Hohle (1978) found that by nine to twelve months after their first exposure to Dutch, English-speaking subjects with the best pronunciation scores also achieved the best performance on a discrimination test for Dutch phonemic contrasts that do not occur in English. This suggests that the accent effect obtained elsewhere may not be a strictly motoric one.

These studies suggest that a decline in phonetic sensitivity may occur at about seven or eight years of age. Recall the results of the study by Tahta, Woods, and Loewenthal (1981) that were displayed in Figure 2.11. The best linguistic performance of their subjects

was at ages five through eight years. Over this range 90 percent of
the subjects were adjudged to be accent-free in English. A sharply
declining number were considered to be accent-free at ages nine,
ten, and eleven, and there was a further reduction at twelve years
and older, when speakers without accents comprised just two percent of the sample at that age.

These studies place the onset of diminishing linguistic or phonetic
sensitivity at about six to eight years of age. Other research seems
to agree. Flege (1991) studied the voice-onset times of American
English stops produced by adults whose native language was Spanish. In the first experiment in his report, one group of subjects had
learned English as five- to six-year-old children, and a second group
was first exposed to English in adulthood. Flege found that the
learners who encountered English as children tended to produce
English /t/ with native properties, while the adult learners produced
that phoneme with voicing values that fell between the short-lags
associated with monolingual Spanish and the long-lags observed in
English monolinguals.

In later experiments, Flege and Fletcher (1992) found that
native Spanish speakers who began learning American English at
five to six years of age had no accent when speaking their second
language, while a group of native Chinese speakers who began
learning English slightly later—at an average of 7.6 years of age—
did have an accent. These groups are not directly comparable, of
course, but the findings confirmed earlier work by Asher and Garcia
(1969), who found that the pronunciation of American English by
native speakers of Spanish was far better if they entered the United
States between the ages of one and six years than if they came in
at seven to twelve years, or thirteen to nineteen years. Their data
break down as follows:

| | Degree of accent | | |
	Nearly native	Slight	Definite
1–6 years	68	32	0
7–12 years	41	43	16
13–19 years	7	27	66

Investigators segregate their age groups in various ways, but
once again it would appear that the period from birth to six or seven

years is one of unusual opportunity for accent-free learning of spoken language. Indeed, no studies seem to disagree on this point. Adolescence may mark the end of the sensitive period for spoken language learning, but this seemingly has obscured "a period within the period."

The reason for the second stage in nonnative language acquisition—from seven or eight years to twelve or thirteen—may be that at about that time there is a temporary dip in the ability to store or process "nonlinguistic" vocal cues that is similar in kind to the voice identification dip observed by Mann, Diamond, and Carey (1979) and perhaps linked to hemispheric reorganization. One wonders, in fact, if the acquisition of phonological language reduces the child's ability to process the nonsegmental cues associated with voice recognition, affect, and "accent."

Research focusing on linguistic judgments has reported age effects for morphology and syntax. Where speech expression is concerned, however, we have seen that nonnative effects for language encountered in the postinfancy period generally involve *phonology.* At the phonological level, moreover, most of the effects that have been documented are *phonetic,* that is, they pertain to the physical implementation of the sound system. This research suggests that phonetic capacity may decline as a function of changes in supporting perceptuomotor mechanisms or processes. Quite apart from this, disproportionate decline in the expression of phonological knowledge is consistent with the dual specialization hypothesis I present in Chapter 9.

SIGNED LANGUAGES

If "the sensitive period for language" is limited to speech, maturation should affect acquisition of signed languages differently. For one thing, the supporting perceptual and motor mechanisms for vocal and manual systems develop at different rates. For another, spoken language is a cultural universal, suggesting a specific phylogenetic endowment: an apparatus that "does" speech. The relative rarity of sign suggests that it might be learned by general (certainly not modular) mechanisms that may be less likely to shut down with whatever maturation occurs, at least in the first decade or two of life.

Yet this is not what the evidence shows. Elissa Newport and her associates (see the studies reported in Newport, 1991) studied three groups of deaf adults who had learned American Sign Language (ASL) at one of three ages prior to adulthood. *Native* signers were born to deaf signing parents and exposed to ASL from birth. *Early* signers were first exposed to ASL at the age of four to six years, when they encountered signing peers at a school for the deaf at which they had just been enrolled. *Late* signers were first exposed to ASL after the age of twelve when they were enrolled in the same school for the deaf or began to socialize with active or former students. At the time of test, all subjects had signed on a daily basis for at least thirty years.

Performance measures included production and comprehension of verbs of motion and a series of tests on the syntactic and morphological structures of ASL. Analyses indicated that while basic word order did not differ across the three age-of-learning groups, on the morphological measures Native signers out-performed Early signers, who in turn performed at a higher level than Late learners. This finding reinforces the conclusion that physical aspects of language expression are particularly disadvantaged by a late start, even if they are not exclusively tied to the vocal modality.

WHAT MAKES A SENSITIVE PERIOD FOR LANGUAGE?

What produces these phonetic and nonphonetic changes over the early years of life? Decline in the capacity to reproduce nonnative phonetic patterns seems to presuppose changes in (1) endogenous factors (such as hormone levels relating to brain function), and (2) factors that are associated with social or psychological functioning (whether related or unrelated to endogenous factors), such as independence or autonomy and relationship to the nurturant ones whose superficial behaviors the child previously copied.

What is so linguistically special about the first six or seven years of life? It is an important question to ask, for if we find out which of these factors varies with the ability to learn and to produce spoken languages encountered after infancy, we may discover the specific factors that naturally promote or facilitate the acquisition of native language. According to this logic, capacities that decline or attentional biases that shift in childhood may previously have been influential. There may be several variables at work here. This is the interval during which children acquire their *native* language (Templin, 1957) and, we may suppose, the minimum period that language-learning systems are open for business. I assume that the dip at six to eight years marks that point when a system that must be kept open for linguistic reasons—a phonetic system that accommodates all cues in a spoken language—can first be safely shut down. In motorically precocial animals, motor learning systems begin to close down soon after they become minimally functional. This frequently occurs so soon after birth that motor development seems impervious to the effects of experience.

At six to seven years there is also evidence of growing mastery in other areas. Helplessness and dependency decline; children from widely divergent cultures are thought to be able to assume responsibility at this time and to express capabilities associated with responsible conduct (Super, 1991). In Western societies, children of about this age tend to "leave home" to begin school.

As I mentioned in Chapter 3, the rapid native learning of behaviors used in linguistic communication is linked to the human infant's sensitive period for social and emotional development. Extraordinarily facile learning of adult vocal behaviors occurs during this period. Vocal behavior—including that which attends speaking—is an important means by which mothers and infants establish affiliative and affectionate ties. Those who invented the term "mother tongue" had it right for reasons they may not have intended. Perhaps we should not be surprised that after this intensely personal time, the value of expressive vocal learning is of a different type, as is suggested by humans' ability to learn the lexicon and syntax of languages throughout life but to have islands of difficulty with "accent."

One might also wonder about the purpose of a partial shut-down of the language-learning system, especially that portion of the system that is responsible for accent. I am unable to come up with an answer, but my present inclination would be to look at it as an extension of the link between vocal affect and prosody on the one hand and maternal dependence on the other.

Developmental Disorders in Childhood
Affective Implications

Comparative studies suggest that the phylogenetically older parts of the brain are more likely to produce a limited range of behavior (Omenn and Motulsky, 1972). The most strongly canalized of all human behaviors, then, may be those we share with nonhuman primates, which would include the communication of intentions and feelings by face and by voice. It should therefore be easier to locate children who fail to speak but do convey affect vocally than to find children with the opposite pattern, and of course this is exactly what we do encounter.

Several developmental brain disorders involve facial and vocal motor systems. One, originally described by Gilles de la Tourette, is a motor disorder in which facial and vocal activity occurs involuntarily in the form of tics (Bruun, 1988; Leckman and Cohen, 1988). Unfortunately, it is not clear where the abnormalities are in Tourette's syndrome; some speculation is that they may be in the basal ganglia and substantia nigra (Leckman, Riddle, and Cohen, 1988). This area, stroke studies suggest, is associated with affective prosody (Cancelliere and Kertesz, 1990).

A second developmental disorder, autism, involves deficits of facial affect, vocal affect, and spoken language. In a continuing effort to understand the biological bases of communication and language, I will take a selective look at some facial, vocal, and neurological findings in this disorder.

THE FACE AND THE VOICE IN AUTISM

Many observers have noted that autistic children seem to display reduced expression and awareness of facial affect. This is interesting in view of the fact that autistic children generally do not acquire spoken language fully or according to the usual schedule. It is even more relevant to my thesis that some autistic children also display reductions of vocal prosody. Neurologically, these deficits are likely bedfellows, since both visuofacial processing and the control of prosody are primarily right hemisphere functions and research attempting to establish a left hemisphere basis to autism has been unsuccessful (Fein et al., 1984).

FACE PROCESSING IN AUTISM   In autism, face-processing mechanisms in the brain may be dysfunctional or hypofunctional, and much of autistic children's response to faces and their own expressions will ultimately be traced to neurological impairment. But first we need to examine what is known about the reactions of autistic children to faces. Clinically, it has long been noted that autistic children look less at other people's faces than do normally developing children (Kanner, 1943), but there is a limited amount of support for this observation in the scientific literature. For example, Hutt and Ounsted (1966) found that autistic children spend significantly less time than normal controls looking at drawings of human faces but about the same amount of time looking at a facial contour, a monkey face, and a dog face. Other studies have explored the facial looking patterns of autistic children, but as Weeks and Hobson (1987) observed, the artificiality or other weaknesses of the early face studies makes them "relatively unenlightening." What one would really like to see, of course, is quantified reactions to live displays of facial emotion, and here the literature has been sparse.

In any case, if we assume for the moment that clinical impressions are correct and that autistic children spend little time looking at faces, is it because they are indifferent to them or do they actively avoid looking at faces? This is an important distinction, for if autistic children are indifferent—giving faces the same attention as inanimate objects—then for them faces lack a species-characteristic appeal that is normally observed from birth, when faces are preferred over other visual patterns (Goren et al., 1975). Weeks and Hobson (1987) seem to lean toward this hypothesis, suggesting that autistic children lack "a biologically based attentiveness and emotional responsiveness to certain of the bodily features of others, including features of emotional expression" (p. 148).

It is possible that for some as yet unexplained reason autistic children actively avoid looking at faces because they wish to keep from witnessing facial displays of social or emotional behavior. However, I have found no reports indicating that autistic children look less long at an actively emoting face than at a poker face. A second possibility is that autistic children cannot reliably discriminate, detect, categorize, or identify facial activity. Hobson (1986) has compared the facial expression judgments of fourteen-year-old autistic children with those of normal and retarded children of the same mental age. In the gestures task, subjects saw a videotape of a masked actor depicting various emotions strictly through body language (for example, to convey happiness, the actor skipped, danced, and leapt into the air). Subjects then selected the schematized or photographed facial expression that best represented the emotion conveyed in the tape. In two other tasks, subjects were to select facial expressions that went with vocalizations (such as the sound of a person humming happily) or contexts (for example, a film clip of a person receiving a birthday cake). On all three tasks, the autistic children were relatively unsuccessful in picking the appropriate photograph or drawing, and they scored significantly below the other two groups.

A third possibility is that facial expressions are correctly apprehended but are not salient, or carry no special meaning, for the autistic child. In Weeks and Hobson (1987), autistic children were compared to retarded children of similar mental age on their sorting of face pictures differing by gender, facial expression, and the presence or absence of a hat. All subjects sorted by gender, but whereas affectively normal children were far more likely to categorize photos by facial expression than by the presence of a hat, for the autistic children precisely the opposite result was obtained.

There is evidence, then, to support several face hypotheses, and we are unable to sort through them more effectively here than others have done elsewhere (Weeks and Hobson, 1987). Higher quality information is needed. Ideally, observations of looking behaviors would be performed on children not yet diagnosed as autistic but regarded differently by their family members. There is one (partially flawed) study of this sort. For ten autistic children, Massie (1978) managed to obtain and analyze home movies made when the children were infants and their autism had not yet been diagnosed. His analyses indicate that in the first year of life, five of the infants repeatedly looked away from or failed to pursue other people visually, or avoided their mother's gaze. However, these findings must be replicated, since Massie had no comparison sample and knew each child's diagnosis.

We would also be aided by studies that examine autistic children's scanpaths and looking time as a function of the degree and type of facial emotion that is revealed. In the interim, what can be said on the basis of present data? Certainly one can suspect a basic disturbance of face perception, since autistic children seem to process facial information in a qualitatively different way. Recall that normally developing children, and adults, too (Shepherd, Davies, and Ellis, 1981) are more aware of the upper face than the lower face. This finding was confirmed by Langdell (1978), who also made some interesting comparisons of normal children's performance with the processing patterns of autistic and retarded children. Langdell began by photographing the face of ten- and fourteen-year-old autistic children. He also took black and white photos of two groups of normally developing children, one matched for chronological age and the other for mental age, as well as of retarded subjects with similar mental age scores. These photos were shown to the children in each group for identification. Pictures were presented either in the normal upright fashion, inverted, or masked in seven different ways to reveal the nose or eyes only; everything below the mouth, nose, or eyes; or everything above the eyebrows or eyes.

Consistent with other research, Langdell's finding revealed that normal and retarded subjects were able to recognize their friends better from the upper half of facial displays than from the bottom half. The two groups of autistic subjects differed somewhat from each other, but on the whole they performed in precisely the opposite fashion, recognizing far more friends from the lower half of their photographs. Langdell's data indicate that normal subjects made half as many errors when scanning faces revealed from the eyes up as when they saw faces exposed from the eyes down. Autistic children, on the other hand, made three times as many errors on the "eyes up" photos as on the "eyes down" photos.

It is not obvious how these data should be explained. Langdell's own speculations embraced the prospect that autistic children do not view the face as a social stimulus and therefore would not be particularly drawn to socially expressive eyes. He also wondered if autistic children might focus upon the mouth area in an attempt to compensate for unusual difficulties in comprehending the auditory components of speech.

One might suppose from Langdell's work that autistic individuals would be fairly good lipreaders, but this was not found in some research (de Gelder, Vroomen, and van der Heide, 1991) in which autistic children and adolescents were given two face recognition tests. In both tasks, subjects were briefly shown photographs of individuals with neutral facial expressions and then asked to find that individual in a group or partial-group photo. Subjects were also given three speech recognition tasks. In the audio-visual task, subjects were given a McGurk task in which audible and visible components of VCV syllables were always in conflict (for example, where the subject might see an individual saying [ata] but hear

[apa]). In the audio-only task subjects heard syllables while viewing the speaker's still face, and in the video-only task they merely saw the speaker producing syllables without sound. Analyses revealed that the autistic subjects performed significantly worse than mental age–matched nonautistic controls on both face memory tasks. On the speech tasks, the groups performed at similarly high levels of accuracy on audio-only and video-only conditions, but the autistic subjects were significantly less likely to produce phonetic fusions on the McGurk task. Autistic subjects who did poorly on the face recognition tasks were not less likely to produce fusions, however. Indeed, their failure to fuse on the McGurk task seemed unrelated to either face recognition ability or performance on either of the other speech recognition tasks. From Langdell's study, one might have expected the autistic subjects to be superior in lipreading and fusion rates. This was not the case, although, as expected from other work, the autistic subjects were inferior in recognizing faces from short-term memory.

If some features of autism reflect a more primary face-processing disorder (Kendrick and Baldwin, 1987b), one might expect some behavioral similarities between children who are autistic and children who are congenitally blind. Hobson (1990) has noted that both populations have a delay in the achievement of symbolic play, confusion of personal pronouns, impairment in production and comprehension of narrative, and difficulty in deictic word forms, and both populations are well known for their rampant echolalia. He commented that "there may be a common psychological deficit underlying the specific constellation of impairments common to autistic and congenitally blind children" (p. 119).

In work more directly related to the association of facial and vocal characteristics, Hobson (1987) compared fourteen-year-old autistic subjects to mental age–matched normally developing young people on their awareness of a number of age- and sex-related measures. In one task, subjects heard the voice of an eight-year-old girl, a boy of similar age, and a woman and a man who were recorded while reading a prose passage and were asked to identify a line drawing of a male or female child or an adult face that corresponded to the voice. The autistic subjects performed significantly below the controls; 42 percent of their errors were age-inappropriate (for example, selecting the boy's face for the man's voice), 28 percent were sex-inappropriate (for example, selecting the boy's face for the girl's voice), and the remaining 30 percent were inappropriate on both counts. Assuming that the response drawings and task were interpreted correctly, it would appear that these autistic adolescents had difficulty negotiating either or both of the two most significant channels of human identification and affective communication. There have been many studies of facial expression; how much do we really know about the vocal processing of autistic children?

Vocal Prosody in Autism   Reflecting the general neglect of prosody, there has been remarkably little work on the vocal quality and intonation of autistic children. Most of the published research has been reviewed by Baltaxe and Simmons (1985). In her own research, Baltaxe (1981) studied eight verbal autistic children of unspecified age and compared them with affectively normal children matched for sex, dialect, and level of language development. Using a sentence imitation task, she elicited connected speech material that was then subjected to acoustic analysis. Baltaxe found, among other things, that autistic children spoke with a restricted frequency range when repeating questions but displayed somewhat greater vocal intensity swings when repeating questions and negative commands.

Other work reviewed by Baltaxe and Simmons reveals considerable heterogeneity in autism. On an individual basis, autistic children's prosody tends either to be unusually flat or wildly exaggerated. Warren Fay has analyzed the spontaneous speech of a number of autistic children, including the nature of their numerous echoic responses (Fay and Schuler, 1980). He reports that the speech of autistic children is characteristically delivered in a monotone and is lacking in affective qualities.

In some research (Van Lancker, Cornelius, and Kreiman, 1989), autistic children performed less well than schizophrenic and affectively normal children on a task requiring comprehension of spoken sentences and interpretation of emotional intonation patterns (such as happy, sad, angry, surprised). However, since subjects had to understand and perform a cross-modal matching task in order to demonstrate their interpretation of emotional intonation, it is not clear that the autistic children were inferior on vocal affect.

VOICE AVOIDANCE?

We are left with many questions. In parallel with their avoidance of the face, we might ask if autistic children ever "avoid the human voice." This may seem a strange question, but there is evidence from very early postnatal life that infants look in the direction of sound that amuses them (such as rattles and voices). For all of us, a normal response to unwanted sound is to look or turn away from its source. In fact, as we saw earlier, normal infants characteristically *turn away* from a perfectly likable face when its mouth movements clash with sounds the infants hear (Dodd, 1979). Because sights are easier to avoid than sounds, a desire to block vocal information could be manifested as gaze aversion. Now, all we need is for normally sociable individuals to look at the person they are addressing most of the time, which they do, and the ingredients exist for a "face avoidance" hypothesis. This is all speculative of course, but it deserves to be checked out.

Field (1982) studied high risk infants with respiratory distress syndrome who were relatively less alert, less attentive to stimulation, and less active than normal term infants on the interaction items of the Brazelton Scale. She found that these infants cooed less and displayed sad faces more frequently than normal infants. Interestingly, high risk and normal infants revealed equal amounts of looking and a similar tonic heart rate when presented with an inanimate Raggedy Ann doll. But when the doll was animated— nodding its head and emitting previously recorded speech ("Hi there, baby. How are you?")—the high risk infants displayed more gaze aversion and higher levels of tonic heart rate than the normal controls. Wouldn't it be interesting to attempt similar comparisons with autistic children?

What we are asking, then, is whether reduced or disturbed facial affect in autistic children is an isolated abnormality or a correlate of dysprosodia? Regardless of the correct explanation of autistic children's behavior in terms of face and voice, these effects would seem to implicate anomalous brain function. What, then, can be said about the operation and structure of the brain in clear-cut cases of autism?

CEREBRAL MALFORMATIONS IN AUTISM

At one time, autism might have been attributed to the misbehavior of parents or other environmental factors, but there is now reasonably good evidence that autism is associated with abnormal brain morphology and cell structure. This possibility is suggested by studies identifying a pattern of autosomal recessive inheritance in multiple-incidence families (Ritvo et al., 1985), a higher frequency of maternal illness and other prenatal risk factors in single-incidence families (Mason-Brothers et al., 1987), and a higher concordance for autism in monozygotic than dizygotic twins (Ritvo et al., 1985).

Aware of the high frequency of language disorder in autism, Hier, LeMay, and Rosenberger (1978) used computerized brain tomography to look for hemispheric asymmetries in autistic adolescents and adults in relation to retarded adults and a variety of neurological patients. They reported that the left parieto-occipital region was equal to or wider than the right in 77 percent of the retarded subjects and 75 percent of the neurological patients. However, this pattern was observed in no more than 44 percent of the autistic patients.

Other research (Damasio et al., 1980) has failed to observe the hemispheric differences reported above, and a review of brain studies prior to 1983 suggests, in any case, that structural asymmetry is not the best place to look for the primary deficit associated with autism (Fein et al., 1984). Instead, noting wide variation in the form and severity of autistic symptoms, Fein et al. became suspicious of "corresponding heterogeneity in the timing, locus and severity of CNS insult" (p. 277).

Bauman and Kemper (1985) were the first to report a comprehensive neuropathologic examination of a carefully documented case of autism. Differences were of several types and were widely scattered. According to the report, the patient's forebrain was characterized by several types of cytoarchitectonic abnormalities, including reduced neuronal size, increased cell-packing density, or both (relative to a control brain). There were also some abnormalities in the cerebellum, which other research now suggests may participate in a range of cognitive activities (Schmahmann, 1991). In the amygdaloid complex, there were increases in cell-packing density in the central, medial, and cortical nuclei, and cell size was reduced.

Bauman has since found similar abnormalities in five additional cases. The amygdala was malformed in every case, and it is interesting that this was the structure that was differently configured. In experiments by Arthur Kling and his colleagues (Dicks, Myers, and Kling, 1969; Kling, Lancaster, and Benitone, 1970) the amygdala was removed from monkeys who were then returned to their social group. The animals were perceptibly fearful and isolated, and seemed unable to socialize. In other work, Kling has found a direct connection between the electrical output of the amygdala and the affective content of vocalization (Lloyd and Kling, 1988). He also found that conspecific calls produced a response in the amygdala, which was greater if the animal was socially integrated at the time of the stimulation than if it was isolated from other animals. This finding is congruent with research suggesting that the amygdala participates in some parallel operations in the areas of cognitive evaluation and emotional appraisal (Halgren, 1992).

Recently, a group at Johns Hopkins (Piven et al., 1990) used magnetic resonance imaging to locate cortical abnormalities in thirteen eight- to fifty-three-year-old high functioning autistic males. Controls were individuals of comparable age and nonverbal IQ. Scans were analyzed blindly and rated for the presence or absence of specific developmental malformations of the cortex. The investigators reported malformations in seven of the autistic subjects and in none of the controls. Five autistic subjects had polymicrogyria[9] in a frontal lobe (2), parietal lobe (1), temporal-occipital area (1), or in both temporal and parietal-occipital lobes (1). One had schizencephaly with bilateral parietal macrogyria and one had unilateral frontal macrogyria. The lateral locus of abnormalities was scattered; three of the subjects had left, two had right, and two had bilateral malformations. Embryologically, these abnormalities were thought to have arisen prior to the sixth month of gestation. This had been suggested earlier by Bauman and Kemper (1985).

In looking at the neurology of the developing infant, I have examined the growth of brain systems that participate in affective vocal and facial communication, including experience-expectant systems

9. Defined as the focal or diffuse presence of an excessive number of cerebral convolutions with or without cortical thickening. Schizencephalic abnormalities were defined as the presence of bilateral, symmetrical clefts in the cerebral cortex, with evidence of lining by gray matter, with or without extension into the ventricles. Macrogyria were defined as the presence of broad, flat, and shallow gyri associated with an underlying area of increased cortical thickness with one gyrus involved.

that are in a partial state of readiness at birth. These systems are designed by nature to process and store sensory information and seem to require nothing more than ubiquitous perceptual experience in order to be brought up to full capacity. It is likely that the initial processing of facial and vocal information by neonates draws upon experience-expectant resources. Richer interpretations of affective communication in these modalities probably require participation by experience-dependent systems, which can only be activated by specific social experience.

The maturing brain prescribes a limited range of activity that, in turn, challenges the brain to develop a broader range of sensory and motor functions. The development of motor systems is hastened by movement, and the stabilization and elaboration of sensory systems are encouraged by relevant stimulation. It is clear from recent research that the brain has the authority to begin remodeling itself the moment some function is unstimulated or inactive.

There is a correlation between overall brain size and the capacity for complex behavior. The nonhuman primate's brain is far closer to its ultimate size at birth than is the brain of the human infant, and while all primates are helpless, monkeys and apes are motorically more advanced than the human newborn. Consequently, the sensorily precocial human infant has an extended period during which sensory information can be taken in and interpreted prior to action. This encourages the development of a sophisticated emotional capability.

No one doubts that maturation is a critical factor in development, and yet the truth of this statement is almost too general to have any useful meaning. It is an oversimplification to say, for example, that nerve tracts must myelinate if there is to be full and efficient function. To some degree, myelination is stimulated or paced by usage, and the amount needed for particular behaviors is unknown. The same goes for experience. Effective experience is different from actual exposure, but lacking knowledge of the infant's attentional habits it is impossible to differentiate the two. Both maturation and exposure imply a level of passivity and reactivity that belies the facts. Infants are proactive; they play a major role in the development of their own neural capabilities by seeking out certain types of sensory stimulation and motor acts during intervals in which their brain is particularly likely to benefit. Whether the brain responds differently to self- and externally-produced stimulation is unclear, but this seems possible inasmuch as some cells appear to respond only to one type of stimulation and other cells seem to respond only to the other type.

Although we are accustomed to thinking about genes as though they worked from within and about the environment as though it operated from outside the organism, the human infant is also exposed to behavior that is shaped by genes, and aspects of the environment are coded into the genes. The evidence now suggests that subtle cognitive factors such as attitudes and beliefs may have a genetic component. How this operates is unclear, but the suggestion is that genes in collaboration with environmental stimulation may set infants into patterns of behavior that influence the way they see the world.

There is another indication of the effects of activity and environmental stimulation upon brain development. The brain develops on a competitive basis. If one modality is unusually "busy" during an interval in which there is relatively little stimulation in a different modality, the former may colonize regions normally associated with the latter. This suggests that individuals with unusual developmental histories or life circumstances may, when they learn language, perform its various operations with a different allocation of neural and cognitive resources.

Spoken language develops during a maximally sensitive period that appears to run from birth to six or seven years. This period seems to be less sensitive to grammar than vocal or phonological factors. The age range corresponds to the interval over which one's native language is typically acquired, and decreases somewhat as infants become increasingly independent of maternal influence. Whether there is a hormonal or neurochemical basis to the unusually efficient language learning in early childhood is unclear at present. A second period, in which language learning is less efficient than it is during the early period but more native-like than later, runs from about eight years until adolescence.

In neurophysiological studies, the right hemisphere appears to develop in advance of the left. By itself, this suggests that the right hemisphere may be more responsible than the left for the infant's vocal and facial expressions of emotionality, and research supports this. In infancy, the familiar, affective, and heavily prosodic voice is probably substantially lateralized to the right hemisphere compared to speech delivered in an unfamiliar monotone. Some left hemisphere dominance for speech processing may be artificially induced by the experimental use of "lab speech," which in infant terms is noncommunicative—the infant's version of "nonverbal"—because it is usually designed to be free of familiar or affective properties.

Affective disorders in childhood interfere with the development of spoken language. Autistic children seem to be less interested in or aware of the human face and its activities than nonautistic children and to be less aware of prosodic variation. Though abnormal cells and cell-packing densities are rather generally distributed in the autistic brain, the amygdala seems invariably to be involved, which is unsurprising in light of its probable role in emotion and social responding.

If we pause at this point to examine the infant's progress along the path to spoken language, where do we find it, and where must it go next? The infant's perceptual system and vocal tract are sufficient for vocal mimicry, and its functional systems of social cognition inform it of meaning cues—the stuff of which lexical semantics is made. It can say a few words and phrases. But other factors must come in—this business will not proceed as it must unless the child develops the urge to convey and a fuller capacity for reference.

8

THE URGE TO CONVEY AND
THE CAPACITY FOR REFERENCE

It has been claimed that in humans the capacity for spoken language began with, or was significantly enhanced by, the evolution of the pharynx (Lieberman, 1984). In my judgment, this view overemphasizes mechanical factors and virtually ignores the functional value of a sound-making system in social communication. The physical configurations of the vocal tract are far less important to spoken language than the desire to use the vocal tract to communicate. Individuals who are born with a small tongue, or with no tongue at all, or who lose their tongue to surgery in adulthood, may still speak with surprisingly high levels of intelligibility (Ferrier, Johnston, and Bashir, 1991; MacKain, 1984). Aphonic infants have been observed to make sounds using a variety of labial, buccal, and glottal actions (Ross, 1983; Simon et al., 1983; Tucker, Rusnov, and Cohen, 1982). But no one without the urge to communicate fully develops the species-specific capacity to speak.

Over the first few years of life, the vocal tract matures and the infant's repertoire of movements and sound patterns expands. In affiliative acts, the infant will use his maturing vocal tract to mimic utterances, and may even achieve a few phonetically consistent forms that, with appropriate deployment, will be apprehended as "words." At this level, the vocal imitation ability of young humans may be no more impressive than the accomplishments of some talking birds. The desire to communicate undoubtedly plays some role at this level, and indeed, the developing infant has many reasons to communicate with adults. These include regulation of behavior, calling attention to itself, and directing adults' attention to objects or events (Prizant, 1992). These acts can be carried out without compromising prelinguistic motor routines. But the vocal tract must be given incentives, must, in effect, be *driven* to do what complex linguistic expression requires. This will not happen without an underlying urge to convey. Indeed, the fact that some children naturally learn to speak *in spite of* theoretically staggering obstacles—aglossia, for example—underscores the power of the human reason to speak.

Others have asked why apes and monkeys lack the rich system of vocal communication possessed by humans. But it makes little sense to question the lack of linguistic capacity in animals having no evident desire to communicate and no ingrained habits of social communication. It is more logical, according to George Miller (1990), that we would find something of the complexity of human language "in a species that was already actively communicating—that had a need to communicate and could take immediate advantage of improvements in its communicative system. Otherwise, a capacity to map meanings into sounds would have offered little selective advantage" (p. 12).

In ontogeny, most of us would not be terribly surprised to find that a child who sits calmly for hours staring into space, evincing no interest in people and objects, does not speak. Speech is something we expect from *interested parties,* who are curious, inclined to explore, amused by novelty, frightened by the unfamiliar, and frequently brimming with excitement and the impulse to speak.

Neonates will start down the path to language on a species-characteristic initiative, encouraged by their attachment to a nurturant mother and attracted and reassured by the salience of vocal, facial, and other social cues. But to proceed past the first few turns, to keep moving along the linguistic path, other things must enter in. Chief among these, in my judgment, is the urge to convey, followed by the growth of communicative capacity and the capability for reference, and ultimately by the actions of a specialization for grammatical analysis.

The urge to convey is so primary in our functional makeup that it is difficult even to ask about it, but not to ask about this attribute is to ignore the fundamental motivation for language and all the preliminary behaviors that lead infants to its door. A theoretical linguist may be able to do that without embarrassment but a biolinguist or psycholinguist cannot. It would be the ontogenetic equivalent of saying, as neo-Darwinian evolutionists never could, "and then, suddenly, there was X," where X is whatever structure or function that is to be explained.

Questioning the motivation to speak is like probing the reasons for other standard human activities. Why do we walk? Common sense says we walk in order to get around. But is getting around the infant's motivation for walking or a natural benefit of ambulation? I think we might usefully begin to creep up on the urge to convey by addressing its origins, which I believe lie somewhere in the conjoint (and essentially inseparable) action of cognition and affect.

Cognition and Affect

Cognition and affect are so intimately interrelated that it is impossible to say which comes first and which is more likely to drive the other into additional elaborations. The evidence suggests that each capacity influences the other, and I take the position that cognition and affect must work together if infants are fully to experience the urge to convey, and therefore to learn and use spoken language.

COGNITION

Some developmentalists use the word *cognition* narrowly in reference to concept development, but I prefer the broader definition offered up some years ago by Ulric Neisser (1967): "all the processes by which . . . sensory input is transformed, reduced, elaborated, stored, recovered, and used . . . even when they operated in the absence of relevant stimulation" (p. 4). Traditionally, developmental theories have valued several major connections between language and cognition. At one time, psychologists and philosophers were interested in knowing whether language was used in, perhaps even needed for, cognitive operations. Some asked if it was possible to think without language (Furth, 1966) or if one's thinking was fundamentally different when implicit verbal responses were impossible (Brown and Lenneberg, 1954; Lantze and Stefflre, 1964; Whorf, 1940).

A second connection involves the search for developmental parallels between language and underlying concepts. The range of these concerns extends from grand questions about Piagetian stages of concept development (for example, Bates et al., 1979) to more focal investigations of selected mental concepts and linguistic structures (for example, Gopnik and Meltzoff, 1986) and—on the extreme "micro" end of the continuum—developmental correlations between particular words and concepts (Gopnik, 1984; Gopnik and Meltzoff, 1985).

A third connection between language and cognition involves the growth of enabling systems for perceiving, analyzing, representing, and retrieving linguistic information. For example, to refer to objects and actions the infant must be aware of their existence and therefore have adequate perception and long-term memory. To produce complex utterances, fledgling speakers must be able to keep several propositions in mind simultaneously, and therefore have adequate immediate memory.

Finally, we have asked if the cognition required by language is inextricably linked to it or or if it exists independently, to be drawn upon as needed when linguistic activity commences. Although questions of this sort have been asked for more than a few years, they have been raised anew in the modularity debate and aired rather fully in recent years (see Chomsky, 1980; Fodor, 1983, 1985; Mattingly and Studdert-Kennedy, 1991). In light of this protracted interest in cognition and language, it is surprisingly rare to find any serious mention of affect in connection with either cognitive or linguistic development. And yet, as I will demonstrate, when affect is left out of the equation it is impossible to account adequately for either cognition or language.

Most models of adult performance entertain emotionally "cold" conceptions of cognition. Consider Figures 8.1 and 8.2, taken from Norman (1981). Figure 8.1 depicts a "pure cognitive system" that consults but certainly is not driven by a regulatory system whose function is essentially biological: to detect danger, mate and reproduce, seek nourishment, and secure other basic needs. Norman saw two fundamental problems with this model. One is that the pure cognitive system is responsible for immediate decisions about it's

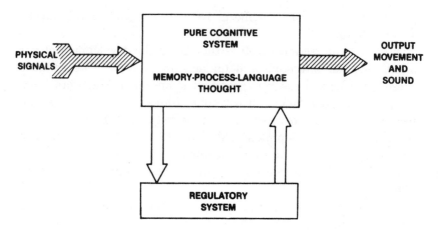

Figure 8.1. Norman's model of cold cognition, which he called "an obvious one, but probably wrong."

own priorities. The other is that phylogenetically, the regulatory system would have been in place first and thus have pressed the cognitive system into service, and in this way shaped it. Norman therefore preferred the depiction shown here in Figure 8.2, in which the cognitive system is subservient to the regulatory system. Ac-

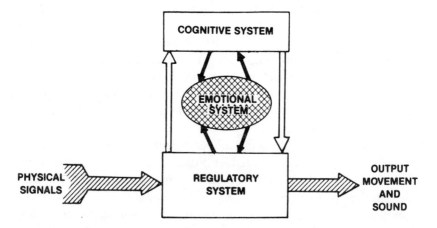

Figure 8.2. Norman's preferred view of cognition, in which the regulatory system, in consultation with the emotional system, processes sensory signals and effects motor responses.

cording to this "warm" model of cognition, the organism's regulatory and emotional systems make the initial decisions about what cognitive processing is needed. I agree with Norman that this model is closer to the adult truth, and there is no question that it fits better with ontogenetic facts.

AFFECT

Cognition also exerts a tremendous influence upon affect. Indeed, it has been argued that "only with recognition is there pleasure and disappointment; only with some development of causality, object permanence, intentionality, and meaning are there joy, anger, and fear; only with self-awareness is there shame" (Sroufe, 1979, p. 491). Emotion has been defined as "a subjective reaction to a salient event, characterized by physiological, experiential, and (usually) overt behavioral change" (Sroufe et al., 1984, p. 317). The expression of emotion—affect—is thought to play a central role in the organization of consciousness and behavior in individuals and their social interactions.[1]

I pointed out earlier that the human infant is sensorily precocial and motorically altricial. This circumstance would seem to favor the development of emotion, for as Pribram (1967) said, "motivation and emotion occur when the organism attempts to extend his control to the limits of what he perceives. To the extent that this attempt is appraised as feasible at any moment the organism is motivated; to the extent that the attempt is appraised infeasible at any moment, the organism—unless he is to 'give up'—becomes of necessity emotional, that is, he relies on self-regulatory mechanisms: either to participate in the uncontrollable or to prepare for another attempt" (p. 837). Thus it appears that one of the reasons our young may be particularly disposed to emotionality is that they are born sensing much about their environment and themselves but are unable to act effectively for many months.

There can be little wonder that when motor action is finally available to the infant, it is inclined to go charging here and climb-

---

1. Though *emotion* refers mainly to the subjective experience and *affect* to any displays associated with that experience, in literary practice the words are used inconsistently. Because I quote from several individuals who use *affect* when *emotion* might be a better choice, and also to avoid repetitiousness, I will occasionally use these words interchangeably.

ing there, twisting this and pulling that. Robert White (1959), at
Harvard, was among the first to invoke a motivation for "effectance," which is essentially "what the neuromuscular system wants
to do when it is otherwise unoccupied or is gently stimulated by
the environment" (p. 321). Harter (1974, 1978a, 1978b, 1980) and
Bronson (1974) picked up on this concept, the latter defining effectance as behavior "which has as its goal the attainment of an effect
upon the environment that is contingent upon the organism's own
action" (Bronson, 1971, p. 270). As for the ontogeny of effectance,
Bronson suggested that "the impetus for achieving contingent effects is intrinsic to the structure of the human organism. Experience
merely determines the degree to which this impetus is developed
and the way in which it becomes integrated with other motivational
systems . . . not to be intrinsically motivated to attain effects that
are contingent upon one's own actions in a species whose members
go out to meet life equipped with little but a neocortex and an
opposable thumb would seem to be the height of maladaptiveness"
(1971, p. 271).

Effectance and affect play several major roles in human communication. Certainly they expand the infant's capacity for intelligent behavior by pushing it to explore and to interact with the
people and objects in its environment. Affective displays provide
parents with a basis for social responding and cues they may use
in adjusting the psychological and physical care of their infant. The
experience of emotion fills infants with energies that are dissipated
by behaviors (such as squealing), which are by their very nature
communicative.

Before looking at the empirical evidence, we might briefly sample
the comments of theorists who see strong connections between affect
and intelligence. According to Jean Piaget (1972), "affect plays an
essential role in the functioning of intelligence. Without affect there
would be no interest, no need, no motivation; and consequently,
questions or problems would never be posed, and there would be no
intelligence. Affectivity is a necessary condition in the constitution
of intelligence" (p. 167). Similarly, Sroufe and Waters (1976) have
commented that cognitive advances "promote exploration, social
development, and the differentiation of affect; and affective-social
growth leads cognitive development . . . Neither the cognitive nor

the affective system can be considered dominant or more basic than the other; they are inseparable manifestations of the same integrated process . . . It is as valid to say that cognition is in the service of affect as to say that affect reflects cognitive processes" (p. 187).

If these statements are correct, the uninformed may suppose that linguists and psycholinguists make a great deal out of affect and build their theories of language on a solid affective base. But a glance at developmental theories reveals exactly the opposite: we seem to have thrown everything into theories of language *except* affect.

Why has this important disposition been so systematically excluded from developmental psycholinguistic theory? How can we deal with linguistic cognition without taking on affective communication? Some clues exist in the research of Haviland (1976), who pointed out that "there have not been acceptable categories of events to call 'affect' until very recently . . . We have not known how to say, 'This baby has a trait or habit of being "interested" or "cheerful" or "frightened"' in a way that would prove satisfactory for research or behaviorally based theory" (p. 437).

What theoretical rewards might we reap if we learn how to observe and classify affective states? How will the consideration of affect enrich developmental theory? It is an oversimplification to say so, but I believe affect does for language acquisition what motivation does for learning. Affect moves infants to socialize and to assimilate the behavior of others; it gives them important personal information to convey before they have language and complex thoughts. Affect moves infants to restructure the environment and to create their own niche within that environment. It is the force that energizes them to explore, observe, examine, and puzzle over a range of phenomena. Affect drives and is sustained by cognition.

EMOTIONAL COGNITION AND COGNITIVE EMOTION

If emotion and cognition are so intimately interrelated, is it possible to separate them? Possibly not. In Haviland's (1976) research, two experienced testers examined the Bayley Scales of Infant Development, classifying each item as affect-related or affect-independent. An item was considered affective if it required the child's interest. The two testers were 100 percent in agreement when classifying items independently as to the affect required for their expression. For "motor and sensorimotor behaviors," they found that dependence on affect was very high from birth to three months, diminishing with age:

	Definitely require affect	Probably require affect	Do not require affect
	(%)	(%)	(%)
0–3 months	40	58	2
3–8 months	25	17	57
8–18 months	1	33	75

From an analysis of the Infant Behavior Record, whose items are designed to assess the child's "social and objective orientations" toward its environment, all items turned out to be dependent on affect! "Every single item on this test," Haviland learned, "relies on an assessment of infant affect and an inference about which affect it is and whether or not it is appropriate. It is not possible to rate an infant without affect on this scale." She concluded that "the best cue to early infant development is affect," which "is either necessary to or is the common method for determination of awareness, interest, recognition, cooperation, anticipation, and change of state." These cognitive states, she added, "cannot be determined or inferred from any source other than affect" (pp. 427–429).

Although some neural substrates for language may develop in anticipation of appropriate stimulation, affect is logically necessary—it impels the child to exploit and therefore to develop linguistic capacity. A considerable threat to language development, then, would be posed by reduced affect (revealed facially and vocally) early in infancy. According to this view, tests of affective expression promise to be more prognostic linguistically than scores on most intelligence tests, for it is unlikely that language will develop without a felt need to communicate. I question the urgency of this need in children who cannot readily detect differences between the way things ought to be, physically and socially, and the way things actually are. Let us, then, look at the elaboration of affective displays in normally developing infants and examine the communication and early language of infants with reduced or atypical affect.

Communicativeness Intensified

To acquire and use language, infants need to understand that their own activity can influence external events, an ability that is typically present very early in postnatal life (Sameroff, 1968; Siqueland and Lipsitt, 1966). Indeed, if effectance motivation theory is valid, infants will do a lot of things merely for the satisfaction they get from the perception that they in some way have made a difference. They must also have the capacity to understand that other people have different feelings and thoughts than they themselves do and they must be able to recognize their own intentions and read the intentions of others. One gets sneak previews of these capacities from several spontaneous behaviors, including those cases in which infants respond empathically, pretend, or practice acts of deception.

OTHER HEARTS: EMPATHY

A feeling of empathy means that one appreciates the feelings of other individuals. Empathy is therefore properly regarded as a communicative matter, relevant to interpersonal communication and at some level, we must assume, the effective use of linguistic knowledge.

At one time, empathy had a meaning approximately equivalent to that of the German *Einfuhlung* or "feeling oneself into."[2] However, the word also meant or came to mean "motor mimicry," which denotes any overt action by an observer that mimics the behavior of the person observed. In the short history of research on empathy, most of it in this century, scholars have been unable to decide whether empathy is an affective construct, a cognitive construct, or both (Strayer, 1987).

I think this natural confusion about the meaning of empathy may be telling us something rather interesting. Since the voice is a major channel for the display of emotion, empathic feelings will frequently be induced through vocalization. Izard (1978) has argued that one's own emotions are amplified, perhaps even to some degree *experienced,* by way of feedback from the affective organs spontaneously activated by the situation that gave rise to the feelings. These organs are taken to be the facial muscles involved in affective

2. For more on the early history of scholarship on empathy, see Brothers (1989).

expressions, although there is no reason to exclude the sound production system and the feedback to one's own ears. Therefore, the
movements that convey emotionality to others are the same as those
that enhance and perhaps confirm the experience of emotion arising
within oneself.

Success in the interpretation of affect is a necessary condition for
attachment, in some cases perhaps even survival, because it includes the infant's ability to read the intentions and emotional
dispositions of others toward it (as well as their identity). Since
affect is vocally encoded, the interpretation of affect may be facilitated when infants engage in vocal accommodation. Viewed in this
context, vocal accommodation is a *perceptual mechanism.*

It is not surprising that "motor mimicry" would be a possible
interpretation of empathy, given current feedback theories of emotion (such as Izard, 1977). If the capacity to feel one's own emotions
is enhanced by sensory feedback from the organs of affective expression, then motor mimicry might be the process that enhances
the individual's capacity to feel the emotions of others. But more
important, there would be a link between the interpretation of
vocally encoded affect in the speech of others—utterances being the
conventional vehicle for vocally expressed emotion—and vocal accommodation as a form of motor mimicry.

Although in the first instance vocal accommodation is an important way to express the fact that one is receiving and properly
interpreting the affective signals of others, it may also be one of
the better ways of understanding their emotional states. That accommodations capture some speech material along with the cues to
emotionality is a beneficial consequence, though arguably one that
is unintended by Nature.

VOICE: A GREAT PLACE TO PUT LANGUAGE   These observations
on affect lead us inexorably to the conclusion that the phonological
mode of language would be culturally optional if the vocal-facial
transmission of feeling and empathy were not biologically imperative. Humans, like other animals, tend to learn about the things to
which they naturally attend, and phylogenetically this would have
made the vocal-facial complex an appropriate place to put gestures
of social significance.

If our species is to survive, our young must thrive. This means that at some point in our evolutionary history we must have developed ways of *warning* the young. In light of the fact that non-human primates have alarm calls, we may assume that our ancestral hominids vocally informed their associates of predators and perhaps other dangers. If we were to have a culture, we also had to invent ways of *instructing* the young. To be sure that warning and instructing were effective, it made sense to use an existing channel with a proven track record. Moreover, it made good biological sense that the sender's identity and social intentions were encoded in the same cue complex as the nominal message. This gave the overwhelming advantage to languages that were spoken. And now, in ontogeny, since the cues to phonological language are embedded in a stream of vocal variations and facial movements, the infant observer's natural orientation to that affective stream satisfies a condition on the learning of speech.

If, as a form of motor mimicry, empathy is related to vocal accommodation, as perspective-taking it is linked to communicative efficiency. It is important, therefore, that we ask how empathy initially manifests itself and changes over the course of infancy. We might begin by asking how much conceptual sophistication is needed to respond empathically. Presumably one must be able to sense what another individual is experiencing. But is this deeply analytical or superficially contagious?

DEVELOPMENT OF EMPATHIC RESPONDING   It appears that in the human infant empathic responding gets off to a very early start. Studies show that the sound of crying causes newborn babies to cry, and that this contagious crying is more frequently set off by the cries of other newborns than by those of older infants or a computer-synthesized cry or noise (Martin and Clark, 1982; Sagi and Hoffman, 1976; Simner, 1971). Some are disinclined to accept contagious crying as empathic since it is not obviously a response to another's "situation" (Thompson, 1987). To do so, however, seems legitimate to me, for if distress produces crying that evokes other distress vocalization, might this not be the route by which humans learn about the state, and therefore the "situation," of others?

Later in development, infants begin to respond sympathetically. At just over a year, infants appear to offer assistance of one form or another when a person in their company begins to cry (Zahn-

Waxler and Radke-Yarrow, 1982). Children with affective disorders may give less evidence of empathic responding than affectively normal children. According to some recent research, high functioning autistic children are less able to label emotions felt by others (Yirmiya et al., 1992). As we will see later, autistic children also seem less aware of the minds as well as the hearts of other individuals.

EMPATHY IN OTHER ANIMALS   There are reasons to expect empathy in other animals. As we saw in Chapter 6, the neural structures associated with phonatory control in nonhuman primates are localizable mainly to the limbic system, which takes a major responsibility for the feeling and display of emotion, including empathy (Brothers, 1989). Monkeys respond readily to a range of vocal alarm calls by retreating to a place of safety and looking in the direction of the expected predator. Group defenses seem to have survival value for individuals. The behaviors that promote group defense among nonhuman primates, and undoubtedly among other mammals as well, communicate emotional state.

Some animals appear to demonstrate empathic responding. De Waal's (1989) detailed description of social behavior in bonobos, a close relative of the common chimpanzee, suggests that they discern and respond to emotionality. Brothers (in submission) presents examples of empathic responding in a variety of species and suggests that in many cases emotion may spread contagiously, propagating through a herd or flock by the mechanism of *entrainment*. According to this account, identical emotional states and acts are transmitted from one individual to another. One presumes the flow of information to be

> *Animal 1*   *Animal 2*
> {feeling → display}   →   {feeling → display} or {display → feeling}

where it is left unclear whether the initial display evokes feeling directly, resulting in a separately evoked display, that is, an exact reproduction of the prior action in Animal 1; or whether the transmission is, in effect, display-to-display with feeling derived from the reproduced motor activity. In any case, Brothers argues convincingly that these behavioral reproductions extend beyond mere imitations, free of feeling.

OTHER MINDS: PRETENDING AND DECEPTION

Although the empathic child appreciates the experience of another person, the mechanisms by which it comes to know that experience are unclear. It seems possible that empathic feelings spread contagiously through displays of emotion that fairly directly evoke like responses in observers. This may be more reflexic than interpretive, as we would expect of an encapsulated system. We cannot therefore be certain that the child believes others *must be* feeling sad because it knows what they experienced. In that sense, empathy may not be the strictest test of a child's appreciation of another's mental experience. However, there is another realm in which the stricter test may be met, pretending and deception.

"Rarely a day goes by when people do not engage in some sort of deceptive interaction," say Friedman and Tucker (1990) realistically and perhaps cynically. "Deception seems to be a stable in our communication repertoire" (p. 257). What are the origins of the capacity to deceive or pretend? How much conceptual sophistication do these acts require? Presumably, to be pulled off convincingly these behaviors required the capacity to form second-order or metarepresentations (Leslie, 1987). According to Malatesta et al. (1989), the capacity for deception is revealed in at least one relatively simple way, when children uncouple feelings from expressive behavior, for example, smiling despite the experience of displeasure or feigning distress. Evidently this capacity is normally first seen during the second year of life (Belsky and Most, 1981; Leslie, 1987; Watson and Fischer, 1977).

In one study, it was found that sixteen- and twenty-nine-month-old infants imitate a variety of affective behaviors, seemingly pretending to cry, laugh, yawn, sigh, and exhibit other such actions (Kuczynski, Zahn-Waxler, and Radke-Yarrow, 1987). However, maternal reports indicate that in the younger infants these reproductions occurred very naturally; the corresponding behaviors among infants in the older group surfaced in a more contrived fashion, with evidence of self-awareness or faking. This observation was reinforced by the finding of fewer delayed than immediate reproductions of affect behavior, which raises questions about a different mechanism, that of contagion, and suggests that it is not that imitations become more contrived at twenty-nine months but that the more genuinely imitative behaviors emerge at this age.

Children's capacity to attribute mental states to others, including the ability to detect discrepancies between their own knowledge and that of other individuals, is usually revealed sometime between the second (Bretherton, McNew, and Beeghly-Smith, 1981; Mac-Namara, Baker, and Olson, 1976) and the fourth year of life (Sodian et al., 1991). But most autistic children appear to be deficient in the capacity to act on the inferred mental states of others, or even to talk about mental states (Tager-Flusberg, 1992). In one study (Baron-Cohen, Leslie, and Frith, 1985), autistic, Down syndrome, and normally developing young children were shown a girl doll putting a marble in a basket. Then, when the doll walked off, the child was allowed to see the experimenter transfer the marble to another location. When the doll was brought back, the children were asked where she would look for her marble. The retarded subjects and the young normals pointed to the basket, the place the doll had last seen it, but the autistic children indicated the place where they (but not the doll) had seen the marble go. In other words, the autistic children seemed unable to dissociate their own knowledge from that of the doll. In effect, they failed to apply a theory of mind.

There is reason to believe that some animals have difficulty taking their own point of view. Having and being aware of one's own viewpoint requires—and perhaps operationally defines—a *sense of self*. This seems to be lacking in most species of nonhuman primates, at least to the degree that the mirror test is a valid indication of the self. In that paradigm, a spot of rouge is put on the nose or forehead of the subject, who is then given the chance to look in a mirror. It is assumed that animals that know the image is their own will touch or attempt to rub off the spot. It appears that normally developing infants but not those with Down syndrome do this by about twenty-two months of age (Mans, Cicchetti, and Sroufe, 1978), although Down infants do express this "sense of self" later on (Hill and Tomlin, 1981). As a group, three- to twelve-year-old autistic children pass the mirror recognition test; the minority that fail it are significantly more likely to be mute (Spiker and Ricks, 1984).

As for nonhuman primates, a review of the literature (Gallup, 1982) suggests that chimpanzees and orangutans recognize themselves in the mirror, but that the vast majority of primate species, including gorillas and several species of gibbons and monkeys, seem incapable of figuring out that the movements they see in the mirror were initiated by them and therefore that the animal they see *is* themselves. Nonhuman primates do have some propensity to practice deception, however. There are several published accounts (Byrne and Whiten, 1991; Cheney and Seyfarth, 1990; Steklis and Raleigh, 1979; Whiten and Byrne, 1988) of interactions in which one nonhuman primate deceived another. But in many of these cases it is not clear that the deceiver intended the deception and attributed intentions to its victim (Byrne and Whiten, 1991; Cheney and Seyfarth, 1992).

Nonhuman primates seem to have some capacity for pretend play, though the evidence here is also anecdotal (Byrne, 1990). More research is needed on second-order representations, but what we have in hand suggests that nonhuman primates and human children reveal different degrees of knowledge of other individuals' mental states, that is, in their conceptions of other minds (Premack and Woodruff, 1978).

Other Levels of Emotion
Hypoaffective Children

What about children who are affectively lacking? Haviland (1976) has said that in development, she "would predict that less affective response would result in less cognition and hence a deficient development of the affective system as well . . . If the cognitive system does not process well, there is less to be excited about, less to enjoy, and on occasion less to be distressed about" (p. 447). It would be interesting to follow a representative population of ostensibly normally developing infants, evaluating them for their degree of spontaneous display of affect and then documenting their cognitive and linguistic development, but I am not aware of precisely such a study (though see Bloom et al., 1988, which I discuss below).

What, then, of retarded children, who, as we saw earlier, have greatly reduced vocal and facial affect? Ganiban, Wagner, and Cicchetti (1990) recently reviewed the literature on the biological factors that may contribute to reduced affect in Down syndrome infants. They describe studies suggesting that within the central nervous system there is a reduced number of cholinergic cells and levels. For example, postmortem examinations of adolescents and adults with Down syndrome reveal less than normal numbers of cells in the nucleus basalis of Meynart, a structure that contains acetylcholine-producing neurons that project to the cortex (Casanova et al., 1985). Concordantly, other research has turned up decreased acetylcholine levels in the central nervous system of individuals with Down syndrome (Yates et al., 1980).

Infants with Down syndrome may also have reduced levels of another neurotransmitter, noradrenaline. Some research has shown reductions of DBH, an enzyme that facilitates conversion of dopamine to noradrenaline (Weinshilbaum et al., 1971), or of noradrenaline itself. Thompson et al. (1985) speculated that these neurotransmitter deficiencies may underlie Down syndrome infants' reduced capacity to interpret new situations rapidly, causing slower or less efficient processing of social alterations. It is interesting that postmortem studies of individuals with Down syndrome have reported dendritic spine abnormalities and a decrease in neurons in the limbic system, that part of the brain responsible for the quality and intensity of the affect we normally experience (Purpura, 1975).

HYPOTONICITY

These neurotransmitter data fit with behavioral observations that Down syndrome infants generally tend to be hypotonic, demonstrating little resistance on tests of passive movement. In their study of elicited humor responses, Cicchetti and Sroufe (1976) found that the four most hypotonic Down syndrome infants in their study never laughed before the age of thirteen months and rarely laughed even then. They assumed that hypotonic infants have difficulty "processing incongruity fast enough to generate the tension required for laughter" (p. 923). This difficulty was thought to be the joint result of biochemical and cognitive factors.

Hypotonicity, then, may retard emotional and cognitive development and contribute to the motoric delays observed in Down syndrome (Henderson, 1985). Since there are reasons to believe that motor delay may retard cognitive development, hypotonicity may be involved in both motoric and intellectual development (Cicchetti and Beeghly, 1990). For this reason, we need to ask if infants with Williams syndrome have similar neurotransmitter deficiencies and similar reductions in the tonicity required for alertness and quick response. And we need to ask if children with Williams syndrome have biochemical abnormalities such as reduced output of norepinephrine, for although these children are incapable of dealing adequately with the items on intelligence tests, from all reports they appear to be emotionally responsive and congenial participants in social, even conversational interactions. If Williams syndrome infants, unlike those with Down syndrome, are not reduced in noradrenaline and other neurotransmitters, we might speculate that these neurochemical factors may, in ways not currently understood, normally contribute to levels or types of social communication that facilitate language. However, as I suggested earlier, there are other possible explanations for the loquaciousness of infants with Williams syndrome. One of these involves their seemingly normal appreciation of facial structure and activity. At present, one can only wonder if biochemical and perceptuofacial explanations are independent of each other or interrelated.

THE LANGUAGE OF HYPOAFFECTIVE
(NONRETARDED) CHILDREN

If affect is so important to language, then why do infants who usually have little or no expression on their face typically learn language more rapidly than infants who are facially expressive (Bloom and Capatides, 1987; Bloom, Beckwith, and Capatides, 1988)? In one study, two groups of nine-month-old infants were followed to the age of twenty-one months or more. One group included children who were subsequently identified as early word learners, the other included those who were subsequently identified as late word learners. With age, both groups increased the frequency of affective display. But the early word learners also increased the frequency of saying words, whereas the late word learners increased the frequency of emotional expression, not word production. There was, then, a positive correlation between time spent in neutral affect expression and quality of early language learning. Bloom and her colleagues concluded that "the experiences and processes that contribute to emotional expression may compete for the cognitive resources required for language learning. In contrast, neutral affect expression, which we have suggested is a continuation of the 'quiet alert states' of early infancy, would allow the

reflective, contemplative stance that is required for learning words"
(1988, p. 171).

This explanation cannot be ruled out with existing evidence.
Indeed, a correlation was recently reported between the ability to
regulate, that is, to suppress vagal tone, and the ability to attend
for prolonged periods. DeGangi et al. (1991) found an association
between vagal tone suppression in eight- to ten-month-olds and
scores on the Mental Development Index of the Bayley Scales of
Infant Development. Infants who suppressed vagal tone during the
test achieved higher test scores.

A related explanation is also neurophysiological, although not
necessarily attentional. In very young infants, emotional expressivity appears to be a function of brainstem activity (Stifter, Fox, and
Porges, 1989). Suppression of facial expressivity is enabled by maturation of cortical control mechanisms (Best and Queen, 1989). In
Malatesta's (1982) study of mother-infant dyads, it was reported
that facial expressions changed every seven seconds in three-month-
olds and every nine seconds in six-month-olds. She also found a
reduction in knit brow and pain expressions from three to six
months. Because deintensification of affect can result in neutrali-
zation (Malatesta et al., 1989), it becomes apparent that Bloom et
al.'s affectively neutral subjects may simply have had the cortical
capacities required for emotional inhibition *and* lexical acquisition.
The plausibility of this explanation is suggested by the observation
that when pointing first appears, it is frequently associated with a
neutral affective state that seems to be both attentive and part of
an orienting response (Thelen and Fogel, 1989).

INFORMATION THEORY IN INFANCY

While not necessarily ruling out either of these explanations, I favor
an alternative account that is inspired by data in Bloom et al. (their
Figure 2) showing a decrease in nonneutral facial expression in
early *and* late word groups during that period in which there was
a dramatic increase in vocabulary (an increase of twelve new words
in children who already had twenty). For the early word group, this
diminution took place between thirteen and seventeen months,
their vocabulary spurt occurring near the end of that period. Later
word learners experienced their decrease in nonneutral expressions
between seventeen and twenty-one months, their spurt occurring
near the end of that interval.

Bloom et al. thought this dip reflected competition between mental resources, but these trends also make sense if one assumes that infants are shifting from purely affective communication by way of the voice and face to affective and lexical communication. Inasmuch as words do affective work—expressing intentions, desires, and attitudes—their availability takes pressure off the facial-vocal (nonlexical) signaling system. The generalization that emotion lies between perception and action applies to lexical action that would be unavailable to prelexical children.

According to this explanation, the diminution of affective expression is important not because of what it indexes—attentional or neurophysiological states that favor word learning—but because in children who are using their voice and face to express something about themselves, the emergence of words causes collateral changes in the nature of affective display. Words add a second signaling system, and thus the possibility of redundancy, so that for the first time in their young lives children are free to relax the intensity of their facial and vocal displays without loss of communicative efficiency. This conception favors redundancy of display over competition between cognitive resources.

Information theory (Shannon and Weaver, 1949) tells us that communicators nearly always do what Bloom et al.'s subjects did: they cut back on the effort and precision dedicated to one set of cues whenever social or physical context or other cue systems are available to do the work. When speakers believe that their message is redundant and therefore predictable, they invest less effort in communication, frequently truncating, abbreviating, and slurring signals that would otherwise be articulated fully and carefully (see Lieberman, 1963; Poplack, 1980; Zipf, 1932, 1949). This practice should hold even where the information conveyed is not of the "rational" sort associated with lexical semantics but is, rather, of the phatic type that targets social and emotional responses in the child's observers. The young speaker can now induce delight, surprise, and humor with the well-timed utterance of a new word as well as with a smile or a playful vocalization.

The Emergence of Reference

We have seen that vocal communication does not have to await language. In the first year of life, the fundamental frequency and

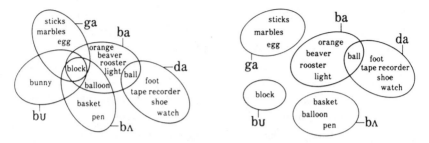

Figure 8.3. Prenegotiated (left) and negotiated (right) labeling patterns of a seventeen-month-old boy.

other physical properties of infants' vocalizations may vary with communicative context (D'Odorico, 1984). Low-level referencing may not wait for words. In the second year of life, sound-meaning associations may occur at the segmental level, embedded in utterances that sound very much like babbling (Blake and Fink, 1987), suggesting the presence of de facto sound-meaning associations prior to the expression of words. These are what developmental psycholinguists have called "phonetically consistent forms" (Dore, 1974) and "protolanguage" (Halliday, 1975).

My colleague in the Neurolinguistics Laboratory at the Massachusetts General Hospital, Michael Smith (1988), reported on a seventeen-month-old boy he observed just as he was embarking on the construction of an initial lexicon. Figure 8.3 depicts an early labeling pattern the child demonstrated one day. On the left are the sound-meaning relationships revealed in the child's spontaneous labeling, and on the right, the more distinct patterns that occurred in the same session when adults sought to resolve ambiguities. Just as the early expression of sound-meaning correspondences may occur independent of words, to be communicative a behavior need not be intended to convey. Some social contexts may threaten or delight, and these feelings will automatically be differentially conveyed because that simply is the way the emotion-vocalization channel works.

Words can come to the surface by different routes and may be deployed with varying degrees of consciousness. They may emerge through acts of vocal accommodation, which the child performs in order to share in or interpret emotional behavior or to appear *simpatico* or masterfully adult. They also may arise by imitation to empower the child who is seeking to engage in lexical communication. In such instrumental uses of sound patterns, the child puts currently available phonetic material to referential work.[3]

Of course, these scenarios are not unique to language. Thelen (1985) has witnessed growth in the ability of maturing infants to use simple patterned movements as instrumental responses. For example, in the activity of kicking she has noticed that "a 1-month-old might kick when distressed, a 3-month-old infant might kick during social play with the mother, a 4-month-old infant might kick against a squeaky toy to reactivate the noise, and a 6-month-old infant might kick apparently to signal the mother to continue the feeding" (p. 234). In the area of vocal development, Papousek and Papousek (in press) think such developmental changes come about as the result of feedback from adults. They have noted that crying and noncrying vocalizations evoke different reactions: "when parents respond only to crying and discomfort sounds," they say, "the infant develops instrumental crying as the only effective means to attract parental attention" (p. 18). Some theorists hold that intentional acts have a natural flow in development: the infant experiences and displays an emotional state that is observed and reacted to by the mother, whose reactions are, in turn, observed by the infant. It is, according to Chappell and Sander (1979), "the response of the mother appropriate and contingent to the infant's 'symptoms of underlying status' that gives meaning to her response for the infant and elevates the infant's expression of underlying status to the level of a goal-directed signal that allows the infant to reveal internal state *in order* to bring about the desired environmental outcome" (p. 107, italics theirs). Although it is difficult to say which early words children produce with the intention of communicating, analyses of children's initial lexicons suggest that they may deploy some words for this reason. Chief among these are the words nearly all children use in pragmatic circumstances as requests and refusals (see Bretherton, 1988).

In my judgment, developmental psychologists have been so eager

3. Piagetians have attempted to relate such "means-ends" capabilities to lexical development. Ironically, such comparisons tend to fail at the grossest levels, since most conceptual advances correlate nonsignificantly with age of first words. On occasion, these comparisons have succeeded at the "micro" level, however, since the awareness of a concept seems to be co-timed with use of the corresponding words (Gopnik and Meltzoff, 1986, 1987).

to demonstrate the relationship between Piagetian stages of concept development and language that they have totally ignored some critical concepts. For example, as I indicated earlier, infants need some level of conceptual sophistication just to know that the object of their mother's attention when she vocalizes is the subject of her reference. In order to acquire lexical information that corresponds to nonlinguistic realities, infants must have the capacity to understand that when their mother looks at an object while vocalizing, she—part of the time, at least—is *naming* that object. And if they do not know this, it is hard to see how they will become full-fledged talkers.

Being able to affiliate and socialize with someone who talks, having the ability to perceive and produce voice, and feeling the desire to communicate are individually necessary but collectively insufficient to launch an initial lexicon. There also must be the lexical and nonlinguistic conceptual capabilities for reference. Infants must become aware that words refer to "categories of similar objects" (Markman and Hutchinson, 1984).

CATEGORIZATION: PRECURSOR TO THE MEANINGFUL DEPLOYMENT OF NAMES

To show that infants *put* objects in the same category, it is necessary to show that the items are discriminable. In some studies that have done this, certain types of low-level categorization were performed by infants as young as four months of age. Using exemplars of the category *bird,* Roberts and Horowitz (1986) obtained evidence for categorization beginning between seven and nine months. Using drawings of faces, Sherman (1985) found that at ten months—one to several months before the usual appearance of words—infants demonstrate the ability to abstract category-level information from their perceptual experience with discriminable objects.

When a child names a novel thing, we can argue that it has figured out what the thing is and that the emergence of expressive vocabulary reflects the growth of the ability to categorize (Reznick and Goldfield, 1990). Reznick (1989) points out that there are at least three levels of categorization (see also Backscheider and Markman, in submission; Markman, 1991; and Markman and Hutchinson, 1984). In level one categorization, the members of a category are perceptually indiscriminable, as in the case of elements that are categorically perceived (for example, stop consonants). In level two categorization, the elements share a perceptual feature that causes them to be seen as members of a set but are discriminable from one another (persons). In level three categories, the members are similar not necessarily perceptually but interpretively—by way of their similar function, cultural value, or some other association (household objects, vehicles).

Reznick believes that the development of categorization ability is difficult to study because some categorizations are modality-sensitive, and there are no clear-cut procedures for measuring the relevant behaviors. Nevertheless, he reviews literature suggesting that level one and level two categorizations emerge under a variety of measurement conditions by the middle of the first year of life. Some level three categorizations are evident by the end of the first year. This would suggest that categorization ability is functioning by the twelve- to eighteen-month interval, when lexical knowledge and use are first revealed. The ability to categorize is almost certainly precursive and prerequisite to the ability to name and creatively use the names of things.

Receptive vocabulary can develop before the child's categorial abilities are adequate for language production, and Benedict (1979) has shown that the child's receptive lexicon exceeds its expressive vocabulary by a certain amount at different ages. Lexical comprehension begins around nine months and reaches the fifty-word level at thirteen months. Lexical expression begins around twelve months and reaches the fifty-word level at eighteen months. It is likely then that lexical comprehension drives expressive word development.

For those interested in knowing what children's first words are, the thirteen-month-olds studied by Bretherton (1988) used words to refer to the categories listed below in decreasing order of frequency (the number of children using the word, based on a sample of thirty-two children):

Parents: 27	Relational/functional words: 17
Requests and refusals: 26	Food: 13
Greetings: 22	Objects: 13
Environmental sounds: 18	Animals: 12

When similar analyses are carried out on the words children comprehend, it is found that receptive vocabularies typically contain more action words.

WHAT DO CHILDREN'S WORDS MEAN?

Children learn their first words through ostensive definition when, to take the typical case, a parent points to a thing and says its name. So far, so good. But as child language researchers have recently asked, how does the child know precisely what the name refers to? How do children pin down the best meaning of a term from a broad range of possible meanings? How can children between eighteen months and six years learn nine new words a day, as has been estimated (Carey, 1978), if they have no interpretive biases that constrain the assignment of meanings to words?

A semantically unbiased child would be in an impossible position where word-learning is concerned. On what grounds would the child

> conclude that a new unfamiliar word, e.g., "dog", refers to dogs? What is to prevent a child from concluding that "dog" is a proper name for that particular dog? What prevents the child from concluding that "dog" means "four-legged object" or "black object" or any number of other characteristics that dogs share? And finally, what prevents the child from concluding that "dog," in addition to referring to that particular dog, also refers to the bone the dog is chewing on or to the tree the dog is lying under? (Markman and Hutchinson, 1984, p. 2)

This latter inference is plausible, since infants tend to be very sensitive to the things objects are used for or associated with. In a series of experiments by Ellen Markman and her colleagues at Stanford (Markman, in submission, 1991; Markman and Hutchinson, 1984), children were shown pictures and asked to indicate to which other pictures they were *taxonomically* or *thematically* related. For example, the child might be handed a picture of a dog and asked to "find another one that is the same kind of thing" (or merely to "find another one") from a set containing a cat (the taxonomic alternative) and a bone (the thematic choice).

Children as young as eighteen months chose the thematic alternative on this task, which is oriented around *objects*. But Markman has used an interesting control, which shifts the focus to (nonce) *words*. For example, the experimenter will say "See this? It's a kind of dax. Can you find another kind of dax?" Just hearing this new term in reference to the same object (dog) greatly increases the number of taxonomic responses. It is as though children know intuitively that words refer to collections of similar objects, that is, to taxonomies. Merely naming an object seems to weaken the thematic associations the child would normally call to mind for that object and for its name. This makes it possible, Markman noted, for words to achieve their fullest flexibility and combinatorial power, for as the names of categories of similar objects, words stand free of associative baggage and are eligible to be linked with other words (taxonomic labels) to yield the desired associations and only those associations.

These findings have been replicated by Waxman and Kosowski (1990), who also found that children's taxonomic bias may be associated solely with nouns; no such effect was observed for adjectives. They also found that children as young as two years have some sense of subordinate-supraordinate relations, revealing in their first and second choices for novel nouns the awareness that perceptually disparate objects such as bird and mouse belong to a single (animal) class. This sort of "vertical" taxonomic organization does not really develop until much later in childhood, however (Lucariello et al., 1992).

Markman and her colleagues have also determined that when an unfamiliar object has component parts, any name that is supplied is taken by children to identify the whole object and not the parts. When the object and its name are familiar, however, and children are supplied with a novel word, they treat the new term as the name of one of the object's parts. This tendency, which Markman calls the *whole object* assumption, constrains the range of possible meanings entertained for new words.

Semantic constraints are also offered by the *mutual exclusivity* assumption. Evidence for such an assumption is usually produced when children see a familiar and an unfamiliar object and hear an unfamiliar word. Almost invariably they select the unfamiliar object rather than assume that the novel word might be another name for the familiar thing or the name of an attribute of the object that they know.

These interpretive biases operate as early as eighteen to twenty-four months, when word-learning takes a dramatic step forward. Newport (1990) proposed that another type of constraint—inadequate memory—limits the utterance data to which children are *effectively* exposed. In effect, this allows children to concentrate on the smaller stretches of language that are likely to comprise functional units, eliminating the need to search through extensive mental corpora in order to locate critical linguistic cues.

As infants move along the path that leads to spoken language, their vocal tracts mature and their perceptual experiences accumulate. Maternal-infant interactions now include vocal turn taking, joint attention, and vocal accommodation, which permit a certain superficial competence in lexical communication within restricted contexts. But to plunge more deeply and creatively into language, infants must have incentives. Linguistic progress requires a series of articulatory negotiations, massive storage of lexical items and phrases, and componential grammatical analyses.

The child is hastened along the path to these more complex operations by an urge to communicate, which at the most general level is produced by parallel and converging developments in the domains of affect and cognition. More specifically, the persistent desire to convey stems from the child's discovery that other individuals have an emotional and mental life that differs from its own. In formal terms, this discovery of "other hearts" and "other minds" makes communication possible, for the child now senses that it has information others lack and vice versa. It is my hypothesis that children speak in order to reduce these discrepancies.

The emergence of lexical reference requires other cognitive advances, of course, especially those associated with object categorization. The child needs to recognize the shared physical and functional properties of the nonlinguistic world and, hence, to appreciate the conceptual basis of categorizations that are built into lexical assignments. Moreover, the child needs to recognize the concept of word, that is, that a label is implicitly taxonomic.

The infant who has made it this far uses single words and stereotyped phrases to refer to things in restricted social contexts. Very few of its utterances are creative and none of them is rule-governed. But the child is now a talker standing at the threshold of grammatical language.

9

DEVELOPMENT
OF SPOKEN LANGUAGE

The path begun in Chapter 2 has now brought the child to the threshold of phonological language, a readiness to use its oral sound-making potential to convey information others are judged to lack. Progress in acquiring a usable lexicon will depend, in large measure, on the efficiency of phonetic analysis and phonological processing, and on the child's ability to subsume nonlinguistic knowledge under appropriate linguistic categories.

The Duality of Linguistic Specialization

Much has been written recently about the existence in human cognition of functionally autonomous capacities that are to some degree independent of other neural and cognitive capabilities. This notion is traceable back through the days of Faculty Psychology to the time, nearly two centuries ago, of Franz Joseph Gall (Gross, 1985). The present incarnation of this idea—the module—has been characterized as

> an informationally encapsulated computational system—an inference-making mechanism whose access to background information is constrained by general features of cognitive architecture, hence relatively rigidly and relatively permanently constrained. One can conceptualize a module as a special-purpose computer with a proprietary database,

under the conditions that: (a) the operations that it performs have access *only* to the information in its database (together, of course, with specifications of currently impinging proximal stimulations); and (b) at least some information that is available to at least some cognitive process is *not* available to the module. (Fodor, 1985, p. 3)

Fodor also proposed the existence of a particular module, one that deals only with the perception and production of language and not with analysis of nonspeech auditory signals. Evidence for the autonomy of the language module includes aphasia, a "proprietary, domain-specific" pathology according to Fodor.

When one considers language from ontogenetic and comparative perspectives, certain roles and functions of a linguistic specialization become evident. In this chapter I will argue from developmental and interspecific data that children could not acquire language through the action of a language module as presently described. Rather, several specializations are responsible for the development of language.

Ironically, Fodor and others embracing modularity have said very little about the actual linguistic properties of a language module. But we must consider the primary responsibility of such a module to be grammatical analysis. We see this in a recent paper by Pinker (1991), in which English morphology is demonstrated to be computational as well as associative; it is the nonassociative property that makes morphology modular.

To carry out morphological operations, the module must deal in rules and representations, computing regular past tense verb forms by application of a rule that concatenates affixes with stem endings (such as *walk-walked*). On the other hand, irregular forms such as *run-ran,* which abound in English speech, are handled associatively; learners commit these forms to memory by rote, though some generalization by analogy is possible. For this reason, it is possible for "came" to precede, and temporarily to be replaced by, "comed" in the utterances of a grammatically developing child.

Pinker sees that only the computational part of morphology requires the operations of a language module. According to him, this part is at least partially distinct from the hardware underlying the associative memory system and whichever of our neural resources deal with irregular forms. In support of his view, Pinker commandeers data from aphasic patients and reaction time experiments with normal subjects. He also refers to data from children with a form of specific language impairment in which irregular verb forms are handled more competently than regular forms.

Because this and other work on grammatical processing support the existence of a specialization that is analytical in development, enabling the extraction of abstract organizational principles, and computational in practice, I cannot merely conceive of this specialization as the *language* module. To do so would also be to tacitly accept notions that I straightforwardly reject, that language equals grammar and that pregrammatic children are incapable of language behavior. I therefore think of our species-unique linguistic specialization as a particular kind of language module, and I propose to call it the *Grammatical Analysis Module* (GAM).

DUPLEX PERCEPTION

The modularity of linguistic perception was endorsed by many of those who contributed chapters to a recent monograph dealing explicitly with this question (Mattingly and Studdert-Kennedy, 1991), as well as a number of colleagues responding in an open peer commentary to Fodor's (1985) précis of *Modularity of Mind*. Though the arguments for a speech perception module are broadly-based, one small piece of behavior that has been offered as evidence for perceptual modularity is the intriguing phenomenon known as duplex perception (Liberman and Mattingly, 1985). This effect is produced dichotically by presenting the critical cue to consonantal place of articulation, a formant transition, to one ear and the remaining portion of the syllable to the other ear. For computer synthesized [da] and [ga], normally the transition by itself resembles a "chirp" and the remaining portion is heard as a syllable initiated by a consonant of ambiguous place of articulation. But in the dichotic mode, listeners tend to hear both a chirp *and* an intact syllable with clear consonantal place cues.

Since the function of the GAM is exclusively computational and analytical (at all levels of language), it cannot function without access to relevant data, that is, utterances and supporting referential behaviors. This requires exposure to and possibly even active solicitation of raw data. These functions are performed by a quasi-linguistic (and richly communicative) accomplice, a specialization that develops prior to the GAM, as it evolved at a far earlier time in the history of the species.

The "proprietary database" of which Fodor spoke is an enormous sample of linguistically relevant data. For reasons I will explain below, I think this is supplied by a specialized information processing system with specific responsibilities that pertain to language. In proposing this specialization, I am not unmindful of the premium on parsimony—most theoreticians are loath to impute structure or process where it is not strictly required. And we would do well to keep in mind Howard Gardner's admonition that "if one posits a second type of system, it becomes necessary to trace two evolutions, two forms of hardware, systems of connections and communications, and so on" (1985, p. 13). Yet I think that when the logical requirement of a second specialization is explained and its functions described, we will record a net theoretical gain, for a range of currently unexplained psycholinguistic phenomena can be handled by a dual specialization hypothesis.[1] Let us look, then, at the specialization I have in mind, and see if it meets any of the tests suggested by Gardner and by Fodor.

As we have seen, infants are aware of the human voice before birth and are most certainly aware of the face from birth. This is revealed neonatally in indexical communication, in which caregivers and other family members become known by their facial structure, and later in affective communication, through which the feelings and intentions of social partners become known. Both vocal and facial activity, independently or more commonly in collaboration, convey emotions and attitudes. Movements of the eyes express affect and degree of attentiveness. They are also referential, either as facial gestures analogous to pointing or, in connection with speech, as cues to object labels.

This rich preserve of intersubjectively communicative behavior meets many of the tests for a neural specialization. One sees this in Brothers (1990), who pointed to evolutionarily significant behaviors in nonhuman primates. These reveal their ability to "read" and act upon the intentions (that is, goal-directed behaviors) of conspe-

---

1. Al Liberman (1992) has argued persuasively that it is ultimately more parsimonious to posit a language module than not to do so, for there is now a sea of experimental phonetic data that cannot be handled by "horizontal" accounts of cognition.

cific animals and suggest the presence of a specialization for social cognition that operates differently from other information processing systems. In her paper, support for a specialized capability in social cognition was also adduced from neurophysiological studies exposing socially dedicated (for example, "face") neurons and ontogenetic data from human infants showing a fairly uniform unfolding of social processing capabilities (as well as neuroanatomical and clinical findings).

It is clear that humans possess a specialization in social cognition (SSC) that meets many of the criteria set down by Fodor and by Gardner.[2] It is domain-specific, since certain kinds of social interactions evoke behaviors that are not otherwise displayed. It is heavily influenced by genetic factors and its activation requires no more than a minimal role for experience. It contains some hardwiring: there are brain cells that fire mainly to faces or to specific facial expressions, and different parts of the brain are responsible for linguistic and nonlinguistic prosody. And it is arguably autonomous; witness clinical entities such as Capgras syndrome, a disorder in which friends are indiscriminable from strangers, and autism (Brothers, 1990). If certain of the functions I am subsuming under the SSC were not fully automatic, the consequences would be very grave indeed. We could die before deciding whether an approaching individual was friend or foe. As Jerry Fodor has said, if approached by a panther he would not want to have to consider everything he knows about panthers "in the course of perceptual panther identification" (1983, p. 71).

In previous chapters, I have argued that social cognition plays a precursive and enabling role in the development of spoken language. We saw that neonates orient to facelike stimuli just minutes after birth and seem to study the expressive face. Infants and their mothers gaze together at the same things, a practice that leads to shared reference. In the first week of life, infants reveal listening preferences for their mother's voice and patterns of maternal prosody capable of distinguishing languages. In vocal turn taking the interactive framework is laid down for vocal learning and dialogue.

---

2. Fodor refers to face recognition as modular, but since we share with nonhuman primates many of the processes and mechanisms of social cognition, I have chosen to identify this very special and coherent collection of capabilities as a *specialization*.

While recognizing the specialness of our capabilities of social cognition, I think it must also be noted that nonhuman primates have a social specialization that has some of the properties of our SSC although they have no GAM. The reason various theorists think nonhuman primates are almost linguistic is that the human SSC can carry out a certain amount of verbal behavior on its own, (such as context-appropriate use of words), mocking the actions of an explicitly linguistic module especially, one might suppose, when the latter is slow to kick in. For the moment, I will take "slow" to mean sometime after twenty-eight months (plus or minus a half year), a rough guess as to when the GAM first conspicuously operates in the typical case.

I base this estimate on several things. Children initially string words together at about twenty-four months. Bickerton (1990) puts two years as the age at which the utterances of human children diverge from those of nonhuman primates trained in sign language. Tucker (1992) takes the same age as the beginning of a cerebral reorganization affecting emotional as well as motor and linguistic behavior. And most directly to the point, Marcus et al. (1992) found that all seven children in their sample, drawn from previously reported data, began to overregularize irregular verbs between twenty and thirty-five months, with a mean of 28.7 months.

One might wonder why I am not calling our specialization in social cognition a module, especially if the functions performed by face cells are modular. After all, there certainly are major differences between the SSC of human and nonhuman primates that relate to vocal turn taking, vocal accommodation, and shared gaze. In each of these areas we exceed anything documented in the other primates. We are also unlike nonhumans in other ways, most noticeably in our very keen awareness that our fellow conspecific experiences a range of private mental activities—an awareness which other primates seem to lack (Cheney and Seyfarth, 1990; Premack and Woodruff, 1978). Little wonder that our young manifest an intense urge to convey ideas while their young never do.

It is clear that our social cognition capabilities are highly specialized and unique to the species *Homo sapiens*. However, I have reasons for resisting the allure of "module." These include the fact that we share many of our social capabilities with other primates, and I have no desire to argue that the SSC is "mostly unique" and "mostly modular" to our species. The GAM is protected from this complication, since we would have difficulty supporting the claim that other primates have components of the capability that allows us to parse sentences, generate syntax, and compute morphology.

DUPLEX PERCEPTION REVISITED

We saw earlier that listeners presented with intact stop consonant plus vowel syllables never hear the chirp representing the critical formant transition that is embedded in the overall pattern. They only hear, for example, [da] or [ga]. Liberman and Mattingly (1989) suppose the reason is that the "closed module" that handles speech perception is preemptive, taking the chirp for its own segmental purposes and denying an "open module" that is concerned with prosody the chance to process this sound for its pitch, loudness, and timbre.

If duplex perception argues for a speech perception module, the converging but separable results of social cognition and grammatical analysis operations argue for the existence of a *dual* specialization. We process the segmental stream and the emotionality of spoken language in parallel, and we are simultaneously mindful of the lexical and the emotional content of speech. Listeners can hear words that, by themselves, would suggest a particular meaning, but simultaneously they pick up a tone of voice that implies a different interpretation altogether. And these cues seem to be prioritized differently than the consonantal place cues discussed earlier.

Developmentally, the additivity of language becomes conspicuous when the GAM turns on, for it is then that a multiplicity of categorial phonetic cues are piled on top of the prosodic, affective and speaker-identifying cues infants already value. In the real speech of sophisticated speakers, where both linguistic content and vocal affect are present, one type of cue does not preempt the other. And for speech to work this must be the case. Listeners must know both what the speaker is saying *and* what he intends by saying it. We duplexly pick up information about linguistic content and speaker affect because the cues to these things are of different sorts and are processed by different brain mechanisms. The listener is thus able to hear conflicts between "the words" and "the music" of spoken language. I am unsure how often listeners pick up linguistic content but miss tone of voice; my own listening experience tells me the opposite circumstance occurs with some frequency.

The proposed dual action of these specializations seems to map onto hemispheric functions as currently understood. If the left hemisphere is disproportionately responsible for phonetic processing we may assume it is coldly and asocially analytical. We know that the right hemisphere is warmly social and emotional, and is seemingly dominant for the processing of personally relevant information, no matter the modality (Van Lancker, 1991).

When I spoke earlier of the contribution of affect to cognitive development (see Chapter 8), in effect I was arguing for a system having "hot" components that acquire information and convey it to "cold" components for processing. We might recall Norman's (1981) rejection of emotionally cold conceptions of cognition that lack a regulatory system and therefore have no way to become aroused, interpret and react to danger, select and secure a mate, act surprised, or be curious. Norman, as we saw, identified two serious problems with such models: one was that cold cognitive systems were in the illogical position of setting their own priorities; the other was that in reality, the regulatory system would have to have been in place first. Otherwise, there would be no force pushing and shaping the cognitive system. Norman therefore argued for a cognitive system that is subordinate to the regulatory system. In such hot models of cognition, the organism's emotional systems make the initial decisions about what cognitive processing is needed and thus play a major role in regulating cognition. What I am saying about the specializations for human language is that they, too, divide along a "thermal" dimension. The SSC is the warmer of the two. It knows which sensory cues are the most interesting and which social behaviors offer its infant host the experience required to implement the developmental plan of the species.

A DISSENTING VIEW?

I am suggesting two specializations, but some researchers question the existence of any kind of modular capability for language. Bates, Bretherton, and Snyder (1988) studied children from ten to twenty-eight months of age and found no evidence of a discontinuity between grammar and semantics at the earliest stages of language development. They concluded from this that language is a strictly horizontal matter, one requiring no special informational system with modular properties. Without going into their data or reasoning, in my judgment Bates et al. did more to support language modularity than to refute it. For example, they repeatedly go to great lengths to distinguish between "the emergence of single words and their meanings" and the "more 'strictly linguistic' areas of phonology and grammar" (p. 12).

Bates et al. cause problems for themselves partly because they restrict their focus to intraspecific matters (individual differences among children), which are unlikely to show huge or easily measurable variations in social cognition. The SSC is revealed with unusual clarity in comparative studies of human and nonhuman primates, since we share many processes of social cognition with them, but we do not share language. They also doubt that there could be a "late-maturing syntax module" (1988, p. 283) because of the range of variation in the age at which syntax is acquired, but this skepticism is groundless since it is based on a failure to appreciate the variation that occurs naturally in biology and neural development.

Communicative Applications of the SSC

Evidence from disparate sources indicates that the SSC preorients infants to the social and facial-vocal cues associated with speaking. Through its specific operations—especially vocal accommodation, shared gaze, and vocal turntaking—this specialization is responsible for the infant's first words and stereotyped phrases. It also feeds utterances to the GAM, which has no data acquisition device of its own but does abstract grammatical rules from utterances that language-acquiring children attend to and seek to incorporate into their own social repertoires.

The most linguistically relevant operations of the SSC are those identified above—vocal accommodation, shared gaze, vocal turn taking—plus the emergent awareness of other minds. Vocal accommodation, as we have seen, involves convergence. Apparently spurred on by the desire for social approval, individuals tend to converge with both the linguistic and the nonlinguistic behaviors of their more seasoned associates. Language is intensely analytical, so one might presume that low-level vocal operations are irrelevant.

But when infants throw themselves into sound-making—when they are, as one says, "talkative"—it can have favorable linguistic consequences. We saw earlier that the sheer frequency of speech events is related to the development of words as well as longer utterances. In studies of shared gaze, mothers' eye movements were found to serve as reliable referential cues, and this, too, is positively related to the development of expressive vocabulary.

We saw earlier that mothers and infants treat each other's vocalizations as social signals when they coordinate and shape their own utterances to complement those of their partner. This practice facilitates vocal imitation by encouraging learners to attend to and reproduce modeled utterances, and by providing mothers with the opportunity to monitor the phonetic quality and semantic significance of reproductions. This skill building process will come in handy when infants become aware that they know things that we do not know, and vice versa.

The Manifestation of a Dual Specialization in Language Development

There are several ways in which dual specialization reveals itself in language development. These include (1) the frequent and heavily context-bound use of formulaic phrases; (2) qualitative differences in lexical development between children; (3) the development of phonological operations and its effect on previously stored forms; (4) differences in the rate of lexical development in signed and spoken languages; and (5) the nature of language delay in otherwise normally developing children.

As I indicated earlier, the SSC does more than feed utterance data to the GAM. By itself, it is also responsible for a great deal of behavior that is communicative and taken to be linguistic. The principle intake mechanisms of the SSC—referential looking and vocal accommodation—take in a lot of speech, and with it, a variety of high-frequency words and phrases. This specialization is slavishly vocal and socially sensitive. That is why it, like the vocal mimicry system of talking birds (Pepperberg, 1990), can reproduce words and stereotyped phrases. It is obvious that Savage-Rumbaugh's (1990) bonobo chimp, Kanzi, has this specialization but lacks the vocal control needed for the production of speechlike sounds.

FORMULAICITY

In her monograph, Ann Peters (1983) commented that "the first units of language acquired by children do not necessarily correspond to the minimal units (morphemes) of language described by conventional linguistics. They frequently consist of more than one (adult) word or morpheme." It is now widely accepted that the earliest utterances of children are *formulaic*. They are, to use Pinker's (1991) terms, associative, noncomputational, and nonrule governed. Formulaic utterances are thought to be holistically perceived and stored, and irreducible to their syllabic or segmental parts. Presumably, formulas reflect the infant's prosodic orientation, perhaps combined with its inability to analyze speech into segment-sized elements. If irreducible to discrete sound elements, the infant's utterances contain no phonemic contrasts and no possibility of recombination, principle features of linguistic systems. Accordingly, one may safely regard such forms as nonlinguistic.

Peters was among the first to systematically catalogue early formulas, which she called "long units." She found that formulas tend to form around overexposed phrases ("I'm gonna," "you'll hafta") and longer utterances, especially when used in restricted contexts. It is counterintuitive that long stretches of speech would precede short ones until one considers the infant's love of melody and prosody. To the young prosodist, long units have more contour to grab onto perceptually.

On a functional level, formulas are legitimately a part of spoken language. First, listeners naturally recognize them as phrases and sentences. Second, formulas are not at all rare: recent research (Lieven, Pine, and Dressner Barnes, 1992) suggests that the first fifty words of children usually include about nine formulas, on average; the first hundred words typically contain about twenty formulas. For some children, nearly half the items in their lexicon are these frozen phrases. Third, we have no reason to assume that children acquire and reproduce formulaic units with anything but the usual perceptual and speech-motor systems that are responsible for words. Indeed, Lieven, Pine, and Dressner Barnes (1992) have speculated that phrases provide children with templates that, following analysis, are converted into lexically based patterns.

Williams syndrome has been offered as an argument for language modularity, since those afflicted measure poorly on cognitive measures but seem able to speak well. However, many of the utterances of Williams syndrome victims seem to be vacuous formulas that have been overheard in the speech of others, including clichés and idioms, social phrases and fillers (Udwin and Yule, 1990). Williams individuals are also known to fabricate many of the things they say. This is exactly what one would expect if the preeminent desire is social convergence in the absence of communicable experience.

But although the literature is still a bit hazy on this point, there do seem to be some linguistically "ruly" behaviors (such as over-regularizations of past tense forms) embedded in the utterances of individuals with Williams syndrome. I think this condition may be telling us two things about modularity. First, it is saying that a great deal of speech can develop without language if the child is sufficiently accommodative vocally. Second, the cases of true linguistic behavior evinced by Williams syndrome sufferers indicate that some grammatical ability can exist without the kind of intelligence that is measured by IQ tests. In other words, Williams syndrome tends to support dual specialization.

MEANING OPTIONAL

As I mentioned earlier, a long-time colleague of mine, Warren Fay (1975), once tried out a few meaningless utterances (that he nevertheless intoned normally) on some three-year-old English-speaking children. When he said "El camino real," a number of them responded verbally. Moreover, their response was influenced by the form of the utterance. When Warren *stated* the phrase declaratively, 24 percent said "yes." But when the children were *asked* "El camino real?" using the rising intonation associated with questions in American English, the frequency of affirmative responses rose to 62 percent. It would appear that these normally developing children were not particularly bothered by the lack of lexical meaning. Indeed, those providing other than yes-no responses to the stated form of this nonsense phrase had a few counter comments of their own, for example, "Just Jerry" and "Because anyhow Mom said." I think these interactions remind mature language-users that much of what the linguistically naive child hears each day must not make particular sense and cannot, given the lack of world knowledge enjoyed by three-year-olds. "Does it make sense?" may not be among the questions that young children particularly concern themselves with. But the linguistically naive are no less adept socially, so any in-kind responses may be guided more by considerations of context-appropriateness and social conformity than linguistic correctness.

CONTINUITY OF BABBLE AND FIRST WORDS

Other evidence that early words may not be particularly linguistic comes from studies of the transition from babbling to speaking. Spoken language is sufficiently robust that we have a preadaptation to its mode of implementation that appears precursively in the form of babbling, the rhythmic repetition of syllables. Babbling resembles speech to such a degree, especially our "baby lexicon" of kinship terms, bodily functions, and so on, that listeners—even very discerning phoneticians—are frequently unclear as to the status of speechlike forms. This enables hopeful mothers to count them as words and causes conservative theorists to discount their lexical status.

Emergence of a Linguistic System

QUALITATIVE DIFFERENCES IN LEXICAL DEVELOPMENT

The socially convergent, vocally accommodative ways of the SSC explain several known developmental trajectories. Young children in the first fifty-word stage (approximately eighteen to twenty months of age) seem to have two different language learning styles. These children have been called, variously, analytical and holistic (Peters, 1977), noun lovers and leavers (Horgan, 1980), and referential and expressive (Nelson, 1973, 1981).

Nelson's data reveal that the initial lexicon of referential children contains a large number of object-oriented words. The early vocabulary of expressive children, on the other hand, is more self-oriented. In place of object words in the lexicons of expressive children is a supply of personal-social terms for expressing feelings, needs, and social forms. At an early age, these children produce a number of socially conventional phrases such as "go away," "stop it," "thank you," and "I want it." Referential children produce

shorter phrases than expressive children, and they say fewer function words and personal-social terms.

Expressive children are heavily formulaic; at an early age they
appear to produce phrases and sentences as single units, and their
speech contains functors and pronouns as well as nouns. According
to Nelson (1981), these gestalts "have the characteristic of being
wholistically produced without pauses between words, with reduced
phonemic articulation, and with the effect of slurred or mumbled
speech but with a clear intonation pattern" (p. 174).

Because little more than vocal accommodation and shared gaze
are needed for the production of situation-appropriate words and
phrases (as we assume for talking birds), and social terms are the
currency of interpersonal commerce, it seems likely that expressive
children's utterances are due primarily to their SSC. The differences
between them and referential children may be due, at least in part,
to the age of the child when the GAM is fully activated.

DEVELOPMENT OF PHONOLOGICAL OPERATIONS

Something that may have obscured the dual existence of these
conjoint modules and their actions is the presumption that phonology precedes the lexicon, and that first words imply the prior
existence of a phonological system. Because phonology is a part of
language, first words, in this view, would signify that language had
already developed, even though the child had not yet advanced to
morphology, syntax, and more complex form-meaning relationships.
However, the proper question is not whether phonology is a component of language but whether the child's first words and stereotyped phrases are evidence of phonology. I claim that they are not.

Studdert-Kennedy (1991) has argued this too. He believes that
phonemes, like other differentiations, fall out of lexical behavior
rather than precede it. Phonology tends not to develop until a
moderate inventory of words is stored and in use. If the initial
lexicon has no phonology, there is no reason to interpret first words
as the onset of the GAM. This makes it logical to suppose that
phonology, morphology, and syntax are a function of the GAM. And
there is an immediate benefit: phonology, which is frequently relegated to the periphery of language, is now joined with its other
components (Liberman, 1970).

The earliest utterances are prephonological, products of the processes of vocal accommodation, which are heavily influenced by the child's relationship with speakers and familiarity with social contexts. These forms are heavily biased perceptually and motorically but relatively free of environmentally induced top-down constraints. Very little of this business should get phonological credit because there is little evidence of systemic behavior; no utterances are transformed by the application of phonological principles. The rise of the phonological system, as well as morphological errors (for example, over-regularization), signal the activation of the GAM.

Some of the better phonetic evidence for activation of the GAM comes from studies of consonant-vowel interactions. We mentioned earlier reports (Davis and MacNeilage, 1990; Stoel-Gammon, 1983) of adjacency effects in young children's early words. For example, a particular consonantal closure may never occur before particular vowels that other closures frequently precede. The movements travel together, as though indivisible and not, therefore, combinable. Nittrouer, Studdert-Kennedy, and McGowan (1989) observed two parallel trends in the production of fricative-vowel syllables by three- to seven-year-old children. As the spectral energy in [s] and [ʃ] became increasingly distinct, the degree of their coarticulation with following vowels decreased. At the production level, this would seem operationally to define the discovery of the phonemic principle, or at least a productive application of that principle. Nittrouer et al. also speculated about how this process occurs. At first, they said, the young child has a few meaningful phonetic sequences that have an acoustically coherent structure. These items, one assumes, have been submitted to analyses that emphasize prosodic contour and skip over constituent parts. They continue: "As the number and diversity of the words in a child's lexicon increase, words with similar acoustic and articulatory patterns begin to cluster. From these clusters there ultimately precipitate the coherent units of sounds and gesture that we know as phonetic segments. Precipitation is probably a gradual process perhaps beginning as early as the second to third year of life when the child's lexicon has no more than 50–100 words. But the process is evidently still going on in at least some regions of the child's lexicon and phonological system as late as 7 years of age" (p. 131).

PROGRESSIVE AND REGRESSIVE IDIOMS

In the literature on developmental phonology various observers have commented on the existence of *progressive idioms* in children's speech. These words are more advanced than would be expected from an analysis of the child's phonological system at the time. Examples include an eight-month-old boy who said "clock" and "truck" correctly but revised their pronunciation to [kak] at fourteen months; and an eight-month-old girl who expressed the word "pretty" with an adultlike [prəti] but had transformed this to [pɪti] by twenty months (Moskowitz, 1980).

Regressions also occur at other levels of language. In English, these include "correction" of plural and past tense forms in which, for example, *feet* may be changed to *foots, mice* to *mouses,* and *went* to *goed.* A more extensive treatment and interpretation of these errors of overregularization is available in Bowerman (1982). I would argue that regressions index the activation of the GAM. They do not represent a fall back of any kind but the beginning of a new way of doing linguistic business.

Regressive idioms are the ontogenetic equivalent of fossilized forms. They seem primitive compared to similar items in the child's lexicon at the time. It is as though these items have been immunized to the application of phonological rules otherwise in effect at the time. This can happen if the child fails to recognize that a lexical entry contains a sound that has been systematically upgraded elsewhere. There are fewer examples of regressive idioms, probably because precocious forms are more likely to come to the listener's attention.

Moskowitz (1980) observed that whether an idiom is progressive or regressive "is in some sense inconsequential: what is common to these various forms is that they are encoded in a phonological unit which is more primitive than the one which forms the basis of the regular items" (p. 78). She also noted that the rapid spread of sound change through a child's lexicon provides the young speaker with "two separate lexical encodings" for all items in the process of change, a dual registration that one would presume ultimately reduces to a single (standard) form. Dual representation of early word forms is exactly what we would predict if infants begin to speak by dint of their SSC's processes of vocal accommodation and then undertake componential analysis of their lexicon, courtesy of the GAM.

It is possible that formulaic phrases and idiomatic words are processed and stored differently than fully analyzed forms. The most appropriate developmental psycholinguistic data are unavailable, but there is some evidence in adults that "automatic speech" is more likely to be represented in the brain bilaterally (Van Lancker, 1991). If true in children as well, we might be even more confident that early formulas and idioms are a function of the SSC, for the neurophysiology of social cognition tends to be bilaterally distributed, whereas segmental phonetic analysis is performed primarily by the left cerebral hemisphere.

NONPRODUCTIVE UTTERANCES

It follows from our understanding of formulaicity that there must be numerous linguistically unproductive phrases in young children's speech. The morphemic elements in phrases cannot be freely recombined if their existence is unknown to the speaker. Kelly and Dale (1989) studied normally developing children at different ages in the second year of life. Using observation and interviews, the researchers classified children as Single Word Users if they produced isolated words or as Productive or Nonproductive Syntax Users if they had an MLU above 1.0. Utterances were considered productive if each word was grammatically free, that is, if it occurred in at least two utterances and if it carried the same semantic associations and occupied the same position within the utterance. In nonproductive utterances, there was no indication that the child knew that the constituent words could be combined in different ways and thus were separable from the utterance.

Each child was given two cognitive measures, a symbolic play task and an imitation task in which children were presented with nonce words made up of sounds that were either in their lexicon at that time or not present in their lexical inventory. On the imitation task, it was found that Single Word Users never imitated sounds falling outside their lexical segment inventory, but that multiword users did by a significant margin. The Single Word Users' unwillingness or inability to reproduce a novel form suggests that they had not yet constructed an internal system from exposure to ambient stimulation. This is additional support for the notion that early words are not necessarily linguistic.

Kelly and Dale commented that many children demonstrated language skills that exceeded expectations based on cognitive measures. Overall, their data reveal no striking relationship between children's linguistic stage and their performance on object permanence and means-end tasks. There was, however, a tendency for productive syntax users to outperform those with nonproductive syntax on the means-end measure. If there was to be a difference between any nonlinguistic cognitive measure and a language measure, this is exactly where one would expect to find it, since the other subjects provide no evidence in their utterances that they know anything about linguistic principles of organization.

SIGNED AND SPOKEN LANGUAGES

Comparative studies by John Bonvillian and his colleagues (Bonvillian and Folven, 1987; Bonvillian, Orlansky, and Novack, 1983; Orlansky and Bonvillian, 1984) suggest that in manual languages first signs may appear several months before first words, but that morphology and syntax tend to appear at about the same ages in speakers and in signers. Semantic relations, verb agreement, deictic pronouns, and morphologically complex verbs of motion and location all seem to develop at the same rate in both speech and sign.

It does not surprise me that there would be one "age" for the onset of spoken words as phonetically sensitive components of language, and another for linguistic elements that are phonetically less sensitive, since the production of words depends heavily upon mechanisms of perception and production. Productive control emerges according to a biological schedule that could easily differ for visual-manual and auditory-vocal systems of communication. Once these perceptuomotor mechanisms are functioning, it becomes possible to express all other linguistic structures, but the advent of additional linguistic material must await the activation of the grammatical analysis module.

The "two age" situation outlined above suggested to Meier and Newport (1990) the possibility of *"two (or more) largely independent timing mechanisms . . .* one controlling the onset of lexical acquisition and another controlling the acquisition of grammar (that is, syntax and morphology)" (p. 13, italics mine). I take this observation as support for dual specialization.

If human infants acquire syntax and morphology at about the same age in manual as well as spoken languages, the GAM may be amodal, as Meier and Newport suggest. Many of the subsystems of the SSC are amodal, too, but this specialization places a very high value on facial-vocal activity. We may assume that it also values movements of the hands. Manual activity can signal intentions, (including threat), and there is evidence that nonhuman primates have cells that are attuned to hand movements. There is also evidence that human infants are aware of finger movements (Meltzoff and Moore, 1977).

Because the SSC operates on physical cues, it is not unlikely that components of a language in one modality might be expressed earlier or later than the corresponding structures in languages occupying other modalities. In humans, the first specialization to develop, the SSC, also enables and activates the second specialization, the GAM, which handles phonology, morphology and syntax. Because the first specialization feeds the second, the timing of the two (in the form of developmental "milestones") is coordinated.

Social preadaptations orient infants to displays that identify individuals and their intentions. They are therefore preset to process movements of the facial-vocal complex as well as the hands. Because movements of the face and eyes figure significantly in signed languages, it is not surprising that these languages are learned at about the same rate as spoken ones. But since sign presumably bears a different relationship to presign manual activity than speech does to babble, signs may be detected earlier. In word studies (for example, Caputo et al., 1986; Gesell and Thompson, 1934), some investigators eliminate the words *dada* and *mama* from consideration. This may be a reasonable thing to do, since babies produce lots of [dada] and [mama] sounds which could be falsely credited (Locke, 1985, 1990c). But this gives rise to two additional concerns. First, what configurations, if any, are routinely eliminated from the sign data? Second, are there any manual or facial behaviors that look like signs but have to be discarded because they occur in prelinguistic infants? Sign language investigators say little or nothing about these matters.

LANGUAGE-DELAYED CHILDREN

Serious language delay exists in children who, from our best estimates, are socially, cognitively, and motorically normal. When such children speak, they do so with few intelligible words or phrases, but they may sound fairly normal otherwise. One's clinical impression is that many of these children "converse" with conventional levels of affect and native-sounding prosody, and this is what we should expect if the SSC is fully operational long before the GAM is activated. With abnormal delays in the analytical and computational aspects of language, there will be an extended period in which formulaic phrases are these children's only utterances.[3]

Pinker (1991) points to research suggesting that children with specific language impairments handle irregular verb forms better than regular ones. This underscores the superior functioning of a system that handles associative, noncomputational items, as we would expect of children with a reasonably intact SSC. As we will see in Chapter 10, the families of children with language delays tend toward elevated histories of similar problems, and recent studies of brain morphometry have found abnormalities in the brains of language-delayed children. The GAM of these kids appears to be deficient,[4] but there is little evidence to suggest that the majority have a dysfunctional SSC.

Comparative analyses of nonhuman primates suggest to me that the majority of human children who experience language delay will do so not because of a hypofunctional SSC but because of GAM deficiency, though there could be problems in both systems. Colleagues at the Massachusetts General Hospital tell me that it is not uncommon for children to acquire a handful of words without particular difficulty but then falter, as though their lexical acquisition system has shut down. These children who are loquacious but, except for formulaic phrases, still asyntactic at three years of

3. This is reminiscent of children who are taught to recognize an initial vocabulary of "sight words" before any initial training in phonics. If they cannot get the hang of letter-sound translation, all the words recognized by these children will be apprehended holistically, their identification by analogy based on visual contours and shape cues—a sort of visual prosody.

4. Many of these same children have a very difficult time learning to read alphabetic languages in which they must learn and apply phoneme-grapheme correspondence rules (Kamhi and Catts, 1989), as might be expected if they are analytically deficient at the phonological level of language.

age seem to justify the label "GAM-deficient." Those presumably less common children who are affectively and socially flat, and essentially mute, may be SSC-deficient and therefore behind in many areas of language.

By definition, those with autism have a dysfunctional SSC. Autistic children are known for their avoidance of faces and possibly deficient face processing. Earlier, I raised questions about a collateral lack of interest in the human voice. Such characteristics reduce the felt urge to convey and deprive the GAM of the utterance data and referential information needed for the induction of grammatical principles.

What of the retarded? There are two findings of relevance to language behavior. The first has to do with Down syndrome infants' reduced level of affective behaviors, which normally signal the presence of attachment to the mother by her young. The second language-relevant finding in retarded infants pertains more directly to the development of affect. The detection of incongruity—leading to laughter—appears to require a level of tonus that is often lacking in infants with Down syndrome. Though Down syndrome infants are generally assumed to have a "cognitive" disorder, these results suggest that retarded infants may have a deficient affective system, and perhaps a hypofunctional SCM (as well as a deficient GAM). These are not necessarily contradictory statements, considering the exceedingly intimate connection, an almost perfect overlap, between affective and cognitive development in the very young.

COORDINATION OF SPECIALIZATIONS

As I mentioned earlier, for infants to thrive the SSC must kick in at the first postnatal moment. Maternal affiliation and emotional development vitally depend on its doing so. The GAM, as we know, does not become conspicuously active until later, when by dint of shared emotional experience mother and infant are nicely attached to each other and the infant is socialized. A reason for supposing that activation of the two specializations is coordinated is the generally continuous nature of language development (Golinkoff, 1983). The coordination of specializations is also supported by evidence reviewed previously that early advances in the initial expression of language behavior usually point to early progress in areas that normally develop later.

BENEFITS OF A DUAL SPECIALIZATION FOR LANGUAGE

With the addition of the SSC, the idea of a "language module" makes more sense than it does standing nakedly, with no database or motivational system, or when so many pseudo-linguistic behaviors, shared with the other primates, are crammed into a module that logically can only do grammatical analyses and computations. Indeed, overloading is probably one of the better ways to sink the idea of a language module. That some psycholinguists have been inclined to overload is dramatized by Robin Chapman's lament that "classical accounts left out of the language module . . . intentions, emotions, personal history of the self and other, and world knowledge generally . . . the very stuff of which linguistic knowledge is made" (1988). It should be obvious that I agree with Chapman—all these things *are* developmentally necessary—I merely question whether they should be treated as components of a system that is specialized for grammatical analysis.

This tendency to "overload" may reflect nothing more than confusion among psycholinguists, which arises from the recognition that some language is not communicative and much communication is not linguistic. Not always sure when confronted with linguistic or pseudolinguistic behavior, observers have put all words and phrases in the "language" column, chalking up those behaviors to a language module. But if the attention to and initial storage of utterances are the responsibility of a different specialization, the GAM is left in the clear to do with purity the only language things that it does at all—grammatical analysis and computation.

At the other end there are associated benefits. First, we are spared the necessity of believing that nonhuman primates have about a third of a language module—I leave it to readers to decide how much sense that makes! Second, with the addition of the SSC, early sound making is seen as purely phonetic, governed by no abstract principles of phonological organization. This puts phonology, a rule-based system, back where it belongs, with the other products of the GAM, morphology and syntax.

To summarize, the theoretical yield of the dual specialization hypothesis for which I have argued here includes the following extensions of developmental theory: With dual specialization, we have a way to deal with formulaic utterances, including why they occur in the first place and why they subsequently diminish. We are in a better position to understand why there might be qualitative differences in lexical development between children, as have been documented. The dual specialization hypothesis provides us with principled explanations for a prephonological period of speaking as well as for the development of a phonological system and the application of phonological rules. The presumption of a single specialization for language has made it hard to understand observed differences in the development of signed and spoken languages, but these differences at the early lexical stage, and the similarities at later stages, are handled easily by a conjoint system. Finally, we have seen why it is that many language-delayed children get as far as an initial lexicon and repertoire of stock phrases before they stumble.

When it became evident that the SSC has the capability to attend to, holistically process, and reproduce words and stereotyped phrases, it began to seem anomalous that an analytical-computational system would repeat these same capabilities and that nature would be so wasteful of our neural resources as to redundantly represent this function. Recently, Lightman and Gingerich (1992) published a fascinating article about anomalies in science. An anomalous fact, they said, is one that is unexpected and difficult to explain within any existing theoretical framework. Ironically, an anomalous fact tends not to be seen as anomalous until a new conceptual framework becomes available. At that time, theoreticians become psychologically free to view the fact as anomalous, since it no longer threatens the only available explanation. Simultaneously, the old conceptual framework begins to appear inadequate and the new framework superior. I bring this matter up here because I think it is now psychologically "safe" to recognize that the GAM does not collect utterances for its own analysis precisely because it is now clear that the SSC does do this.

Processes of Phonological Development

At one time, cognitive development was thought to be discontinuous, primarily because investigators measured nonequivalent behaviors in infancy and childhood (Bornstein and Sigman, 1986). In some cases, "cognitive" measures in infancy were heavily loaded motorically while cognitive measures in childhood were more conceptually oriented. With more nearly equivalent measures, the continuity that naturally exists in human development has become more readily apparent.

The situation in language development is similar. Jakobson (1968) and other scholars thought there was a clear break between babbling and speech (for a review see Locke, 1983). The reason, however, had nothing to do with the measurement of nonequivalent behaviors. Observers listened to utterances in both cases, but in the babbling of babies they seemed to think they could hear a little bit of everything while in the speech of young children they heard no more than a handful of sounds. No one systematically tabulated babies' actual sounds, so this misconception prevailed for a time.

In Chapter 2 I described the processes by which perceptual categories come to exist. We saw that sound contrasts present immediately after birth could be maintained and stabilized by appropriate stimulation or relinquished if such stimulation was not available and that new perceptual contrasts are learned following systematic exposure to ambient stimulation. In Chapter 7 I described parallel processes in brain development in which there is stabilization of synapses, an increase in synapses or synaptic efficacy associated with environmental stimulation, or neuronal atrophy brought on by underexposure to appropriate sensory stimulation. As we will see, similar distinctions apply to phonetic production as well.

PRUNING

Ironically, perhaps the first and most reliable indication that children are acquiring phonology is not the sound patterns they gain or increasingly master but the phonetic behaviors they gradually relinquish. The reason is that "prespeech" does not perfectly anticipate the target language; more sounds are present in the repertoire of babbling than will be needed for words. For motoric reasons, it ought to be easier to signal an increasing awareness of the units of phonology by letting go of the ones that do not belong than by tackling more complex movement patterns.

What becomes of these sounds that the infant makes but its parents never say? Obviously, a certain amount of pruning is necessary, whether actively or through benign neglect. Infants born into English-speaking homes produce several sound-movement patterns that will not be needed to converse in their native language. Eventually they will need to quit making "raspberries" (bilabial trills) and prevocalic glottal stops. They may not know it at seven and eight months, but these sounds are slated for demolition. We need only consider the fate of glottal stops and fricatives. Both are abundant in babbling, but only the fricative occurs prevocalically in American English.

Loss of babbled sounds can also be associated with phonological delay or disorder. Carol Stoel-Gammon and her colleagues have reported on a child who produced English sounds in his babbling at nine months that were not found in his speech at twenty-three months. As it turned out, most of the sounds that were wrongly discarded were lingual; the child tended to retain sounds of labial articulation (Stoel-Gammon, Burkardt, and Huffman, 1990). The possible reasons for this are various, including lack of motor control over linguals in babbling and misperception of English words that contain lingual consonants.

STABILIZATION

Many communicative behaviors get their start early on. These behaviors include facial expressions (Ekman and Friesen, 1969), which are preserved by the culture. Similarly, pre-imitative patterns of vocal affect and prosody are transformed by cultural influence into culturally consistent modes of vocal expression (Malatesta, 1981). In Japanese macaques, anecdotal reports suggest that there may be an "innate" vocal repertoire in infancy from which later vocal forms and functions are derived, with maintenance of some infantile forms (Takeda, 1965, 1966).

Pre-imitative manual activity may exhibit a pattern comparable to the one observed for vocal activity. Hannan (1982) has described a variety of hand and finger configurations that occur over the first year of life. Exposure to signed languages presumably keeps some of these configurations alive and, as Hannan observed, "some of the hand expressions would be expected to either cease to be displayed or to become reorganized into new behaviors as development proceeds" (p. 264).

Some babbled sounds are also preserved and stabilized. In the preservation of babbled sounds, a phonetic behavior, such as pressing the apex of the tongue against the alveolar ridge while vocal-

izing, is done throughout the period during which the infant progresses from babbling to speaking. This perceptibly yields, for
example, [na] or [da] in babbling and /na/ or /da/ in words. The
perceptual capacity needed for preservation is probably very low—
essentially the ability to recognize in one's own repertoire phonetic
material that corresponds approximately to what one hears in the
utterances of others. Grossly, such ability probably exists somewhat
before children produce their first words.

There is no shortage of evidence for preservation and stabilization. In several studies, Vihman and her associates (Vihman et al.,
1985; Vihman, 1986; Vihman and Miller, 1988) observed a significant degree of continuity between the sounds of babbling and the
sounds of speech. Stoel-Gammon and Cooper (1984) observed that
many words and nonwords in the vocal output of their infant subjects were constructed with the same phonetic segments. Later, I
will provide more specific evidence on this.

This continuity has an interesting consequence. To be sure that
lexical credit is not falsely assigned, one must be conservative,
discounting—along with the "mama" and "dada" sounds—all such
phonetically natural utterances that have not been used with semantic or contextual consistency. Attempting to make precisely this
effort with his twin daughters, one perfectly good phonetician (Cruttenden, 1970) threw up his hands in frustration, calling the identification of the first word "pointless": "If the child habitually uses
[dada] in his babbling and sometimes uses it in the presence of his
father, when can it be said that 'Daddy' is uttered to designate his
father? For example both twins went through a period lasting 3–4
months during which [baba] [dada] [gaga] were used indiscriminately but could on occasions have been interpreted as bye-bye and
Daddy. Indeed I found it extremely difficult and perhaps rather
pointless to pin down the occurrence of the first word" (p. 114).
Cruttenden's frustration is a direct consequence of the naturalness
of spoken languages, a property that arises from the human endowment of oral movement patterns, which is waiting to be tinkered
with in babbling and appropriated for speech.

When sounds are stabilized by experience, the culture may de-
serve much of the credit. Nurturant speakers in the child's environment all but guarantee the preservation of babbled sounds and

syllables by custom-tailoring their utterances to fit the child's evident capabilities. This tendency, of course, is the origin of *daedae, peepee, kaka, bye-bye* and many of the other reduplications that conform so nicely to the child's proclivities to repeat open syllables and, indeed, may originate with the child (Locke, 1985).

Stabilization is also encouraged by the practice of contingent responding, that is, phonetic mimicry by the mother and other caregivers. Mothers of babblers commonly respond to their infants' word-like forms by reproducing their utterances, sometimes inserting the closest equivalent words the infant could conceivably be trying to say. There is some indication that this process has the effect of encouraging infant reproductions of the original behavior, both at the prelexical, and the early lexical and phrasal levels of vocal expression (Bloom, Russell, and Wassenberg, 1987; Hardy-Brown, Plomin, and DeFries, 1981; Veneziano, 1988). It is probable that contingent responding and culturally fossilized baby words are expressions of the same underlying tendency to present babies with behaviors that coincide with their own.

Because infants begin to refer to things while their phonetic capabilities are still in the process of developing, their first words can only be produced with the motor ability that exists at the time vocal reference becomes useful. Words are interesting, but not so interesting that young speakers will adopt a supply of completely new articulatory patterns just to produce them. Some evidence for this was reported by Messick (1984), who analyzed the segmental inventories of infants still in the later stages of babbling and several months later presented to each child two sets of nonce words. One set of nonce words was constructed with the child's own babbling sounds. These were termed IN words. OUT words were made up of material not heard in the child's samples of babbling. Messick found that children attempted more of the nonce words that contained babbling sounds; they also acquired these items earlier and produced them more frequently.

The sounds that figure prominently in babbling are generally accurate in speech from the beginning. We simply have no acquisition curve for these phones; in the youngest children tested these sounds are already there. Indeed, there is abundant evidence from various quarters (such as Labov and Labov, 1978) that when sounds are appropriated for speech, they are not pruned out of the concurrent babbling repertoire but are now displayed or used in both activities.

In young speakers stabilization produces a segmental repertoire that looks very much like infant babble. Where syllable structure is concerned, there is an exceedingly strong relationship between babble and early speech. In the speech of fifteen-month-olds, word-initial consonants are nearly six times more plentiful than word-final ones (Stoel-Gammon, 1985), a tendency also evident in babbling. And there is a common core of consonantlike sounds that shows up both in babbling *and* in children's first fifty words (Locke, 1983).

The stabilization of babbled sounds, as I have said, is not a "learning-free" concept. Some of the learning is very much under the control of the active infant; it involves exposure to the feel and sound of the infant's own oral-motor activity. Some learning also involves comparative analyses by infants, which allow them to recognize that sounds they make in their own oral activities also exist in the utterances of others. Other aspects of stabilization involve the infant's discovery of the phonetic environments in which individual segments occur—and therefore, *can* occur—in ambient phonological systems. Finally, preservation of segments left over from babbling undoubtedly requires some articulatory adjustments, but this may occur so quickly and spontaneously as to escape our notice.

EARLY PHONOLOGICAL LEARNING

Children's perception of speech generally precedes their production of it. And as Pribram (1967) observed, "when the variety of perceptions exceeds to some considerable extent the repertory of action available to the organism he is motivated to, that is, attempts to, extend this repertory" (p. 836). One hallmark of phonological development is the child's steadily increasing mastery of sounds that are rare in babbling and poorly controlled in the initial words of young speakers. Attempts to reproduce words (if not to speak) may encourage changes in the form of existing phonetic behaviors and the achievement of novel movements. Stoel-Gammon and Cooper (1984) inventoried the consonantlike sounds heard in three children's babbling and speaking. All clusters and most fricatives—categories of late-developing phonetic elements on anyone's survey—occurred only in speech. Since some of these sounds do not occur in English phonemically, their occurrence suggests an added expenditure of effort or an exercise in creativity at a time when articulatory capability was exceeded by the desire to accommodate to caregivers' speech.

Clusters and fricatives and final obstruents are late to develop and sometimes need additional environmental support because of the fundamental mismatch between the natural sound-making dispositions of children and certain of the requirements of English phonology. Clinicians spend a great deal of time working on cluster reduction, and babbling contains virtually no clusters. They devote hours to final omissions, and babbling contains relatively few VC syllables. Speech pathologists contribute more of their time to fricatives, affricates, and liquids, of which babblers produce few, than stops, nasals, and glides, which are the consonantal core of babbling. We may suppose that these elements either require articulatory activity that is physically late to mature or involve additional perceptual or other experience.

How does the infant with controllable sound-movement patterns make the transition from affective communication and babbling to the meaningful use of words? For years, the appearance of words was interpreted as the beginning of language. But some lexically adaptive phonetic changes may occur prephonologically—prior to the emergence of words.

First Words

MODALITY EFFECTS: WORDS AND SIGNS

Studdert-Kennedy (1991) has argued that ontogenetic factors play a role in evolution and have probably contributed to the development of our species' capacity for language. I believe that humans' uniformly early and natural use of voice to convey indexical and affective information gives vocal communication an ontogenetic primacy that prehistorically influenced evolution of phonological capacity in hominids. Except for the deaf, no culture has ever evolved or adopted anything but a *spoken* language as a primary system of communication. And yet various studies attest that signed languages are learned as rapidly as spoken languages and carry information that is equally complex. This has prompted Meier and Newport (1990) to declare that "there is neither an overall evolutionary advantage for speech nor an overall evolutionary disadvantage for sign" (p. 2).

If there truly were *no* advantage to those who speak and listen, this should make us all the more suspicious that it was in ontogeny that phonological communication assumed its predominance, and that ontogeny thereby played a key role in phylogeny. The determining ontogenetic factor would be the neonatal human primacy of voices and vocalizing faces, in large part owing to prenatal vocal stimulation and learning. In spoken language, the identity of the speaker and his or her illocutionary intentions conveniently and efficiently occupy the same channel as the nominal message.

Over the years there have been several claims of "manual babbling" by infants reared in signing homes. Let us examine these claims. Among hearing infants, current evidence suggests that the onset of "vocal babbling" is heavily influenced by and precisely timed with the maturation of neuromotoric control mechanisms. Babbling follows very rigidly on the heels of repetitive hand banging. In hearing infants reared in speaking homes, the onset of rhythmic vocal activity coincides with the onset of *rhythmic manual activity.* Now, if the human infant is equally able to learn speech and sign, as seems certain, and if babbling truly is a precursor to language, which seems no less certain, one need not look only in signing homes to see "manual babbling." We can take the simultaneous onset of rhythmic hand and vocal activity at six to seven months as evidence that the brain is ready to control either type of activity.

An elevated incidence of manual activity was recently reported in children reared in signing homes (Petitto and Marentette, 1991). I assume that this observation correctly reflects a tendency by all infants to assimilate environmental stimulation. If reared by people who place great importance on the communicative movements of the hands, infant observers will join in, indulging in manual accommodations of the type that lead to, and may be interpreted as, legitimate signing. This activity would reflect the child's natural tendency to respond in kind, and one would expect that many of the hand movements of an infant reared in signing homes would be copied and used meaningfully, whether analysts discern them or not. But this would not be babbling in any sense in which the word is currently used by developmental phoneticians, and it certainly has little resemblance to the repetitive, self-reinforcing form of asocial play that I imagine babbling to be.

If there is little in the manual area that is closely analogous to syllabic babbling, this may also be telling us something about why our species evolved spoken rather than manual languages. Where in evolution new capacities reflect the novel use of some preexisting structure, so might we suppose that speech in the species, and in developing infants, was and is an elaboration of behaviors that are topographically and functionally similar to speech and to speaking—the sound of babble, the behavior of babbling (Locke, 1989). The infant's disposition to use the vocal channel for the exchange of information about personal identity, feelings, and intentions, joined now with a syllabically (and ultimately segmentally) organized signaling system, put the infant, as I believe it placed our species, on a path to languages that are spoken.

PHONETIC EFFECTS IN SPOKEN LANGUAGE

If our social cognition specialization can produce languagelike behaviors, some of the patterning in first words and utterances may be traced to this specialization. For example, we would expect vocally accommodating infants to reproduce selectively those words that are physically stressed in speech directed to them, since there is nothing semantic in vocal accommodation. This is clearly what happens; young speakers do eliminate unstressed syllables, a practice that masquerades as "difficulty with grammatical morphemes." Indeed, much of the patterning in delayed language belies rate difficulties—problems in processing phonetically encoded lexical information at rates preferred by speakers. In English, these problems include a variety of plurality, tense, and possession markers, articles, copulas and auxiliaries, and other morphemes. Steven Pinker (1984) believes it may be grammatically significant that these morphemes are low in phonetic substance and perceptually inconspicuous.

A variety of other ostensibly morphological and syntactic effects in child language may, in actuality, reflect phonetic factors. Branigan (1979) and Waterson (1978) have argued that two-word utterances would come somewhat sooner in development if the child's articulatory prowess were further along than it is at, say, twelve to eighteen months. Donahue's (1986) report is interesting in this regard. She described the speech of her son Sean between eleven and twenty-two months. Analyses of single word utterances revealed that Sean had a consonant harmony constraint that prohibited utterances in which there were two different places of consonant articulation. As a result, he could and did say "preharmonized" words such as "daddy" [daedae], but he attempted relatively few words that had heterorganic places of articulation. On the rare occasion when he did, the dissimilar consonants were harmonized (for example, "Katie" was [titi]). Moreover, this constraint seemed to extend beyond the word level to sequences of words. Sean's attempt at "Big Bird" was realized as [bɪboeb], but he refused to attempt "big dog." Donahue argued that Sean's application of this harmony rule held down the number of word combinations, delaying for phonological reasons the onset of the two-word stage in his development of language.

Some "syntactic" effects may in actuality be phonetic stress effects (Gleitman et al., 1988). As we saw earlier, infants seem to notice when prosodic interruptions fall within rather than between phrase boundaries, and this may help them to learn where word and syllable boundaries fall (Jusczyk et al., in Jusczyk, 1992; Fernald, 1985; Fernald and Kuhl, 1987).

VISUAL EFFECTS IN EARLY PHONOLOGY

Earlier, I described studies in which infants were more likely to imitate speakers they could see and hear than those they could only hear. If the sight of a moving face elicits vocal imitation, there may also be visual effects in the infants' utterances, perhaps even in their lexical learning.

Randa Mulford (1983, 1988) has discovered some interesting effects of vision on the contents of children's initial vocabulary. It turns out that sighted infants are more likely to attempt words that contain labial consonants relative to nonlabials than are blind infants. Figure 9.1 is a graph of her data. It suggests that sighted infants can see how "labial words" are produced and are thus more likely, other things being equal, to reproduce them. The larger point here is that children in general may be more inclined to attempt a word if they have some confidence that they'll be able to pull it off.

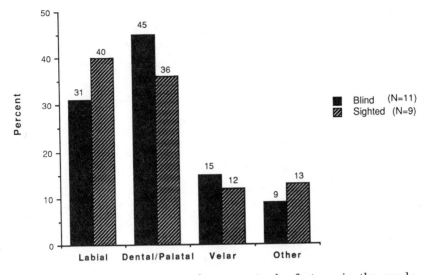

Figure 9.1. Relative frequency of consonants, by feature, in the words targeted by sighted and blind children.

This effect would be the reciprocal of lexical avoidance (Ingram, 1978), in which young children make systematically fewer attempts at words whose articulatory requirements they perceive to exceed their present capabilities or which are underspecified in the child's internal representation.

EXPANSION OF THE INITIAL LEXICON

At some point after they have learned a number of words, probably as relatively unanalyzed wholes, children make the discovery that words differ by bits of phonetic substance that correspond to consonants and vowels. From this point on, one presumes that existing "long words" are reorganized and that new lexical items are stored in a fundamentally different form and executed differently. Dating from its discovery of the phoneme, the child is phonological: it has an inventory of sounds, a set of rules governing their distribution, and an emerging sense of the combinatorial possibilities.

I believe that words precede the acquisition of phonology, which then enables additional word learning. This fits with the established ontogenetic pattern of growth and differentiation whereby parts

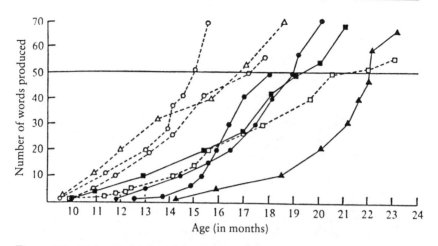

Figure 9.2. Rate at which eight children added new words to their expressive vocabulary. Unfilled symbols refer to males, filled symbols to females.

emerge from wholes (Studdert-Kennedy, 1991). And apparently the eighteen- to twenty-two-month-old child is prepared for words, for at that age there is typically a very sharp increase in the rate of lexical learning. Figure 9.2 shows the rate at which new words were added to the expressive vocabulary of one group of normally developing children.

There are usually just under fifty words in the expressive vocabulary of children at the age when they experience this spurt, as Figure 9.3 shows. One might suppose that at this age something happens to production mechanisms to account for this rapid increase, but investigators (Reznick and Goldfield, 1990) have found that single-word comprehension also surges at about the same time. This suggests an explosion of lexical knowledge and perhaps, therefore, an extra-motoric explanation. It could even be an extra-phonological explanation. Reznick and Goldfield suggested that the spurt reflects a reference-oriented discovery that "names refer to things," that "words have reference outside the immediate context, or can be used to stand for another object." These authors also identify an object-oriented alternative discovery made by children at this age that "all things can be named" and, indeed, that all things *require* names. Reznick and Goldfield see this second hy-

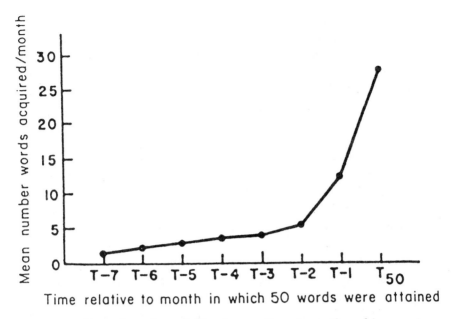

Figure 9.3. Rate of word acquisition by months prior to the achievement of a fifty-word vocabulary.

pothesis as a corollary of the discovery that objects belong to categories and posit that naming explodes because the general tendency to categorize sharply increases.

DEVELOPMENT OF PHONETIC CODE AND PHONOLOGY

Phonemes are frequently referred to as the "building blocks" of language since they constitute every word and every morpheme. This may tempt us to believe that the phoneme is the first unit to fall into place developmentally, followed by the syllable, the word, the morpheme, and so on. But this would be incorrect. The phoneme is a later discovery, occurring after some dozens of words have joined the child's expressive vocabulary. On biological grounds it can only be thus, for "it is a general rule of both phylogeny and ontogeny that complex structures evolve by differentiation of smaller structures from larger. Accordingly . . . we should expect phonemes to emerge from words" (Studdert-Kennedy, 1991, p. 16). Let us take a look at how this differentiation might occur.

Bjorn Lindblom (1989) has speculated that children do not discover phonemes in the acoustic data. Rather, he said, "minimal pairs identify nodes of 'gestural overlap'" (p. 41). The child who learns *boy* and *toy, my* and *pie,* has been "set up" to discover minimally distinctive differences. When the child traces overlapping articulatory gestures upstream to their common source, it finds the phoneme in its storage of other people's words. The phoneme does not fall out of auditory analyses performed on the speech of others, but analyses—presumably kinesthetic—of the child's own articulatory activity or stored commands. Because overlapping motor gestures need less storage space than disparate ones, there are important benefits here for lexical storage, but the discovery of phonemes seems less a cause than a consequence of vocabulary growth.[5]

Supporting acoustic data are available. We have seen (Nittrouer, Studdert-Kennedy, and McGowan, 1989) that as the spectral energy in consonantal phones becomes increasingly distinct in children's speech, the coarticulation between these sounds and their following vowels tends to decrease. At the production level, this signals the discovery of the phonemic principle, or at least the articulatory expression of that principle.

The message to mothers and fathers is this: If you want your children to discover the phoneme early, teach them minimal pairs! Give them a teddy named Freddy, a snake named Jake. There may also be a semantic twist to this story. David Premack, the comparative psychologist, has expressed a view that is worth entertaining here: children cannot discover that sounds combine to have meanings until they discover that individual sounds have *no* meaning. This, he believes, is fostered by the polysemous nature of language, for "if a sound can have arbitrarily many meanings—and meanings that are unrelated—then it can also have no meaning" (1972, p. 65). The presence of minimal pairs would accomplish essentially the same thing. But a semantic hypothesis seems to add something to Lindblom's "gestural overlap" notion, and both may be needed

---

5. Abler (1989) has published a fascinating paper on "particulate systems" in nature, which include languages that are phonological. Although individual gestures are blended together in speech, listeners are always able to retrieve the original elements from the mixture, just as chemists can retrieve constituent elements from chemical compounds.

to explain the child's phonemic discovery. With a burgeoning vocabulary, the child feels itself making the same movement in the expression of lexical items that have nothing semantically in common.

THE NATURE OF PHONOLOGICAL LANGUAGES

It has been said that "it is impossible profitably to discuss changes in a system unless one has some picture of what the system is like" (Waddington, 1975, p. 11). What, then, are phonologies like? What do infants have to grapple with to gain access to and control over spoken words?

If it is to meet all the requirements of lexical transmission, speech has a great deal of work to do. However, humans are not without output constraints, and speakers generally do little more than they must to satisfy their communicative ends. As a result, in the historical development of languages, consonant inventories tended to evolve so that maximum perceptual distinctiveness was achieved at minimum articulatory cost (Lindblom, 1984; Lindblom and Engstrand, 1989; Lindblom and Maddieson, 1988). Lindblom and Maddieson metaphorically depicted this process in the display that appears in Figure 9.4.

The figure suggests that, left to their own devices, speakers will produce mainly neutral articulations. The exigencies of large-inventory lexical communication require a number of perceptually distinctive units, which act as magnets to attract speakers into a number of articulatory forays. The dashed lines represent forces that oppose these magnetic (segmental) excursions. The greater the departure from articulatory neutrality, the greater the tension on the system. When its limits are exceeded, tension is manifested phonologically in the form of various simplifying processes that are heard as "errors."

This model was devised to account for the evolved phonological structure of established languages, but it also fits the problem facing the child: how to achieve all the distinct stored phonetic targets with an immature, overburdened, and relatively unpracticed speech apparatus. Thanks to dozens of very insightful developmental phonologists, we now know something about how children "handle the tension." Not talking is no solution for those with an urgent need

PHONETIC SPACE

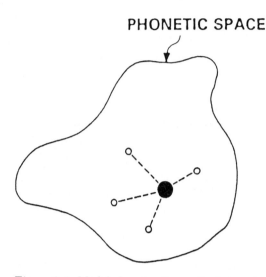

Figure 9.4. Model showing forces that operate to expand phonological systems while keeping them at a manageable size.

to communicate. Selective word avoidance gets a child only so far, especially if its stock of synonyms is limited. So children are destined to fall short of their articulatory targets, an accidental phenomenon that generally happens in motorically predictable ways, or substitute for themselves alternative targets that are more achievable. The latter action may rightfully be considered a strategy, like that which occurs in the second year of life when otherwise monosyllabic children reduplicate syllables to achieve adultlike contours for disyllabic words, or in desperation use one phonetic form homonymously to represent several words (Vihman, 1978, 1981).

It has been proposed and generally affirmed that there is an autonomous, encapsulated specialization for human language. Because humans are the only species with this specialization, its properties must be limited to the capabilities that we have and other animals lack. This, and other evidence, argues for a language module that is coldly analytical and computational. Such a module cannot operate without a data base, and I have argued that our specialization for social cognition feeds utterances to the grammatical analysis module. Specifically, when the infant attends to and stores the things people do while talking, it collects data whose patterning will be discerned by the analytical module.

Some of the evidence for a phonetic processing module includes duplex perception, that phenomenon by which a person hearing a spectrally fragmented syllable, presented dichotically, perceives both the individual pieces and the fully integrated whole. Something similar to duplex perception occurs in natural speech conversations. It is commonplace for those hearing well-formed linguistic material that is directed at and of great relevance to them to be aware of the meaning of both a linguistic message and the speaker's tone of voice. This duality reflects the fact that we have a conjoint specialization for language, a dual specialization that includes social cognition and grammatical analysis, and processors that are separately sited in the two cerebral hemispheres.

Duality of specialization accounts for a number of heretofore disparate and incompletely explained phenomena. For example, if one assumes that the child's initial utterances are produced by a social cognition module, their formulaic, underanalyzed nature is predictable. And when these early forms appear to regress, this also is to be expected, for if a grammatical module has kicked in or now has enough to "chew on," holistic words and phrases will be subject to reanalysis. That spoken and signed languages should be learned at different rates, but only until the onset of grammatical behavior, makes sense because the social cognition specialization is modality sensitive and the GAM is amodal. We should not be surprised that some children develop speech up to a point, perhaps an initial vocabulary of several dozen words, before slowing down.

The development of phonological languages follows certain principles that link and detach speech from the speechlike behaviors that come before words. The processes of segmental pruning, preservation, and learning that occur in perceptual development also occur in speech. For this reason, the child's first words may be built entirely of prelinguistic stock, and ambient experiences only gradually and subtly reveal themselves. These trenchant phonetic biases are carried over into all phases of language and are frequently confused with deficits of a morphological or syntactic type.

Although we are used to being told that phonemes are the building blocks of words, in fact words come to the child first. Systems that develop are systems that differentiate, and phonology is no exception. When the child with a small lexicon discovers the phonemic principle, it automatically discovers the combinatorial privilege of phonemes. What could only have been stored as a series of prosodically analyzed templates can now be organized phonologically and stored more efficiently. Unfortunately, not all children proceed through this process smoothly.

10

OTHER PATHS:
THE NEUROBIOLOGY OF
LINGUISTIC VARIATION

If we can learn how to read her, Nature has a great deal to say. Her variations are among the few clues that naturalistic observers can use to identify developmentally influential factors. What then accounts for the variability in language development from one child to the next? Which structural characteristics and nonlinguistic behaviors distinguish children with delays and disorders of language from those who learn to speak "on time"? What is the relative contribution of cognitive, motoric, social, and other factors?

Observers of child speech immediately notice that each child's phonetic profile is unique. For some reason, this interchild variability has been interpreted as evidence for underlying "cognitive factors" that are "not biological" (Ferguson and Macken, 1983; Goad and Ingram, 1987). To my knowledge, these "cognitive factors," which presumably include variations in perceptual style, creativity, and other organizing principles, have neither been described nor cognitively localized. On the surface, these variations may seem "elective" or relatively unconstrained structurally, but there are several reasons for questioning the validity of such interpretations.

If interchild differences in phonetic patterning are to be considered evidence for a "cognitive" model of phonological development, it follows that no interchild differences exist independent of cognition or prior to phonetic learning. There is evidence, however, that children's speech mechanisms are observably different, as are their patterns of performance in producing oral-motor movements on nonspeech tasks. There is also abundant evidence that individual children begin to babble at different ages and that they manifest this behavior differently (Vihman, Ferguson, and Elbert, 1986). Moreover, these interchild variations appear during a developmental period when the evidence for phonetic learning is scanty and during a type of vocal behavior that has about the same featural patterns in both normally developing infants and those with severe cognitive deficits (Dodd, 1972; Smith and Oller, 1981).

But there are more fundamental aspects to variability. Let us examine this construct as it applies to the human sound-making potential. Evolutionary mechanisms cannot operate unless a species is composed of genetically diverse individuals—this variation gives natural selection something to chew on, whether it occurs by adaptation or exaptation. Human infants will differ genetically, therefore, as well as in their social environments and individual patterns of behavior. Many of the so-called "individual differences" in children's behavior are undoubtedly an expression of their genetic and epigenetic differences.

Studdert-Kennedy (1986) has said that "a structure (e.g. the vocal apparatus) permits an unspecifiable, though presumably limited, range of functions, and the natural variability of behavior offers this range for selection" (p. 71). Because children's brains and vocal tracts vary, there is no logical need to attribute phonetic variations across children to anything but differences in anatomy and physiology. Studies of the vocal tract reveal wide variations in lingual morphology and lingual function in speech and speechlike motor activity. Fletcher and Daly (1974) measured the tongues of fifty children ranging in age from one month to five years. From these measurements they calculated an index of lingual agility, a ratio based on the length of the free part of the tongue (frenulum insertion to tongue tip) and the total sublingual length. As a ratio, this measure ignores differences in absolute size and therefore might be expected to be relatively invariant from one child to the next. And yet, as Figure 10.1 reveals, there was a great deal of vertical scatter not attributable to age or, presumably, to head size. In other research, Fletcher found that this ratio correlates significantly with

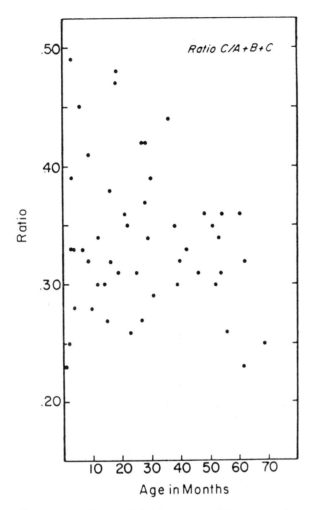

Figure 10.1. Ratio of the free part of the tongue (measurement C) to total sublingual length (measurements A + B + C) in fifty children.

the speed of repetitive oral movements (diadochokinesis) and performance on a test of speech articulation (Fletcher and Meldrum, 1968).

Neuroanatomical differences also reveal wide variation from subject to subject. Geschwind and Levitsky (1968) dissected one hundred adult brains, making bilateral measurements of the *planum temporale,* a cortical structure buried in the sylvian fissure that appears to have linguistic responsibilities. They found shape differences, with the posterior border sloping backward more sharply on the left in 57 percent of the cases and on the right in 18 percent of the cases (with symmetry in the remaining 25 percent). A sharper anterior border was also found on the left in 40 percent of the cases and on the right in 24 percent of the cases (with symmetry in the remaining 36 percent). Geschwind and Levitsky also found size differences. Overall, the left *planum* was larger than the right in 65 percent of the cases, smaller in 11 percent, and equal in 24 percent. Recently, Ojemann (1991) reported that in ninety subjects undergoing electrical stimulation mapping during object naming, no frontal perisylvian essential areas could be identified in 15 percent and only frontal areas could be identified in another 17 percent. Instead of a universally invariant speech mechanism that produces variable utterances, we seem to have a broad range of language control structures that express very similar utterances some three or four years after children begin to speak.

We can now revisit the relationship between individual differences and cognition. There is no reason to believe that environmental or "cognitive" factors are more or less responsible for variability than neurogenetic ones. These factors represent two different levels of organization. Each level affects the other, and both are susceptible to certain common influences. The fact is that genes contain the seeds of variability, while environments typically provide whatever minimal stimulation is needed to build linguistic capacity; and humans are roughly the same constitutionally in all the important ways, but every home is different from every other.

Instinct and learning serve complementary functions in insects and birds, but which stimuli (or portions thereof) an infant pays attention to is influenced by species-specific perceptual biases. It is therefore not surprising that individual differences in cognitive development may be transmitted genetically (Bouchard and McGue, 1981; also see Chapter 7).

Disorders in Children's Spoken Language

I have suggested that the greatest threats to language are a weak canalization for language and a linguistically unsupportive environment. Each year at least one in twenty children fails to develop language at the usual pace. How best to characterize these children and their problems is a question of some currency. Theorists have debated whether developmental dyslexia is a separate disorder or merely the low end of an acquisition curve (Geschwind, 1985; Shaywitz et al., 1992). Similarly, some speech pathologists conceptualize children with specific language impairment (SLI) as "not disordered in the sense of damage to a system . . . but less skilled in language" (Leonard, 1991, p. 68). According to this notion, the factors that cause language disorders are the same ones that regulate the pace of language acquisition in the normally developing child. Others think that SLI has etiologies, or malfunctions of language-enabling mechanisms, a conception that appeals particularly to those who are concerned with the treatment of disabled children (Aram, 1991; Tomblin, 1991) or read the literature identifying the neurophysiological correlates of language delay (Johnston, 1991). However, these etiologies, if they exist, rarely include hearing loss, mental retardation, brain damage, and primary emotional problems. Nor is the child's physical and social environment usually at fault.

There are several types of children who begin to develop language late. Some may have a slowly maturing brain. This is suggested by the fact that they speak like chronologically younger, normally developing children rather than in some altogether deviant way, and perform poorly on a range of tasks that have little to do with language. Additionally, they learn new words in the laboratory as quickly as normal children and progress linguistically at about the same rate as their normally developing peers. Other children may have a differently configured brain that works inefficiently. This is suggested by studies documenting a brain architecture in linguistically delayed children that differs from that of children who learn to speak at the normal rate. More will be said about these distinctions shortly.

It is important to ask how best to assist linguistically delayed children, and therefore to ask about the functional basis of developmental language disorders. Such research, ongoing at present, suggests a large phonetic component: language delayed speakers have difficulty with the processing of phonetically encoded lexical information at normal rates of presentation.

There are several reasons to suspect difficulties in phonetic processing. First, children with SLI have serious problems with grammatical morphemes. In English, according to Leonard (1989), these problems include the word-final plural, past tense, and possessive markers, the third person singular -s, the articles, the copula, and auxiliary be forms, the modal will, the infinitive particle to, and the complementizer that. Some consider these perceptually inconspicuous morphemes to be low in phonetic substance (Pinker, 1984). In general, low phonetic-substance morphemes are "nonsyllabic consonant segments and unstressed syllables, characterized by shorter duration than adjacent morphemes, and, often, lower fundamental frequency and amplitude" (Leonard, 1989, p. 186). Second, almost every SLI child has problems at the phonological level of language (Ingram, 1975; Leonard, 1982) with substitution patterns that are predictable independent of perceptual data (Tallal, Stark, and Curtiss, 1976).

Genetic Factors

Several epidemiologic factors seem to be consistent with a hereditary basis for SLI. SLI children characteristically do poorly on perception tasks in which the contrasts involve brief, transient information, even if the material is nonphonetic (Tallal and Piercy, 1975). Among SLI children there is also a higher ratio of males to females. Some research shows a reduced tendency toward right-handedness among the more severely language-delayed children (Neils and Aram, 1986), although several other studies have failed to observe manual laterality differences (Bishop, 1990a, 1990b), and there is no evidence for atypical cerebral lateralization patterns in the data from tapping (Hughes and Sussman, 1983) and dichotic listening experiments (Obrzut et al., 1980). In Hughes and Sussman's tapping experiment there was a noncompeting control condition in which subjects were simply to tap on a telegraph key as fast as possible without speaking concurrently. It is of interest that in this condition, language-delayed children tapped much more slowly with right and left hands than age-matched children who were developing language at a normal rate. This suggests that manual, and perhaps other cortical control mechanisms, may be less developed in children with developmental linguistic deficits, independent of any differences in hemispheric specialization.

FAMILY STUDIES

Less than a decade ago, a multiauthored book called *Genetic Aspects of Speech and Language Disorders* appeared (Ludlow and Cooper, 1983). In their own chapter, the editors called attention to a possible genetic basis for developmental language disorders, although at that time they had access to very little evidence they could interpret with confidence. A few years later, *Genetic Syndromes in Communication Disorders* was published (Jung, 1989). Its chapters dealt with genetic disorders whose symptoms include communicative difficulties but, ironically, they contained nothing on any genetic disorders whose phenotype *is* linguistic pathology.

Fortunately, in the last few years research addressing these shortcomings has mushroomed. Numerous investigations have identified a positive family history exceeding that of normally developing control subjects (Lewis, 1990; Lewis, Ekelman, and Aram, 1989; Neils and Aram, 1986; Tallal, Ross, and Curtiss, 1989; Tomblin, 1989). In most of these studies no hard data were available on parents' developmental history, but in one remarkable study the investigators (Parlour and Broen, 1989) tracked down subjects who, as preschoolers several decades earlier, had participated in a language development study. As expected, their children were also linguistically delayed.

TWIN STUDIES

The most trustworthy research in the area of behavioral genetics, of course, are the adoptive twin studies. In one such study, Hardy-Brown, Plomin, and DeFries (1981) administered a number of vocal, gestural, and other communicative measures to a group of fifty twelve-month-old infants and also administered several cognitive tests to both the infants' birth mothers and their adoptive mothers. The findings were that the birth and adoptive mothers both had a significant influence on children's communicative development, but in different ways. The biological mothers' scores on a cognitive battery (especially on a visual memory subtest) were predictive of communicative performance, as were the adoptive mothers' contingent vocal responding practices.

At older ages, measures of phonology, syntax, and receptive vocabulary have been far more concordant between monozygotic than dizygotic twins (Matheny and Bruggemann, 1973; Mather and Black, 1981; Munsinger and Douglass, 1976). But it is a mistake to expect children who are genetically identical and raised in the same home to speak in identical ways. Leonard et al. (1980) examined the utterances of identical twin girls in their second year of life. Phone tree analyses showed that the girls had very different sound systems, as different as those of children who were neither related nor reared by the same parents.

To date, most behavioral genetic studies of developmental language delay have focused on the frequency of such problems in family members in probands and normally developing control subjects. But at some level it is important to pin down the biological basis of such congruent disorders. Toward that end, we might ask if the phonological patterns of twins are also more similar qualitatively. One might suppose that the biological basis of human speech would be revealed in development by shared difficulties between genetically identical individuals, that is, that children with presumptively identical vocal tracts would be similarly troubled by the requirements of certain articulatory movement patterns but would not necessarily resolve their difficulties in exactly the same fashion. This is what Patricia Mather and I (Locke and Mather, 1989) found in a study of phonetic patterning in the speech of normally developing four-year-olds from monozygotic and same-sex dizygotic twins. We looked at the articulation test results obtained on eleven identical twin sets and an equal number of same-sex fraternal twins from the same socioeconomic class and dialect region. Figure 10.2 shows the percentage of shared errors.

Statistical analyses revealed a significantly higher rate of qualitative concordance between monozygotic than dizygotic twins. The identical twins were more likely to err on the same words on the test, although their articulatory problems were manifested in ways that were no more concordant than the misarticulations of fraternal twins. Though it is possible that the monozygotics were influenced to a greater degree by their co-twins, there is no evidence of this in our data, since the superficial speech habits of monozygotic twins

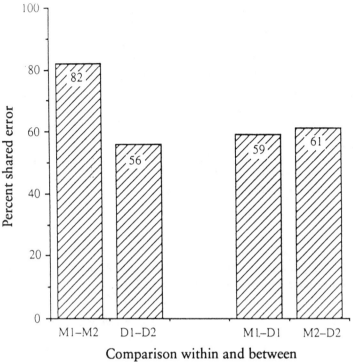

Figure 10.2. Percent shared error within monozygotic twins (M1–M2), dizygotic twins (D1–D2) and between monozygotic and dizygotic twin sets (M1–D1, M2–D2).

were not more similar than those of their dizygotic controls. I think, then, that our findings imply a genetic influence. But we certainly need more qualitative studies of twins using phonetically and acoustically rigorous methods of analysis.

To my knowledge, there is only one report of developmental language delay using the twin design, and it was just conducted (Lewis and Thompson, 1992). In this research, the concordance rate for speech and language delay was compared in monozygotic and dizygotic twin sets. As had been expected, probandwise[1] concordance

1. In calculating probandwise concordance, one divides the number of affected individuals in concordant pairs by the total number of probands in which the feature selected for (in this case, speech or language delay) is identified.

for monozygotic twins was significantly higher than for dizygotic twins, by a margin of 86 percent to 48 percent. Lewis and Thompson also found greater concordance for the type of speech or language disorder manifested by the monozygotic twins, as grossly classified by school personnel. This was particularly true for those with articulation disorders, though the other categories ("learning disorders," "delayed speech onset") were infrequently represented in the total twin sample.

The Brain of Children with Spoken Language Disorders

I am not surprised that research has identified a family background in cases of SLI, though I am unsure of what this means. Because genes indirectly contribute to children's social capacities and, therefore, their relationships with linguistically stimulating caregivers, it would be unwise to presume that familial language disorders are either strictly or straightforwardly neurolinguistic. However, it would not be surprising to find that many cases of specific language impairment are associated with an unorthodox brain structure. For one thing, children with developmental dyslexia typically have difficulty with certain types of phonological operations and judgments, and they tend toward atypical brain architectures. In fact, neuroanatomical findings in dyslexia may say less about inefficient processes of printed word recognition than about the biological correlates of underlying difficulties with phonetic representation.

MORPHOMETRIC STUDIES

Earlier we saw that in the majority of adults, the *planum temporalis* is larger on the left side than it is on the right. A study using magnetic resonance imaging recently reported symmetrical *plana* in a child who had developmental delay of spoken language. In a recent study, this result was obtained in a child with delayed oral language. Plante, Swisher, and Vance (1989) used MRI to measure language areas in both hemispheres of a four-year-old dizygotic right-handed twin male with specific language impairment. In this child, the perisylvian areas were bilaterally symmetrical. The left side was not larger than the right. This was in contrast to the finding of normally asymmetric *plana* in his normally developing fraternal twin and in a control group of linguistically normal children.

In a second study, Plante and her colleagues (1991) imaged eight boys with developmental language disorders. Six of the eight had atypical perisylvian asymmetries, the left side either equal to or smaller than the right. In contrast, only two of the eight controls had an atypical pattern; in those cases, the right and left perisylvian areas were equal. Abnormal asymmetries also were found in twenty language-delayed and learning-disabled children by Jernigan et al. (1991). The right prefrontal region was larger than the left in these subjects but not in normal controls.

Like others before her, Plante (1991) has found that the parents of boys with developmental language disorders generally experienced difficulty with speech, language or academic skills when they themselves were children. Her MRI analyses revealed that these parents, and also the siblings of probands, had atypical perisylvian asymmetries. In other words, developmental language disorders and atypical perisylvian asymmetries seem to aggregate in families. This is surely the strongest evidence to date of a transmittable neurobiological factor that is expressed communicatively and linguistically. Plante observed that since perisylvian asymmetries typically exist prior to birth, there would be little reason to be suspicious of "the environment" in these cases.

Anyone reading to this point might draw the conclusion that we have found the neurobiological basis of developmental language disorders: that there is a genetic basis paired with a neuromorphometric pattern that deviates from the normal. But of course there is nothing "abnormal" about perisylvian symmetry—it is simply not the most prevalent arrangement. In their classic parametric study, Geschwind and Levitsky (1968) found that about 35 percent of the adult brains dissected did not have a larger *planum* on the left. One presumes that most of these subjects had no history of developmental linguistic abnormalities.

A way out of this dilemma may lie in the fact that there is more to the biology of developmental language disorders than cerebral symmetry. In Galaburda's work on developmental dyslexia, reviewed elsewhere, most of those with symmetrical *plana* also had a variety of cellular abnormalities—atypical patterns of cellular size and shape. Whether their literacy disorders were associated with these neural ectopias, their structural symmetry, or both is unclear. Obviously, we need a great many more studies of brain structure and function in those with developmental language disorders.

WHAT EXPLAINS DEVELOPMENTAL LANGUAGE DEFICITS?

How do we get from asymmetries and ectopias to language deficits? One would think that children with linguistic deficits and atypical brain organization would speak like no other humans. It is surprising, therefore, that a number of investigators have found that children with delayed language have *normal* linguistic patterning (Curtiss, Katz, and Tallal, 1992). That is, analyses of utterances, and the order in which various linguistic structures are mastered, do not distinguish these subjects from younger children who are developing language apace. Indeed, even the cerebral palsied produce phonological errors not unlike those of normally developing young people (see Locke, 1983), and phonology is arguably more sensitive to motoric factors than any other area of language. These types of data suggest that developmental linguistic deficits—even those associated with extreme organic deviations—are best characterized as *delays*. But then how do we harmonize cortical deviation with linguistic delay?

To see the larger picture, it will be best if we temporarily put this question aside and turn to a different matter. A fair amount of research shows that children with language deficits, as a group, score poorly on measures of abilities that logically or theoretically support language learning, such as auditory memory, motor coordination, and phonetic perception. Viewing these findings, one might assume that many children are delayed *because* systems that presumptively facilitate or enable language have been functioning at subnormal levels of efficiency. On this view, there must be some reason for language delay, and we will find it when glitches are uncovered in one or more of the putatively acquisitive mechanisms.

This story has a logical ring to it, and I do not honestly know that it is wrong. However, I am unconvinced that we know enough to proclaim its truth either. In practice we usually test only for the functions that logically or theoretically relate to language. Certainly, granting agencies would be disinclined to fund studies of theoretically irrelevant capacities. We are therefore unlikely to know if children with specific language impairments also have delayed (or deviant) development of olfactory, gustatory, visual, or tactile processing. Consequently, the deficits we uncover will automatically appear to be specifically linked to the observed linguistic delay.

But there are reasons to believe that other functions may be impaired or delayed, too, ones that have little or nothing directly linking them with language. Studies over the last fifty years reveal that language-delayed children tend to do worse than control subjects on tasks as diverse as auditory attention, gross and fine motor development, diadochokinesis (rapid repetition of articulatory gestures), oral kinesthesis, two-point lingual discrimination, auditory memory span, tone perception, and a host of other behavioral capabilities that are related or marginally related to spoken language.

Spoken language is not unique in this regard. A team of British researchers (Johnson, Goddard, and Ashurst, 1990) found that of the children not walking independently at eighteen months, 56 percent were diagnosed with an associated abnormality by three years of age. But the cause of the late walking was not always clear. "Failure to achieve this milestone may be associated with neurological abnormality, or impairment in other systems," wrote Johnson et al., "but in many late walkers there is no obvious cause. They could represent the limit of normal biological variation in the age of independent walking" (p. 486).

Language-delayed children also tend to do worse on tasks that by present theories have nothing to do with speech. How one would know this is a matter of some interest in its own right. In some unusual experiments, the linguistically underdeveloped group fell down on control measures that were selected specifically because they were theoretically unrelated to language. For example, in the tapping task used by Hughes and Sussman (1983), language-delayed children tapped at significantly slower rates even in the non-concurrent control condition, that is, when silent.

In other cases, research has simply strayed into areas in which deficits would not necessarily have been expected. Paula Tallal and her colleagues have found that developmentally language-disordered children perform inferiorially on tactile and visual perception tasks as well as on measures of auditory and phonetic perception

(Johnston et al., 1981). Are these deficits related to any kinds of developmental delay? Possibly. As a group, linguistically under-achieving children score lower on IQ tests administered concurrently with language evaluations (Stark et al., 1983) or some years later (Aram, Ekelman, and Nation, 1984; Felsenfeld, Broen, and McGue, 1992; Silva, Williams, and McGee, 1987).

Tallal and Stark (1983) saw an element of causality in these connections. Observing a high correlation between the comprehension scores of language delayed children and their verbal and nonverbal temporal processing abilities, they concluded that "developmental language delay may be related, at least in part, to deficits in lower level processing that may be *prerequisite* to the normal development of speech and language skills" (p. 104, italics mine). I am not sure that this position is justified, though on present evidence it would be hard to prove that deficits in theoretically related areas are *not* causally related to language development.

In any case there are other, neurodevelopmental factors to be considered. Though there is a neural specialization for language, there is no reason to believe that development of this specialization is immune to general constraints on neurodevelopmental growth (such as metabolic factors). Deficits on a variety of sensory, cognitive, and motor tasks may mean that entire areas of the cortex are developing slowly. If so, some language-delayed children may have a slowly maturing brain and commensurately reduced processing in several modalities. These deficits would merely coexist with delayed language. Since correlations do not prove causality, we need not accept that there is anything to deal with here but language delay secondary to neurodevelopmental delay.

Others may have disorders that are masked by the strength of natural language habits. For example, our species' natural disposition to produce certain categories of oral gesture, such as stop consonants, is so strong that in clinical practice we rarely see children with more errors on stops than fricatives or affricates. So, one could argue, no wonder those with disorders do not necessarily sound different. To sound abnormal they must obviate basic human dispositions.

My thinking is that some children, like some of the late walkers discussed above, are merely on the low end of a normal distribution (Leonard, 1991). They are analogous to school children with developmental reading delay (Shaywitz et al., 1992), many of whom also

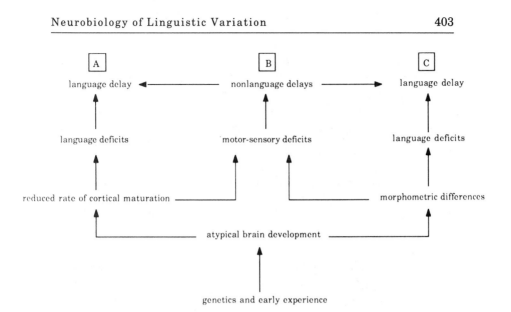

Figure 10.3. Neurodevelopmental model by which atypical brain development produces a range of behavioral deficits, including language and processing capabilities that potentially affect linguistic development, but also capacities that have nothing to do with language.

have underlying deficits of phonological processing and language comprehension. But other children with delayed development of spoken language undoubtedly are maturationally delayed or structurally deviant. There seems to be some support for this in family history studies. When researchers question the parents of children with developmental language difficulties, many of them claim that they themselves had delayed language in their youth. Of these adults, some speak normally and some seem to have residual deficits of one kind or another. Research designs tend to reflect these differences. In some studies (such as Tallal, Ross, and Curtiss, 1989), "affected" family members are taken to be those with a history of language (or academic) problems. In other studies (Felsenfeld, Broen, and McGue, 1992; Lewis, Ekelman, and Aram, 1989; Tomblin, 1989), "affected" is defined by contemporaneous evaluation. If a parent is affected, by these definitions, interpretation becomes complicated because the child is susceptible to exogenous as well as endogenous sources of error.

I have modeled the "slow maturation" and "deviant structure" scenarios in Figure 10.3. In the figure, genetics and early experience produce atypical brain development, as revealed in scenario A, a reduced rate of cortical maturation, and scenario C, morphometric differences. In A, abnormally slow brain development retards development of a variety of behavioral capacities, which include language and a number of motor and sensory capabilities that support or are independent of language. Language delay of the type occurring in A is primarily due to slow maturation of a language organ in a slowly growing brain, although it may be complicated by converging deficits in related areas. This conception has a direct bearing on an issue raised in Chapters 1 and 5, the existence of "precursors" to language.

Figure 10.3 also imagines, in scenario C, a deviant brain structure that, like the immature brain, produces simplified utterances. It is proposed that some trace of these behaviors, like those in A, remains in adulthood, to be observed either in the superficial phonetics of speech or experimental tests of related functions. Scenario B refers to a variety of other delays and deviations produced by motor and sensory deficits associated with atypical brain function. These nonlinguistic differences may, to some degree, affect language delays and deviations that draw upon other systems for support. Interestingly, in our present state of ignorance, differential diagnosis may be less likely to succeed if based on performance in childhood, when the deficits are at their peak, than in adulthood, when behaviors either linger or abate. There is more to be said about these distinctions, and I have begun to say more elsewhere (Locke, 1992b, in preparation).

ACQUIRED DISORDERS IN CHILDHOOD

I have already discussed the plasticity of the developing human brain and noted that human children have a broadly sensitive (and not narrowly critical) period for the development of spoken language. Does this mean, then, that the language chreod is deep enough to survive neonatal brain damage? Does damage to affective, social, or linguistic areas of the brain knock infants out of the chreod, producing developmental linguistic deviations as they struggle to assume their place on the path to spoken language? Or, does brain damage just freeze infants in their tracks, producing language delays not qualitatively different from those of children with developmental language disorders (and normally developing young children)?

Various investigators have looked at the language of children who incurred unilateral brain damage in the first several years of life (Aram and Ekelman, 1987; Aram, Ekelman, and Whitaker, 1986; Dennis and Kohn, 1975; Feldman et al., 1992). These studies reveal that many infants who experience significant damage to neural tissue in the left cerebral hemisphere may nonetheless go on to acquire a normal or nearly normal command of spoken language. Precisely how this result comes about is unknown, and whether there are any qualitative differences between their linguistic processing and that of neurologically normal children is uncertain, since most of the evaluations have been based on standardized performance tests.

The studies by Dorothy Aram and her colleagues are nevertheless enlightening, since they were able to compare the language of subjects with unilateral left and right hemisphere lesions, cortical and subcortical lesions, and relatively early onset with later onset of damage. My affective hypothesis makes specific predictions about the effects upon language of unilateral left and unilateral right hemisphere strokes at different points in brain development. Specifically, most infant strokes seem not to leave lasting linguistic impairments. However, the transitory effects of right hemisphere stroke, relative to left, should be greater in infants under a year than in children who are significantly older. This should be true at least if the yearling, guided by vocal and facial (and other) person-identifying and affective cues, processes this information mainly in the right hemisphere. Damage to this hemisphere would be expected to disturb the infant's orientation to or ability to interpret things people do when talking. It would knock the infant off the language track.

Aram et al. (1986) measured the spoken syntax of eight children who had sustained left-hemisphere damage, and an equal number of children who had incurred right-hemisphere damage, between the ages of one month and six years. The length of time between the damage and testing ranged from two days to two years. Measures included the percentage of sentences produced correctly, the mean length of utterance (MLU), developmental sentence score (DSS), percentage of simple sentences attempted and produced correctly, and performance on a variety of grammatical markers and more complex utterances. I separated the data from subjects who had right-hemisphere damage in the first year of life (N = 6) or later (N = 2), and the findings on children whose left-hemisphere lesions occurred in the first year of life or later (N = 4 per group). This categorization produced small and uneven samples but the comparisons were still of interest.

The younger right hemisphere–lesion subjects performed *worse* than the older right hemisphere–lesion subjects on tests of MLU, DSS, percentage of all sentences produced correctly, percentage of simple sentences attempted, and percentage of simple sentence produced correctly. They were also measurably inferior on the use of personal pronouns, main verbs, interrogatives, WH questions, and negatives. The children whose left-hemisphere lesions occurred in the first year of life performed better than children whose left hemisphere damage occurred later on MLU, DSS, personal pronouns, main verbs, and interrogatives. The younger subjects performed worse on the percentage of all sentences produced correctly, percentage of simple sentences attempted and produced correctly, and main verbs. Though these data were too limited to analyze statistically, the general direction of the outcome lends some support to my hypothesis regarding age and side of lesion.

There is also evidence for the hypothesis linking age of damage and side of lesion in a recent study by Feldman et al. (1992). One of their subjects had sustained unilateral right hemisphere damage prior to birth. At twenty-seven months, when the study ended, she had just one word and was communicating nonverbally. The investigators concluded that "both cerebral hemispheres may play critical roles in the very earliest stages of language acquisition" (p. 89).

The study population of Aram et al. (1987) also included some subjects whose damage was localized to subcortical and cortical areas in the left and right hemispheres. However I was unable to observe any greater linguistic deficits among the right subcortical cases. In other work by Aram (Aram and Ekelman, 1987), right-lesioned subjects were slightly more impaired on a measure of language comprehension (the modified token test) than were left-lesioned subjects, relative to the controls. The right-lesioned subjects, however, were faster to respond, and the investigators considered them "impulsive."

My age-and-side hypothesis seems to be disconfirmed by these studies; children with left lesions prior to a year had as much or more difficulty comprehending sentential commands than those with later damage, and children with early right-hemisphere damage out-performed children with later damage on that side of the brain. Whether this reflects a genuine difference between linguistic comprehension and expression or the variability associated with small populations is difficult to tell.

A NOTE ON THE EPIGENESIS OF LANGUAGE DEVELOPMENT

The term "epigenesis" has been with us a long time. Originally, it referred to "the emergence of new structures and functions during the course of development," where the cause of the changes was left unspecified (Gottlieb, 1992, p. 159). Because development of new structures and functions implicated an environmental role, the meaning of "epigenesis" took on an interactive connotation. According to Gottlieb:

> That epigenetic development is probabilistically determined by active interactions among its constituent parts is now so well accepted that epigenesis itself is sometimes defined as the interactionist approach to the study of individual development . . . the new definition of epigenesis would say that *individual development is characterized by an increase of complexity of organization—i.e., the emergence of new structural and functional properties and competencies—at all levels of analysis . . . as a consequence of horizontal and vertical coactions among its parts, including organism-environment coactions.*" (pp. 159–160, italics his)

The evidence for interactivity is even greater than Gottlieb may have thought. There is now evidence in animals that cortical cells are influenced as much by the activity of other cells as they are by genes (Walsh and Cepko, 1992). This adds even more flexibility to the development of neural systems that are already known to be massively influenced by experience.

For Gottlieb, development is a bidirectional process in which genes interact with stimulation to create structure, and thereby to produce a capacity for behavior. Behavior, in turn, additionally influences the development of structure. How does epigenesis work in the case of language?

Consider the family history studies referenced above. Though it typically is unstated, the implicit logic in these studies is that since probands were exposed to normal speech (the parents having somehow achieved this, in spite of their own developmental difficulties), their problems must not be "environmental" and must therefore be of endogenous origin. The endogenous view is reinforced by congruent brain findings on affected family members, but a reason for caution is that children do indeed have the capacity to influence their linguistic environment and then to be influenced by the patterns of stimulation they themselves have set in motion. Precisely how this occurs is unknown, but neither is it known how it is that monozygotic twins separated at birth tend to hold similar views on religion and politics. One possibility is that general (that is, phonetically nonspecific) effects operate in association with globally social factors. This would not be altogether different, by analogy, from the finding that social behaviors expressed toward strangers may be heritable (Kagan, Reznick, and Snidman, 1988; Plomin and Rowe, 1979).

Given that language development is a collaborative affair requiring genetic and environmental teamwork, children who acquire language with difficulty are likely to have deficits at several levels. There is evidence that parents, siblings, and caregivers talk to language-delayed children with shorter and simpler utterances than they use in addressing normally developing children of the same age (see review in Leonard, 1987). Presumably these individuals are attempting, in their nurturant or pragmatic ways, to talk to delayed children in language they think will be understood. A model of linguistic epigenesis was presented earlier in Figure 3.6. That figure envisions several developmental relationships, including those bidirectional effects whereby maturation influences function, which in turn affects behavior, and behavior affects function, which in turn influences maturation.

Children with limitations on the neural capacity to socialize and "cognize" in ways that facilitate spoken language may be confronted with a less than age-appropriate level of linguistic stimulation. If children with hereditary language deficits are systematically exposed to linguistically deprived environments, then "linguistic genes" interact with "linguistic environments" in ways that at least relate to, and at most produce or confound, language delay. In this sense the disorders of language—just as much as the normal development of language—are an epigenetic affair.

DEVELOPMENTAL DYSLEXIA

Analogous to specific language impairment, developmental dyslexia results in difficulty in learning to read and write in spite of broadly normal sensory, cognitive, and linguistic capabilities, and adequate instruction and motivation to acquire literacy skills. At one time it was thought that dyslexia affected males more frequently than females and appeared more often in left-handed individuals (Geschwind and Behan, 1982). Recent studies question the gender bias (Shaywitz et al., 1990) and raise serious questions about the manual laterality hypothesis (Locke et al., in preparation). But surveys continue to show a strong family history (DeFries and Decker, 1982), and dyslexia is far more commonly shared by monozygotic than dizygotic twins (Decker and Vandenberg, 1985; DeFries, Fulker, and LaBuda, 1987).

One study of familial patterning has estimated an occurrence of dyslexia in 40 percent of the sons and 20 percent of the daughters of affected fathers, and 35 percent of the sons and 15 percent of the daughters of affected mothers (Vogler, DeFries, and Decker, 1984). There is a higher than normal incidence of reading disorder in the siblings of dyslexic children, and even where the siblings read normally, they may still be more prone to immune disorders (Geschwind and Behan, 1982) and slower in symbolic processing (Denckla and Rudel, 1976). Regions of the brain, especially those not critically related to reading, may therefore be similar in dyslexic males and their unaffected brothers. Familial patterns in the Colorado Study (DeFries, 1985) are consistent with a polygenic threshold model in which there is a predisposition toward reading disability that is a function of both genetic and environmental influences. It is therefore conceivable that familial and nonfamilial reading disability have different neuroanatomical bases.

In light of these findings, it is not surprising that research has revealed abnormalities of brain *function* in developmentally dyslexic individuals on a variety of measures. Research on regional cerebral blood flow in dyslexic men has revealed reduced anteroposterior asymmetry during a line orientation task and exaggerated hemispheric asymmetries during a semantic classification task (Rumsey et al., 1987). However, results from such studies, as well as auditory event-related potentials (Shucard, Cummins, and McGee, 1984) and EEG-BEAM (Duffy et al., 1980), have failed to produce a unitary conception of dyslexic brain function.

Studies of brain *structure,* on the other hand, have produced at least one generalization: hemispheric asymmetries seen in normal individuals are reduced in dyslexics. Findings from CT scans suggest that in dyslexia there is a reduction or a reversal of the tendency in normal readers for the left parieto-occipital region to be wider than the homologous area in the right hemisphere (Hier et al., 1978). Postmortem measurements of individuals with a history of reading difficulty have revealed reductions in the typical patterns of asymmetry across the hemispheres.

In all dyslexic brains reported to date, the left and right *plana* have been found to be symmetrical (Galaburda et al., 1985; Kemper, 1984). In the majority of these cases, a variety of cytoarchitectonic abnormalities has also been reported, including ectopias, dysplasias, and micropolygyria, primarily in the perisylvian areas. That there should be such findings in the perisylvian region accords well with accepted models of developmental reading disorder, which attribute word recognition failure to inefficient use of grapheme-phoneme correspondence rules (Liberman et al., 1977), secondary to impairment in *phonological* processing (Scarborough, 1990; Vellutino, 1979; Wagner and Torgeson, 1987). It is known, for example, that adult dyslexics from three-generation kindreds (and who may therefore have a heritable form of dyslexia) make predominantly phonological misspellings (which change the pronunciation of the word; Pennington et al., 1986). It is not surprising that regions of the brain associated with phonological processing would be morphometrically deviant from the corresponding regions in normal readers.

Although it is unfortunate that some children experience trenchant difficulties in the acquisition of language, the natural range of variation in rate and quality of learning in our young makes possible the identification of facilitating and retarding factors. Interchild variation is to be expected because the human genome specifies a range of variation upon which the environment is unusually free to act. Except for identical twins, all humans have a different set of genes, and all of us, including identical twins, have a different brain and vocal tract architecture. Those who witness the range of natural variation in the general population frequently express astonishment that we speak so very similarly. On the other hand, for all the differences from one home to the next, social environments tend to be fairly similar in linguistically significant ways.

Children who are "functionally" delayed in the development of language—that is, have nothing else that is obviously wrong with them—are characteristically poor in the reproduction of elements that are low in phonetic power. Because these include unstressed syllables, children with these problems are inclined to delete weak syllables from words. On the surface, this appears to be a phonological problem. However, these children tend to eliminate weak material from phrases as well, giving the illusion that they have a specifically grammatical problem rather than a pervasive difficulty in dealing with phonetic material.

Research in the last few years has begun to document an elevated incidence of similar problems in the families of language-delayed children, including a higher concordance rate in monozygotic twins. These kinds of data suggest the presence of an underlying genetic contribution. Morphometic studies using magnetic resonance imaging are beginning to show neuroarchitectural variations in children with delayed language. There is, then, a conspicuous biology to developmental language disorders as well as to the development and execution of linguistic capacity as it occurs more normally.

11

REFLECTIONS ON
THE PATH TO LANGUAGE

If the antecedents to human speech are to be found in the graded calls of nonhuman primates, we must look to the sounds used by the younger, still-maturing subadults of a species, for freed from the roles of sexual partner, troop defender, and status seeker, they have the greatest opportunity for learning and friendly social interactions. The adult members of a primate group, on the other hand, serve as teachers by providing, in the consistency of their vocalizations and their behavioral responses to the calls of others, a set of "rules" for subadults to learn.

J. D. Newman and D. Symmes, "Inheritance and Experience
in the Acquisition of Primate Acoustic Behavior"

I cannot resist some speculations on the evolution of our species' capacity for languages that are spoken. In this concluding chapter, I will take up some possible links between ontogeny and phylogeny and end with a revisitation of ontogenetic questions I raised earlier.

Mother Tongue:
A Note on Some Possible
Links between Ontogeny and Phylogeny

I came to this challenge prepared to ask how human infants develop an interest in, and capability for, complex vocal communication. Little did I suspect at the outset that along the way I would be so frequently struck by an irrepressible urge to speculate about the evolution of our species' capacity for spoken language. But this was not idle speculation. Indeed, I would like to have been able to avoid it. We all know the matter cannot be resolved one way or the other, and many scholars have their own well-formed views on the subject. To take an optional foray into phylogeny seemed to represent a risky venture, and it still does. Yet, to me, now, speculation on this matter not only seems helpful, but even a necessary step in the effort to think lucidly about linguistic ontogeny. The reason is that maternal-infant interaction was arguably as instrumental in the evolution of our species-specific capacity for language as it is in the modern-day infant's development of speech. Because of this, the infant's approach to language is fundamentally different from what it would have been had ontogeny not influenced evolution.

The properties of established languages are fairly well aligned with the phonetic proclivities of the human infant. I used to think this was because the vocal-motor system of adults—those who design and continually redesign languages—possesses many of the same biases and constraints as the infant's vocal-motor system (Locke, 1983). I continue to believe this, but I can now see that language is the way it is because it evolved in an ontogenetic framework. The early prelinguistic and linguistic forms of the species were probably much like the infant's early forms because the hominid mother paid particular attention to what phonetic material "went over" best with the infant in her audience.

I am suggesting that certain of the maternal-infant interactions that characterize ontogeny today may have occurred in the final stages of prelinguistic history, fostering growth of our species' capacity for spoken language. I think it is safe to assume that contact and alarm calls would have suited the needs of hominids as they do those of nonhuman primates. One might assume, further, that hominids were already exchanging vocal affect with their babies when motor capabilities evolved. But they came to possess a great deal more phonatory control than alarm calls require, possibly as a by-product of advances in manual motor coordination. Accordingly, our ancestors became increasingly articulate and used articulated voice with their young and with each other. Now they could transmit more complex information. In effect, they could *advise* their infant as well as warn it. With increasing levels of vocal complexity and vocal reference being displayed for and reciprocated by infants during the period of maximum cortical plasticity, they would have carried increasingly complex vocal forms into childhood and adulthood with them. This would have materially enhanced their own and our species' capability for language.

How would this have worked at the level of the individual maternal-infant dyad? The human mother who wishes to nurture now *speaks*. She knows that her words will mean nothing but that her voice and dancing eyes can easily tell the story she needs to tell and her infant needs to hear. I suspect that when hominid parents noticed their progeny's interest in the face and voice, they, too, realized that they had an open channel and used it to convey emotionality. Accordingly, they put their messages—in the form of modulated vocal sounds—in the same channel. In effect, the creation of spoken language by our ancestors received encouragement from the same discovery that is made anew by each primiparous mother who emotes facially and vocally, and learns from the reciprocal acts of her baby that her messages were received and appreciated.

My speculation is that spoken language grew out of the mother's desire to nurture and the baby's need to be securely attached. Infants liked their mothers' sounds and facial expressions, and mothers kept these displays coming. The mother's tongue became the mother tongue of her child; maternal vocal behavior and contingent responding collaborated with other factors to shape our species' capacity for spoken language. In practically every culture studied, there is some form of baby language (Ferguson, 1964). If we could roll back linguistic history, I would not be in the least surprised to find "mama" among our forebears' first words. Indeed, this and other so-called "baby words" may have been the core of the earliest lexicons. I am not the first to wonder along these lines, for nearly a century ago Johnston (1896) said that "the human race began to talk as babies begin to talk . . . in the prattle of every baby, we have a repetition in a minor key of the voice of the earliest man . . . by watching the first movements of speech in a baby, we can see once more the first steps in articulate language, which the whole world of man once took in dim ages long ago" (p. 499).

Such a prospect is not implausible; 80 percent of the names for "mother" in the languages of the world contain a nasal consonant (Locke, 1985), for example, *mama, mati, maama, majka, nana, meme, maman,* and *mae.* Why this nonarbitrary association between sound and meaning? The eminent linguist, Roman Jakobson (1960) offered some conjecture on this matter, observing that often "the sucking activities of a child are accompanied by a slight nasal murmur, the only phonation which can be produced when the lips are pressed to mother's breast or to the feeding bottle and the mouth is full." Later, Jakobson speculated, "this phonatory reaction to nursing is reproduced as an anticipatory signal at the mere sight of food and finally as a manifestation of a desire to eat" (p. 542).

Jakobson believed these ancestors of ours were already talking at the time this scenario took place. I think it more likely that these unintended nasalizations were appropriated for maternal use very early on. Mother—*la grande dispensatrice*—called the tune, and indexical and affective cues made up the melody. Instead of assuming that such terms are created especially for use with children, we might speculate that baby words were there at the beginning and merely survived as other lexical assignments were made.

The intersubjective processes that develop in the human infant are the fruits of phylogeny. At the most basic level, it seems reasonable to suppose that selection processes applied to maternal-infant dyads that were able to use vocal and other indexical information to maintain or regain contact, and that infants particularly responsive to vocal cues were less likely to lose maternal contact and perish. In our evolutionary history, one imagines that the ancestral infant also communicated affect by way of vocal and facial activity, took vocal turns, and shared gazes with its mother. If the early months and years of life are critical learning opportunities in humans, they would have been at least as important to hominids who, like nonhuman primates, may have had a shorter period of postnatal brain development. Anything as complex as language would logically have had to get its start during this period in the infant's life. Mother-infant interactions would have been indispensible to the development of linguistic capacity in individual children and thus to the creation of spoken language in the species.

Generally, theories on the evolution of language have referred to pressures associated with adults' need to communicate information related to work, hunting, tool making, and the like. But if such factors entered the picture, I think they must have done so in parallel with the ontogenetic processes I have discussed, or even somewhat later. To be drawn upon by adults, the capacity for complex vocal referencing would necessarily have existed already, and in my judgment this capacity would have come from a mixture of species-specific predispositions and very early rearing experiences, as it does now.

Neurologically there may be parallels, too. Since certain of the nonhuman primates process indexical vocal information bilaterally, we might speculate that in the attempt to identify their fellow hominid and to infer its motives, our prehistoric ancestors also relied on both hemispheres more or less equally. In hominids, both hemispheres may have handled vocal information of all types before there was anything as complex as modern languages. When our ancestors began to interrupt voice with articulatory movements, their vocal repertoire differentiated into a series of segmental constituents whose mode of production required precise timing and coordination. These unfamiliar, transient patterns with little affective force or indexical value were naturally processed in the hemisphere that produced them and was better able to sequence and coordinate precise movements in any reproductions that might be attempted. This hemisphere, accustomed now to relating movements and sounds, became coolly analytical, able to decompose larger stretches of vocal material into parts that corresponded to oral gestures. Vocal affect was driven out by the competition, as it were, leaving the right hemisphere to deal with this important communicative function. In ontogeny, correspondingly, our expectation is that this right hemisphere specialization for vocal affect will develop before the left hemisphere takes on the responsibility for phonetic operations, and, indeed, this is what the evidence suggests does happen.

With the ability to superimpose articulate movements upon phonation, and a desire to nurture and teach, the hominid would have been able to take a step on his own path to spoken language. But did hominids have didactic dispositions? For clues, we might examine the record of nonhuman primates in this regard.

Studies of maternal teaching in nonhuman primates have been undertaken, but only very recently, and it seems too soon to judge their didactic tendencies. Negative indications were reported in some of the earlier studies. For example, Bard and Vauclair (1984) observed two mother-child dyads, one involving chimpanzees and the other humans, in the same situation with identical objects. The investigators were struck by the nearly complete lack of teaching efforts by the chimpanzee mother relative to the human one. Tomasello et al. (1987) observed the use of tools in chimpanzees who had been exposed to a demonstration and in a control group of chimps who had been denied this experience. Eight- to nine-year-old animals showed no evidence of learning, though four- to six-year-olds did learn to use the tools in the manners demonstrated. However, none of the younger animals in the experimental group learned either of two more complex strategies. Tomasello and his colleagues concluded that there had been no imitation per se, but that animals exposed to the demonstration had become more aware of the tool—and the activities that could be accomplished by its use—and that they then used their own rather than the demonstrated strategies. In a later review paper, Tomasello (1991) concluded from various tool use studies, including his own, that "in no case is there reproduction of behavior from one animal to another, and thus, by my definition, in no case is there cultural transmission."

Roger Fouts and his colleagues (Fouts, 1983; Fouts, Fouts, and Van Cantfort, 1989) placed a ten-month-old male chimpanzee named Loulis with a foster mother. However, this particular foster mother was different from other chimps. In fact, she was a celebrity—the infamous "Washoe"—who had been taught to sign some years earlier and was the subject of several research reports. Loulis was allowed to see humans producing no more than seven different signs; all others observed were made by Washoe and three other signing chimpanzees living in the area. Fouts et al. found that Loulis assimilated many of Washoe's signs spontaneously, the first just eight days after his introduction to Washoe. More important in the present context, on occasion Washoe was seen molding Loulis's hands into a sign, that is, she appeared to be giving "articulatory training."

The research carried out in these studies was contextually somewhat constrained and perhaps not the best indication of what nonhuman primates can do in their natural circumstance. Under more ethologically natural circumstances, Hannah and McGrew (1987) observed the propagation of tool use among sixteen chimpanzees who had been liberated from captivity to an island off the coast of Liberia. The practice of cracking palm nuts with two stones—a hammer and an anvil—seemed to originate in one of the animals, then spread horizontally to the other adults. This suggested to the authors a "limited cultural diffusion" (p. 31).

That the younger subjects in Tomasello et al. (1987) benefited more from tool use demonstration suggests that vertical instruction—the transmission of information from parent to child—may be more effective than horizontal diffusion. In our own species, vertical teaching is a key element in the propagation of culture. Our elementary and secondary schools are supposed to play a major role in this. Among nonhuman primates, mother-infant relationships are such that teaching would appear to be possible—several ethologists have documented what might be called "good mothering" by wild chimpanzees (Plooij, 1984). In laboratory experiments, even monkeys separated from their mothers at birth and raised in social isolation, never observing an instance of mothering in other animals, still offer attentive care upon the birth of their own infant (Meier, 1965).

There are also indications that maternal teaching does, in fact, occur. For example, Boesch (1991) has described several cases in which Tai chimpanzee mothers encouraged nut cracking in their young. They tended to stimulate nut cracking in their younger offspring and to facilitate this behavior among older infants. In a recent review, Caro and Hauser (in press) noted several cases of "discouragement" among nonhuman primates in which mothers prevented their young from eating a substance that was not part of that species' normal diet or threatened young animals who approached some fruit known from experience to be poisonous. Caro and Hauser also reviewed a study by Hauser in which "encouragement" (contingent responding) occurred when a younger animal produced an alarm call appropriately.

There is a huge mitigating circumstance, however. Nonhuman primate mothers have little need to nurture their young over an extended period; the rapid motor development and self-sufficiency of infant apes and monkeys makes this unnecessary. Hinde and Simpson (1975) noted that at four weeks of age rhesus monkey infants frequently left their mothers' company in order to explore and play. The chimpanzee infant frequently can stand by eight weeks and tends to separate himself from his mother at about four to six months of age (Plooij, 1984). Chism (1991) has observed that patas monkey infants are able to survive the loss of their mother, without adoption, as early as seven months of age. As a result of this early self-sufficiency, nonhuman primate infants, in general, have a shorter period in which close contact with their mother is

needed or available. This undoubtedly threatens the vertical transmission of behavior.

There is, then, some evidence of maternal demonstration, facilitation, and the like, but it is proffered over a short period of time,
and there is little evidence of explicit vertical teaching among nonhuman primates. Nonhuman primates appear to lack a strong disposition to instruct their young, and their system of contact and
alarm calls clearly is better suited to needs that have less to do
with culture than survival. In other words, one sees little evidence
in nonhuman primates that maternal voice is used freely to provide
information irrelevant to survival.

Ontogeny Revisited

At long last, we seem to have arrived at an appropriate time for a
progress report. I speak not of a report on the child's progress toward
spoken language but on our own efforts to understand how ontogenetic linguistic progress occurs.

At the beginning of this book I wondered about a number of
things. How, I asked, does the human infant discern linguistic from
nonlinguistic behavior? This seemed an important basic question
to be asked at the outset, for how, lacking some mechanism that
permits this discrimination, would the infant be able to allocate the
proper amount of time attending to stimulation that is of linguistic
import? Now this seems to have been the wrong question. The infant
need not tell linguistic from nonlinguistic. It need only tune in to
the sights and sounds that are personally relevant—those that identify and convey the feelings of caregivers. In the first instance, this
allows the infant to recognize and therefore to become attached to
appropriate parties. If the infant stays with this, if it continues to
track the personally relevant cues of recognizance and emotionality,
we need not worry about its attention to linguistically relevant
information. The infant is already listening in the right places, and
it may have the potential to pick out many of the segmental variations that may be embedded in the vocal stream.

We need to be careful about how we interpret research based on
infants' processing of these phonetic equivalents of the black-on-
white line drawing. By sending to their ears signals that are de-

prived of all affective and indexical significance, we elicit responses from infants that tell us little of value about their development of language. Indeed, I would argue that these studies give us a very distorted picture of what really happens. The need of rigorous experimental control is not in question here. What is in question is what behavior means when it is elicited by ethologically unnatural events. When we select stimuli that are likely to be of equal value to everyone—the disposition of those trained in the methods and paradigms of experimental psychology (the present author included)—I think, without intending to, we ensure that the stimuli will be of no particular value to anyone, especially the infant.

With naturally intoned material, infants will at some point develop the capability of analyzing the stream of indexical and affective vocal cues at the level at which linguistic entities are signaled. As long as they do not compete for resources, these two propensities—one to listen for vocal resonance and prosody, the other to attend to transient frequency sweeps—will keep the infant in the queue to languages that are implemented phonologically.

We have likewise wondered how we theorists are to tell the infant's linguistic from its nonlinguistic behaviors. Are the wordlike forms that it uses appropriately to be considered linguistic? This would seem to be one of the more basic judgments to be made. But now I think we see that the situation is more complicated than we might have supposed. Even animals and prelinguistic children may sound linguistic, owing to mechanisms that are socially and vocally specialized but without grammatical capability. Yet we do not impute linguistic knowledge to parrots for good reason, and we should not confer linguistic status upon infants' formulaic words and phrases for the same good reason, among others.

Understanding that language develops more or less continuously, and seeing some of the preparatory, facilitating, and enabling behaviors that occur along the way, I think we are now in an advantaged position to identify factors that place certain infants at risk for delay or disorder. We would be concerned should a child not respond favorably to the configuration and movement of faces and voices from the earliest postnatal moments or, after a certain age, not defer vocalization until others are done. Uneasiness will arise if we encounter an infant whose attention cannot be swung to ambient objects and events with eye movements, or who assimilates none of the vocal, facial, or manual gestures of individuals to whom the infant has become attached. We surely would have great concern for the child who fails to understand that other people have feelings and thoughts not exactly like its own or the infant whose vocal behavior remains relatively undifferentiated over the first year of life.

We cannot be sure of the reasons the human infant spends so much time pleasantly and softly vocalizing when there is no signaling to be done and no audience in the immediate vicinity. In the long run, however, this activity is likely to be richly functional, paradoxically, precisely because there is no immediate communicative need or objective. This releases the infant to engage in vocalization playfully, allowing for the vocal self-exploration that fosters growth and elaboration of speech monitoring systems. At the neural level, it now seems likely that the loquacious human infant regularly contributes to the vocal processing capacity of its developing brain. Vocalizing is something that infantile apes and monkeys do far less of, and one can only wonder if their lack of vocal control as adults will to any degree reflect this relative quiescence—a missed opportunity—at a time when the brain is impressionable to self-activity.

It will be clear by now that language does not begin to develop with the first appearance of utterances. The word is a significant event to the infant's family but no more significant to language acquisition than many other accomplishments, and there is no evidence that the word launches some new stage in the larger process. The birth of the infant is not as significant an event on the continuum of life as it was once thought to be. For the fetus, the uterus is a stimulating place that allows for the exercise of emergent motor ability. That it also allows for linguistically relevant learning is also becoming evident. In the final three months of gestation, the normal fetus can hear and respond to auditory stimulation and is probably aware of its mother's voice. It is likely that some vocal learning commences in the weeks before birth, learning that predisposes the newborn infant to attend particularly to sound patterns whose resonance and prosody resemble sounds it has heard earlier. This encourages selective attention both to its mother and to the language that will become its mother tongue. Indeed, we are unable to dismiss the possibility that the universal primacy of languages that are spoken is a reflection of this early and prolonged access to the voice at a time when visual stimulation is unavailable.

I mentioned earlier the infant's need to track both prosodic and segmental alterations. One might speculate that a value of the father's voice (and the voice of others less known to the infant than the mother) is that it has the same kinds of fluctuations as the mother's but is initially unfamiliar. To a degree, this may facilitate or reinforce the perceptual impression that there are levels of processing that are somewhat distinct.

The composite of behaviors subsumed under "language" includes some abstract, amodal concepts, but the physical stuff that language is wrapped up in accounts for much of what we know about its development. This may be the reason that traditional linguistic classifications distort or mislabel the infant's continuously changing communicative repertoire. To be sure, if we are to engage in scholarly discussions of language, we will need to refer to phonology, syntax, morphology, semantics, and pragmatics, but in the infant's case, how can we be sure at any given moment which of these domains we *should* be talking about? In the infant's initial expression of words and phrases we hear individually recognizable sounds coming out of its mouth that are almost certainly not represented in its mind. We hear phrases of two and three words that, for all intents and purposes, have no constituent parts. Children with an "obvious" syntactic deficit—selectively deleting articles, determiners and other functors—are also heard to omit unstressed syllables from the words they do say. Phonemes are the building blocks of language, but their existence and the recombinatory principle of phonological systems appear to be among the final insights in a progression that begins with communication and dialogue and advances to words and phrases before this linguistically critical discovery. I presume that the first linguistic analyses, those that lead the infant into grammatical behavior, are performed not on newly heard linguistic material but on stock words and phrases that have long been in the infant's expressive repertoire.

The human infant is not a machine that coldly collects linguistic material which will someday be analyzed in an effort to derive structural rules, nor is it in any way passive. Rather, to develop lexical and grammatical knowledge the infant must hotly pursue utterances and their referents, eliciting exemplars, testing hypotheses, trying out pronunciations. And then, when enough has literally been said and done, it can calmly sort through the yield of these pursuits looking for patterns and searching for constituent elements. The infant's incorporation of new lexical forms probably goes on best by day, face to face with the mother, but I suspect much of the analysis takes place after dark, in the crib, when the interactions have died down.

The classic opposition—genes versus the environment—now appears to be rather shopworn and empty. In reality, there never was a *versus* in this artificial dichotomy and there never were just two factors in the equation. Instead, we see that early brain developments beget others, that the child is an active agent in the creation of its brain and neurolinguistic capacity, that environments are themselves the expression of genes which are also inherited by the infant, that brain systems develop competitively, that behavior influences function and function influences structure, and that experience produces lasting changes in the architecture and function of the brain.

In a nurturant society, paradoxically, learning is not directed by those that are nurturant but by the human subject of their nurturance. That, indeed, is the idea of nurturance. When affectionate and caring parents watch, listen to, and smell their infant—literally taking their cues from it—they place themselves at the infant's disposal. From the beginning the infant, even while helpless, directs the activities of its caregivers. And that is the biological point to helplessness. With neoteny automatically comes nurturance, and that puts infant self-determination squarely in the middle of the developmental picture.

The development of linguistic communication is a story about the preoccupation among the human young with things that move—faces that wrinkle, eyes that dance, voices that undulate, and hands that wiggle through the air. Parents obviously understand this and, correctly believing that more is better, exaggerate their facial and vocal movements when addressing their young. And to good developmental effect, for the cues to phrase boundaries are prosodic, and the cues to vocal turn taking include variations of pitch and gaze.

REFERENCES

Abler, W. L. 1989. On the particulate principle of self-diversifying systems. *Journal of Social and Biological Structure, 12,* 1–13.

Alberts, J. R., and Decsy, G. J. 1990. Terms of endearment. *Developmental Psychobiology, 7,* 569–584.

Allman, J. 1977. Evolution of the visual system in the early primates. In Sprague, J. M., and Epstein, A. N. (eds.), *Progress in psychobiology and physiological psychology, 7,* 1–53. New York: Academic Press.

Andrew, R. J. 1963a. Evolution of facial expression. *Science, 141,* 1034–1041.

Andrew, R. J. 1963b. The origin and evolution of the calls and facial expressions of the primates. *Behaviour, 20,* 1–109.

Andrew, R. J. 1964. The displays of the primates. In Buettner-Janusch, J. (ed.), *Evolutionary and genetic biology of primates.* Vo. 2. New York: Academic Press.

Andrew, R. J. 1965. The origins of facial expressions. *Scientific American, 213,* 88–94.

Anthoney, T. R. 1968. The ontogeny of greeting, grooming and sexual motor patterns in captive baboons (superspecies *Papio cynocephalus*). *Behaviour, 31,* 358–372.

Antinucci, F. 1990. The comparative study of cognitive ontogeny in four primate species. In Parker, S. T., and Gibson, K. R. (eds.) *"Language" and intelligence in monkeys and apes: Comparative developmental perspectives.* New York: Cambridge University Press.

Aoki, C., and Siekevitz, P. 1988. Plasticity in brain development. *Scientific American, 256,* 56–64.

Aram, D. M. 1991. Comments on specific language impairment as a clinical category. *Language, Speech, and Hearing Services in Schools, 22,* 66–68.

Aram, D. M., and Ekelman, B. L. 1987. Unilateral brain lesions in childhood: Performance on the Revised Token Test, *32*, 137–158.

Aram, D. M., Ekelman, B. L., and Nation, J. E. 1984. Preschoolers with language disorders: 10 years later. *Journal of Speech and Hearing Research, 27*, 232–244.

Aram, D. M., Ekelman, B. L., and Whitaker, H. A. 1986. Lexical retrieval in left and right brain lesioned children. *Brain and Language, 27*, 75–100.

Aram, D. M., Ekelman, B. L., and Whitaker, H. A. 1987. Spoken syntax in children with acquired unilateral hemisphere lesions. *Brain and Language, 31*, 61–87.

Archer, L. A., Campbell, D., and Segalowitz, S. J. 1988. A prospective study of hand preference and language development in 18- to 30-month-olds: II. Relations between hand preference and language development. *Developmental Neuropsychology, 4*, 93–102.

Argyle, M., and Cook, M. 1976. *Gaze and mutual gaze.* New York: Cambridge University Press.

Argyle, M., Lalljee, M. and Cook, M. 1968. The effects of visibility on interaction in a dyad. *Human Relations, 21*, 3–17.

Armstrong, E. 1982. Mosaic evolution in the primate brain: Differences and similarities in the hominoid thalamus. In Armstrong, E., and Falk, D. (eds.), *Primate brain evolution: Methods and concepts.* New York: Plenum Press.

Arnold, S. J. 1990. Inheritance and the evolution of behavioral ontogenies. In Hahn, M. E., Hewitt, J. K., Henderson, N. D., and Benno, R. H. (eds.), *Developmental behavior genetics: Neural, biometrical, and evolutionary approaches.* New York: Oxford University Press.

Aronson, E., and Rosenbloom, S. 1971. Space perception in early infancy: Perception within a common auditory-visual space. *Science, 172*, 1161–1163.

Asher, J., and Garcia, R. 1969. The optimal age to learn a foreign language. *Modern Language Journal, 38*, 334–341.

Aslin, R. N., and Pisoni, D. B. 1980. Some developmental processes in speech perception. In Yeni-Komshian, G. H., Kavanagh, J. F., and Ferguson, C. A. (eds.), *Child phonology.* Vol. 2. *Perception.* New York: Academic Press.

Assal, G., Zander, E., Kramin, H., and Buttet, J. 1976. Discrimination des voix lors des lesions du cortex cerebral. *Archives Suisses de Neurologie, Neurochirurgie et de Psychiatrie, 119*, 307–315.

Atkinson, J. 1984. Human visual development over the first 6 months of life: A review and a hypothesis. *Human Neurobiology, 3*, 61–74.

Atkinson, K., MacWhinney, B., and Stoel, C. 1968. An experiment on the recognition of babbling. In *Language Behavior Research Laboratory Working Paper #14.* Berkeley: University of California.

Atkinson, M. 1982. *Explanations in the study of child language development.* New York: Cambridge University Press.

Attwood, A., Frith, U., and Hermelin, B. 1988. The understanding and use of interpersonal gestures by autistic and Down's syndrome children. *Journal of Autism and Developmental Disorders, 18*, 241–257.

Bahrick, H. P., Bahrick, P. O., and Wittlinger, R. P. 1975. Fifty years of memory for names and faces: A cross-sectional approach. *Journal of Experimental Psychology: General, 104,* 54–75.

Baker, C. 1977. Regulators and turn-taking in American Sign Language discourse. In Friedman, L. (ed.), *On the other hand: New Perspectives in American Sign Language.* New York: Academic Press.

Baldwin, J. D., and Baldwin, J. I. 1976. Effects of food ecology on social play: A laboratory simulation. *Zeitschrift fur Tierpsychologie, 40,* 1–14.

Balogh, R. D., and Porter, R. H. 1986. Olfactory preferences resulting from mere exposure in human neonates. *Infant Behavior and Development, 9,* 395–401.

Baltaxe, C. A. M. 1981. Acoustic characteristics of prosody in autism. In Mittler, P. (ed.), *Frontiers of knowledge in mental retardation. Vol. 1. Social, educational, and behavioral aspects.* Baltimore, Md.: University Park Press.

Baltaxe, C. A. M., and Simmons, J. Q. 1985. Prosodic development in normal and autistic children. In Schopler, E., and Mesibov, G. (eds.), *Communication problems in autism.* New York: Plenum Press.

Baptista, L. F., and Petrinovich, L. 1984. Social interaction, sensitive phases, and the song template hypothesis in the white-crowned sparrow. *Animal Behaviour, 32,* 172–181.

Baptista, L. F., and Petrinovich, L. 1986. Song development in the white-crowned sparrow: Social factors and sex differences. *Animal Behaviour, 34,* 1359–1371.

Bard, K. A., Platzman, K. A., Lester, B. M., and Suomi, S. J. 1992. Orientation to social and nonsocial stimuli in neonatal chimpanzees and humans. *Infant Behavior and Development, 15,* 43–56.

Bard, K., and Vauclair, J. 1984. The communicative context of object manipulation in ape and human adult-infant pairs. *Journal of Human Evolution, 13,* 181–190.

Barlow, G. W. 1977. Modal action patterns. In Sebeok, T. A. (ed.), *How Animals Communicate.* Bloomington: Indiana University Press.

Baron-Cohen, S., Leslie, A. M., and Frith, U. 1985. Does the autistic child have a "theory of mind"? *Cognition, 21,* 37–46.

Barrett, K. C., and Campos, J. J. 1983. Cited in Bertenthal, B. I., Campos, J. J., and Barrett, K. C. 1984. Self-produced locomotion: An organizer of emotional, cognitive, and social development in infancy. In Emde, R. N., and Harmon, R. J. (eds.), *Continuities and discontinuities in development.* New York: Plenum.

Barrett-Goldfarb, M. S., and Whitehurst, G. J. 1973. Infant vocalizations as a function of parental voice selection. *Developmental Psychology, 8,* 273–276.

Bartholomeus, B. 1973. Voice identification by nursery school children. *Canadian Journal of Psychology, 27,* 464–472.

Bates, E., Bretherton, I., and Snyder, L. 1988. *From first words to grammar: Individual differences and dissociable mechanisms.* New York: Cambridge University Press.

Bates, E., Benigni, L., Bretherton, I., Camaioni, L., and Volterra, V. 1979. *The emergence of symbols: Cognition-communication in infancy*. New York: Academic Press.

Bates, H., and Busenbark, R. 1969. *Parrots and related birds*. Neptune City, N.J.: T. F. H. Publications.

Bateson, P. 1979. How do sensitive periods arise and what are they for? *Animal Behaviour, 27,* 470–486.

Bauman, M., and Kemper, T. L. 1985. Histoanatomic observations of the brain in early infantile autism. *Neurology, 35,* 866–874.

Bavelas, J. B., Black, A., Lemery, C. R., and Mullett, J. 1986. "I *show* how you feel": Mimicry as a communicative act. *Journal of Personality and Social Psychology, 50,* 322–329.

Bavelas, J. B., Black, A., Lemery, C. R., and Mullett, J. 1987. Motor mimicry as primitive empathy. In Eisenberg, N., and Strayer, J. (eds.), *Empathy and its development*. New York: Cambridge University Press.

Baylis, G. C., Rolls, E. T., and Leonard, C. M. 1985. Selectivity between faces in the responses of a population of neurons in the cortex in the superior temporal sulcus of the monkey. *Brain Research, 342,* 91–102.

Beggs, W. D. A., and Foreman, D. L. 1980. Sound localization and early binaural experience in the deaf. *British Journal of Audiology, 14,* 41–48.

Bekoff, M. 1972. The development of social interaction, play, and metacommunication in mammals: An ethological perspective. *Quarterly Review of Biology, 47,* 412–434.

Bekoff, M. 1984. Social play behavior. *BioScience, 34,* 228–233.

Bekoff, M., and Fox, M. W. 1972. Postnatal neural ontogeny: Environment-dependent and/or environment-expectant? *Developmental Psychobiology, 5,* 323–341.

Bell, W. L., Davis, D. L., Morgan-Fisher, A., and Ross, E. D. 1990. Acquired aprosodia in children. *Journal of Child Neurology, 5,* 19–26.

Bellugi, U., Bihrle, A., Jernigan, T., Trauner, D., and Doherty, S. 1990. Neuropsychological, neurological, and neuroanatomical profile of Williams syndrome. *American Journal of Medical Genetics Supplement, 6,* 115–125.

Bellugi, U., Bihrle, A., Neville, H., Doherty, S., and Jernigan, T. 1992. Language, cognition, and brain organization in a neurodevelopmental disorder. In Gunnar, M. R., and Nelson, C. A. (eds.) *Developmental behavioral neuroscience. The Minnesota Symposia on Child Psychology, Vol. 24.* Hillsdale, N.J.: Erlbaum.

Belmore, N. F., Kewley-Port, D., Mobley, R. L., and Goodman, V. E. 1973. The development of auditory feedback monitoring: Delayed auditory feedback studies on the vocalizations of children aged six months to 19 months. *Journal of Speech and Hearing Research, 16,* 709–720.

Belsky, J., and Most, R. K. 1981. From exploration to play: A cross-sectional study of infant free play behavior. *Developmental Psychology, 17,* 630–639.

Bel'tyukov, V. I., and Salakhova, A. D. 1973. Babbling in the hearing child. *Voprosy Psikhologii, 2,* 587–605.

Bench, J. 1969. Some effects of audio-frequency stimulation on the crying baby. *Journal of Auditory Research, 9,* 122–128.

Benedict, H. 1979. Early lexical development: Comprehension and production. *Journal of Child Language, 6,* 183–200.

Benevento, L. A., Fallon, J., Davis, B. J., and Rezak, M. 1977. Auditory-visual interaction in single cells in the cortex of the superior temporal sulcus and the orbital frontal cortex of the macaque monkey. *Experimental Neurology, 57,* 849–872.

Benno, R. H. 1990. Genetic approaches to the developing nervous system. In Hahn, M. E., Hewitt, J. K., Henderson, N. D., and Benno, R. H. (eds.), *Developmental behavior genetics: Neural, biometrical, and evolutionary approaches.* New York: Oxford University Press.

Benowitz, L. I., and Routtenberg, A. 1987. A membrane phosphoprotein associated with neural development, axonal regeneration, phospholipid metabolism, and synaptic plasticity. *Trends in Neuroscience, 10,* 527–532.

Benzaquen, S., Gagnon, R., Hunse, C., and Foreman, J. 1990. The intrauterine sound environment of the human fetus during labor. *American Journal of Obstetrics and Gynecology, 163,* 484–490.

Berger, J., and Cunningham, C. C. 1981. The development of eye contact between mothers and normal versus Down's syndrome infants. *Developmental Psychology, 17,* 678–689.

Berger, J., and Cunningham, C. C. 1983. Development of early vocal behaviors and interactions in Down's syndrome and nonhandicapped infant-mother pairs. *Developmental Psychology, 19,* 322–331.

Berger, K. W., Garner, M., and Sudman, J. A. 1971. The effect of degree of facial exposure and the vertical angle of vision on speechreading performance. *Teacher of the Deaf, 69,* 322–326.

Bergman, T., Haith, M. M., and Mann, L. 1971. In Mendelson, M. J., and Haith, M. M. 1976. The relation between audition and vision in the human newborn. *Monographs of the Society for Research in Child Development, 41* (Serial No. 167).

Berkson, G. 1983. Repetitive stereotyped behaviors. *American Journal of Mental Deficiency, 88,* 239–246.

Berkson, G., and Gallagher, R. J. 1986. Control of feedback from abnormal stereotyped behaviors. In Wade, M. G. (ed.), *Motor skill acquisition of the mentally handicapped: Issues in research and training.* New York: Elsevier.

Berkson, G., and Mason, W. A. 1964. Stereotyped behaviors of chimpanzees: Relation to general arousal and alternative activities. *Perceptual and Motor Skills, 19,* 635–652.

Berkson, G., Mason, W. A., and Saxon, S. 1963. Situation and stimulus effects on stereotyped behaviors of chimpanzees. *Journal of Comparative and Physiological Psychology, 56,* 786–792.

Berntson, G. G., and Boysen, S. T. 1989. Specificity of the cardiac response to conspecific vocalizations in chimpanzees. *Behavioral Neuroscience, 103,* 235–245.

Berntson, G. G., Boysen, S. T., Bauer, H. R., and Torello, M. S. 1990. Conspecific screams and laughter: Cardiac and behavioral reactions of infant chimpanzees. *Developmental Psychobiology, 22,* 771–787.

Bertenthal, B. I., and Bai, D. L. 1989. Infants' sensitivity to optical flow for controlling posture. *Developmental Psychology, 25,* 936–945.

Bertenthal, B. I., and Campos, J. J. 1990. A systems approach to the organizing effects of self-produced locomotion during infancy. In Rovee-Collier, C., and Lipsitt, L. P. (eds.), *Advances in infant research,* Vol. 6. Norwood, N.J.: Ablex.

Bertenthal, B. I., Campos, J. J., and Barrett, K. C. 1984. Self-produced locomotion: An organizer of emotional, cognitive, and social development in infancy. In Emde, R. N., and Harmon, R. J. (eds.), *Continuities and discontinuities in development.* New York: Plenum Press.

Bertoncini, J., Bijeljac-Babic, R., Blumstein, S. E., and Mehler, J. 1987. Discrimination in neonates of very short CVs. *Journal of the Acoustical Society of America, 82,* 31–37.

Bertoncini, J., Morais, J., Bijeljac-Babic, R., McAdams, S., Peretz, I., and Mehler, J. 1989. Dichotic perception and laterality in neonates. *Brain and Language, 37,* 591–605.

Best, C. T. 1988. The emergence of cerebral asymmetries in early human development: A literature review and a neuroembryological model. In Segalowitz, S., and Molfese, D. L. (eds.), *Developmental implications of brain lateralization.* New York: Guilford Press.

Best, C., Hoffman, H., and Glanville, B. 1982. Development of infant ear asymmetries for speech. *Perception and Psychophysics, 31,* 75–85.

Best, C. T., and Queen, H. F. 1989. Baby, it's in your smile: Right hemiface bias in infant emotional expressions. *Developmental Psychology, 25,* 264–276.

Bever, T. G., Carrithers, C., Cowart, W., and Townsend, D. J. 1989. Language processing and familial handedness. In Galaburda, A. (ed.), *From reading to neurons.* Cambridge, Mass.: MIT Press.

Beyn, E. S., and Knyazeva, G. R. 1962. The problem of prosopagnosia. *Journal of Neurology, Neurosurgery and Psychiatry, 25,* 154–158.

Bickerton, D. 1990. *Language and species.* Chicago: University of Chicago Press.

Bickley, C., Lindblom, B., and Roug, L. 1986. Acoustic measures of rhythm in infants' babbling, or "All God's children got rhythm." Proceedings of the 12th International Congress on Acoustics.

Birnholz, J. C., and Benacerraf, B. R. 1983. The development of human fetal hearing. *Science, 222,* 516–518.

Birns, B., Blank, M., Bridger, W. H., and Escalona, S. K. 1965. Behavioral inhibition in neonates produced by auditory stimuli. *Child Development, 36,* 639–645.

Bishop, D. V. M. 1990. Handedness, clumsiness and developmental language disorders. *Neuropsychologia, 28,* 681–690.

Blair, R. G. 1965. Vagitus uterinus: Crying in utero. *Lancet, 11,* 1164–1165.

Blake, J., and Fink, R. 1987. Sound-meaning correspondences in babbling. *Journal of Child Language, 14,* 229–253.

Bloom, K. 1974. Eye contact as a setting event for infant learning. *Journal of Experimental Child Psychology, 17,* 250–263.

Bloom, K., Russell, A., and Wassenberg, K. 1987. Turn taking affects the quality of infant vocalizations. *Journal of Child Language, 14,* 211–227.

Bloom, L. 1973. *One word at a time.* The Hague: Mouton.

Bloom, L., Lightbown, P., and Hood, L. 1975. Structure and variation in child language. *Monographs of the Society for Research in Child Development, 40,* Serial No. 160.

Bloom, L., and Capatides, J. 1987. Expression of affect and the emergence of language. *Child Development, 58,* 1513–1522.

Bloom, L., Beckwith, R., and Capatides, J. B. 1988. Developments in the expression of affect. *Infant Behavior and Development, 11,* 169–186.

Boesch, C. 1991. Teaching among wild chimpanzees. *Animal Behaviour, 41,* 530–532.

Bolinger, D. 1989. *Intonation and its uses.* Stanford: Stanford University Press.

Bondurant, J. L., Romeo, D. J., and Kretschmer, R. 1983. Language behaviors of mothers of children with normal and delayed language. *Language, Speech, and Hearing Services in Schools, 14,* 233–242.

Bonvillian, J. D., and Folven, R. J. 1987. The onset of signing in young children. Paper presented at the Fourth International Symposium on Sign Language Research, Lappeenranta, Finland, July 15–19, 1987.

Bonvillian, J. D., Orlansky, M. D., and Garland, J. B. 1982. Handedness patterns in deaf persons. *Brain and Cognition, 1,* 141–157.

Bonvillian, J. D., Orlansky, M. D., and Novack, L. L. 1983. Developmental milestones: Sign language acquisition and motor development. *Child Development, 54,* 1435–1445.

Bornstein, B., and Kidron, D. P. 1959. Prosopagnosia. *Journal of Neurology, Neurosurgery and Psychiatry, 22,* 124–131.

Bornstein, B., Sroka, H., and Munitz, H. 1969. Prosopagnosia with animal face agnosia. *Cortex, 5,* 164–169.

Bornstein, M. H. 1985. How infant and mother jointly contribute to developing cognitive competence in the child. *Proceedings of the National Academcy of Science, 82,* 7470–7473.

Bornstein, M. H., Pecheux, M-G., and Lecuyer, R. 1988. Visual habituation in human infants: Development and rearing circumstances. *Psychological Research, 50,* 130–133.

Bornstein, M. H., and Sigman, M. D. 1986. Continuity in mental development from infancy. *Child Development, 57,* 251–274.

Borod, J. C., Koff, E., Lorch, M. P., and Nicholas, M. 1985. Channels of emotional expression in patients with unilateral brain damage. *Archives of Neurology, 42,* 345–348.

Bortolini, U., and Leonard, L. 1990. Phonological disorders in Italian-speaking children. Paper delivered at the Eleventh Annual Child Phonology Conference, Madison, Wis.

Bouchard, T. J., Lykken, D. T., McGue, M., Segal, N. L., and Tellegen, A. 1990.

Sources of human psychological differences: The Minnesota study of twins reared apart. *Science, 250,* 223–250.

Bouchard, T. J., and McGue, M. 1981. Familial studies of intelligence: A review. *Science, 212,* 1055–1059.

Bowerman, M. 1982. Starting to talk worse: Clues to language acquisition from children's late speech errors. In Strauss, S. (ed.), *U-shaped behavioral growth.* New York: Academic Press.

Bowlby, J. 1969. *Attachment and loss.* Vol. 1. *Attachment.* New York: Basic Books.

Bowman, S. A., Shanks, J. C., and Manion, M. W. 1972. Effect of prolonged nasotracheal intubation on communication. *Journal of Speech and Hearing Disorders, 37,* 403–406.

Boysson-Bardies, B. de, Halle, P., Sagart, L., and Durand, C. 1989. A crosslinguistic investigation of vowel formants in babbling. *Journal of Child Language, 16,*1–18.

Boysson-Bardies, B. de, Vihman, M. M., Roug-Hellichius, L., Durand, C., Landberg, I., and Arao, F. 1992. Material evidence of infant selection from the target language: A cross-linguistic phonetic study. In Ferguson, C., Menn, L., and Stoel-Gammon, C. (eds.), *Phonological development: Models, research, implications.* Parkton, Md: York Press.

Branigan, G. 1979. Some reasons why successive single word utterances are not. *Journal of Child Language, 6,* 411–421.

Brazelton, T. B. 1961. Psychophysiologic reactions in the neonate. I. The value of observation of the neonate. *Journal of Pediatrics, 58,* 508–512.

Brazelton, T. B., Tronick, E., Adamson, L., Als, H., and Wise, S. 1975. Early mother-infant interaction. In *Parent-infant interaction* (CIBA Foundation Symposium 33). New York: Elsevier.

Bretherton, I. 1988. How to do things with one word: The ontogenesis of intentional message making in infancy. In Smith, M. D., and Locke, J. L. (eds.), *The emergent lexicon: The child's development of a linguistic vocabulary.* New York: Academic Press.

Bretherton, I., McNew, S., and Beeghly-Smith, M. 1981. Early person knowledge expressed in gestural and verbal communication: When do infants acquire "theory of mind"? In Lamb, M., and Sherrod, L. (eds.), *Infant social cognition.* Hillsdale, N.J.: Erlbaum.

Bretherton, I., McNew, S., Synder, L., and Bates, E. 1983. Individual differences at 20 months: Analytic and holistic strategies in language acquisition. *Journal of Child Language, 10,* 293–320.

Bricker, P. T., and Pruzansky, S. 1966. Effects of stimulus content and duration on talker identification. *Journal of the Acoustical Society of America, 40,* 1441–1449.

Brodbeck, A. J., and Irwin, O. C. 1946. The speech behaviour of infants without families. *Child Development, 17,* 145–156.

Bronson, W. C. 1971. The growth of competence: Issues of conceptualization and measurement. In Schaffer, H. R. (ed.), *The origins of human social relations.* New York: Academic Press.

Bronson, W. C. 1974. Mother-toddler interaction: A perspective on studying the development of competence. *Merrill-Palmer Quarterly, 20,* 275–301.

Brooks-Gunn, J., and Lewis, M. 1982. Affective exchanges between normal and handicapped infants and their mothers. In Field, T., and Fogel, A. (eds.), *Emotion and early interaction.* Hillsdale, N.J.: Erlbaum.

Brothers, L. 1989. A biological perspective on empathy. *American Journal of Psychiatry, 146,* 10–19.

Brothers, L. 1990. The social brain: A project for integrating primate behavior and neurophysiology in a new domain. *Concepts in Neuroscience, 1,* 27–51.

Brothers, L. In submission. A further perspective on empathy: Contagious acts.

Brothers, L., Ring, B., and Kling, A. 1991. Selective responses of macaque temporal neurons to complex social stimuli.

Browman, C. P., and Goldstein, L. 1989. Articulatory gestures as phonological units. *Phonology, 6,* 201–251.

Brown, J. W. 1988. Cingulate gyrus and supplementary motor correlates of vocalization in man. In Newman, J. D. (ed.), *The physiological control of mammalian vocalization.* New York: Plenum Press.

Brown, R., and Lenneberg, E. 1954. A study in language and cognition. *Journal of Abnormal and Social Psychology, 49,* 454–462.

Bruce, C., Desimone, R., and Gross, C. G. 1981. Visual properties of neurons in a polysensory area in superior temporal sulcus of the macaque. *Journal of Neurophysiology, 46,* 369–384.

Bruner, J. S. 1977. Early social interaction and language acquisition. In Schaffer, H. R. (ed.), *Studies in mother-infant interaction.* New York: Academic Press.

Bruner, J. S. 1981. The social context of language acquisition. *Language and Communication, 1,* 155–178.

Bruner, J. S. 1983. The growth of cognitive psychology: Developmental psychology. In Miller, J. (ed.), *States of mind.* New York: Pantheon Books.

Bruun, R. D. 1988. The natural history of Tourette's syndrome. In Cohen, D. J., Bruun, R. D., and Leckman, J. F. (eds.), *Tourette's syndrome and tic disorders: Clinical understanding and treatment.* New York: John Wiley and Sons.

Buchwald, J. S., and Shipley, C. 1985. A comparative model of infant cry. In Lester, B. M., and Boukydis, C. F. Z. (eds.), *Infant crying: Theoretical and research perspectives.* New York: Plenum Press.

Burnham, D. K. 1986. Developmental loss of speech perception: Exposure to and experience with a first language. *Applied Psycholinguistics, 7,* 207–240.

Bushnell, I. W. R., Sai, F., and Mullin, J. T. 1989. Neonatal recognition of the mother's face. *British Journal of Developmental Psychology, 7,* 3–15.

Butterworth, G., and Hopkins, B. 1988. Hand-mouth coordination in the newborn baby. *British Journal of Developmental Psychology, 6,* 303–314.

Byrne, R. W., and Whiten, A. 1991. Computation and mindreading in primate tactical deception. In Whiten, A. (ed.), *Natural theories of mind.* Oxford: Blackwell.

Calvin, W. H. 1983. Timing sequencers as a foundation for language. *Behavioral and Brain Sciences, 2,* 210–211.

Cameron, J., Livson, N., and Bayley, N. 1967. Infant vocalizations and their relationship to mature intelligence. *Science, 157,* 331–333.

Camhi, J. M. 1984. *Neuroethology: Nerve cells and the natural behavior of animals.* Sunderland, Mass.: Sinauer Associates.

Camp, B. W., Burgess, D., Morgan, L. J., and Zerbe, G. 1987. A longitudinal study of infant vocalization in the first year. *Journal of Pediatric Psychology, 12,* 321–331.

Campbell, D. 1973. Sucking as an index of mother-child interaction. In Bosma, J. F. (ed.), *Fourth symposium on oral sensation and perception: Development in the fetus and infant.* Bethesda, Md.: DHEW Publication No. NIH 75–546.

Campbell, R., Landis, T., and Regard, M. 1986. Face recognition and lipreading. *Brain, 109,* 509–521.

Campos, J. J., and Bertenthal, B. I. 1989. Locomotion and psychological development in infancy. In Morrison, F., Lord, K., and Keating, D. (eds.), *Applied developmental psychology.* New York: Academic Press.

Cancelliere, A. E. B., and Kertesz, A. 1990. Lesion localization in acquired deficits of emotional expression and comprehension. *Brain and Cognition, 13,* 133–147.

Caplan, P., and Kinsbourne, M. 1976. Baby drops the rattle: Asymmetry in duration of grasp by infants. *Child Development, 47,* 532–534.

Cappella, J. N., and Greene, J. O. 1982. A discrepancy-arousal explanation of mutual influence in expressive behavior for adult and infant-adult interaction. *Communication Monographs, 49,* 89–114.

Capute, A. J., Palmer, F. B., Shapiro, B. K., Wachtel, R. C., Schmidt, S., and Ross, A. 1986. Clinical linguistic and auditory milestone scale: Prediction of cognition in infancy. *Developmental Medicine and Child Neurology, 28,* 762–771.

Carey, S. 1978. The child as word learner. In Halle, M., Bresnan, J., and Miller, A. (eds.), *Linguistic theory and psychological reality.* Cambridge, Mass.: MIT Press.

Carey, S. 1981. The development of face perception. In Davies, G., Ellis, H., and Shepherd, J. (eds.), *Perceiving and remembering faces.* London: Academic Press.

Carey, S., and Diamond, R. 1977. From piecemeal to configurational representation of faces. *Science, 195,* 312–314.

Carey, S., and Diamond, R. 1980. Maturational determination of the developmental course of face encoding. In Caplan, D. (ed.), *Biological studies of mental processes.* Cambridge, Mass.: MIT Press.

Carey, S., Diamond, R., and Woods, B. 1980. Development of face recognition—a maturational component? *Developmental Psychology, 16,* 257–269.

Carmichael, L. 1926. The development of behavior in vertebrates experimentally removed from the influence of external stimulation. *Psychological Review, 33,* 51–58.

Carmichael, L. 1927. A further study of the development of behavior in verte-brates experimentally removed from the influence of external stimulation. *Psychological Review, 34,* 34–47.

Carmichael, L. 1970. The onset and early development of behavior. In Mussen, P. (ed.), *Carmichael's manual of child psychology.* Vol. 1. New York: Wiley.

Carmon, A., and Nachshon, I. 1973. Ear asymmetry in perception of emotional non-verbal stimuli. *Acta Psychologica, 37,* 351–357.

Caro, T. M., and Hauser, M. D. 1992. Is there evidence of teaching in nonhuman animals? *Quarterly Review of Biology, 67,* 151–174.

Caron, A. J., Caron, R. F., Caldwell, R. C., and Weiss, S. J. 1973. Infant perception of the structural properties of the face. *Developmental Psychology, 9,* 385–399.

Caron, A. J., Caron, R. F., and MacLean, D. J. 1988. Infant discrimination of naturalistic emotional expressions: The role of face and voice. *Child Development, 59,* 604–616.

Carpenter, G. 1974. Mother's face and the newborn. *New Scientist, 61,* 742–744.

Carpenter, R. L., Mastergeorge, A. M., and Coggins, T. E. 1983. The acquisition of communicative intentions in infants eight to fifteen months of age. *Language and Speech, 26,* 101–116.

Carr, J. 1953. An investigation of the spontaneous speech sounds of five-year-old deaf-born children. *Journal of Speech and Hearing Disorders, 18,* 22–29.

Casanova, M., Walker, L., Whitehouse, P., and Price, D. 1985. Abnormalities of the nucleus basalis in Down's syndrome. *Annals of Neurology, 18,* 310–313.

Cernoch, J. M., and Porter, R. H. 1985. Recognition of maternal axillary odors by infants. *Child Development, 56,* 1593–1598.

Changeux, J.-P. 1985. *Neuronal man: The biology of mind.* New York: Oxford University Press.

Changeux, J.-P., and Danchin, A. 1976. Selective stabilization of developing synapses as a mechanism for specification of neuronal networks. *Nature, 264,* 705–712.

Chapman, R. S. 1988. Child Talk: Assumptions of a developmental process model for early language learning. Paper delivered to the Wisconsin Child Language Disorders Symposium, Madison, Wisconsin, June.

Chappell, P. F., and Sander, L. W. 1979. Mutual regulation of the neonatal-maternal interactive process: Context for the origins of communication. In Bullowa, M. (ed.), *Before speech: The beginning of interpersonal communication.* New York: Cambridge University Press.

Chavez, A., Martinez, C., and Yaschine, T. 1975. Nutrition, behavioral development, and mother-child interaction in young rural children. *Federation proceedings, 34,* 1574–1582.

Cheney, D. L., and Seyfarth, R. M. 1980. Vocal recognition in free-ranging vervet monkeys. *Animal Behaviour, 28,* 362–367.

Cheney, D. L., and Seyfarth, R. M. 1990. *How monkeys see the world: Inside the mind of another species.* Chicago: University of Chicago Press.

Cheney, D. L., and Seyfarth, R. M. 1992. Precis of *How monkeys see the world*. *Behavioral and Brain Sciences, 15,* 135–182.

Cheney, D., Seyfarth, R., and Smuts, B. 1986. Social relationships and social cognition in nonhuman primates. *Science, 234,* 1361–1366.

Chevalier-Skolnikoff, S. 1989. Spontaneous tool use and sensorimotor intelligence in *Cebus* compared with other monkeys and apes. *Behavioral and Brain Sciences, 12,* 561–627.

Chism, J. 1991. Ontogeny of behavior in humans and nonhuman primates: The search for common ground. In Loy, J. D., and Peters, C. B. (eds.), *Understanding behavior: What primate studies tell us about human behavior.* New York: Oxford University Press.

Chomsky, N. 1980. *Rules and representations*. New York: Columbia University Press.

Cicchetti, D., and Beeghly, M. 1990. An organizational approach to the study of Down syndrome: Contributions to an integrative theory of development. In Cicchetti, D., and Beeghly, M. (eds.), *Children with Down syndrome: A developmental perspective*. New York: Cambridge University Press.

Cicchetti, D., and Sroufe, L. A. 1976. The relationship between affective and cognitive development in Down's syndrome infants. *Child Development, 47,* 920–929.

Cicchetti, D., and Sroufe, L. A. 1978. An organizational view of affect: Illustration from the study of Down's syndrome infants. In Lewis, M., and Rosenblum, L. A. (eds.), *The development of affect*. New York: Plenum Press.

Clayton, N. S. 1988. Song tutor choice in zebra finches and Bengalese finches: The relative importance of visual and vocal cues. *Behaviour, 104,* 281–299.

Clifton, R. K., Clarkson, M. G., Gwiazda, J., Bauer, J., and Held, R. M. 1988. Growth in head size during infancy: Implications for sound localization. *Developmental Psychology, 24,* 477–483.

Cobb, K., Goodwin, R., and Saelens, E. 1966. Spontaneous hand positions of newborn infants. *Journal of Genetic Psychology, 108,* 225–237.

Coe, C. L. 1990. Psychobiology of maternal behavior in nonhuman primates. In Krasnegor, N. A., and Bridges, R. S. (eds.), *Mammalian parenting: Biochemical, neurobiological, and behavioral determinants*. New York: Oxford University Press.

Cohen, A., and Starkweather, J. 1961. Vocal cues to language identification. *American Journal of Psychology, 74,* 90–93.

Cohn, J. F., and Elmore, M. 1988. Effect of contingent changes in mothers' affective expression on the organization of behavior in 3-month-old infants. *Infant Behavior and Development, 11,* 493–505.

Cohn, J. F., and Tronick, E. Z. 1983. Three-month-old infants' reaction to simulated maternal depression. *Child Development, 54,* 185–193.

Collis, G. M. 1977. Visual co-orientation and maternal speech. In Schaffer, H. R. (ed.), *Studies in mother-infant interaction*. New York: Academic Press.

Collis, G. M., and Schaffer, H. R. 1975. Synchronization of visual attention in mother-infant pairs. *Journal of Child Psychology and Psychiatry, 16,* 315–320.

Colombo, J., and Bundy, R. S. 1981. A method for the measurement of infant auditory selectivity. *Infant Behavior and Development, 4,* 219–223.

Conel, J. 1939–1967. *The postnatal development of the human cerebral cortex,* Vols. 1–8. Cambridge, Mass.: Harvard University Press.

Conrad, R. 1979. *The deaf schoolchild.* London: Harper and Row.

Cosmides, L. 1983. Invariances in the acoustic expression of emotion during speech. *Journal of Experimental Psychology: Human Perception and Performance, 9,* 864–881.

Coupland, N., and Giles, H. 1988. Communicative accommodation: Recent developments. *Language and Communication, 8,* 175–182.

Courchesne, E., Yeung-Courchesne, R., Press, G. A., Hesselink, J. R., and Jernigan, T. L. 1988. Hypoplasia of cerebrellar vermal lobules VI and VII in autism. *New England Journal of Medicine, 318,* 1349–1354.

Cowan, W. M., Fawcett, J. W., O'Leary, D. D. M., and Stanfield, B. B. 1984. Regressive events in neurogenesis. *Science, 225,* 1258–1265.

Cramblit, N. S., and Siegel, G. M. 1977. The verbal environment of a language-impaired child. *Journal of Speech and Hearing Disorders, 42,* 474–482.

Creutzfeldt, O., Ojemann, G., and Lettich, E. 1989a. Neuronal activity in the human lateral temporal lobe. I. Responses to speech. *Experimental Brain Research, 77,* 451–475.

Creutzfeldt, O., Ojemann, G., and Lettich, E. 1989b. Neuronal activity in the human lateral temporal lobe. II. Responses to the subjects' own voice. *Experimental Brain Research, 77,* 476–489.

Cruttenden, A. 1970. A phonetic study of babbling. *British Journal of Disorders of Communication, 5,* 110–117.

Cullen, J. K., Fargo, N., Chase, R. A., and Baker, P. 1968. The development of auditory feedback monitoring: I. Delayed auditory feedback studies on infant cry. *Journal of Speech and Hearing Research, 11,* 85–93.

Culp, R. E., and Boyd, E. F. 1975. Visual fixation and the effect of voice quality and content differences in 2-month-old infants. In Horowitz, F. D. (ed.), Visual attention, auditory stimulation, and language discrimination in young infants. *Monographs of the Society for Research in Child Development, 39,* 78–91.

Curtiss, S., Katz, W., and Tallal, P. 1992. Delay versus deviance in the language acquisition of language-impaired children. *Journal of Speech and Hearing Research, 35,* 373–383.

Cutler, A., and Carter, D. M. 1987. The predominance of strong initial syllables in the English vocabulary. *Computer Speech and Language, 2,* 133–142.

Cutler, A., and Norris, D. 1988. The role of strong syllables in segmentation for lexical access. *Journal of Experimental Psychology: Human Perception and Performance, 14,* 113–121.

Damasio, A. R. 1989. Reflections on visual recognition. In Galaburda, A. M. (ed.), *From reading to neurons.* Cambridge, Mass.: MIT Press.

Damasio, H., Maurer, R. G., Damasio, A. R., and Chui, H. C. 1980. Computerized tomographic scan findings in patients with autistic behavior. *Archives of Neurology, 37,* 504–510.

Darwin, C. 1872. *The expression of emotions in man and the animals*. London: Murray.

Davis, B. L., and MacNeilage, P. F. 1990. Acquisition of correct vowel production: A quantitative case study. *Journal of Speech and Hearing Research, 33,* 16–27.

De Beer, G. 1958. *Embryos and ancestors*. New York: Oxford University Press.

DeCasper, A. 1990. Paper delivered to the American Psychological Association, Boston, August.

DeCasper, A., and Fifer, W. P. 1980. On human bonding: Newborns prefer their mothers' voices. *Science, 208,* 1174–1176.

DeCasper, A., and Sigafoos, D. 1983. The intrauterine heartbeat: A potent reinforcer for newborns. *Infant Behavior and Development, 6,* 19–25.

DeCasper, A., and Spence, M. 1986. Prenatal maternal speech influences newborns' perception of speech sounds. *Infant Behavior and Development, 9,* 133–150.

Decker, S. N., and Vandenberg, S. G. 1985. Colorado twin study of reading disability. In Gray, D. B., and Kavanagh, J. F. (eds.), *Biobehavioral measures of dyslexia*. Parkton, Md.: York Press.

Decker, S. N., Vogler, G. P., and DeFries, J. C. 1989. Validity of self-reported reading disability by parents of reading-disabled and control children. *Reading and Writing: An Interdisciplinary Journal, 1,* 327–331.

DeFries, J. C. 1985. Colorado reading project. In Gray, D. B., and Kavanagh, J. F. (eds.), *Biobehavioral measures of dyslexia*. Parkton, Md.: York Press.

DeFries, J. C., and Decker, S. N. 1982. Genetic aspects of reading disability: A family study. In Malatesha, R. N., and Aaron, P. G. (eds.), *Reading disorders: Varieties and treatments*. New York: Academic Press.

DeFries, J. C., Fulker, D. W., and LaBuda, M. C. 1987. Evidence for a genetic aetiology in reading disability of twins. *Nature, 329,* 537–539.

DeGangi, G., DiPietro, J. A., Greenspan, S. I., and Porges, S. W. 1991. Psychophysiological characteristics of the regulatory disordered infant. *Infant Behavior and Development, 14,* 37–50.

de Gelder, B., Vroomen, J., and van der Heide, L. 1991. Face recognition and lip-reading in autism. In Bruce, V. (ed.), *Face recognition*. Hillsdale, N.J.: Erlbaum.

Delack, J. B. 1976. Aspects of infant speech development in the first year of life. *Canadian Journal of Linguistics, 21,* 17–37.

Denckla, M. B., and Rudel, R. 1976. Naming of pictured objects by dyslexic and other learning disabled children. *Brain and Language, 39,* 1–15.

Denenberg, V. H. 1969. The effects of early experience. In Hafez, E. S. E. (ed.), *The behaviour of domestic animals*. Baltimore, Md.: Williams and Wilkins.

Dennis, M., and Kohn, B. 1975. Comprehension of syntax in infantile hemiplegics after cerebral hemidecortication: Left-hemisphere superiority. *Brain and Language, 2,* 472–482.

Dennis, W. 1941. Infant development under conditions of restricted practice and of minimum social stimulation. *Genetic Psychology Monographs, 23,* 143–189.

Deputte, B. L. 1982. Duetting in male and female songs of the white-cheeked gibbon *(Hylobates concolor leucogenys)*. In Snowdon, C. T., Brown, C. H., and Petersen, M. R. (eds.), *Primate communication*. New York: Cambridge University Press.

Desimone, R. 1991. Face-selective cells in the temporal cortex of monkeys. *Journal of Cognitive Neuroscience, 3,* 1–8.

Desimone, R., Albright, T. D., Gross, C. G., and Bruce, C. 1984. Stimulus selective properties of inferior temporal neurons in the macaque. *Journal of Neuroscience, 4,* 2051–2062.

de Vries, J. I. P., Visser, G. H. A., and Prechtl, H. F. R. 1982. The emergence of fetal behavior. I. Qualitative aspects. *Early human development, 7,* 301–322.

de Waal, F. 1989. *Peacemaking among primates*. Cambridge, Mass.: Harvard University Press.

Dewson, J. H. 1977. Preliminary evidence of hemispheric asymmetry of auditory function in monkeys. In Harnad, S. R., Doty, R. W., Goldstein, L., Jaynes, J., and Krauthamer, G. (eds.), *Lateralization in the nervous system*. New York: Academic Press.

Diamond, M. C. 1988. *Enriching heredity: The impact of the environment on the anatomy of the brain*. New York: Free Press.

Dicks, D., Myers, R. E., and Kling, A. 1969. Uncus and amygdala lesions: Effects on social behavior in the free-ranging rhesus monkey. *Science, 165,* 69–71.

Dilts, C. V., Morris, C. A., and Leonard, C. O. 1990. Hypothesis for development of a behavioral phenotype in Williams syndrome. *American Journal of Medical Genetics, Supplement 6,* 126–131.

Dimitrovsky, L. 1964. The ability to identify the emotional meaning of vocal expressions at successive age levels. In Davitz, J. R. (ed.), *The communication of emotional meaning*. New York: McGraw-Hill.

Dinger, M. C., and Blom, J. G. 1973. An investigation of infant babbling. *Proceedings from the Institute of Phonetic Sciences*, University of Amsterdam, *3,* 42–50.

DiPietro, J. A., and Porges, S. W. In press. Vagal responsiveness to gavage feeding as an index of preterm stress. *Pediatric Research*.

Dobbing, J., and Sands, J. 1979. Comparative aspects of the brain spurt. *Early Human Development, 3,* 79–83.

Dodd, B. 1972. Effects of social and vocal stimulation on infant babbling. *Developmental Psychology, 7,* 80–83.

Dodd, B. 1979. Lip reading in infants: Attention to speech presented in- and out-of-synchrony. *Cognitive Psychology, 11,* 478–484.

D'Odorico, L. 1984. Nonsegmental features in prelinguistic communications: An analysis of some types of infant cry and noncry vocalizations. *Journal of Child Language, 11,* 17–27.

Dodwell, P. C., Timney, B. N., and Emerson, V. F. 1976. Development of visual stimulus-seeking in dark-reared kittens. *Nature, 260,* 777–778.

Doehring, D. G., and Bartholomeus, B. N. 1971. Laterality effects in voice recognition. *Neuropsychologia, 9,* 425–430.

Donahue, M. 1986. Phonological constraints on the emergence of two-word utterances. *Journal of Child Language, 13,* 209–218.

Donovan, W. L., and Leavitt, L. A. 1985. Physiology and behavior: Parents' responses to the infant cry. In Lester, B. M., and Boukydis, C. F. Z. (eds.), *Infant crying: Theoretical and research perspectives.* New York: Plenum Press.

Donovan, W. L., Leavitt, L. A., and Balling, J. D. 1978. Maternal physiologic response to infant signals. *Psychophysiology, 15,* 68–74.

Dordain, M., Degos, J.-D., and Dordain, G. 1971. *Revue de Laryngologie Otologie-Rhinologie, 92,* 178–188.

Dore, J. 1974. A pragmatic description of early language development. *Journal of Psycholinguistics Research, 4,* 343–350.

Dudek, S. M., and Bear, M. F. 1989. A biochemical correlate of the critical period for synaptic modification in the visual cortex. *Science, 246,* 673–675.

Duffy, F. H., Denckla, M. B., Bartels, P. H., and Sandini, G. 1980. Dyslexia: Regional differences in brain electrical activity by topographic mapping. *Annals of Neurology, 7,* 412–420.

Dunn, J. F. 1975. Consistency and change in styles of mothering. In *Parent-infant interaction* (CIBA Foundation Symposium 33). New York: Elsevier.

Eady, S. J. 1980. The onset of language-specific patterning in infant vocalization. M.A. thesis, University of Ottawa.

Eales, L. A. 1987. Do cross-fostered zebra finches still tend to select a conspecific song tutor to learn from? *Animal Behaviour, 35,* 1347–1355.

Eckerman, C. O., Sturm, L. A., and Gross, S. J. 1985. Different developmental courses for very-low-birthweight infants differing in early head growth. *Developmental Psychology, 21,* 813–827.

Eichorn, D. H., and Bayley, N. 1962. Growth in head circumference from birth through young adulthood. *Child Development, 33,* 257–271.

Eilers, R. E., and Minifie, F. D. 1975. Fricative discrimination in early infancy. *Journal of Speech and Hearing Research, 18,* 158–167.

Eilers, R. E., Wilson, W. R., and Moore, J. M. 1977. Developmental changes in speech discrimination in infants. *Journal of Speech and Hearing Research, 20,* 766–780.

Eimas, P. D., Siqueland, E. R., Jusczyk, P., and Vigorito, J. 1971. Speech perception in infants. *Science, 171,* 303–306.

Eisenberg, J. F. 1966. The social organization of mammals. *Handbuch der Zoologie Berlin, 8,* 1–92.

Eisenberg, L. 1990. The biosocial context of parenting in human families. In Krasnegor, N. A., and Bridges, R. S. (eds.), *Mammalian parenting: Biochemical, neurobiological, and behavioral determinants.* New York: Oxford University Press.

Ekman, P. 1973. Cross-cultural studies of facial expression. In Ekman, P. (ed.), *Darwin and facial expression.* New York: Academic Press.

Ekman, P., and Friesen, W. V. 1969. The repertoire of nonverbal behavior: Categories, origins, usage, and coding. *Semiotica, 1,* 49–98.

Elias, G., and Broerse, J. 1989. Timing in mother-infant communications: A comment on Murray and Trevarthen 1986. *Journal of Child Language, 16,* 703–706.

Elliott, D., and Weeks, D. J. 1990. Cerebral specialization and the control of oral and limb movements for individuals with Down's syndrome. *Journal of Motor Behavior, 22,* 6–18.

Ellis, A. W., and Young, A. W. 1988. *Human cognitive neuropsychology.* Hillsdale, N.J.: Erlbaum.

Enstrom, D. H. 1982. Infant labial, apical and velar stop productions: A voice onset time analysis. *Phonetica, 39,* 47–60.

Etcoff, N. L. 1984a. Selective attention to facial identity and facial emotion. *Neuropsychologia, 22,* 281–295.

Etcoff, N. L. 1984b. Perceptual and conceptual organization of facial emotions: Hemispheric differences. *Brain and Cognition, 3,* 385–412.

Fagen, R. M. 1981. *Animal play behaviour.* New York: Oxford University Press.

Falk, D. 1978. External neuroanatomy of Old World monkeys *(Cercopithecoidea). Contributions to Primatology, 15.* Basel: Karger.

Farran, D. C., and Kasari, C. 1990. A longitudinal analysis of the development of synchrony in mutual gaze in mother-child dyads. *Journal of Applied Developmental Psychology, 11,* 419–430.

Farentinos, R. C. 1971. Some observations on the play behavior of the Stellar sea lion *(Eumetopias jabata). Zeitschrift fur Tierpsycholgie, 28,* 428–438.

Fay, W. H. 1969. On the basis of autistic echolalia. *Journal of Communication Disorders, 2,* 38–47.

Fay, W. H. 1975. Occurrence of children's echoic responses according to interlocutory question types. *Journal of Speech and Hearing Research, 18,* 336–345.

Fay, W. H., and Butler, B. V. 1968. Echolalia, I.Q., and the developmental dichotomy of speech and language systems. *Journal of Speech and Hearing Research, 11,* 365–371.

Fay, W. H., and Butler, B. V. 1971. Echo-reaction as an approach to semantic resolution. *Journal of Speech and Hearing Research, 14,* 645–651.

Fay, W. H., and Schuler, A. L. 1980. *Emerging language in autistic children.* Baltimore: University Park Press.

Fein, D., Humes, M., Kaplan, E., Lucci, D., and Waterhouse, L. 1984. The question of left hemisphere dysfunction in infantile autism. *Psychological Bulletin, 95,* 258–281.

Feldman, H. M., Holland, A. L., Kemp, S. S., and Janosky, J. E. 1992. Language development after unilateral brain injury. *Brain and Language, 42,* 89–102.

Felsenfeld, S., Broen, P. A., and McGue, M. 1992. A 28-year follow-up of adults with a history of moderate phonological disorder: Linguistic and personality results. *Journal of Speech and Hearing Research, 35,* 1114–1125.

Fentress, J. C., and McLeod, P. J. 1986. Motor patterns in development. In Blass, E. M. (ed.), *Handbook of Behavioral Neurobiology.* Vol. 8. *Developmental Psychobiology and Developmental Neurobiology.* New York: Plenum Press.

Ferguson, C. A. 1964. Baby talk in six languages. *American Anthropologist,*
66, 103–114.

Ferguson, C. A., and Macken, M. A. 1983. The role of play in phonological
development. In Nelson, K. E. (ed.), *Children's language.* Vol. 4. Hillsdale,
N.J.: Erlbaum.

Fernald, A. 1985. Four-month-old infants prefer to listen to motherese. *Infant*
Behavior and Development, 8, 181–195.

Fernald, A. 1989. Intonation and communicative intent in mothers' speech to
infants: Is the melody the message? *Child Development, 60,* 1497–1510.

Fernald, A. 1991. Prosody and focus in speech to infants and adults. *Develop-*
mental Psychology, 27, 209–221.

Fernald, A. 1992a. Meaningful melodies in mothers' speech to infants. In Papousek, H., Jurgens, U., and Papousek, M. (eds.), *Origins and development*
of nonverbal vocal communication: Evolutionary, comparative, and meth-
odological aspects. Cambridge: Cambridge University Press.

Fernald, A. 1992b. Human maternal vocalisations to infants as biologically
relevant signals: An evolutionary perspective. In Barkow, J. H., Cosmides,
L., and Tooby, J. (eds.), *The adapted mind: Evolutionary psychology and*
the generation of culture. New York: Oxford University Press.

Fernald, A., and Kuhl, P. 1987. Acoustic determinants of infant prererence for
motherese speech. *Infant Behavior and Development, 10,* 279–293.

Fernald, A., and Simon, T. 1984. Expanded intonation contours in mothers'
speech to newborns. *Developmental Psychology, 20,* 104–113.

Fernald, A., Taeschner, T., Dunn, J., Papousek, M., Boysson-Bardies, B. de, and
Fikui, I. 1989. A cross-language study of prosodic modifications in mothers'
and fathers' speech to preverbal infants. *Journal of Child Language, 16,*
477–501.

Ferrier, L. J., Johnston, J. J., and Bashir, A. S. 1991. A longitudinal study of
the babbling and phonological development of a child with hypoglossia.
Clinical Linguistics & Phonetics, 5, 187–206.

Field, T. 1979. Differential behavioral and cardiac responses of 3-month-old
infants to a mirror and peer. *Infant Behavior and Development, 2,* 179–184.

Field, T. 1982. Affective displays of high-risk infants during early interactions.
In Field, T., and Fogel, A. (eds.), *Emotion and early interaction.* Hillsdale,
N.J.: Erlbaum.

Field, T. M., Cohen, D., Garcia, R., and Greenberg, R. 1984. Mother-stranger
face discrimination by the newborn. *Infant Behavior and Development, 7,*
19–25.

Field, T. M., Woodson, R., Greenberg, R., and Cohen, D. 1982. Discrimination
and imitation of facial expressions by neonates. *Science, 218,* 179–181.

Fifer, W. P., and Moon, C. 1988. Auditory experience in the fetus. In Smotherman, W., and Robertson, S. (eds.), *Behavior of the fetus.* West Caldwell,
N.J.: Telford Press.

Fifer, W., and Moon, C. 1989. Early voice discrimination. In Von Euler, C.,
Forssberg, H., and Lagercrantz, H. (eds.), *The neurobiology of early infant*
behavior. New York: Stockton Press.

Fillmore, L. W. 1977. Individual differences in second language acquisition. In Fillmore, C. J., Kempler, D., and Wang, W. S-Y. (eds.), *Individual differences in language ability and language behavior.* New York: Academic Press.

Finkelstein, N. W., and Ramey, C. T. 1977. Learning to control the environment in infancy. *Child Development, 48,* 806–819.

Fischer, K. W., and Bidell, T. 1991. Constraining nativist inferences about cognitive capacities. In Carey, S., and Gelman, R. (eds.), *The epigenesis of mind: Essays on biology and cognition.* Hillsdale, N.J.: Erlbaum.

Fischer, K. W., and Bidell, T. R. 1992. Ever younger ages: Constructive use of nativist findings about early development. *SRCD Newsletter,* Winter Issue, 1992.

Fishman, M. C. 1989. Genes of neuronal growth and plasticity. In Landmesser, L. (ed.), *Assembly of the nervous system.* New York: Liss.

Flege, J. E. 1991. Age of learning affects the authenticity of voice-onset time VOT in stop consonants produced in a second language. *Journal of the Acoustical Society of America, 89,* 395–411.

Flege, J. E., and Fletcher, K. L. 1992. Talker and listener effects on the perception of degree of foreign accent. *Journal of the Acoustical Society of America, 91,* 370–389.

Fleming, A. S. 1990. Hormonal and experiential correlates of maternal responsiveness in human mothers. In Krasnegor, N. A., and Bridges, R. S. (eds.), *Mammalian parenting: Biochemical, neurobiological, and behavioral determinants.* New York: Oxford University Press.

Fletcher, S. G., and Daly, D. A. 1974. Sublingual dimensions in infants and young children. *Archives of Otolaryngology, 99,* 292–296.

Fletcher, S. G., and Meldrum, J. R. 1968. Lingual function and relative length of the lingual frenulum. *Journal of Speech and Hearing Research, 11,* 382–390.

Fodor, J. 1983. *Modularity of mind.* Cambridge, Mass.: MIT Press.

Fodor, J. 1985. Precis of *Modularity of Mind. Behavioral and Brain Sciences, 8,* 1–42.

Fogel, A. 1977. Temporal organization in mother-infant face-to-face interaction. In Schaffer, H. R. (ed.), *Studies in mother-infant interaction.* New York: Academic Press.

Fogel, A., and Hannan, T. E. 1985. Manual actions of nine- to fifteen-week-old human infants during face-to-face interaction with their mothers. *Child Development, 56,* 1271–1279.

Formby, D. 1967. Maternal recognition of infant's cry. *Developmental Medicine and Child Neurology, 9,* 293–298.

Fotheringham, J. B. 1987. Facial recognition cells and autism. *Science, 238,* 1496–1497.

Fouts, R. S. 1983. Chimpanzee language and elephant tails: A theoretical synthesis. In de Luce, J., and Wilder, H. T. (eds.), *Language in primates: Perspectives and implications.* New York: Springer-Verlag.

Fouts, R., Fouts, D. H., and Van Cantfort, T. E. 1989. The infant Loulis learns signs from cross-fostered chimpanzees. In Gardner, R. A., Gardner, B. T., and Van Cantfort, T. E. (eds.), *Teaching sign language to chimpanzees*. Albany: State University of New York Press.

Fox, M. W. 1971. Towards a comparative psychopathology. *Zeitschrift fur Tierpsychologie, 29,* 416–437.

Fox, N. A., and Davidson, R. J. 1986. Taste-elicited changes in facial signs of emotion and the asymmetry of brain electrical activity in human newborns. *Neuropsychologia, 24,* 417–422.

Fox, N. A., and Gelles, M. 1984. Face to face interaction in term and preterm infants. *Infant Mental Health Journal, 5,* 192–205.

Fraiberg, S. 1979. Blind infants and their mothers: An examination of the sign system. In Bullowa, M. (ed.), *Before speech: The beginning of interpersonal communication*. New York: Cambridge University Press.

Francis, P. L., Self, P. A., and Noble, C. A. 1982. Maternal verbal control techniques with young infants during mutual gaze and visual co-orientation episodes. *Internal Journal of Behavioral Development, 5,* 317–327.

Freedle, R., and Lewis, M. 1977. Prelinguistic conversations. In Lewis, M., and Rosenblum, L. A. (eds.), *Interaction, conversation and the development of language*. New York: Wiley.

Freedman, D. G. 1964. Smiling in blind infants and the issue of innate vs. acquired. *Journal of Child Psychology and Psychiatry, 5,* 171–184.

Freudenberg, R. P., Driscoll, J. W., and Stern, G. S. 1978. Reactions of adult humans to cries of normal and abnormal infants. *Infant Behavior and Development, 1,* 224–227.

Fridlund, A. J. 1991. Evolution and facial action in reflex, social motive, and paralanguage. *Biological Psychology, 32,* 3–100.

Fried, I., Katz, A., McCarthy, G., Sass, K. J., Williamson, P., Spencer, S. S., and Spencer, D. D. 1991. Functional organization of human supplementary motor cortex studied by electrical stimulation. *Journal of Neuroscience, 11,* 3656–3666.

Friedlander, B. Z. 1968. The effect of speaker identity, voice inflection, vocabulary, and message redundancy on infants' selection of vocal reinforcement. *Journal of Experimental Child Psychology, 6,* 443–459.

Friedman, H. S., and Tucker, J. S. 1990. Language and deception. In Giles, H., and Robinson, W. P. (eds.), *Handbook of language and social psychology*. New York: John Wiley and Sons.

Fromkin, V. A., Krashen, S., Curtiss, S., Rigler, D., and Rigler, M. 1974. The development of language in Genie: A case of language acquisition beyond the "critical period." *Brain and Language, 1,* 81–107.

Frost, D. O. 1989. Transitory neuronal connections in normal development and disease. In von Euler, C., Lundberg, I., and Lennerstrad, G. (eds.), *Brain and reading*. London: Macmillan.

Frost, D. O., and Innocenti, G. M. 1986. Effects of sensory experience on the development of visual callosal connections. In Lepore, F., Petito, M., and Jasper, H. H. (eds.), *Two hemispheres – one brain: Functions of the corpus callosum*. New York: Liss.

Fry, D. B. 1966. The development of the phonological system in the normal and deaf child. In Smith, F., and Miller, G. A. (eds.), *The genesis of language.* Cambridge, Mass.: MIT Press.

Fry, D. B., Abramson, P., Eimas, P., and Liberman, A. M. 1962. The indentification and discrimination of synthetic vowels. *Language and Speech, 5,* 171–189.

Furth, H. G. 1966. *Thinking without language: Psychological implications of deafness.* New York: Free Press.

Galaburda, A. M., Sherman, G. F., Rosen, G. D., Aboitiz, F., and Geschwind, N. 1985. Developmental dyslexia: Four consecutive patients with cortical anomalies. *Annals of Neurology 18,* 222–223.

Gallois, C., and Callan, V. J. 1988. Communication accommodation and the prototypical speaker: Predicting evaluations of status and solidarity. *Language and Communication, 8,* 271–283.

Gallup, G. G. 1982. Self-awareness and the emergence of mind in primates. *American Journal of Primatology, 2,* 237–248.

Ganiban, J., Wagner, S., and Cicchetti, D. 1990. Temperament and Down syndrome. In Cicchetti, D., and Beeghly, M. (eds.), *Children with Down syndrome: A developmental perspective.* New York: Cambridge University Press.

Gardner, H. (1985). The centrality of modules. *Behavioral and Brain Sciences, 8,* 12–14.

Gardner, R. A., and Gardner, B. T. 1969. Teaching sign language to a chimpanzee. *Science, 165,* 664–672.

Gardner, R. A., Gardner, B. T., and Drumm, P. 1989. Voiced and signed responses of cross-fostered chimpanzees. In Gardner, R. A., Gardner, B. T., and Van Cantfort, T. E. (eds.), *Teaching sign language to chimpanzees.* Albany, N.Y.: State University of New York Press.

Geschwind, N. 1985. The biology of dyslexia: The after-dinner speech. In Gray, D. B., and Kavanagh, J. F. (eds.), *Biobehavioral measures of dyslexia.* Parkton, Md.: York Press.

Geschwind, N., Behan, P. 1982. Left-handedness: Association with immune disease, migraine, and developmental learning disorder. *Proceedings of the National Academy of Science, 79,* 5097–5100.

Geschwind, N., and Levitsky, W. 1968. Human brain: Left-right asymmetries in temporal speech region. *Science, 161,* 186–187.

Geschwind, N., Quadfasel, F. A., and Segarra, J. M. 1968. Isolation of the speech area. *Neuropsychologia, 6,* 327–340.

Gesell, A., and Thompson, H. 1934. *Infant behavior: Its genesis and growth.* New York: McGraw-Hill.

Gibbs, R. W., and Gonzales, G. P. 1985. Syntactic frozenness in processing and remembering idioms. *Cognition, 20,* 243–259.

Gibson, C. J., and Bryden, M. P. 1984. Cerebral laterality in deaf and hearing children. *Brain and Language, 23,* 1–12.

Gibson, J. J. 1966. *The senses considered as perceptual systems.* Boston: Houghton Mifflin.

Gibson, K. R. 1990. New perspectives on instinct and intelligence: Brain size and the emergence of hierarchical mental constructional skills. In Parker, S. T., and Gibson, K. R. (eds.), *"Language" and intelligence in monkeys and apes: Comparative developmental perspectives*. New York: Cambridge University Press.

Gibson, K. R. 1991. Myelination and behavioral development: A comparative perspective on questions of neoteny, altriciality and intelligence. In Gibson, K. R., and Petersen, A. C. (eds.), *Brain maturation and cognitive development: Comparative and cross-cultural perspectives*. New York: Aldine de Gruyter.

Giles, H. (ed.) 1984. The dynamics of speech accommodation. *International Journal of the Sociology of Language, 46,* 1–155.

Giles, H., Mulac, A., Bradac, J. J. and Johnson, P. 1987. Speech accommodation theory: The next decade and beyond. In McLaughlin, M. (ed.), *Communication yearbook*. Oxford: Blackwell.

Ginsburg, G. P., and Kilbourne, B. K. 1988. Emergence of vocal alternation in mother-infant interchanges. *Journal of Child Language, 15,* 221–235.

Glanville, B., Best, C., and Levenson, R. 1977. A cardiac measure of cerebral asymmetries in infant auditory perception. *Developmental Psychology, 13,* 54–59.

Gleitman, L. R., Gleitman, H., Landau, B., and Wanner, E. 1988. Where learning begins: Initial representations for language learning. In Newmeyer, F. J. (ed.), *Linguistics: The Cambridge survey*. Vol. 3. *Language: Psychological and biological aspects*. New York: Cambridge University Press.

Glenn, S. M., and Cunningham, C. C. 1983. What do babies listen to most? A developmental study of auditory preferences in nonhandicapped infants and infants with Down's syndrome. *Developmental Psychology, 19,* 332–337.

Goad, H., and Ingram, D. 1987. Individual variation and its relevance to a theory of phonological acquisition. *Journal of Child Language, 14,* 419–432.

Goldfield, B. A., and Reznick, J. S. 1990. Early lexical acquisition: Rate, content, and the vocabulary spurt. *Journal of Child Language, 17,* 171–183.

Goldman-Rakic, P. S. 1987. Development of cortical circuitry and cognitive function. *Child Development, 58,* 601–622.

Golinkoff, R. M. (ed.) 1983. *The transition from prelinguistic to linguistic communication*. Hillsdale, N.J.: Erlbaum.

Golinkoff, R. M., Hirsh-Pasek, K., Cauley, K. M., and Gordon, L. 1987. The eyes have it: Lexical and syntactic comprehension in a new paradigm. *Journal of Child Language, 14,* 23–45.

Gollin, E. S. 1981. Development and plasticity. In Gollin, E. S. (ed.), *Developmental plasticity: Behavioral and biological aspects of variations in development*. New York: Academic Press.

Gomez, J. C. 1990. The emergence of intentional communication as a problem-solving strategy in the gorilla. In Parker, S. T., and Gibson, K. R. (eds.),

"Language" and intelligence in monkeys and apes: Comparative developmental perspectives. New York: Cambridge University Press.

Goodall, J. 1965. Chimpanzees of the Gombe Stream Reserve. In DeVore, I. (ed.), *Primate behavior: Field studies of monkeys and apes.* New York: Holt, Rinehart and Winston.

Goodall, J. 1971. *In the shadow of Man.* Boston: Houghton Mifflin.

Gopnik, A. 1984. The acquisition of *gone* and the development of the object concept. *Journal of Child Language, 11,* 273–292.

Gopnik, A., and Meltzoff, A. N. 1985. From people, to plans, to objects: Changes in the meaning of early words and their relation to cognitive development. *Journal of Pragmatics, 9,* 495–512.

Gopnik, A., and Meltzoff, A. N. 1986. Relations between semantic and cognitive development in the one-word stage: The specificity hypothesis. *Child Development, 57,* 1040–1053.

Gopnik, A., and Meltzoff, A. N. 1987. The development of categorization in the second year and its relation to other cognitive and linguistic developments. *Child Development , 58,* 1523–1531.

Gorelick, P. B., and Ross, E. D. 1987. The aprosodias: Further functional-anatomical evidence for the organisation of affective language in the right hemisphere. *Journal of Neurology, Neurosurgery, and Psychiatry, 50,* 553–560.

Goren, C. C., Sarty, M., and Wu, P. Y. K. 1975. Visual following and pattern discrimination of face-like stimuli by newborn infants. *Pediatrics, 56,* 544–549.

Gottlieb, G. 1961. The following-response and imprinting in wild and domestic ducklings of the same species *(Anas platyrhynchos). Behaviour, 18,* 205–228.

Gottlieb, G. 1970. Conceptions of prenatal behavior. In Aronson, L. R., Tobach, E., Lehrman, D. S., and Rosenblatt, J. S. (eds.), *Development and evolution of behavior.* San Francisco: Freeman.

Gottlieb, G. 1971a. Ontogenesis of sensory function in birds and mammals. In Tobach, E., Aronson, L. R., and Shaw, E. (eds.), *The biopsychology of development.* New York: Academic Press.

Gottlieb, G. 1971b. *Development of species identification in birds: An inquiry into the prenatal determinants of perception.* Chicago: University of Chicago Press.

Gottlieb, G. 1975. Development of species identification in ducklings: I. Nature of perceptual deficit caused by embryonic auditory deprivation. *Journal of Comparative and Physiological Psychology, 89,* 387–399.

Gottlieb, G. 1978. Development of species identification in ducklings: IV. Change in species-specific perception caused by auditory deprivation. *Journal of Comparative and Physiological Psychology, 92,* 375–387.

Gottlieb, G. 1980. Development of species identification in ducklings: VI. Specific ambryonic experience required to maintain species-typical perception in Peking ducklings. *Journal of Comparative and Physiological Psychology, 94,* 579–587.

Gottlieb, G. 1991a. Experiential canalization of behavioral development: The-
    ory. *Developmental Psychology, 27,* 4–13.

Gottlieb, G. 1991b. Experiential canalization of behavioral development: Re-
    sults. *Developmental Psychology, 27,* 35–39.

Gottlieb, G. 1992. *Individual development and evolution: The genesis of novel
    behavior.* New York: Oxford University Press.

Gould, E. 1975. Experimental studies of the ontogeny of ultrasonic vocalizations
    in bats. *Developmental Psychobiology, 8,* 333–346.

Gould, J. L. 1984. Natural history of honey bee learning. In Marler, P., and
    Terrace, H. S. (eds.), *The biology of learning.* New York: Springer-Verlag.

Gould, J. L., and Marler, P. 1987. Learning by instinct. *American Scientist, 255,*
    74–85.

Gould, S. J. 1977a. *Ontogeny and phylogeny.* Cambridge, Mass.: Harvard Uni-
    versity Press.

Gould, S. J. 1977b. *Ever since Darwin: Reflections in natural history.* New York:
    Norton.

Gould, S. J., and Lewontin, R. C. 1984. The spandrels of San Marco and the
    panglossian paradigm: A critique of the adaptionist programme. In Sober,
    E. (ed.), *Conceptual issues in evolutionary biology: An anthology.* Cam-
    bridge, Mass.: MIT Press.

Graber, J. A., and Petersen, A. C. 1991. Cognitive changes at adolescence:
    Biological perspectives. In Gibson, K. R., and Petersen, A. C. (eds.), *Brain
    maturation and cognitive development: Comparative and cross-cultural per-
    spectives.* New York: Aldine de Gruyter.

Graham, F., Leavitt, L., Strock, B., and Brown, J. 1978. Precocious cardiac
    orienting in a human anencephalic infant. *Science, 199,* 322–324.

Green, S. 1975. Variation of vocal pattern with social situation in the Japanese
    monkey *(Macaca fascata):* A field study. In Rosenblum, L. A. (ed.), *Primate
    behavior: Developments in field and laboratory research.* New York: Aca-
    demic Press.

Greenberg, H. J., and Bode, D. L. 1968. Visual discrimination of consonants.
    Journal of Speech and Hearing Research, 11, 869–874.

Greenberg, J. H. (ed.) 1978. *Universals of human language. Vol. 2. Phonology.*
    Stanford: Stanford University Press.

Greenfield, P. M. 1991. Language, tools and brain: The ontogeny and phylogeny
    of hierarchically organized sequential behavior. *Behavioral and Brain Sci-
    ences, 14,* 531–595.

Greenfield, P. M., and Savage-Rumbaugh, E. S. 1990. Grammatical combination
    in *Pan paniscus:* Process of learning and invention in the evolution and
    development of language. In Parker, S. T., and Gibson, K. R. (eds.), *"Lan-
    guage" and intelligence in monkeys and apes: Comparative developmental
    perspectives.* New York: Cambridge University Press.

Greenough, W. T., and Chang, F.-L. F. 1985. Synaptic structural correlates of
    information storage in mammalian nervous systems. In Cotman, C. W.
    (ed.), *Synaptic plasticity.* New York: Guilford Press.

Greenough, W. T., Black, J. F., and Wallace, C. S. 1987. Experience and brain
    development. *Child Development, 58,* 539–559.

Greenough, W. T., Larson, J. R., and Withers, G. S. 1985. Effects of unilateral and bilateral training in a reaching task on dendritic branching of neurons in the rat motor-sensory forelimb cortex. *Behavioral and Neural Biology, 44,* 301–314.

Grieser, D. L., and Kuhl, P. K. 1988. Maternal speech to infants in a tonal language: Support for universal prosodic features in motherese. *Developmental Psychology, 24,* 14–20.

Groos, K. 1898. *The play of animals.* New York: D. Appleton.

Groos, K. 1901. *The play of Man.* New York: D. Appleton and Company.

Gross, C. G. 1985. On Gall's reputation and some recent "new phrenology." *Behavioral and Brain Sciences, 8,* 16–18.

Hafez, E. S. E., Schein, M. W. and Ewbank, R. 1969. The behaviour of cattle. In Hafez, E. S. E. (ed.), *The behaviour of domestic animals.* Baltimore, Md.: Williams and Wilkins.

Haggard, M. P., and Parkinson, A. M. 1971. Stimulus and task factors as determinants of ear advantages. *Quarterly Journal of Experimental Psychology, 23,* 68–177.

Hahn, M. E. 1990. Approaches to the study of genetic influence on developing social behavior. In Hahn, M. E., Hewitt, J. K., Henderson, N. D., and Benno, R. H. (eds.), *Developmental behavior genetics: Neural, biometrical, and evolutionary approaches.* New York: Oxford University Press.

Hahn, M. E., and Benno, R. H. 1990. Issues of integration. In Hahn, M. E., Hewitt, J. K., Henderson, N. D., and Benno, R. H. (eds.), *Developmental behavior genetics: Neural, biometrical, and evolutionary approaches.* New York: Oxford University Press.

Haith, M. M., Bergman, T., and Moore, M. J. 1977. Eye contact and face scanning in early infancy. *Science, 198,* 853–855.

Halgren, E. 1992. Emotional neurophysiology of the amygdala within the context of human cognition. In Aggleton, J. P. (ed.), *The amygdala: Neurobiological aspects of emotion, memory, and mental dysfunction.* New York: Wiley-Liss.

Halle, P. A., Boysson-Bardies, B. de, Vihman, M. M. 1991. Beginnings of prosodic organization: Intonation and duration patterns of disyllables produced by Japanese and French infants. *Language and Speech, 34,* 219–238.

Halliday, M. A. K. 1975. *Learning how to mean.* London: Edwin Arnold.

Hamburger, V. 1934. The effects of wing bud extirpation on the development of the central nervous system in chick embryos. *Journal of Experimental Zoology, 68,* 449–494.

Hamilton, C. R., and Vermeire, B. A. 1988a. Complementary hemisphere specialization in monkeys. *Science, 242,* 1691–1694.

Hamilton, C. R., and Vermeire, B. A. 1988b. Cognition, not handedness, is lateralized in monkeys. *Behavioral and Brain Sciences, 11,* 723–725.

Handbook of Phonological Data from a Sample of the World's Languages: A Report of the Stanford Phonology Archive. 1979. Stanford University, Department of Linguistics.

Hannah, A. C., and McGrew, W. C. 1987. Chimpanzees using stones to crack open oil palm nuts in Liberia. *Primates, 28,* 31–46.

Hannan, T. E. 1982. Young infants' hand and finger expressions: An analysis of category reliability. In Field, T., and Fogel, A. (eds.), *Emotion and early interaction*. Hillsdale, N.J.: Erlbaum.

Hannan, T. E., and Fogel, A. 1987. A case-study assessment of "pointing" during the first three months of life. *Perceptual and Motor Skills, 65,* 187–194.

Harding, C. G. 1983. Setting the stage for language acquisition: Communication development in the first year. In Golinkoff, R. M. (ed.), *The transition from prelinguistic to linguistic communication*. Hillsdale, N.J.: Erlbaum.

Harding, C. G., and Golinkoff, R. M. 1979. The origins of intentional vocalizations in prelinguistic infants. *Child Development, 50,* 33–40.

Hardy-Brown, K., Plomin, R., and DeFries, J. 1981. Genetic and environmental influences on the rate of communicative development in the first year of life. *Developmental Psychology, 17,* 704–717.

Harrison, R. G. 1904. An experimental study of the relation of the nervous system to the developing musculature in the embryo of the frog. *American Journal of Anatomy, 3,* 197–220.

Harter, S. 1974. Pleasure derived from cognitive challenge and mastery. *Child Development, 45,* 661–669.

Harter, S. 1978a. Effectance motivation reconsidered: Toward a developmental model. *Human Development, 21,* 34–64.

Harter, S. 1978b. Pleasure derived from optimal challenge and the effects of extrinsic rewards on children's difficulty level choices. *Child Development, 49,* 788–799.

Harter, S. 1980. A model of intrinsic motivation in children: Individual differences and developmental change. In Collins, A. (ed.), *Minnesota symposium on child psychology*. Hillsdale, N.J.: Erlbaum.

Harter, S., and Zigler, E. 1974. The assessment of effectance motivation in normal and retarded chidren. *Developmental Psychology, 10,* 169–180.

Harvey, P. H., and Clutton-Brock, T. H. 1985. Life history variation in primates. *Evolution, 39,* 559–581.

Hasselmo, M. E., Rolls, E. T., and Baylis, G. C. 1989. The role of expression and identity in the face-selective responses of neurons in the temporal visual cortex of the monkey. *Behavioural Brain Research, 32,* 203–218.

Hauser, M. 1989. Ontogenetic changes in the comprehension and production of Vervet monkey *(Cercopithecus aethiops)* vocalizations. *Journal of Comparative Psychology, 103,* 149–158.

Hauser, M. 1992a. Articulatory and social factors influence the acoustic structure of rhesus monkey vocalizations: A learned mode of production? *Journal of the Acoustical Society of America, 91,* 2175–2179.

Hauser, M. 1992b. *Homo unicus* or *Homo diversus*. Review of "Uniquely human: The evolution of speech, thought, and selfless behavior" by Philip Lieberman. *Applied Psycholinguistics, 13,* 237–243.

Hauser, M. D. 1992c. A mechanism guiding conversational turn-taking in vervet monkeys and rhesus macaques. *Topics in primatology*. Vol. 1. *Human Origins*. Tokyo: Tokyo University Press.

Hauser, M. D., and Fowler, C. 1992. Fundamental frequency declination is not unique to human speech: Evidence from nonhuman primates. *Journal of the Acoustical Society of America, 91,* 363–369.

Haviland, J. 1976. Looking smart: The relationship between affect and intelligence in infancy. Species patterns and individual variations. In Lewis, M. (ed.), *Origins of intelligence: Infancy and early childhood.* New York: Plenum Press.

Hawn, P. R., and Harris, L. J. 1983. Hand differences in grasp duration and reaching in two- and five-month-old infants. In Young, G., Segalowitz, S. J., Corter, C. M., and Trehub, S. E. (eds.), *Manual specialization and the developing brain.* New York: Academic Press.

Hayes, C. 1951. *The ape in our house.* New York: Harpers.

Hayes, K. J., and Nissen, D. H. 1971. Higher mental functions of a home-raised chimpanzee. In Schrier, A. M., and Stollnitz, F. (eds.), *Behavior of nonhuman primates.* New York: Academic Press.

Hayes, K. J. 1962. Genes, drives and intellect. *Psychological Reports, 10,* 299–342.

Hebb, D. O. 1949. *The organization of behavior: A neuropsychological theory.* New York: Wiley.

Hecaen, H., and Angelergues, R. 1962. Agnosia for faces (prosopagnosia). *Archives of Neurology, 7,* 92–100.

Heffner, H. E., and Heffner, R. S. 1984. Temporal lobe lesions and perception of species-specific vocalizations by macaques. *Science, 226,* 75–76.

Heilman, K. M., Bowers, D., Speedie, L., and Coslett, H. B. 1984. Comprehension of affective and nonaffective prosody. *Neurology, 34,* 917–921.

Hein, A., and Held, R. 1967. Dissociation of the visual placing response into elicited and guided components. *Science, 158,* 390–392.

Hein, A., Held, R., and Gower, E. C. 1970. Development and segmentation of visually controlled movement by selective exposure during rearing. *Journal of Comparative and Physiological Psychology, 73,* 181–187.

Held, R. 1961. Exposure-history as a factor in maintaining stability of perception and coordination. *Journal of Nervous and Mental Disease, 132,* 26–32.

Held, R., and Bauer, J. A. 1967. Visually guided reaching in infant monkeys and restricted rearing. *Science, 155,* 718–720.

Held, R., and Bossom, J. 1961. Neonatal deprivation and adult rearrangement: Complementary techniques for analyzing plastic sensory-motor coordinations. *Journal of Comparative and Physiological Psychology, 54,* 33–37.

Held, R., and Hein, A. 1963. Movement-produced stimulation in the development of visually guided behavior. *Journal of Comparative and Physiological Psychology, 56,* 872–876.

Hellyer, N. L., and Farmer, A. 1982. A comparison of vowel formant measurements between posttracheostomy and postbabbling children. *Folia Phoniatrica, 34,* 17–20.

Henderson, S. 1985. Motor skill development. In Lane, D., and Stratford, B. (eds.), *Current approaches to Down's syndrome.* New York: Praeger.

Hendrick, I. 1942. Instinct and the ego during infancy. *Psychoanalytic Quarterly, 11,* 33–58.

Hendrick, I. 1943a. Work and the pleasure principle. *Psychoanalytic Quarterly, 12*, 311–329.

Hendrick, I. 1943b. The discussion of the 'instinct to master.' *Psychoanalytic Quarterly, 12*, 561–565.

Hewes, G. W. 1981. Pointing and language. In Myers, T., Laver, J., and Anderson, J. (eds.), *The cognitive representation of speech*. New York: North-Holland.

Hier, D. B., LeMay, M., and Rosenberger, P. B. 1979. Autism and unfavorable left-right asymmetries of the brain. *Journal of Autism and Developmental Disorders, 9*, 153–159.

Hier, D. B., LeMay, M., Rosenberger, P. B., and Perlo, P. 1978. Developmental dyslexia: Evidence for a subgroup with a reversal of cerebral asymmetry. *Archives of Neurology, 35*, 90–92.

Hill, S. D., and Tomlin, C. 1981. Self-recognition in retarded children. *Child Development, 52*, 145–150.

Hinde, R. A. 1970. *Animal behaviour*. New York: McGraw-Hill.

Hinde, R. A., and Simpson, M. J. A. 1975. Qualities of mother-infant relationships in monkeys. In *Parent-infant interaction* (CIBA Foundation Symposium 33). New York: Elsevier.

Hirsh-Pasek, K., Kemler Nelson, D. G., Jusczyk, P. W., Cassidy, K. W., Druss, B., and Kennedy, L. 1987. Clauses are perceptual units for young infants. *Cognition, 26*, 269–286.

Hiscock, M., and Kinsbourne, M. 1978. Ontogeny of cerebral dominance: Evidence from time-sharing asymmetry in children. *Developmental Psychology, 14*, 321–329.

Hittelman, J. H., and Dickes, R. 1979. Sex differences in neonatal eye contact time. *Merrill-Palmer Quarterly, 25*, 171–184.

Hobson, R. P. 1986. The autistic child's appraisal of expressions of emotion. *Journal of Child Psychology and Psychiatry, 27*, 321–342.

Hobson, R. P. 1987. The autistic child's recognition of age- and sex-related characteristics of people. *Journal of Autism and Developmental Disorders, 17*, 63–79.

Hobson, R. P. 1990. On acquiring knowledge about people and the capacity to pretend: Response to Leslie (1987). *Psychological Review, 97*, 114–121.

Holmes, M. D., Ojemann, G. A., Cawthon, D. F., and Lettich, E. 1991. Neuronal activity in nondominant human lateral temporal cortex related to short term spatial memory and visuospatial recognition. Poster presented at the 21st Annual Meeting of the Society for Neuroscience, New Orleans.

Holmgren, K., Lindblom, B., Aurelius, G., Jalling, B., and Zetterstrom, R. 1986. On the phonetics of infant vocalization. In Lindblom, B., and Zetterstrom, R. (eds.), *Precursors of early speech*. New York: Stockton Press.

Holzman, P. S., Rousey, C., and Snyder, C. 1966. On listening to one's own voice: Effects on psychophysiological responses and free associations. *Journal of Personality and Social Psychology, 4*, 432–441.

Hopkins, B., Lems, W., Janssen, B., and Butterworth, G. 1987. Postural and motor asymmetries in newlyborns. *Human Neurobiology, 6*, 153–156.

Horgan, D. 1980. Nouns: love 'em or leave 'em. In Teller, V., and White, S. J. (eds.), Studies in child language and multilingualism. *Annals of the New York Academy of Sciences, 345,* 5–25.

Hubbard, C. A., and Asp, C. W. 1991. Vocalized emotions of infants: A perceptual and acoustic analysis. Paper presented at the American Speech-Language-Hearing Association convention, Atlanta, November.

Huber, H. 1970. A preliminary comparison of English and Yucatec infant vocalization at nine months. *Papers from the Sixth Regional Meeting of the Chicago Linguistic Society.* Chicago: Chicago Linguistic Society.

Hughes, M., and Sussman, H. M. 1983. An assessment of cerebral dominance in language-disordered children via a time-sharing paradigm. *Brain and Language, 19,* 48–64.

Hunt, J. McV. 1963. Motivation inherent in information processing and action. In Harvey, O. J. (ed.), *Motivation and social interaction.* New York: Ronald Press.

Hunt, J. McV. 1965. Intrinsic motivation and its role in psychological development. In Levine, D. (ed.), *Nebraska symposium on motivation* Vol. 13. Lincoln: University of Nebraska Press.

Hursh, D. E., and Sherman, J. A. 1973. The effects of parent-presented models and praise on the vocal behavior of their children. *Journal of Experimental Child Psychology, 15,* 328–339.

Hutt, C., and Ounsted, C. 1966. The biological significance of gaze aversion with particular reference to the syndrome of infantile autism. *Behavioral Science, 11,* 346–356.

Ingram, D. 1978. The production of word-initial fricatives and affricates by normal and linguistically deviant children. In Caramazza, A., and Zurif, E. B. (eds.), *Language acquisition and language breakdown: Parallels and divergencies.* Baltimore: Johns Hopkins University Press.

Ingram, T. 1975. Speech disorders in childhood. In Lenneberg, E. H., and Lenneberg, E. (eds.), *Foundations of language development.* Vol. 2. New York: Academic Press.

Irvine, J. T. 1990. Registering affect: Heteroglossia in the linguistic expression of emotion. In Lutz, C. A., and Abu-Lughod, L. (eds.), *Language and the politics of emotion.* New York: Cambridge University Press.

Irwin, O. C. 1947. Infant speech: Consonantal sounds according to place of articulation. *Journal of Speech Disorders, 12,* 397–401.

Izard, C. E. 1977. *Human emotions.* New York: Plenum Press.

Izard, C. E. 1978. On the ontogenesis of emotions and emotion-cognition relationships in infancy. In Lewis, M., and Rosenblum, L. A. (eds.), *The development of affect.* New York: Plenum Press.

Jakobson, R. 1960. Why 'Mama' and 'Papa'? In Kaplan, B., and Wapner, S. (eds.), *Perspectives in psychological theory: Essays in honor of Heinz Werner.* New York: International Universities Press.

Jakobson, R. 1968. *Child language, aphasia, and phonological universals.* The Hague: Mouton (originally published, 1941).

Jasnow, M., and Feldstein, S. 1986. Adult-like temporal characteristics of mother-infant vocal interactions. *Child Development, 57,* 754–761.

Jenkins, W. M., Merzenich, M. M., Ochs, M. T., Allard, T., and Guic-Robles, E. 1990. Functional reorganization of primary somatosensory cortex in adult owl monkeys after behaviorally controlled tactile stimulation. *Journal of Neurophysiology, 63,* 82–104.

Jenkins, W. M., Merzenich, M. M., and Recanzone, G. 1990. Neocortical representational dynamics in adult primates: Implications for neuropsychology. *Neuropsychologia, 28,* 573–584.

Jensen, T. S., Boggild-Andersen, B., Schmidt, J., Ankerhus, J., and Hansen, E. 1988. Perinatal risk factors and first-year vocalizations: Influence on pre-school language and motor performance. *Developmental Medicine and Child Neurology, 30,* 153–161.

Jergens, U. 1987. Primate communication: Signaling, vocalization. In Adelman, G. (ed.), *Encyclopedia of Neuroscience.* Boston: Birkhauser.

Jernigan, T. L., and Bellugi, U. 1990. Anomalous brain morphology on magnetic resonance images in Williams syndrome and Down syndrome. *Archives of Neurology, 47,* 529–533.

Jernigan, T. L., Hesselink, J. R., Sowell, E., and Tallal, P. A. 1991. Cerebral structure on magnetic resonance imaging in language- and learning-impaired children. *Archives of Neurology, 48,* 539–545.

Johnson, A., Goddard, O., and Ashurst, H. 1990. Is late walking a marker of morbidity? *Archives of Disease in Childhood, 65,* 486–488.

Johnson, J. I., Hamilton, T. C., Hsung, J-C. and Ulinski, P. S. 1972. Gracile nucleus absent in adult opossums after leg removal in infancy. *Brain Research, 38,* 421–424.

Johnson, K. 1990. The role of perceived speaker identity in F0 normalization of vowels. *Journal of the Acoustical Society of America, 88,* 642–654.

Johnson, M. H., Dziurawiec, S., Bartrip, J., and Morton, J. 1992. The effects of movement of internal features on infants' preferences for face-like stimuli. *Infant Behavior and Development, 15,* 129–136.

Johnson, M. H., Dziurawiec, S., Ellis, H., and Morton, J. 1990. Newborns preferential tracking of face-like stimuli and its subsequent decline. *Cognition, 40,* 129–136.

Johnson, M. H., and Morton, J. 1991. *Biology and cognitive development: The case of face recognition.* Cambridge, Mass.: Blackwell.

Johnston, C. 1896. The world's baby-talk and the expressiveness of speech. *Fortnightly Review, 60,* 494–505.

Johnston, J. R. 1991. The continuing relevance of cause: A reply to Leonard's "specific language impairment as a clinical category." *Language, Speech, and Hearing Services in Schools, 22,* 66–68.

Johnston, R. B., Stark, R. E., Mellits, E. D., and Tallal, P. 1981. Neurological status of language-impaired and normal children. *Annals of Neurology, 10,* 159–163.

Jones, M. C. 1965. An investigation of certain acoustic parameters of the crying vocalization of young deaf children. Ph.D. diss., Northwestern University.

Jones, O. H. M. 1977. Mother-child communication with pre-linguistic Down's syndrome and normal infants. In Schaffer, H. R. (ed.), *Studies in mother-infant interaction*. New York: Academic Press.

Jones, S. J., and Moss, H. A. 1971. Age, state and maternal behavior associated with infant vocalizations. *Child Development, 42,* 1039–1051.

Jung, J. H. 1989. *Genetic syndromes in communication disorders*. Boston: Little, Brown.

Jurgens, U. 1979. Neural control of vocalisation in nonhuman primates. In Steklis, H. D., and Raleigh, M. J. (eds.), *Neurobiology of social communication in primates*. London: Academic Press.

Jurgens, U. 1985. Implication of SMA in phonation. *Experimental Brain Research, 58,* A12–14.

Jurgens, U., and Pratt, R. 1979. Role of the periaqueductral grey in vocal expression of emotion. *Brain Research, 167,* 367–378.

Jusczyk, P. W. 1992. Developing phonological categories from the speech signal. In Ferguson, C., Menn, L., and Stoel-Gammon, C. (eds.), *Phonological development: Models, research, implications*. Parkton, Md.: York Press.

Jusczyk, P. W., Pisoni, D. B., and Mullennix, J. 1989. Effects of talker variability on speech perception by 2-month-old infants. *Research on Speech Perception*. Progress Report No. 15, Indiana University.

Jusczyk, P. W., and Thompson, E. 1978. Perception of a phonetic contrast in multisyllabic utterances by 2-month-old infants. *Perception and Psychophysics, 23,* 105–109.

Kagan, J. 1971. *Change and continuity in infancy*. New York: Wiley.

Kagan, J., Kearsley, R. B., and Zelazo, P. R. 1978. *Infancy: Its place in human development*. Cambridge, Mass.: Harvard University Press.

Kagan, J., Reznick, J. S., and Snidman, N. 1988. Biological bases of childhood shyness. *Science, 240,* 167–171.

Kamen, R. S., and Watson, B. C. 1991. Effects of long-term tracheostomy on spectral characteristics of vowel production. *Journal of Speech and Hearing Research, 34,* 1057–1065.

Kamhi, A. G., and Catts, H. W. (eds.) 1989. *Reading disabilities: A developmental language perspective*. Boston: Little, Brown.

Kanner, L. 1943. Autistic disturbances of affective contact. *Nervous Child, 2,* 217–250.

Kaslon, K. W., and Stein, R. E. 1985. Chronic pediatric tracheostomy: Assessment and implications for habilitation of voice, speech and language in young children. *International Journal of Pediatric Otorhinolaryngology, 9,* 165–171.

Kaye, K. 1977. Toward the origin of dialogue. In Schaffer, H. R. (ed.), *Studies in mother-infant interaction*. New York: Academic Press.

Kaye, K. 1979. Thickening thin data: The maternal role in developing communication and language. In Bullowa, M. (ed.), *Before speech*. Cambridge: Cambridge University Press.

Kaye, K. 1982. *The mental and social life of babies: How parents create persons*. Chicago: University of Chicago Press.

Kaye, K., and Charney, R. 1980. How mothers maintain "dialogue" with two-year-olds. In Olsen, D. (ed.), *The social foundations of language and thought.* New York: Norton.

Kaye, K., and Fogel, A. 1980. The temporal structure of face-to-face communication between mothers and infants. *Developmental Psychology, 16,* 454–464.

Kaye, K., and Wells, A. 1980. Mothers' jiggling and the burst-pause pattern in neonatal sucking. *Infant Behavior and Development, 3,* 29–46.

Keating, C. F., and Keating, E. G. 1982. Visual scan patterns of rhesus monkeys viewing faces. *Perception, 11,* 211–219.

Kellogg, W. N. 1968. Communication and language in the home-raised chimpanzee. *Science, 162,* 423–427.

Kelly, C. A., and Dale, P. S. 1989. Cognitive skills associated with the onset of multiword utterances. *Journal of Speech and Hearing Research, 32,* 645–656.

Kemler Nelson, D. G., Hirsh-Pasek, K., Jusczyk, P. W., and Cassidy, K. W. 1989. How the prosodic cues in motherese might assist language learning. *Journal of Child Language, 16,* 55–68.

Kemper, T. L. 1984. Asymmetrical lesions in dyslexia. In Geschwind, N., and Galaburda, A. M. (eds.), *Cerebral dominance: The biological foundations.* Cambridge, Mass.: Harvard University Press.

Kendon, A. 1967. Some functions of gaze direction in social interaction. *Acta Psychologica, 26,* 22–63.

Kendrick, K. M., and Baldwin, B. A. 1987a. Cells in temporal cortex of conscious sheep can respond preferentially to the sight of faces. *Science, 236,* 448–450.

Kendrick, K. M., and Baldwin, B. A. 1987b. Facial recognition cells and autism: Response to Fotheringham. *Science, 238,* 1496–1497.

Kennell, J. H., Trause, M. A., and Klaus, M. H. 1975. Evidence for a sensitive period in the human mother. In *Parent-infant interaction* (CIBA Foundation Symposium 33). New York: Elsevier.

Kenney, M. D., Mason, W. A., and Hill, S. D. 1979. Effects of age, objects, and visual experience on affective responses of rhesus monkeys to strangers. *Developmental Psychology, 15,* 176–184.

Kent, R. D. 1981. Articulatory-acoustic perspectives on speech development. In Stark, R. (ed.), *Language behavior in infancy and early childhood.* Amsterdam: Elsevier/North Holland.

Kent, R. D., and Bauer, H. R. 1985. Vocalizations of one-year-olds. *Journal of Child Language, 12,* 491–526.

Kent, R. D., Osberger, M. J., Netsell, R., and Hustedde, C. G. 1987. Phonetic development in identical twins differing in auditory function. *Journal of Speech and Hearing Disorders, 52,* 64–75.

Kermoian, R., and Campos, J. J. 1988. Locomotor experience: A facilitator of spatial cognitive development. *Child Development, 59,* 908–917.

Kessen, W., Levine, J., and Wendrich, K. 1979. The imitation of pitch in infants. *Infant Behavior and Development, 2,* 93–100.

Kidd, K. H. 1983. Recent progress on the genetics of stuttering. In Ludlow, C. L., and Cooper, J. A. (eds.), *Genetic aspects of speech and language disorders*. New York: Academic Press.

Kimura, D. 1973a. Manual activity during speaking–I. Right-handers. *Neuropsychologia, 11,* 45–50.

Kimura, D. 1973b. Manual activity during speaking–II. Left-handers. *Neuropsychologia, 11,* 51–55.

King, A. P., and West, M. J. 1988. Searching for the functional origins of cowbird song in eastern brown-headed cowbirds *(Molothrus ater ater)*. *Animal Behaviour, 36,* 1575–1588.

King, F. L., and Kimura, D. 1972. Left-ear superiority in dichotic perception of vocal nonverbal sounds. *Canadian Journal of Psychology, 26,* 111–116.

King, M. C., and Wilson, A. C. 1975. Evolution at two levels in humans and chimpanzees. *Science, 188,* 107–116.

Kinsbourne, M., and McMurray, J. 1975. The effect of cerebral dominance on time sharing between speaking and tapping by preschool children. *Child Development, 46,* 240–242.

Klaus, M. H., Trause, M. A., and Kennell, J. H. 1975. Does human maternal behaviour after delivery show a characteristic pattern? In *Parent-infant interaction* (CIBA Foundation Symposium 33). New York: Elsevier.

Kling, A. S., and Brothers, L. A. 1992. The amygdala and social behavior. In Aggleton, J. P. (ed.), *The amygdala: Neurobiological aspects of emotion, memory, and mental dysfunction*. New York: Wiley.

Kling, A., Lancaster, J., and Benitone, J. 1970. Amygdalectomy in the free-ranging vervet *cercopithecus aethiops*. *Journal of Psychiatric Research, 7,* 191–199.

Kluender, K. R. 1991. Effects of first formant onset properties on voicing judgments result from processes not specific to humans. *Journal of the Acoustical Society of America, 90,* 83–96.

Knapp, M. L. 1972. *Nonverbal communication in human interaction*. New York: Holt, Rinehart and Winston.

Knudsen, E. I. 1985. Experience alters the spatial tuning of auditory units in the optic tectum during a sensitive period in the barn owl. *Journal of Neuroscience, 5,* 3094–3109.

Knudsen, E. I., and Knudsen, P. F. 1990. Sensitive and critical periods for visual calibration of sound localization by barn owls. *Journal of Neuroscience, 10,* 222–232.

Kohler, W. 1917. Intelligenzprufungen an Anthropoiden. *Abhandlungen der Preussische Akademie der Wissenschaften. Physikalische-Mathematische Klasse*. Nr. 1. Described briefly in Gomez, J. C. 1990. The emergence of intentional communication as a problem-solving strategy in the gorilla. In Parker, S. T., and Gibson, K. R. (eds.), *"Language" and intelligence in monkeys and apes: Comparative developmental perspectives*. New York: Cambridge University Press.

Konner, M. 1991. Universals of behavioral development in relation to brain myelination. In Gibson, K. R., and Petersen, A. C. (eds.), *Brain maturation and cognitive development: Comparative and cross-cultural perspectives.* New York: Aldine de Gruyter.

Koopmans-van Beinum, F. J., and van der Stelt, J. M. 1986. Early stages in the development of speech movements. In Lindblom, B., and Zetterstrom, R. (eds.), *Precursors of early speech.* New York: Stockton Press.

Korner, A. F. 1969. Neonatal startles, smiles, erections, and reflex sucks as related to state, sex, and individuality. *Child Development, 40,* 1039–1053.

Korner, A. F. 1973. Sex differences in newborns with special reference to differences in the organization of oral behavior. *Journal of Child Psychology and Psychiatry, 14,* 19–29.

Korner, A. F., Chuck, B., and Dontchos, S. 1968. Organismic determinants of spontaneous oral behavior in neonates. *Child Development, 39,* 1145–1157.

Krasnegor, N. A., and Bridges, R. S. (eds.) 1990. *Mammalian parenting: Biochemical, neurobiological, and behavioral determinants.* New York: Oxford University Press.

Kravitz, H., and Boehm, J. J. 1971. Rhythmic habit patterns in infancy: Their sequence, age of onset, and frequency. *Child Development, 42,* 399–413.

Kuczynski, L., Zahn-Waxler, C., and Radke-Yarrow, M. 1987. Development and content of imitation in the second and third years of life: A socialization perspective. *Developmental Psychology, 23,* 276–282.

Kuhl, P. K., and Meltzoff, A. N. 1982. The bimodal perception of speech in infancy. *Science, 218,* 1138–1141.

Kuhl, P. K., and Meltzoff, A. N. 1988. Speech as an intermodal object of perception. In Yonas, A. (ed.), *Perceptual development in infancy.* Minnesota Symposia on Child Psychology. Hillsdale, N.J.: Erlbaum.

Kuhl, P., and Miller, J. 1975. Speech perception by the chinchilla: Voiced-voiceless distinction in alveolar plosive consonants. *Science, 190,* 69–72.

Kuhl, P., and Miller, J. 1982. Discrimination of auditory target dimensions in the presence or absence of variation in a second dimension by infants. *Perception and Psychophysics, 31,* 279–292.

LaBarbera, J. D., Izard, C. E., Vietze, P., and Parisi, S. A. 1976. Four- and six-month-old infants' visual responses to joy, anger, and neutral expressions. *Child Development, 47,* 535–538.

Labov, W., and Labov, T. 1978. The phonetics of *cat* and *mama. Language, 54,* 816–852.

Ladd, D. R., Silverman, K. E. A., Tolkmitt, F., Bergmann, G., and Scherer, K. R. 1985. Evidence for the independent function of intonation contour type, voice quality, and F0 range in signaling speaker affect. *Journal of the Acoustical Society of America, 78,* 435–444.

Lamendella, J. T. 1977. The limbic system in human communication. In Whitaker, H., and Whitaker, H. (eds.), *Studies in neurolinguistics.* Vol. 3. New York: Academic Press.

Lancaster, J. B. 1986. Human adolescence and reproduction: An evolutionary perspective. In Lancaster, J. B., and Hamberg, B. A. (eds.), *School-age pregnancy and parenthood: Biosocial dimensions.* New York: Aldine de Gruyter.

Landau, B., and Gleitman, L. R. 1985. *Language and experience: Evidence from the blind child.* Cambridge, Mass.: Harvard University Press.

Langdell, T. 1978. Recognition of faces: An approach to the study of autism. *Journal of Child Psychology and Child Psychiatry, 19,* 255–268.

Landon, S. J., and Sommers, R. K. 1979. Talkativeness and children's linguistic abilities. *Language and Speech, 22,* 269–275.

Langer, S. K. 1942. *Philosophy in a new key.* Cambridge, Mass.: Harvard University Press.

Langer, S. K. 1988. *Mind: An essay on human feeling.* Abridged edition. Baltimore: Johns Hopkins University Press.

Lantze, D., and Stefflre, V. 1964. Language and cognition revisited. *Journal of Abnormal and Social Psychology, 69,* 472–481.

Larson, C. R. 1985. The midbrain periaqueductal gray: A brainstem structure involved in vocalization. *Journal of Speech and Hearing Research, 28,* 241–249.

Larson, C. R. 1988. Brain mechanisms involved in the control of vocalization. *Journal of Voice, 2,* 301–311.

Larson, C. R., and Kistler, M. K. 1984. Periaqueductal gray neuronal activity associated with laryngeal EMG and vocalization in the awake monkey. *Neuroscience Letters, 46,* 261–266.

Larson, C. R., and Kistler, M. K. 1986. The relationship of periaqueductal gray neurons to vocalization and laryngeal EMG in the behaving monkey. *Experimental Brain Research, 63,* 596–606.

Lazarus, R. S. 1991. *Emotion and adaptation.* New York: Oxford University Press.

LeBarre, W. 1954. *The human animal.* Chicago: University of Chicago Press.

LeBarre, W. 1973. The development of mind in man in primitive cultures. In Richardson, F. (ed.), *Brain and intelligence: The ecology of child development.* Hyattsville, Md.: National Educational Press.

Lecanuet, J.-P., Granier-Deferre, C., and Busnel, M.-C. 1989. Differential fetal auditory reactiveness as a function of stimulus characteristics and state. *Seminars in Perinatology, 13,* 421–429.

Lecanuet, J.-P., Granier-Deferre, C., Cohen, H., Le Houezec, R., and Busnel, M.-C. 1986. Fetal responses to acoustic stimulation depend on heart rate variability pattern, stimulus intensity and repetition. *Early Human Development, 13,* 269–283.

Leckman, J. F., and Cohen, D. J. 1988. Descriptive and diagnostic classification of tic disorders. In Cohen, D. J., Bruun, R. D., and Leckman, J. F. (eds.), *Tourette's syndrome and tic disorders: Clinical understanding and treatment.* New York: John Wiley and Sons.

Leckman, J. F., Riddle, M. A., and Cohen, D. J. 1988. Pathobiology of Tourette's syndrome. In Cohen, D. J., Bruun, R. D., and Leckman, J. F. (eds.), *Tourette's syndrome and tic disorders: Clinical understanding and treatment.* New York: John Wiley and Sons.

Lecours, A. R. 1975. Myelogenetic correlates of the development of speech and language. In Lenneberg, E. H., and Lenneberg, E. (eds.), *Foundations of language development: A multidisciplinary approach*. Vol. 1. New York: Academic Press.

LeDoux, J. E. 1986. Sensory systems and emotion: A model of affective processing. *Integrative Psychiatry, 4,* 237–248.

LeDoux, J. E. 1989. Cognitive-emotional interactions in the brain. *Cognition and Emotion, 3,* 267–289.

LeDoux, J. E. 1992. Emotion and the amygdala. In Aggleton, J. P. (ed.), *The amygdala: Neurobiological aspects of emotion, memory, and mental dysfunction*. New York: Wiley.

Lee, G. P., Loring, D. W., Meader, K. J., and Brooks, B. B. 1990. Hemispheric specialization for emotional expression: A reexamination of results from intracarotid administration of sodium amobarbital. *Brain and Language, 12,* 267–280.

Leehey, S. C. 1976. Face recognition in children evidence for the development of right hemisphere specialization. Ph.D. diss., Massachusetts Institute of Technology.

Leehey, S. C., and Cahn, A. 1979. Lateral asymmetries in the recognition of words, familiar faces and unfamiliar faces. *Neuropsychologia, 17,* 619–625.

Leehey, S. C., Moscowitz-Cook, A., Brill, S., and Held, R. 1975. Orientational anisotropy in infant vision. *Science, 190,* 900–902.

Legerstee, M. 1990. Infants use multimodal information to imitate speech sounds. *Infant Behavior and Development, 13,* 343–354.

LeMay, M., and Geschwind, N. 1975. Hemispheric differences in the brains of great apes. *Brain, Behavior and Evolution, 11,* 48–52.

Lenneberg, E. H. 1962. Understanding language without ability to speak: A case report. *Journal of Abnormal Social Psychology, 6,* 419–425.

Lenneberg, E. H. 1967. *Biological foundations of language*. New York: Wiley.

Lenneberg, E. H., Rebelsky, F. G., and Nichols, I. A. 1965. The vocalizations of infants born to deaf and to hearing parents. *Human Development, 8,* 23–37.

Leonard, L. 1982. Phonological deficits in children with developmental language impairment. *Brain and Language, 16,* 73–86.

Leonard, L. 1987. Is specific language impairment a useful construct? In Rosenberg, S. (ed.), *Advances in applied psycholinguistics*. Vol. 1. *Disorders of first-language development*. New York: Cambridge University Press.

Leonard, L. 1989. Language learnability and specific language impairment in children. *Applied Psycholinguistics, 10,* 179–202.

Leonard, L. B. 1991. Specific language impairment as a clinical opportunity. *Language, Speech, and Hearing Services in Schools, 22,* 66–68.

Leonard, L. B., Newhoff, M., and Mesalam, L. 1980. Individual differences in early child phonology. *Applied Psycholinguistics, 1,* 7–30.

Leonard, L. B., Schwartz, R. G., Chapman, K., Rowan, L. E., Prelock, P. A., Terrell, B., Weiss, A. L., and Messick, C. 1982. Early lexical acquisition in children with specific language impairment. *Journal of Speech and Hearing Research, 25,* 554–564.

Leopold, W. F. 1949. Original invention in infant language. *Symposium, 3,* 66–75.

Leslie, A. M. 1987. Pretense and representation: The origins of 'theory of mind'. *Psychological Review, 94,* 412–426.

Leung, E. H., and Rheingold, H. L. 1981. Development of pointing as a social gesture. *Developmental Psychology, 17,* 215–220.

Leutenegger, W. 1974. Functional aspects of pelvic morphology in Simian primates. *Journal of Human Evolution, 3,* 207–222.

Leutenegger, W. 1980. Encephalization and obstetrics in primates with particular reference to human evolution. In Armstrong, E., and Falk, D. (eds.), *Primate brain evolution: Methods and concepts.* New York: Plenum Press.

Levine, M. H., and Sutton-Smith, B. 1973. Effects of age, sex, and task on visual behavior during dyadic interaction. *Developmental Psychology, 9,* 400–405.

Levine, S. C. 1985. Developmental changes in right-hemisphere involvement in face recognition. In Best, C. T. (ed.), *Hemispheric function and collaboration in the child.* Orlando, Fl.: Academic Press.

Levine, S. L., Fishman, L. M., Oller, D. K., Lynch, M. P., and Basinger, D. L. 1991. The relationship between infant motor development and babbling in normally developing, at risk, and handicapped infants. Paper presented at the Gatlinburg Conference on Research and Theory in Mental Retardation and Developmental Disabilities, Key Biscayne, Fla., May.

Levitt, E. A. 1964. The relationship between abilities to express emotional meanings vocally and facially. In Davitz, J. R. (ed.), *The communication of emotional meaning.* New York: McGraw-Hill.

Lewedag, V. L., Lynch, M., Levine, S., and Oller, D. K. 1991. A comparison of language production in the home and laboratory environment. Paper presented to the Gatlinburg Conference on Research and Theory in Mental Retardation and Developmental Disabilities, Key Biscayne, Fla., May.

Lewis, B. A. 1990. Familial phonological disorders: Four pedigrees. *Journal of Speech and Hearing Disorders, 55,* 160–170.

Lewis, B. A., Ekelman, B. L., and Aram, D. M. 1989. A familial study of severe phonological disorders. *Journal of Speech and Hearing Research, 32,* 713–724.

Lewis, B. A., and Thompson, L. A. 1992. A study of developmental speech and language disorders in twins. *Journal of Speech and Hearing Research, 35,* 1086–1094.

Lewis, M. 1969. Infants' responses to facial stimuli during the first year of life. *Developmental Psychology, 1,* 75–86.

Lewis, M., and Freedle, R. 1973. Mother-infant dyad: The cradle of meaning. In Pliner, P., Krames, L., and Alloway, T. (eds.), *Communication and affect: Language and thought.* New York: Academic Press.

Lewis, M. M. 1936. *Infant speech: A study of the beginnings of language.* New York: Harcourt, Brace.

Ley, R. G., and Bryden, M. P. 1982. A dissociation of right and left hemispheric effects for recognizing emotional tone and verbal content. *Brain and Cognition, 1,* 3–9.

Liberman, A. M. 1970. The grammars of speech and language. *Cognitive Psychology, 1,* 301–323.

Liberman, A. M. 1992. Plausibility, parsimony, and theories of speech. In Alegria, J., Holender, D., Junca de Morais, J., and Radeau, M. (eds.), *Analytic approaches to human cognition.* New York: North-Holland.

Liberman, A. M., and Mattingly, I. M. 1989. The motor theory of speech perception revised. *Cognition, 21,* 1–36.

Liberman, A. M., and Mattingly, I. M. 1991. A specialization for speech perception. *Science, 243,* 489–494.

Liberman, A. M., Cooper, F. S., Shankweiler, D. P., and Studdert-Kennedy, M. 1967. Perception of the speech code. *Psychological Review, 74,* 431–461.

Liberman, I. Y., Shankweiler, D., Liberman, A. M., Fowler, C., and Fischer, F. W. 1977. Phonetic segmentation and recoding in the beginning reader. In Reber, A. S., and Scarborough, D. (eds.), *Toward a psychology of reading: The proceedings of the CUNY Conferences.* Hillsdale, N.J.: Erlbaum.

Lickliter, R. 1990. Premature visual experience facilitates visual responsiveness in Bobwhite Quail neonates. *Infant Behavior and Development, 13,* 487–496.

Lieberman, P. 1963. Some effects of semantic and grammatical context on the production and perception of speech. *Language and Speech, 6,* 172–187.

Lieberman, P. 1967. *Intonation, perception, and language.* Cambridge, Mass.: MIT Press.

Lieberman, P. 1984. *The biology and evolution of language.* Cambridge, Mass.: Harvard University Press.

Lieberman, P. 1991. *Uniquely human: The evolution of speech, thought, and selfless behavior.* Cambridge, Mass.: Harvard University Press.

Lieberman, P., and Michaels, S. B. 1962. Some aspects of fundamental frequency and envelope amplitude as related to the emotional content of speech. *Journal of the Acoustical Society of America, 34,* 922–927.

Liederman, J., and Kinsbourne, M. 1980a. The mechanism of neonatal rightward turning bias: A sensory or motor asymmetry? *Infant Behavior and Development, 3,* 223–238.

Liederman, J., and Kinsbourne, M. 1980b. Rightward motor bias in newborns depends upon parental right-handedness. *Neuropsychologia, 18,* 579–584.

Lieven, E., and McShane, J. 1978. Language is a developing social skill. In Chivers, D. J., and Herbert, J. (eds.), *Recent advances in primatology.* Vol. 1. *Behaviour.* New York: Academic Press.

Lieven, E. V. M., Pine, J. M., and Dresner Barnes, H. 1992. Individual differences in early vocabulary development: redefining the referential-expressive distinction. *Journal of Child Language, 19,* 287–310.

Lightman, A., and Gingerich, O. 1992. When do anomalies begin? *Science, 255,* 690–695.

Lindblom, B. 1984. Can the models of evolutionary biology be applied to phonetic problems? In Van den Broecke, M. P. R., and Cohen, A. (eds.), *Proceedings of the Tenth International Congress of Phonetic Sciences*. Dordrecht, Holland: Foris Publications.

Lindblom, B. 1989. Some remarks on the origin of the phonetic code. In Euler, C., Lundberg, I., and Lennerstrand, G. (eds.), *Brain and reading*. New York: Stockton Press.

Lindblom, B., and Engstrand, O. 1989. In what sense is speech quantal? *Journal of Phonetics, 17,* 107–121.

Lindblom, B., and Maddieson, I. 1988. Phonetic universals in consonant systems. In Hyman, L. M., and Li, C. N. (eds.), *Language, speech and mind: Studies in honour of Victoria Fromkin*. New York: Routledge.

Lindblom, B., and Zetterstrom, R. 1986. (eds.). *Precursors of early speech*. New York: Stockton Press.

Lindburg, D. G. 1982. Primate obstetrics: The biology of birth. *American Journal of Primatology,* Supplement 1, 193–199.

Lloyd, R. L., and Kling, A. S. 1988. Amygdaloid electrical activity in response to conspecific calls in squirrel monkey (S. Sciureus): Influence of environmental setting, cortical inputs, and recording site. In Newman, J. D. (ed.), *The physiological control of mammalian vocalization*. New York: Plenum Press.

Lock, A. 1980. *The guided reinvention of language*. New York: Academic Press.

Locke, J. 1690. *An essay concerning human understanding*. Book 3. IX. 9.

Locke, J. L. 1978. Selective loss of phonetic production and perception. *Journal of the National Student Speech Language Hearing Association, 6,* 3–11.

Locke, J. L. 1980a. The prediction of child speech errors: Implications for a theory of acquisition. In Yeni-Komshian, G. H., Kavanagh, J. F., and Ferguson, C. (eds.), *Child phonology*. Vol. 2. *Production*. New York: Academic Press.

Locke, J. L. 1980b. Mechanisms of phonological development in children: Maintenance, learning and loss. *Papers from the Sixteenth Regional Meeting of the Chicago Linguistic Society,* 220–238.

Locke, J. L. 1983. *Phonological Acquisition and Change*. New York: Academic Press.

Locke, J. L. 1985. The role of phonetic factors in parent reference. *Journal of Child Language, 12,* 215–220.

Locke, J. L. 1986a. The linguistic significance of babbling. In Lindblom, B., and Zetterstrom, R. (eds.), *Precursors of early speech*. New York: Stockton Press.

Locke, J. L. 1986b. Review of The biology and evolution of language, by Philip Lieberman. *Asha, 28,* 73–74.

Locke, J. L. 1988. Variation in human biology and child phonology: A response to Goad and Ingram. *Journal of Child Language, 15,* 663–668.

Locke, J. L. 1989. Babbling and early speech: Continuity and individual differences. *First Language, 9,* 191–206.

Locke, J. L. 1990a. Structure and stimulation in the ontogeny of spoken language. *Developmental Psychobiology, 23,* 621–643.

Locke, J. L. 1990b. "Mama" and "Papa" in child language: Parent reference or phonetic preference? In Metuzale-Kangere, B., and Rinholm, H. D. (eds.), *Symposium Balticum: A Festschrift to honour Professor Velta Ruke-Dravina*. Hamburg: Helmut Buske Verlag.

Locke, J. L. 1992a. Neural specializations for language: A developmental perspective. *Seminars in the Neurosciences, 4,* 425–431.

Locke, J. L. 1992b. Learning spoken language in time to speak it well. Paper presented to the ASHA convention, San Antonio, November.

Locke, J. L., Bekken, K., Wein, D., McMinn-Larson, and Ruzecki, V. 1991. Neuropsychology of babbling: Laterality effects in the production of rhythmic manual activity. Paper delivered to the Society for Research in Child Development, Seattle.

Locke, J. L., and Mather, P. 1989. Genetic factors in the ontogeny of spoken language: Evidence from monozygotic and dizygotic twins. *Journal of Child Language, 16,* 553–559.

Locke, J. L., and Pearson, D. M. 1990. Linguistic significance of babbling: Evidence from a tracheostomized infant. *Journal of Child Language, 17,* 1–16.

Locke, J. L., and Pearson, D. M. 1992. Vocal learning and the emergence of phonological capacity: A neurobiological approach. In Ferguson, C., Menn, L., and Stoel-Gammon, C. (eds.), *Phonological development: Models, research, implications.* Parkton, Md.: York Press.

Locke, J. L., Smith, S., Macaruso, P., and Powers, S. In preparation. Manual laterality in dyslexic and normally reading populations.

Lockman, J. J., and McHale, J. P. 1989. Object manipulation in infancy: Developmental and contextual determinants. In Lockman, J., and Hazen, N. (eds.), *Action in a social context: Perspectives on early development.* New York: Plenum Press.

Loizos, C. 1967. Play behavior in higher primates: A review. In Morris, D. (ed.), *Primate ethology.* London: Weidenfeld and Nicolson.

Lovejoy, C. O. 1981. The origin of man. *Science, 211,* 341–350.

Loy, J. 1970. Behavioral responses of free-ranging rhesus monkeys to food shortage. *American Journal of Physical Anthropology, 33,* 263–272.

Lucariello, J., Kyratzis, A., and Nelson, K. 1992. Taxonomic knowledge: What kind and and when? *Child Development, 63,* 978–989.

Ludlow, C. L., and Cooper, J. A. 1983. *Genetic aspects of speech and language disorders.* New York: Academic Press.

Lykken, D. T., Bouchard, T. J., McGue, M., and Tellegen, A. 1990. The Minnesota Twin Family Registry: Some initial findings. *Acta Geneticae Medicae et Gemellologiae, 39,* 35–70.

Lykken, D. T., McGue, M., Bouchard, T. J., and Tellegen, A. 1990. Does contact lead to similarity or similarity to contact? *Behavior Genetics, 20,* 547–561.

MacFarlane, A. 1975. Olfaction in the development of social preferences in the human neonate. In *Parent-Infant Interaction* (CIBA Foundation Symposium 33). New York: Elsevier.

MacKain, K. S. 1982. Assessing the role of experience on infants' speech discrimination. *Journal of Child Language, 9,* 527–542.

MacKain, K. S. 1984. Speaking without a tongue. *Journal of the National Student Speech Language Hearing Association, 12,* 46–71.

MacKain, K., Studdert-Kennedy, M., Spieker, S., and Stern, D. 1983. Infant intermodal speech perception is a left-hemisphere function. *Science, 219,* 1347–1349.

Macken, M. A., and Barton, D. 1980. The acquisition of the voicing contrast in English: A study of voice onset time in word-initial stop consonants. *Journal of Child Language, 7,* 41–74.

MacNamara, J., Baker, E., and Olson, C. L. 1976. Four-year-olds' understanding of *pretend, forget,* and *know:* Evidence for propositional operations. *Child Development, 47,* 62–70.

MacNeilage, P. F. 1986. Bimanual coordination and the beginnings of speech. In Lindblom, B., and Zetterstrom, R. (eds.), *Precursors of early speech.* New York: Stockton Press.

MacNeilage, P. F. 1991. The "postural origins" theory of primate neurobiological asymmetries. In Krasnegor, N., Rumbaugh, D., Studdert-Kennedy, M., and Schiefelbusch, R. (eds.), *Biological foundations of language development.* Hillsdale, N.J.: Erlbaum.

MacNeilage, P. F., and Davis, B. 1990a. Acquisition of speech production: Frames, then content. In Jeannerod, M. (ed.), *Attention and Performance 13: Motor Representation and Control.* Hillsdale, N.J.: Erlbaum.

MacNeilage, P. F., and Davis, B. 1990b. Acquisition of speech production: The achievement of segmental independence. In Hardcastle, W. J., and Marchal, A. (eds.), *Speech production and speech modelling.* Dordrecht: Kluwer.

MacNeilage, P. F., Studdert-Kennedy, M., and Lindblom, B. 1984. Functional precursors to language and its lateralization. *American Journal of Physiology, 246* (Regulatory, Integrative and Comparative Physiology 15), R 912–914.

MacNeilage, P. F., Studdert-Kennedy, M., and Lindblom, B. 1987. Primate handedness reconsidered. *Behavioral and Brain Sciences, 10,* 247–263.

Maddieson, I. 1980. Phonological generalizations from the UCLA Phonological Segment Inventory Database. *UCLA Working Papers in Phonetics, 50,* 57–68.

Malatesta, C. Z. 1981. Infant emotion and the vocal affect lexicon. *Motivation and Emotion, 5,* 1–23.

Malatesta. C. Z. 1982. The expression and regulation of emotion: A lifespan perspective. In Field, T., and Fogel, A. (eds.), *Emotion and early interaction.* Hillsdale, N.J.: Erlbaum.

Malatesta, C. Z., Davis, J., and Culver, C. 1984. Emotion in the infant voice: Its relation to facial expression. Poster presentation at the International Conference on Infant Studies, New York, April.

Malatesta, C. Z., Culver, C., Tesman, J. R., and Shepard, B. 1989. The development of emotion expression during the first two years of life. *Monographs of the Society for Research in Child Development, 54* (Serial No. 219).

Mann, V. A., Diamond, R., and Carey, S. 1979. Development of voice recognition:

Parallels with face recognition. *Journal of Experimental Child Psychology, 27,* 153–165.

Mans, L., Cicchetti, D., and Sroufe, L. A. 1978. Mirror reactions of Down's syndrome infants and toddlers: Cognitive underpinnings of self-recognition. *Child Development, 49,* 1247–1250.

Marchman, V. A., Miller, R., and Bates, E. A. 1991. Babble and first words in children with focal brain injury. *Applied Psycholinguistics, 12,* 1–22.

Marcotte, A. C., and LaBarba, R. C. 1987. The effects of linguistic experience on cerebral lateralization for speech production in normal hearing and deaf adolescents. *Brain and Language, 31,* 276–300.

Marcus, G. F., Pinker, S., Ullman, M., Hollander, M., Rosen, T. J., and Xu, F. 1992. Overregularization in language acquisition. *Monograph of the Society for Research in Child Development, 57* (Serial No. 228).

Margoliash, D. 1987. Neural plasticity in birdsong learning. In Rauschecker, J. P., and Marler, P. (eds.), *Imprinting and cortical plasticity: Comparative aspects of sensitive periods.* New York: John Wiley and Sons.

Markman, E. M. 1991. The whole object, taxonomic, and mutual exclusivity assumptions as initial constraints on word meanings. In Byrnes, J. P., and Gelman, S. A. (eds.), *Perspectives on language and cognition: Interrelations in development.* New York: Cambridge University Press.

Markman, E. M. In submission. Constraints on word meaning in early language acquisition.

Markman, E. M., and Hutchinson, J. E. 1984. Children's sensitivity to constraints on word meaning: Taxonomic vs. thematic relations. *Cognitive Psychology, 16,* 1–27.

Marler, P. 1970. A comparative approach to vocal learning: Song development in white-crowned sparrow. *Journal of Comparative and Physiological Psychology, 71,* 1–25.

Marler, P. 1975. An ethological theory of the origin of vocal learning. *Annals of the New York Academy of Sciences, 280,* 386–395.

Marler, P. 1977. The evolution of communication. In Sebeok, T. A. (ed.), *How animals communicate.* Bloomington: Indiana University Press.

Marler, P. 1987. Sensitive periods and the roles of specific and general sensory stimulation in birdsong learning. In Rauschecker, J. P., and Marler, P. (eds.), *Imprinting and cortical plasticity: Comparative aspects of sensitive periods.* New York: John Wiley and Sons.

Marler, P., and Peters, A. 1982a. Developmental overproduction and selective attrition: New processes in the epigenesis of birdsong. *Developmental Psychobiology, 15,* 369–378.

Marler, P., and Peters, A. 1982b. Long-term storage of learned birdsongs prior to production. *Animal Behaviour, 30,* 479–482.

Marler, P., and Peters, A. 1982c. Structural changes in song ontogeny in the swamp sparrow *Melospiza georgiana. Auk, 99,* 446–458.

Marler, P., and Sherman, V. 1983. Song structure without auditory feedback: Emendations of the auditory template hypothesis. *Journal of Neuroscience, 3,* 517–531.

Marler, P., and Tenaza, R. 1977. Signaling behavior of apes with special reference to vocalization. In Sebeok, T. A. (ed.), *How animals communicate.* Bloomington: Indiana University Press.

Marler. P., and Waser, M. S. 1977. Role of auditory feedback in canary song development. *Journal of Comparative and Physiological Psychology, 91,* 8–16.

Martin, G. B., and Clark, R. D. 1982. Distress crying in neonates: Species and peer specificity. *Developmental Psychology, 18,* 3–9.

Martin, P., and Caro, T. M. 1985. On the functions of play and its role in behavioral development. *Advances in the Study of Behavior, 15,* 59–103.

Martin, N. G., Eaves, L. J., Heath, A. C., Jardine, R., Feingold, L. M., and Eysenck, H. J. 1986. Transmission of social attitudes. *Proceedings of the National Academy of Sciences, 83,* 4364–4368.

Masangkay, Z. S., McCluskey, K. A., McIntyre, C. W., Sims-Knight, J., Vaughn, B. E., and Flavell, J. H. 1974. The early development of inferences about the visual percepts of others. *Child Development, 45,* 357–366.

Masataka, N. 1992. Pitch characteristics of Japanese maternal speech to infants. *Journal of Child Language, 19,* 213–223.

Maskarinec, A. S., Cairns, G. F., Butterfield, E. C., and Weamer, D. K. 1981. Longitudinal observations of individual infant's vocalizations. *Journal of Speech and Hearing Disorders, 46,* 267–273.

Mason, W. A. 1965. The social development of monkeys and apes. In DeVore, I. (ed.), *Primate behavior: Field studies of monkeys and apes.* New York: Holt, Rinehart and Winston.

Mason, W. A. 1968. Scope and potential of primate research. In Masserman, J. H. (ed.), *Animal and human.* New York: Grune and Stratton.

Mason, W. A. 1985. Experiential influences on the development of expressive behaviors in rhesus monkeys. In Zivin, G. (ed.), *The development of expressive behavior: Biology-environment interactions.* New York: Academic Press.

Mason-Brothers, A., Ritvo, E. R., Guze, B., Mo, A., Freeman, B. J., Funderburk, S. J., and Schroth, P. C. 1987. Pre-, peri-, and postnatal factors in 181 autistic patients from single and multiple incidence families. *Journal of American Academy of Child and Adolescent Psychiatry, 26,* 39–42.

Massaro, D. W. 1987. *Speech perception by ear and by eye: A paradigm for psychological inquiry.* Hillsdale, N.J.: Erlbaum.

Massie, H. N. 1978. The early natural history of childhood psychosis: Ten cases studied by analysis of family home movies of the infancies of the children. *Journal of the American Academy of Child Psychiatry, 17,* 29–45.

Matheny, A. P., and Bruggemann, C. E. 1973. Children's speech: Hereditary components and sex differences. *Folia Phoniatrica, 25,* 442–449.

Matheny, A. P., Dolan, A. B., and Wilson, R. S. 1974. Bayley's infant behavior record: Relations between behaviors and mental test scores. *Developmental Psychology, 10,* 696–702.

Mather, P. L., and Black, K. N. 1984. Hereditary and environmental influences on preschool twins' language skills. *Developmental Psychology, 20,* 303–308.

Mattingly, I. G., and Studdert-Kennedy, M. (eds.) 1991. *Modularity and the motor theory of speech perception.* Hillsdale, N.J.: Erlbaum.

Maurer, D., and Lewis, T. L. 1979. A physiological explanation of infants' early visual development. *Canadian Journal of Psychology, 33,* 232–252.

Maurer, D., and Salapatek, P. 1976. Developmental changes in the scanning of faces by young infants. *Child Development, 47,* 523–527.

Maurus, M., Barclay, D., and Streit, K.-M. 1988. Acoustic patterns common to human communication and communication between monkeys. *Language and Communication, 8,* 87–94.

Maurus, M., Kuehlmorgen, B., Wiesner, E., Barclay, D., and Streit, K. M. 1985. 'Dialogues' between squirrel monkeys. *Language and Communication, 5,* 185–191.

Maurus, M., Kuehlmorgen, B., Wiesner, E., Barclay, D., and Streit, K. M. 1987. Interrelations between structure and function in the vocal repertoire of Saimiri: Asking the monkeys themselves where to split and where to lump. *European Archives of Psychiatric and Neurologic Science, 236,* 35–39.

Maurus, M., Streit, K. M., Barclay, D., Wiesner, E., and Kuehlmorgen, B. 1986. Vocal interactions between squirrel monkeys out of visual, tactile and olfactory contact. *Language and Communication, 7,* 39–45.

Mayr, E. 1976. Behavior programs and evolutionary strategies. In *Evolution and the diversity of life: Selected essays.* Cambridge, Mass.: Harvard University Press.

McCall, R. B. 1974. The development of intellectual functioning in infancy and the prediction of later I.Q. In Osofsky, J. (ed.), *Handbook of infant development.* New York: Wiley.

McCall, R. B. 1981a. Exploratory Manipulation and Play in the Human Infant. *Monographs of the Society for Research in Child Development, 39* (Serial No. 155).

McCall, R. B. 1981b. Nature-nurture and the two realms of development: A proposed integration with respect to mental development. *Child Development, 52,* 1–12.

McDonald, T. J., and Nathanielsz, P. W. 1991. Bilateral destruction of the fetal paraventricular nuclei prolongs gestation in sheep. *American Journal of Obstetrics and Gynecology, 165,* 764–770.

McDonnell, P. M., Anderson, V. E. S., and Abraham, W. C. 1983. Asymmetry and orientation of arm movements in three- to eight-week-old infants. *Infant Behavior and Development, 6,* 287–298.

McGowan, J. S., Marsh, R. R., Fowler, S. M., Levy, S. E., and Stallings, V. A. 1991. Developmental patterns of normal nutritive sucking in infants. *Developmental Medicine and Child Neurology, 33,* 891–897.

McEwen, B. S. 1989. The role hormones acting on the brain play in linking nature and nurture. In Galaburda, A. M. (ed.), *From reading to neurons.* Cambridge, Mass.: MIT Press.

McGue, M., and Bouchard, T. J. 1989. Genetic and environmental determinants of information processing and special mental abilities: A twin analysis. In Sternberg, R. J. (ed.), *Advances in the psychology of human intelligence, 5,* 7–45.

McGurk, H., and MacDonald, J. 1976. Hearing lips and seeing voices. *Nature, 264*, 746–748.

McHenry, H. M. 1975. Biomechanical interpretation of the early hominid hip. *Journal of Human Evolution, 4*, 343–355.

McLuhan, M. 1964. *Understanding media*. London: Routledge and Kegan Paul.

Mead, M., and Hayman, K. 1965. *The family*. London: Macmillan.

Meadows, J. C. 1974. The anatomical basis of prosopagnosia. *Journal of Neurology, Neurosurgery, and Psychiatry, 37*, 489–501.

Mebert, C. J. 1983. Laterality in manipulatory and cognitive-related activity in four- to ten-month-olds. In Young, G., Segalowitz, S. J., Corter, C. M., and Trehub, S. E. (eds.), *Manual specialization and the developing brain*. New York: Academic Press.

Mehler, J. 1989. Language at the initial state. In Galaburda, A. M. (ed.), *From reading to neurons*. Cambridge, Mass.: MIT Press.

Mehler, J., Bertoncini, J., Barriere, M., and Jassik-Gerschenfeld, D. 1978. Infant recognition of mother's voice. *Perception, 7*, 491–497.

Mehler, J., Jusczyk, P., Lambertz, G., Halsted, N., Bertoncini, J. and Amiel-Tison, C. 1988. A precursor of language acquisition in young infants. *Cognition, 29*, 143–178.

Mehrabian, A., and Wiener, M. 1967. Decoding of inconsistent communications. *Journal of Personality and Social Psychology, 6*, 109–114.

Meier, G. W. 1965. Maternal behaviour of feral- and laboratory-reared monkeys following the surgical delivery of their infants. *Nature, 206*, 492–493.

Meier, G. W. 1975. Behavioral development viewed in terms of conspecific communication. In Ellis, N. R. (ed.), *Aberrant development in infancy: Human and animal studies*. Hillsdale, N.J.: Erlbaum.

Meier, R. P., and Newport, E. L. 1990. Out of the hands of babes: On a possible sign advantage in language acquisition. *Language, 66*, 1–23.

Meltzoff, A. N. 1986. Imitation, intermodal representation, and the origins of mind. In Lindblom, B., and Zetterstrom, R. (eds.), *Precursors of early speech*. New York: Stockton Press.

Meltzoff, A. N., and Borton, R. W. 1979. Intermodal matching by human neonates. *Nature, 282*, 403–404.

Meltzoff, A. N., and Gopnik, A. 1989. On linking nonverbal imitation, representation, and language learning in the first two years of life. In Speidel, G. E., and Nelson, K. E. (eds.), *The many faces of imitation in language learning*. New York: Springer-Verlag.

Meltzoff, A. N., and Moore, M. K. 1977. Imitation of facial and manual gestures by human neonates. *Science, 198*, 75–78.

Mendelson, M. J., Haith, M. M., and Goldman-Rakic, P. S. 1982. Face scanning and responsiveness to social cues in infant rhesus monkeys. *Developmental Psychology, 18*, 222–228.

Menzel, E. W. 1963. The effects of cumulative experience on responses to novel objects in young isolation-reared chimpanzees. *Behaviour, 21*, 1–12.

Meredith, M. A., and Stein, B. E. 1986. Visual, auditory, and somatosensory convergence on cells in superior colliculus results in multisensory integration. *Journal of Neurophysiology, 56*, 640–642.

Merzenich, M. M., Nelson, R. J., Stryker, M. P., Cynader, M. S., Schoppmann, A., and Zook, J. M. 1984. Somatosensory cortical map changes following digit amputation in adult monkeys. *Journal of Comparative Neurology, 224,* 591–605.

Messer, S. 1967. Implicit phonology in children. *Journal of Verbal Learning and Verbal Behavior, 6,* 609–613.

Messick, C. K. 1984. Phonetic and contextual aspects of the transition to early words. Ph.D. diss., Purdue University.

Mesulam, M.-M. 1990. Large-scale neurocognitive networks and distributed processing for attention, language, and memory. *Annals of Neurology, 28,* 597–613.

Michel, G. F., and Goodwin, R. 1979. Intrauterine birth position predicts newborn supine head position preferences. *Infant Behavior and Development, 2,* 29–38.

Michelsson, K. 1986. Cry analysis in clinical neonatal diagnosis. In Lindblom, B., and Zetterstrom, R. (eds.), *Precursors of early speech.* New York: Stockton Press.

Miller, C. L., Younger, B. A., and Morse, P. A. 1982. The categorization of male and female voices in infancy. *Infant Behavior and Development, 5,* 143–159.

Miller, G. A. 1965. Some preliminaries to psycholinguistics. *American Psychologist, 20,* 15–20.

Miller, G. A. 1990. The place of language in a scientific psychology. *Psychological Science, 1,* 7–14.

Miller, J. 1990. Communication without words. In Mellor, D. H. (ed.), *Ways of communicating.* New York: Cambridge University Press.

Mills, A. E. 1983. Acquisition of speech sounds in the visually-handicapped child. In Mills, A. E. (ed.), *Language acquisition in the blind child: Normal and deficient.* San Diego: College-Hill Press.

Mills, M., and Melhuish, E. 1974. Recognition of mother's voice in early infancy. *Nature, 252,* 123–124.

Milner, B. 1962. Laterality effects in audition. In Mountcastle, V. B. (ed.), *Interhemispheric relations and cerebral dominance.* Baltimore: Johns Hopkins Press.

Mittelmann, B. 1954. Motility in infants, children, and adults: Patterning and psychodynamics. *The Psychoanalytic Study of the Child 9,* 142–177.

Miyamoto, M. M., Koop, B. F., Slightom, J. L., Goodman, M., and Tennant, M. R. 1988. Molecular systematics of higher primates: Genealogical relations and classification. *Proceedings of the National Academy of Science, 85,* 7627–7631.

Molfese, D. L., Freeman, R. B., and Palermo, D. S. 1975. The ontogeny of brain lateralization for speech and nonspeech stimuli. *Brain and Language, 2,* 356–368.

Montagu, M. F. A. 1962. Time, morphology, and neoteny in the evolution of man. In Montagu, M. F. A. (ed.), *Culture and the evolution of man.* New York: Oxford University Press.

Moody, D. B., Stebbins, W. C., and May, B. J. 1990. Auditory perception of communication signals by Japanese monkeys. In Stebbins, W. C., and Berkley, M. A. (eds.), *Comparative perception*. Vol. 2. *Complex signals*. New York: John Wiley and Sons.

Moon, C., and Fifer, W. P. 1988. Newborn response to a male voice. Paper presented at the International Conference on Infant Studies, April 21–24, Washington, D.C.

Moon, C., and Fifer, W. P. 1990. Syllables as signals for 2-day-old infants. *Infant Behavior and Development, 13,* 377–390.

Moran, G., Krupka, A., Tutton, A., and Symons, D. 1987. Patterns of maternal and infant imitation during play. *Infant Behavior and Development, 10,* 477–491.

Morgan, J. L. 1986. *From simple input to complex grammar.* Cambridge, Mass.: MIT Press.

Morikawa, H., Shand, N., and Kosawa, Y. 1988. Maternal speech to prelingual infants in Japan and the United States: Relationships among functions, forms and referents. *Journal of Child Language, 15,* 237–256.

Morton, E. S. 1977. On the occurrence and signficance of motivation-structural rules in some bird and mammal sounds. *American Naturalist, 111,* 855–869.

Moses, P. J. 1954. *The voice of neurosis.* New York: Grune and Stratton.

Moskowitz, B. A. 1980. Idioms in phonology acquisition and phonological change. *Journal of Phonetics, 8,* 69–83.

Mount, R., Reznick, J. S., Kagan, J., Hiatt, S., and Szpak, M. 1989. Direction of gaze and emergence of speech in the second year. *Brain and Language, 36,* 406–410.

Mowrer, O. H. 1952. Speech development in the young child: 1. The autism theory of speech development and some clinical applications. *Journal of Speech and Hearing Disorders, 17,* 263–268.

Mowrer, O. H. 1960. *Learning theory and the learning process.* New York: John Wiley and Sons.

Moynihan, M. H. 1964. Some behavior patterns of platyrrhine monkeys. I. The night monkey *(Aotus trivargatus). Smithsonian Miscellaneous Collections, 146,* 1–84.

Muir, D., Abraham, W., Forbes, B., and Harris, L. 1979. The ontogenesis of an auditory localization response from birth to four months of age. *Canadian Journal of Psychology, 33,* 320–333.

Mulford, R. 1983. Referential development in blind children. In Mills, A. E. (ed.), *Language acquisition in the blind child: Normal and deficient.* London: Croom Helm.

Mulford, R. 1988. First words of the blind child. In Smith, M. D., and Locke, J. L. (eds.), *The emergent lexicon: The child's development of a linguistic vocabulary.* New York: Academic Press.

Mullennix, J. W., Pisoni, D. B., and Martin, C. S. 1989. Some effects of talker variability on spoken word recognition. *Journal of the Acoustical Society of America, 85,* 365–378.

Muller, E., Hollien, H., and Murry, T. 1974. Perceptual response to infant crying: Identification of cry types. *Journal of Child Language, 1,* 89–95.

Muller-Preuss, P. 1988. Neural correlates of audio-vocal behavior: Properties of anterior limbic cortex and related areas. In Newman, J. D. (ed.), *The physiological control of mammalian vocalization.* New York: Plenum Press.

Mundy, P., and Sigman, M. 1989. The theoretical implications of joint-attention deficits in autism. *Development and Psychopathology, 1,* 173–183.

Mundy, P., Sigman, M., and Kasari, C. 1990. A longitudinal study of joint attention and language development in autistic children. *Journal of Autism and Developmental Disorders, 20,* 115–128.

Munsinger, H., and Douglass, A. 1976. The syntactic abilities of identical twins, fraternal twins, and their siblings. *Child Development, 47,* 40–50.

Murphy, C. M. 1978. Pointing in the context of a shared activity. *Child Development, 49,* 371–380.

Murphy, C. M., and Messer, D. J. 1977. Mothers, infants and pointing: A study of gesture. In Schaffer, H. R. (ed.), *Studies in mother-infant interaction.* New York: Academic Press.

Murphy, K. P., and Smyth, C. N. 1962. Response of foetus to auditory stimulation. *Lancet, 5,* 972–973.

Murray, A. D. 1985. Aversiveness is in the mind of the beholder: Perception of infant crying by adults. In Lester, B. M., and Boukydis, C. F. Z. (eds.), *Infant crying: Theoretical and research perspectives.* New York: Plenum Press.

Murray, L., and Trevarthen, C. 1986. The infant's role in mother-infant communications. *Journal of Child Language, 13,* 15–29.

Myers, R. E. 1976. Comparative neurology of vocalization and speech: Proof of a dichotomy. *Annals of the New York Academy of Sciences, 280,* 745–757.

Nagel, T. 1974. What is it like to be a bat? *Philosophical Review, 83,* 435–450.

Nash, L. T., and Wheeler, R. L. 1982. In Firzgerald, H. E., Mullins, J. A., and Gage, P. (eds.), *Child nurturance.* Vol. 3. *Studies of development in non-human primates.* New York: Plenum Press.

Natale, M. 1975. Convergence of mean vocal intensity in dyadic communication as a function of social desirability. *Journal of Personality and Social Psychology, 32,* 790–804.

Neils, J. R., and Aram, D. M. 1986. Handedness and sex of children with developmental language disorders. *Brain and Language, 28,* 53–65.

Neisser, U. 1967. *Cognitive psychology.* New York: Appleton-Century-Crofts.

Nelson, C. A. 1987. The recognition of facial expressions in the first two years of life: Mechanisms of development. *Child Development, 58,* 889–909.

Nelson, K. 1973. Structure and strategy in learning to talk. *Monographs of the Society for Research in Child Development, 38,* 1–2 (Serial No. 149).

Nelson, K. 1981. Individual differences in language development: Implications for development and language. *Developmental Psychology, 17,* 170–187.

Nelson, K. 1985. *Making sense: The acquisition of shared meaning.* New York: Academic Press.

Neville, H. J. 1991. Neurobiology of cognitive and language processing: Effects of early experience. In Gibson, K., and Petersen, A. C. (eds.), *Brain matur-*

ation and behavioral development: Comparative and cross-cultural perspectives. New York: Aldine de Gruyter.

Neville, H. J., Schmidt, A., and Kutas, M. 1983. Altered visual-evoked potentials in congenitally deaf adults. *Brain Research, 266,* 127–132.

Newman, J. D. 1985. The infant cry of primates: An evolutionary perspective. In Lester, B. M., and Boukydis, C. F. Z. (eds.), *Infant crying: Theoretical and research perspectives.* New York: Plenum Press.

Newman, J. D., and Symmes, D. 1982. Inheritance and experience in the acquisition of primate acoustic behavior. In Snowdon, C. T., Brown, C. H., and Petersen, M. R. (eds.), *Primate communication.* New York: Cambridge University Press.

Newport, E. L. 1990. Maturational constraints on language learning. *Cognitive Science, 14,* 11–28.

Newport, E. L. 1991. Contrasting concepts of the critical period for language. In Carey, S., and Gelman, R. (eds.), *The epigenesis of mind: Essays on biology and cognition.* Hillsdale, N.J.: Erlbaum.

Newport, E., Gleitman, L., and Gleitman, H. 1977. Mother, I'd rather do it myself: Some effects and non-effects of maternal speech style. In Snow, C. E., and Ferguson, C. A. (eds.), *Talking to children: Language input and acquisition.* New York: Cambridge University Press.

Nicolson, N. A. 1991. Maternal behavior in human and nonhuman primates. In Loy, J. D., and Peters, C. B. (eds.), *Understanding behavior: What primate studies tell us about human behavior.* New York: Oxford University Press.

Nittrouer, S., Studdert-Kennedy, M., and McGowan, R. S. 1989. The emergence of phonetic segments: Evidence from the spectral structure of fricative-vowel syllables spoken by children and adults. *Journal of Speech and Hearing Research, 32,* 120–132.

Norman, D. A. 1981. Twelve issues for cognitive science. In Norman, D. A. (ed.), *Perspectives on cognitive science.* Hillsdale, N.J.: Erlbaum.

Nottebohm, F. 1975. A zoologist's view of some language phenomena with particular emphasis on vocal learning. In Gibson, K., and Petersen, A. C. (eds.), *Foundations of language development: A multidisciplinary approach,* Vol. 1. New York: Academic Press.

O'Gara, M. M., and Logemann, J. A. 1985. Phonetic analysis pre- and postpalatoplasty. Paper presented to the American Speech-Language-Hearing Association, Washington, D.C.

Ohala, J. J. 1978. Production of tone. In Fromkin, V. (ed), *Tone: A linguistic survey.* New York: Academic Press.

Ohala, J. J. 1980. The acoustic origin of the smile. Paper delivered to the Acoustical Society of America, Los Angeles, Calif., November.

Ojemann, G. A. 1984. Common cortical and thalamic mechanisms for language and motor functions. *American Journal of Physiology, 246* (Regulatory Integrative and Comparative Physiology 15), R901–R903.

Ojemann, G. A. 1991. Cortical organization of language. *Journal of Neuroscience, 11,* 2281–2287.

Olivos, G. 1967. Response delay, psychophysiologic activation, and recognition of one's own voice. *Psychosomatic Medicine, 29,* 433–440.

Oller, D. K. 1980. The emergence of sounds of speech in infancy. In Yeni-Komshian, G. H., Kavanagh, J. F., and Ferguson, C. A. (ed.), *Child phonology.* Vol. 1. *Production.* New York: Academic Press.

Oller, D. K. 1981. Infant vocalizations: Exploration and reflexivity. In Stark, R. (ed.), *Language behavior in infancy and early childhood.* New York: Elsevier/North Holland.

Oller, D. K. 1986. Metaphonology and infant vocalizations. In Lindblom, B., and Zetterstrom, R. (eds.), *Precursors of early speech.* New York: Stockton Press.

Oller, D. K., and Eilers, R. E. 1982. Similarity of babbling in Spanish- and English-learning babies. *Journal of Child Language, 9,* 565–577.

Oller, D. K., and Eilers, R. E. 1988. The role of audition in infant babbling. *Child Development, 59,* 441–449.

Oller, D. K., Eilers, R., Bull, D., and Carney, A. 1985. Prespeech vocalizations of a deaf infant: A comparison with normal metaphonological development. *Journal of Speech and Hearing Research, 28,* 47–63.

Oller, D. K., Wieman, L. A., Doyle, W. J., and Ross, C. 1976. Infant babbling and speech. *Journal of Child Language, 3,* 1–11.

Olney, R. L., and Scholnick, E. K. 1976. Adult judgments of age and linguistic differences in infant vocalization. *Journal of Child Language, 3,* 145–155.

Omenn, G. S., and Motulsky, A. G. 1972. Biochemical genetics and the evolution of human behavior. In Ehrman, L., Omenn, G. S., and Caspari, E. (eds.), *Genetics, environment, and behavior.* New York: Academic Press.

Orlansky, M. D., and Bonvillian, J. D. 1984. The role of iconicity in early sign language acquisition. *Journal of Speech and Hearing Disorders, 49,* 287–292.

Overman, W. H., and Doty, R. W. 1982. Hemisphere specialization displayed by man but not macaques for analysis of faces. *Neuropsychologia, 20,* 113–128.

Owren, M. J., Dieter, J. A., Seyfarth, R. M., and Cheney, D. L. 1990. Vocalizations of rhesus *Macaca mulatta* and Japanese *M. fuscata* macaques cross-fostered between species show evidence of only limited modification. Paper presented to the Thirteenth Annual Meeting of the American Society of Primatologists, Davis, Calif.

Oyama, S. 1976. A sensitive period for the acquisition of a non-native phonological system. *Journal of Psycholinguistic Research, 5,* 261–285.

Oyama, S. 1978. The sensitive period and comprehension of speech. *Working Papers on Bilingualism, 16,* 1–17.

Oyama, S. 1985. *The ontogeny of information: Developmental systems and evolution.* New York: Cambridge University Press.

Panneton, R. K., and DeCasper, A. J. 1984. Newborns prefer intrauterine heartbeat sounds to male voices. Poster presented at the International Conference for Infant Studies, New York.

Papousek, H., and Papousek, M. 1974. Mirror image and self-recognition in young human infants: I. A new method of experimental analysis. *Developmental Psychobiology, 7,* 149–157.

Papousek, H., and Papousek, M. 1975. Cognitive aspects of preverbal social interaction between human infants and adults. In *Parent-infant interaction* (CIBA Foundation Symposium 33). New York: Elsevier.

Papousek, H., and Papousek, M. 1977. Mothering and the cognitive head-start: Psychobiological considerations. In Schaffer, H. R. (ed.), *Studies in mother-infant interaction*. New York: Academic Press.

Papousek, H., and Papousek, M. 1984. Learning and cognition in the everyday life of human infants. *Advances in the Study of Behavior, 14,* 127–163.

Papousek, M., and Papousek, H. 1989. Forms and functions of vocal matching in interactions between mothers and their precanonical infants. *First Language, 9,* 137–158.

Papousek, M., and Papousek, H. 1991. Preverbal vocal communication from zero to one: Preparing the ground for language acquisition. In Lamb, M. E., and Keller, H. (eds.), *Perspectives on infant development: Contributions from German speaking countries*. Hillsdale, N.J.: Erlbaum.

Parker, S. T. 1990. Why big brains are so rare: Energy costs of intelligence and brain size in anthropoid primates. In Parker, S. T., and Gibson, K. R. (eds.), *"Language" and intelligence in monkeys and apes: Comparative developmental perspectives*. New York: Cambridge University Press.

Parker, S. T., and Gibson, K. R. (eds.) 1990. *"Language" and intelligence in monkeys and apes: Comparative developmental perspectives*. New York: Cambridge University Press.

Parkin, A. J., and Williamson, P. 1986. Patterns of cerebral dominance in wholistic and featural stages of facial processing. In Ellis, H. D., Jeeves, M. A., Newcombe, F., and Young, A. (eds.), *Aspects of face processing*. Boston: Martinus Nijhoff.

Parlour, S. F., and Broen, P. A. 1989. Familial risk for articulation disorder: A 25-year follow-up. Paper presented at the Nineteenth Annual meeting of the Behavior Genetics Association, Charlottesville, Va., June.

Parrott, W. G., and Gleitman, H. 1989. Infants' expectations in play: The joy of peek-a-boo. *Cognition and Emotion, 3,* 291–311.

Passingham, R. E. 1979. Specialization and the language areas. In Steklis, H. D., and Raleigh, M. J. (eds.), *Neurobiology of social communication in primates*. New York: Academic Press.

Pauls, M. D. 1947. Speechreading. In Davis, H., and Silverman, S. R. (eds.), *Hearing and deafness*. New York: Rinehart and Company.

Pawlby, S. J. 1977. Imitative interaction. In Schaffer, H. R. (ed.), *Studies in mother-infant interaction*. New York: Academic Press.

Pedersen, P. E., and Blass, E. M. 1981. Olfactory control over suckling in albino rats. In Aslin, R. N., Alberts, J. R., and Petersen, M. R. (eds.), *Development of perception*. Vol. 1. *Psychobiological perspectives*. New York: Academic Press.

Pennington, B. F., McCabe, L. L., Smith, S. D., Lefly, D., Bookman, M., Kimberling, W., and Lubs, H. 1986. Spelling errors in adults with a form of familial dyslexia. *Child Development, 57,* 1001–1013.

Pepperberg, I. M. 1990. Referential mapping: A technique for attaching functional significance to the innovative utterances of an African Grey parrot *(Psittacus erithacus)*. *Applied Psycholinguistics, 11,* 23–44.

Perrett, D. I., Harries, M. H., Mistlin, A. J., Hietanen, J. K., Benson, P. J., Bevan, R., Thomas, S., Oram, M. W., Ortega, J., and Brierley, K. 1990. Social signals analyzed at the single cell level: Someone is looking at me, something touched me, something moved! *International Journal of Comparative Psychology, 4,* 25–55.

Perrett, D. I., Mistlin, A. J., and Chitty, A. J. 1987. Visual neurones responsive to faces. *TINS, 10,* 358–364.

Perrett, D. I., Rolls, E. T., and Caan, W. 1982. Visual neurones responses to faces in the monkey temporal cortex. *Experimental Brain Research, 47,* 329–342.

Perrett, D. I., Smith, P. A. J., Potter, D. D., Mistlin, A. J., Head, A. S., Milner, A. D. and Jeeves, M. A. 1984. Neurones responsive to faces in the temporal cortex: Studies of functional organization, sensitivity to identity and relation to perception. *Human Neurobiology, 3,* 197–208.

Perrett, D. I., Smith, P. A. J., Potter, D. D., Mistlin, A. J., Head, A. S., Milner, A. D., and Jeeves, M. A. 1985. Visual cells in the temporal cortex sensitive to face view and gaze direction. *Proceedings of the Royal Society of London, B 223,* 293–317.

Peters, A. M. 1977. Language learning strategies: Does the whole equal the sum of the parts? *Language, 53,* 560–573.

Peters, A. M. 1983. *The units of language acquisition.* New York: Cambridge University Press.

Petersen, M. R., Beecher, M. D., Zoloth, S. R., Moody, D. B., and Stebbins, W. C. 1978. Neural lateralization of species-specific vocalizations by Japanese macaques *(Macaca fuscat)*. *Science, 202,* 324–327.

Petersen, M. R., Zoloth, S. R., Beecher, M. D., Green, S., Marler, P. R., Moody, D. B., and Stebbins, W. C. 1984. Neural lateralization of vocalizations by Japanese macaques: Communicative significance is more important than acoustic structure. *Behavioral Neuroscience, 98,* 779–790.

Peterson, G. E., and Barney, H. L. 1952. Control methods used in the study of vowels. *Journal of the Acoustical Society of America, 24,* 175–184.

Petrie, B. F., and Peters, M. 1980. Handedness: Left/right differences in intensity of grasp response and duration of rattle holding in infants. *Infant Behavior and Development, 3,* 215–221.

Petitto, L. A., and Marentette, P. F. 1991. Babbling in the manual mode: Evidence for the ontogeny of language. *Science, 251,* 1493–1496.

Piaget, J. 1962. *Play, dreams and imitation in childhood.* New York: Norton.

Piaget, J. 1972. The relation of affectivity to intelligence in the mental development of the child. In Harrison, S., and McDermott, J. (eds.), *Childhood psychopathology.* New York: International Universities Press.

Piatelli-Palmarini, M. 1989. Evolution, selection and cognition: From "learning" to parameter setting in biology and in the study of language. *Cognition, 31,* 1–44.

Piazza, D. M. 1977. Cerebral lateralization in young children as measured by dichotic listening and finger tapping tasks. *Neuropsychologia, 15*, 417–425.

Pinker, S. 1984. *Language learnability and language development.* Cambridge, Mass.: Harvard University Press.

Pinker, S. 1991. Rules of language. *Science, 253*, 530–535.

Pinker, S., and Bloom, P. 1990. Natural language and natural selection. *Behavioral and Brain Sciences, 13*, 707–784.

Piven, J., Berthier, M. L., Starkstein, S. E., Nehme, E., Pearlson, G., and Folstein, S. 1990. Magnetic resonance imaging evidence for a defect of cerebral cortical development in autism. *American Journal of Psychiatry, 147*, 734–739.

Plante, E. 1991. MRI findings in the parents and siblings of specifically language-impaired children. *Brain and Language, 41*, 67–80.

Plante, E., Swisher, L., and Vance, R. 1989. Anatomical correlates of normal and impaired language in a set of dizygotic twins. *Brain and Language, 37*, 643–655.

Plante, E., Swisher, L., Vance, R., and Rapcsak, S. 1991. MRI findings in boys with specific language impairment. *Brain and Language, 41*, 52–66.

Plomin, R., Corley, R., DeFries, J. C., and Fulker, D. W. 1990. Individual differences in television viewing in early childhood: Nature as well as nurture. *Psychological Science, 1*, 371–377.

Plomin, R., and Daniels, D. 1987. Why are children in the same family so different from one another? *Behavioral and Brain Sciences, 10*, 1–60.

Plomin, R., and Rowe, D. C. 1979. Genetic and environmental etiology of social behavior in infancy. *Developmental Psychology, 15*, 62–72.

Plomin, R., DeFries, J. C., and Loehlin, J. C. 1977. Genotype-environment interaction and correlation in the analysis of human behavior. *Psychological Bulletin, 84*, 309–322.

Ploog, D. 1979. Phonation, emotion, cognition, with reference to the brain mechanisms involved. *Brain and Mind* (CIBA Foundation Symposium 69), 79–98.

Ploog, D. 1988. An outline of human neuroethology. *Human Neurobiology, 6*, 227–238.

Plooij, F. 1979. How wild chimpanzee babies trigger the onset of mother-infant play—and what the mother makes of it. In Bullowa, M. (ed.), *Before speech: The beginnings of interpersonal communication.* Cambridge: Cambridge University Press.

Plooij, F. X. 1984. *The behavioral development of free-living chimpanzee babies and infants.* Norwood, N.J.: Ablex.

Pons, T. P., Garraghty, P. E., Ommaya, A. K., Kaas, J. H., Taub, E., and Mishkin, M. 1991. Massive cortical reorganization after sensory deafferentation in adult macaques. *Science, 252*, 1857–1860.

Poplack, S. 1980. Deletion and disambiguation in Puerto Rican Spanish. *Language, 56*, 371–385.

Porges, S. W. 1991. Vagal tone: A mediator of affect. In Garber, J., and Dodge,

K. A. (eds.), *The development of affect regulation and dysregulation.* New York: Cambridge University Press.

Porges, W. W., and Humphrey, M. M. 1977. Cardiac and respiratory responses during visual search in non-retarded children and retarded adolescents. *American Journal of Mental Deficiency, 82,* 162–169.

Porter, R. H., Balogh, R. D., and Makin, J. W. 1988. Olfactory influences on mother-infant interactions. In Rovee-Collier, C., and Lipsitt, L. P. (eds.), *Advances in infancy research.* Vol. 5. Norwood, N.J.: Ablex.

Porter, R. H., Cernoch, J. M., and Balogh, R. D. 1985. Odor signatures and kin recognition. *Physiology and Behavior, 34,* 445–448.

Porter, R. H., Makin, J. W., Davis, L. B., and Christensen, K. M. 1992. Breast-fed infants respond to olfactory cues from their own mother and unfamiliar lactating females. *Infant Behavior and Development, 15,* 85–94.

Poulson, C. L. 1988. Operant conditioning of vocalization rate of infants with Down syndrome. *American Journal of Mental Retardation, 93,* 57–63.

Powell, R. P., and Bishop, D. V. M. 1992. Clumsiness and perceptual problems in children with specific language impairment. *Developmental Medicine and Child Neurology, 34,* 755–765.

Prather, E. M., Hedrick, D. L., and Kern, C. A. 1975. Articulation development in children aged two to four years. *Journal of Speech and Hearing Disorders, 40,* 179–191.

Prechtl, H. F. R., Theorell, K., Gramsbergen, A., and Lind, J. 1969. A statistical analysis of cry patterns in normal and abnormal infants. *Developmental Medicine and Child Neurology, 11,* 142–152.

Premack, D. 1972. Two problems in cognition: Symbolization, and from icon to phoneme. In Alloway, T., Krames, L., and Pliner, P. (eds.), *Communication and affect: A comparative approach.* New York: Academic Press.

Premack, D. 1990. Words: What are they, and do animals have them? *Cognition, 37,* 197–212.

Premack, D., and Woodruff, G. 1978. Does the chimpanzee have a theory of mind. *Behavioral and Brain Sciences, 1,* 515–526.

Prescott, P. A., and DeCasper, A. J. In submission. Human perception of speech and nonspeech is functionally lateralized at birth.

Preston, M. S., Yeni-Komshian, G. H., Stark, R. E., and Port, D. K. 1969. Certain aspects of the development of speech production and perception in children. Paper presented at the 77th Meeting of the Acoustical Society of America, April.

Pribram, K. H. 1967. The new neurology and the biology of emotion: A structural approach. *American Psychologist, 22,* 830–838.

Prizant, B. 1992. Profiling communication and symbolic abilities in infants and toddlers. Neurolinguistics Laboratory Colloquium, MGH Institute of Health Professions, February.

Provine, R. R. 1989a. Contagious yawning and infant imitation. *Bulletin of the Psychonomic Society, 27,* 125–126.

Provine, R. R. 1989b. Faces as releasers of contagious yawning: An approach to face detection using normal human subjects. *Bulletin of the Psychonomic Society, 27,* 211–214.

Provins, K. A., Dalziel, F. R., and Higginbottom, G. 1987. Asymmetrical hand usage in infancy: An ethological approach. *Infant Behavior and Development, 10,* 165–172.

Purpura, D. 1975. Dendritic differentiation in human cerebral cortex: Normal and aberrant developmental patterns. In Kretzberg, G. (ed.), *Advances in neurology.* New York: Raven Press.

Querleu, D., and Renard, X. 1981. Les perceptions auditives du foetus humain. *Medecine et Hygiene, 39,* 2102–2110.

Querleu, D., Renard, X., and Crepin, G. 1981. Perception auditive et reactivite foetale aux stimulations sonores. *Journal de Gynecologie, Obstetrique et Biologie de la Reproduction, 10,* 307–314.

Querleu, D., Renard, X., and Versyp, F. 1985. Vie sensorielle du foetus. In Levy, G., and Tournaire, M. (eds.), *L'environnement de la naissance.* Paris: Vigot.

Rakic, P. 1989. Competitive interactions during neuronal and synaptic development. In Galaburda, A. M. (ed.), *From reading to neurons.* Cambridge, Mass.: MIT Press.

Ramey, C. T., and Ourth, L. L. 1971. Delayed reinforcement and vocalization rates of infants. *Child Development, 42,* 291–298.

Ramsay, D. S. 1984. Onset of duplicated syllable babbling and unimanual handedness in infancy: Evidence for developmental change in hemispheric specialization? *Developmental Psychology, 20,* 64–71.

Rasmussen, K. L. R., Fellowes, J. R., Byrne, E., and Suomi, S. J. 1988. Heart rate measures associated with early emigration in adolescent male rhesus macaques *(Macaca mulatta). American Journal of Primatology, 14,* 439 abstract.

Rauschecker, J. P. 1987. What signals are responsible for synaptic changes in visual cortical plasticity. In Rauschecker, J. P., and Marler, P. (eds.), *Imprinting and cortical plasticity: Comparative aspects of sensitive periods.* New York: John Wiley and Sons.

Rauschecker, J. P., and Marler, P. 1987. Cortical plasticity and imprinting: Behavioral and physiological contrasts and parallels. In Rauschecker, J. P., and Marler, P. (eds.), *Imprinting and cortical plasticity: Comparative aspects of sensitive periods.* New York: John Wiley and Sons.

Redican, W. K. 1975. Facial expressions in nonhuman primates. In Rosenblum, L. A. (ed.), *Primate behavior: Developments in field and laboratory research.* New York: Academic Press.

Reznick, J. S. 1989. Research on infant categorization. *Seminars in Perinatology, 13,* 458–466.

Reznick, J. S., and Goldfield, B. A. 1990. Rapid change in language acquisition during the second year: Naming explosion or knowing explosion? Unpublished manuscript.

Ricks, D. 1979. Making sense of experience to make sensible sounds. In Bullowa, M. (ed.), *Before speech: The beginning of interpersonal communication.* New York: Cambridge University Press.

Ritvo, E. R., Freeman, B. J., Mason-Brothers, A., Mo, A., and Ritvo, A. M. 1985. Concordance for the syndrome of autism in 40 pairs of afflicted twins. *American Journal of Psychiatry, 142,* 74–77.

Ritvo, E. R., Spence, M. A., Freeman, B. J., Mason-Brothers, A., Mo, A., and Marazita, M. L. 1985. Evidence for autosomal recessive inheritance in 46 families with multiple incidences of autism. *American Journal of Psychiatry, 142,* 187–192.

Rizzo, M., Hurtig, R., and Damasio, A. R. 1987. The role of scanpaths in facial recognition and learning. *Annals of Neurology, 22,* 41–45.

Roberts, K., and Horowitz, F. D. 1986. Basic level categorization in seven- and nine-month-old infants. *Journal of Child Development, 13,* 191–208.

Roe, A. W., Pallas, S. L., Kwon, Y. H., and Sur, M. 1990. Visually innervated auditory cortex in ferrets generates visual response properties similar to those in normal visual cortex. *Society for Neuroscience Abstracts, 16,* 984.

Roe, K. V. 1975. Amount of infant vocalization as a function of age: Some cognitive implications. *Child Development, 46,* 936–941.

Roe, K. V. 1978. Infants' mother-stranger discrimination at 3 months as a predictor of cognitive development at 3 and 5 years. *Developmental Psychology, 14,* 191–192.

Roe, K. V., McClure, A., and Roe, A. 1982. Vocal interaction at 3 months and cognitive skills at 12 years. *Developmental Psychology, 18,* 15–16.

Rose, R. J., Koskenvuo, M., Kaprio, S., Sarna, S., and Langinvainio, H. 1988. Shared genes, shared experiences, and similarity of personality: Data from 14,288 adult Finnish co-twins. *Journal of Personality and Social Psychology, 54,* 161–171.

Rosenblatt, J. S. 1975. Prepartum and postpartum regulation of maternal behavior in the rat. In *Parent-infant interaction* (CIBA Foundation Symposium 33). New York: Elsevier.

Rosenblum, L. A. 1978. Affective maturation and the mother-infant relationship. In Lewis, M., and Rosenblum, L. A. (eds.), *The development of affect.* New York: Plenum Press.

Rosenfeld, S. A., and Van Hoesen, G. W. 1979. Face recognition in the rhesus monkey. *Neuropsychologia, 17,* 503–509.

Rosenthal, M. K. 1982. Vocal dialogues in the neonatal period. *Developmental Psychology, 18,* 17–21.

Rosenzweig, M. R. 1971. Effects of environment on development of brain and of behavior. In Tobach, E., Aronson, L. R., and Shaw, E. (eds.), *The biopsychology of development.* New York: Academic Press.

Rosner, B. S., and Doherty, N. E. 1979. The response of neonates to intrauterine sounds. *Developmental Medicine and Child Neurology, 21,* 723–729.

Ross, E. D. 1981. The aprosodias: Functional-anatomic organization of the affective components of language in the right hemisphere. *Archives of Neurology, 38,* 561–569.

Ross, E. D., and Mesulam, M.-M. 1979. Dominant language functions of the right hemisphere? Prosody and emotional gesturing. *Archives of Neurology, 36,* 144–148.

Ross, G. S. 1983. Language functioning and speech development of six children receiving tracheostomy in infancy. *Journal of Communication Disorders, 15,* 95–111.

Routh, D. K. 1967. Conditioning of vocal response differentiation in infants. *Developmental Psychology, 1,* 219–226.

Ruhlen, M. 1976. *A Guide to Languages of the World.* Stanford, Calif: Language Universals Project, Stanford University.

Rumsey, J. M., Berman, K. F., Denkla, M. B., Hamburger, S. D., Kruesi, M. J., and Weinberger, D. R. 1987. Regional cerebral blood flow in severe developmental dyslexia. *Archives of Neurology, 44,* 1144–1150.

Rumsey, J. M., Dorwart, R., Vermess, M., Denkla, M. B., Kruesi, M. J. P., and Rapoport, J. L. 1986. Magnetic resonance imaging of brain anatomy in severe developmental dyslexia. *Archives of Neurology, 43,* 1045–1046.

Ryder, G. H. 1943. Vagitus uterinus. *American Journal of Obstetrics and Gynecology, 46,* 867–872.

Sacher, G. A. 1980. The role of brain maturation in the evolution of the primates. In Armstrong, E., and Falk, D. (eds.), *Primate brain evolution: Methods and concepts.* New York: Plenum Press.

Sacher, G. A., and Staffeldt, E. F. 1974. Relation of gestation time to brain weight for placental mammals: Implications for the theory of vertebrate growth. *American Naturalist, 108,* 593–615.

Sachs, J., Bard, B., and Johnson, M. L. 1981. Language learning with restricted input: Case studies of two hearing children of deaf parents. *Applied Psycholinguistics, 2,* 33–54.

Sackett, G. P. 1966. Monkeys reared in isolation with pictures as visual input: Evidence for an innate releasing mechanism. *Science, 154,* 1468–1473.

Sackett, G. P., Holm, R. A., and Landesman-Dwyer, S. 1975. Vulnerability for abnormal development: Pregnancy outcomes and sex differences in macaque monkeys. In Ellis, N. (ed.), *Aberrant development in infancy.* Hillsdale, N.J.: Erlbaum.

Sackett, G. P., and Ruppenthal, G. C. 1974. Some factors influencing the attraction of adult female macaque monkeys to neonates. In Lewis, M., and Rosenblum, L. A. (eds.), *The effect of the infant on its caregiver.* New York: John Wiley and Sons.

Sackett, G. P., Suomi, S. J., and Grady, S. 1970. Species preferences by macaque monkeys. Cited by Sackett, G. P. Unlearned responses, differential rearing experiences, and the development of social attachments by rhesus monkeys. In Rosenblum, L. A. (ed.), *Primate behavior.* Vol. 1. New York: Academic Press.

Safer, M. A., and Leventhal, H. 1977. Ear differences in evaluating emotional tones of voice and verbal content. *Journal of Experimental Psychology: Human Perception and Performance, 3,* 75–82.

Sagi, A., and Hoffman, M. L. 1976. Empathic distress in the newborn. *Developmental Psychology, 12,* 175–176.

Salk, L. 1962. Mothers' heartbeat as an imprinting stimulus. *Transactions of the New York Academy of Science, 24,* 753–763.

Salzen, E. A., and Cornell, J. M. 1968. Self-perception and species recognition in birds. *Behaviour, 30,* 44–65.

Sameroff, A. J. 1968. The components of sucking in the human newborn. *Journal of Experimental Child Psychology, 6,* 607–623.

Sameroff, A. J. 1973. Reflexive and operant aspects of sucking behavior in early infancy. In Bosma, J. F. (ed.), *Fourth symposium on oral sensation and perception: Development in the fetus and infant.* Bethesda, Md: DHEW Publication No. (NIH) 75–546.

Sameroff, A., and Chandler, M. 1975. Reproductive risk and the continuum of caretaking causality. In Horowitz, F., Hetherington, M., Scarr-Salapatek, S., and Siegel, G. (eds.), *Review of child development research.* Vol. 4. Chicago: University of Chicago Press.

Saudino, K. J., and Eaton, W. O. 1991. Infant temperament and genetics: An objective twin study of motor activity level. *Child Development, 62,* 1167–1174.

Savage-Rumbaugh, E. S. 1988. A new look at ape language: Comprehension of vocal speech and syntax. In Leger, D. (ed.), *Comparative perspective in modern psychology, Nebraska Symposium on Motivation, 35,* 201–256.

Savage-Rumbaugh, E. S. 1990. Language acquisition in a nonhuman species: Implications for the innateness debate. *Developmental Psychobiology, 23,* 599–620.

Saxby, L., and Bryden, M. P. 1984. Left-ear superiority in children for processing auditory emotional material. *Developmental Psychology, 20,* 72–80.

Scaife, M., and Bruner, J. S. 1975. The capacity for joint visual attention in the infant. *Nature, 253,* 265–266.

Scarborough, H. S. 1990. Very early language deficits in dyslexic children. *Child Development, 61,* 1728–1743.

Scarr, S. 1983. An evolutionary perspective on infant intelligence. In Lewis, M. (ed.), *Origins of intelligence: Infancy and early childhood.* New York: Plenum Press.

Scarr, S. 1992. Developmental theories for the 1990s: Development and individual differences. *Child Development, 63,* 1–19.

Scarr, S., and McCartney, K. 1983. How people make their own environments: A theory of genotype → environment effects. *Child Development, 54,* 424–435.

Schaffer, H. R., Collis, G. M., and Parsons, G. 1977. Vocal interchange and visual regard in verbal and pre-verbal children. In Schaffer, H. R. (ed.), *Studies in mother-infant interaction.* New York: Academic Press.

Scherer, K. 1979a. Acoustic concomitants of emotional dimensions: Judging affect from synthesized tone sequences. In Weitz, S. (ed.), *Nonverbal communication.* New York: Oxford University Press.

Scherer, K. R. 1979b. Nonlinguistic vocal indicators of emotion and psychopathology. In Izard, C. E. (ed.), *Emotion in personality and psychopathology.* New York: Plenum Press.

Schiff, N. 1979. The influence of deviant maternal input on the development of language during the preschool years. *Journal of Speech and Hearing Research, 22,* 581–603.

Schmahmann, J. D. 1991. An emerging concept: The cerebellar contribution to higher function. *Archives of Neurology, 48,* 1178–1187.

Schonen, S. de, Gil de Diaz, M., and Mathivet, E. 1986. Hemispheric asymmetry in face processing in infancy. In Ellis, H. D., Jeeves, M. A., Newcombe, F., and Young, A. (eds.), *Aspects of face processing.* Boston: Martinus Nijhoff.

Schwartz, M. L., and Goldman-Rakic, P. 1990. Development and plasticity of the primate cerebral cortex. *Clinics in Perinatology, 17,* 83–102.

Schwartz, R. G. 1988. Phonological factors in early lexical acquisition. In Smith, M. D. and Locke, J. L. (eds.), *The emergent lexicon: The child's development of a linguistic vocabulary.* New York: Academic Press.

Schwartz, R. G., and Leonard, L. B. 1982. Do children pick and choose: An examination of phonological selection and avoidance in early lexical acquisition. *Journal of Child Language, 9,* 319–336.

Scollon, R. 1976. *Conversations with a one year old.* Honolulu: University Press of Hawaii.

Scott, J. P. 1977. Social genetics. *Behavior Genetics, 7,* 327–346.

Segalowitz, S. J., and Chapman, J. S. 1980. Cerebral asymmetry for speech in neonates: A behavioral measure. *Brain and Language, 9,* 281–288.

Seligman, M. E. P. 1970. On the generality of laws of learning. *Psychological Review, 77,* 406–418.

Sergent, J., and Villemure, J.-G. 1989. Prosopagnosia in a right hemispherectomized patient. *Brain, 112,* 975–995.

Seyfarth, R. M., and Cheney, D. L. 1982. How monkeys see the world: A review of recent research on East African vervet monkeys. In Snowden, C. T., Brown, C. H., and Petersen, M. R. (eds.), *Primate communication.* New York: Cambridge University Press.

Seyfarth, R., and Cheney, D. 1986. Vocal development in vervet monkeys. *Animal Behaviour, 34,* 1640–1658.

Shannon, E. C., and Weaver, W. 1949. *The mathematical theory of communication.* Urbana: University of Illinois Press.

Shapiro, B. E., and Danly, M. 1985. The role of the right hemisphere in the control of speech prosody in propositional and affective contexts. *Brain and Language, 25,* 19–36.

Shatz, M. 1985. An evolutionary perspective on plasticity in language development: A commentary. *Merrill-Palmer Quarterly, 31,* 211–222.

Shaywitz, S. E., Escobar, M. D., Shaywitz, B. A., Fletcher, J. M., and Makuch, R. 1992. Evidence that dyslexia may represent the lower tail of a normal distribution of reading ability. *New England Journal of Medicine, 326,* 145–150.

Shaywitz, S. E., Shaywitz, B. A., Fletcher, J. M., Escobar, M. D. 1990. Prevalence of reading disability in boys and girls: Results of the Connecticut Longitudinal Study. *Journal of the American Medical Association, 264,* 998–1002.

Shepherd, J., Davies, G., and Ellis, H. 1981. Studies of cue saliency. In Davies, G., Ellis, H., and Shepherd, J. (eds.), *Perceiving and remembering faces.* New York: Academic Press.

Sherman, T. 1985. Categorization skills in infants. *Child Development, 56,* 1561–1573.

Sherrod, L. R. 1981. Issues in cognitive-perceptual development: The special case of social stimuli. In Lamb, M. E., and Sherrod, L. R. (ed.), *Infant social cognition: Empirical and theoretical considerations.* Hillsdale, N.J.: Erlbaum.

Shucard, D. W., Cummins, K. R., and McGee, M. G. 1984. Event-related brain potentials differentiate normal and disabled readers. *Brain and Language, 21,* 318–334.

Shultz, T. R., and Zigler, E. 1970. Emotional concomitants of visual mastery in infants: The effects of stimulus movement on smiling and vocalizing. *Journal of Experimental Child Psychology, 10,* 390–402.

Siegel, G. M., Cooper, M., Morgan, J. L., and Brenneise-Sarshad, R. 1990. Imitation of intonation by infants. *Journal of Speech and Hearing Research, 33,* 9–15.

Silva, P. A., Williams, S., and McGee, R. 1987. A longitudinal study of children with developmental language delay at age three: Later intelligence, reading and behaviour problems. *Developmental Medicine and Child Neurology, 29,* 630–640.

Simner, M. L. 1971. Newborn's response to the cry of another infant. *Developmental Psychology, 5,* 136–150.

Simon, B. M., Fowler, S. M., and Handler, S. D. 1983. Communication development in young children with long-term tracheostomies: Preliminary report. *International Journal of Pediatric Otorhinolaryngology, 6,* 37–50.

Simonds, R. J., and Scheibel, A. B. 1989. The postnatal development of the motor speech area: A preliminary study. *Brain and Language, 37,* 42–58.

Sinnott, J. M., Stebbins, W. C., and Moody, D. B. 1975. Regulation of voice amplitude by the monkey. *Journal of the Acoustical Society of America, 58,* 412–414.

Siqueland, E. R., and Lipsitt, L. P. 1966. Conditioned headturning behavior in newborns. *Journal of Experimental Child Psychology, 3,* 356–376.

Slobin, D. I. 1973. Cognitive prerequisites for the development of grammar. In Ferguson, C. A., and Slobin, D. I. (eds.), *Studies of child language development.* New York: Holt, Rinehart and Winston.

Small, M. 1986. Hemispheric differences in the evoked potential to face stimuli. In Ellis, H. D., Jeeves, M. A., Newcombe, F., and Young, A. (eds.), *Aspects of face processing.* Boston: Martinus Nijhoff.

Smith, B. L., Brown-Sweeney, S., and Stoel-Gammon, C. 1989. A quantitative analysis of reduplicated and variegated babbling. *First Language, 9,* 175–190.

Smith, B. L. and Oller, D. K. 1981. A comparative study of pre-meaningful vocalizations produced by normally developing and Down's syndrome infants. *Journal of Speech and Hearing Disorders, 46,* 46–51.

Smith, H. J., Newman, J. D., and Symmes, D. 1982. Vocal concomitants of affiliative behavior in squirrel monkeys. In Snowdon, C. T., Brown, C. H., and Petersen, M. R. (eds.), *Primate communication.* New York: Cambridge University Press.

Smith, M. D. 1988. The meaning of reference in emergent lexicons. In Smith, M. D., and Locke, J. L. (eds.), *The emergent lexicon: The child's development of a linguistic vocabulary.* New York: Academic Press.

Smotherman, W. P., and Robinson, S. R. 1988. The uterus as environment: The ecology of fetal behavior. In Blass, E. M. (ed.), *Handbook of behavioral neurobiology.* Vol. 9. *Developmental psychobiology and behavioral ecology.* New York: Plenum Press.

Snow, C. 1987. Relevance of the notion of a critical period to language acquisition. In Bornstein, M. H. (ed.), *Sensitive periods in development: Interdisciplinary perspectives.* Hillsdale, N.J.: Erlbaum.

Snow, C. E. 1989. Imitativeness: A trait or a skill? In Speidel, G. E., and Nelson, K. E. (eds.), *The many faces of imitation in language learning.* New York: Springer-Verlag.

Snow, C., and Hoefnagal-Hohle, M. 1978. The critical period for language acquisition: Evidence from second language learning. *Child Development, 49,* 1114–1128.

Snow, C. E., and Pan, B. A. 1993. Ways of analyzing the spontaneous speech of children with mental retardation: The value of cross-domain analyses. In Bray, N. (ed.), *International Review of Research in Mental Retardation.* New York: Academic Press.

Sodian, B., Taylor, C., Harris, P. L., and Perner, J. 1991. Early deception and the child's theory of mind: False trails and genuine markers. *Child Development, 62,* 468–483.

Speidel, G. E. 1989. A biological basis for individual differences in learning to speak. In Speidel, G. E., and Nelson, K. E. (eds.), *The many faces of imitation in language learning.* New York: Springer-Verlag.

Spelke, E. S., and Cortelyou, A. 1981. Perceptual aspects of social knowing: Looking and listening in infancy. *Infant social cognition: Empirical and theoretical considerations.* Hillsdale, N.J.: Erlbaum.

Spelke, E. S., and Owsley, C. J. 1979. Intermodal exploration and knowledge in infancy. *Infant Behavior and Development, 2,* 13–24.

Spence, M. J., and DeCasper, A. J. 1987. Prenatal experience with low-frequency maternal-voice sounds influence neonatal perception of maternal voice samples. *Infant Behavior and Development, 10,* 133–142.

Sperber, D., and Wilson, D. 1988. *Relevance: Communication and cognition.* Cambridge, Mass.: Harvard University Press.

Spiker, D., and Ricks, M. 1984. Visual self-recognition in autistic children: Developmental relationships. *Child Development, 55,* 214–225.

Spreen, O., and Gaddes, W. H. 1969. Developmental norms for 15 neuropsychological tests age 6 to 15. *Cortex, 5,* 170–191.

Sroufe, L. A. 1979. Socioemotional development. In Osofsky, J. D. (ed.), *Handbook of infant development.* New York: John Wiley and Sons.

Sroufe, L. A., and Waters, E. 1976. The ontogenesis of smiling and laughter: A perspective on the organization of development in infancy. *Psychological Review, 83,* 173–189.

Sroufe, L. A., and Wunsch, J. P. 1972. The development of laughter in the first year of life. *Child Development, 43,* 1326–1344.

Sroufe, L. A., Schork, E., Motti, F., Lawroski, N., and LaFreniere, P. 1984. The role of affect in social competence. In Izard, C. E., Kagan, J., and Zajonc, R. B. (eds.), *Emotions, cognition, and behavior*. New York: Cambridge University Press.

Stark, R. E. 1980. Stages of speech development in the first year of life. In Yeni-Komshian, G. H., Kavanagh, J. F., and Ferguson, C. A. (ed.), *Child phonology*. Vol. 1. *Production*. New York: Academic Press.

Stark, R. E., Tallal, P., Kallman, C., and Mellits, E. D. 1983. Cognitive abilities of language-delayed children. *Journal of Psychology, 114,* 9–19.

Stassen, H. H., Lykken, D. T., and Bomben, G. 1988. The within-pair EEG similarity of twins reared apart. *European Archives of Psychiatry and Neurological Sciences, 237,* 244–252.

Stebbins, S. 1990. Natural acts: Doing what we do when we talk. In Bekoff, M., and Jamieson, D. (ed.), *Interpretation and explanation in the study of animal behavior*. Vol. 1. *Interpretation, intentionality, and communication*. Boulder, Colo.: Westview Press.

Stechler, G., and Carpenter, G. 1973. A viewpoint on early affective development. In Harrison, S. I., and McDermott, J. F. (eds.), *Childhood psychopathology: An anthology of basic readings*. New York: International Universities Press.

Steklis, H. D., and Raleigh, M. J. 1979. Requisites for language: Interspecific and evolutionary aspects. In Steklis, H. D., and Raleigh, M. J. (eds.), *Neurobiology of social communication in primates*. New York: Academic Press.

Stein, B. E., Huneycutt, W. S., and Meredith, M. A. 1988. Neurons and behavior: The same rules of multisensory integration apply. *Brain Research, 448,* 355–358.

Stern, D. N. 1974. Mother and infant at play: The dyadic interaction involving facial, vocal, and gaze behaviors. In Lewis, M., and Rosenblum, L. A. (eds.), *The effect of the infant on its caregiver*. New York: John Wiley and Sons.

Stifter, C. A., Fox, N. A., and Porges, S. W. 1989. Facial expressivity and vagal tone in 5- and 10-month-old infants. *Infant Behavior and Development, 12,* 127–137.

Stoel-Gammon, C. 1983. Constraints on consonant-vowel sequences in early words. *Journal of Child Language, 10,* 455–457.

Stoel-Gammon, C. 1985. Phonetic inventories, 15–24 months: A longitudinal study. *Journal of Speech and Hearing Research, 28,* 505–512.

Stoel-Gammon, C. 1988. Prelinguistic vocalizations of hearing-impaired and normally hearing subjects: A comparison of consonantal inventories. *Journal of Speech and Hearing Disorders, 53,* 302–315.

Stoel-Gammon, C. 1989. Prespeech and early speech development of two late talkers. *First Language, 9,* 207–224.

Stoel-Gammon, C. 1990. Issues in phonological development and disorders. In Miller, J. (ed.), *Research on child language disorders: A decade of progress*. Austin, Tex.: Pro-Ed.

Stoel-Gammon, C., Burkardt, A., and Huffman, D. 1990. Individual differences in the phonology of first words. Eleventh Annual Child Phonology Conference, Madison, Wisc., May 30.

Stoel-Gammon, C., and Cooper, J. 1984. Patterns of early lexical and phonological development. *Journal of Child Language, 11,* 247–271.

Stoel-Gammon, C., and Herrington, P. B. 1990. Vowel systems of normally developing and phonologically disordered children. *Clinical Linguistics and Phonetics, 4,* 145–160.

Stoel-Gammon, C., and Otomo, K. 1986. Babbling development of hearing-impaired and normally hearing subjects. *Journal of Speech and Hearing Disorders, 51,* 33–41.

Strayer, J. 1987. Affective and cognitive perspectives on empathy. In Eisenberg, N., and Strayer, J. (eds.), *Empathy and its development.* New York: Cambridge University Press.

Street, R. L. 1982. Evaluation of noncontent speech accommodation. *Language and Communication, 2,* 13–31.

Street, R. L., Street, N. J., and Van Kleek, A. 1983. Speech convergence among talkative and reticent three-year-olds. *Language Sciences, 5,* 79–96.

Studdert-Kennedy, M. 1986. Sources of variability in early speech development. In Perkell, J. S., and Klatt, D. H. (eds.), *Invariance and variability in speech processes.* Hillsdale, N.J.: Erlbaum.

Studdert-Kennedy, M. 1991. Language development from an evolutionary perspective. In Krasnegor, N., Rumbaugh, D., Schiefelbusch, R., Studdert-Kennedy, M. (eds.), *Language acquisition: Biological and behavioral determinants.* Hillsdale, N.J.: Erlbaum.

Sullivan, J. W., and Horowitz, F. D. 1983. The effects of intonation on infant attention: The role of the rising contour. *Journal of Child Language, 10,* 521–534.

Summerfield, Q. 1979. Use of visual information for phonetic perception. *Phonetica, 36,* 314–331.

Suomi, S. J., Sackett, G. P., and Harlow, H. F. 1970. Development of sex preferences in rhesus monkeys. *Developmental Psychology, 3,* 326–336.

Super, C. M. 1991. Developmental transitions of cognitive functioning in rural Kenya and metropolitan America. In Gibson, K. R., and Petersen, A. C. (eds.), *Brain maturation and cognitive development: Comparative and cross-cultural perspectives.* New York: Aldine de Gruyter.

Sutton, D., Larson, C., and Lindeman, R. C. 1974. Neocortical and limbic lesion effects on primate phonation. *Brain Research, 71,* 61–75.

Sutton, D., Larson, C., Taylor, E. M., and Lindeman, R. C. 1973. Vocalization in rhesus monkeys: Conditionability. *Brain Research, 52,* 225–231.

Sutton, D., Samson, H. H., and Larson, C. R. 1978. Brain mechanisms in learned phonation of *Macaca mulatta.* In Chivers, D. J., and Herbert, J. (eds), *Recent advances in primatology.* London: Academic Press.

Sutton, D., Trachy, R. E., and Lindeman, R. C. 1981. Primate phonation: Unilateral and bilateral cingulate lesion effects. *Behavioural Brain Research, 3,* 99–114.

Suzuki, S., and Yamamuro, T. 1985. Fetal movement and fetal presentation. *Early Human Development, 11,* 255–263.

Sweeney, S. 1973. The importance of imitation in the early stages of speech acquisition: A case report. *Journal of Speech and Hearing Disorders, 38,* 490–494.

Swoboda, P., Morse, P., and Leavitt, L. 1976. Continuous vowel discrimination in normal and at-risk infants. *Child Development, 47,* 459–465.

Sykes, J. L. 1940. A study of the spontaneous vocalizations of young deaf children. *Psychological Monographs, 52,* 104–123.

Tager-Flusberg, H. 1992. Autistic children's talk about psychological states: Deficits in the early acquisition of a theory of mind. *Child Development, 63,* 161–172.

Tahta, S., Wood, M., and Loewenthal, K. 1981. Age changes in the ability to replicate foreign pronunciation and intonation. *Language and Speech, 24,* 363–372.

Takeda, R. 1965. Development of vocal communication in man-raised Japanese monkeys I. From birth until the sixth week. *Primates, 6,* 337–380.

Takeda, R. 1966. Development of vocal communication in man-raised Japanese monkeys II. From the 7th to the 30th week. *Primates, 7,* 73–116.

Tallal, P. 1976. Rapid auditory processing in normal and disordered language development. *Journal of Speech and Hearing Research, 19,* 561–571.

Tallal, P., and Piercy, M. 1975. Developmental aphasia: The perception of brief vowels and extended stop consonants. *Neuropsychologia, 13,* 69–74.

Tallal, P., Ross, R., and Curtiss, S. 1989. Familial aggregation in specific language impairment. *Journal of Speech and Hearing Disorders, 54,* 167–173.

Tallal, P., Stark, R., and Curtiss, B. 1976. Relation between speech perception and speech production impairment in children with developmental dysphasia. *Brain and Language, 3,* 305–317.

Tallal, P., and Stark, R. 1983. Perceptual prerequisites for language development. In Kirk, U. (ed.), *Neuropsychology of language, reading, and spelling.* New York: Academic Press.

Tallal, P., Stark, R., Kallman, C., and Mellits, D. 1981. A reexamination of some nonverbal perceptual abilities of language-impaired and normal children as a function of age and sensory modalities. *Journal of Speech and Hearing Research, 24,* 351–357.

Tallal, P., Townsend, J., Curtiss, S., and Wulfeck, B. 1991. Phenotypic profiles of language-impaired children based on genetic/family history. *Brain and Language, 41,* 81–95.

Tamis-Lemonda, C. S., and Bornstein, M. H. 1989. Habituation and maternal encouragement of attention in infancy as predictors of toddler language, play, and representational competence. *Child Development, 60,* 738–751.

Tanner, J. M. 1974. Variability of growth and maturity in newborn infants. In Lewis, M., and Rosenblum, L. A. (eds.), *The effect of the infant on its caregiver.* New York: John Wiley and Sons.

Tartter, V. C. 1980. Happy talk: Perceptual and acoustic effects of smiling on speech. *Perception and Psychophysics, 27,* 24–27.

Taub, E., Goldberg, I. A., and Taub, P. 1975. Deafferentation in monkeys: Pointing at a target without visual feedback. *Experimental Neurology, 46,* 178–186.

Telzrow, R. W., Campos, J. J., Shepherd, A., Bertenthal, B. I., and Atwater, S. 1987. Spatial understanding in infants with motor handicaps. In Jaffe, K. (ed.), *Childhood powered mobility: Developmental, technical, and clinical perspectives*. Washington, D.C.: RESNA.

Templin, M. C. 1957. *Certain language skills in children*. Minneapolis: University of Minnesota Press.

Terrace, H. S. 1979. *Nim: A chimpanzee who learned sign language*. New York: Columbia University Press.

Terrace, H. S., Petitto, L. A., Sanders, R. J., and Bever, T. G. 1979. Can an ape create a sentence? *Science, 206*, 891–902.

Thal, D. J., Marchman, V., Stiles, J., Aram, D., Trauner, D., Nass, R., and Bates, E. 1991. Early lexical development in children with focal brain injury. *Brain and Language, 40*, 491–527.

Thatcher, R. W., Walker, R. A., and Giudice, S. 1987. Human cerebral hemispheres develop at different rates and ages. *Science, 236*, 1110–1113.

Thelen, E. 1981. Rhythmical behavior in infancy: An ethological perspective. *Developmental Psychology, 17*, 237–257.

Thelen, E. 1985. Expression as action: A motor perspective of the transition from spontaneous to instrumental behaviors. In Zivin, G. (ed.), *The development of expressive behavior: Biology-environment interactions*. New York: Academic Press.

Thelen, E. 1991. Motor aspects of emergent speech: A dynamic approach. In Krasnegor, N., Rumbaugh, D., Studdert-Kennedy, M., and Schiefelbusch, R. (eds.), *Biological foundations of language*. Hillsdale, N.J.: Erlbaum.

Thelen, E., and Fogel, A. 1989. Toward an action-based theory of infant development. In Lockman, J., and Hazen, N. (eds.), *Action in a social context: Perspectives on early development*. New York: Plenum Press.

Thevenin, D., Eilers, R. E., Oller, D. K., and LaVoie, L. 1985. Where's the drift in babbling drift? A cross-linguistic study. *Applied Psycholinguistics, 6*, 3–15.

Thoden, C.-J., and Koivisto, M. 1980. Acoustic analyses of the normal pain cry. In Murry, T., and Murry, J. (eds.), *Infant communication: Cry and early speech*. Houston, Tex.: College-Hill Press.

Thompson, R., Cicchetti, D., Lamb, M., and Malkin, C. 1985. The emotional responses of Down syndrome and normal infants in the Strange Situation: The organization of affective behavior in infants. *Developmental Psychology, 21*, 828–841.

Thompson, R. A. 1987. Empathy and emotional understanding: The early development of empathy. In Eisenberg, N., and Strayer, J. (eds.), *Empathy and its development*. New York: Cambridge University Press.

Tiberghien, G., and Clerc, I. 1986. The cognitive locus of prosopagnosia. In Bruyer, R. (ed.), *The neuropsychology of face perception and facial expression*. Hillsdale, N.J.: Erlbaum.

Timney, B. N., Emerson, V. F., and Dodwell, P. C. 1979. Development of visual stimulus-seeking in kittens. *Quarterly Journal of Experimental Psychology, 31*, 63–81.

Tobach, E., and Schneirla, T. C. 1968. The biopsychology of social behavior of animals. In Cooke, R. E., and Levin, S. (eds.), *Biologic basis of pediatric practice*. New York: McGraw-Hill.

Todd, G. A., and Palmer, B. 1968. Social reinforcement of infant babbling. *Child Development, 39*, 591–596.

Tomasello, M. 1990. Cultural transmission in the tool use and communicatory signalling of chimpanzees? In Parker, S. T., and Gibson, K. R. (eds.), *"Language" and intelligence in monkeys and apes*. New York: Cambridge University Press.

Tomasello, M., and Farrar, M. J. 1986. Joint attention and early language. *Child Development, 57*, 1454–1463.

Tomasello, M., and Todd, J. 1983. Joint attention and lexical acquisition style. *First Language, 4*, 197–212.

Tomasello, M., Gust, D., and Frost, G. T. 1989. A longitudinal investigation of gestural communication in young chimpanzees. *Primates, 30*, 35–50.

Tomasello, M., Mannle, S., and Kruger, A. C. 1986. Linguistic environment of 1- to 2-year-old twins. *Developmental Psychology, 22*, 169–176.

Tomasello, M., George, B. L., Kruger, A. C., Farrar, M. J., and Evans, A. 1985. The development of gestural communication in young chimpanzees. *Journal of Human Evolution, 14*, 175–186.

Tomasello, M., Davis-Dasilva, M., Camak, L., and Bard, K. 1987. Observational learning of tool-use by young chimpanzees. *Human Evolution, 2*, 175–183.

Tomblin, J. B. 1989. Familial concentration of developmental language impairment. *Journal of Speech and Hearing Research, 54*, 287–295.

Tomblin, J. B. 1991. Examining the cause of specific language impairment. *Language, Speech, and Hearing Services in Schools, 22*, 66–68.

Tooby, J., and Cosmides, L. 1988. Can non-universal mental organs evolve? Constraints from genetics, adaptation, and the evolution of sex. *Institute for Evolutionary Studies Technical Report 88–2*.

Trachy, R. E., Sutton, D., and Lindeman, R. C. 1981. Primate phonation: Anterior cingulate lesion effects on response rate and acoustical structure. *American Journal of Primatology, 1*, 43–55.

Tranel, D., and Damasio, A. R. 1985. Knowledge without awareness: An autonomic index of facial recognition by prosopagnosics. *Science, 228*, 1453–1454.

Tranel, D., and Damasio, A. R. 1988. Non-conscious face recognition in patients with face agnosia. *Behavioural Brain Research, 30*, 235–249.

Tranel, D., Damasio, A. R., and Damasio, H. 1988. Intact recognition of facial expression, gender, and age in patients with impaired recognition of face identity. *Neurology, 38*, 690–696.

Trauner, D. A., Bellugi, U., and Chase, C. 1989. Neurologic features of Williams and Down syndromes. *Pediatric Neurology, 5*, 166–168.

Tronick, E. Z., Als, H., and Adamson, L. 1979. Structure of early face-to-face interactions. In Bullowa, M. (ed.), *Before speech: The beginnings of interpersonal communication*. Cambridge: Cambridge University Press.

Tronick, E., Als, H., Adamson, L., Wise, S., and Brazelton, T. B. 1978. The infant's response to entrapment between contradictory messages in face-to-face interaction. *Journal of the American Academy of Child Psychiatry, 17,* 1–13.

Tuaycharoen, P. 1977. The phonetic and phonological development of a Thai baby: From early communicative interaction to speech. Ph.D. diss., University of London.

Tucker, D. M. 1992. Developing emotions and cortical networks. In Gunnar, M. R., and Nelson, C. A. (eds.), *Developmental behavioral neuroscience.* The Minnesota Symposia on Child Psychology, vol. 24. Hillsdale, N.J.: Erlbaum.

Tucker, H. M., Rusnov, M., and Cohen, L. 1982. Speech development in aphonic children. *Laryngoscope, 92,* 566–568.

Tulkin, S. R. 1973. Social class differences in infants' reactions to mother's and stranger's voices. *Developmental Psychology, 8,* 137.

Turkewitz, G., and Creighton, S. 1974. Changes in lateral differentiation of head posture in the human neonate. *Developmental Psychobiology, 8,* 85–89.

Turner, S., and Macfarlane, A. 1978. Localisation of human speech by the newborn baby and the effects of pethidine ('meperidine'). *Developmental Medicine and Child Neurology, 20,* 727–734.

UCLA Phonological Segment Inventory Database: Data and Index. 1981. *UCLA Working Papers in Phonetics, 53,* 1–242.

Udwin, O., and Yule, W. 1990. Expressive language of children with Williams syndrome. *American Journal of Medical Genetics, Supplement 6,* 108–114.

Ulvund, S. E. 1980. Cognition and motivation in early infancy: An interactionist approach. *Human Development, 23,* 17–32.

Uzgiris, I. C., Benson, J. B., Kruper, J. C., and Vasek, M. E. 1989. Contextual influences on imitative interactions between mothers and infants. In Lockman, J., and Hazen, N. (eds.), *Action in a social context: Perspectives on early development.* New York: Plenum Press.

van der Knapp, M. S., Valk, J., Bakker, C. J., Schooneveld, M., Faber, J. A. J., Willemse, J., and Gooskens, R. H. J. M. 1991. Myelination as an expression of the functional maturity of the brain. *Developmental Medicine and Child Neurology, 33,* 849–857.

van der Stelt, J. M., and Koopmans-van Beinum, F. J. 1986. The onset of babbling related to gross motor development. In Lindblom, B., and Zetterstrom, R. (eds.), *Precursors of early speech.* New York: Stockton Press.

Van Lancker, D. 1991. Personal relevance and the human right hemisphere. *Brain and Cognition, 17,* 64–92.

Van Lancker, D. R., and Canter, G. J. 1982. Impairment of voice and face recognition in patients with hemispheric damage. *Brain and Cognition, 1,* 185–195.

Van Lancker, D., Cornelius, C., and Kreiman, J. 1989. Recognition of emotional-prosodic meanings in speech by autistic, schizophrenic, and normal children. *Developmental Neuropsychology, 5,* 207–226.

Van Lancker, D., Kreiman, J., and Emmorey, K. 1985. Familiar voice recognition: Patterns and parameters. Part I: Recognition of backward voices. *Journal of Phonetics, 13,* 19–38.

Van Lancker, D., Kreiman, J., and Wickens, T. D. 1985. Familiar voice recognition: Patterns and parameters. Part II: Recognition of rate-altered voices. *Journal of Phonetics, 13,* 39–52.

Van Lancker, D. R., Cummings, J. L., Kreiman, J., and Dobkin, B. H. 1988. Phonagnosia: A dissociation between familiar and unfamiliar voices. *Cortex, 24,* 195–209.

van Lawick-Goodall, J. 1967. Mother-offspring relationships in free-ranging chimpanzees. In Morris, D. (ed.), *Primate ethology.* London: Weidenfeld and Nicolson.

Vellutino, F. R. 1979. *Dyslexia: Theory and research.* Cambridge, Mass.: MIT Press.

Veneziano, E. 1988. Vocal-verbal interaction and the construction of early lexical knowledge. In Smith, M. D., and Locke, J. L. (eds.), *The emergent lexicon: The child's development of a linguistic vocabulary.* New York: Academic Press.

Vihman, M. M. 1978. Consonant harmony: its scope and function in child language. In Greenberg, J. H. (ed.), *Universals of human language.* Stanford: Stanford University Press.

Vihman, M. M. 1981. Phonology and the development of the lexicon: evidence from children's errors. *Journal of Child Language, 8,* 239–264.

Vihman, M. M. 1986. Individual differences in babbling and early speech: Predicting to age three. In Lindblom, B., and Zetterstrom, R. (eds.), *Precursors of early speech.* New York: Stockton Press.

Vihman, M. M., and Miller, R. 1988. Words and babble at the threshold of language acquisition. In Smith, M. D., and Locke, J. L. (eds.), *The emergent lexicon: The child's development of a linguistic vocabulary.* New York: Academic Press.

Vihman, M. M., Ferguson, C. A., and Elbert, M. 1986. Phonological development from babbling to speech: Common tendencies and individual differences. *Applied Psycholinguistics, 7,* 3–40.

Vihman, M. M., Macken, M. A., Miller, R., Simmons, H., and Miller, J. 1985. From babbling to speech: A reassessment of the continuity issue. *Language, 61,* 397–446.

Vince, M. A. 1979. Postnatal effects of prenatal sound stimulation in the guinea pig. *Animal Behavior, 27,* 908–918.

Vince, M. A., Billing, A. E., Baldwin, B. A., Toner, J. N., and Weller, C. 1985. Maternal vocalizations and other sounds in the fetal lamb's sound environment. *Early Human Development, 11,* 179–190.

Visalberghi, E., and Fragaszy, D. M. 1990. Do monkeys ape? In Parker, S. T., and Gibson, K. R. (eds.), *"Language" and intelligence in monkeys and apes: Comparative developmental perspectives.* New York: Cambridge University Press.

Vogler, G. P., DeFries, J. C., and Decker, S. N. 1984. Family history as an indicator of risk for reading disability. *Journal of Learning Disabilities, 17,* 616–618.

von Holst, E. 1954. Relations between the central nervous system and the peripheral organs. *British Journal of Animal Behavior, 2,* 89–94.

Vygotsky, L. S. 1981. The development of higher forms of attention in childhood. In Wertsch, J. V. (ed.), *The concept of activity in Soviet psychology.* Armonk, N.Y.: M. E. Sharpe.

Waddington, C. H. 1940. *Organisers and genes.* Cambridge: Cambridge University Press.

Waddington, C. H. 1975. *The evolution of an evolutionist.* Ithaca: Cornell University Press.

Wagner, R., and Torgeson, J. 1987. The nature of phonological processing and its causal role in the acquisition of reading skills. *Psychological Review, 101,* 192–212.

Wahler, R. G. 1969. Infant social development: Some experimental analyses of an infant-mother interaction during the first year of life. *Journal of Experimental Child Psychology, 7,* 101–113.

Walker, A. S. 1982. Intermodal perception of expressive behaviors by human infants. *Journal of Experimental Child Psychology, 33,* 514–535.

Walker-Andrews, A. S., and Grolnick, W. 1983. Discrimination of vocal expressions by young infants. *Infant Behavior and Development, 6,* 491–498.

Walker, D., Grimwade, J., and Wood, C. 1971. Intrauterine noise: A component of the fetal environment. *American Journal of Obstetrics and Gynecology, 109,* 91–95.

Walker-Smith, G. J., Gale, A. G., and Findlay, J. M. 1977. Eye movement strategies involved in face perception. *Perception, 6,* 313–326.

Waller, N. G., Kojetin, B. A., Bouchard, T. J., Lykken, D. T., and Tellegen, A. 1990. Genetic and environmental influences on religious interests, attitudes, and values: A study of twins reared apart and together. *Psychological Science, 1,* 138–142.

Walley, A. C., Pisoni, D. B., and Aslin, R. N. 1981. The role of early experience in the development of speech perception. In Aslin, R. N., Alberts, J., and Peterson, M. J. (eds.), *The development of perception: Psychobiological perspectives.* New York: Academic Press.

Walsh, C., and Cepko, C. L. 1992. Widespread dispersion of neuronal clones across functional regions of the cerebral cortex. *Science, 255,* 434–440.

Waser, P. M. 1977. Individual recognition, intragroup cohesion and intergroup spacing: Evidence from sound playback to forest monkeys. *Behaviour, 60,* 28–74.

Washburn, S. L. 1960. Tools and human evolution. *Scientific American, 203,* 63–75.

Waterson, N. 1971. Child phonology: A prosodic view. *Journal of Linguistics, 7,* 179–211.

Waterson, N. 1978. Growth of complexity in phonological development. In

Waterson, N., and Snow, C. (eds.), *The development of communication.* New York: Wiley.

Watson, J. S. 1972. Smiling, cooing and "the game." *Merrill-Palmer Quarterly, 18,* 323–339.

Watson, M. W., and Fischer, K. W. 1977. A developmental sequence of agent use in late infancy. *Child Development, 48,* 828–832.

Waxman, S. R., and Kosowski, T. D. 1990. Nouns mark category relations: Toddlers' and preschoolers' word-learning biases. *Child Development, 61,* 1461–1473.

Weaver, D. R., and Reppert, S. M. 1989. Direct in utero perception of light by the mammalian fetus. *Developmental Brain Research, 47,* 151–155.

Webster, R. L. 1969. Selective suppression of infants' vocal responses by classes of phonemic stimulation. *Developmental Psychology, 1,* 410–414.

Wedenberg, E. 1965. Prenatal tests of hearing. *Acta Oto-Laryngology, 206,* 27–32.

Weinshilbaum, R., Thoa, N., Johnson, D., Kopin, I., and Axelord, J. 1971. Proportional release of norepinephrine and dopamine-beta-hydroxylase from sympathetic nerves. *Science, 174,* 1349–1351.

Weeks, S. J., and Hobson, R. P. 1987. The salience of facial expression for autistic children. *Journal of Child Psychology and Psychiatry, 28,* 137–152.

Welker, W. I. 1971. Ontogeny of play and exploratory behaviors: A definition of problems and a search for new conceptual solutions. In Moltz, H. (ed.), *The ontogeny of vertebrate behavior.* New York: Academic Press.

Werker, J. F., and Pegg, J. E. 1992. Infant speech perception and phonological acquisition. In Ferguson, C., Menn, L., and Stoel-Gammon, C. (eds). *Phonological development: Models, research, implications.* Parkton, Md.: York Press.

West, M. J., and King, A. P. 1988a. Coming to terms with the everyday language of comparative psychology. In Leger, D. (ed.), *Nebraska Symposium on Motivation, 35,* 51–89. Lincoln: University of Nebraska Press.

West, M. J., and King, A. P. 1988b. Female visual displays affect the development of male song in the cowbird. *Nature, 334,* 244–246.

West, M. J., King, A. P., and Duff, M. A. 1990. Communicating about communicating: When innate is not enough. *Developmental Psychobiology, 23,* 585–598.

Whalen, D., and Liberman, A. 1987. Speech perception takes precedence over nonspeech perception. *Science, 237,* 169–171.

White, B. L., and Held, R. 1966. Plasticity of sensorimotor development in the human infant. In Rosenblith, J. F., and Allinsmith, W. (eds.), *The causes of behavior: Readings in child development and educational psychology.* Boston: Allyn and Bacon.

White, N., and Kinsbourne, M. 1980. Does speech output control lateralize over time? Evidence from verbal-manual time-sharing tasks. *Brain and Language, 10,* 215–223.

White, R. W. 1959. Motivation reconsidered: The concept of competence. *Psychological Review, 66,* 297–333.

Whitehurst, G. J., Smith, M., Fischel, J. E., Arnold, D. S., and Lonigan, C. J. 1991. The continuity of babble and speech in children with specific language delay. *Journal of Speech and Hearing Research, 34,* 1121–1129.

Whiteley, A. M., and Warrington, E. K. 1977. Prosopagnosia: A clinical, psychological, and anatomical study of three patients. *Journal of Neurology, Neurosurgery, and Psychiatry, 40,* 395–403.

Whiten, A. 1977. Assessing the effects of perinatal events on the success of the mother-infant relationship. In Schaffer, H. R. (ed.), *Studies in mother-infant interaction.* New York: Academic Press.

Whiten, A., and Byrne, R. W. 1988. Tactical deception in primates. *Behavioral and Brain Sciences, 11,* 233–244.

Whorf, B. L. 1940. Science and linguistics. *Technological Review, 42,* 207–219.

Wiegerink, R., Harris, C., Simeonsson, R., and Pearson, M. E. 1974. Social stimulation of vocalizations in delayed infants: Familiar and novel agent. *Child Development, 45,* 866–872.

Wiesel, T. N., and Hubel, D. H. 1963. Effects of visual deprivation on morphology and physiology of cells in the cat's lateral geniculate body. *Journal of Neurophysiology, 26,* 978–993.

Wilcox, B. M., and Clayton, F. L. 1968. Infant visual fixation on motion pictures of the human face. *Journal of Experimental Child Psychology, 6,* 22–32.

Williams, C. E., and Stevens, K. N. 1972. Emotions and speech: Some acoustical correlates. *Journal of the Acoustical Society of America, 52,* 1238–1250.

Wimer, C., 1990. Genetic studies of brain development. In Hahn, M. E., Hewitt, J. K., Henderson, N. D., and Benno, R. H. (eds.), *Developmental behavior genetics: Neural, biometrical, and evolutionary approaches.* New York: Oxford University Press.

Winnega, M., and Berkson, G. 1986. Analyzing the stimulus properties of objects used in stereotyped behavior. *American Journal of Mental Deficiency, 91,* 277–285.

Witelson, S. F., and Pallie, W. 1973. Left hemisphere specialization for language in the newborn. Neuroanatomical evidence of asymmetry. *Brain, 96,* 641–646.

Wittgenstein, L. 1980. *Remarks on the philosophy of psychology.* Oxford: Blackwell.

Wolf, J. J. 1972. Efficient parameters for speaker recognition. *Journal of the Acoustical Society of America, 51,* 2044–2056.

Wolff, A. B., and Thatcher, R. W. 1990. Cortical reorganization in deaf children. *Journal of Clinical and Experimental Neuropsychology, 12,* 209–221.

Wolff, P. H. 1969. The natural history of crying and other vocalization in early infancy. In Foss, B. M. (ed.), *Determinants of infant behaviour.* Vol. 4. London: Methuen.

Wolff, P. H. 1971. Mother-infant relations at birth. In Howells, J. C. (ed.), *Modern perspectives in international psychiatry.* New York: Brunner/Mazel.

Wollberg, Z., and Newman, J. D. 1972. Auditory cortex of squirrel monkey: Response patterns of single cells to species-specific vocalizations. *Science, 175,* 212–214.

Wood, C. C., Goff, W. R., and Day, R. S. 1971. Auditory evoked potentials during speech perception. *Science, 173,* 1248–1251.

Wu, H. M. H., Holmes, W. G., Medina, S. R., and Sackett, G. P. 1980. Kin preference in infant *Macaca nemestrina. Nature, 285,* 225–227.

Yakovlev, P. L., and Lecours, A. R. 1967. The myelogenetic cycles of regional maturation of the brain. In Minkowski, A. (ed.), *Regional development of the brain in early life.* Oxford: Blackwell.

Yamane, S., Kaji, S., and Kawano, K. 1988. What facial features activate face neurons in the inferotemporal cortex of the monkey? *Experimental Brain Research, 73,* 209–214.

Yarrow, L. J., and Messer, D. J. 1976. Motivation and cognition in infancy. Species patterns and individual variations. In Lewis, M. (ed.), *Origins of intelligence: Infancy and early childhood.* New York: Plenum Press.

Yates, C., Simpson, J., Maloney, A., Gorden, A., and Reid, A. 1980. Alzheimer-like cholinergic deficiency in Down's syndrome. *Lancet, i,* 979.

Yeni-Komshian, G. H., and Benson, D. A. 1976. Anatomical study of cerebral asymmetry in the temporal lobe of humans, chimpanzees, and rhesus monkeys. *Science, 192,* 387–389.

Yirmiya, N., Sigman, M. D., Kasari, C., and Mundy, P. 1992. Empathy and cognition in high-functioning children with autism. *Child Development, 63,* 150–160.

Young, A. W., and Bion, P. J. 1980. Absence of any developmental trend in right hemisphere superiority for face recognition. *Cortex, 16,* 213–221.

Young, G., and Decarie, T. G. 1977. An ethology-based catalogue of facial-vocal behavior in infancy. *Animal Behaviour, 25,* 95–107.

Young, A. W., and Ellis, H. D. 1976. An experimental investigation of developmental differences in ability to recognize faces presented to the left and right cerebral hemispheres. *Neuropsychologia, 14,* 495–498.

Zahn-Waxler, C., and Radke-Yarrow, M. 1982. The development of altruism: Alternative research strategies. In Eisenberg, N. (ed.), *The development of prosocial behavior.* New York: Academic Press.

Zeskind, P. S., and Collins, V. 1987. Pitch of infant crying and caregiver responses in a natural setting. *Infant Behavior and Development, 10,* 501–504.

Zigler, E. 1973. Motivational factors in the performance of the retarded child. In Richardson, F. (ed.), *Brain and intelligence: The ecology of child development.* Hyattsville, Md.: National Educational Press.

Zigler, E., Levine, J., and Gould, L. 1966. The humor response of normal, institutionalized retarded, and noninstitutionalized retarded children. *American Journal of Mental Deficiency, 71,* 472–480.

Zinober, B., and Martlew, M. 1985. Developmental changes in four types of gesture in relation to acts and vocalizations from 10 to 21 months. *British Journal of Developmental Psychology, 3,* 293–306.

Zipf, G. K. 1932. *Selected studies of the principle of relative frequency in language.* Cambridge, Mass.: Harvard University Press.

Zipf, G. K. 1949. *Human behavior and the principle of least effort.* New York: Hafner.

Zurif, E. 1974. Auditory lateralization: Prosodic and syntactic factors. *Brain and Language, 1,* 391–404.

Zurif, E., and Mendelsohn, M. 1972. Hemispheric specialization for the perception of speech sounds: The influence of intonation and structure. *Perception and Psychophysics, 11,* 329–332.

CREDITS

Figure 2.1. From D. Querleu, X. Renard, and G. Crepin, "Perception auditive et reactivite foetale aux stimulations sonores," *Journal de Gyncologie, Obstetrique et Biologie de la Reproduction* 10 (1981): 307–314.

Figure 2.2. From S. Benzaquen et al., "The interuterine sound environment of the human fetus during labor," *American Journal of Obstetrics and Gynecology* 163 (1990): 484–490.

Figure 2.3. From B. Z. Friedlander, "The effect of speaker identity, voice inflection, vocabulary, and message redundancy on infants' selection of vocal reinforcement," *Journal of Experimental Child Psychology* 6 (1968): 443–459.

Figure 2.4. From C. C. Goren, M. Sarty, and P. Y. K. Wu, "Visual following and pattern discrimination of face-like stimuli by newborn infants," *Pediatrics* 56 (1975): 544–549. Reproduced by permission of *Pediatrics*, vol. 56, page 544, copyright 1975.

Figure 2.5. From A. N. Meltzoff and M. K. Moore, "Imitation of facial and manual gestures by human neonates," *Science* 198 (1977): 75–78. Copyright © 1977 by the AAAS.

Figure 2.8. From S. Carey and R. Diamond, "Maturational determination of the developmental course of face encoding," in D. Caplan, ed., *Biological Studies of Mental Processes* (Cambridge, Mass.: MIT Press, 1980).

Figure 2.10. From V. A. Mann, R. Diamond, and S. Carey, "Development of voice recognition: Parallels with face recognition," *Journal of Experimental Child Psychology* 27 (1979): 153–165.

Figure 2.11. From S. Tahta, M. Wood, and K. Lowenthal, "Age changes in the ability to replicate foreign pronunciation and intonation," *Language and Speech* 24 (1981): 363–372.

Figure 2.13. From A. M. Liberman, "The grammars of speech and language," *Cognitive Psychology* 1 (1970): 301–323.

Figure 3.3. From K. Kaye, *The Mental and Social Life of Babies: How Parents Create Persons* (Chicago: University of Chicago Press, 1982).

Figure 3.4. From K. Kaye and A. Wells, "Mothers' jiggling and the burst-pause pattern in neonatal sucking," *Infant Behavior and Development* 3 (1980): 29–46.

Figure 3.5. From J. Berger and C. C. Cunningham, "Development of early vocal behaviors and interactions in Down's syndrome and nonhandicapped infant-mother pairs," *Developmental Psychology* 19 (1983): 322–331. Copyright © 1983 by the American Psychological Association. Reprinted by permission.

Figure 4.1. From J. B. Delack, "Aspects of infant speech development in the first year of life," *Canadian Journal of Linguistics* 21 (1976): 17–37.

Figure 4.2. Data from B. Dodd, "Effects of social and vocal stimulation on infant babbling," *Developmental Psychology* 7 (1972): 80–83.

Figures 5.1 and 5.2. From F. J. Koopmans-van Beinum and J. M. van der Stelt, "Early stages in the development of speech movements," in B. Lindblom and R. Zetterstrom, eds., *Precursors of Early Speech* (New York: Stockton Press, 1986).

Figure 5.3. From E. Thelen, "Rhythmical behavior in infancy: An ethological perspective," *Developmental Psychology* 17 (1981): 237–257. Copyright © 1981 by the American Psychological Association. Reprinted by permission.

Figure 5.4. From D. S. Ramsay, "Onset of duplicated syllable babbling and unimanual handedness in infancy: Evidence for developmental change in hemispheric specialization?" *Developmental Psychology* 20 (1984): 64–71.

Figures 5.6 and 5.7. From D. K. Oller and R. E. Eilers, "The role of audition in infant babbling," *Child Development* 59 (1988): 441–449. © The Society for Research in Child Development, Inc.

Figures 5.8 and 5.9. From J. L. Locke and D. M. Pearson, "Linguistics significance of babbling: Evidence from a tracheostomized infant," *Journal of Child Language* 17 (1990); 1–16.

Figure 5.10. From B. I. Bertenthal, J. J. Campos, and K. C. Barrett, "Self-produced locomotion: An organizer of emotional, cognitive, and social development in infancy," in R. N. Emde and R. J. Harmon, eds., *Continuities and Discontinuities in Development* (New York: Plenum, 1984).

Figure 5.11. From R. W. Telzrow et al., "Spatial understanding in infants with motor handicaps," in K. Jaffe, ed., *Childhood Powered Mobility: Developmental, Technical, and Clinical Perspectives* (Washington, D.C.: RESNA, 1987).

Figure 5.12. From R. Held, "Exposure-history as a factor in maintaining stability of perception and coordination," *Journal of Nervous and Mental Disease* 132 (1961): 26–32, © by Williams & Wilkins, 1961.

Figure 5.13. From J. Loy, "Behavioral responses of free-ranging rhesus monkeys to food shortage," *American Journal of Physical Anthropology* 33 (1970): 263–272.

Figure 5.14. From P. Martin and T. M. Caro, "On the functions of play and its role in behavioral development," *Advances in the Study of Behavior* 15 (1985): 59–103.

Figure 6.1. From G. A. Sacher and E. F. Staffeldt, "Relation of gestation to brain weight for placental mammals: Implications for the theory of vertebrate growth," *American Naturalist* 108 (1974): 593–615.

Figure 6.2. From W. H. Overman and R. W. Doty, "Hemisphere specialization displayed by man but not macaques for analysis of faces," *Neuropsychologia* 20 (1982): 113–128. Copyright © 1982, Pergamon Press Ltd.

Figure 6.3. From J. C. Borod et al., "Channels of emotional expression in patients with unilateral brain damage," *Archives of Neurology* 42 (1985): 345–348. Copyright © 1985, American Medical Association.

Figure 7.1. From J. Dobbing and J. Sands, "Comparative aspects of the brain spurt," *Early Human Development* 3 (1979): 79–83.

Figure 7.2. From W. Leutenegger, "Encephalization and obstetrics in primates with particular reference to human evolution," in E. Armstrong and D. Falk, eds., *Primate Brain Evolution: Methods and Concepts* (New York: Plenum, 1980).

Figure 7.3. From C. Wimer, "Genetic studies of brain development," in M. E. Hahn et al., eds., *Developmental Behavior Genetics: Neural, Biometrical, and Evolutionary Approaches* (New York: Oxford University Press, 1990).

Figure 7.4. From P. Rakic, "Competitive interactions during neuronal and synaptic development," in A. M. Galaburda, ed., *From Reading to Neurons* (Cambridge, Mass.: MIT Press, 1989).

Figures 7.5 and 7.6. From B. N. Timney, V. F. Emerson, and P. C. Dodwell, "Developmental of visual stimulus-seeking in kittens," *Quarterly Journal of Experimental Psychology* 31 (1979): 63–81.

Figure 7.7. From C. T. Best and H. F. Queen, "Baby it's in your smile: Right hemiface bias in infant emotional expressions," *Developmental Psychology* 25 (1989): 264–276. Copyright © 1989 by the American Psychological Association. Reprinted by permission.

Figure 7.8. From P. Bateson, "How do sensitive periods arise and what are they for?" *Animal Behaviour* 27 (1979): 470–486.

Figure 7.9. From E. L. Newport, "Maturational constraints on language learning," *Cognitive Science* 14 (1990): 11–28.

Figure 7.10. From C. Snow and M. Hoefnagal-Hohle, "The critical period for language acquisition: Evidence from second language learning," *Child Development* 49 (1978): 1114–1128.

Figures 8.1 and 8.2. From D. A. Norman, "Twelve issues for cognitive science," in D. A. Norman, ed., *Perspectives on Cognitive Science* (Hillsdale, N.J.: Erlbaum, 1981).

Figure 8.3. From M. D. Smith, "The meaning of reference in emergent lexicons," in M. D. Smith and J. L. Locke, eds., *The Emergent Lexicon: The Child's Development of a Linguistic Vocabulary* (New York: Academic Press, 1988).

Figure 9.2. From H. Benedict, "Early lexical development: Comprehension and production," *Journal of Child Language* 6 (1979): 183–200.

INDEX